Forensic Criminology

This text provides an examination of the aetiological development of forensic criminology in the UK. It links the subjects of scientific criminology, criminal investigations, crime scene investigation, forensic science and the legal system and it provides an introduction to the important processes that take place between the crime scene and the courtroom. These processes help identify, define and label the 'criminal' and are crucial for understanding any form of crime within society. The book includes sections on:

- the epistemological and ontological philosophies of the natural sciences;
- the birth of scientific criminology and its search for the criminal 'body';
- the development of early forms of forensic science and crime scene investigation;
- investigating crime;
- information, material and evidence;
- crime analysis and crime mapping;
- scientific support and crime scene examination; and
- forensic science and detection methods and forensics in the courtroom.

The text combines coverage of historical research and contemporary criminal justice process and provides an introduction to the most common forensic practices, procedures and uses that enable the identification and successful prosecution of criminals. *Forensic Criminology* provides a framework for understanding the varieties of information work that exist within current criminal justice practice.

Forensic Criminology is essential for students of criminology, criminal justice, criminal investigations and crime science. It is also useful to those criminal justice practitioners wishing to gain a more in-depth understanding of the links between criminology, criminal investigations and forensics techniques.

Andy Williams is Principal Lecturer and Programme Area Leader in the Institute of Criminal Justice Studies at the University of Portsmouth. His main research areas are forensic criminology; forensic techniques and their uses and interpretation in court; dangerous offenders; public protection and offender profiling. His previous books include: *The Anatomy of Serious Further Offending* (Oxford University Press, with Mike Nash); *The Handbook Of Public Protection* (Willan, co-edited with Mike Nash); and *The Myth of Moral Panics* (Routledge, with Bill Thompson).

'This long-awaited book will become part of the foundational literature in forensic criminology. It is essential reading for students, practitioners, and academics who wish to fully appreciate the interplay between theoretical/substantive criminology and the practical world of forensic science, as well as everyday investigative and legal decision-making. Fortunately for both criminal justice professionals and general citizenry alike, the gap between theory and practice has just been substantially narrowed.'

Daniel B. Kennedy, Ph.D., Oakland University and President, Forensic Criminology Associates, Inc., USA

'This is a very timely and important book for the progression of forensic criminology. It uses an impressive array of literature and sources to provide a rigorous and robust overview of the historical and theoretical contexts that underpin contemporary forensic practice and relevant criminology. It demonstrates the tangible links between the evolution of criminological thought and its utilisation in forensic practice without adhering to a formulaic description of tasks, science and technologies. Instead, this book offers an interesting and insightful overview of developments in regards to the relevant science, techniques and ideologies, which is augmented by a detailed commentary on their underlining application and development.'

Dr Paul Smith, Institute of Criminal Justice Studies, University of Portsmouth, UK

'A useful point of reference for all students of forensic criminology. This book concisely summarises historical developments and research through to current thinking in a logical framework from crime scene to court room.'

Terry Lowe, Head of Scientific Services Department, Hampshire Constabulary, UK

Forensic Criminology

Andy Williams

Routledge
Taylor & Francis Group

LONDON AND NEW YORK

First published 2015
by Routledge
2 Park Square, Milton Park, Abingdon, Oxon, OX14 4RN

and by Routledge
711 Third Avenue, New York, NY 10017

Routledge is an imprint of the Taylor & Francis Group, an informa business

British Library Cataloguing-in-Publication Data
A catalogue record for this book is available from the British Library

Library of Congress Cataloging in Publication Data
Williams, Andy, 1973–
Forensic criminology / Andy Williams.
    pages cm
  1. Forensic sciences. 2. Criminology. 3. Criminal investigation. I. Title.
  HV8073.W52537   2014
  363.250941—dc23   2014005573

ISBN13: 978-0-415-67267-2 (hbk)
ISBN13: 978-0-415-67268-9 (pbk)
ISBN13: 978-0-203-10114-8 (ebk)

Typeset in Times New Roman
by Keystroke, Station Road, Codsall, Wolverhampton

Printed and bound in Great Britain by
CPI Group (UK) Ltd, Croydon, CR0 4YY

For Dad (1939–2013)

For Eve

Contents

Figures

Tables

Case studies

Acknowledgments

This has been a difficult book to write and has taken much longer than expected. Thanks go to Routledge for putting up with constant deadline changes that stretched over a year. Particular thanks go to Nicola and Heidi for their immense patience.

I would like to thank key members of the University of Portsmouth, who were open enough to see the potential in developing a forensic strand to an already impressive criminal justice department; and who also gave me the space to develop the Criminology and Forensic Studies course as well as help me through the early 'sociopathic years'. In particular I would like to thank Mike Nash, Steve Savage and Dave Russell for all their support; and Val and the admin girls who are the best and covered my ass on many occasions! Merging practical policing with academic social science is always difficult, but, with the help of ex-practitioners, it has been fun; and over the last seven years it has been great working with a good bunch of 'insiders'. Thanks go to Paul, Adrian, Brian and Claire; I hope you have learned as much from me as I have from you (academics are not entirely useless). I would also like to say a big thanks to all the undergraduate Criminology and Forensic Studies students who have passed through the door: you have been entertaining and every day remind me why I do the job I do. Particular thanks to PT and KH for all their help over the last year; a debt I can only repay through copious amounts of wine and pool (10–2)!

As ever, Eve has been my guiding force of strength; as well as providing me with the necessary breaks whilst putting up with the never-ending story that has been this book. Thanks to Mazzy and Star for constantly stopping my work at the most inconvenient times.

The ultimate academic debt once again goes to BT.

I would also like to thank the College of Policing for allowing me to reproduce Figure 6.5, which was reproduced from Authorised Professional Practice (APP) for Investigation with permission from the College of Policing Ltd. I would also like to thank Paul Smith, University of Portsmouth, and Barbara Ann O'Donoghue and Kenneth Andrews of Leicestershire Constabulary Scientific Support department, who gave me permission to reproduce the crime scene report found in Figure 9.7. Thanks also to Jonas Claesson, who kindly granted me permission to use his sketch of Heisenberg in Figure 10.6.

Chapter 1

Introduction

A brave old world

The subject of criminology is regarded as both fascinating and enthralling. The excitement and apparent *sexiness* around the notion of crime and deviant behaviours is of course not new, neither could it be called monolithic. Burke (1994:149–177) highlights how, in early modern Europe, *villains* revealed the standards of the culture in which they belonged. Furthermore, public executions were not only part of the repertoire of public rituals but they were also endowed with a carnivalesque atmosphere (Burke, 1994:196–197; also see Foucault, 1977). Over the last 150 years, the excitement and interest in crime and the criminal have not only been linked but also matched to ideas and developments around *forensics*. Indeed, the mix of crime, criminals and forensics is so potent that it has spawned vast educational, economic, and technological industries that have increasingly influenced our social, cultural and political worlds. When people meet individuals who are *criminologists* or practitioners that deal with offenders, a common response is, 'oh criminology is very interesting'. Of course, when asked for a cogent augmentation of this statement, further elucidation is often lacking or is distinctly opaque. Criminology does not simply deal with crime and horrific acts of behaviour against human beings; it also has to deal with a broad gamut of social problems – from poverty and injustice (Wilkinson and Pickett, 2010; Dorling, 2011; Jones, 2011) through substance misuse (Stevens, 2011) and violence (Flannery *et al.*, 2007) to mental health issues (Maden, 2007). Despite such issues being intrinsic to much that is studied within criminology, people still vicariously enjoy a good murder mystery or hearing about a violent serial sexual killer. Indeed, serial sexual killers often draw the most attention from the general public and students, with countless undergraduate dissertations entitled 'Mad or bad' or 'Theoretical explanations of serial killing'. It is actually quite surprising that the prevalence and reductive repetitiveness of these issues does not result in supervisors becoming killers themselves! Within the last 50 years, however, the apparent *seductive nature* of the criminal world has influenced a dramatic expansion in the three interlinked areas of criminal investigations, forensic science and criminology. It is not only cultural artefacts such as books, movies and TV shows that have proliferated in these years (can any reader remember when there were no crime, police, forensic or pro- filing dramas on TV?); educational programmes, professional bodies and organisations, and the resultant 'exploitative culture' (Cohen, 1972:139) have rapidly expanded during this period as well. The underlying thesis in Wiener's *Reconstructing the Criminal* (1994) suggests it is not possible to think about crime and offenders and the subsequent societal responses without thinking about sociocultural influences. Furthermore, what is designated as a crime as well as components of physical evidence, the narrative of *crimes* and the resultant understanding of offenders and their behaviour are all determined by social and cultural discourses which intersect the areas of criminal investigations, forensic science, the legal system and criminology. This book is about these four areas.

The goal of this book

This book is intended as an introductory text for those wishing to develop a *critical* theoretical and applied understanding of *forensic criminology*, an inter- disciplinary field within the social science subject of criminology. It attempts to introduce both students and practitioners to some of the core ideas, theories/ concepts and issues that link four different academic subjects and professions – *criminal investigations, forensic science, the legal system* and *criminology*. It critically examines some of the core processes that take place in these four areas and assesses the usefulness that forensic criminology has for the various proc- esses from crime scene to courtroom. In doing so, it discusses the underlying investigative and forensic epistemologies that will aid those who wish to under- take casework in the wide variety of occupations that currently exist within the criminal justice sector, and in related occupations outside of the sector. The core objectives are to *provide social science students with a meaningful understanding of the interplay between forensic science and the legal system; and, through the lens of a criminological analysis, demonstrate the effects of forensic science on the criminal justice system and understandings of criminality*. In recent years the market for *forensically* focused science and social science undergraduate courses has increased dramatically (see below for an expansion on this issue). Forensic elements have been relatively easy to develop and *drop into* the traditional natural science degree programmes; for example, in the last five years, lots of biology departments in UK universities have created 'forensic biology' or 'forensic science' degrees. What has been more difficult is creating forensic units for social science subjects such as criminology. The reasons behind these difficulties are numerous and include: jurisdictional boundary fighting over the *ownership* of forensics (Abbott, 1998 and 2001; Cohen, 1985); venomous criticism by specific academic disciplines, such as sociology and criminology, of any subject that could be construed as being even vaguely positivistic; and, finally, the lack of knowledge of forensic specialisms within criminology.[1] Despite these inherent difficulties, what has been quite remarkable in the last seven years is the huge growth in the provision of forensics in criminology and criminal justice degrees in the UK. This, of course, mirrors our closest Western educational systems: the US, Canada and Australia. This text has been written because of this increased interest, and it attempts to synthesise four crucial areas – *forensics, criminal investigations, the legal system and criminology* – into an introductory UK undergraduate text. My hope is that it will serve as a useful introduction that can be used by both students and practitioners in the UK who have an interest in criminal investigations, crime scene examinations, concepts of forensic science and their application to resolving legal problems. It will also be of use to international students and practitioners who wish to learn about our successes and failures. The closest rival to this text would be Petherick *et al.*'s (2010) *Forensic Criminology*; readers who are interested in this subject are advised to seek out this source.

Before discussing more about the contents of the book and introducing a working definitional parameter, it is important to mention what this book is *not* going to do. This book will not provide an in-depth overview of forensic science and criminal investigative techniques for those wishing to be forensic scientists or criminal investigators. It does, of course, critically discuss some of the core ideas, theories and concepts that forensic scientists and criminal investigators use, and the text includes a comprehensive bibliography for readers who wish to go into more detail vis-à-vis the science and the investigative techniques. However, as previously mentioned, the main audience are students and professionals who do not wish to be stuck in a lab, testing evidence – in the UK, these are the men and women in the white coats. Instead, this text is primarily aimed at those who wish to become, or already are, involved in the criminal justice process. For those readers studying criminology and criminal justice for the first time, it will soon become apparent just how broad the subject area is. To be sure, due to the breadth of the aforementioned four thematic areas, it will not be possible in this text to cover every aspect or caveat in the detail necessary to do each subject the academic justice it deserves. Laughlin's (2008:28–29) concept of *knowledge degradation* is very pertinent at this juncture:

> The nontechnical version of knowledge degradation is sadly familiar to most of us. It's the basis of the famous party game in which you whisper a rumor into someone's ear, let it travel from person to person, and see how it changes. After about thirty such transfers, *the final version of the rumor usually has little resemblance to the original one. The knowledge degrades with each retelling because each person, in internalizing the information, isolates what he or she believes to be parts that don't matter and then retells the story with these parts changed*, thereby making it more interesting to the listener. [My emphasis.]

In short, knowledge loses its value every time someone retells the *story*. Whilst this text primarily deals with written, technical knowledge as opposed to the oral transfer of information,[2] the analogy still holds. Academic writers are necessarily selective and use information to fit their own objectives. In doing so, they selectively choose which parts of knowledge to discuss, emphasising particular elements over others. Furthermore, as Laughlin (2008:31) also notes, when it comes to technical knowledge, this loses its value in another way. Technical knowledge tends to be buried under mountains of irrelevant technical information. Being able to identify and apply the right knowledge becomes the equivalent of trying to find a needle in a haystack. This second aspect produces a catch-22 situation for many academics. On the one hand there is a lot of technical knowledge available on any given academic subject; and for many subjects an in-depth understanding of this knowledge should be required, especially at undergraduate level and in the practitioner world. On the other hand, the enormity of trying to understand all of the available technical knowledge on any given subject often results in enforced selectivity. The analyses and discussions undertaken in the following chapters *are* selective, and this point will undoubtedly be a bitter pill for some readers to swallow. In order to avoid the effects of knowledge degradation, this text includes case studies and examples, footnotes and an extensive bibliography that provide additional material to the critique interwoven into each chapter. As a final obvious point, for a fuller understanding of any aspect of what is written in the following chapters, go to and forensically dissect the original sources that are provided in the footnotes and bibliography.

Defining forensic criminology

Whilst the term *forensic criminology* is relatively new, the core elements of forensic criminology are not new and have a long history across many different countries. As far back as the mid nineteenth century, there were a small number of scientists, doctors and criminal investigators who utilised a mix of scientific methods and techniques to resolve investigative and legal problems (Rafter, 2004 and 2009; Davie, 2005; Evans, 2006). In 1906, Hans Gross, one of the founding fathers of forensic criminology, was the first to bring criminology, forensic science, criminal investigations and the law together under one analytical and educational framework (Gross, 1962). He used the term *Kriminalistik*, which, in the US, has often been thought to mean *criminalistics*.[3] Primarily because of the work of Kirk (1974), this term became very popular in the US from the 1960s and is still widely used today. Other countries, especially the UK, have avoided the wholesale use of the term criminalistics and have instead opted for placing the term *forensic* in front of pre-existing academic subjects and practitioner roles. In educational terms, the result has been an explosion in the number of courses that have *forensic* somewhere in the title. The point I am trying to make is simple: new terms are actually not that new. Instead, they become caught up in the academic game of differentiation, fractal differentiation and fractal cycles, with each dominant paradigm eventually becoming involved in generational conflict with 'defeat of one side, division of the winners, and remapping of the losers' concerns onto the equivalent descendant of the winners' (Abbott, 2001:23). An obvious criminological example is *cultural criminology*, which has attempted to subsume the cultural relativism and ethnographies of the Chicago School (e.g. Sutherland, 1956; Wirth, 1956; Shaw, 1966; Polsky, 1971; Cressey, 2008) as well as UK subcultural theories (Hebdige, 1979). In short, this concept isn't new at all but is just the rebranding of old ideas. The notion of fractal differentiation and fractal cycles can also be seen in contemporary criminological and sociological postgraduate theses. Abbott, using the eloquent words of T. S. Eliot, spells out the crux of the matter: 'For last year's words belong to last year's language. And next year's words await another voice' (Eliot, 1943, cited in Abbott, 2001:27).

We are currently in a fractal cycle whereby both the market demand and the generational paradigm have shifted towards the umbrella term *forensics*. The effects of market demand on higher education have been a dominant force in shaping the forensics agenda, with many academic subjects using the term *forensics* in their degree programme or unit (module) titles. Unfortunately, since 2010, the coalition government has initiated policies that have put the provision of forensic science in the UK at risk (Lawless, 2011). Forensic criminology is no different and this should be met with a combination of critical scepticism but also enthusiasm. But what do we mean by the term forensic criminology?

A multidisciplinary approach

Definitional parameters can be crucial but also very problematic. They are crucial for attempting to conceptualise the subject area under examination and for setting the necessary boundaries that any scientific and academic endeavour must operate within.[4] They also affect the way concepts, theories, research and ideas are operationalised in practice. Unfortunately, definitional parameters can also produce developmental and operational difficulties for those that use them, and this occurs for the following reasons. First, the concept of *moral panic* has led a plethora of academics and researchers down theoretical *blind alleys* (see Thompson, 1989 and 1994a; Williams, 2004; Thompson and Williams, 2014). Second, definitions can become either too inclusive or exclusive. Third, definitions can be so poorly conceptualised that attempts to operationalise them result in badly conducted studies that produce empirical knowledge that is evidentially and scientifically weak. Trying to define forensic criminology involves the same problems. In fact, it is much more difficult, due to the multidisciplinary nature of the parent subject within which it sits.

Forensic criminology is a discipline within the broader subject of criminology (Turvey and Petherick, 2010:xxi). Depending on the starting point of any particular academic position, it can also be a science, a behavioural science and a forensic science. Turvey and Petherick's (2010:xix–xxxix) ambitious conceptualisation is an attempt to remind contemporary criminologists of the scientific basis and origins of the development of criminology – something that usually produces disdain from those who belong to the qualitative/interpretive paradigm. A quick historical review of the development and evolution of criminology creates the following list of contributing disciplines (see Bonger, 1936; Rhodes, 1936; Sutherland and Cressey, 1960; Wiener, 1994; Rafter, 2004 and 2009; Davie, 2005; Lilly *et al.*, 2011):

- medicine
- alienists/psychiatry
- psychology
- penology
- mathematics and statistics
- anthropology

- natural sciences
- sociology
- history
- philosophy
- geography

Turvey and Petherick point out that 'because the study of crime and criminals is multidisciplinary, no one profession, discipline or type of scientist may lay a sole claim to the vestments of criminology' (2010:xx). This multidisciplinary aspect is both a strength *and* a weakness. It is a strength because it does not (or should not) easily fit into a traditional academic silo, so typical of the division of expert labour reproduced within academic disciplines and faculties (Durkheim, 1984; Abbott, 1998). Indeed, its very multidisciplinary nature presupposes a wider epistemological philosophy that *should* move criminologists beyond their *comfort zones* and into other interrelated disciplines.[5] On the other hand it is also a weakness for with multidisciplinarity there comes the potential for contradictory clashes in epistemological and ontological philosophies, especially around the areas of theoretical explanations and research methodologies. This is very relevant to discussions of definitional parameters, as different disciplines tend to have different epistemological foundations as well as have different goals and objectives. This issue is discussed in more detail below.

Towards a definition

In the only other textbook on forensic criminology, Turvey and Petherick define forensic criminology as 'the scientific study of crime and criminals for the purposes of addressing investigative and legal issues' (Turvey and Petherick, 2010:xxi). This is a good starting point despite the obvious weaknesses. It has three clear components that have a good operational base on which to develop. First, it includes the idea of *scientific study*, which incorporates both the social and natural sciences. Second, it identifies its target area of study and research – *crime and criminality*. The final element of this definition places a context within which the scientific study and target areas should be located, namely *investigative* and *legal issues*. This definition expands the original Latin meaning of forensics – *public forum* – to incorporate a wider usage that covers criminal investigations as well as the criminal trials. Turvey and Petherick clearly state their main objective for developing forensic criminology:

> This [textbook] is intended to educate students in an applied fashion regarding the nature and extent of forensic casework that is supported by, dependent on, and interactive with research, theory and knowledge derived from criminology. It is also intended to act as a preliminary guide for criminologist practitioners working with and within related criminal justice professions – particularly when they are involved with assisting investigations, administrative inquiries, legal proceedings or providing expert findings or testimony under oath.
>
> (2010:xxi)

It is important to stress that whilst Petherick *et al.*'s (2010) text is an important contribution to the development of forensic criminology, and their definition (Turvey and Petherick, 2010) is a good starting point, there are a number of conceptual and operational weaknesses that need to be discussed. The first problem is that the definition is very inclusive. A quick review of the contents of their text reveals some obvious topics but also some bizarre ones for an introductory text of this kind. For example, chapters on miscarriages of justice and the role of DNA are obvious areas to include under the umbrella of forensic criminology; whereas topics such as premises *liability* are much more difficult to comprehend. Their inclusion appears to be the authors' attempt to broaden their already impressive business portfolio rather than developing a rigorous critique of forensic criminology. Inclusive definitional boundaries can be problematic to scientists, whether they belong to the social or natural sciences. Kennedy (2013) also considers how the boundaries of *forensics* have increased in recent years, and his review of the growth in use of forensic expertise in civil cases is in line with the fundamental 'purposes of addressing investigative and legal issues' (Turvey and Petherick, 2010:xxi). However, we need to be careful here, as definitions like Turvey and Pentherick's are so broad it is difficult to think of a subject that could not be included. Not all criminology is directed at or suited to addressing investigative and legal issues. For example, individuals who study victimology and the growth and development of the victims' movement in the UK are undoubtedly concerned with how victims are dealt with during the investigation and the trial processes (see Rock, 2004; Hoyle, 2012). However, this addresses both investigative and legal issues and, despite their obvious importance for criminological and criminal justice matters, it is unlikely that individuals studying this topic could be regarded as forensic criminologists. Nor would some of them want to. Rock's excellent work *Constructing Victims' Rights* (2004) could hardly be construed as *forensic*, and, given Rock's epistemological roots, he might be rather perturbed at the thought of being placed within such a positivist category. In short, the terminology used by Turvey and

Petherick needs clarification, as 'purposes of addressing investigative and legal issues' is too vague.

A second problem relates to the term *scientific study*. As will be shown in this introductory chapter, the majority of definitions of criminology use this term. However, this concept is not easily comprehensible. Just what exactly do we mean by the term *scientific study*? This is a question that is usually suited to philosophical debates about the nature of science and scientific knowledge. Most criminal justice practitioners, despite the fact they utilise the epistemological results on a daily basis, do not usually discuss these debates in any detail. However, such discussions can take place in the courtroom, especially when new methods or knowledge are introduced. Indeed, US rulings such as those in *Frye v. United States [293 F. 1013, D. C. Cir. 1923], Daubert V. Merrell Dow Pharmaceuticals, Inc. [509 U.S. 579, 1993]* and *Kumho Tire Co. v. Carmicheal [526 U.S. 137, 1999]* set out rules regarding the uses and determination of expert testimony, scientific testimony and technical and specialist knowledge. Chapter 2 examines the origin and development of science and demonstrates that much of the scientific knowledge that we assume as *objective fact* actually depends upon human interpretation, which is influenced and determined by a myriad of social and cultural factors such as belief systems and political ideologies and agendas. Therefore, underlying themes that are developed throughout this text are the notions of constructed and contested knowledge (Anderson *et al.*, 2005; Golinksi, 2005; Burke, 2008; Durston, 2008; Fritze, 2009; Kaptein *et al.*, 2009) and how forensic criminology has a crucial role to play in reducing the external effects that influence knowledge production. Another important aspect of this element of the definition is the fact that criminal investigations, the legal system and forensic science all have very different epistemological and ontological bases (Jasanoff, 1997; Redmayne, 2004; Golan, 2007). For instance, forensic scientists tend to operate using inductive logic and reasoning, observation and hypothesis testing through falsification (Popper, 2002:3–34), which is taken from the natural scientist's philosophical position of the 'intellectual honesty of science, on its uncompromising probing of the evidence unhindered by dogma' (Gaukroger, 2009:31). The legal system, on the other hand, does not operate under the same philosophy. The legal system in the UK is adversarial, with defence and prosecution solicitors and barristers operating from the perspective of abductive reasoning (Anderson *et al.*, 2005), which is a different position to that of the forensic scientist. It is therefore right that forensic criminology should develop an informed critique of the effects of the conflict within the epistemological and ontological positions of criminal investigators, forensic scientists, criminologists and the legal system. However, using the work of Thornton (1994), Turvey and Petherick make a convincing argument for separating the underlying theories and methods of forensic criminology from the legal system when they suggest that, 'like any other scientific practice, it exists beyond legal or national boundaries as a realm unto itself as it must be a true discipline' (2010:xxi).

A third problem with Petherick and Turvey's definition, which is also connected to the second problem outlined above, is their very basic, if not poor, understanding of criminology itself. This is discussed in greater detail in Chapter 3, which examines the epistemological origins, growth and development of criminology. For now, it is enough to highlight that Petherick *et al.*'s understanding of the historical origins and paradigmatic shifts is too simplistic. It also doesn't provide any discussion regarding what they mean by their assertion that forensic criminology should be 'supported by, dependent on, and interactive with research, theory and knowledge derived from criminology' (Turvey and Petherick, 2010:xxi). In fact, their text does not provide any chapters on criminological research that examines the concepts of crime and criminality. In many chapters it is not clearly discussed just where the practical and applied elements of forensic criminology have been supported by, dependent on or interactive with criminological research. Figure 1.1 shows the core components of Turvey and Petherick's definition of forensic criminology.

An integrated approach

The previous section outlined the core definitional components of forensic criminology as outlined by Petherick *et al.* (2010). This conceptualisation needs further development, as it is necessary to expand their definition to include more integrated links between the four core areas of criminology, criminal investigations, forensic science and the legal system. The definition used throughout this text is as follows: *forensic criminology is the applied use of scientific and criminological research and analytical techniques for the purposes of addressing proactive and reactive investigative work, and for aiding legal cases and issues.* Whilst this definition has the same elements as outlined by Turvey and Petherick, it attempts to extend and provide clarity to the precise nature and interaction of the four core

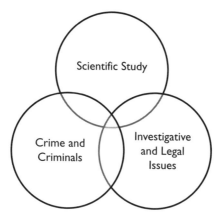

Figure 1.1 The core components of forensic criminology

areas. It also incorporates the inclusion of the potential separation that sometimes exists between activities of a criminal investigation and the forensic scientist *and* what ends up in the courtroom. There are many forensic elements of criminal investigations and forensic science that do not become part of a legal trial as there are lots of investigative, scientific and evidential filtering processes that take place between the crime scene and the courtroom. This does not mean these issues should be ignored, and oftentimes they play a crucial role in aiding investigative and legal issues. Therefore, with every attempt at a definition, a detailed expansion and critical examination is required. Figure 1.2 outlines the elements of the working definition presented above and used throughout this text.

It is important to recognise that there are a number of strands to this definition, but all of them are within a practical and applied framework that covers scientific and criminological research and analysis, proactive and reactive elements, and operational and strategic issues for investigative and legal frameworks. Not only is this a useful way to approach understanding the work of forensic criminologists, and their usefulness to the society's epistemological knowledge base as well as the criminal justice system, but it is also a useful framework in which to develop

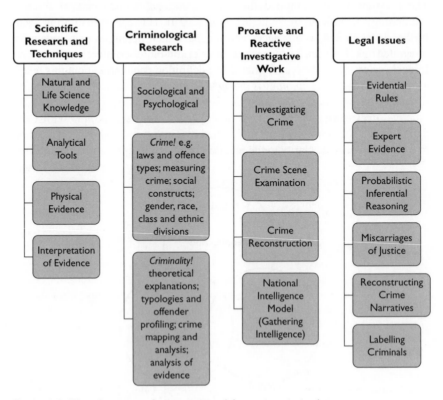

Figure 1.2 The elements of an integrated forensic criminology

a forensic stream within the academic discipline of criminology. Fundamentally, forensic criminology should be about getting involved in cases; it should be about trying to provide justice based upon robust empirical evidence; and finally, it should be about using strong data and methodological triangulation in developing knowledge about crime and criminality.

Before moving onto an in-depth discussion of these important areas, it is perhaps useful to examine some of the core challenges that anyone faces when trying to develop the type of educational programme briefly examined above. These issues may seem trivial or unimportant; however, they form the educational, political and social backdrop to the development and application of science and knowledge to one of the most important social problems facing society – crime and criminality.

A case for forensic criminology

So far this introduction has identified the core themes and aims of the book, discussed the problem with knowledge degradation and outlined some definitional parameters for forensic criminology. The context of the topic is that it is an educational stream based within the social sciences, and this section examines the case for such a development. Forensic criminology sits within what has become labelled as *forensic studies*, as opposed to *forensic science*, and this book argues the case for the need to develop a forensic studies stream within criminology and criminal justice undergraduate programmes. So what makes this both important and necessary?

Increased popularity and forensic awareness

Over the last 20 years the criminal justice system in the UK has recognised the increasing importance of the role of forensic analysis of physical evidence in supporting a democratic and due process model of justice (Caddy and Cobb, 2004; Pepper, 2005; Fradella *et al.*, 2007:261). When viewing different types of evidence along a continuum, physical evidence that has been forensically analysed tends to be located at the higher end (Canter and Youngs, 2009:203–204) and assigned a higher weight of what is known as *probative value* (Anderson *et al.*, 2005:246–261). This is a concept readers will become familiar with as they progress through this text. Unfortunately, many *lay* individuals tend to have a poor understanding of what forensic science can achieve in reality: for instance, what the strength of a particular piece of evidence actually is, or what it enables us to prove or disprove in a criminal trial. There are numerous reasons as to why the general public, in many instances, inappropriately place such faith in forensic evidence; after all, they are usually not experts and have obtained their *knowledge* from watching TV. Recently, research has introduced the concept of the 'CSI Effect' (Bergslien, 2006; Podlas, 2006 and 2009; Tyler, 2006; Cavender and Deutsch, 2007; Deutsch and Cavender, 2008) whereby audiences are provided

Hollywood blockbusters and a plethora of popular prime-time television with forensics at their core and which construct 'the illusion of science' through a 'strategic web of forensic facticity' (Deutsch and Cavender, 2008:36). Research suggests that the popularity of programmes such as *CSI* (in all three of its incarnations); *Waking the Dead*; and *Silent Witness*, to name just a few, tends to distort the reality of what forensic science can actually do.

It's not only *lay* individuals that suffer from a misunderstanding of forensics. More seriously, perhaps, many *practitioners* suffer from what has been called a lack of *forensic awareness*. Police officers who are first to arrive on scene have historically been accused of a widespread lack of awareness about forensic science (Tilley and Ford, 1996:v), whilst magistrates and Crown Courts are littered with examples where magistrates and judges have made assumptions regarding the strength of the forensic evidence being presented (see Sekar, 1998; Fielding, 2006). I return to this issue in Chapter 11. Whilst basic forensic training has improved in recent years, it is still noticeable that new police recruits only get token forensic awareness preparation (the Forensics 21 programme) during their two-year training, which includes approximately 35 weeks of supported learning materials. Numerous schemes have attempted to address the issues of inadequate forensic training for police officers: for example, the NPIA (National Policing Improvement Agency) worked closely with the Forensic Science Regulator, Skills for Justice, and higher *education* organisations to provide a range of forensic investigative training courses,[6] as shown in table 1.1 (Source: NPIA, 2009:17–20):

Table 1.1 Types of investigative training course

Crime Scene Training	Fire Investigation
Refresher Crime Scene Investigator	Digital Photography
Crime Scene Managers Development Programme	Forensic Physicians
Scientific Support Coordinators	Footwear Marks Coding and Intelligence Course
Fingerprint Evidence Recovery and Recording Techniques (FERRT) FERRT Development	Fingerprints (Foundation, Intermediate and Advanced)

These courses are available to both national and international law enforcement agencies. However, they are usually targeted at individuals in specific roles or who are advancing along a specific career path. There are few opportunities for forensic awareness training for people who have just joined their particular organisation. As readers will see in later chapters, one of the fundamental problems faced by both criminal investigators and forensic scientists is that of evidence. In citing Osterburg's (1968) study of crime laboratories, Fradella *et al.* (2007:262) note that '[a] lack of [forensic] awareness can cause officers to disregard certain types of evidence, or cause overconfidence in (or misunder-standing of) laboratory abilities, potentially leading to sloppiness, frustration, and disappointment'.

It has, therefore, become increasingly important that the educational curricula respond to this problem. The majority of individuals who attend crime scenes (as first responders, for instance) are usually individuals from one of the following four groups:

1   police officers of junior rank (for example, police constables are more often than not first responders);
2   junior detectives;
3   a member of one of the other emergency services (ambulance, fire and rescue); and
4   a member of a criminal justice organisation (for example, a prison officer).

In relation to the police, more often than not, the FOA (first officer attending) will have an educational background in the social sciences and *not* the natural sciences; or, instead, they will have professional training and on-the-job experience relevant to their particular occupation. Having an understanding not just of physical evidence but also of crime scene examination, forensic science techniques, and the interplay these areas have with investigations and the legal system is crucial for successful and *just* outcomes in the criminal justice system. It also potentially enhances the chances of achieving these two outcomes.

There are many occupations from other organisations, inside and outside the criminal justice system, that attend crime scenes; for example, prison officers and paramedics. Prison officers are often confronted with a number of crimes that occur in their prison; GBH (grievous bodily harm), ABH (actual bodily harm), stabbings, rape and drug misuse are obvious examples.[7] If reported or identified by officers, an investigation must be undertaken; but, because of the extreme internal conditions of prisons, while proper examination of crime scenes is important, this is difficult to undertake. The tragic case of the murder of Zahid Mubarek (see Case study 1.1) attests to the importance of the need for increased forensic awareness within the wider criminal justice family.

When it comes to the issue of forensic awareness, it is also important to consider alternative organisations that *are* aware of the issues surrounding the preservation of evidence and the crime but whose very organisational objectives differ from those of crime scene examiners and forensic scientists. For instance, paramedics and police officers have, as central to their professional ethic, the objective to preserve and maintain life (Berg, 2008; Beaufort-Moore, 2009; Stelfox, 2009). This is often counter-intuitive to the central ethos of forensics – the complete preservation and non-contamination of the crime scene and physical evidence (Turvey, 2001:86-87; Pepper, 2005; Beaufort-Moore, 2009; Gardner and Bevel, 2009; Miller, 2009; Sutton and Trueman, 2009). In an applied/

CASE STUDY 1.1 ZAHID MUBAREK

On 21st March 2000, Zahid Mubarek was brutally murdered in his cell at Feltham Young Offender Institution, aged just 19. He was bludgeoned to death by his cellmate Robert Stewart (also 19). Of specific importance here is ethnicity – Mubarek was of Pakistani origin, whilst Stewart was white. Stewart clubbed Mubarek 'several times about the head with a wooden table leg. . . . Such was the ferocity of the attack . . . his head looked like a huge balloon. He was almost unrecognisable. His face was full of blood with bruising all over it' (Keith, 2006a:xvii). After a number of investigations, and the conviction of Stewart for murder, a public inquiry into Mubarek's death was eventually established by the then Home Secretary David Blunkett, on 29th April 2004. One of the core issues investigated was the fact that Stewart was a known racist, and a violent offender. A note in Stewart's 'temporary wing file', dated 12th January 2000, made reference to him stating there were 'a lot of niggers on the wing plus other similar references' (Keith, 2006a:187). On the same day, and written in red (assuming for emphasis), was the following:

STAFF ARE ADVISED TO SEE THE SECURTY FILE ON THIS INMATE (HELD IN SECURITY). VERY DANGEROUS INDIVI-DUAL. *BE CAREFUL.*

The core question that was asked in relation to this issue was why a violent racist was placed in the same cell as Mubarek, who was clearly of a non-white ethnicity. Mubarek's case is pertinent to forensic criminology for the following reasons:

1 the need for prison officers to adequately deal with, and be forensi-cally aware at, a crime scene – i.e. understand the issues of control of the crime scene, crime scene examination, preservation and contamination of evidence, Locard's principle of exchange and so forth (see Chapter 4);
2 to understand *evidence dynamics* and to be able to identify core types of evidence pertinent to the alleged crime in question;
3 to understand the importance of evidence for proactive investi-gations to prevent crimes (i.e. there were a number of evidential clues that should have been examined to produce an informed risk assessment vis-à-vis Stewart's known extreme racism); and
4 to use physical and behavioural evidence analysis to understand levels of dangerousness such as risk of harm, seriousness of harm and imminence.

practitioner sense, the development of forensic criminology can help address important knowledge areas not only for FOAs but also for the wider forensic family, whose activities cross over into the realm of forensics and criminal investigations. Table 1.2 provides some examples of those individuals and organisations that belong to the *forensic family*.

Table 1.2 The forensic family

Occupation/ Organisation	Forensic link
Police Service	• Undertaking criminal investigations – both proactive and reactive • Identifying and gathering evidence • Identification (inclusion) or exclusion of suspects • Corroboration of witness statements • Producing a fully formed 'investigation' file for the CPS • Giving evidence in court
Probation Service	• Undertaking risk assessment review of offence(s) for pre-sentence reports • Risk assessment and risk management planning for noncustodial and/or released offenders • Understanding levels of seriousness and dangerousness • Understanding patterns and dynamics of criminality • Proactive crime prevention • Potential witness – i.e. giving evidence in court
Prison Service	• Understanding risk and patterns of criminality through analysis of physical evidence • Undertaking in-house investigations • Control and maintenance of crime scene • Aiding criminal investigators • Potential witness – i.e. giving evidence in court
Crown Prosecution Service	• Advising police on criminal investigations • Aiding the development of the 'investigation file' • Assessing the probative value and weight of the physical and behavioural evidence
Fire Service	• Undertaking fire investigations • Identifying and gathering evidence • Preservation of crime scene (where possible) • Potential witness – i.e. giving evidence in court
Ambulance Service	• Responding to emergency (crime) situations • Dynamic involvement in crime scenes • Dynamic involvement with witnesses, victims and suspects • Potential witness – i.e. giving evidence in court
Forensic Health Teams	• Risk assessment and risk management • Understanding levels of seriousness and dangerousness • Understanding patterns and dynamics of criminality • Proactive crime prevention • Potential witness – i.e. giving evidence in court

(Continued)

Table 1.2 (Continued)

Occupation/ Organisation	Forensic link
Youth Offending Teams	• Risk assessment and risk management • Understanding levels of seriousness and dangerousness • Understanding patterns and dynamics of criminality • Proactive crime prevention • Potential witness – i.e. giving evidence in court
Forensic Criminologists	• Aiding reactive police investigations – i.e. offender profiling, crime analysis, etc. • Assessment of physical and behavioural evidence • Aiding prosecution and/or defence teams in legal cases and appeals • Understanding levels of seriousness and dangerousness • Understanding patterns and dynamics of criminality • Understanding patterns and dynamics of victimology • Proactive crime prevention • Undertaking research
Forensic Psychologists	• Aiding reactive police investigations – i.e. offender profiling, crime analysis, investigative interviewing, etc. • Assessment of physical and behavioural evidence • Aiding prosecution and/or defence teams in legal cases and appeals • Understanding levels of seriousness and dangerousness • Understanding patterns and dynamics of criminality • Understanding patterns and dynamics of victimology • Proactive crime prevention • Undertaking research

Of course, this list is not exhaustive: I have not included all relevant duties and responsibilities for each organisation, and there may be lots of other organisations or occupations that become involved in forensic issues. The point here is that, with such a broad range of individuals coming into contact with criminal cases, there is an urgent need to develop what Fredella *et al.* (2007:271) call a 'baseline of forensic knowledge'. As suggested by the authors, this should be located within the social science disciplines of criminology and criminal justice – something which this text aims to achieve. Furthermore, any attempt to combine interdisciplinary subjects such as criminology, forensic investigations and science, criminal investigations and legal approaches should also take into account the three models of criminal justice education – *training, professional* and *social sciences* – which are becoming increasingly important in the academic/scientific and practitioner worlds.

Models of criminal justice education

The overriding objective within this text is to introduce students to the meaning and significance of scientific evidence, its uses and limitations, and the role it plays in the criminal justice system. In order to achieve this, educators need to consider the *end user*; and, as discussed in the previous section, the *end users* of forensic information are both numerous and varied. A useful way of conceptualising criminal justice education has been proposed by Lindquist (1994, cited in Fradella *et al.*, 2007:263–264), who refers to three models of criminal justice education – what he calls the *training, professional* and *social sciences* models. The training model tends to place emphasis on the core skills aspect of criminal justice. For example, many criminology and criminal justice courses have skills *benchmarks*, which, at the time of writing were determined by the Quality Assurance Agency for Higher Education (QAA).[8] Many policing units on degree courses, for instance, provide some elementary skills for police officers (i.e. understanding the Police and Criminal Evidence Act 1984). The *professional model* examines the 'internalization of standards appropriate to role-specific behavior in a particular career ladder' (Lindquist, 1994:61, cited in Fradella *et al.*, 2007:263). An example of professional model education would be accredited forensic training programmes such as those in Table 1.1, which aim to heighten the awareness of forensic processes and evidentiary standards. Finally, the *social science* model emphasises the 'acquisition of broad-based knowledge' (Fradella *et al.*, 2007:263). This final type is what we know to be the traditional university social science degree programmes, which might be subject specific but do not generally prepare an individual for a particular career. These might involve, for example, training in understanding the needs of justice, human rights issues and miscarriages of justice. Forensic criminology is an attempt to bring these three models together – following Lindquist's suggestion that the models can be uniquely tailored to fit forensic subjects to social science criminology and criminal justice programmes – and to advocate that the development of bespoke social-science-based forensic programmes is desirable if we wish to create a higher level of criminal justice professionals.

Lindquist's suggestions also need to be considered in light of current debates about higher education. As Furedi (2006:11) suggests, education has 'acquired a formidable influence over society'; with more and more people participating in higher education, it appears there is a never-ending thirst for the acquisition of knowledge. The increase in higher education over the last 40 years has generated much debate about what higher education is supposed to provide. For many years, secondary and higher education across the UK has been dumbing down; and, as a result, we expect less and less of our students nowadays. Anecdotal evidence collected from many colleagues across the higher education sector suggests that many students consistently moan about the fact that you ask them to think for themselves using such alien practices as the application of empirical evidence and logical reasoning. They are astonished when you ask them to read some books *cover to cover*; and don't even suggest asking students to move beyond the realms of *wiki-google-pedia*! They are even more outraged at the thought of having to read more than one text.[9] Many stories are told around the *academic campfire* about individual tutorials where students get rather agitated when tutors don't *give them the answer*. Students want the quick fix, path-of-least-resistance, one-textbook-fits-all answer to their assignments. Whilst the benefits of the Internet are immense, many undergraduate students would rather use Wikipedia than go to a library or museum and hunt sources down, so I strongly believe the art of academic research has slowly been eroded in many areas. Unfortunately, the claim that society is dumbing down usually produces a vitriolic response from those defenders of the academic status quo. Why does the claim to dumbing down generate such a response? A short answer would be: because the ones responding in such a way are the ones primarily involved in the dumbing down; for instance, through setting the *standards*, *learning outcomes* and the near fetishistic turn to *modularisation*. This 'Macdonaldization' of higher education in the UK has not resulted in the raising of standards in universities. Furedi's analysis is useful here, for he links the dumbing down of higher education to the 'dogmatic commitment to instrumentalism' (2006:12). He highlights the age-old conflict between market-driven economic determinism[10] and intellectual and artistic knowledge production. With one eye on the market, many university degrees are being tailored to provide market-driven programmes and content rather than to provide students with a decent academic knowledge of their chosen subject. On the one hand, this text may appear not to be any different for, as mentioned above, any form of academic subject that has the word *forensics* in its title has become immensely popular and the academic world has pandered to these market forces. On the other hand, this text strives to take a different perspective, as it is not aimed at a particular profession or role. It provides students and practitioners with a sound knowledge base and understanding of some of the core theories, ideas and skills that can be applied to a broad range of jobs that relate to the developing discipline of forensic criminology. The word *generalist* often comes to mind with any attempt to move away from the division of academic labour that has been created over the last 150 years (Durkheim, 1984). Both Hans Gross (1962) and Paul Kirk (1974) – who were early pioneers of integrating the subjects of criminology, forensic science and criminal investigation – extolled the virtues of being a generalist forensic practitioner. However, I prefer the more classic term of *intellectual speculator*, used by Pareto (1935) to describe the Jewish intellectuals as referenced in Veblen's (1919) excellent paper 'The intellectual pre-eminence of Jews in modern Europe'. The intellectual speculator tends to sit between the borders of two or more academic paradigms, 'a position which encourages skepticism and detachment' (Burke, 2008:33). Pareto's idea can be contrasted against the *intellectual rentiers* – an idea, associated with Bourdieu's (2000) notion of cultural capital, whereby academic institutions tend to reproduce themselves through the continuation of academic disciplines, creating centres of cultural capital that have highly guarded vested interests around their subjects (also see Abbott's 1988 thesis on *jurisdictional boundaries*). The position of intellectual speculator allows for greater flexibility or, as Mannheim (1925 cited in Burke, 2008:32) suggested, a *free-floating intelligentsia* that 'are less subject to social pressures than the beliefs of other groups'. The intellectual speculator also fits more closely with the idea of intellectual morality (Gaukroger, 2009:30–31), which is an underlying foundation of Popper's (2002:57–73) suggestion that 'the aim of the scientific enterprise is to try and falsify theories' (Gaukroger, 2009:30).

The text that follows is for those who wish to move beyond the role of intellectual rentier and into the realm of the intellectual speculator. It wants students to get involved in the rich eclecticism of the four underlying themes running throughout each chapter, and it demands that students use the pedagogical features to further enhance their understanding of the subjects within. In many places, the text will be challenging, especially to those students approaching the subjects for the first time. Stick with it; higher education should be challenging, and we should not bow down to the instrumental dumbing down of human beings' intellect for the sake of generating profit for somebody else (Furedi, 2006 and 2009; Laughlin, 2008). For those who want to be just another *brick in the wall*, move along, go back to the *reality* of *Eastenders* and *Jersey Shore* – there's nothing of interest for you here.

A second issue that has been (and is at the time of writing) prominent in higher education is the coalition government's policy regarding the funding of higher education. This has created a large amount of uncertainty across the university sector in England and Wales. In England, HEFCE[11] funding was slashed, which left a gap that had to be filled.[12] The response was, of course, to raise the cap on fees that universities could charge students (from around £3,000 to £9,000). What is remarkable is that the government seemed *surprised* by the fact that most universities have elected to charge close to the upper threshold (*The Independent*, 30th April 2011).[13] The new fees system started in 2012, so, at the time of writing, it is difficult to predict the effect this increase will have on university departments and degree programmes over the long term. Based on the experience at my educational institution (as well as speaking to others across the higher education sector), one thing is certain: we have been forced to make radical (and, in some places, unnecessary) changes to the curriculum in order to provide a more *value for money* service. Whilst this is a valid idea in principle, as usual, it has been rushed through by university senior management and politicians and without adequate consultation with those who have to implement and teach the new format. The issue of funding has been briefly mentioned here to highlight the fact that the format and structure of education, learning and knowledge is influenced and determined by a wide range of political, economic, social and technological trends. These areas of influence need to be considered when attempting to synthesise the three models of education discussed above. Indeed, combining these models is challenging; especially if we consider the economic, political and social difficulties we currently face.

Challenges

There are three core challenges to implementing forensic studies programmes within a social science framework that have been outlined by Fradella *et al.* (2007:276–280). The first challenge, briefly introduced in the previous section, is *market demand*. The majority of studies on the subject highlight the fact that the criminal justice system often relies on forensic evidence, so it is highly unlikely that it will abandon its use. Even if we take important developments such as the 2012 closure of the UK's Forensic Science Service into account, forensic evidence still needs to be collected, analysed and interpreted. Indeed, Fradella *et al.* (ibid.:276) suggest that 'the demand for criminal justice professionals with a basic working knowledge of forensics will certainly remain constant, if not increase'. Readers may have already identified the obvious question – if we know that the market is out there, where is the challenge? The core challenges in responding to market demand for forensic courses are: (i) avoiding hastily or poorly constructed programmes; and (ii) ensuring courses are properly marketed. Hastily constructed forensic degrees, whether based in the paradigms of the social or the natural sciences, often quickly develop without adequate conceptualisation of the term *forensics*. Fradella *et al.* warn that '[p]rograms should not be a mere assortment of courses, sharing in common only the word "forensic" in course titles or descriptions, cobbled together without concern for overall program thematic coherence' (ibid.).

Forensic courses should also be properly marketed, with clarity and transparency over what they *are* and what they *are not*. For example, forensic studies based within social science degrees should be clear that the courses do *not* train students to become forensic scientists. Likewise, forensic science programmes should state that hard science subjects *do not* provide adequate criminological and legal understandings of crime and criminality. At the time of writing, Internet research into the number and types of forensic courses revealed around 386 higher education courses available in England, Wales and Scotland. This is quite a substantial number, and the government is rightly concerned that this could create excessive labour that far outstrips demand; or, even worse, that the next generation is being educated for jobs that will not exist in the future. This is of concern especially for the more specialist forensic courses, such as forensic biology, forensic accounting or forensic photography. Whilst these services (and others) are important, there are only a finite number of jobs available at any given time; and, with the rapidly decreasing amount of funding, this is a situation that is not likely to change anytime soon. This is coupled with current investigative ideology, which still places interviews and witnesses' statements as the *prima facie* evidence, despite mounting psychological research identifying numerous problems with such evidence (for example, see Eysenck, 1998; Gross, 2005).

Figure 1.3 provides a breakdown of the spread of the subject areas in which forensic courses can be found. These undergraduate courses are still predominantly

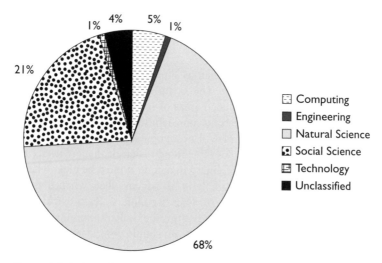

Figure 1.3 A disciplinary breakdown of higher education forensic science courses (England, Wales and Scotland)

natural science based (68 per cent), however more and more are being spread over social science, computing, engineering and technology faculties/departments.

What is of interest is that 21 per cent of forensic courses are now based within social science departments. Over the last six years or so, criminology departments have developed a variety of forensic courses to keep up with market demand, and the challenge of marketing these degrees should be of constant concern. On the one hand, there is a possibility of students coming into these programmes thinking they will become forensic scientists (which should not be the aim of such courses). On the other hand, you may end up with a number of students who do not want to learn the *harder* aspects of forensics. Managing student expectations becomes a core marketing issue.

The second major challenge to developing forensic studies programmes within a social science framework concerns *resources* and *academic politics*. Resource problems include set-up costs and locating qualified people to teach and develop forensic units. Setting up any new degree, let alone an entire subject stream, can be costly. Having the support and backing of sympathetic and motivated key personnel such as the Head of Department and Dean of Faculty is beneficial. However, resource issues are nothing compared to academic politics. Most academic disciplines are traditionally quite insular and there can often be some very malicious defending of the ownership of knowledge jurisdictions, both intra- and inter-discipline (Abbott, 1988). With this in mind, attempting to implement a social science programme that utilises elements of the natural sciences will undoubtedly bring out the paranoid and myopic insecurities of some members of the academic world. In short, there is a possibility that *turf wars* could develop and, where possible, these need careful handling (Fradella *et al.*, 2007). To achieve the successful development of any forensic social science programme, getting people of different skill sets *on board* is crucial (ibid.:278).

The final major challenge identified by Fradella *et al.* (2007) comes under the very fashionable term *pedagogy*. The complexity of synthesising theory and application with the four interrelated areas of forensics, criminal investigations, criminology and the law needs careful consideration and is a key theme throughout this entire text. The two fundamental pedagogical obstacles are the concept of forensic studies itself and the types of learning materials that are used (ibid.:279). As forensic studies are interdisciplinary in nature, it must be clear what is meant by the term forensic studies. Fradella *et al.* suggest that, when thinking about pedagogical issues, the concept of interdisciplinary team-teaching must be encouraged and that, by doing so, this permits the 'holistic examination of a topic' (ibid.:280). Ideally, an interdisciplinary team should consist of the following:

- **Forensic Criminologist** – generalist who has academic and applied understandings of the four epistemological areas;
- **Ex-Police Officer** – who has the necessary practical experience of undertaking criminal investigations;
- **Ex-Crime Scene Manager** – who has the necessary practical experience of undertaking crime scene examinations and managing crime scenes;
- **Ex-Scenes of Crimes Officer** – who has the necessary practical experience of undertaking crime scene examinations;
- **Forensic Scientist** – generalist in forensic science (who may also have one or two specialisms in forensic areas);
- **Behavioural 'Scientist'** – who has an understanding of the dynamics between crime scene actions, behaviour and patterns in criminality (i.e. forensic criminologists and/or investigative psychologists);
- **Crime Analyst** – who has an understanding of crime mapping and crime analysis; and
- **Ex-members of the legal profession** – those who have an applied knowledge and understanding of the legal system (i.e. barristers and/or solicitors).

The benefits of developing a forensic studies course using an interdisciplinary team such as that listed above are numerous and include: (i) providing an holistic understanding of all aspects of the process from crime scene to courtroom to rehabilitation and recidivism; (ii) enabling the different team members to enhance their understanding of the different elements of cases and how they are processed in other disciplines; and (iii) enhancing the development of integrated epistemologies and ontologies. To reiterate a point made a number of times earlier, forensic studies requires a balance between theory and application. Whilst this can be achieved through developing educational streams such as forensic studies and forensic criminology, it is crucial that the next generation is taught how forensic science intersects with the law, criminal justice system, science and technology.

Outline of the book

In an attempt to synthesise the three models of criminal justice education identified by Lindquist (1994, cited in Fradella *et al.*, 2007), and discussed above, the following text has a mixture of chapters that follow training and professional elements with the more traditional academic social science format of history, theory and critical analysis. It should be highlighted that the dominant framework of the analysis presented here is the social science model, and every attempt has been made to strike the right balance between theory and application. The hope is that what follows covers the subject in enough introductory detail to satisfy a broad range of readers' expectations and requirements. As this is the first UK text of its kind, I have been able to discuss many *forensic* issues from a criminological vantage point; however, the subjects that follow in this text are by no means exhaustive, and, of course, I would like to highlight that many issues have been omitted due to lack of space rather than my own academic incompetence.

This text is composed of three parts that cover the core areas of the four interrelated themes relevant to forensic criminology. In order to provide readers with a richness and depth of detail that is missing from many of the standard forensic and criminology textbooks, part 1 examines the history, epistemological development and origins of scientific knowledge, criminology and early forms of forensic investigation. In doing so, it provides the necessary historical context to our current knowledge of crime, criminality and forensic science. Chapter 2 begins in a rather non-traditional way for a social science text, as it discusses the broad issue of *scientific* knowledge. It examines the epistemological origins and development of scientific knowledge and criminology, and it considers some of the major developments that have occurred over the last 350 years and which are relevant to forensic criminology. It also discusses the different disciplines that can be linked to forensic criminology and introduces the concept of *paradigms*, which often frame knowledge in specific ways. Chapter 3 provides an overview of the beginnings of what has been labelled *scientific* criminology (Davie, 2005) and locates and traces the development of criminology to a broad range of disciplines and practitioners in the eighteenth and nineteenth centuries. This chapter is crucial for readdressing the epistemological fractal imbalance (Abbott, 2001) that has taken place within criminology due to the dominance of sociologically oriented perspectives during the twentieth century. Chapter 4 examines the historical development of early forms of forensic investigation, tracing these developments to early Chinese legal medicine. The main bulk of this chapter concentrates on the important developments that took place in the eighteenth, nineteenth and early twentieth centuries; this is crucial as it demonstrates that many of the ideas and concepts that are used in forensic investigations today originated within this eclectic period. Chapter 5 has a similar objective to Chapter 4, but the topic is criminal investigations. It charts some of the important historical developments, issues and concepts around policing and criminal investigations. In doing so, it sets the practical and structural backdrop for understanding criminal investigations in the UK.

Following from Chapter 5, part 2 looks at contemporary criminal and forensic investigations and consists of four chapters that are geared more towards the concepts, structures and processes that guide current criminal investigation techniques. Chapter 6 continues the theme of policing by examining modern criminal investigations and includes issues such as defining criminal investigations, detecting crime and the structure of policing in the UK. It also discusses the National Intelligence Model, which is underpinned by a broader inclusive use of the term *forensics*, as outlined in the definition section above. Chapter 7 provides the link between criminal investigations, crime scene examination and forensic science by discussing the differences between the terms material, information and evidence. It examines the structural conditions that enabled the development of crime scene examination techniques and the increased use of forensic evidence. It provides an in-depth, critical examination of the concepts of trace evidence, transference and persistence, highlighting their importance to criminal investigations. Chapter 8 introduces the processes of crime analysis and crime mapping, which have become useful tools for both reactive and proactive criminal investigations. It describes how current crime analysis and mapping techniques have their historical origins and links within early criminology, as discussed in Chapter 3. By examining analysis and mapping processes and structures, this chapter highlights the increasing use of these techniques in developing intelligence around crime and criminality, which are crucial for resolving forensic problems. I argue that these types of developments are clearly an indication of the inclusionary expansion of the term *forensics* within the UK's criminal justice system and proffer some critical reflection on this issue. The final chapter in part 2 is Chapter 9, which deals with scientific support and crime scene examination. It discusses the fundamentals of crime scene investigation, including definitions, key concepts such as chain of quality/evidence and contamination; as well as examining the core processes of scene preservation, the searching, recording, recovery and packaging of evidence. It reflects on all these practices in light of the structures and processes of crime scene investigation, such as national and ISO standards, forensic strategies and submissions.

Part 3 moves the criminal justice process along by critically considering the uses and abuses of forensic evidence. Chapter 10 introduces the basic concepts pertaining to scientific analysis and detection methods; for instance, class characteristics and individualisation. It also examines the actual uses of forensic science within the criminal justice system, reviewing evidence from UK government committees and research into the effectiveness of such evidence. It does all this in light of the closure of the UK's Forensic Science Service in 2012. Chapter 11 finishes the criminal justice process by looking at the criminal trial process. It examines how forensic practices and evidence are used in court, discussing concepts such as abductive reasoning, legal and expert evidence and proof, and the construction of cases using forensic science. It also reviews the numerous forensic evidence abuses that have been made during criminal trials by examining miscarriages of justice resulting from poor forensic investigative practice. I conclude the book with a short discussion of its key themes, but also a look towards future directions that forensic criminology could take.

Whilst all of the chapters can be read in isolation, it is not advisable. I have attempted to place the chapters in a logical, sequential order as they also have elements that link to each other's epistemological basis; or, to put it another way, common threads of *knowledge themes* that run through them. For instance, in part 1, the historical chapters are linked together as the majority of the processes, structures and concepts are historically located within the eighteenth, nineteenth and early twentieth centuries. Whilst it may take some readers time to get to grips with some of the more challenging ideas and concepts, this book is best read as a composite whole.

Part I

The historical and epistemological backdrop

Chapter 2

Constructed knowledge and the philosophy of science

> If you would understand anything, understand its beginning and its development.
>
> Aristotle (4th century BC)

Introduction

How do we know the Earth and other planets in our solar system revolve around the Sun? How did Newton develop the theory that gravity is a universal force, acting in an inverse-square relation to the distances between bodies (Shapin, 1998:61)? If the crime scene assessment at a murder scene indicates an offender is *disorganised* (Ressler *et al.*, 1995:130–131) what does that mean, and what evidence supports such an inference? If an *expert* is interviewed on TV about looting youths and uses the term *disaffected*, or makes claims as to a causal link between government cuts and crime, what evidence are they using? How do we distinguish between empirical evidence, ideology or political rhetoric? Indeed, is that even important?

It is often said that we are living in a *knowledge society* or in the *age of information* which is dominated by experts, some of whom utilise scientific methods and tools. All of us use information and knowledge to negotiate everyday life, whether it's to solve problems (well, at least sidestep them) or to undertake the tasks required to fulfill our daily obligations (i.e. professional, family or leisure activities). However, in using knowledge, most of us do not consider where this knowledge comes from, how it was developed or what technology is involved in its application. This is because, generally, we don't need this information in order to function in our daily lives. This chapter examines some of the epistemological and ontological origins of the natural and social sciences that are most relevant to the field of forensic criminology. To borrow a phrase from Oscar Wilde 'any fool can make history, but it takes a genius to write it' (cited in Szasz, 1974:553). Wilde's prose highlights the difficulty one faces when attempting to write a historically coherent account of the growth of science. It is not possible to cover the entire scope and depth of the epistemological and ontological developments of the social and natural sciences in one whole text, let alone one chapter. What follows is therefore highly selective: it concentrates on defining some core concepts that are still useful for today's sciences; it then moves on to provide a brief overview of some of the key (relevant) developments in science and knowledge that help *set the scene* for understanding the development of forensic science and criminology; specifically, it examines the notions of epistemology, ontology, induction, deduction, taxonomies and natural kinds.

The importance of history

Henry Adams once wrote that 'history will die if not irritated. The only service I can do to my profession is to serve as a flea' (cited in Szasz, 1974:560). Whilst my students may enjoy the idea of me as the *epistemological flea*, distant cousin to Geoff Goldblum's portrayal in *The Fly*, the point Adams makes is very pertinent. History, for non-history students, is often an annoyance, like the scratching brought on from the bite of a flea (although I have never understood why this is the case). Yet it is one of the most important elements of any academic discipline. Knowing what's come before allows us to learn from the mistakes of the past as well as providing the context for the present. To some extent it also enables us to guide future directions and developments. Unfortunately, teaching history to the uninterested or ignorant is challenging, regardless of how interesting you make it.

That which precedes it determines all science, as it does with all knowledge. As mentioned in Chapter 1, forensic criminology utilises knowledge, theories and techniques from a number of subjects within the social and natural sciences. It is therefore important to understand the historical origins and developments of such knowledge and techniques. Historical analysis enables us to put the present knowledge in context. It also enables an understanding of how disciplinary boundaries are drawn and redrawn, how they develop and the ways in which different knowledge is often hotly contested. In short, historical analysis helps to demonstrate the fluidity of knowledge over time. This is crucial because it casts a critical eye over the subject matter one is studying. Turvey is right when he argues that history is for critical thinkers:

> The study of history is for critical thinkers – those who will not blindly and politely accept what they have been handed by someone claiming to be an authority. It is for those who would rather come to understand things and their relationships for themselves. It is for those who understand the value of hunting down information and sourcing it, *and who would prefer not to be led by the hand into intellectual servitude. It is a bold and dangerous journey that can educate, inspire, and inflame a lifetime of study.* [My emphasis.]
>
> (2008:2)

It is important to know the history behind forensic criminology not only for understanding the context of knowledge but also for understanding the work undertaken within the criminal justice system. Let's take criminal investigation, for instance, which attempts to reconstruct the past using bits of physical, witness and behavioural evidence. These pieces of information, when reconstructed, form the historicised narrative of the criminal event or events that have taken place. History also plays a key role in the everyday working of the criminal justice system. Police officers often use the PNC (Police National Computer) and PND (Police National Database) during proactive and reactive police investigations. Such databases contain much historical information about offenders, victims and the circumstances and context in which the crime event occurs (Scott, 1977). Depending on which probation trust one works for, probation officers in court will also use several sources of historical information (e.g. the Delius and OASys databases) to produce their reports, assisting in the sentencing and punishment of offenders. Much of this information contains history; for example, pre-convictions and their respective details are perhaps the most commonly used historical pieces of information in determining future events such as likelihood of reoffending.[1] Decisions about what went on during the crime, the risk assessment of offenders and what punishment is appropriate are all made with the help of historical information. The importance of the need to have a firm grasp of historical information in order to make appropriate criminological decisions in the present is no more apparent than in the tragic cases of Victoria Climbié and Peter Connelly.

CASE STUDY 2.1 UNNECESSARY DEATHS – VICTORIA CLIMBIÉ AND PETER CONNELLY

The physical abuse and murder of two young children has raised major concerns about social care and child protection in the UK. The first case was that of Victoria Climbié who, on 25th February 2000, at the age of eight years and three months, died from multiple injuries caused by 'months of ill-treatment and abuse by her great-aunt, Marie-Therese Kouao and her great aunt's partner, Carl John Manning' (House of Commons Health Committee, 2003:3). During the year prior to her death, there was intensive contact between Kouao, Manning and Climbié, and Haringey Social Services, NHS and police staff. This contact was a result of a number of instances where Victoria showed up with 'injuries'. For example, on one occasion a distant relative of Victoria, Esther Ackah, and her childminder, Priscilla Cameron, began to notice several marks on Victoria; and, when looking after Victoria overnight, Cameron identified several marks on her face which Kouao claimed to be 'self-inflicted' (ibid.:7). She was taken to the A&E department of Central Middlesex hospital where the registrar identified a large number of injuries, 'some of which it was thought could be non-accidental' (ibid.:7). This was just one in a line of 'mysterious' injuries that were dealt with by local authorities yet failed to result in direct action being taken to remove Victoria from an abusive environment. Things got so bad for her that, by 2000, she was 'being given her food on a piece of plastic in the bathroom. Her hands were tied with masking tape and she would be pushed towards the food to eat it like a dog' (ibid.:8). She was burnt with cigarettes and hit with bike chains, hammers and wires. After becoming incredibly ill, and futile attempts made claiming that evil spirits possessed her, Victoria was sent in a minicab to hospital. She eventually ended up at St Mary's hospital with hypothermia and multi-system failure and a temperature of 27 degrees Celsius. She went into respiratory, cardiac and renal systems failure and was declared dead, ironically, on the same day 'that Haringey Social Services formally closed her case' (ibid.:9). On 12th January 2001, Kouao and Manning were sentenced to life imprisonment. With the death of Victoria, Lord Laming was asked to undertake an *independent* inquiry to investigate why there were so many failures by key agencies in their duty of care towards her. His final report, which received widespread public and media attention, was wide-sweeping in its criticism and condemnation of a child protection *system* that had failed Victoria so comprehensively.

The second case was frighteningly similar to the case of Victoria Climbié – even more so given the fact that it was another one within the jurisdiction of Haringey Council. On 3rd August 2007, paramedics took 17-month Peter Connelly, aka Baby P, to North Middlesex University Hospital where he was pronounced dead at 12.10pm. An initial examination of his body found 'bruising to his body, a tooth missing, a torn frenum and marks to his head' (Haringey Local Safeguarding Children Board, 2009:3). On 6th August, a post mortem revealed that a tooth was found in Peter's colon, he had 'eight fractured ribs on the left side and a fractured spine' (ibid.:3). At the time of his death, Peter was living with his mother Tracey Connelly, her boyfriend Steven Barker, and his brother Jason Owen. They were all acquitted of murder but were convicted, in November 2008, of causing or allowing the death of a child. Haringey's Local Safeguarding Children Board initiated a serious case review in December 2008 as, at the time of his death, Peter was 'subject of a child protection plan' and 'his name had been on Haringey's child protection register under the category of physical abuse and neglect since 22nd December 2006' (ibid.:4). The case review found that the following agencies were involved: Haringey's Children and Young People's Service (CYPS); Haringey's Teaching Primary Care Trust (HtPCT); Whittington Hospital NHS; North Middlesex University Hospital (NMUH); Great Ormond Street Hospital (GOSH); Metropolitan Police Service (MPS); the Epic Trust and Family Welfare Association (FWA); two Haringey schools; Haringey's Legal Services; and Haringey's Strategic & Community Housing. All of these agencies and services failed in their duty of care towards Peter.

Whilst both cases have been simplified in the above account, and it is not possible to go into the detail of the findings and recommendations of both Laming's independent inquiry and Haringey's Local Safeguarding Children Board's serious case review, it is clear that common themes running through both cases were those of poor communication and lack of direct action. Both children were *known* to the local authorities for an extended period when the physical abuse was taking place, yet several opportunities to identify and communicate crucial information were missed. This meant that direct action was not taken to remove the children from their abusive environments, meaning the historical data was not acted upon.

- Lord Laming's report can be downloaded free from the Department of Health's website – www.dh.gov.uk/prod_consum_dh/groups/dh_digitalassets/documents/digitalasset/dh_110711.pdf.
- Haringey's Local Safeguarding Children Board's Serious Case Review can be downloaded from their website – www.haringeylscb.org/executive_summary_peter_final.pdf.

Definitional parameters

Before moving on to the history of scientific knowledge, it is perhaps useful to define some of the core *concepts* that are used in this and subsequent chapters. As the majority of this text deals with *knowledge, information* and *science,* this section provides working definitions for each of these and discusses some of the important epistemological and philosophical issues surrounding them. The importance behind definitions of *things* was clearly laid down 170 years ago by John Stuart Mill (1806–1873). In *A System of Logic*, Mill argued that:

> It is not expected that there should be agreement about the definition of anything, until there is agreement about the thing itself. To define, is to select from among all the properties of a thing, those which shall be understood to be designated and declared by its name; and the properties must be well known to us before we can be competent to determine which of them are fittest to be chosen for this purpose.
>
> (Mill, [1843]2011, loc. 476)

Mill goes on to suggest that we must follow the logic that because the sciences and our knowledge of them are imperfect, so too must be our definitions. He does stipulate that definitions should be placed at the beginning of the subject being studied, and that they should define the scope of the authors' inquiries (Mill, [1843]2011, loc. 476-480). It is in the spirit of Mill that the following definitions are outlined.

Knowledge and information

It is very difficult to answer the question 'what is knowledge?' (Burke, 2008: 11–13). Perhaps the first issue to consider is the distinction between *knowledge* and *information* as understanding the difference between these two concepts is especially important when it comes to both forensic science and criminal investigations. For example, physical evidence identified at a crime scene consists of an object that contains a multitude of information about that object (i.e. its chemical or compound structure). The forensic scientist, however, applies his or her knowledge in order to access the information within the object – by identifying its component parts, for instance. So, if police officers find a white substance at the home of a suspected drug dealer, the white substance contains information only, *not knowledge*. The forensic scientist will utilise his or her knowledge of particular techniques to classify that information and identify the substance – for example by using gas or high-pressured liquid chromatographic techniques (Bayne and Carlin, 2010; Jackson and Jackson, 2011). Information about the object is only accessed using knowledge. This conceptual difference between knowledge and information fits Burke's conceptualisation (2008:11–13). For Burke, the difference between *knowing how* and *knowing what* is important. He uses the term '"information" to refer to what is relatively "raw", specific and practical, while "knowledge" denotes what has been "cooked", processed or systematised by thought' (ibid.:11). Burke states that this distinction is only 'a relative one, since our brains process everything we perceive' (ibid.:11). What is important for Burke's social history of knowledge is the elaboration and classification of knowledge from the early modern period.[2] Another issue must be briefly mentioned before we move on to the history of scientific knowledge: when examining the growth and development of knowledge, it should be recognised that, in every culture, whilst there exists *dominant* knowledge, usually generated and controlled by the elites, there also exist *knowledges* in the plural. What is of specific interest for the purposes of this book, and in particular this chapter, is the 'competition, conflict and exchange between intellectual systems of academic elites and what might be called "alternative knowledges"' (ibid.:14). We see, for example, a number of conflicts between different *sites of knowledge* when reviewing the development of scientific ideas used for the purposes of resolving legal problems.

Science, the scientist and the scientific revolution

The second important definition for this text is that of *science* and its subsidiary concepts. What is regarded as *science* has gone through a number of definitional changes and developments over the last 500 years. A core question that should be considered is what we include under the banner of *science*. Today, the lay public's perception of *forensics* tends to be limited to the *science* that is often simplified in TV programmes such as *CSI Las Vegas, Miami or New York*. In short, the term forensics is often associated with a scientific technique of some kind. However, as noted in the introductory chapter, in recent years the term forensics has been added to a wide variety of disciplines or practices that are not technically part of what has traditionally been thought to be science: forensic accounting being an obvious example. So what do we mean by the term science?

Historically, the term *natural philosophy* was used to designate a group of disciplines that included subjects such as physics, chemistry, biology and physiology. This conceptualisation tended to exclude the disciplines of mathematics and medicine; the primary reason for this exclusion being the way Aristotle defined science, as 'those things that are independent of us and undergo change' (Gaukroger, 2009:1). Natural philosophy was therefore anything that developed knowledge about nature or natural objects on Earth. Today's forensic scientists make great use of the *knowledge* generated by the last 500 years of investigations undertaken by natural philosophers. Their work is the reason why the different elements of compounds found at a crime scene can be identified, which sometimes enables scientists to link a suspect to a victim or crime scene (White, 2004; Jackson and Jackson, 2011). It is because of the research and classification of the different species of plants that scientists can link particular batches of drugs to particular regions of the world (Saferstein, 2007; Jackson and Jackson, 2011). Natural philosophers, in short, engaged in *science*; and the origin of the word is from the Latin *scientia*, meaning *knowledge* or *wisdom*. According to Shapin (1998:5–6), in the seventeenth century the word science 'tended to designate any body of properly constituted knowledge (that is, knowledge of necessary universal truths)'. Furthermore, research on the objects of nature and the causal structure of the natural world were referred to, respectively, as *natural history* and *natural philosophy* (ibid.:6).

Gaukroger (2009:2) argues that the modern meaning of the term science is a form of professional activity, which is very different from the Latin term. The conceptualisation of the term *science* today is thus different from the past, as we would expect. According to van Doren (1991:187–189), there are three characteristics of modern science, and these three characteristics explain not only the concept *science* but also the term *scientist*. First, a certain type of individual with a specific perspective of the world practices science. Scientists are 'objective, unsentimental, unemotional' (ibid.:188). They are supposed not to let their emotions get in the way of their observations, and they carefully control their research using strict methods and controls and report findings so others can verify (or falsify) their results. Van Doren also notes that scientists should not claim more than they can prove (ibid.:188), and this has become an important mantra that forensic scientists should also adhere too. Unfortunately, later chapters will demonstrate where this is not always the case, with some forensic experts going beyond what they can actually prove. The second characteristic of science is that it deals almost exclusively with things or objects within the external world. It does not deal with feelings or what van Doren calls 'inner states' (ibid.:188), which is why psychology has had difficulty in establishing itself as a science, and is perhaps the reason why, in recent years, they have resorted to a fetishistic use of SPSS![3] Another aspect of dealing with objects in the natural world is the required ability to measure them. In short, the external world is anything that scientists can describe and measure using mathematics and statistics. Finally, science utilises 'special methods and a language for reporting results that is unique' (ibid.:188–189). The most common scientific method is the *experiment*, which consists of having an idea, framing it into a testable hypothesis and testing the hypothesis in a controlled environment which either verifies or falsifies the hypothesis (Conze, 1935:39–48; van Doren, 1991:188–189). The idea behind the experiment is so other scientists can follow the work and test the hypothesis and theory time and time again. According to Conze (1935:39), scientific methods are designed to uncover the 'most general laws of thinking and of reality'. He identified four laws or rules of scientific method (ibid.:40–48):

Table 2.1 Four laws of scientific method

1 Think concretely; for everything is concrete	3 Wherever we may find opposites we must look for their unity. Opposites are always in unity
2 Everything must be studied in its movement and development; for everything changes continually	4 We must seek the contradictions in the processes of nature and society; for everything is put into motion by contradictions

Below is an expanded discussion on the methodology of science, including the epistemological debate that arose between Mill and Whewell. The term *scientist* was only invented in the nineteenth century by William Whewell (1794–1866) and was not routinely used until the early twentieth century (Shapin, 1998; Gaukroger, 2009). Whewell invented the term in 1833 in response to a challenge by the poet S. T. Coleridge. Before this, the only expressions in use were 'natural philosopher' and 'man of science' (Shapin, 1998:5–6 fn. 3; Golinski, 2005; Snyder, 2006:2). What the above indicates is that whilst these are useful terms that contemporary commentators can retrospectively apply to specific historical activities, they were not used at the time when science and scientific knowledge was being constructed; it is an entirely modern term.

Epistemology and ontology

A final important definitional parameter that requires attention is related to philosophical issues of knowledge itself, involving two concepts that consider the *what, how* and *who* questions of knowledge construction. The first concept is called *epistemology* and is the branch of philosophy that studies the nature, scope and limitations of knowledge. It questions *what* we know and *how* we know it. Latour (2008:94) defines epistemology as 'the discipline that tries to understand how we manage to bridge the gap between representations and reality'. As I expand upon below, all human knowledge is a social construct, with some members of society in each generation creating knowledge that aids in solving – or at least trying to minimise – the social problems we face (Basalla, 1999; Golinski, 2005). Because of this, what we know and how we know it, or the epistemological basis of knowledge, is determined by social, cultural, economic, technological and political factors. When it comes to the history of science, there has been some general agreement that understanding the epistemological roots of scientific knowledge is necessary if one is to grasp current theories and methods. Some of the important questions asked by epistemology include: What is knowledge?; How is knowledge constructed?; How is knowledge acquired? A further area covered by epistemology is the extent to which it is possible for a given subject or entity to be known.

The second concept is *ontology*. Ontology often sits beside the concept of epistemology, with the assumption being that they are two peas in a similar *knowledge pod*. Ontology is the science of the principles of pure being; or, to put it another way, ontology is the metaphysics concerning the nature or essence of knowledge classification schemes. Not only does ontology study the categories of things that exist or may exist in some domain, but it also considers the specific language used to describe such categories. I think Karl Pearson summed up ontology best when he stated, in the preface to the third edition of his famous work *The Grammar of Science* ([1919]2007), that ontological categories such as the atom and ether 'are merely intellectual concepts solely useful for the purpose of describing our perceptual routine' (ibid., loc. 10). In this respect there is a clear relationship between our ontological categories and the language created to conceptualise them. For example, the periodic table of elements is a catalogue of everything tangible that is currently known to exist or, as Theodore Gray amusingly puts it, 'everything that can be dropped on your foot' (2009:5). The periodic table classifies the elements on the basis of their ontological essence. So, to begin with, the elements are determined by *universal* laws of quantum mechanics and are listed according to their atomic number.[4] The elements are placed into the following ontological categories: alkali metals, alkali earth metals, transition metals, poor metals, non-metals, halogens, noble gases and rare earth metals (see Figure 2.1). Each of these categories has its own physical characteristics that determine its *essence*, and we have created descriptive ontological categories for each of these characteristics (e.g. atomic radius, atomic weight, density, melting point and boiling point). As each element has different *essences* we have built up an entire ontological system that enables the identification of the elements even at the microscopic level. For example, it is known that Fluorine has the atomic number of 9; an atomic weight of 18.9984032; a density of 1696 g/l; a melting point of −219.6 degrees Celsius; and a boiling point of −188.12 degrees Celsius (ibid.). As will become apparent in later chapters, it is these ontological schemes that allow forensic science to aid criminal investigations through the analysis of trace evidence.

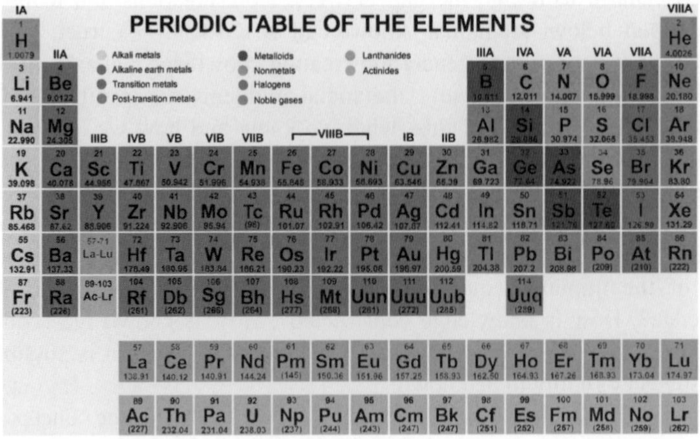

PERIODIC TABLE OF THE ELEMENTS

- Alkali metals
- Alkaline earth metals
- Transition metals
- Post-transition metals
- Metalloids
- Nonmetals
- Halogens
- Noble gases
- Lanthanides
- Actinides

(Periodic table of elements showing groups IA–VIIIA, IIIB–IIB, with element symbols H, He, Li, Be, B, C, N, O, F, Ne, Na, Mg, Al, Si, P, S, Cl, Ar, K, Ca, Sc, Ti, V, Cr, Mn, Fe, Co, Ni, Cu, Zn, Ga, Ge, As, Se, Br, Kr, Rb, Sr, Y, Zr, Nb, Mo, Tc, Ru, Rh, Pd, Ag, Cd, In, Sn, Sb, Te, I, Xe, Cs, Ba, La-Lu, Hf, Ta, W, Re, Os, Ir, Pt, Au, Hg, Tl, Pb, Bi, Po, At, Rn, Fr, Ra, Ac-Lr, Rf, Db, Sg, Bh, Hs, Mt, Uun, Uuu, Uub, Uuq; lanthanide series La, Ce, Pr, Nd, Pm, Sm, Eu, Gd, Tb, Dy, Ho, Er, Tm, Yb, Lu; actinide series Ac, Th, Pa, U, Np, Pu, Am, Cm, Bk, Cf, Es, Fm, Md, No, Lr)

Figure 2.1 The periodic table of elements[5]

Source: © www.shutterstock.com

Young has argued that there is no ontological reality when it comes to the concept of *crime* (Young, 1999:17–18); an argument that derives from his work within the critical criminology and left realist paradigms (Taylor and Taylor, 1973). He uses the concept of relativism to argue that 'the "same" behaviour can be constructed totally differently. Thus, for example, a serial killer could be either a psychopathic monster or a hero if dropping bombs daily in the Afghan War' (Young, 2002:254). To a certain degree Young is correct: behaviours can be viewed differently in different cultures, at different times and under different social contexts. Unfortunately, Young never informs us what definition of 'serial killer' he is using or of the simple fact that, if one took the common definitions which tend to include a cooling off period of more than 30 days (ibid.:254), this would not fit as a suitable definition to describe his example of daily bomb dropping. He also ignores the fact that ontological categories are merely intellectual concepts that we create in order to make sense of something so we can visualise and measure the *thing* we are interested in. What Young is advocating is a pure form of relativism, and he either refuses or fails to engage with the epistemological and ontological works of Whewell, Mill, Locke, James and Fleck. He has also not considered the more contemporary ontological debates of Quine (1969) or indeed the ontological ethnography of Latour (2008; also see Latour and Woolgar, 1986). What Young really fails to grasp is the time reliant, *bush-branch* conceptualisation of ontology (described below) as well as the link between ontology and language. Just because a US or UK soldier defines his or her actions as heroic does not preclude an ontological reality to this label.

Over the last 200 years or so, there have been numerous epistemological and ontological debates about the nature of knowledge, especially *scientific knowledge* and whether it is indeed possible to have *objective* knowledge of any-thing. Victorian society saw the height of these debates with some of the most important scientific minds developing their philosophies of science over the period of Queen Victoria's reign. These debates were especially important as they were intertwined with broader economic, technological and political develop-ments and, more specifically, the advent of capitalism and the rapid urbanisation and industrialisation that took place across the UK in the eighteenth and nine-teenth centuries (Marx, [1867]1990; Marx and Engels, [1892]1987; Thompson, 1991). In particular, the epistemological dispute over the methods of the sciences between Mill and Whewell is said to have captured the 'spirit of the age' enabling a contextual understanding of the 'intellectual spirit of Victorian Britain' (Snyder, 2006:3). These were important times, especially given Mill's claim that Britain was 'in a state of "intellectual anarchy," in which old systems of thought were being abandoned and new ones were yet to be fully accepted' (Snyder, 2006:2). Within the social sciences this epistemological debate has been framed as an attack on the positivist paradigm. Positivism developed out of the work of Auguste Comte (see below and Chapter 3), and was an attempt to develop the science of society – Comte's *sociology* – using the same methods that were being developed for the natural sciences ([1865]2009). At the end of the nineteenth century and into the twentieth century, critics of positivist methods and theories began to question the so-called *objectivity* of such theories from researchers such as Lombroso, Ferri, and Quetelet (Davie, 2005; Rafter, 2009). In particular, relativ-ism, interpretivism and social constructionism questioned our very ability to know things. I pick up on positivist ontology in relation to the development of criminology in the following chapter. In this chapter some of the core epistemo-logical and ontological developments relating to scientific knowledge are exam-ined. Before moving on to these, it is important to briefly discuss some of the important philosophical questions that have been raised since the Enlightenment period and the *age of reason* began in the seventeenth century.

How do we know our ontological categories are sufficient or, indeed, if they accurately reflect the true nature of the world we inhabit? We tend to use episte-mology, as defined above, to question knowledge itself. However, as Latour (2008) notes, epistemological debates are actually redundant; and in his chapter entitled 'A textbook case revisited – knowledge as a mode of existence' he attempts to 'de-epistemologize and to re-ontologize knowledge activity' (ibid.:87). In essence, the epistemological debate can be summarised from two orthogonal positions for what Latour calls 'knowledge-making pathways' (ibid.:94). The first position, labelled the *teleportation scheme*, stipulates a separation between the *object known* and the *knowing subject*, and knowledge within this system consists of two clear points of reference. The gap between object and subject, so what humans know about objects in nature, can move backwards and forwards, towards the object known or backwards towards the knowing subject. Latour, following the ideas laid down by James ([1907]1912) and Fleck ([1935]1981), is very criti-cal of any move towards the knowing subject for that indicates that we 'are thrown back to the prison of prejudices, paradigms, or presuppositions' (2008:95). As a result, we have to engage in *gap-bridging* by using our perceptions of things (the knowing subject) through the bias of our own presuppositions – or, teleporting between the two frames of reference. According to Latour, the epistemological problem with the teleportation scheme is bridging the 'gap between two distinct domains totally unrelated to one another, mind and nature' (ibid.:95). He suggests that it is not possible to bridge this gap as it is 'artificial' and has been created 'due to the wrong positioning of the knowledge acquisition pathway' (ibid.:94). The implication of this was succinctly expressed in a personal communication with Berkeley philosopher John Searle, who stated that 'science raises no epistemological question' (2000, cited in Latour 2008:94). The evidence supporting this is the simple fact that science is only concerned with *what* is known and *how* society can use this knowledge; it is certainly not bothered by constructionist questions of '*whether* it knows objectively or not' (ibid.:94) as, in the end, *tangible and useful* results attest to the accuracy of knowledge.

Another problem with the teleportation approach is that it fails to account for knowledge as travelling across the vector of time: that knowledge is part of the Heraclitean[6] flow of time is perhaps one of its most important elements. As Latour points out, when it comes to an unknown statement or entity, once you 'allow for the addition of *time, instrument, colleagues* and *institutions*, you come to certainty' (ibid.:88 – original emphasis). The American philosopher William James (1842–1910), in *Essays in Radical Empiricism* ([1907]1912), introduced the notion of knowledge as a *trajectory* or *vector* to illustrate the fact that when it comes to our knowledge about any *object* under study, our initial perceptions of it cannot be known; however, eventually we *will* know if our initial perceptions were right. The concept of *rectification* is used here to describe the process of retroactive certification of knowledge by others across 'a continuous vector where *time* is of the essence' (Latour, 2008:88 – original emphasis). This is explained as follows:

> Take any knowledge at any time: you don't know if it's good or not, accurate or not, real or virtual, true or false. Allow for a successive, continuous path to be drawn between several versions of the knowledge claims and you will be able to decide fairly well. At time *t* it cannot be decided, at time *t* + 1, *t* + 2, *t* + *n*, it has become decidable provided of course you engage along the path leading to a 'chain of experiences'.
>
> (Ibid.: 88)

Where James saw knowledge generation as a result of rectification by 'chain[s] of experience' along the continuous vector of time, Ludwig Fleck used the term *thought collective*. In *Genesis and Development of a Scientific Fact* ([1935]1981), Fleck introduces us to the notion of science as being like an 'excited conversation' that takes place across time ([1935]1981:15 cited in Latour, 2008:91).

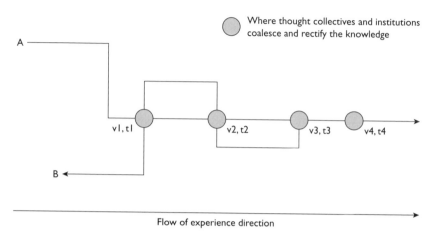

A

Where thought collectives and institutions
coalesce and rectify the knowledge

v1, t1

v2, t2

v3, t3

v4, t4

B

Flow of experience direction

Figure 2.2 The continuous scheme of knowledge

This conversation is a continuous scheme and involves many different voices with many different *branches*, speaking simultaneously, trying to get their voices heard and, over a period of time, eventually creating a consensus about a domain of knowledge. Fleck's conceptualisation of *thought collective* is essentially the 'heterogeneous practices laboratory studies have since rendered familiar to us' (Latour, 2008:91).

The notion of a continuous scheme for ontological developments in science does not mean a linear directionality. Instead, knowledge acquisition pathways originate from all sorts of different points and travel in different directions; however, these pathways must intersect to allow for the thought collective to rectify the knowledge. For example, under Latour's continuous scheme, knowledge version 1 (v1) at time 1 (t1) will continue to move forward and, under the right circumstances will intersect with version 4 at time 4. Thus, at t4, v4 rectifies the initial conceptualisation of v1 that was made at t1; but it has to have passed through versions v2 and v3 at t2 and t3 in order to be rectified at v4/t4. It should be remembered that versions 1 to 4 at times 1 to 4 usually would have involved other individuals and institutions – or the chains of experience/thought collective. As can be seen from the simplified example illustrated in Figure 2.2 (see Latour, 2008:95–99), there are two knowledge acquisition pathways (A and B) that move forward through time and which intersect at given points. At each intersection, networks of people and institutions coalesce, and this is when knowledge is rectified (or not rectified). The usefulness of the model proposed by Latour is that it accounts for the continuous development of knowledge through time, with little need for the epistemological questions raised above. When it comes to creating accurate ontological categories for scientific knowledge, Latour identifies six elements that are required (ibid.:94).

1   Knowledge is a *vector* through time.
2   *Ideas* are there and have to be taken seriously but only at the *beginning of a chain of experience*.
3   *Successive rectification* is the substantial part of the knowledge acquisition pathways.
4   *Rectification* by colleagues is essential.
5   *Institutionalisation* is a requirement and consists of 'becoming familiar, black-boxing novelty in instruments, tuning, standardizing, getting used to the state of affairs'.
6   *Direct perception* is the end not the beginning of fact genesis.

The remainder of this chapter deals with some of the key ontological issues within the history and philosophy of science whilst the rest of the chapters in part 1 consider some of the key knowledge acquisition pathways that have taken place within the domains of criminology, forensic and criminal investigations.

Knowledge as reification

All human activity tends to be social activity so it is impossible to think about developments in scientific knowledge and practice without locating them in their social context. This social context is influenced by a myriad of factors such as religious belief systems, political ideologies, gender and social class to name just a few (Berger and Luckmann, 1991; Burke, 2008; Latour, 2008). Early conceptualisations of science removed the nature of its methodology from any form of context or social/political influence. Gaukroger (2009:11) argues that the 'gradual assimilation of all cognitive values to scientific ones' is a distinctive feature of Western modernity. He suggests that the West's sense of superiority in the early nineteenth century was largely based upon a conceptualisation of science as appealing 'solely to reason and experience, and is as a consequence untinged by historical or cultural factors' (ibid.:11). In short, science was supposed to have no context or history and was answerable only to reason. Thinking about science in this way led to the association between scientific values, morality and democracy (see below for an expansion of this issue). Unfortunately, there have been some dark episodes in human history that demonstrate that science and the application of scientific knowledge are not, as Weber suggested, *value free* (Gerth and Mills, 1993) or separate from historical or cultural factors (for example, the eugenics movement and Nazi experimentation – see Soloway, 1990; Lifton, 2000; Black, 2004; Bashford and Levine, 2012).

For the purpose of this book, it is a given that science is historically situated and that its development and the ideas and theories produced, as well as its practice, are all historically embedded in the social activity undertaken within a specific historical context. However, as Latour (2008:84) amusingly notes, stating that science is historically situated will usually produce nothing more than a bored, yawning acceptance, similar to the fear of the death slide to intellectual entropy that one might feel watching Saturday night TV and its production of yet another group of failed singers, one of which will inevitably produce a moronic Christmas no. 1 *hit-parade* single (the anomaly of the wonderful 'Killing in the name' aside)! What is required is a more sophisticated theoretical understanding of our constructed scientific knowledge. To this end, I find Berger and Luckmann's (1991) concept of reification extremely useful. In their famous treatise on the sociology of knowledge, entitled *The Social Construction of Reality* ([1966]1991), they outline reification as:

> The apprehension of human phenomena as if they were things, that is, in non-human or possibly supra-human terms. Another way of saying this is that reification is the apprehension of the products of human activity *as if* they were something other than human products – such as facts of nature, results of cosmic laws, or manifestations of devine will. Reification implies that man is capable of forgetting his own authorship of the human world, and, further, that the dialectic between man, the producer, and his products is lost to consciousness. The reified world is, by definition, a dehumanized world. It is experienced by man as a strange facticity, an *opus alienum* over which he has no control rather than as the *opus proprium* of his own productive activity.
>
> (Ibid.:106)

This passage illustrates that all human knowledge is *made* by humans, and even when we construct our *objective reality* through the creation of ontological categories, reification of those objects 'is never far away' (ibid.:106). Thus, knowledge, 'however objectivicated' is still made by humans and can therefore be 'remade by them' (ibid.:106); and it is this fact that ultimately fits with the underlying philosophy of scientific knowledge – that it changes and develops as our conceptions of the world are tested and empirically tested. I return to this issue later in the chapter. I also return to the concept of reification in Chapter 7 when I discuss the concepts of information, material and evidence.

Science is collectively practiced within specific social contexts (van Doren, 1991; Shapin, 1998; Burke, 2008; Gaukroger, 2009), and it is exactly the same for forensic science and forensic criminology. Forensic scientists operate within a number of specific contexts – for example, the laboratory and sometimes within the courtroom. As I will illustrate in chapters 10 and 11, both these contexts are different and have different cultural and organisational rules that affect the way scientific knowledge is developed and interpreted. The context in which scientific knowledge operates is therefore important. Take what we know about crime and criminality for example: criminological knowledge is largely determined by a complex interplay between the social circumstances and context within which a crime is committed, the individual psychology of offenders and victims, as well as structural forces such as legal definitions of crime, police resources and political agendas (Sutherland and Cressey, 1960; Wilson and Herrnstein, 1998; Andrews and Bonta, 2003; Bartol and Bartol, 2008; Jones, 2008). Just like debates about scientific knowledge, explanations about crime and criminality are historically and contextually situated. One can find numerous criminological examples throughout history to illustrate this point – for instance, homosexuality and rape within marriage. The Sexual Offences Act 1967 legalised gay sex and this had a dramatic social and cultural impact on lifestyle choices as well as altering elements of criminological and psychiatric conceptions of sexual deviance (Davies, 1975; Plummer, 1992; Thompson, 1994b). Indeed, many of these changes took place and were contested against within the courtroom, the Spanner Case being one example (Thompson, 1994b). Marital rape was not criminalised in England until 1991, but the reconceptualisation of this previously legal act as a crime has added a further contextual and behavioural dimension to typologies of rapists, thereby adding to our stock of knowledge and understanding of this crime. These examples and many others illustrate the importance of examining how knowledge is constructed and the context in which it is constructed.

A brief history of the development of scientific knowledge

Any history of the development science could go as far back as ancient Greece. Discussions of Greek philosophy are usually the domain of philosophers or historians of science; and some may even argue that such ideas should be left in the past and are of no use today, especially in an applied sense for practitioners. However, historical scholarship on the sciences informs us of a great deal. For example, historical research has noted that the ideas of Aristotle and Plato played a key role in the emergence of what could be loosely called a *scientific culture*. I am thinking here of Magnus and Aquinas' attempt to establish a Christianised form of Aristotelianism in the thirteenth century (van Doren, 1991:119–126; Shapin, 1998:15–64; Gaukroger, 2009:47–70). There are so many important historical figures, ideas, theories and developments that it is not possible to cover them all in any great depth here. Just where should a history of this kind begin? I have opted to provide a very simple overview of some the core ideas and developments that drove scientific knowledge and which became important for criminology, criminal investigations and forensic science. Of particular interest to forensic criminology is the development of a *scientific culture*, the creation of the multitude of *academic disciplines* and the different types of techniques that produce ideas and theories about the natural and social worlds. I move around different time periods, but the rest of this chapter concentrates mainly on the developments from the Renaissance period up until the end of the nineteenth century. Chapters 3, 4 and 5 examine the basic history of forensic science, criminal investigation and criminology, and these chapters review some of the core individuals who, either on their own or collectively, developed *scientific* knowledge and practice in order to detect and solve crime and to punish offenders.

The history that follows is the epistemological and ontological foundation of these criminological and forensic developments.

The scientific 'revolution'

Before moving on to the components of the scientific revolution, a brief word on the term is required. Shapin (1998:2) has rightly pointed out that the term 'scientific revolution' was not in common usage until 1939, and it was not until 1954 that the term was used in the main titles of two important books – A. Rupert Hall's *The Scientific Revolution* (1966) and J. D. Bernal's *The Scientific and Industrial Revolutions* (1977) (both cited in Shapin, 1998). Seventeenth-century practitioners who actually undertook activities that developed scientific methods and knowledge certainly did not use the term scientific revolution. There are specific parts of forensic criminology that operate within the framework of a scientific culture. Obviously, forensic science is one element, but there are also elements of criminology that derive from the scientific paradigm. This section examines the aetiological origins of scientific knowledge through the historical lens of the scientific revolution. Many writers have used the term *scientific revolution* to denote a period in which specific forms of knowledge were created that were significantly different from previous forms of knowledge, such as religious doctrine and metaphysics (van Doren, 1991; Couvalis, 1997; Shapin, 1998; Burke, 2008; Gaukroger, 2009). As a period in human history, the scientific revolution has been regarded by many as one of the most important so far. Butterfield, for instance, thought that the scientific revolution outshone 'everything since the rise in Christianity and reduces the Renaissance and Reformation to the rank of mere episode' (cited in Shapin, 1998:1). For Hall (1954), the scientific revolution was nothing short of 'an *a pirori* redefinition of the objects of philosophical and scientific inquiry' (cited in Shapin, 1998:2). It is also the period where there was a fundamental shift in intellectual values in the Western world, with physics and mathematics becoming the 'pre-eminent form of learning' (Gaukroger, 2009:1) and where the cognitive values of the West generally came to be shaped around scientific ones. This shift was said to have taken place from around the seventeenth century onwards. Today, forensic criminology and its disciplinary components rely heavily on the scientific ideas, theories, methods and knowledge developed during this period.

Mechanical corpuscularianism

The scientific revolution is said to have happened sometime between the late sixteenth and the early eighteenth century and has been viewed by some as the beginning of the modern period for the Western world (van Doren, 1991; Shapin, 1998; Burke, 2008; Gaukroger, 2009). It is also the period where what was known, how we knew it and how we applied this knowledge went through dramatic changes. In short, the epistemological and ontological base of knowledge was altered. During the Enlightenment period, from the seventeenth to the eighteenth century, philosophers began to believe that the scientific method would lead to a greater understanding of the external physical world as well as human nature itself (Couvalis, 1997:1). Faith was placed in the ability of scientific knowledge to provide humankind with guidance on the ethical principles that would enable us to lead better lives and create a better social system. More importantly, science would replace metaphysics, ethics and political philosophy (ibid.:1) and become the dominant form of knowledge. Shapin (1998:13) identifies four interrelated aspects that, from the late sixteenth century, not only changed knowledge about the natural world but also brought about changes in the way knowledge was secured. First was the increasing use of mechanical metaphors to describe processes that occur in the natural world, which Shapin calls the 'mechanization of nature' (ibid.:13). It was here that Aristotle's teleology was replaced by a conceptualisation of nature based upon the characteristics of a machine (ibid.:30). This became so central to modern scientific thinking that many referred to it as the *mechanical philosophy*. Two examples in the seventeenth century illustrate the importance of seeing nature as possessing machine-like qualities – the invention of the clock and the development of the suction pump. The development of the clock, Shapin (ibid.:32) argues, appealed to many early natural philosophers and is thus central to the scientific revolution: '[t]he hours told by the mechanical clock were constant over space and time, taking no heed of the natural rhythms of the universe or of the varying situated practices of human life' (ibid.:33).

Many scientists used the mechanical nature of the clock in their work. In 1605 the German Astronomer Kepler noted that the machine of the universe was 'not similar to a divine animated being, but similar to a clock' (ibid.:33). In the 1630s the French philosopher and mathematician René Descartes produced a number of causal analogies between the 'movements of mechanical clocks and those of all natural bodies' (ibid.:33). Today it might seem a tad odd to think of the mechanics of a clock as being analogous to the workings of the natural world. However, many philosophers at the time thought it was an appropriate metaphor to use for various reasons. For example, the clock 'was an exemplar of uniformity and regularity' (ibid.:36), which mirrored the orderly patterns of the natural world. Francis Bacon's *Novum Organon Scientiarum* (1620) used the mechanical analogy within his empiricist epistemology when he suggested that there could be a 'mechanical method of discovery' (Snyder, 2006:78; also see Bacon, [1620]2009). Shapin's important analysis suggests that the mechanisation of nature differed significantly from the seventeenth-century conceptualisation of traditional natural philosophy, which focused on anthropomorphism and animism and 'ascribed to nature and its components the capacities of purpose, intention, or sentience' (1998:37).

The second aspect of changes in knowledge was the *depersonalisation* of natural knowledge. This is where a noticeable and 'growing separation between human subjects and the natural objects of their knowledge' began to take shape (ibid.:13) – in particular, the distinction between mundane human experience and views of what nature is really like. Third, there was a shift towards the *mechanisation of knowledge*. This included the development and application of explicitly formulated rules of method whose aim was the systematisation of knowledge production that eliminated the effects of human interests and emotions (ibid.:13). A classic historical example of this is Descartes' use of geometry as a model of how best to conduct an inquiry (Couvalis, 1997:1). The fourth and final aspect is the expectation that this new natural knowledge would be used to *achieve moral, social and political ends*. The caveat here is that because of the nature of dispassionate scientists, using explicitly formulated rules of methods without emotive interests, the knowledge that is produced is itself disinterested (ibid.:13). These four aspects not only challenged the epistemological basis of knowledge but they also enabled thinkers to expand their horizons and conceptualise a whole new type of knowledge that would soon overtake old conceptualisations about the natural world.

Renaissance and Enlightenment conceptualisations of science and knowledge

Having relevant *knowledge* means we can solve problems, and the education system – from school to university – is still the most common way that knowledge is systematised and taught from generation to generation. Much of the history of science therefore examines the debates and discussions between the dominant theorists of the time and examines competing ideas and theories. Whilst these issues are important, they tend to downplay or ignore the social, cultural and political context in which such debates arise. As mentioned above, all *knowledge* is a social construction by humans and is therefore based on how individuals formulate or conceptualise problems, how they collect data to *prove* their conceptualisations and how they eventually place *things* into labelled *categories*. The social context is therefore crucial to any understanding of knowledge, as it will often have a direct influence and shape what sort of knowledge is produced and reified. This is especially true when it comes to criminological knowledge (Wiener, 1994). Why do certain ideas develop and take hold at particular times, whilst others do not? For example, why did Lombroso's theories regarding the *criminal man* receive so much positive attention during the late nineteenth century? As will be demonstrated in Chapter 3, the broader social context and the organisation of science throughout Europe as well as the political meaning of scientific ideas helped Lombroso's theories gain momentum and *scientific* credibility (Davie, 2005; Rafter, 2009). The same can also be said for the 'harder' sciences. Kuhn (1996:7) notes, for instance, how Maxwell's equations were as revolutionary as Einstein's, yet were strongly resisted at the time. Some of the key moments of relevance are discussed below, but, before examining these, it is wise to consider some of the core ideas that came from early social studies of science. The reason why this is important will become obvious to the more attuned reader, for the ideas briefly discussed below form some of the ideological basis of today's understanding of core scientific principles in forensic practice.

In his groundbreaking work on the structure of scientific revolutions, Kuhn suggested that normal science 'is predicated on the assumption that the scientific community knows what the world is like' (1996:5). However, he also 'denied the possibility of a rational account of conceptual revolutions', seeing groups of scientific theories and concepts more in terms of a *collective psychology* than proof of the existence of an objective reality (Kuhn, 1996; Turner, 2008). For centuries, literature on the social character of science has debated practical problems regarding the organisation of science as well as the political meaning of science (Turner, 2008:33). These debates have tended to form one of two conflicting positions: the first stipulates that science is a distinctive 'method that can be extended to social and political life'; whilst the second saw science 'as a distinctive form of activity with its own special problems' that did not 'provide a model for social and political life' (ibid:33).

To begin with, the *fons et origo* of the social explanatory interest in science is found in Francis Bacon (1561–1626). Bacon was an English philosopher, scientist, jurist and author and is largely remembered for his ideas about the *inductive method,* which he started to outline in his early text *Cogitata et Vista* (1607). Unfortunately, the Renaissance period in which Bacon was writing had an absurd style whereby political arguments were presented in terms of 'fiction' and 'allegory' and often 'shrouded in ambiguities' (Turner, 2008:34). Bacon's vision of a political order saw scientists given 'power by an enlightened ruler in his House of Solomon in "The New Atlantis"' (cited in Turner, 2008:33). As Turner points out, this political 'fiction' had a 'practical effect on the attempts by the Royal Society in London to distinguish itself by its methodological practices and internal governance as a type of political body in relation to the Crown' (Turner, 2008:33). For Bacon, the methodological practice that distinguished science was that it was a 'technique of assembling facts, generalizing about them, and ascending to higher level generalizations from them' (ibid.:34). He argued that science should be pursued collectively and cooperatively; that the scientific mind should be free from prejudices or assumptions; and that a social science was also possible (ibid.:34). It was within *Novum Organum Scientiarum*[7] (1620) that Bacon fully developed a method of scientific experimentalism and discovery through the process of induction. In the preface to *Novum* he outlined his concern over two arguments relating to knowledge of the natural world:

> Those who have taken upon them to lay down the law of nature as a thing already searched out and understood, whether they have spoken in simple assurance or professional affection, have therein done philosophy and the sciences great injury.

> (Bacon, [1620]2009, loc. 2)

The second group that concerned him were those that 'asserted that absolutely nothing could be known' (ibid., loc. 2). Bacon's *Novum* project was an attempt to move away from Aristotle's 'syllogistic method', or deductive reasoning, which consisted of a major premise, a minor premise and a conclusion; for example, all humans are mortal (major), I am human (minor), therefore I am mortal (conclusion). In short, Bacon was attacking the classic logicians. He rejected the classic method of science called the 'anticipation of nature' (*anticipatio naturae*), which was the cultivation of 'the most general axioms' from 'the senses and particulars' which were taken for granted and 'immovable' (ibid., 104). This involved the following process: starting from senses and particulars and moving quickly to general axioms, which 'proceeds to judgments and to the discovery of middle axioms' (ibid., loc. 104). Bacon rejected this method on the basis of his belief that 'logic fixes errors instead of disclosing truths' (ibid., loc. 13) and that logical deduction was practically useless as it was often predicated on faulty notions that were founded upon hastily abstracted facts (ibid., loc. 62–104). He argued that anticipation logic and knowledge was beset by four idols – *idols of the tribe, cave, market place and theatre*; and each of these idols played a role in refracting, distorting and discolouring the laws of nature (ibid., loc. 146–169). To put it more succinctly, what Bacon highlighted through his 'idols' thesis was simply that scientific knowledge using the deductive/syllogistic method alone created false axioms that were based upon faulty dogmas, beliefs and prejudices as well as the individual's own sensory failings. Indeed, he even suggested that any knowledge predicated purely on the human senses, and which did not move beyond what can be observed, was destined to fail because the senses were dull, incompetent and deceptive (ibid., loc. 216). However, Bacon did recognise that anticipation knowledge was more powerful because observable phenomena were psychologically easier for humans to understand: what can be seen is familiar, and what is familiar is more easily accepted.

The problems Bacon saw with anticipation knowledge motivated the development of his *Novum*, or new instrument, which became known as the inductive method. Bacon labelled this the 'interpretation of nature' (*interpretatio naturae*), which was a means by which we can ascend to axioms. Bacon proposed that as man was 'the servant and interpreter of nature' he should establish the laws of nature through 'progressive stages of certainty' that involved evidence gathered by the senses (observations) and solidified through the process of correction (testing and experimentation) (ibid., loc. 62). In Book I, part X of 'Aphorisms', Bacon notes how the underlying laws of nature are more subtle 'than the subtlety of the senses and understanding' (ibid., loc. 83). The process of science, therefore, should be slow and involve the toil of gathering information through the use of the new *instrument* that invigorates that which the senses cannot sense (ibid., loc. 83–104). The double starting point for this new instrument was empiricism and rationality, and, as with *anticipatio naturae*, the process begins with the senses and particulars. However, instead of a direct move to general axioms, there is a middle stage that consists of the 'gradual and unbroken ascent' to general axioms through painstaking study and experimentation. Bacon noted how 'axioms duly and orderly formed from particulars easily discover the way to new particulars' and that this was the very essence of 'active science' (ibid., 115). Therefore, he wanted to replace our reliance on anticipation knowledge with an inductive interpretation of nature. In order to do this, Bacon suggested that science should move away from the examination of forms and should concentrate on looking at the particles and structure of matter (ibid. 216–250). This, for Bacon, was the true task of science, and his method was one of openness and fluidity towards this task:

> He believed that theories should be advanced to explain whatever data were available in a particular domain. These theories should preferably concern the underlying physical, causal mechanisms and ought, in any case, to go beyond the data which generated them. They are then tested by drawing out new predictions, which, if verified in experience, may confirm the theory and may eventually render it certain, at least in the sense that it becomes very difficult to deny.
>
> (Urbach, 1987:49)

Within these ideas is the germ of what would become experimental science, which was famously epitomised in the work of the English natural philosopher, chemist, physicist and inventor, Robert Boyle (1627–1691). If you took Bacon's conclusions about the dullness and incompetence of the senses to their logical conclusion, the only way to move beyond these problems was to develop measuring instruments and techniques that could be used in experiments that would properly visualise and measure the components of the natural world. For example, in 1660, Boyle published *New Experiments Physico-Mechanical, Touching the Spring of the Air, and its Effects*, which was a landmark in experimental science. In this text he described the first controlled experiments of the effects of reducing the pressure of the air in which, for the first time, it was possible to observe physical and physiological processes at both normal and reduced barometric pressures. As Hunter (2009:2) suggests:

> Boyle was extraordinarily ingenious in devising experiments which would reveal significant information about phenomena. . . . he was also ever alert to instruments which would enable him to manipulate nature and thus draw conclusions about it that would not be available in normal circumstances.

Whilst both Bacon and Boyle's role in the history of science was the development of experimentalist science, others have criticised Bacon's conceptualisation of syllogistic logic and induction. For example, De Maistre has recently argued syllogism and induction 'differ essentially in name only' (1998:16), and that Bacon's inductive method was not actually a 'new instrument', but was really a 'shortened syllogism' and nothing more (ibid.:15).

In the eighteenth century, the Marquis de Condorcet (1743–1794) reworked the Baconian vision in his *Outlines of a Historical View of the Progress of the Human Mind* (1795) and raised the idea of science as an 'engine of human progress' (Turner, 2008:34). Condorcet saw scientific rivalry as a normal product of the 'passions of scientists for their work', but he also noted how these passions could take on 'pathological institutional forms', with institutions such as universities creating dictatorial centres of knowledge that fail to fully realise talented individuals who do not follow the paradigmatic visions set out by their professors (ibid., 34). He was also concerned with the need for science to be autonomous from the political process and free from political control, and this idea was largely based on the politics of financing and 'on the consideration that only scientists have the capacity to govern scientific activity' (ibid.:34). Despite his views on the need for the autonomy of science, Condorcet was aware that, in order to maximise the benefits of science, state action was required. He also saw the importance of education as a way to extend the benefits of science and enable citizens to 'think on their own' (cited in Turner, 2008:35); although he did recognise that there would always be an epistemic difference between citizens and scientists. Condorcet effectively foresaw the development of the *expert* who would rule over the general public, albeit with a non-authoritarian hand.

With Condorcet's ideas came the implication that social knowledge based upon scientific evidence would supersede politics, and this placement of politics against science became problematic for many (Turner, 2008:35). After the French revolution and the restructuring of French society between 1789 and 1799, France restored the primacy of politics and began to suppress what was regarded as 'dangerous science', thereby rejecting the 'extension of science to politics' (ibid.:35). One of the consequences of this newly found dominance from left-wing political groups was 'that social and political speculation, and in particular speculation on science and politics' fell to those outside the new establishment and on the 'margins of science' (ibid.:35). One such thinker was fellow Frenchman Saint-Simon, who took many of Condorcet's ideas and radicalised them: for instance, his anti-liberal and anti-political idea that future rule 'of man over man would be replaced by "the administration of things"' where 'capacities were fitted to tasks' determined by scientific rationality (ibid.:35). His secretary, Auguste Comte, properly formulated Saint-Simon's ideas and generated a complete intellectual system from his mentor's ideas, which became the basis of positivism and are discussed in the following chapter. In particular, he added some venomous hostility to the liberal squeamishness over authority and consent, introducing the simple idea that 'if science is correct, and science includes knowledge of the social worlds and politics, why shouldn't scientists rule over the ignorant' (ibid.:36). This went against a central liberal tenet that 'everyone should be permitted to have their opinion heard' (ibid.:37). The catch-22 created by this epistemological debate was that if science were to rule the ignorant, in order to better the lives of everyone, then the rules of science must be imposed like the dogmas of religion. Comte's logic was sound, although it sat uncomfortably with those who were trying to move away from years of religious and state repression from the Dark and Middle Ages (Gaukroger, 2009). Despite these debates, the Renaissance and Enlightenment periods should be regarded as the beginning of a rich period in the discovery and construction of scientific knowledge; most of which centred on the uncovering of *natural kinds*.

The naming of names and the creation of *natural kinds*

When it comes to the history of the development of scientific knowledge, the creation of ontological classification systems of animals, mammals, plants and elements has to be one of the most important aspects that impact upon forensic investigations. Without a classification scheme, including information about the characteristics of known animal/mammal species, plants or materials found on earth, there would be no forensic science: and there would be no ability to identify trace evidence found at a crime scene. Furthermore, our ability to undertake micro-biological and micro-chemical analyses for comparison and identification purposes, owes everything to the work of natural philosophers. For centuries, some of the most brilliant minds have engaged in what can only be described as an immense measuring and cataloguing of the natural world, all in an attempt to find the underlying laws of nature. The concept of universal laws of nature dates back to the early Greek philosophies of Socrates and his ontological heirs Plato and Aristotle. These great thinkers used the idea of natural laws in a slightly different way: in order to argue for the development of laws of society that were natural and free from the ideology of the political economy (ibid.). Others used the idea to try and uncover universal laws of nature, or, to put it another way, to find out about what nature actually consists of.

The taxonomic mission

In *Dry Store Room No. 1*, Fortey (2008) discusses some of the secrets behind the history of the 'taxonomic mission' of the Natural History Museum. In wonderfully eloquent prose, Fortey highlights the importance of the work of natural philosophers in creating a 'reference system for nature' (ibid.:31) and the vast collections of animal, plant and elements which attest to the project of the 'naming of names'. He outlines the taxonomic[8] mission as simply 'to make known all the species on Earth' (ibid.:31) and argues that recognising and naming of species is the first step to 'understanding the complex interactions of the biological world' (32). For over 2,000 years, work on developing a comprehensive taxonomic system of the natural world has involved the observation and collection of millions of species of animals, mammals, plants and elements. These observations have led to the naming of *natural kinds* and their placement into classification or taxonomic schemes based on their observable characteristics. Some of these collections are huge and continue to grow as new species are identified. For example, Fortey notes that 'according to William T. Stearn the insect collections had grown from 2,250,000 specimens in 1912 to some 22,500,000 in 1980' (ibid.:45). Much like the natural world of their discoveries, the history of the taxonomists is rich and varied: too varied to comprehensively cover here. I will provide a couple of examples simply to illustrate the importance of the 'naming of names' (ibid.:30–72) for the history of scientific knowledge and more specifically the development of forensic science.

The importance of the taxonomic mission is that it was driven by the single belief that there is order to the 'dizzying variety of the natural world' (Pavord, 2009:19), and this belief is still present today. One of the biggest issues facing taxonomists is how to create ontological categories that accurately describe whatever natural kind is under investigation. For this you need both a *method* and a naming *system*, and some methods and systems take many years to develop and sometimes involve intense critical debate. An excellent example to illustrate the importance of the taxonomic mission is the creation of plant names for all known plant species. One of the first individuals to undertake a serious attempt at this 'naming plant names' was Theophrastus (371–287 BC). He attempted to answer two big questions: 'What have we got?' and 'How do we differentiate between these things?' (ibid.:19). In this sense, he was the 'first person to discuss plants in relationship to each other, not just in terms of their usefulness to man' (ibid.:19). He spent an entire lifetime observing and collecting different species of plants in order to answer the questions: 'How do we define plants?'; and 'Which parts of the plants are most useful when it comes to classifying them?' (ibid.:24). Between the third and second century, BC Theophrastus published *Enquiry into Plants* and *On the Causes of Plants*, both of which constitute the most important early contributions to botanical science. These works were the first systematisation of the botanical world, and his observations and research laid the groundwork for the next 1,600 years of research, experimentation and naming of plants – important work that was taken up by alchemists, herbalists and natural philosophers (ibid.). In the seventeenth century, John Ray provided an answer to Theophrastus' second question (how to differentiate), when he outlined six rules for the classification of plants in *Methodus plantarum emendata* (1703). He suggested a classification scheme based upon their 'natural affinities' (cited in Pavord, 2009:303):

- plant names must be changed as little as possible to avoid confusion and mistakes;
- the characteristics of a group must be clearly defined and not rely on comparison;
- characteristics must be obvious and easy to grasp;

- groups approved should be preserved;
- related plants should not be separated; and
- the characteristics used to define should not be unnecessarily increased.

Ray strongly argued for the importance of method before system, primarily because of a belief in the idea that any classification system is only as good as the method used to produce it. His method was simple; the classification of names should identify and describe plants as a first step (Pavord, 2009:290). Once the plants were described, identification and 'agreement of the principal parts' could take place (ibid.:296). For Ray, the principal parts included the 'number of seeds and seed-vessels developed from each flower,' the form of the flower, the corolla[9] and the calyx[10]. He created the terms 'monocotyledon' and 'dicotyledon', which describe plants whose seeds produce seedlings with one leaf (mono) or those that sprout two (di), and these terms are still in use today (ibid.:296). Just to give an indication as to the depth of Ray's work, his *Historia planatarum* (1686–1704) consisted of three volumes running to 'more than 2,000 pages' (ibid.:297). According to Pavord (ibid.:304–305), Ray provided a 'more solid foundation for future scholars to build on' and 'shifted the study of plants away from superstition and towards science'. Unfortunately, however sophisticated Ray's *method* was, taxonomists still faced a major problem when it came to creating classification schemes. Taxonomic systems are systematic ways to distinguish names and groups of species in the natural world: 'in effect, a register of biodiversity' (ibid.:307). However, any taxonomy must 'operate in a universal language' (ibid.:307). Ray provided the *method* for naming, but it was the Swedish botanist, physician and zoologist Carl von Linné (1701–1778) who would provide the unifying scheme.

Von Linné created the scientific system for naming and classifying plants and animals in the eighteenth century. Commonly known as the Linnaeus system, it brought standardisation to how plants and animals are named by using a Latinised binomial model. Scientific names have traditionally taken 'Latin or Greek form' (Fortey, 2008:48) largely because scientific communication and the 'language understood by the intellectual classes across Europe' was Latin (ibid.:48). Linné introduced his system in *Species planatarum*, which was published in 1753, and it was here that he put forward the argument that 'all the name had to do was designate. It did not have to describe' (Pavord, 2009:306). His Latin binomial system was actually not his invention, but was haphazardly used by Theophrastus in terms such as '"mekon e melaina," "mekon e keratitis," "mekon e rhoias"' as well as by other natural philosophers such as Brunfels, Fuchs, Cesalpino and Bauhin (ibid.:306). Linné's system is well known today, despite the fact that many people using the words may not know of its creator; for example, *Homo sapiens* uses Linné's system, consisting of a simple binomial which incorporates a two-module word made up of the *genus* and *species* name. First is the genus name, the plural of which is genera, from the word generic. Second is the species name, taken from the word specific (Fortey, 2008:48-51; Pavord, 2009:308–310).

What is especially interesting is that Linné not only suggested a system of naming but he also attempted to produce a method for describing plants based upon 'the number and arrangement of the stamens and carpels within a flower' (Pavord, 2009:308). Unfortunately, this method was nowhere near as useful as Ray's (ibid.:308), so what we end up with is Ray's classification method and Linné's naming system. Pavord goes on to note that the method and system for naming plants, which thereby creates our ontological categories, remained fluid because 'nobody could agree on the most convincing indicator of their similarities and differences' (ibid.:310). This led to alternative ways to identify and name plants:

> Phytochemical properties have been proposed as the key. By bringing together nasturtium and oil-seed rape (both contain mustard oil), taxonomists have returned to the method of the earliest herbals: grouping by use. So, species have continued to shift from one genus to another.
>
> (Ibid:310)

There is even a committee that sits at Kew and discusses naming issues, which is, quite amusingly, called the 'Family Planning Committee' (ibid.:311). More recently, the human genome project and the mapping of the DNA structure have resulted in the technology being used in other areas, including the development of the twenty-first-century taxonomy system. As Pavord (ibid.:311) notes, 'by ana-lysing the DNA of plants, scientists can now work out a kind of evolutionary tree, and make clear relationships that no outward character could ever suggest'. This example illustrates the dynamic and fluid nature of scientific knowledge as well as providing evidence that such knowledge is constantly evolving as our ways of observing and measuring become more sophisticated. Regardless of the fluidity of taxonomic systems, one thing is certain – on a forensic level, these classifica-tion systems allow for the identification of known species of plants, animals and physical material. For instance, the method and system of Ray and Linné allows us to compare botanical samples and identify place of origin of cannabis plants, which is important if one is trying to trace the likely importation routes of drug smugglers (Saferstein, 2007; Jackson and Jackson, 2008). Taxonomic systems such as the ones described above contribute greatly to our understanding of the natural world for they create ontological categories of objects that exist in nature: what are commonly called 'natural kinds'.

Natural kinds

The concept of natural kinds and their place in the development of scientific knowledge cannot be underestimated. The concept has been met with both enthusiasm and scepticism but has managed to maintain enough evidential support to be of great use to natural and forensic scientists over the last 300 years. Koslicki (2008:789) defines natural kinds as 'categories or taxonomic classifications into which particular objects may be grouped on the basis of shared characteristics of some sort'. *Natural kinds* are therefore kinds that are found in nature. It should be obvious that most of this chapter has been about the development of knowledge around natural kinds. This has been the lifeblood of natural philosophy and science, and their taxonomic mission since the beginning of the Renaissance period. There is, however, some debate as to who invented the term. Bird and Tobin (cited in Magnus, 2011:1), for instance, claim that Mill used the term in *A System of Logic* (1843); however, anyone who has ever read *Logic* will realise that this is actually incorrect. Mill uses the term *kind*, for instance, in Book I, Chapter VII (entitled 'Of the Nature of Classification'), but he does not use the term *natural kind* (see also Magnus, 2011). Snyder (2006:18) states that that the concept was first used by the English mathematician and philosopher John Venn (1834–1923), who introduced the term in 1866 in his famous text *The Logic of Chance*. On the other hand, Kornblith (1995:13–34) suggests that the English philosopher and physician John Locke (1632–1704) was the first major Enlightenment thinker who grappled with the concept of natural kinds. Locke's *An Essay Concerning Human Understanding* (1690) presents at least two philosophical 'pictures' concerning natural kinds in relation to the way we know about the natural world. Kornblith (ibid.:14–15) labels the first type the *realist* perspective, which sees the world consisting 'not merely of individuals, but of kinds of individuals as well' and notes that 'this division of the world into kinds is not of our own invention' (ibid.:14). The scientific mission of four millennia was seen by many as an attempt to 'discover the kinds which actually exist in nature' (ibid.:14), and our taxonomies are attempts (sometimes successful, sometimes not) to match up with real natural kinds. The second 'picture' is that of the *conventionalist*, which presents nature as the creator of things but not as the creator of kinds (ibid.:14). So, horses, dogs and cats are things created by nature; the classification of these things into separate species of animals, however, is a human construct and 'has been found to be convenient' as 'it answers to human interests' (ibid.:15). The metaphysical question, then, is whether the taxonomic schemes are 'grounded in the world or are they instead merely products of our own minds' (ibid.:15)? For around 200 years this question has tested those of even the strongest faith in science. More specifically, this question became central to the Whewell-Mill debate around induction and deduction and the entire philosophy of science that took place in the Victorian era.

Methods of reasoning: induction, deduction or a third way?

The taxonomic mission to identify natural kinds opened up what has become one of the most important debates in the philosophy of science. This debate was about the whole notion of epistemology and ontology and whether or not it was possible to truly know anything about the natural world. Those who advocated scientific knowledge over religious and mystical explanations based their claims that science provided a more truthful/realistic knowledge on the very 'notion of the scientific method itself' (Turner, 2008:37). As previously discussed, a common debate that derived from the Baconian vision of science was that science, when properly applied and exhausted, would yield a distinctive method or a 'spiritual despotism' that would mean an ever decreasing reliance on politics. However, this logic created an inescapable philosophical conflict. John Stuart Mill's (1806–1873) famous text *On Liberty* (1859) with its examination of free discussion was juxtaposed against his *A System of Logic* ([1843]2011), which proffered the inescapable logic that if the scientific canons of induction led to proven knowledge then indoctrination into such canons would easily override democratic discussion through politics. Turner eloquently sums up Mill's conflict thus: '[i]f science is distinguished by the possession of a consensus-producing method, its reliance on human institutions is incidental or inessential and the authority of science overrides free discussion' (2008:37).

Mill never resolved the conflict between science and free discussion. Others, however, were less ambivalent to this apparent conflict. William Whewell (1794–1866) was one such individual. Whewell was a famous polymath, and, whilst his portfolio of works covers a broad range of interests including mechanics, physics, geology, economics and poetry, he is best remembered for his work on the philosophy and history of the sciences. His work was an attack on the liberal position of individuals such as Mill; indeed Mill attacked Whewell's philosophy of science in *A System of Logic*, producing an interesting debate between the two of them over deduction versus induction (Mill, [1843]2011; Snyder, 2006).

Deduction and induction are pervasive elements in critical thinking and form the basis of the majority of all research methods in the natural and social sciences (Gilbert, 1993). *Deductive reasoning* is based on logic and typically moves from general truths, usually starting with a statement or statements (premises) known or believed to be true, to specific conclusions. In this sense, deductive reasoning is narrow and is concerned with testing or confirming hypotheses, so it is dependent on its premises; a false premise can lead to a false conclusion, and inconclusive premises will yield an inconclusive conclusion. In doing so, as Turvey (2001:38–41) points out, it guarantees the correctness of a conclusion. *Inductive reasoning*, on the other hand, moves from specific observations and uses these instances to create more general underlying principles or laws to explain the observations. The inductive process is open-ended and exploratory and creates premises which are believed to support the conclusion but do not ensure it. An inductive conclusion is often regarded as a hypothesis, which has to go through the process of falsification before it moves into the realm of scientific *fact*. However, even then, scientific fact is open to change as new data becomes available that changes what is known.

Reforming philosophy

Both deductive and inductive forms of reasoning became a core issue for scientists in the eighteenth and nineteenth centuries. Many budding natural philosophers thought long and hard about the epistemological and ontological knowledge that was created through each type of reasoning, and some intense debates used induction/deduction as a means to critically assess the validity of the taxonomic classification schemes as being accurate representations of natural kinds. In his *The Philosophy of the Inductive Sciences* (1857), Whewell traced at great length the major inductive ideas of what he called the *physical sciences* and demonstrated 'the difficulties that major ideas had in becoming accepted' (Turner, 2008:37; see Books I and II in Whewell, [1857]2012:16–164). This went against the dominant idea advocated from Bacon to Mill that scientific 'truth was readily recognised' (Turner, 2008:38). Whewell was a strong believer in Bacon's method as being the proper inductive method and at the same time was very critical of the deductive method despite having a deep respect for it: he even called advocates of deduction 'deductive savages' (cited in Snyder, 2006:34). He saw the need to combine 'empirical and a priori elements of science' which he achieved rather successfully in a method he called *fundamental antithesis* (ibid.:37). Whewell saw that there was a natural synergy between deductive (*a priorism*) and inductive (*empiricism*) lines of reasoning. He wrote extensively on the need to combine observation (empirical induction) with reason (a priori deduction). For example, in his 1831 review of Herschel's *Preliminary Discourse on the Study of Natural Philosophy* (1830), Whewell wrote:

> Induction agrees with mere Observation in accumulating facts, and with Pure Reason in stating general propositions; but she does *more* than Observation, inasmuch as she not only collects facts, but catches some connexion or relation among them; and *less* than pure Reason . . . because she only declares that there *are* connecting properties, without asserting that they *must* exist of necessity and in all cases. [Original emphasis.]
>
> (Whewell, 1831:379, cited in Snyder, 2006:38)

Whewell strongly asserted that both induction/deduction were needed for the creation and understanding of scientific knowledge as 'both facts and ideas are requisite for the "formation of science"' (Snyder, 2006:40). He used the term *fundamental ideas* as being the subjective element that governed his antithetical epistemology, arguing that ideas 'enable us to have real knowledge of the empirical world. They do so by connecting the facts of our experience. . . . Ideas provide the general relations that really exist in the world between objects and events' (ibid.:41). In short, Whewell's fundamental ideas give structure to our empirical senses. For example, ideas such as space, time, causation and resemblance are the relations to sensory data and enable us to make sense of our sensations (ibid.:41). In presenting the union between deductive *a priorism* and inductive *empiricism*, Whewell rejected Kant's claim that 'we can only have knowledge of our "categorized experience"' (ibid.:44) as well as highlighting his dislike for Locke's version of knowledge. He effectively wanted to create a third way, seeking a middle ground between the systems of Kant and Locke (ibid.:46). He invented the term *colligation* as a way to describe how the act of intellectual thought requires the merging of *observation* and *reasoning*. We use our reasoning to create fundamental ideas, which help make sense of and structure our empirical observations. Furthermore, Whewell highlighted the fact that poor science was often a result of unsuitable fundamental ideas or, as they're now referred to, *conceptions*. Whewell stated that it was impossible to separate observations from our reasoned ideas/conceptions (Whewell, [1857]2012). For Whewell, this was how scientific knowledge was *made*:

> Scientific discoveries are made not merely when accurate observations are obtained, as was the case after Tycho Brahe's observations of the orbit of Mars, but when in addition to accurate observations the appropriate conception is used, as when Kepler applied the conception of the ellipse rather than the epicycle.
>
> (Synder, 2006:54)

Mill accused Whewell of belonging to the '"Germano-Coleridgian" school' of epistemology and criticised him for building a bridge between *a priorism* and *empiricism* (Snyder, 2006:51). Despite this, Whewell was undeterred in demonstrating that the key to valid scientific knowledge was predicated upon finding the appropriate conception, which was created through the colligation of facts. However, as with the case of Kepler's first law of planetary motion, scientific laws[11] were also created through the making of inferences about unobserved entities using observations of what *has* been observed. When Kepler used Brahe's observations and looked through his telescope, he was only able to observe what was within his line of sight and, of course, this was determined by the available technology. His theory became a scientific law because he used accurate observations (i.e. the trajectory of planetary motion) combined with inferences about what he (or Brahe) couldn't observe (i.e. the unobserved mathematically calculated continued trajectory pathway of planetary motion) with an *appropriate conception* (i.e. an ellipse). Whewell used examples such as Kepler to illustrate that the scientific method could be successful, as there was often the need to make inferences because inductive reasoning moved beyond the realm of the senses to the consideration of unobservable entities. In doing so, he reverted back to Bacon's vision of science:

> laborious observation, narrow and modest inference, caution, slow and gradual advance, limited knowledge, are all unwelcome efforts and restraints to the mind of man, when his speculative spirit is once roused: yet they are the necessary conditions of all advance in the Inductive Sciences.
>
> (Whewell, cited in Synder, 2006:67)

Mill openly criticised Whewell on a number of points – too many to mention here (for a full review of the debate see Yeo, 2003, and Snyder, 2006). For instance, he suggested that Whewell's concept of *colligation* was little more than observation and description. He was also critical of Whewell's type of inductive science, what he called *intuitionist philosophy*, because it often led to political and social conservatism (Snyder, 2006:26–28, 95–155). Mill argued that intuitionism 'allowed "every inveterate belief and every intense feeling" to be "its own all-sufficient voucher and justification"' (cited in Snyder, 2006:27). Other differences between Mill and Whewell's conceptualisation and operationalisation of science include Whewell's belief that it was possible to 'make reliable probable inferences to empirical truths about unobserved causes and entities' whilst Mill denied the possibility of 'even probable knowledge or unobserved causes and entities' (Snyder, 2006:27).

Scientific renovatum

The Mill-Whewell debate set the stage for intense discussions about whether science was a product of distinctive 'routinizable methods' and these discussions enabled a reformulation of 'the basic Baconian picture of science' (Turner, 2008:38). At the end of the nineteenth and beginning of the twentieth centuries, the two grand narratives of positivism and Communist theories of science were brought closer together by Ernst Mach (1838–1916) and Karl Pearson (1857–1936) (ibid. 2008). Mach was an Austrian physicist and philosopher who developed the philosophy of science and was a strong advocate of Comte's logical positivism. Pearson, on the other hand, was an English mathematician who developed statistics and founded the first university statistics department. He was also a proponent of eugenics, an interesting by-product of rational science and something that had important links with the development of positivist criminology (see Chapter 3). Both of these influential thinkers had a major influence on the way science developed, especially 'their ideas about the relation of theory to data' (ibid.:38). Both were against the notion that science could (or should) move beyond the data, which, as we saw earlier, was a key idea in Whewell's *fundamental antithesis* (Snyder, 2006:37–42). Furthermore, Mach and Pearson held the view that science was '"economical" or oriented to "efficiency"' (Turner, 2008:38). In his *Grammar of Science*, Pearson ([1919]2007) linked science to 'national efficiency', the unintended chilling results of which were used to such powerfully negative effect under Hitler's Nazi Germany (Burleigh, 2001:343–404; also see Lifton, 2000) and Stalinist Russia. For Pearson, science's purpose 'was the same as that of any other human activity: to promote the welfare of human society, to increase social happiness, and to strengthen social stability' (Turner, 2008:38). However, it was only able to do this by achieving *consensus* within society, yet again returning to the philosophical quandary of the eighteenth and nineteenth centuries. Pearson thought that education and popularisation would be the 'right way to inculcate the scientific, unbiased cast of mind' (ibid.:39), and he thought the best way to achieve this was not by a broad reading of science alone but by the 'close scientific study of some small area' (ibid.:39; also see Chapters 1 and 2 of Pearson, [1917]2007). What Pearson effectively established here was the idea of the specialisation of scientific knowledge or, to use Durkheimian parlance, the division of expert-knowledge labour. To be truly scientific, one should concentrate one's efforts on minute areas of study. Study of these *areas* need not simply be restricted to the study of natural objects, or natural philosophy, but should be extended to beyond the normal subject matter. Turner (2008:39) lists the possible areas of expansion as including: 'technology and engineering', the '"social and mental" sciences', policy sciences and so forth. He also argues that Pearson's notion of science incorporated a passing of the method and ideas to others and that this was 'deeply imbedded' in the culture and social context of the time (ibid.:39). The idea of science being culturally embedded within society led to the development of a liberal view of science that raised the issue of whether science was culturally significant. This soon became a hotly con-tested debate, with scientific conceptions of the natural world attempting to distinguish themselves from 'mere "world views"' (Richardson, 2003:68–69, cited in Turner, 2008:40). More recently, this debate has become more con-fusing given the changes to the nature and structure of academia, with its increased emphasis on market-driven specialisation of knowledge acquisition pathways.

Academic disciplines and paradigms

The period from the Renaissance until the twentieth century saw the rapid development of scientific and academic specialisation, with the establishment of centres and peripheries, curricula, libraries and encyclopedias on an immense range of scientific subjects (Burke, 2008:53–115). As knowledge bases, evidence and theories increased, the ability to continue as a generalist or polymath became increasingly impossible; there was just too much information to handle. The solution for science and academia has been to break subjects into smaller manageable blocks called academic disciplines; and within these blocks *paradigms* have emerged to create further specialisation. This has been most clearly explained in Kuhn's ([1962]1996) *The Structure of Scientific Revolutions*. His suggestion that scientific revolutions have occurred throughout history and that they have similar embryonic and developmental structures shocked many. He courted controversy by doubting that practitioners of the natural sciences possessed firmer knowledge than those practitioners of the social sciences (ibid.:x). He also noticed that there were quite a large number of disagreements between social scientists 'about the nature of legitimate scientific problems and methods' (ibid.:x), arguing that these disagreements were more pronounced in the social sciences than controversies about the fundamental ideas in the natural sciences (using astronomy, physics, chemistry and biology as examples). In an attempt to find the source of this difference, Kuhn discovered *paradigms,* which he defined as 'universally recognized scientific achievements that for a time provide model problems and solutions to a community of practitioners' (ibid.:x). A scientific revolution starts with dissatisfaction with the dominance of a particular *paradigm*, with those who are expressing dissatisfaction developing new theories that becomes a new paradigm. Eventually, this new paradigm becomes the orthodox science until another generation of researchers becomes dissatisfied and the cycle begins all over again (Burke, 2008; Kuhn, 1996). Kuhn's work is a useful way to think about the way criminological theory and research has been generated since the mid nineteenth century (see Chapters 3 and 4). However, we should not forget the warning given by Latour (2008), who argues that using paradigms as the ontological basis for knowledge forces us back towards the prejudices and presuppositions of the knowing subject in the teleportation scheme of knowledge acquisition. Throughout history, paradigms have played an interesting role in the development of scientific knowledge for they have both moved knowledge forward and have restricted new or embryonic ideas from emerging.

The disciplines of forensic criminology

The academic and knowledge domain of forensic criminology is very broad and, in recent years, just like one theory of the universe, appears to be constantly expanding (Kennedy, 2013). It incorporates the scientific study of crime and criminality (Bonger, 1936:1; Wolfgang and Ferracuti, 1967:19) and examines these two areas from a number of different perspectives. In modern Western society, *knowledge* is constructed through many different means and sources including universities and colleges, government departments, non-governmental organisations (NGOs), quasi-autonomous non-governmental organisations (QUANGOs), numerous political *think tanks* and private businesses. With the involvement of so many organisations, employing millions of people across the globe, it is near impossible to have a full gasp of all the available data, research and knowledge on any given subject. There are one or two exceptions of course. Collaborations such as the one at the impressive CERN, the European Organization for Nuclear Research (*Conseil Européen pour la Recherche Nucléaire*), which started in 1954 and currently sits astride the Franco-Swiss border near Geneva, is one of the world's largest centres for scientific research. Run by 20 European Member States, CERN involves the collaboration of many scientists from across the scientific spectrum, some of whom, no doubt, have epistemological differences yet share the same underlying purposes of developing research, technology, collaboration and education which originate from a purely 'scientific and fundamental character'.[12] CERN is unique in its scope and depth, but it should be remembered that it has been in existence for some 60 years so has had time to build and develop its impressive portfolio of research, technology and collaboration. Unlike the activities of CERN, the majority of scientific and social scientific research is on a much smaller scale and often involves sole individuals locked away in university offices and libraries working with limited resources yet still managing to produce an impressive variety of knowledge. Reckless succinctly explains this as follows:

> Although criminology is a behavioural science as well as an applied science, it is also a highly synthetic science and not at all an exact science like physics or mathematics. It receives its contributions from experts in such disciplines as biology, anthropology, physiology, medicine, psychiatry, psychology, social administration, sociology, economics, law, political science, and penology and corrections.
>
> (Reckless, 1955:7, cited in Turvey and Petherick, 2010:14)

To this list, many other disciplines could be added; for instance, philosophy, history, economics, social work, physics, genetics, neurochemistry and neurophysiology to name just a few. All of these sciences and professionals, including their methods/techniques, 'comprise or inform the multi-disciplinary fabric of criminology as a composite field of study' (Turvey and Petherick, 2010:14), which makes criminology and forensic criminology unique. Table 2.2 outlines a typical list of disciplines that are within the radex of the four areas of forensic criminology identified in Chapter 1. This list is not exhaustive, but simply provides a basic threshold of the most pertinent disciplines and professional activity that, when combined, contribute to forensic criminology as a body of knowledge that is applied to resolve issues within the criminal justice system.

Table 2.2 The interdisciplinary universe of forensic criminology

Main discipline	Subject/Topic streams
Criminology and Criminal Justice	– Crime and deviance – Crime types and statistics – Theoretical explanations and offender motivations – Police science and criminal investigations – Crime analysis and case linkage – Crime scene examination – Offender profiling – The law and legal frameworks – Victimology – Penology – punishment and rehabilitation
Biology	– Serology – DNA analysis – Hair analysis – Entomology – Blood pattern analysis – Fingerprint analysis

(Continued)

Table 2.2 (Continued)

Main discipline	Subject/Topic streams
Chemistry	– Chemical analysis – Drug, paint, glass and fibre analysis – Gunshot residue analysis – Toxicological analysis – Fingerprint analysis – Soil analysis – Fire debris analysis
Physics	– Theories of optics, light, sound and heat – Glass analysis – Blood pattern analysis
Medicine	– Pathology – Anthropology – Dentistry and Odontology – Nursing
Computing	– Digital evidence analysis – Network analysis
Psychiatry and Psychology	– Offender risk assessment – Offender evaluation, diagnoses and treatment – Counselling and therapy – Investigative interviewing – Offender profiling

Paradigmatic myopia

One last issue needs to be highlighted in relation to the epistemological and ontological foundation of forensic criminology. The majority of academic subjects in science tend to be focused and do not often cross over into other domains. Even within different disciplines many academics/scientists do not often venture out of their preferred paradigmatic bubbles – what I call *paradigmatic myopia*. Judith Harris has noticed and discussed this problem in the excellent *The Nurture Assumption* (1999). She suggests that academics rarely read works from other disciplines and suggests two main reasons for this: first, they know they won't agree; and, second, they don't have the time (1999:14–15). Harris' specialty is psychology, and she rightly points out the paradigmatic myopia of current academic psychology:

> Socialization researchers and behavioural geneticists earn a living by teaching college undergraduates and graduate students and by doing research. heir status depends on the success of their research and the quantity and quality of their publications. They are specialists: neither side spends much time reading what the other has written, partly because they know they won't agree with it, partly because they don't have time. In general, academicians

read mostly the publications in their own area and perhaps a few closely related areas.

(1999:14)

Others have also encountered the problem of paradigmatic myopia. Bunge (2006:14) argues that, when it comes to understanding offender behaviour, reliance on one's preferred paradigm could result in one seizing 'on certain features and pretend[ing] others do not exist or are less important'. What forensic criminology aims to do is draw from multiple perspectives so it does not worship at the altar of just one paradigm. In essence it juxtaposes the necessity of specialist knowledge in all four areas of forensic criminology whilst at the same time gently pushing the idea of the beauty in being an intellectual speculator with archeological skills.

Summary

Whilst it has not been possible to cover all of the important developments in this very selective and brief history of the development of science, this chapter aimed to discuss some of the more relevant concepts and issues which have a bearing on the overall subject of forensic criminology. The concepts of epistemology and ontology are important for understanding the types of knowledge that exist and the fact that human beings construct classification (taxonomic) schemes that attempt to reflect the real structure of *things* that exist in the natural world. The taxonomic mission of the last 2,000 years has connections and important implications not only for forensic science but also criminology, criminal investigations and the legal system. With the advent of the Renaissance and Enlightenment periods and the move to a scientific knowledge system based upon rationality and reasoning, we have been able to understand more and more about the planet we all inhabit. In particular, classification of plant and animal species as well as the study of the chemical composition of the elements since the sixteenth century has created the scientific culture that all contemporary forensic science is based upon today. With the emergence of the scientific culture, came the need for logic and critical thinking; and, over the last 400 years or so, Western culture in particular has harnessed the early scholasticism of the Greek philosophers, creating debates regarding the epistemological and ontological basis of human knowledge and interpretation. This is not merely an academic debate. Since the nineteenth century, discussions around science have created two methods of reasoning, both of which are still crucial and applied to today's natural and social scientific community. They have also played an important role in the development of scientific criminology and forensic science, which is dealt with in the next two chapters.

Chapter 3

The beginnings of scientific criminology

The Beast and the Whore rule without control.

(Blake, 1798)

Introduction

The multidisciplinary approach to forensic criminology and the application of casework or research into understanding the crime event is not a new phenomenon. For centuries, as scientific and technological ideas developed and advanced, more and more uses of this new knowledge were found and applied; and some of this knowledge was found to be useful for resolving criminal justice problems. In particular, developments in medicine, biology and chemistry over 2,000 years began to be systematised into a structured body of knowledge, and the epistemological and ontological roots of forensic criminology can be located in the core areas of the scientific revolution, some of which were discussed in the previous chapter. This chapter provides a slightly more focused-down approach, by looking at how these ideas and paradigms led to the creation of scientific criminology in the eighteenth, nineteenth and early twentieth centuries. It is no coincidence that scientific criminology, which can be regarded as an early form of forensic criminology, developed in the same historical epoch as policing and criminal investigations (Morris, 2007) as well as early forms of forensic science (Gross, 1962; Kirk, 1974; Evans, 2006).

This chapter charts the development of scientific criminology. In order to achieve this aim, brief histories of criminology, criminal investigations and forensic science will be developed and placed within their historical context. The chapter begins by introducing a microanalysis framework for understanding the social and cultural context within which scientific criminology developed. It begins with scientific criminology because this is where numerous micro-pockets of practice created the structural conditions under which criminology developed (Davie, 2005; Rafter, 2009). It then highlights how these conditions were influenced by wider social and cultural fears regarding issues of self-control, by respect for order and by concerns over the habitual criminal. These fears led many practitioners to study criminals and criminality using the deductive and inductive methods of the *new* science. Using the *positivist* paradigm, the chapter then discusses some of the important ideas and theories within early criminology, including: moral insanity, evolution and biological determinism, criminal anthropology and the *criminal man*. Such ideas galvanised researchers in the eighteenth and nineteenth centuries and effectively *invented the criminal*.

Micro-contextual developments

No-one knows for sure who first applied science to aid in the solving of crime. As discussed in Chapter 2, even the concept and definition of *science* as we know and use it today has gone through many changes over the centuries (van Doren, 1991; Gaukroger, 2009). Caddy and Cobb (2004:2) argue that an early form of forensic science shows up in the sixth century, especially in the legal medicine practiced by the Chinese. In the year 1000, Roman Attorney Quintilian showed how bloody palm prints were used to try to frame a blind man with his mother's murder (Inman and Rudin, 2000). As we shall see in the following chapter, in 1247 the Chinese book *Hsi Yuan Yu* (The Washing Away of Wrongs) contained a description of how to distinguish drowning from strangulation (Nickell and Fischer, 1999:6) as well as medical information on wound characteristics, poison and forensic dentistry (Bell, 2008:26). What these few examples demonstrate is that the construction of the scientific and criminological disciplines covered in this text has not been a linear, progressive movement. For many years, the history of science sought a 'centre-periphery' model of scientific knowledge construction (Golinski, 2005; Raj, 2010:516). As Raj (2010:513) notes, the positivist notion of science as a progressive movement, that saw scientific knowledge, instruments, texts and practitioners as disembodied and universal, began to weaken in the 1970s. More and more we came to see the importance of the role of localised historical, social, cultural, gendered and geographical contexts in the production of scientific knowledge. Therefore, contingencies of place (Raj, 2010:513) are of crucial importance if one is to understand the epistemological and ontological development of scientific criminology. If one is to successfully practice this knowledge, one needs an appreciation of its origins and development. This chapter takes the post-postivist view, as outlined by Raj (2010:514) who states that:

> Science is locally created, and only subsequently, through a series of investments and deliberate strategies, does it become transferrable to the outside world . . . the primacy of universality over locality has been reversed: the question of science's claim to universality – the process of the spread of ideas, texts, practices, norms, instruments, procedures and protocols from their site of invention to other parts of the globe – has been reformulated and has itself become an object of historical, social and political inquiry.

This micro-contextual analysis is especially important for understanding forensic criminology for a number of reasons. First, during the reconstruction of the crime event – which, as we will see in later chapters, is the core business of forensic science and criminal investigations – the knowledge that is utilised and produced during the crime reconstruction process is determined by the localised social, cultural, political and economic practices of those involved in the process. For instance, the amount and types of forensic evidence collected at the scene will be determined by a number of local economic and structural factors, such as budget constraints (Roberts and Willmore, 1993:25–28). Following this is the idea that the process of crime reconstruction is itself based upon the people that construct it. Contingencies of people working within their local environments must also be considered in the process of the construction of scientific criminology. A third reason for a micro-level analysis relates to the context in which the crime event occurs. Crimes consist of the interactions between offenders and victims within a specific environmental circumstance and context (Scott, 1977). Our analysis and understanding of such events will obviously be affected by such micro-level factors (Brantingham and Brangtingham, 1984: 332–336).

The social and cultural context of scientific developments

Scientists use empirical evidence to support their fundamental ideas/conceptions and theories in an attempt to provide a strong basis on which to solve problems as well as make claims about objects in the natural and social worlds. What is often underemphasised is the social context in which such knowledge is created and used. All knowledge has an historical context and is constructed within specific cultural milieus that, in part, determine what Geertz (1980, cited in Wiener, 1994:10) describes as constellations of 'enshrined ideas'. The epistemological and ontological developments within forensic science, criminal investigations and scientific criminology are all affected by the social context in which the knowledge is produced. Take the words of Henry Maudlsey, for instance:

> Lunatics and criminals are as much manufactured articles as are steam engines and calico-printing machines, only the processes of the organic manufactory are so complex that we are not able to follow them. They are neither accidents nor anomalies in the universe, but come by law and testify to causality; and it is the business of science to find out what the causes are and by what laws they work.
>
> (Maudsley, 1874:30, cited in Davie, 2005:15)

The underlying social context in which the three subject areas of criminology, forensic science and criminal investigations originally intersect was the Victorian age. This was an age that was characterised by a deep commitment to social reform (Bristow, 1977; Wiener, 1994) and of major scientific advancement, especially within the realms of technological and medical investment, where the British insisted on practical, value-free solutions to penal problems (Lightman, 1997; Davie, 2005). As mentioned in the previous chapter, the Renaissance and

Enlightenment periods brought major developments in scientific methods and techniques, which brought changes to the epistemological and ontological basis of knowledge. These scientific developments continued and increased rapidly in the nineteenth century and, coupled with the resultant advancements in technology, created the necessary conditions for the major social changes of industrialisation and urbanisation (Thompson, 1991; Wiener, 1994). For example, using an evolutionary theory of technological change, Basalla (1999) has demonstrated how three themes emerge throughout human history in relation to technological advances. First, humans have used a *diverse* range of *things* readily available to humankind; second, humans are driven out of *necessity* to create new *things* to meet basic needs; third, that *technological evolution* explains the drive to develop *novel artefacts* that are selected by society and incorporated into its social life. So the move from feudalism to industrialism changed the agrarian mode of production to a manufacturing mode of production, which led to the dramatic rise of capitalism and urbanisation (Thompson, 1991), creating diversity, increased necessity and technological evolution. Enshrined in this evolution of human society was the rise in a distinct group of individuals, later to become known as the middle classes. The Victorian middle classes were highly organised, and, as the capitalist mode of production took a foothold and began to dominate the production and sale of goods in the marketplace, the middle classes owned a large proportion of the private property and wealth created from this advancement and dominance of capitalism (Thompson, 1991; Weber, [1930]1992; Engels, [1845]1987).

The Victorian age was also the period in which a centralised bureaucratic state was formed, and this could be viewed as a major attempt to separate state business from royal and religious interference. At the same time, many charitable, philanthropic and moral crusader groups were formed – for example, the National Vigilance Association, the Society for the Suppression of Vice and the Temperance Society – and the majority of these had strong religious ideological undertones that dominated their constructions of human action and behaviours, which ultimately influenced the creation of criminal justice policy during this period (Pearl, 1955; Bristow, 1977; Roberts, 1983; Wiener, 1994). Victorian criminal policy, its justice organisations and the knowledge produced and used were all 'molded in the midst of these developments' (Wiener, 1994:11; Davie, 2005). The criminal justice system, including practical criminological, investigative and forensic knowledge production, often responds to social and cultural concerns that are historically specific and localised. Indeed as Wiener notes (1994:6), 'even the most practical men do not act in a conceptual or moral vacuum'.

Perhaps the most visible and dominant social and cultural concerns during this period were the need to build character and the issue of maintaining the social order (Wiener, 1994:14–45; Davie, 2005:27–123). Rising fears and anxieties about individual impulses as well as individuals being out of control were the common components of the stereotypical image of the criminal during this period (Pearson, 1983; Wiener, 1994; Davie, 2005). Crime became the central metaphor of this loss of control, but also for the wider public disorder that took place during this period of massive social change and upheaval. The two phenomena of *crime* and the *criminal* became the dominant symptoms of the perceived wider social malaise, and such social constructs were generated through a mesh of political, religious and practitioner interests, values and sensibilities that were dominant during the Victorian period. Criminal justice policy was largely created on the basis of such images, so this subjective or sociocultural dimension, as Wiener argues, is inescapable. Unfortunately, this type of contextual analysis has been lacking in much of the criminological discourse on the historical development of criminal policy (Wiener, 1994:7). The main reason for this is because of the dominance of the political paradigm. Primarily, the likes of Foucault ([1977]1991), Ignatieff (1978) and Garland (1991) argue that penal policy and constructs of crime and the criminal have been determined by those wishing to reproduce existing social power relations. The main theoretical influence of such ideas can be traced to Foucault's widely read *Discipline and Punish* ([1977]1991). Unfortunately, as with Foucault's work on *The History of Sexuality* (1978, 1985), *Discipline and Punish* largely ignores the complexities that a micro-contextual historical analysis is able to highlight. The central problem with the works of Foucault, Ignatieff and Garland is that they see criminal policy in terms of increasing success in social domination or social control. This forms the basis of Foucault's thesis on the move away from public punishments to punishing more deeply into the body (Foucault, [1977]1991:135–228). The social control paradigm has proved to be both powerful and useful, especially for expanding the *police state* thesis. However, as Wiener (1994:8) argues, 'human motives and even interests are more complex and more problematic, and the institutions of criminal justice have responded to a greater variety of motives and served a wider array of interests than that of "social control"'. Wiener's claims certainly have social and cultural resonance, especially if we consider the early moral crusades and social panics over crime and criminals that came to dominate nineteenth-century Victorian Britain.

Self-control, respect for order and the habitual criminal

Criminal policy in the Victoria era was largely created to counter the widespread concerns and moral crusades over the perceived loss of self-control and fears about public disorder and the habitual criminal (Pearl, 1955; Bristow, 1977; Pearson, 1983; Boyer, 1992; Wiener, 1994; Morone, 2003; Davie, 2005). The advancement of capitalist society, with its increasing urbanised populace, and the move to a more 'individualistic spirit' had the effect of dismantling many of the traditional restraints on an individual's 'freedom of action' (Wiener, 1994:11) and at the same time weakened the traditional structures of authority (Weber, 1978:212–301). According to Wiener all these developments had the effect of 'multiplying the effective force of human desires and will'; and, when this was placed within the structure of an 'uprooted, rapidly growing, and youthful populace', middle-class concerns about 'regulating one's passions and planning one's life' soon followed (1994:11). Individuals were beginning to be more reflective of their surrounding environment, leading some to claim that the modernisation project of industrial society had created a great deal of anxiety, especially amongst the burgeoning middle classes (Harvey, 1990). The three themes of *self-control, order* and the *habitual criminal* provide a micro-contextual vantage point of such attitudes and their links to the epistemological development of scientific criminology.

First, the beginning of the nineteenth century saw concerns over the excesses of upper classes, especially the English and French aristocracies (Pearl, 1955; Bristow, 1977). The perceived moral and material depravity of the rich was juxtaposed with the moral restraint of the capitalist middle classes (Wiener, 1994:14–45). For early Victorians, there was a need to build character which was both moral and industrious. More importantly, the material growth of the capitalist upper and middle classes was predicated on the exploitation of the lower class's labour (Thompson, 1991; Marx, [1867]1990; Engels, [1845]1987). In order to maximise industriousness, one had to control one's desires; and the 'problem of human desires' was part of the broader philosophy of utilitarianism which was introduced by Jeremy Bentham and expanded upon by the Enlightenment philosopher John Stuart Mill (Tierney, 2010; Lilly *et al.*, 2011) – and included ideas regarding the nature of human beings. The basic idea outlined by Mill ([1879]2012:9) was 'pleasure itself, together with exemption from pain'; or, to put it another way, that most people generally act in a way that maximises their pleasure and minimises their pain. The implication of Mill's conceptualisation of men and women was they exercised *free will* in making decisions about how to behave which, of course, included whether to commit criminal, immoral or deviant acts. The premise that criminals made calculated decisions, or as Lilly *et al.* (2011) suggest, were 'criminal calculators', became a fundamental idea of *Classicism* (Beccaria, [1764]1986; Jones, 2001; Tierney, 2010). Unfortunately, it was the *free will* and *utility* aspects of human nature that frightened the upper and middle classes the most. If the working classes maximised their happiness primarily, it was thought, through drink and sexual promiscuity, then their productivity would diminish considerably. What was needed was restraint of the utility principle: restraint of self-control, therefore, served as the 'focus for middle and upper-class fears of working-class insubordination' (Wiener, 1994:16).[1] It was during the eighteenth and nineteenth centuries that this focus was channelled into a number of moral crusades using intensive moral entrepreneurial activity to promote the religious and ideological agendas of the middle and upper classes (Becker, 1963). For example, crusades against sexual promiscuity, vice, manners and poor social hygiene were staples of the professional activities of groups such as the Society for the Reformation of Manners, the Society for the Suppression of Vice, the Society for the Prevention of Venereal Disease and the Society for Promoting Christian Knowledge (Pearl, 1955; Bristow, 1977; Boyer, 1992). These groups were part of the burgeoning social purity movements of

Queen Victoria's reign and appeared at a time when the aforementioned capitalist changes were altering our economic and social relations.

The *unrestrained* leisure pursuits of the working classes, that became the target and focus of the crusading groups, were not only seen as a threat to the Protestant work ethic (Weber, [1930]1992) but they were also often connected to the major pockets of *public disorder* that emerged throughout major cities, towns and villages of Victorian England (Mayhew, [1851]1985; Hobsbawm, 1965, 2012). Protest movements developed during the nineteenth century as the middle and working classes became more educated, and a number of different groups emerged to fight for more control of the way their lives were run. Groups such as the Chartists and the Luddites, whilst created for different reasons and with different aims, were all perceived by the middle and upper classes to be a part of a common trend towards dangerous political activism (Thompson, 1991; Hobsbawm, 2012). Added to such movements were outbreaks of disorder – for example, The Swing Riots in 1830, which saw farm labourers react angrily to years of high taxes and low wages as riots broke out when their livelihood was threatened by the introduction of threshing machines; threshing machines were wrecked, and those farmers who owned them were also threatened (Thompson, 1991; Hobsbawm, 2012). Apart from increasingly harsh punishments being levied against those who protested in demonstrations such as The Swing Riots – which we also saw 180 years later with the disproportionately severe punishments being handed out to those who took part in the 2011 riots in London (Ministry of Justice, 2012) – the *criminal conversations* that took place around the notions of self-restraint, respectability and disorder were also linked to aspects of crime and criminality through the lens of the *habitual criminal*.

Throughout the Victorian age, criminal conversations and public and private discourses were full of fears and concerns over the *new* social phenomena of the habitual or repeat offender (Pearson, 1983; Wiener, 1994; Rowbotham and Stevenson, 2003, 2005; Davie, 2005). Taylor (2005:4) argues that, whilst the notion of the criminal 'outsider' threatening the health of the nation was a common theme throughout the nineteenth century, the concept of the dangerous, habitual criminal was solidified in the latter half of the century. Thus, the 'threat from below', tied to the language of class conflict during a time of urbanisation and industrialisation, meshed very nicely with the middle- and upper-class focus on respectability and loss of self-control. Not only that, but the image of the criminal as being noticeably *different* from the rest of society also became part of the common-sense parlance of criminal conversations that were taken place during this time (ibid.:3–20). Henry Mayhew's works *London Labour and the London Poor* ([1851]1985) and *The London Underworld in the Victorian Period* ([1862]2005) demonstrate the common-sense, journalistic language of the criminal *other* – especially the latter work, which attempted what is perhaps one of the first ethnographic studies of crime in a major city. In *The London Underworld*, Mayhew and his team of researchers were able to produce a taxonomic scheme of the different varieties of criminals, their habits and descriptions of their local environments (Mayhew, [1862]2005). As Taylor (2005:6) points out, Mayhew stressed that criminals needed to be studied closely because they were 'such strange members of the human family'. This excerpt, describing a 'youth of the vagrant class' provides an excellent example of the image of the criminal as the other:

> The youths of the vagrant class are particularly distinguished for their libidinous propensities. They frequently come to the gate with a young prostitute, and with her they go off in the morning . . . the vagrant is totally distinct, having propensities not less vicious, but of a very different kind. He considers the young tramps to be generally a class of lads possessing the keenest intellect, and of a highly enterprising character. . . . They generally are of a most restless and volatile disposition. They have great quickness of perception, but little power of continuous attention or perseverance. . . . Being repeatedly committed to prison for disorderly conduct and misdemeanour, the gaol soon loses all terrors for them.
>
> (Mayhew, [1862]2005:371–372)

Wiener (1994:23–24) highlights how Mayhew's view of the 'unrespectable poor blended imperceptibly into the antisociety of criminality', which is also an image that underpins some twenty-first-century perceptions of criminals. In addition to this, in the last quarter of the nineteenth century, the image of the separate, definable other was also linked to the perception of the decline of Britain's economic and imperial power. However, ideas began to circulate that changed perceptions of such individuals. No longer were they automatically assigned as belonging to the 'dangerous classes' (Davie, 2005; Taylor, 2005): instead, society's perceptions began to see criminal classes as weak, pathetic creatures (Wiener, 1994:12). In particular, it was largely thought that the defective and criminal residuum of British society, personified by the physically and mentally weak habitual criminal, were creatures to be pitied rather than feared. The reality of Victorian society then, and one which differs from Foucault's (1978, 1985) myopic vision of Victorian sexuality, was of a vibrant, pluralistic, and multi-discursive society that was attempting to find answers to some of the social problems created by the industrial revolution.

It was in this period that the concept of degeneration, especially decay into a lower form of evolution, became a dominant theme, image and discourse, not only in criminal conversations amongst the upper and middle classes but also within discourses of such eminent individuals as Francis Galton and Charles Goring (Davie, 2005; Taylor, 2005). Of course, it should come as no surprise that the ideas of criminals being weak or *less evolved* followed the themes outlined by Charles Darwin's theory of evolution (ideas extrapolated from Herbert Spencer), which was also published in the same period. Perhaps the most relevant point to make here though is the fact that the threat of the habitual criminal generated a strong impetus for what could be regarded as a human taxonomic mission to clearly identify those problem groups to 'prevent them from contaminating the rest of society' (Taylor, 2005:17). Consequently, as Wiener (1994:12) has articulated:

> Fears of a dam-bursting anarchy began to be replaced by opposite fears of a disabled society of ineffectual, devitalised, and over-controlled individuals molded by environmental and biological forces beyond their control. . . . At the same time that upper-middle-class individuals began to feel less autonomous and less vital, they began to perceive criminal offenders as less threatening and less responsible for their behaviour and instead saw them as social wreckage and stepchildren of nature, rather than willful enemies of society.

It was within these contexts and discourses that the project of scientific criminology really took shape with the identification and classification of criminals and the subtypes that existed within them; alongside the biopsychological theories of offending behaviour that were created to explain them. Scientific thinking about criminal behaviour profoundly changed to reflect this general social consciousness, and criminal policy and the links to the developing sciences were both influenced and determined by these discourses. As Rowbotham and Stevenson (2005:1) point out, this context had an important and crucial influence on the identification of appropriate evidence as well as raising questions as to what constituted a competent witness. Such issues were established through the dominant gender, age, class and racial fault lines that existed within Victorian society. It is this context in which a broad range of theoretical, technological and practical developments in scientific criminology, criminal investigations and forensic techniques occurred. This was a crucial period in the development of criminological knowledge, much of which was generated through a prism that refracted the observation, measurement and classification of criminals, their physical, mental and social characteristics. These methods created and, for a time, cemented some fundamental ideas about the causal nature of criminal behaviours, which became known as *scientific criminology* (Davie, 2005).

The birth of scientific criminology

Turvey and Petherick (2010:xxii) mention, in the preface to their *Forensic Criminology* text, that 'criminology in general suffers from a number of ills' that they 'have long observed and now recognize as both serious and pathological'. They identify three major 'ills' with the epistemological position of criminology. First, they claim that criminologists 'no longer have a sense of where they came from' (ibid.:xxii). Second, they suggest that criminology has been 'conceptualized and presented at university' in the same way for the last 60 years (ibid.:xxii). The main reason for this has to be the dominance of the left-wing sociological theories that have become part of mainstream criminology departments over the last 60 years. Finally, they suggest that the vast majority of university teaching largely ignores the forensic element of criminology, as the subject is mainly taught by 'theoretical social scientists' (ibid.:xxii). The result, according to these forensic practitioners, is that students only get a 'limited picture of criminology', which often misses out the importance of forensic issues (ibid.:xxii). This situation has created a noticeable level of forensic ignorance within the subject of criminology, especially regarding the effects of forensics on 'the nature, extent, and implications of criminological research and opinions' (ibid.:xxii). Perhaps the most disparaging comments Turvey and Petherick level at contemporary criminology, however, is that criminologists 'have repeatedly chosen the path of least political resistance and consequently the least intellectual advancement within the study of crime and criminals' (ibid.:xii). Unfortunately, much of what they say is true; however, there are some tangential caveats involving sociological explanations of crime that explain why many contemporary criminologists suffer from paradigmatic myopia.

It was during the twentieth century that sociologically oriented explanations of crime were developed to add a supposedly missing element to the criminological puzzle – that of social and environmental factors. These ideas became fully realised within the Chicago School, with their extensive work on the ecological approach and on social disorganisation, and the numerous deviant and criminal ethnographies undertaken (Sutherland, 1956; Wirth, 1956; Thomas and Znaniecki, 1958; Shaw, 1966; Park and Burgess, [1925]1967; Polsky, 1971; Blumer, 1984; Downes and Rock, 2007). As the Chicago School developed their ideas, sociologists at Harvard also constructed explanations of society that incorporated some ideas about the social structural aspects of criminal behaviour. The Harvard work of Parsons (1967) and Merton (1968) also trained and influenced writers of subcultural explanations (Cohen, 1956), and in the UK others began to examine criminal groups through the lens of subcultural theory (Downes, 1966). With the development of the interactionist paradigm (Tannenbaum, 1938; Lemert, 1951; Becker, 1963), a number of *sociologists of deviance* criticised the medical/positivist dominance over criminological jurisdictional boundaries. In the 1950s, subcultural groups – so wonderfully explored by Chicago School social theorists of the 1920s and 1930s (Sutherland, 1956; Wirth, 1956; Thomas and Znaniecki, 1958; Shaw, 1966; Park and Burgess, [1925]1967; Polsky, 1971) – became a real threat to the *establishment*, resulting in discursive themes such as 'it's like a disease' and 'social malaise' being used to explain everything from rock 'n' roll misogynist thuggery and Teddy Boy violence in the 1950s to the Mods and Rockers skirmishes in Clacton in 1964 through to Skinhead homophobic and racist violence in the 1970s (Cohen, 1972; Hall and Jefferson, 1975; Brake, 1980; Thompson and Williams, 2014). The creation of the sociology of deviance, especially in the UK, with its critical juxtaposition with positivism, eventually led a number of sociologists to break away from the British Society of Criminology to form the National Deviancy Conference (NDC) (Cohen, 1971; Taylor and Taylor, 1973; Clarke, 1980) and create interactionist explanations of countercultural criminality. Some members of the NDC then went on to to develop critical criminology (Taylor *et al.*, 1994) using neo-Marxist theories linked to social structural explanations of crime (Bonger, [1916]2012; Sellin, 1937, 1938; Vold, 1958; Dahrendorf, 1959; Quinney, 1970). Whilst it is not within the scope of this text to examine this vast body of work in any detail, the importance of the dominance of sociological paradigm in relation to Petherick and Turvey's concerns cannot be emphasised enough. Since the 1960s, criminological university courses, academic journals, conferences, research monographs and textbooks have been dominated by sociological explanations of crime and criminality. Unfortunately, such dominance has resulted in paradigmatic myopia, with those preferring sociological explanations tending to be dismissive or, worse, engage in vitriolic attacks on anything remotely scientific or positivistic. Rightly or wrongly, such blind devotion to all things sociological has resulted in a tendency to ignore the more practical and applied scientific origins of criminology. This is the true cause of the epistemological and ontological historical 'amnesia' that concerns Turvey and Petherick (2010).

Multidisciplinary roots

The very roots of criminology are multidisciplinary, and this has its advantages and disadvantages. The most obvious advantage is that criminology is not based upon a single subject or paradigm, but its very epistemological and ontological roots are a result of what I call *paradigmatic pluralism*. Criminology incorporates many subjects, some of which include:

* sociology;
* psychology;
* history;
* political science;
* anthropology;
* law; and
* penology.

The advantage with having a wide range of subjects as a knowledge base is that it creates a more holistic understanding of the crime event as well as an understanding of the offender's criminality; and it also potentially allows for more critical and reflexive thinking around the subject matter. It makes logical sense that, if you are dealing with human behaviour, you utilise an holistic, multidisciplinary approach, because human behaviour consists of a complex mix of historical, biological, psychological and sociological stimuli, cues and environmental factors and influences (Blackburn, 1995; Andrews and Bonta, 2003; Bartol and Bartol, 2008). If you then factor in the notion that the human behaviour under examination is a transgression of some legal rule, you have even more issues to consider (Davies *et al.*, 2005). As a criminologist, it is important to be an intellectual *speculator* and tap into the wealth of knowledge that has been generated by the different disciplines over the last 200 years. One core disadvantage of a multidisciplinary approach is that, in practice, the subject of criminology has simply produced a number of paradigmatic pockets of subject-specific research. For example, what is often taught on undergraduate pro-grammes in the UK is the juxtaposition between sociological theories of crime and deviance and positivist theories of criminality (Jones, 2001; Downes and Rock, 2007; Tierney, 2010; Lilly *et al.*, 2011). Despite the subtle nuances of whether one adopts or rejects a particular paradigmatic perspective, the dominance of one paradigm over the other is not necessarily the best way to achieve a full understanding of crime and criminality. This is the critical issue missed by Petherick *et al.*, (2010) for, whilst they rightly attempt to address the lack of forensic analysis in criminological work, they themselves largely ignore the other paradigms involved – if they had reconstructed the past a little better, the answer to their concerns would be obvious.

Forensic criminology's epistemological and ontological roots can be located within nineteenth-century attempts to control order, control people and deal with habitual offenders (Wiener, 1994; Davie, 2005). More specifi-cally, the medical and psychiatric professions took the first steps in classifying criminals, their behaviours and actions and linking them to biological and/or psychological explanations. However, to begin with, these developments were not systematic or very organised. Rafter's term 'cottage industries' (2009:xiii) is a useful way to denote the micro-centres of criminological knowledge production that sprang up throughout Europe and the United States. Scattered thinly around Italy, Scotland, London, Germany, Paris, Vienna and New York (ibid.:xiii), a number of individuals started to look into the problem of crime and criminality. These small outlets of locally produced knowledge were largely contingent on place, yet some were eventually able to break free from the fetters of locality and 'establish professional journals, organize international conferences, and lay the foundations for a new field of knowledge' (ibid.:xiii). However, as with the development of the natural sciences, these initial forays into creating crimino-logical knowledge were also non-linear in their progression. Indeed, because of the multidisciplinary nature of those involved in criminology in its embryonic stage – which primarily consisted of statisticians, penologists, psychiatrists and medical doctors (Davie, 2005) – the development of the body of knowledge that today we call criminology did not really occur until the twentieth century.

The main disciplines involved in early studies were all relatively new themselves. This created a situation where newly formed disciplines began to fight for control and dominance over the issues they were interested in. As Abbott has ably demonstrated (1988, 2001), groups that dominate intellectual landscapes also attempt to dominate the jurisdictional boundaries and ownership over whatever knowledge centre, issue or problem they wish to control. Early forms of scientific criminology, therefore, consisted of a number of disciplines studying crime and criminality throughout different areas of society. This contextual aspect created localised centres of criminological knowledge production typified by differentiation that included competing focuses, competing agendas, rival theories, varieties of methodologies and different political orientations (Garland, 1997; Rafter, 2004, 2009; Davie, 2005). Despite these many differences and epistemological chasms, there are some common themes or ideas that threaded together to create both criminological theory and practice. Rafter (2009), who provides an excellent *reader* in the origins of criminology, identifies nine thematic streams in early criminological research:

1 physiognomy and phrenology;
2 moral and mental insanity;
3 evolution, degeneration and heredity;
4 ethnographic approaches to the underclass and underworld;
5 criminal anthropology;
6 habitual criminals;
7 eugenic criminology;
8 criminal statistics; and
9 sociological approaches to crime.

All nine of the themes incorporate a vast body of research, writing and applied use throughout the nineteenth and early twentieth centuries. Of direct relevance for the history of forensic criminology, however, are those early theories that link to a broader project called positivism.

The positivist paradigm

Positivistic studies of criminality are perhaps the most persistent types found in early criminological studies, involving the underlying premises of evolutionary and degeneracy theories discussed in more detail below. Positivist philosophy believed that one could analyse human behaviour using the same methods that had proved so successful in the natural sciences (primarily through inductive reasoning). It was believed that the scientific method – observation, recording and measurement, hypothesis testing through falsification and verification, and theory generation – could be applied to the social sciences and their attempts to understand human behaviour and solve social problems.

Auguste Comte (1798–1857) was the first to develop the system of what he called positive philosophy, which was both a philosophical and political movement. He wanted to develop a philosophy of mathematics, physics, chemistry and biology, which effectively makes him one of the first individuals to attempt a systematised philosophy of science. Comte was interested in the social dimensions of science and this theme resonates through his key works. A good starting point is to consider his famous dictum 'we have no knowledge of anything but phenomena; and our knowledge of phenomena is relative not absolute' (cited in Mill, 1961:6). For Comte, positivism had two primary objectives. The first was to generalise our scientific conceptions of phenomena, and the second was to systematise the art of social life (Comte, [1865]2009:3); and these objectives run through Comte's series *The Course of Positive Philosophy* (1830–1842) and his *A General View of View of Positivism* (1865). Within this work Comte pursued two goals. The first was to create a foundation for *social physics*, or what is now called socio-logy. The second goal was the coordination of the whole of positive knowledge. The first three volumes of *The Course* examined the five natural sciences that existed at the time of Comte (physics, chemistry, biology, mathematics and astronomy), and the final three volumes dealt with the social sciences. According to Comte, perhaps the best way to explain positive philosophy was through the law of three stages. Human development and knowledge passes through three successive stages – the theological, metaphysical and the positive ([1865]2009). The first stage is the starting point for the human mind, the second a transitory stage and the last is its *normal* state. In the theological stage, the mind searches for primary and final causes of phenomena and finds answers within the supernatural realm. It is within this phase that humans view objects as being created and manipulated by religious agents. The second stage is a slight modification of the first with supernatural agents being replaced by abstract entities. In the positive stage, characterised by the scientific method, the mind stops looking for absolute causal explanations of things, and instead we concentrate on finding out the physical laws that govern phenomena (ibid.). Knowledge, therefore, becomes relative, fluid and dynamic as opposed to absolute, rigid and dogmatic. It must be remembered that the time in which Comte was writing was truly a time of optimism, and the progress of humanity was a dominant ideology that drove much of the scientific work of the nineteenth century. His ideas were supported by some of the most powerful thinkers of the Victorian age. For example, Darwin remarked that Comte's notion of a theological stage was a 'grand notion'. However, not everyone agreed with Comte's conceptualisation of societal and knowledge development. Whewell criticised Comte's law of three stages, arguing that his arrangement of the progress of science between the metaphysical and positive stages did not follow the actual reality of history ([1865]2009). Despite this criticism, Comte's ideas became very popular, especially within the area of sociological positivism. According to Comte's theory, forensic practice would be a natural part of the positive stage, as it is based upon scientific knowledge and explanations that are used to resolve societal problems (i.e. a criminal justice issue).

The second area of importance for Comte was the classification of the sciences. Comte wanted to show the complex diversity of both the natural and social sciences whilst, at the same time, not losing sight of their unity. Comte's system – which starts from the most general of sciences (mathematics) and, as generality decreases, moves to the most complex (sociology) – was also an attempt to avoid fragmentation of knowledge. Higher education in UK universities over the last 100 years or so has developed its various subjects' curricula, and these have been structured on a strict division of labour, which is ultimately determined by occupational and professional dominance as well as economic or market forces (Abbott, 2001; Furedi, 2006, 2009). In Comteian terms, this is problematic, for it creates knowledge fragmentation, something that has become quite prevalent in the social sciences and which also goes some way to explain Petherick and Turvey's criticism that criminologists 'no longer have a sense of where they came from' (2010:xxii). It appears that many academics and subjects have lost the intellectual speculator element of the classic polymaths.

There are three main types of positivism: biological, psychological and sociological. It is not possible to review all these types in depth here, so I have restricted the discussion to those issues that are directly relevant to the epistemological and ontological development of scientific criminology. We must look towards nineteenth-century positivism as being primarily based upon the search for difference and classification amongst the criminal population. Three features of early positivism help explain what drove the search for difference, and the search for difference aided the development of classification or taxonomic schemes. The first idea is that of *determinism* (Tierney, 2010:58–59). A criminal's behaviour was thought to be determined by factors beyond their control, so a range of biological, psychological and sociological factors *influence* individuals to commit crime. However, there was still the difficult task of answering the question as to how could one identify factors that determined behaviour. The logical first step would be to consider physical difference. As Comte's positive philosophy suggested, our knowledge about things should largely be based upon what we observe, so, regardless of whether you agree or disagree with positivism per se, it was actually quite natural to consider physical difference; and this makes up the second feature of early positivism. Criminals were deemed to be *different* from non-criminals, whether it was differences in physical characteristics, abnormal or negative psychological traits, or socially learned attitudes (ibid.:58–59). Wiener (1994) pointed out that differentiation became important for the scientific study of criminality as research in the Victorian period tended to start from the assumption that criminals constituted a subcategory of the human race. These differences were then susceptible to scientific investigation, for if a difference exists then it should be observable, *ergo* you can measure it. If we then link these ideas to the social context of the dangerous and habitual classes with, say, the vivid descriptions of such individuals in the work of Mayhew and Dickens, the idea of difference becomes firmly entrenched within Victorian criminal conversations (Pearson, 1983; Wiener, 1994; Taylor, 2005).

The third feature of positivism is the idea of *pathology* and is linked to the aspect of biological or psychological disease (Tierney, 2010:58–59). Pathology implies that there is something wrong *within* the criminal; something that can be potentially cured. This idea is, of course, closely aligned with the professional discourses of medicine and psychiatry, which, as we shall see, were amongst the first as well as being the most dominant professions engaged in constructing criminological research during this period. The pathological theme is connected to a broader movement that is often called the medicalisation of deviancy (Conrad and Schneider, 1992). The medicalisation of deviancy suggests that changes to the way we think about criminals and the causes of their criminality can affect the type of knowledge constructed. In the 1950s, for example, explanations about crime took a distinctly medicalised form, similar to those of the nineteenth century. Criminals were deemed to be suffering from pathological illnesses, both biological and psychological in origin and nature. In times where medical discourse dominates our understandings of crime and criminality, behaviours can be redefined to fit such discursive framing. For example, the move from offenders being simply bad to offenders being sick was clearly seen in subjects such as opiate addiction, alcoholism and child abuse (ibid.). Today, medico-pathological discourses still filter through the criminal justice system, for example, in the risk assessment and risk management of *personality-disordered* offenders; and such discourses still play a key role in *inventing* the criminal.

Inventing the criminal

The intellectual backdrop to scientific criminology is placed within the disciplines of psychiatry and medicine, as well as a number of penologists that worked closely with offenders within prisons. Throughout the nineteenth century, psychiatrists interested in crime attempted to explain why some offenders were recidivists and, in many cases, very vicious. As the above section on the micro-contextual issues noted, a common perception of the criminal during this period was that of the repeat or habitual violent offender (Wiener, 1994; Davie, 2005; Taylor, 2005), and this conceptualisation was often linked to the relatively new concept of *moral insanity*.

Moral insanity

The dominance of the concept of moral insanity as an explanation of crime can be linked to the developments within medicine and the rise of the psychiatric profession. Psychiatrists in this period were often referred to as alienists – for they were physicians 'who dealt with alienated minds' (Rafter, 2009:43) – and they made numerous attempts to explain the actions of morally insane offenders. As with a great deal of criminological labels, many different terms other than moral insanity were used to convey the same condition. Some of these included: *moral derangement, mania without delirium, degeneration, moral imbecility, inborn criminality* and *hereditary unfitness* (ibid.). Moral insanity was theorised as a *state* rather than a set of behaviours, so it was conceivable that two people could engage in a particular type of behaviour – let's say a violent attack on another individual – and one be diagnosed as suffering from moral insanity whilst the other diagnosed as *sane*.

Two key examples from the period illustrate some of the core explanatory ideas to come from medicine and psychiatry during this period. In 1786 the physician Benjamin Rush (1746–1813) published *An Inquiry into the Influence of Physical*

Causes upon the Moral Faculty. Rush was particularly interested in mind-body relationships and looked for the physical causes of moral insanity (Runes, 1947, cited in Rafter, 2009:45). He undertook one of the first investigations into biology and crime and examined the capacity of the mind to distinguish and choose between good and evil (virtue and vice). Rush identified ten physical causes that affected the moral faculty, or one's ethical capacity (Rafter, 2009:45). These factors were climate, diet, certain drinks, extreme hunger, disease, idleness, excessive sleep, bodily pain, cleanliness and solitude. Climate, for example, was linked to geographic location and the moral qualities of the local inhabitants. Rush found that 'irascibility, levity, timidity and indolence' were qualities associated with people from warmer climates, whilst 'selfishness, tempered with sincerity and integrity, form the moral character of the inhabitants of cold countries' (Runes, 1947, cited in Rafter, 2009:47). Rush also tied moral sensibilities to the effects of the change in seasons. Another example illustrating the presence and dominance of psychiatry in Victorian discourses on crime and criminality involves the work of James Cowles Pritchard (1786–1848) who published *Researches into the Physical History of Man* (1818) and *Treatise on Insanity* (1835). Pritchard was an English anthropologist, linguist, physician and psychiatrist, and it is suggested that he coined the term moral insanity to bring together Rush's observations on the disease of the moral faculty and Pinel's concept of mania without delirium (Pritchard, 1835, cited in Rafter, 2009:54–59). Pritchard's term was so succinct and clearly defined that it was adopted by American and European psychiatrists and criminologists 'to denote afflictions in which feelings or emotions (the "moral" dispositions) alone are disordered' (Rafter, 2009:54). Furthermore, and as Rafter highlights, Pritchard's conceptualisation of moral insanity also incorporated a set of syndromes that today are linked to *psychopathy*. Apart from identifying the usual aspects of moral insanity – for instance, morbid depression and excitement – Pritchard noted the prevalence of angry and malicious feelings 'which arise without provocation or any of the ordinary incitements' (Pritchard, 1835, cited in Rafter, 2009:54–59). The concept of psychiatric disorders such as moral insanity, then, served to link the biologically determined mental faculties with decisions to commit crime. Such explanations were then used to explain the criminal actions of the habitual offender. Their behaviours were seen as a stable state, indicative of moral insanity, and such ideas also fed the fever surrounding the concept of the dangerous classes (Wiener, 1994; Davie, 2005).

The importance of ideas from people like Rush and Pritchard for the beginnings of scientific criminology should not be underestimated. However, there is a missing piece to the picture. Rush's primary occupation was as a Physician; Pritchard was an Anthropologist. In order to get their ideas on moral insanity applied in practice, they needed the help of individuals who worked with the *morally insane* in hospitals and prisons. When it comes to the aetiological development of scientific criminology, a crucial aspect is how these ideas were transmitted through social institutions and how they became part of criminal justice policy.[2] Individuals such as Philippe Pinel (1745–1826) were highly influential in making moral insanity a key diagnostic tool for the criminally insane. Pinel was a physician and became medical director of the Asylum de Bicetre in Paris and later of a women's asylum Salpêtrière (Rafter, 2004:989). Pinel's *A Treatise on Insanity*, published in 1801, brought together a number of core ideas about how moral insanity should be treated like a disease. He was also specifically interested in repeat offenders. Again the project of classification through observation became the important method for developing a taxonomy of insanity. Pinel identified five types of moral derangement – *melancholy, dementia, idiocy, mania with delirium* and *mania without delirium* – which he then attempted to link to an individual's propensity to commit criminal acts. Pinel's position as medical director no doubt had status and influence and enabled him to study and develop his ideas about criminal causality. As the nineteenth century progressed, ideas about moral derangement and moral insanity took a dominant foothold within explanations of criminality.[3] Perhaps the central reason for this dominance, with consistent links being made between an individual's moral compass and mental faculties and their criminal or deviant behaviour, was the influence of physiognomy and phrenology in the first third of the nineteenth century.

Bumpology – the coming of the criminal man

The first biological and psychological positivistic attempts to find causes of criminality through theories of evolution, degeneration, differentiation, determinism and pathology came from *physiognomy* and *phrenology*, whose influence peaked somewhere in the 1820s and 1830s (Rafter, 1997, 2008, 2009; Davie, 2005). The central idea for both sciences was the need for close observation of the structure, proportions and contours of the skull and face. It had been thought for many years that a criminal's 'face was less pleasing to the eye' (Davie, 2005:34). However, ideas regarding the physical differences between criminals and non-criminals received its first scientific analysis through the work of Swiss poet and theologian Johann Lavater (1741–1801). Lavater developed physiognomy, which he defined as 'the science of knowledge of the correspondence between external and internal man, the visible superficies, and invisible contents' (Lavater quoted in Hartley, 2001:33, cited in Davie, 2005:34). Rafter suggests that what Lavater meant by this was 'reading character and other psychological traits from outer physical signs, especially those of the face' (Rafter, 2009:10). In his *Essays on Physiognomy* (1789), Lavater divided the face into three distinct areas and associated a specific area to an aspect of human nature. The mouth and chin represented *animal life*; the nose and cheeks associated with *moral life*; and finally, the forehead and eyebrows were associated with an individual's *intellectual life*. The aspect of intellectual life was the one that most interested physiognomists such as Lavater as he believed it was superior to the other two forms (Lavater, 1789, cited in Rafter, 2009:10; also see Rafter, 1997, 2008; Davie, 2005). Lavater strongly argued that physiognomy could be developed into a science, for science, in his eyes, is where 'truth and knowledge is explained by fixed principles . . . by words, lines, rules, and definitions' (Lavater, 1789, cited in Rafter, 2009:13). He was sure that:

> Precision in observation is the very soul of physiognomy. The physiognomist must possess a most delicate, swift, certain, most extensive spirit of observation ... to observe, to be attentive, to distinguish what is similar, to discover proportion, and disproportion, is the office of his understanding.
>
> (Lavater, 1789 cited in Davie, 2005:34–35)

Lavater's insistence on observation as the foundation of his method and which aids in the generation of knowledge follows that of the natural scientists as described in the previous chapter. It was this method that linked the propensity to commit criminal acts with the structure and form of the head, and, in the Victorian period, the *head* was frequently cited as possessing identifiable features that *caused* criminality. In order to do this, researchers innovatively linked physical features with theories of evolution and degeneration. British physiognomist W. Hatfield, for example, published *Face Reading* (1870), which described the criminal head as 'low and broad, with wide lips, and a short and thick or "bullish" neck' (Davie, 2005:35). Of course, the disproportionately large lower jaw in relation to the forehead region were directly related to what was perceived to be a regression or recapitulation towards a more primitive form; or, using Lavater's concept, an *animal state*. Figure 3.1 illustrates some of the typical imagery physiognomists used in their work in the nineteenth century.

Whilst physiognomy failed to make a sustained impact on scientific criminology, a similar set of ideas did. A number of physicians and medical doctors took the ideas of Lavater and developed them into what was to be called *phrenology*. Phrenology was one of the first systematic explanations of human behaviour that used external observations of the physical make-up of the skull to make inferences about the 'innermost workings of the human brain' (Davie, 2005:36; also see Rafter, 1997, 2008, 2009). Phrenology had, at its core, three basic assumptions:

> First, that the exterior conformation of the skull matched both its interior surface and the conformation of the brain. Second, that the mind could be analysed in terms of innate faculties or functions. Third, that the shape and size of protuberances on the surface of the skull reflected the development of these faculties.
>
> (Davie, 2005:36)

The creation of phrenology is accredited to the work of Neuroanatomist and physiologist Franz Joseph Gall (1758–1828). Sometime around 1800, Gall invented cranioscopy, which was later rebranded as phrenology. Where Lavater mapped onto the face the *animal, moral* and *intellectual* aspects of human life, Gall identified *propensities, sentiments* and *intellectual* powers and associated

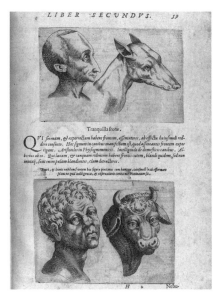

Figure 3.1 The faces of physiognomy[4, 5]
Images courtesy of the National Library of Medicine.

these aspects to areas of the skull. Gall published *On The Functions of the Brain* (1822–1825), and it was this text that introduced the idea that the brain was divided into various mental *faculties* and that behaviour was explained in terms of sentiments or faculties localised to specific parts of the brain. Johann Gaspar Spurzheim (1776–1832) extended Gall's work in his *Phrenology in Connection with the Study of Physiognomy* (1834). Spurzheim's work included a self-improvement element, which then became 'the basis for a theory of criminal behavior and, following from that, a theory of punishment and reformation' (Rafter, 2009:20). Spurzheim provided a map of the location and classification of faculties including selfish sentiments, moral sentiments, reason, semi-intellectual sentiments and perceptive intellect (see figure 3.2).

The Victorian period saw a dramatic increase in research into phrenology as well as the growth in phrenological societies, journals and articles. For example, Edinburgh lawyer George Combes (1788–1858) set up Britain's first phrenological society. In 1828, Combes published *The Constitution of Man and its Relation to External Objects*, and, interestingly, by 1860 it had sold over 100,000 copies, which is twice the amount of Darwin's *Origin of the Species* over a similar period of time (Davie, 2005:37). Again, the importance of moral entrepreneurs in key positions within the criminal justice system is crucial to understanding how such ideas became dominant. In 1840, Alexander Maconochie (1787–1860), the superintendent of the Penal Station, Norfolk Island, Australia, put in place a regime partly based upon phrenological principles. In 1841, Marmaduke B. Sampson

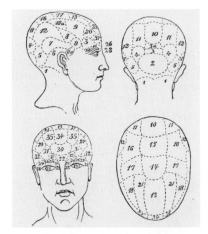
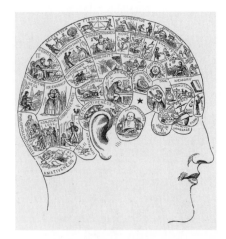

Figure 3.2 The phrenology head[6, 7]

published *Criminal Jurisprudence Considered in Relation to Mental Organisation*, and in 1846 he published the second edition of *Rationale of Crime and its Appropriate Treatment being a Treatise on Criminal Jurisprudence Considered in Relation to Cerebral Organization* – both of which were largely based upon phrenological principles. It is easy to see how moral entrepreneurs such as Combes and Maconochie became influenced by phrenology. One of the fundamental themes of the post-Gall phrenological developments saw the brain as being malleable and capable of change, which heavily influenced neoclassical ideas pertaining to punishment and rehabilitation (Wiener, 1994; Davie, 2005). As Spurzheim noted back in 1828, such developments enabled phrenologists to combine biological determinism with an 'optimistic rehabilitative approach' that conceptualised character traits as 'heritable but not fixed' (Spurzheim, 1828, cited in Davie, 2005:38). If the brain could be changed then an individual's behaviour could be manipulated and changed, and that opened up a number of possibilities regarding punishment and rehabilitation. The influence of phrenology in the epistemological origins of scientific criminology is crucial. It set the agenda in research and theories of criminality at its height in the 1820s and 1830s. However, by the 1850s and 1860s its influence began to wane as these ideas were supplemented with clearer biological explanations of criminality, especially in relation to the theories of evolution, degeneration and determinism (Rafter, 1997, 2008, 2009; Davie, 2005).

Evolution and the deterministic nature of being

At the same time as the physical sciences were developing their ideas regarding the physical nature of objects and the biological sciences were engaged in the taxonomic process of classifying the plant and animal species on the planet, a number of ideas about human nature and its link to evolution were also developed. The introduction of Darwin's theory of evolution in the nineteenth century created much debate between the scientific, religious and social spheres of society, and his ideas created a motivating boost to the natural sciences, especially biology. The taxonomic mission discussed in the previous chapter was also greatly affected by Darwin's theories, as this added an evolutionary dimension to classification schemes and theories. Furthermore, Darwin's theories were also *borrowed* by other natural and social science subject areas, and the links between his ideas and early understandings of criminality were of special influence for the development of scientific criminology. Charles Darwin (1809–1882) was an English naturalist whose work did more to revolutionise our thinking about animal and human development than that of any other thinker of the nineteenth century. The ideas laid out in *The Origin of Species by Means of Natural Selection or The Preservation of Favoured Races in the Struggle for Life* (1859) included some of his most popular; namely, 'the struggle for existence' and the 'survival of the fittest'.[8] Within this work Darwin laid down his ideas on variation amongst all species. Some individuals (whether plants, animals or mammals) differ in terms of hereditary traits, such as being able to digest certain foods, run faster or have greater strength (Wilson, 2006:437). Those with more of these hereditary traits survive longer or breed faster and leave more offspring. There is not only more of this *next generation* but they also inherit the advanced traits. Evolution by natural selection has occurred. As Wilson (2006:437–438) points out, 'the Darwinian calculus of genetic change, pitting variant against variant' also comes juxtaposed against a great deal of evidence that shows us that natural selection 'can also generate hereditary cooperation and self-sacrifice'. Specifically, the creation of social groups that combine to aid in their own self-interest and survival is a Darwinian message that favourably linked with nineteenth-century discourses on the habitual or dangerous criminal classes. If *The Origins of the Species* laid out in great detail the theory of evolution, Darwin's *The Descent of Man and Selection in Relation to Sex* (1871) put forward the notion that man had descended from lower forms. The only problem for Darwin was that he completely lacked fossil evidence. Fortunately for the rest of us, scientific studies over the last 140 years have consistently uncovered a multitude of supporting fossil and genome evidence in support of Darwin's theory (Wilson, 2006:766); often to the detriment of competing theories, such as Lamarck's inherited characteristics and Mendel's units of hereditary particulates (ibid.:438). So how did Darwin's theories link into early explanations of criminal behaviour?

To put it in simple terms, it was proposed that individual humans vary in terms of their evolutionary development and that criminal and deviant behaviour was associated with a lower evolutionary stage (Rafter, 1997, 2009; Lombroso, 2007; Lilly, *et al.*, 2011; Tierney, 2010). Perhaps the most dominant theme within the theory of evolution was the idea of *biological determinism*. It was suggested that an individual's genetic make-up determines every aspect of their biological being and also of their psychological personality. Behaviour and, more importantly, criminal behaviour was thus determined by inherent characteristics which are genetically determined and passed on from generation to generation. One important element of evolutionary theory was *degeneration*, and criminal behaviour was often closely linked to this concept. Criminals broke the law not because of free will but because of degeneration, which was seen as a process of slow decay that left them prey to baser instincts. As degeneration was viewed as a condition that pre-exists and somehow causes behaviour, it was perhaps natural that the theory of evolution would be connected to the ideas and works of those concerned with nineteenth-century criminality. The century is littered with examples of work on evolution and degeneracy within the context of criminal behaviour. For instance, Benedict-August Morel's *Treatise on the Physical, Intellectual and Moral Degenerations of the Human Species* (1857), argues that criminality, imbecility and insanity were symptoms of the underlying condition of degeneration. Morel was a physician, psychiatrist and chief medical officer at St. Yon Insane Asylum in Rouen, France. Another example comes from the work of J. Bruce Thomson, resident surgeon at the General Prison for Scotland, Perth. Thomson published an article entitled 'The Hereditary Nature of Crime' in the *Journal of Mental Health Sciences* in 1870 (Davie, 2005; Rafter, 2009). These two examples illustrate again the importance of motivated moral entrepreneurs (Becker, 1963) in key positions within the criminal justice system. Without these individuals, such ideas would not have been applied and developed and they would not have shaped criminological knowledge during the nineteenth century.

Perhaps the most famous example of the link between theories of evolution and degeneracy and criminality is from the works of Darwin's cousin, Francis Galton. Galton (1822–1911), an English anthropologist, eugenicist, inventor and statistician, took his cousin's ideas and developed them in line with his own interest in quantifying the physical attributes of the different races in South Africa. As Davie notes:

> Galton's interest in anthropological measurement and his preoccupation with racial degeneration came together in his decision to begin measuring what he considered a self-evidently mentally homogenous group of men: the inmates of Britain's convict prisons.

(2005:97)

Galton's *Hereditary Genius: An Inquiry into its Laws and Consequences* (1869) and *Inquiries into Human Faculty and its Development* (1883) linked all these key themes together. Thus, degeneration and evolution became the major themes within positivist explanations of crime and criminality and helped nineteenth-century criminologists[9] understand why crime was more often than not associated with pauperism, insanity and other social ills. A pauper family, for instance, would naturally produce criminals: an idea that still resonates through much sociological research on the transmission of criminal values (Sellin, 1938; Cohen, 1956; Park and Burgess, [1925]1967), research on the reproduction of social inequality (Macleod, 2004), as well as the criminalisation of the working classes (Jones, 2011; Wacquant, 2009). For nineteenth-century policymakers, the beliefs about crime being directly linked with evolution and degeneracy theories had a number of implications. They began to think about different ways to deal with three groups of people: (i) *dependents*, which usually meant the poor; (ii) *defectives*, a rather pejorative term to describe the insane, feeble-minded and deaf and dumb; and finally (iii) *delinquents*, which included adult and juvenile offenders (Davie, 2005). For example, Thomson's article entitled 'Psychology of Criminals' (1870) attempted to build a profile of different types of individuals prone to crime and deviance by bridging the gap between degeneration and criminal anthropology. Thomson claimed that there was a low type of physique indicating a deteriorated character (Davie, 2005). These works, and many like them, on moral insanity, physiognomy and phrenology, degeneration and evolutionary theory laid the foundation for the development of more explicit positivist theories and methods for explaining crime and criminality.

Criminal anthropology

Whilst the ideas presented above can be seen as seminal examples of the major themes running through early criminological knowledge, it took the controversial work of an Italian doctor to put positivism firmly on the criminological map (Rafter, 1997, 2008; Davie, 2005; Gibson, 2009): Cesare Lombroso (1835–1909) developed the discipline of criminal anthropology, which was the scientific study of the physical and psychological traits of criminals. Lombroso's criminal anthropology was an attempt to fuse his medical knowledge, as a doctor and psychiatrist, with the ideas of physiognomy and anthropology within a Darwinist framework of evolution. However, he is most famous for his theory of the *born criminal* (Rafter, 1997, 2008; Davie, 2005; Gibson, 2009). Most standard criminological texts accept, somewhat begrudgingly, Lombroso as being one of the founding fathers of criminology. Unfortunately, they also usually provide nothing but a cursory analysis and criticism of his theories (Jones, 2001; Newburn, 2007; Lilly *et al.*, 2011). There have been many criticisms of Lombroso's work that have accumulated over the years, especially as sociologically oriented theories of crime dominated the British criminological landscape from the 1920s onwards. Before moving on to the core ideas of Lombroso, it is worthwhile exploring in more detail the issues surrounding the criticisms; for it is here we can find yet more possible answers to the problem of epistemological amnesia and paradigmatic myopia. Any worthwhile analysis of the problems around the criticisms of Lombroso's work uncovers a common problem with much contemporary scholarship into crime and criminality. The majority of criticisms of Lombroso's work follow a particular a pattern:

> Disdain for what we understood as the simplemindedness of Lombroso's theory of atavism and with a fear that his biological determinism was

prejudicial to women, blacks, and other social groups that he deemed inferior. Many of his conclusions seemed silly, and his project a particularly frightful example of bad science.

(Lombroso, 2007:1)

Often tied to the disdain for Lombroso is a disdain for general positivistic methods, which is usually transmitted from academic generation to generation without any true critical reflection. The biggest problem with criticisms of Lombroso (which are discussed below) is that they tend to come not from a reading of any of his original works but from watered-down critiques that have become the staple of most undergraduate textbooks in criminology (for example, see Jones, 2001; Newburn, 2007; Tierney, 2010). These are, then, simply regurgitated time and time again, and is simply poor scholarship. Lombroso is best known for his *L'Uomo Delinquente* [*Criminal Man*] (1876), in which he outlined how positivism could be used to link explanations of criminal differentiation and behaviour to physiological development, epitomised through the concept of the *born criminal*. What many texts do not mention in any detail is that this work went through five editions spanning 20 years and including a vast expansion in its comprehensiveness, with additional topics, evidence and theories. As Davie (2005:130) notes, the last edition alone spanned more than 2,000 pages. Indeed, Lombroso's work embodies a multi-causal theory of crime that is not simply based upon biological determinism but also includes psychological and sociological causes as well as the extensive use and analysis of cultural artefacts (Rafter, 1997, 2008; Davie, 2005; Gibson, 2009). Most authors conveniently ignore the sociological positivism and humanistic elements to Lombroso's theory and instead reduce everything to biological determinism. More specifically, humanist/interpretive sociologists have used Lombroso's atavistic theory of the *criminal man* as a stick to flog positivists with over many decades. Gibson and Hann-Rafter (Lombroso, 2007:2) highlight the main reason for this lack of critical reading of Lombroso: they point out that 'no complete English translation exists of any of the five editions' of *Criminal Man*. They go on to suggest that only two English books that can be closely linked to Lombroso's text and each of these 'radically oversimplifies' or 'flattens out the nuances' of Lombroso's complex and comprehensive work (ibid.:3). What this means in real terms is that, whilst the history of Lombroso and his work is presented in criminological texts, it is rarely based on the original works; and because of this, we should be careful that we aren't persuaded by the critical arguments of those who have not bothered to go to the original work.

This problem can be clearly seen in the preface to Petherick *et al.*'s *Forensic Criminology* (2010). Turvey and Petherick simply dismiss examining Lombroso in any detail and instead lazily state that the 'history is presented in every introductory criminology text and does not need repeating here' (2010:xxiii), which is amazing given the fact that throughout their text they espouse skills such as critical thinking, in-depth evidence collection and analysis.[10] It is bemusing that they don't dig a little deeper into the epistemological origins of forensic criminology themselves. Hopefully, this myopic vision of the aetiological origins of criminology has begun to be dispelled by the more in-depth historical works of Rafter (2004, 2009), Davie (2005) and to some extent Wiener (1994), as well as the overview provided in this chapter. Lombroso's work spans 'over thirty books and one thousand articles during his lifetime' (Lombroso, 2007:3). It is, of course, not possible to adequately examine all of this in this current text. It is, however, useful to discuss the ideas that are most relevant to the creation of scientific criminology. Whether or not you're a lover of positivism, it is clear that Lombroso and the Italian school of criminology played a crucial role in the epistemological and ontological development of criminology.

Lombroso was critical of the classical and utilitarian idea of an individual's behaviour being largely a result of rational thinking and free will. He wished to explore the idea that our biological and physiological make-up acted as the driving influence to criminal behaviour. Using the positivist methods of observation, measurement and recording, Lombroso's major claim was to 'have turned the study of crime into a science that draws its conclusions from empirical data and clinical case studies' (ibid.:7). He adopted the core assumption of phrenology, that external features mirror internal moral faculties, and he also accepted and utilised the work on moral insanity as well as the work of French statisticians such as Quetelet and Guerry (see Chapter 8). Through such work, Lombroso argued that crime was natural and not part of free will. Holding posts as an army doctor and then in mental asylums and prisons, Lombroso was able to observe and measure thousands of bodies over the course of his life. In the fourth edition of *Criminal Man*, Lombroso drew conclusions from the study of 52,313 bodies, taken from his own research and that of 'Marro, Ferri, and Rossi' (ibid.:233). This is quite a remarkable sample size that is rarely achieved even by contemporary standards and research.

Delinquente nato

As previously mentioned, Lombroso's concept of the 'born criminal' (*delinquente-nato*) has become *the* primary concept that is emphasised and reproduced time and time again in criminology textbooks. It is also the concept that is used to criticise early positivistic methods. As Gibson and Hann-Rafter suggest:

> For modern readers, Lombroso's methodology appears unscientific and even laughable. Whilst his books are filled with statistical tables, these tables are often sloppy and unsophisticated in their lack of standardization . . . even more questionable is Lombroso's mixture of quantitative data with qualitative evidence such as proverbs, historical anecdotes, and examples drawn from painting and literature.
>
> (Ibid.:8)

Most scientific projects of the eighteenth and nineteenth centuries engaged in developing classification schemes for plants, animals and elements found on Earth. Criminologists such as Lombroso followed suit. Over the five editions of *Criminal Man* he developed an elaborate classification of criminals (Rafter, 1997, 2008; Davie, 2005; Gibson, 2009). However, in the first edition, he simply placed 'all lawbreakers together in a single, undifferentiated group, which he compares to the insane and, sporadically, to control groups of "healthy" men (usually soldiers)' (Lombroso, 2007:9). Lombroso thought that these three groups could be compared and contrasted and that there were clear physical differences between each group. He put forward the concept of *atavism*, which was used to link physical differences between these three groups to degeneracy and evolutionary theories. The atavistic criminal man showed physical characteristics similar to an earlier stage of evolution, and criminal behaviour was linked to these atavistic characteristics. In the first edition, Lombroso outlines some of the main differences between criminals and the healthy:

> Robbers and murderers are taller than rapists, forgers, and especially thieves. As for weight, we can compare findings on 1,331 soldiers, studied by me and Dr. Franchini . . . in most other regions, most notably Naples, Sicily, and Piedmont, criminals' average weight exceeded that of healthy men.
>
> (Ibid.:50)

Lombroso identified a number of atavistic qualities in the various samples he used:

> In general, thieves are notable for their expressive faces and manual dexterity, small wandering eyes that are often oblique in form . . . . Habitual murderers have a cold, glassy stare and eyes that are sometimes bloodshot and filmy; the nose is often hawklike and always large, the jaw is strong, the cheekbones broad.
>
> (Ibid.:51)

Furthermore, Lombroso's sample indicated that 'nearly all criminals have jug ears, thick hair, thin beards, pronounced sinuses, protruding chins, and broad cheekbones' (ibid.:53).

In the second edition, Lombroso began adding to his classification system by introducing the 'criminal of passion'. However, it wasn't until the third edition that he introduced the term *born criminal*, which was actually borrowed from Italian criminologist Enrico Ferri. In the third edition it is clear that Lombroso was attempting to establish a 'Darwinist framework of criminal anthropology' (ibid.:161); for it was here that Lombroso proposed that for an individual to be a full criminal type they needed to exhibit 'a cluster of five or more anomalies' (ibid.10). Lombroso suggested that 40 per cent of all criminals were born criminals, and even a single isolated anomaly 'marked an offender as constitutionally flawed and therefore potentially dangerous' (ibid.:10). In the third edition, Lombroso also highlights that the concept of atavism is inadequate to explain multiple anomalies in all born criminals, so he links disease with atavism in order to explain arrested development (degeneration) in biological and mental functions (ibid.:11). This provided Lombroso with the necessary bridge linking atavism with moral insanity. Throughout all five editions, Lombroso consistently uses atavism as the anchor on which his theory sits. Because of this, it is not surprising that subsequent criticisms tend to overemphasise this aspect and ignore the multi-causal, sociological and cultural elements to his theory. The fourth edition adds to Lombroso's criminal taxonomic mission by including epilepsy as a cause of born criminality as well as returning to examine in more detail the insane criminal, adding three subcategories – the alcoholic criminal, the hysterical criminal, and the mattoid[11] (ibid.:11). In the fifth and final edition, Lombroso introduces yet more categories of criminals – for instance, the political criminal[12] – but he regarded these as being different to born criminals. It is also in the fifth edition that Lombroso introduces more sociological and environmental factors as explanation of the causes of criminality. For example, Lombroso discusses urban density, wealth, religion and education, repeating what he had argued since the first edition of *Criminal Man*: 'there is no crime which is not rooted in multiple causes' (ibid.:12). As already mentioned above, this aspect of Lombroso's work has largely been ignored by those who criticise him.

What makes Lombroso's work part of the aetiological origins of scientific criminology is his use of scientific principles to study the criminal. As the basis of his theory was physical – bodily anomalies were proof of criminal disposition – he needed to find ways to detect these anomalies. In short, he needed to find the appropriate measuring apparatus. For example, he borrowed and altered the following instruments in order to measure criminality (Finn, 2009:15):

- *Plethysmograph* and *hydrophyg-mograph* (invented by Francis Frank) – used to test blood pressure to measure the 'level of affection in subjects';
- *Phonograph* – used to measure speech patterns;
- *Electric Pen* (invented by Thomas Edison) – used for handwriting analysis;
- *Tachyanthropometer* and the *craniograph* (invented by Anfonsi) – used to measure the subject's height and arm length and 'the form and capacity of the skull';
- *Aesthesiometer* (invented by Max von Frey) – used to measure tactile sensibility;
- *Algometer* (invented by Emil du Bois-Reymond) – which measured general sensibility and sensitivity to pain.

Regardless of his somewhat dubious conclusions, Lombroso did attempt to apply a scientific methodology to his studies, including the systematic use of data and methodological triangulation. For example, he used his medical training and experience to study a number of criminal skulls, which were subject to a number of craniometric tests. Anthropologists had been using cranial capacity for many years as a way to classify 'races in the evolutionary hierarchy' (Davie, 2005:132). Lombroso compared the criminal skulls with those of *honest men*. He concluded that there was a concentration of small brains and large brains among his sample of criminal skulls. In his first edition, Lombroso found:

> The cranial sutures or joins in the bones of the skull were normal in only seventeen cases. . . . in another study of fifty-six criminal craniums, I found that thirteen had one of the most serious of all anomalies, a media occipital fossetta[13] or indentation at the base of the skull. . . . Criminals have the following rates of abnormality: 61 percent exhibit fusion of the cranial bones; 92 percent, prognathism or an ape-like forward thrust of the lower face.
>
> (Lombroso, 2007:45–49)

As well as using medical methods to examine the physiology of criminals, Lombroso employed a number of anthropometric tests that were in use at the time. These included measuring the 'relative size of the frontal and occipital regions of the brain, the facial angle. . . . the size of the lower jaw and the cranial index' (Davie, 2005:132). In the 1880s anthropometry was routinely being used as the first systematic method of criminal identification (Nickell and Fischer, 1999; Finn, 2009; Rafter, 2009). This is discussed in greater detail in Chapter 4 as anthropometry is directly linked to the development of forensic science and criminal investigations. Lombroso also used the technique of portrait photography, developed and employed by Galton's use of the composite photograph (also discussed in the following chapter). Lombroso thought portrait photography would be a valuable shortcut to the observation of such outwardly visible stigmata that were signs of atavistic anomalies (Cole, 2002; Finn, 2009).

There are obviously a number of problems with Lombroso's methods and theory. In particular, Lombroso's use of theories of evolution, degeneracy, phrenology and physiognomy, linked to his use of the available scientific apparatus, never reached an adequate level of predictive accuracy, empirical adequacy or explanatory depth. However, it did have heuristic value and unifying power (Ward *et al.*, 2006:8–10). Furthermore, Lombroso's use of anthropometry and photography offer a clear link with the origins and development of forensic science and criminal investigations. There is much to Lombroso's theory, and scholarship into the role Lombroso played in developing scientific criminology is starting to move beyond the usual reductive and sometimes erroneous reading of his core work, *L'Uomo Delinquente [Criminal Man]*.

Summary

This chapter has outlined only a mere fraction of the breadth and depth of the early research into scientific criminology. What hopefully has been achieved is a discussion of some of the core elements relevant to the epistemological and onto-logical development of scientific criminological knowledge. Early forms of criminology were created in the social context of growing fears surrounding the problems of maintaining social order and the lack of self-control amongst the lower classes as well as fears over the habitual criminal, all of which devel-oped in the eighteenth and nineteenth centuries. During the reign of Queen Victoria, a number of individuals attempted to emulate the scientific work of the natural philosophers by copying the taxonomic mission of observation, recording and classifying. They applied similar taxonomic principles to a number of criminal and psychological problems that presented themselves in an attempt to understand the inner states of human beings. Part of this process involved devel-oping and using a number of scientific methods and tools for the observation and measurement of criminals. It was thought that the outward physicality of the *body* would provide sufficient evidence of *criminality*, by looking at physical signs of difference, or any biological anomalies that might exist. These differences were deemed to determine pathological behaviour within individuals, thereby *causing* their criminal behaviour. Such ideas, theories and methods were later collectively labelled as biological and psychological positivism. Tied to this scientific practice was its application to the *real world*, for such ideas only gained in popularity and spread throughout the criminal justice system due to their implementation by a number of key practitioners who worked in prisons. These moral entrepreneurs created the necessary link between scientific theory and practice, which was crucial for the development of scientific criminology. Contemporary forensic criminology has its roots clearly within this historical epoch, research and prac-tice. This claim is further strengthened if one considers how scientific criminol-ogy was also linked to early forms of forensic and criminal investigations.

Chapter 4

The beginnings of forensic investigation

Introduction

Forensic science as embedded in criminal investigations has the contemporary persona of a *sexy* subject and in recent years has become big business within the popular entertainment industry. Countless fictional books, TV programmes and movies have all successfully exploited the general public's thirst for anything that remotely looks like *CSI* or *forensics*. Some students who start forensics courses think they will end up in some investigative role, juxtaposed with scientific work in a state-of-the-art laboratory with blue neon mood lighting included as standard; although I often wonder how the team in *CSI Las Vegas* solve any crime under those lighting conditions! When students begin to study the realities behind forensics and criminal investigations they begin to see the vast differences between these realities and what they've seen on TV. This chapter aims to push past some of these perceptions by examining the aetiological origins and development of forensic investigative methods. A full and complete history of the development of forensic investigations is yet to be written, and although I am wary of Pearson's (1975:x) dislike for academics who often *cop out* by saying there is a need for more research at the end of their work, there *is* a clear need for more historical research in this area.

This chapter provides a selective historical account of some of the key developments in forensic science as directly linked to criminal investigations. These developments are also linked to the growth in scientific criminology that was discussed in the previous chapter. What we understand today as forensic investigations were primarily developed in the Victorian period and are contextually linked to the same social, economic and political discourses that influenced the rise in scientific criminology. However, the application of *scientific* methods to resolve problems within society dates back for thousands of years. Whilst this chapter considers some of these early developments, its main focus is on the eighteenth and nineteenth centuries. This was the age of poison being commonly used in cases of death; of the development of the pathologist; and of the beginnings of a fully formed police force and detective bureau. The developments in scientific criminology outlined in Chapter 3 paralleled the practical developments in catching the criminals. As with science and scientific criminology, the period in which forensic investigations developed was exciting, dynamic and full of innovation, epitomised by close links between the academic and practitioner worlds.

This chapter is divided into four core sections. The first two sections provide a broad historical overview of the early developments in forensic investigations as well as well as a brief discussion on the birth of modern forensic investigations. The final two sections focus down on what were the core influences and themes in the development of forensic investigations in the nineteenth century. The first major theme looks at the development of technologies for measuring and identifying criminals and includes an examination of the developments in anthropometry, photography and fingerprints. The final section looks at the development of what has become the foundation of modern forensic science. It reviews the research on dust particles and how this research generated two of the most enduring fundamental ideas in forensic science: the idea of *trace evidence* and the *principal of exchange*. It examines these concepts in light of the work of Edmond Locard and the use of his pioneering research into dust particles for forensic purposes, becoming the bedrock of all contemporary forensic practice.

Early forensics – the washing away of wrongs

The beginnings of criminal investigations are relatively easy to pinpoint as they can be connected to various advancements in policing that took place during the nineteenth century (Emsley, 2003, 2010; Morris, 2007; Savage, 2007). Any attempt to trace the history of the development of forensic science is more difficult as it spans a longer time period. It wasn't until the end of the nineteenth and the beginning of the twentieth centuries that it was a common occurrence to find scientific methods applied to solve criminal cases, which eventually evolved throughout the twentieth century into what we now consider to be forensic science. However, there is lots of evidence to suggest that at various points throughout human history there have been occasions where elements of *science* have been used to resolve disputes or, indeed, simply used for identification purposes. For example, there is evidence of fingerprints in early paintings and rock carvings of prehistoric humans (Nickell and Fischer, 1999; Caddy and Cobb, 2004). Bell (2008:23) argues that forensic history dates as far back as 3000–2000 BCE and can be linked to the Sumer region.[1] The Sumerians created the concept of private property, and their ruler Ur-Nammu developed 'the first known set of codified laws' (ibid.:23). The Sumerians also developed an intricate educational system that taught students mathematics, medicine and astronomy; and Bell argues that medicine, mixed with pharmaceutical knowledge of primitive drugs obtained from plants, is an important influence in forensic history. Indeed, she goes on to argue that 'more than any other science, medicine is the direct precursor of forensic science' (ibid.:23).

Around the same time as the Sumer civilization, Egyptian culture was developing, and they also played a crucial role in the history of forensic science:

> The Egyptians also had extensive knowledge of plant-based medicines including opium and its derivatives. By 300 B.C.E., they were teaching classes in anatomy and performing the odd dissection on living criminals. They observed and documented the cooling (algor mortis) and stiffening of a body (rigor mortis) after death.
>
> (Ibid.:24)

As knowledge of drugs developed, so too did the links between medicine and law: primarily because of the obvious connection between poisons and death investigations. Ancient China, for example, shared knowledge with Mesopotamia, Egypt and India, with the Chinese developing a rudimentary legal system as far back as 700 BCE. In the sixth century, the Chinese practiced legal medicine to great effect (Caddy and Cobb, 2004:2) and were 'very well versed in medicinal chemistry and pharmacology' (Bell, 2008:26). Recent archaeological research in China has uncovered some early examples of Chinese medicine and the practice of what would now be regarded as forensic crime scene examination. Bamboo slips of Chhin[2] point to the beginnings of forensic medicine, as can be seen in the following case of death by robbery with violence:

> On the left temple there was one knife wound, and on the back of the head some four inches long and one inch wide, with blood oozing from one to the other; the laceration was just like those made by an axe. The chest, temples, cheeks and eye-sockets of the corpse all exuded blood, which covered the body down to the ground, so that nowhere could the length or breadth of the bloodstains be established. Other than this, the corpse was intact.
>
> (cited in Gwei-Djen and Needham, 1988:364)

This example demonstrates that early forms of forensic medicine and crime scene examination were used as far back as the third century BCE. However, despite the Chinese having a system of writing, very few texts from this period have survived. It wasn't until 1247 that a text on legal medicine surfaced. Entitled *Hsi Yuan Chi Lu* (*The Washing Away of Unjust Imputations or Wrongs*), this text was the 'first systematic treatise on forensic medicine in any civilization' (Gwei-Djen and Needham, 1988:361). Written by Sung Tzhu (1181–1249), a Judicial Intendant in Hunan and later a Circuit Judge of Kuangtung, *Hsi Yuan Chi Lu* is a remarkable work. Tzhu's motivation for writing the text was to eradicate the 'dishonesty and inefficiency in inquest procedures' that were common and had resulted in many injustices (ibid.:361). Previous texts available to Tzuh all took the form of case studies, so the importance of his work was that he systematised the entire subject of forensic medicine (ibid.:364). It was noted in the preface by Giles, translator of the 1923 edition, that a copy of Tzhu's text was 'always carried to the scene of an

inquest by the high territorial official on whom the duties of coroner devolved'
(Hall, 2010:7). A quick trawl through the contents of Book One provides further
evidence of this text being perhaps the earliest forensic text of any kind
(Hall, 2010):

Table 4.1 The themes of Hsi Yuan Chi Lu

Chapter	Description
1	General remarks on inquests.
2	General remarks on wounds and the death limit.
3	(1) Printed form for wounds.
	(2) Human skeleton.
4	(1) Examination of the corpse before burial.
	(2) Examination of the corpse after burial.
5	Preparing corpse for examination.
6	(1) The first inquest.
	(2) Further inquest.
7	Decomposition of body at different seasons.
8	Real and counterfeit wounds.
9	Examination of female corpses.
10	Dried up corpses.
11	Examination of decomposed corpses.
12	Human bones.
13	(1) Examination of bones.
	(2) Whether injured before or after death.
14	On the bones and veins of the human body.
15	The blood-dropping test (for kindred).
16	Examination of ground.

The topics indicated in the above list were the sorts of topics that were of
concern to Chinese jurists. According to Bell (2008:26), medico-legal investigators
used this text up until at least the twentieth century, despite physicians playing
only a limited role in death investigation (also see Gwei-Djen and Needham,
1988). Regardless of their limited role in the early history of forensics, death
investigations and the changes that take place on and around the body prior to,
during and after death is clearly prominent during this period. For instance, in
Book Two, which consists of 12 chapters, Tzhu examines a number of different
mechanisms and causes of death, including 'wounds inflicted by hand, foot, and
weapons', 'murder passed off as suicide by strangulation', 'burning' and 'knife-
wounds' (Hall, 2010:47). Book Two also includes a description of how to distinguish drowning from strangulation. It is clear that Tzhu's *Hsi Yuan Chi Lu*
should be regarded as one of the earliest examples of scientific practices being
used during criminal investigations. Alongside these developments, there are
several others that can be identified as being influential forerunners to forensic
science. In the 700s, the Chinese used 'fingerprints to establish the identity of

documents' and, in the year 1000, Roman attorney Quintilian showed that 'bloody palm prints were meant to frame a blind man of his mother's murder' (Inman and Rudin, 2000:329). However, it was the scientific and technological developments in both biology[3] and chemistry that brought a new arsenal to the pursuit of justice. As Basalla (1999) and Gaukroger (2009) point out, techno-logical methods were often developed before the *scientific knowledge* behind the technology was fully understood or even realised. This is often the case in contemporary forensic science, with new technological methods being developed and applied to criminal investigations before the science has been *approved*. In fact, as Golan (2007) notes, the courtroom is often the place where new scientific and technological methods are contested and agreed upon. I expand upon this issue in Chapter 11.

For instance, chemistry evolved from medicine, metallurgy and alchemy and grew out of practical need long before the *science* was known or understood (Bell, 2008:37). It began as the study of precious metals, developing as analytical chemistry, which 'remains at the heart of forensic chemistry today' (ibid.:37; also see Pavord, 2009). Up until the 1700s, fire assay[4] was the only technique available to analyse and separate metals, and this was often used to identify amounts of gold and silver. Another test often used to identify the purity of gold was the *touchstone test*. As explained by Bell (2008:38), this was 'a special stone that would show a gold streak if pure gold were rubbed against it'. The benefit of using the touchstone was that it was non-destructive in comparison to fire assay. The touchstone was used as far back as Ancient Greece, with the likes of Plato and Aristotle mentioning the stone. Another chemical test of importance in the aetiological development of forensic science was the *spot test*. The Roman author and natural philosopher Pliny (23–79) experimented with copper metals that contained iron compounds, and one of these tests was possibly the first record of the spot test. Pliny took a strip of papyrus soaked in extract of pine gallnuts; 'if an extract of the suspected copper salt was placed on the test strip and a black colour developed, it was assumed that the copper was contaminated with iron' (Bell, 2008:39). In modern forensic terms, the spot test has now evolved into the presumptive test or colour test (James and Nordby, 2009; Jackson and Jackson, 2011) and involves 'testing a questioned substance with a specific chemical reagent' and watching for any colour changes (Bell, 2008:39).

Perhaps the most influential developments in early chemistry were the various methods created to separate different elements from a compound. Contemporary analytical chemistry used for forensic purposes relies on its ability to isolate one or more elements from compounds found on crime scenes (Anderson, 2004; Cole, 2004; Saferstein, 2007; James and Nordby, 2009; Houck and Siegel, 2010; Jackson and Jackson, 2011). Early methods of separation did not have the benefit of acids and solvents to dissolve and separate materials or, indeed, machinery such as the gas chromatograph (Bayne and Carlin, 2010); instead they used simple fire and heat as a way to *excite* the electrons into a higher/lower orbit around the atom, which helps determine the rates of absorption (higher) and emission (lower) of specific elements (Saferstein, 2007:169–171). For example, the ancient alchemist's interest in fire applied to metallurgy and their use of heat as a way to separate materials is of interest to forensics (Bell, 2008:40). They also perfected three fundamental means of separation – *sublimation,*[5] *distillation,*[6] and *pyrolysis*[7] – which ultimately provided the necessary technical means through which modern science developed. The major problem with alchemy, which dates back to around 400 BCE, was that it was surrounded by much religious and metaphysical mysticism, which tended to supersede the fact that many alchemists were practical technologists who learned through experience and observation. According to Bell's brief history (ibid.:35–41), the era of ancient alchemy ended with the decline of the Roman Empire.

If we consider the literature on the development of science, Western perspectives would have us believe that the Dark Ages – a period from the fall of Rome in AD 476 that lasted until AD 1000 – saw the stagnation and suppression of scientific ideas in most parts of the Western world (Gaukroger, 2009). However, as Bell (2008:41–43) and Gaukroger (2009) point out, this darkness was not a feature in every part of the world, and there is evidence of fundamental scientific developments in the Moslem Empire during this period. For example, between 750 and 1150 'the Arabs made significant advances in chemistry' by studying chemical reactions which they attempted to classify (Bell, 2008:41; also see Huff, 2003). They also had contact with the Chinese, which led to a wider dissemination of ideas and the advancement of a range of tools critical for the development of both the natural sciences as well as the forensic sciences, including glassmaking expertise that made significant advancement in 'lenses, microscopes, and prisms' (Bell, 2008:42). Other developments made by the Moslem Empire include the isolation of ethanol, a crucial chemical used in distillation, as well as the discovery of mineral acids such as nitric acid, which was often used to detect counterfeit coins; Bell (2008:42) suggests this could have been the origin of phrase *acid test*. It is very interesting that whilst scientific ideas of the Chinese and Arab-Islamists developed in the Dark Ages and continued into the medieval period and beyond, a systematic scientific culture did not fully develop until the Enlightenment period. Using the work of Huff, Gaukroger (1993, cited in Gaukroger, 2009:32–35) offers a unique analysis of the reasons behind this. He points to the need to view the development of science within the 'large-scale social and institutional context that shapes the possibility of an adversarial approach' which is crucially linked to the development of capitalism (2009:32; also see Huff, 2003). Weber (1992, cited in Gerth and Mills, 1993) notes how a number of Eastern cultures, despite having the technology and structures to do so, failed to develop a capitalist mode of production. He also found that the move from pre-industrial to capitalist society tended to result in the abandonment of traditional values. However, Chinese and Arab-Islamic societies lacked the necessary motives and frameworks for development such as this. If we consider the Arab-Islamic culture, for example, while it was an 'atomistic intellectual culture' where adversarial argument could develop (Gaukroger, 2009:32), there was no institutional support available for scientific ideas that were not useful for traditional means. Mathematical astronomy, for instance, received strong institutional support because of its important role in 'determining the direction of Mecca at different locations' (ibid.:32). Chinese culture, on the other hand, had an extensive network for the communication and dissemination of scientific ideas, but their tradition was not set up for adversarial argument. Huff (1993, cited in Gaukroger, 2009:32) argues that the situation in the West was different, as it had many corporate entities, which enabled the establishment of 'neutral zones of free enquiry'. These were crucial, for they allowed science a measure of autonomy, which encouraged the necessary innovation required for its epistemological and ontological development (Huff, 2003).

The social and institutional context of Chinese and Arab-Islamic culture has briefly been highlighted to demonstrate how influential these are in determining the epistemological fate of forensic science, criminal investigations and scientific criminology. By around the 1200s, the Western empire began to break free from the suppression of religious *and* royal ideology and power; and, with the breaking of these chains, the natural sciences re-emerged and began to re-explore avenues of epistemological and ontological development (see Chapter 2). One of the biggest advances made was the development of iatrochemistry, which is the application of chemistry to medicine and biology; and a key figure in its development was the alchemist and philosopher Paracelsus (1493–1541). There are plenty of other examples that could be used to illustrate the important developments made by the thousands of scientists over the last 500 years or so, many of which have added to society's general stock of scientific knowledge as well as creating numerous techno-logical advances that have been used for various practical reasons and tasks. The next section begins the process of focusing in on the development of modern forensic investigation.

The development of modern forensic investigations

What we know from the brief reviews of forensic investigative history that many texts provide is that, up until the nineteenth century, scientific techniques and their application to *criminal* cases were sporadic and did not necessarily yield any systemic organisation or application. Towards the end of the nineteenth century this changed, with a number of crucial developments in both the natural sciences and their application to criminal investigations. It is often suggested that the birth of modern forensics can be traced to the 1880s (Nickell and Fischer, 1999; Inman and Rudin, 2000; Caddy and Cobb, 2004; Evans, 2006), for it was this decade that saw significant advancements in the forensic use of natural science tools, technologies and theories. These advancements go through a number of stages that play a crucial role in the advancement and application of scientific ideas:

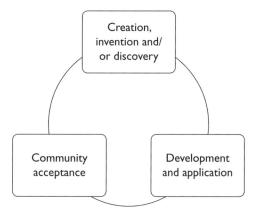

Figure 4.1 The process of scientific advancement

The first step is that scientific ideas are *created, invented* or *discovered* and, through methodological and data triangulation, hypotheses are tested time and time again to either falsify or verify these scientific ideas (Popper, 2002). Once scientific ideas are tested and found to be valid or robust they can be *developed* and *applied* to real-world situations. The *utility* element of scientific ideas is therefore crucial, especially for forensic investigations. The third and final aspect is *acceptance*. Contemporary science operates on the process of peer review, which is the *acceptance* of scientific ideas through reviewing work in artefacts such as articles published in subject-relevant journals. Trawling through the known history of scientific developments, there are many examples whereby scientific technology and tools have arisen from simple ideas that have been used *in situ*. For example, in 1784, in Lancaster, England, John Toms was tried and convicted for murdering Edward Culshaw with a pistol. Upon examining the head wound, a *pistol wad* – which is crushed paper used to secure powder and balls in the muzzle – was found. When Toms was searched, a torn newspaper was found in his pocket which matched the pistol wad. This is regarded as one of the first documented uses of physical matching. Since then, scientists have taken this idea of *matching* and have developed numerous technological tools to aid in the matching of items between offenders, victims and crime scenes. Another example taken from the early nineteenth century is that of German chemists who developed a chemical test for a particular ink dye that became the first recorded use of questioned document analysis when it was applied to a document known as the *konigin hanschritt* (Inman and Rudin, 2000:329).

There are many examples over the last 2,000 years that illustrate the nature of forensic progress. However, it was in the nineteenth century that some of the most important developments in forensic investigations took place. The rest of this chapter examines some of the more practical developments and changes that took place within the realm of forensic science and how they were used in criminal investigations. It is often said that 'history is written by the winners', and, unfortunately, the winners only include the major players or the ones in power. It is, therefore, impossible to include every individual who played a part in developing scientific ideas and methods that would become useful in a forensic setting. Table 4.2 outlines some of the key players in the development of forensic science.

Table 4.2 Key players in forensic science

Key names	Core work/influence
Mathieu Orfila (1787–1853)	Published *Toxicologie Générale* (1813), which introduced forensic toxicology to criminal cases.
Alphonse Bertillon (1853–1914)	Developed the science of measurement of the human body called *anthropometry*. This system became known as *Bertillonage*. He was also known as the father of criminal identification.
Henry Faulds (1843–1930)	In 1880 Faulds noted sweat from skin left faint oily latent (invisible) deposits on surfaces that matched an individuals finger.
William Herschel (1833–1917)	Herschel was a magistrate and administrator in India when he suggested that every prisoner place his fingerprint after his name.
Francis Galton (1822–1911)	Published *Fingerprints* (1892), which was the first systematic and scientific study of the subject of fingerprints. He developed a method for classifying fingerprints for filing.
Hans Gross (1847–1915)	The first true forensic detective. He was the first to bring forensic science and criminal investigations under one broad category, through publications such as *Criminal Investigation: A Practical Textbook for Magistrates, Police Officers and Lawyers* (1893). He also made the term *criminalistics* popular.
Edmond Locard (1877–1966)	Developed the fundamental principle of forensic science – the *principle of exchange*. Instrumental in developing the working *crime laboratory* in police forces.

Key names	Core work/influence
Karl Landsteiner (1868–1943)	In 1900 was the first to discover *blood groups*. Max Richter adapted the technique to *type stains* and this is one of the first instances of performing validation experiments specifically to adapt a method for forensic science.
Paul Uhlenhuth (1870–1957)	Devised a test to distinguish blood origin – i.e. whether blood was animal or human – known as the *precipitin test*.
Leon Lattes (1887–1943)	Took the work of Landsteiner and used it to develop an antibody *blood stain test* (1915).
Colonel Calvin Goddard (1891–1955)	Laid groundwork for the individualisation of weapons. Used comparison microscope to identify and compare firing pin marks on shell casings.
Albert Osborn (1858–1936)	Developed the processes involved in the field of forgery detection. Published the first text in *document analysis* entitled *Questioned Documents* (1910).
Paul Kirk (1902–1970)	Similar to Gross, he began applying knowledge of biochemistry to forensic questions, conducting thousands of studies on blood and hair trace evidence. Sought to combine and systematise crime investigation, physical evidence and the police laboratory. Published seminal text *Crime Investigation* (1953).

Identifying and measuring criminals

Forensic science and criminal investigations intersect with scientific criminology at the crossroads with identifying and measuring the *criminal body*. It has already been suggested that the ideas of early scientific criminology incorporated identifying and classifying types of criminals, and that various physical attributes could attest to the existence of a criminal type. The link between physical attributes and deviant behaviour required numerous methods to record and measure such attributes. The *heroic* (1829–1878) and *organisational specialization* (1878–1932) periods identified by Morris (2007) saw the invention, development and application of many of the tools and techniques used for early forms of identification and measurement, and these were used by the police to develop intelligence records of habitual criminals. However, in the nineteenth century, these techniques were not simply tied to catching criminals; they were also closely connected to the idea that the identification and measurement techniques provided empirical evidence of criminality (Finn, 2009). Therefore, in the nineteenth and early twentieth centuries, forensic methods were much more closely tied to understanding criminality than they are today. To be sure, this is a criticism that could be levelled at many contemporary forensic texts which tend to bypass understanding the crime and an offenders' criminality and instead concentrate only on the pertinent *who* and *how* questions of crime reconstruction. This is the core weakness of Petherick *et al.* (2010), who spend a great deal of time discussing various forensic investigative practices whilst providing only a cursory analysis of why offenders commit the crimes in the first place.

There was also a functional reason why the search for the criminal body became a dominant practice in the Victorian period. In France, there was a 'burgeoning fear of recidivism' in 1851, and the French authorities responded to this fear by 'mandating the deportation of parole violators to penal colonies in New Caledonia and Guyana' (Cole, 2002:18). Furthermore, 1868 saw the end of the UK's transportation of criminals to Australia, and with this came an increased pressure on the judicial system (ibid.:19). As many criminals were transported to the colonies, Britain did not have to concern herself with repeat or habitual offenders. It was no coincidence, therefore, that the fears and concerns over habitual offenders, that were discussed in Chapter 3, coincided with the phasing out of deportation in Britain. This also led to calls for tougher sentencing for recidivists. The core problem, however, was how to identify a recidivist. It soon became clear to many practitioners working in criminal justice organisations that a more accurate knowledge of a criminal's history was required. The year after the cessation of transportation, parliament passed the Habitual Criminals Bill, and Part II, ss5–6 attempted to facilitate identification by establishing 'an annually published Alphabetical Register of Habitual Criminals'[8] (ibid.:19; also, see Wiener, 1994:148–150 and Davie, 2005:91–92). This can be seen as one of the first criminal identification systems and included the development of *photography* merged with the system of *anthropometry*, which was then replaced by the growth in *fingerprinting*.

Photography and the composite criminal

As Finn (2009:1) notes, 'the police mug shot has become an icon in contemporary visual culture. . . . It is an image that is taken to indicate criminality.' Even today the mugshot holds a powerful resonance within local communities. It is no coincidence that the expansion in photographic technologies took place in the same time period as developments in scientific criminology, forensic science and criminal investigations. In 1844, Henry Fox Talbot claimed, in *The Pencil of Nature*, photography held a vast instrumental potential to a 'new legalistic truth, the truth of *indexical* rather than *textual* inventory' (Sekula, 1986:6). Upon reviewing a photograph of several shelves full of china crockery, Talbot speculated that if a thief were to steal such items and 'if the mute testimony of the picture were to be produced against him in court – it would certainly be evidence of a novel kind' (Talbot, 1844, cited in Sekula, 1986:6). As Sekula suggests, Talbot had uncovered the idea that photography could be used as 'a silence that silences':

> The protean oral 'texts' of the criminal and pauper yield to a 'mute testimony' that 'takes down' (that diminishes in credibility, that transcribes) and unmasks the disguises, the alibis, the excuses and multiple biographies of those who find or place themselves on the wrong side of the law. This battle between the presumed denotative univocality of the legal image and the multiplicity and presumed duplicity of the criminal voice is played out during the remainder of the nineteenth century. In the course of this battle a new object is defined – the criminal body – and, as a result, a more extensive 'social body' is invented.
>
> (Sekula, 1986:6)

Sekula introduces the phrase *inclusive archive* as a way to describe this nineteenth-century practice. He positions photography as used by state institutions in the nineteenth century within 'a larger "bureaucratic-clerical-statistical system"' (Finn, 2009:xiii) in which the all-inclusive archive contained traces of the visible body or images of the bodies of 'the unworthy' (Sekula, 1986:10). The unworthy, of course, included criminals and deviants. Interestingly, Sekula links the growth of the all-inclusive archive with the widespread use and prestige of physiognomy and phrenology (ibid.:10–11). With the growth of these areas, as well as the work of the French social statisticians (see Chapter 8) *and* the advent of the Eugenic movement (Rafter, 1997; Black 2004; Finn, 2009; Bashford and Levine, 2012), photography provided a means to scientifically legitimise the 'discourse of the criminal body'; more importantly, 'this discourse held that criminality could be read directly from the body' (Finn, 2009:xiv). We should also turn to Latour and Woolgar's (1986) concept of *inscriptions* as a useful way to view photography as playing a role in the generation of forensic scientific fact. They examined how science laboratories produce *inscription devices*, which are defined as 'any item of apparatus or particular configuration of such items which can transform a material substance into a figure or diagram which is directly usable by one of the members of the office space' (ibid.:51): for example, diagrams, figures, pictures, tables and so forth. Photographic pictures in contemporary forensic investigations are inscriptive devices of high currency in scientific practice. One of the reasons for this is that photographs of evidence, the crime scene, weapons, victim and offender tend to be viewed in terms of 'confirmation or evidence for or against, particular ideas, concepts, or theories' (ibid.:63). On a more functional note, Finn (2009:xvii) suggests that one of the reasons photography played a central role in forensic science, criminal investigations and scientific criminology in the nineteenth century is because of its 'cost-effectiveness, ease of use, rapid means of production, and unique claim to objectivity'.

The 'claim to objectivity' can clearly been seen in the police mugshot, which has its roots in the 'photographic portrait of the mid-to-late-nineteenth century' (ibid.:2). The idea was to capture an accurate representation of an individual's face that would thwart any later attempts to avoid identification. According to Finn (ibid.:2), many criminals tried to avoid this by twisting, turning and changing their facial impressions so a *true representation* could not be captured by the photographic image. As it was a perfect tool 'for the documentation, classification, and regulation of the body within the carceral network' (ibid.:6), the photograph worked to create and enhance the visible criminal body, which Foucault ([1977]1991) saw as being integral to the *new* microphysics of power which had arisen in the nineteenth century. As early as 1841, French police produced 'daguerreotypes[9] of prisoners' (Finn, 2009:6), which was soon adopted by a number of police forces in the USA and Canada. In Britain, the police employed a photographer in the 1840s and there are *ambrotypes*[10] of Birmingham prisoners that date from the 1850s (Cole, 2002:20). By the last decades in the nineteenth century, 'police departments in major metropolitan areas around the world were collecting photographs of criminals' (Finn, 2009:6). These photographs were supplemented with 'textual accounts of criminals' histories and their biographical information and were combined in leather-bound books' called *rogues' galleries* (ibid.:6). Perhaps the most famous rogues' gallery collection was created by 'the legendary Thomas Byrnes, who headed the detective bureau of the NYPD and then served as police chief from 1880 until 1895' (Cole, 2002:21). Byrnes created an album of 204 frontal portraits of criminals, published as *Professional Criminals of America* (1886). Each page consisted of six mugshots with text that described 'each offender, including his or her name alias, biographical and physical description and criminal history' (Finn, 2009:7). The importance of Byrnes' text was that it 'targeted the "professional" criminal, the repeat offender who made a living from crime' as well as using photography as a means of identification (Cole, 2002:21). More importantly, *Professional Criminals in America* was 'a rogues' gallery in coffee-table-book format' which could be carried and used by police officers to identify criminals (ibid.:21).

As photographic technologies developed, the number of mugshots increased. The ease and speed with which the police could photograph criminals led to the accumulation of police records. In part, this increase was fed by the rise in crime rates that took place within the 'industrialized and urban world' (Finn, 2009:10; also see Maguire, 2007:243–257). As Finn notes (2009:10), in the closing decades of the nineteenth century, rogues' galleries had grown from hundreds to thousands, and the leather-bound books were replaced by filing cabinets full of records. The sheer size in numbers of records soon became problematic as they required full-time attendants to simply manage them. Finn (ibid.:10) gives the example of the Berlin collection, which had grown to such an extent that by 1877 it required three attendants: 'in 1880 the Berlin gallery housed 2,135 images, and within three years this has increased to 3,459' (ibid.:10). Unfortunately, as the numbers of the records increased their actual

TegnTengo、 stop

utility decreased, as it was not possible to keep track of so many names and faces. Byrnes provided a unique solution to this problem:

> While the photograph of burglars, forgers, sneak thieves, and robbers of lesser degree are kept in police albums, many offenders are still able to operate successfully. But with their likeness within reach of all, their vocation would soon become risky and unprofitable.
>
> (Byrnes, 1886:v, cited in Finn, 2009:10)

By asking the general public to familiarise themselves with criminals, the photograph became an 'evidentiary document' (Finn, 2009:11). Photographs were also used in conjunction with criminal anthropology and physiognomy (as discussed in the previous chapter), forever linking the inscriptive device of the image with attempts to understand the offenders' criminality. Nowhere can this link be seen better than in the development of *composite photography*.

Like many of his historical age, Francis Galton thought that the camera could capture an objective representation of the body. As the core ideas of criminal anthropology and physiognomy stipulated that signs of criminality could be visibly identified on the criminal body, it is not a huge leap of faith to link such ideas with advancements in photographic technology and developing processes (Cole, 2002; Davie, 2005; Finn, 2009). *Composite photography* was one such technique, and this was devised by Galton when layering 'multiple exposures of a group of criminals onto a single photographic plate' (Cole, 2002:24). Galton hoped that the resultant composite image would reveal the criminal physiognomy, isolating the common physiognomic attributes of the criminal man and woman.

The composite photograph demonstrates just how strongly scientists of the Victorian era believed in the idea of the existence of the *mark of Cain*. In his excellent history of fingerprinting and criminal identification, Cole (ibid.:24–25) notes how some police departments put composite photographs into their practice by training detectives to arrest 'criminal types', even if they hadn't committed a crime. Boston Police Superintendent used a rogues' gallery book, entitled *Our Rival the Rascal: A Faithful Portrayal of the Conflict Between the Criminals of this Age and the Defenders of Society – The Police* (1897), to effectively implement physiognomic profiling 'akin to the racial profiling we hear about today' (ibid.:26). Prospective identification of criminal attributes has become the staple of criminal justice policy that underpins much of the forensic assessment of offenders in criminal justice today.

In the end, composite photography was not successful in uncovering 'any unequivocal physiognomic marker of the criminal type'; nor did the rogues' galleries 'develop into a fully-fledged criminal identification system' (ibid.:26). Furthermore, Galton's work 'did not find significant practical application' (Finn, 2009:23). The main difficulty was how to maximise the utility of

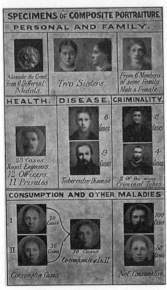

Figure 4.2 Galton's composite criminals[11, 12]

thousands of images of criminals, which was really a problem of ordering and classification. As Cole (2002) and Finn (2009) point out, indexing photographs using simply the face or image was difficult: instead, the photographs were arranged alphabetically based upon the names given by the offender. Unfortunately, this led right back to problem of the use of aliases. If an offender gave an alias, the vast amount of photographic records were rendered useless as a means of identification; so, in the 1870s, the British authorities created 'the first criminal identification register indexed, not according to names, but according to the criminal body itself' (Cole, 2002:26–27). The *Register of Distinctive Marks* (RDM) used the vagaries of the body to attempt to identify unique markings on the body that could be individualised and used for identification purposes. The RDM divided the body into nine general regions (ibid.:27):

1   head and face;
2   throat and neck;
3   chest;
4   belly and groin;
5   back and loins;
6   arms;
7   hands and fingers;
8   thighs and legs; and
9   feet and ankles.

A prisoner would be stripped and examined for any distinguishing marks, such as scars, birthmarks or burns. All distinctive markings would then be entered onto the register. The idea was that when an offender was arrested or entered a prison, he could be physically examined and any marks could be checked against the register; acting as a confirmation of whom they were. Unfortunately, this method was very laborious, and it is no surprise that the *Report of a Committee Appointed by the Secretary of State to Inquire into the Best Means Available for Identifying Habitual Criminals* (1894) found that even those who used the register did not 'by this means make a large number of identifications' (ibid.:27). The RDM, alongside other visual and textual methods of identification, did succeed in linking some subjects to their criminal records; however, this was at great cost in human hours. Scotland Yard estimated that each 'successful identification using the Register of Distinctive Marks required more than eight man-hours, while officials at Holloway Prison estimated a whopping ninety man-hours for each successful identification' (ibid.:29). This was far too time-consuming and expensive, so criminal justice and forensic practitioners sought to find a better method of criminal identification. By the late nineteenth century, two new forensic technologies of identification appeared to resolve these issues.

Measuring the criminal body

The first of the *new* identification technologies was *anthropometry*, which is defined as 'the physical measurement of the size and proportions of the human body' (ibid.:32). In the late 1870s French police official Alphonse Bertillon (1853–1914) developed anthropometric techniques that became the first modern system of criminal identification. As with photography, concerns regarding recidivist criminals fuelled the development of what became known as *Bertillonage*. This was of special concern to Bertillon, who stated that: '[i]t is not enough to make a law against recidivists . . . it is then necessary to enforce it.

In order to condemn a recidivist to relegation, the first requirement is the recognition of his identity' (Ibid.:33).

Bertillon's ideas are perhaps amongst the first that later developed into what is today called *biometrics*.[13] Bertillon's upbringing provides some insight as to why he took this particular direction; for his father was a pioneer of the social sciences, including anthropology, so there were many anthropometric measuring tools around his house when he was growing up. Despite being the perennial underachiever, with the help of his father Bertillon eventually secured a lowly position 'as a clerk at the Paris prefecture of police' (ibid.:34). It was in this position that Bertillon came to realise the 'chaotic state of police recordkeeping' (ibid.:34; Rhodes, 1936) and that the application of his father's scientific method could possibly resolve the problem of filing and retrieving criminal records. The system of Bertillonage was intricate, yet the ideas were simple. The first time a *Bertillon operator* measured a prisoner, 11 different anthropometric measurements were taken 'with specially designed callipers, gauges, and rulers' (Cole, 2002:34). The anthropometric tools used by Bertillon can be seen in Figure 4.3 (Bertillon, 1889:19–20), and the 11 measurements are outlined in Table 4.3 (Rhodes, 1936; Cole, 2002:37; Finn, 2009:23).

According to Cole (2002:37), Bertillon chose these 'specific "osseous[14] lengths" because they were the proportions least likely to be affected by weight change or aging over time'. After measuring the offender, the Bertillon operator would record a physical description, and photographs would also be taken. All of the measurements, physical descriptions and photographs were recorded on a *Bertillon card* (see Figure 4.4), which included 'spaces for descriptions of the prisoner's eyes, ears, lips, beard, hair color, skin color, ethnicity, forehead, nose, build, chin, general contour of head, hair growth pattern, eyebrows, eyeball and orbit, mouth, physiognomic expression, neck, inclination of shoulders, attitude, general demeanor, voice, language, and habiliments' (ibid.:37).

What is especially interesting is that Bertillon took it upon himself to create a specific inscription device (Latour and Woolgar, 1986:51–53) to describe all the varieties of humans. Ordinary human language, according to Cole (2002:37) 'did not provide enough nuance' to describe all the features of humans adequately. It was simply not precise enough, so Bertillon attempted to develop a 'precise "scientific" language' called *morphological vocabulary*. For example, he moved beyond simplistic descriptions of eye colour, defining more than 50 types, each

Table 4.3 Bertillon measurements

Height	Left Little Finger Length
Head Length	Left Foot Length
Head Breadth	Left Forearm Length
Arm Span	Right Ear Length
Sitting Height	Cheek Width
Left Middle Finger Length	

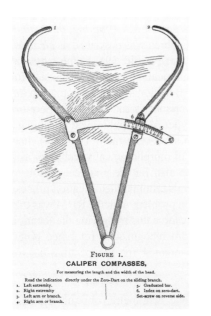

FIGURE 1.
CALIPER COMPASSES,
For measuring the length and the width of the head.

Read the indication directly under the Zero-Dart on the sliding branch.
1. Left extremity.
2. Right extremity
3. Left arm or branch.
4. Right arm or branch.
5. Graduated bar.
6. Index on zero-dart.
    Set-screw on reverse side.

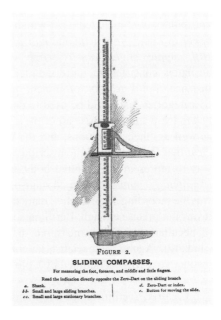

FIGURE 2.
SLIDING COMPASSES,
For measuring the foot, forearm, and middle and little fingers.

Read the indication directly opposite the Zero-Dart on the sliding branch
a. Shank.
b b. Small and large sliding branches.
c c. Small and large stationary branches.
d. Zero-Dart or index.
e. Button for moving the slide.

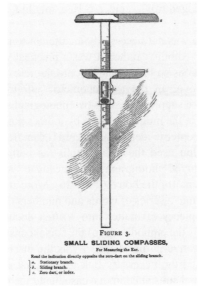

FIGURE 3.
SMALL SLIDING COMPASSES,
For Measuring the Ear.
Read the indication directly opposite the zero-dart on the sliding branch.
a. Stationary branch.
b. Sliding branch.
c. Zero dart, or index.

Figure 4.3 Anthropometric measuring tools[15]

having its own abbreviation (ibid.:38). Other examples of the morphological vocabulary used included: *lips*, which might be described as *pouting, thick, thin, upper* or *lower prominent*; and *hair of a beard*, which was described as *straight, stiff, supple, slightly curly, frizzly* or *very frizzly* (ibid.:39). Some physical attributes consisted of quite detailed morphological vocabulary. The ear, for instance, holds a very prominent place in Bertillon's card system, having 63 categories that could be used to describe a prisoner's ear. Bertillon operators had to learn and memorise all of the different types of morphological vocabulary as well as 'their definitions, and the differences between them' (ibid.:40). It is clear that Bertillon used the inscriptive device of morphological vocabulary as a way to represent the criminal body, but it was also for the practical reason of *identifying criminals*. The final stage of Bertillon's criminal identification process was the recording of distinctive marks. The main problem with the RDM was that it was not precise enough. Bertillon sought to resolve this by 'giving the location of peculiar marks as a measured distance from recognizable reference point' (ibid.:40). Again, a specialist language was created for the peculiarities of distinctive marks, as outlined by Cole (ibid.:43):

> Cicatrix, rectilinear, of a dimension of one centimetre, oblique external, on middle second phalanx of middle finger, left side, posterior face. . . . (which could be abridged to). . . . cic. r. o 1b e, ml. 2d f. M. g.

The use of such language was not necessarily an attempt to provide *Bertillonage* with an air of scientific credibility; rather, it was a practical way to shorten what could be lengthy descriptions so they could fit onto the relatively small Bertillon cards. As mentioned above, all the anthropometric information gathered and recorded on the cards were supplemented by two photographs – one full-face and one profile shot – similar to the mugshots taken by today's police force. Figure 4.4 is Bertillon's own anthropometric identification card (taken from Rhodes, 1936).

As Finn notes, Bertillon used the photographs 'as both representation and inscription', and he employed photography as a means to 'isolate, make visible, and study the various "signs" of the body' (2009:26). More crucially, the criminal body could be translated into a series of words and numbers that act as inscriptive devices that 'transform pieces of matter into written documents' (Latour and Woolgar, 1986:51). This is the embodiment of the social construction of scientific facts as used for investigative purposes, for it was the inscriptive device of the Bertillon card that showed the necessary link to 'original substance' (ibid.:51; Finn, 2009:26); the original substance in this case being the criminal. But would it work? Could Bertillon's system be used to identify the feared habitual and recidivist criminal? Jim Fisher[16] eloquently describes the possible breakthrough moment for Bertillon:

> Late in the afternoon of February 20, 1883, Bertillon was measuring an arrestee who said his name was Dupont, the sixth prisoner that day who had

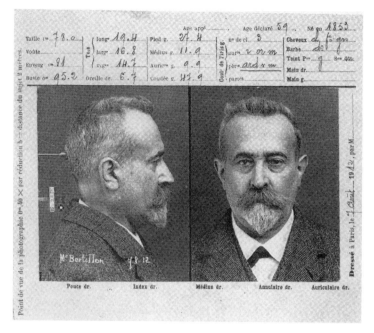

Figure 4.4 A Bertillon identification card[17]

used that name. Bertillon noticed that the man had a mole near his left eyebrow and a face that was vaguely familiar. Excited by the possibility that he had measured this man before under a different name, Bertillon rushed to the filing cabinet to find a match. Dupont had a medium head, therefore only the middle third of the cabinet had to be searched. The width of this prisoner's head narrowed the number of drawers to nine, the length of his middle finger to three, and the measurement of his little finger to one. In that drawer Bertillon found fifty cards. A quick search produced a card containing a set of measurements, to a man who had given the name Martin after being arrested on December 15, 1882, for theft, that were identical to the measurements of the prisoner who had just given the name Dupont. When confronted with the details of his previous arrest under another name, the prisoner insisted that there had to be some kind of clerical error. After Bertillon pressed the issue, the prisoner admitted that he was in fact a repeat offender, and that his name wasn't Martin or Dupont.

Bertillonage was officially accepted for use by the Parisian police force in 1883 and soon after 'was quickly adopted across Europe, Canada, and the United States' (Finn, 2009:28). However, there were a number of flaws that quickly became apparent. At an epistemological and philosophical level, Bertillon's insistence that the inscriptive devices developed by him showed substantive signs of criminality was far from universally accepted. Another problem was teaching and learning the system itself. Bertillon was very clear that his method had to be followed to the letter. Unfortunately, as most individuals learnt this through translated books, many 'skimped on learning the morphological vocabulary, glossed over the precise movements in the measuring process, and contented themselves with sloppily recording a few measurements' (Cole, 2002:52). Even worse, many police departments modified the process without the same number of years of experimentation and testing which had underpinned Bertillon's system. As Cole highlights, Bertillon was not impressed by these modifications, stating that 'we reject in advance every modification, every further change, however slight, either in their form or in the manner of using them' (ibid.:52). Figure 4.5 provides an illustration of the strength in Bertillon's conviction that his precise method should be followed, for he even produced a detailed diagrams of how to measure the head correctly (taken from Bertillon, 1889:29).

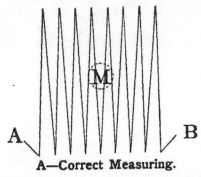

A—Correct Measuring.

A.—B. Course followed by one of the points of the compasses on the side of the head. Point M, centre of Maximum.

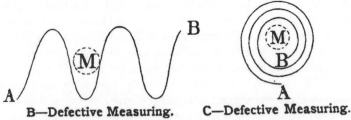

B—Defective Measuring.

A.—B. Course when the zigzag lines described by the compasses are too far apart. Point M, centre of Maximum, not touched by the compasses.

C—Defective Measuring.

A.—B. Circular course described by the compasses around point M, centre of Maximum, not touched by the compasses.

FIGURE 9.

WIDTH OF THE HEAD.

THIRD MOVEMENT.

For general position see Figure 7. See text, § 33, 34 and 35.

Figure 4.5 Measuring the head[18]

Despite these flaws, Cole has argued that Bertillon had developed a system that could visualise criminality in a bureaucratic, 'yet devastatingly effective way' (Cole, 2002:59). As the last decade of the nineteenth quickly approached, others began to find another, more devastating inscriptive device that would make criminal identification technologies even more advanced. As it happens, a new identification technique was also being developed parallel to Bertillonage, and it was this technique that eventually usurped anthropometry and became the driving force within forensic investigations.

The creation of fingerprint identification

Fingerprinting has been the quintessential identification technique for approximately 100 years and was developed around the same time as Bertillonage. Despite the unique differences between the technologies of Bertillonage and fingerprinting, they were both trying to solve the same problem – how to identify and classify criminals. Cole points to the fact that these two technologies developed in 'quite different social and political contexts' with anthropometry developing primarily in European cities whilst fingerprinting emerged 'in the colonies and on the frontiers of the Western imperial states' (2002:32). Bertillon's anthropometry died out in the first third of the twentieth century and was slowly replaced by fingerprinting, which has withstood the test of time despite its obvious problems (Cole, 2002; Bandey, 2004).

It is a misnomer to suggest that fingerprints were *discovered*. Cole rightly asks how is it possible to say who discovered them 'since they have always been right at everyone's fingertips' (Cole, 2002:60)? Most forensic science sources offer only a cursory back-history of fingerprinting; and some do not even bother with the history at all (Nickell and Fischer, 1999; Champod and Chamberlain, 2009; Gaensslen, 2009) which is surprising given that, even with the advent of DNA analysis in the 1980s, fingermark collection and fingerprinting is still one of the most commonly collected and processed types of forensic evidence. Despite the dearth of historical literature on the subject, there are some excellent reviews of the history and development of identification technologies. Simon Cole's *Suspect Identities* (2002) provides an in-depth, yet accessible review of the history of fingerprint and criminal identification. Cole demonstrates how it is impossible to 'pinpoint exactly when the idea of authenticating personal identity through papillary ridges first emerged' (2002:61). Thus, throughout history, we see different uses of fingerprints within a number of different cultures. For instance, in seventh-century China, fingerprints 'embossed in clay seals' were used as a method to sign documents; and, as early as 1303, the Persian historian Rashid-eddin declared that no two individuals have the same fingerprints (ibid.:60–61). Europeans were even later to the party, as descriptions about fingerprints and their uses did not show up in writings until the end of the seventeenth century. In 1684, in one of his many addresses to the Royal Society of London, Nehemiah Grew reported that one could 'perceive innumerable *little Ridges*, of equal bigness and distance, and everywhere running parallel one with another' (cited in Cole, 2002:60; Nickell and Fischer, 1999:113).

At the same time Grew made his observations, two microscopists also noticed papillary ridges: the Dutch anatomist Govard Bidloo and Italian doctor Marcello Malpighi both published work illustrating papillary ridges. Malpighi, one of the founders of embryology, disagreed with Grew on the function of fingerprints; for Grew insisted that the papillary ridges were designed to 'facilitate sweating in order to release the "more noxious" wastes of the blood', whilst Malpighi argued their function was for touch (Cole, 2002:61). Despite the work and observations of such distinguished scientists, it took until 1788 for the uniqueness of finger-prints to be realised. German anatomist J. C. A. Mayer is thought to be the first to state that 'the arrangement of skin ridges is never duplicated in two persons' (cited in Cole, 2002:61). Again, observations like these were very interesting and formed part of the epistemological and ontological backdrop to fingerprint devel-opment, yet they did not yield a fully formed classification scheme. Fingerprinting, therefore, offers a seminal example of the process in which observations come first, leading to ideas about practical applications which results in the develop-ment of the necessary technologies required to apply the ideas. The first attempt at creating a fingerprint classification scheme came from the Czech physician Jan Evangelista Purkyne (1787–1869) in 1823. Purkyne classified fingerprints into nine basic types (ibid.:61). He also adopted Leibniz's position that 'every natural object is identical only to itself' (ibid.:62), which logically led him to the same belief as Mayer: that no two individuals had identical fingerprints. Figure 4.6 shows the nine fingerprint patterns identified by Purkyne (taken from Cummins and Kennedy, 1940:349). The nine types include: the tented arch (no. 8); the loop (no. 10); and the whorl (no. 13), which still exist today as level 1 ridge detail (Champod and Chamberlain, 2009:58–59).

As Cole argues (2002:62), at the end of the nineteenth century and the beginning decades of the twentieth centuries, two Englishmen, their students and descendants would 'spend more than fifty years feuding over which of them had "invented" fingerprinting despite the microscopic and taxonomic work that preceded them'. This was more a feud over who created the classification scheme than over who discovered papillary ridges. Regardless of the often-heated debates between the two camps, credit must be given to William Herschel and Henry Faulds for starting the process that eventually led to the creation of the taxonomic system of fingerprints – a taxonomy that would make Britain the driving force behind forensic identification technologies for much of the twentieth century.

British fingerprinting did not originate, as one might think, in Scotland Yard; and it certainly did not develop for forensic investigative purposes. Instead, British colonial fingerprinting was initially used as a way of controlling the ethnic populations under the control of colonial administrators (Cole, 2002; Sengoopta, 2003; Finn, 2009). More specifically, fingerprinting developed in India – the

Figure 4.6 Purkyne's 9-type fingerprint classification[19]

UK's most valuable imperial asset – but was subject to the major problems of administering such a huge bureaucratic empire 'with a small corps of civil servants outnumbered by hostile natives' (Cole, 2002:63; Sengoopta, 2003; Finn, 2009). Modern fingerprinting came about during a period of heightened social conflict in British India:

> In 1857 Indian conscripts, known as 'sepoys', spurred by rumours that the grease that lubricated their rifle cartridges contained beef and pork fat – thus violating the dietary laws of both Hindus and Muslims – rebelled against their British officers and, for a time, took control of Delhi. . . . Colonial administrators on the ground, meanwhile, knew it was vital to reassert both their own authority and the rule of law.
>
> (Cole, 2002:64)

One such administrator was William Herschel (1833–1917), who was chief administrator of the Hooghly district of Bengal. Herschel, grandson of the famous astronomer, noticed that the violence of the 1857 uprising also led to a great deal of fraud and forgery, especially in relation to native impersonators attempting to obtain the pensions of deceased individuals (Sengoopta, 2003:55–80). At the time, it was deemed by administrators to be very difficult to identify 'one Indian from another', so Herschel began to think of ways to link a pension to the right individual (Cole, 2002:64; Sengoopta, 2003:55; Finn, 2009). In 1858 Herschel asked road contractor Rajyadhar Konai to 'press his handprint in ink on a deed' to ensure that Konai did not renege on a contract (Cole, 2002:65; Sengoopta, 2003:55–60). Because of the success of this method, Herschel tried twice to push for further research into fingerprints as well as the adoption of his method. For example, in *Finger Prints*, Galton notes how Herschel submitted a report to the 'inspector general of gaols' in 1877, asking him to extend the process; however, no results followed (Galton, 1892:29). The second attempt came in 1881 when he sent a description of the method to the governor of the 'gaol at Greenwich in Sidney'. Again no further steps were taken (ibid.:29; also see Sengoopta, 2003). Herschel was undeterred by such setbacks for he had a great belief in the theory that not only were fingerprints unique to each individual, but they also persisted over time and did not change. It is a testament to this belief that, over a 50-year period, Herschel kept records of fingerprints and retested them over time. For example, Figure 4.7 is taken from Herschel's *The Origin of Finger-Printing* (1916), and this depicts the fingerprints of A. C. Howard who was District Superintendent of Police, Nuddea in 1862 and afterwards became Assistant Commissioner at Scotland Yard (Herschel, 1916:13; Sengoopta, 2003). The left image was taken at a dinner party held by Herschel in 1862. The right image is a *repeat* that Howard gave Herschel in London 46 years later and to which Herschel (1916:13) declared 'it will be seen how good the persistence has been'.

Fingerprinting, then, began as a technique for *civil* and not criminal identification which is actually the dominant theme running through debates about

13th April 1862   20th July 1908

Figure 4.7 Fingerprints of Charles Howard[20]

the need to introduce biometric databases, such as the failed attempt to introduce identity cards to the UK.[21] The civil use of fingerprinting in this colonial context was also tied to evolutionary understandings of race. The work of nineteenth-century anthropologists and ethnographers pronounced that certain lower and nomadic Indian castes were criminal tribes, thereby making criminality 'ethnic' (Cole, 2002:67; Sengoopta, 2003). Finger-printing, as an inscriptive device, was a way to produce an accurate identification of habitual criminal castes; and the term *habitual criminal* soon became the *hereditary criminal*, forever making the link between inscriptive devices, scientific (evolutionary) criminality and forensic investigations. In India, these ideas were most sinisterly applied in the Criminal Controls Act 1871 'which called for the "registration, surveillance, and control of certain criminal tribes"' (Cole, 2002:67). Jurist James Fitzjames Stephen (1829–1894), who helped write the *Indian Code of Criminal Procedure*, pronounced that there existed tribes 'whose ancestors were criminals from time immemorial, who are themselves destined by the usages of caste to commit crime' (ibid.:67). As many of the lower castes were nomadic, unpredictable mobility became synonymous with criminality, and fingerprinting offered a potential way to track, monitor and control these so-called criminal classes. Stephen's comments perfectly illustrate the close relationship between criminal anthropology, evolutionary theory and 'surveillance technologies like fingerprinting' (ibid.:69). However, it should be noted that, despite the move towards developing a method of fingerprint classification, administrators were also still using Bertillon's anthropometric system. Edward Henry (1850–1931), Inspector General of Police, was in charge of anthropometric identification in Bengal and became frustrated with trying to use Bertillon's system as a means of identification. However, without a workable classification system for fingerprinting, the Bertillon system was still required (ibid.:73).

Henry Faulds (1843–1930), a Scottish physician working in Tsukiji hospital in Tokyo, was the first individual to attempt to create a fingerprint classification system. In a letter to the periodical *Nature* (1880), Faulds suggested that fingermarks could be used to identify criminals and also noticed that oil and sweat pores resulted in latent fingerprints that could be developed with powders. This letter prompted a response by Herschel who also claimed ownership over the technique. Herschel's claim was then bitterly disputed by Faulds – a dispute that would last 'well into the 1950s' (Cole, 2002:73; Sengoopta, 2003:81–92). According to Cole (2002:73–75) and Sengoopta (2003:88–91), Faulds used a 'syllabic' classification system in which 'consonants represented fingerprint pattern types' (Cole, 2002:74) as well as a subclassification system using vowels, and he envisioned the creation of a criminal identification register catalogued according to such patterns. By describing each fingerprint pattern using consonants and vowels, Faulds was able to index using the structure of the fingerprint itself. In 1880 he wrote to Charles Darwin about his research into fingerprints, and Darwin forwarded the letter to his cousin Francis Galton (Sengoopta, 2003:81). Galton is often credited as the 'first to devise a system for the use of fingerprints for identification' (Nickell and Fischer, 1999:114), and in 1892 he published the first textbook on fingerprints. However, whilst Galton *was* interested in how fingerprint patterns may be used to identify individuals, he was more concerned with how they might provide 'a physical marker of hereditary, ethnicity and race' (Cole, 2002:75). One of the first things Galton achieved was the ten-rolled impression system that is still used today, albeit with different technology. He used 'printer's ink made of lampblack' and a roller to cover a copper or glass slab with the ink (Cole, 2002:75; Sengoopta, 2003:593–119). The subject's right hand would then be taken and the tips of all four fingers would be pressed onto the ink-plate and then pressed onto 'an index card measuring eleven and a half by five inches' (Cole, 2002:75). The process would be repeated with the left hand. The next stage would be to take *rolled impressions* (see Figure 4.8):

> The operator would take hold of the finger or thumb and roll it gently from left to right in the ink, then similarly roll it on a designated spot on the index card. A rolled impression made it possible to record a larger area of the fingerprint pattern; it essentially transformed the curved surface of the fingertip into a flat image.
>
> (Ibid.:75)

Galton viewed this type of fingerprint technique as an essential tool for colonial governance (Sengoopta, 2003). However, there was still no developed classification scheme, so Galton set out to create one and, for him, the key was in the structure of the fingerprint patterns themselves. He noted that 'it is that patterns, especially those of a spiral form, may be apparently similar, yet fundamentally unlike, the unaided eye being frequently unable to analyse them and to discern real differences' (Galton, 1892:66). In *Finger Prints*, Galton (1892) builds upon the work of Bertillon, Herschel, Faulds and Purkyne as he moves through an overview of his own research. The contents of his seminal text illustrates the range and depth of topics covered and include: *previous use of fingerprints, methods of printing, ridges and their uses, patterns, their outlines and cores, evidential value, methods of indexing, personal identification, heredity, races* and *classes*. For Galton, papillary ridges are perhaps the most important of all anthropological data:

> We shall see that they form patterns, considerable in size and of a curious variety of shape, whose boundaries can be firmly outlined and which are little worlds in themselves. They have the unique merit of retaining all their peculiarities unchanged throughout life, and afford in consequence an incomparably surer criterion of identity than any other bodily feature. They may be made to throw welcome light on some of the most interesting biological questions of the day, such as heredity, symmetry, correlation, and the nature of genera and the species.
>
> (Ibid.:2)

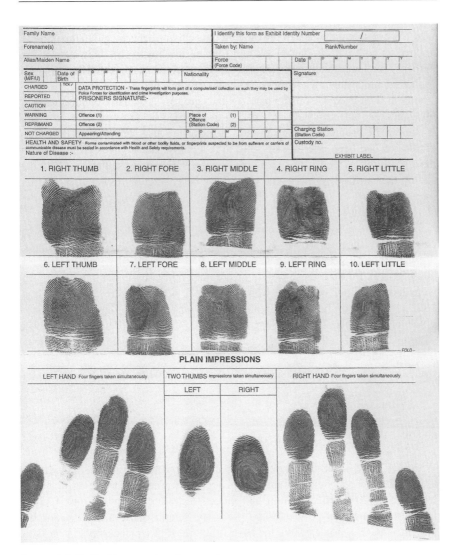

Figure 4.8 Rolled impression fingerprints

These ridges formed the basis of Galton's initial investigations. In Galton's early trials, he collected an aggregate of 504 prints of right thumbs, arranged in a matrix (6 × 6 × 14); but he also discusses his initial attempts at methodology and the fact that he failed many times (1892:66; also see Cole, 2002:77; Sengoopta, 2003:92–119). The problem was in the production of the visual images and identifying and classifying the defined patterns. Bertillon had managed to reduce the body to numbers, but Galton had the problem of trying to classify qualitative data. Importantly, the failures signified a number of influences. For example, 'a complex pattern is capable of suggesting various readings' (Galton, 1892:66), which is a problem that is still prevalent today. Other effects included the pressure applied to both putting on the ink and making the fingerprint. However, it was perhaps the individuality of fingerprints themselves that created most of the problems, muddling any attempt at a classification scheme.

Galton then tried to sort the patterns into groups, eventually coming up with 60 standards. Unfortunately, when Galton returned to these patterns he found a number of problems; for example, 'discovering that the identity of certain duplicates had been overlooked' (ibid.:65). Finally, Galton decided to abandon his 60 patterns, as well as the 9 patterns used by Purkyne. He settled on 3 patterns, stating that all fingerprints could essentially be characterised as being an *arch, loop,* or *whorl*, as outlined by the plates in Galton's *Fingerprint Directories* (1895) in Figure 4.9.

This tripartite system has since become 'the basis for most subsequent classification schemes' (Cole, 2002:79; Sengoopta, 2003:92–119), and it makes up what is called level one general ridge flows (Champod and Chamberlain, 2009:58–59). Because these patterns were not evenly distributed – 67.5 per cent were loops; 26 per cent were whorls; and 6.5 per cent were arches (Galton, 1892:115) – Galton further divided loops into *inner* or *radial* loops and *outer* or *ulnar* loops[22] (Cole, 2002:79; Sengoopta, 2003:92–119). Galton used these four patterns to classify all eight fingers and two thumbs, expressed in the following four-letter alphabet:

- A = Arch
- I = Inner/Radial Loop
- O = Outer/Ulnar Loop
- W = Whorl.

With each finger and thumb being assigned the requisite letter, it was thought that identification cards could be indexed alphabetically according to the resultant ten-letter string. In essence, Galton had indeed 'translated identity from a visual image into language' (Cole, 2002:79). Today, scientists use another four-letter system – ACGT – to designate the base structure of DNA (Jackson and Jackson, 2011:162–167). Galton then went on to suggest that two fingerprints could be matched using what he called *minutiae* (1892:101), noticing that the three core patterns he had identified were not in themselves adequate enough to indivi-dualise. He noted that 'on average, no great reliance can be placed on a general resemblance, in the appearance of two finger prints' (ibid.:101). What was needed was a more careful comparison, 'and [to] collate successively the numerous minutiae, their coincidence throughout would be an evidence of identity' (ibid.:101). It is here that Galton is talking about how the analysis of *ridge characteristics* or *ridge details* can be matched against two finger prints in order to legally identify an individual (Cole, 2002:79–80; Sengoopta, 2003:92–119). Ridge characteristics, also known as *Galton details* are 'points along a papillary

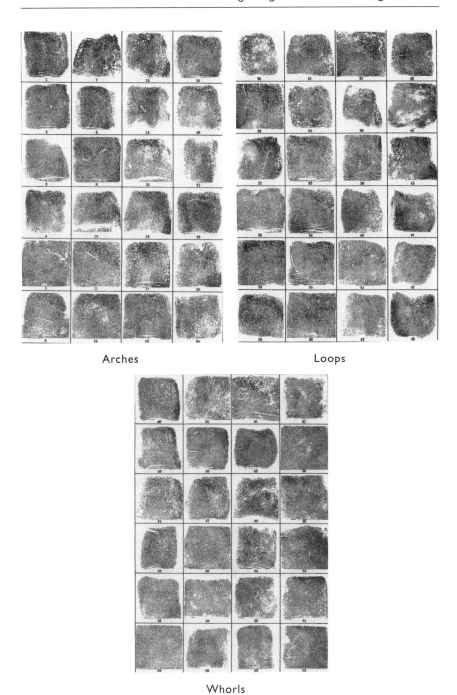

Arches   Loops

Whorls

Figure 4.9 Galton's three core fingerprint patterns[23]

ridge where the right ended abruptly, split in two, or split and then rejoined' (Cole, 2002:79). Whilst there is often some disagreement over terminology, Cole (ibid.:80) identifies the following ridge characteristics:

- ridge termination;
- bifurcation;
- independent ridge;
- dot or island;
- lake;
- spur; and
- crossover.

With these different minutiae, on all eight fingers and two thumbs, combined with the three core patterns, Galton employed the calculus of probability to statistically infer that the probability of two whole fingers matching would be one in 64 billion:

> The result is, that the chance of lineations, constructed by the imagination according to strictly natural forms, which shall be found to resemble those of a single finger print in all their minutiae, is less than 1 to 2(24) x 2(4) x 2(8), or 1 to 2(36), or 1 to about sixty-four thousand millions. The inference is, that as the number of the human race is reckoned at about sixteen thousand millions, it is a smaller chance than 1 to 4 that the print of a *single* finger of any given person would be exactly like that of the same finger of another member of the human race. [Original emphasis]
>
> (Galton, 1892:110–111)

In 1893, in response to these findings, the Home Office appointed a committee to look into both Bertillon's and Galton's systems of identification. Chaired by Charles Troup, the committee heard a review of the Bertillon system and visited Galton's laboratory. One of the biggest problems found by the committee was that Galton had not 'yet devised a working method of subclassification' (Cole, 2002:80), whereas, of course, Bertillon's system was built upon a systematic identification system (Sengoopta, 2003). The Troup Committee thought that without the necessary classification method, Galton's method would become problematic once the number of fingerprints collected 'exceeded 1,000 identi-fication cards' (Cole, 2002:81). Because of this, the committee recommended the continued use of anthropometry. However, there were individuals who were less enthusiastic about this technique, and again we move back to British-controlled India, where one such individual led the way in developing the subclassification system that was much needed to make Galton's system practically useful.

Edward Henry (1850–1931) was Inspector General of Police of Bengal and between 1896 and 1897, with the help of his sub-inspectors Azizul Haque and

Chandra Bose, Henry developed a system of fingerprint classification enabling fingerprint records to be organised and searched with relative ease. One of the major contributions they made to the aetiological development of finger-printing was the creation of a 'scheme for using "ridge counting" and "ridge racing" to sort loops and whorls into smaller groups' (Cole, 2002:81; also see Sengoopta, 2003). Cole (2002:81–85) provides an excellent overview of Henry's complicated system. The first two steps were based on Galton's three pattern types of whorls, arches and loops, to which Henry and his team added a fourth category known as *composites*.[24] These four patterns formed the basis of the *primary classification*, which is where the fingers are examined and the location of the whorls are noted. The fingers and thumbs are numbered 1 to 10, starting with the left little finger moving in a right direction and vice versa for the right hand. The reason for using a numbering system was to enable the qualitative pattern to be numerically expressed, thus making it easier to create a practical identification index. Odd-numbered fingers would be numerators and those with even numbers, denominators (Cole, 2002:82). Next, certain values were assigned depending on whether whorls were found on odd- or even-numbered fingers, and to these values Henry added 1 in order to avoid having zeros. Thus, the primary classification fingerprint fraction could range from 1/1 to 32/32; my fingerprints, for instance, have no whorls, so I would have a primary classification of 1/1. As the largest fraction was 32/32, 'fingerprint cards were stored in a filing cabinet with 32 rows and 32 columns of pigeonholes' (ibid.:82). Unfortunately, this primary classification – what is called today a *level 1* analysis of the main categories of general ridge flow analysis (Champod and Chamberlain, 2009: 57–58) – is not able to individualise to a specific finger of origin. Think of my 1/1 primary classification; how many individuals in the world do not have whorls on any of their fingers or thumbs? Therefore, a second level of analysis, or classification, is required.

The *secondary classification* is a more detailed, intricate characterisation of the core patterns. As whorls were included in the primary classification they were omitted from the secondary analysis. Instead, the other core patterns were analysed in more detail, producing the further subclassifications of arches (A or a);[25] tented arches (T or t); radial loops (R or r); or ulnar loops (U or u). Further subclassification was then conducted on the whorls whereby *ridge tracing* was undertaken between the two *deltas*. If the ridge passed inside the right delta it was classified 'as an "inner" whorl, designated by I. It if passed outside, the pattern was classified as an "outer" whorl, designated by O' (Cole, 2002:82). Henry and his team then used *ridge counting* to subclassify loops. They would count the number of ridges between the delta and the *core* and these values were then added to the secondary classification scheme. Even after this there was still more subclassification, making the Henry system a multilayered classification system that 'greatly speeded up the process of checking whether a suspect's fingerprint had already been registered with the police, perhaps under an alias' (Cole, 2002:84; Sengoopta, 2003). Henry introduced his system in the Bengal police department in 1895 and published *Classification and Uses of Finger Prints* in 1900:[26] a text outlining the fundamental principles of the Henry System. This new method, once fully developed, became know as the *Henry system* and, whilst quite complicated, became the standard classification for fingerprinting in the twentieth century (Sengoopta, 2003). However, as with many developments in forensics, practical acceptance was slow.

In 1897 the colonial government appointed a committee to evaluate Henry's new system. Chaired by General Strahan, the Surveyor General of India, part of the committee's remit was to compare anthropometry to fingerprinting. Strahan was concerned that, whilst the main benefit of Bertillon's system was scientific rigour, the system was predicated on in-depth knowledge, training and skills – something that the warders and policemen of nineteenth-century India often lacked (Cole, 2002:87). Henry had sold the fingerprinting classification system as simplicity itself, especially the fact that 'fingerprints could be taken "without skilled labour, and without instruments"' (ibid.:87). Not only this, the speed and efficiency at which a full set of fingerprints could be taken (approximately five minutes) made it an attractive alternative to the time-consuming method employed by Bertillon. A third advantage identified by the Strahan committee was the ease and speed at which you could search the fingerprint catalogue, with Cole suggesting that 'a search in a file of more than 8,000 cards required less than five minutes' (ibid.:87). The committee provided a clear indication as to which side they were on:

> In conclusion, therefore, we are of opinion that the method of identification of habitual criminals by means of finger prints as worked on the system of recording impressions, and of classification devised by Mr. Henry, may be safely adopted as being superior to the anthropometric method, (1) in simplicity of working, (2) in the cost of apparatus, (3) in the fact that all the skilled work required is transferred to the central or classification bureau, (4) in the rapidity with which the process can be worked, and (5) in the certainty of the results.
>
> (Strahan and Pedler, 1897, cited in Henry, 1900:98)

On 12th June 1897, the Governor General of India switched to Henry's classification system, and it soon spread not only through the provinces in India but also from police and prison departments to other bureaucratic domains of the colonial governance of India. Henry lists the Opium Department, the Emigration Department, the Survey of India, the Post Office, the Medical Department and the Registration Department as some of the colonial bureaucracies that started to use fingerprints as a method of identification (Henry, 1900:5–9; also see Cole, 2002:87–88). In 1897, the system was used in a criminal investigation and, for the first time, moved beyond the realm of record keeping and into the arena of forensic investigation. On 15th August 1897 the manager of a tea garden was stabbed to death. During the incident 'a wooden box belonging to the deceased had been opened and money removed from it ... [and] a bloody fingerprint was found on an almanac that had been removed from the wooden box' (Cole, 2002:88). An ex-servant named Kangali Charan soon became a suspect and as the police already had his fingerprints on record they used Galton's method of comparison by matching the ridge characteristics 'between the bloody print and the inked print' (ibid.:88). In 1898 the first criminal trial using fingerprint evidence began and the importance of this case and its role in the development of fingerprinting for forensic purposes cannot be overemphasised. Up until this point, fingerprints had been used to identify individuals using *all* ten prints taken from an individual. When decisions were made on whether any two sets of fingerprints matched, they were made on the basis of two *full* sets of ten fingerprints. The probability scores of 1 in 64 billion, assigned by Galton, were also predicated upon a ten-set comparison, with the underlying premise that 'no two individuals had identical *sets of ten* fingerprints' (ibid.:88, original emphasis). In a forensic setting, this is not the case. It is very rare that investigators analysing a crime scene find a complete set of ten fingermarks. It is more common to find one or two marks or even to find only a partial mark at a crime scene. Once the forensic context is factored into the analysis it becomes clear that forensic fingerprint identification rests on the very ambitious premise that no two *single* fingerprints are alike; moreover, that *no two partial prints are identical* (ibid.:89). If you then add the fact that partial marks found at crime scenes 'are often blurred, smudged and overlaid upon one another, and distorted by foreign matter' (ibid.:89), it becomes even more difficult to analysis the pattern and ridge detail required for a positive match. These issues are still crucial in relation to contemporary issues in fingerprint identification.

The Charan case was the first known, and crucial, test of the work of Herschel, Galton and Henry. Detectives on the case matched 18 ridge characteristics and pushed forward with the trial. As Cole (ibid.:89) notes, there was no such thing as a fingerprint expert, so the judge and assessors examined the fingerprints themselves. Upon examination of the prints, they were unwilling to convict him of the murder, and instead the prints were enough to place him in the room of the deceased on the night in question. Charan was acquitted of the murder and charged with burglary (ibid.:89). Whilst this was not the ideal result for the police, it did establish that fingerprints could be used to convict; and it also influenced the creation of the Indian Evidence Act of 1899 (ibid.:90), which amended the Law of Evidence 'to the extent of declaring relevant the testimony of those who by study have become proficient in finger-print decipherment, such testimony not having been admissible under the unamended law' (Henry, 1900:9). It is within this passage, taken from Henry's *Classification and Uses of Finger Prints*, and also the passing of the Act that we see the legal precedent of expert forensic fingerprint identification witnesses being formally accepted. In the 1904 case *Emperor v. Sahdeo*, the government found that fingerprint evidence was legitimate, ratifying 'the still unproven assumption that no two fingerprints were alike' (Cole, 2002:90).

However, as Cole notes, this type of evidence was clearly within the realms of inductive reasoning:

> There had 'never yet been found any case in which the pattern made by one finger exactly resembled the pattern made by any other finger of the same or any other hand.' The absence of disproof was taken as proof.
>
> (Ibid.:90)

The success of fingerprinting in what Cole calls the 'colonial laboratory' (ibid.:96) established the Henry system as a viable alternative to Bertillonage. The same year that Henry published his *Classification and Uses*, the British Home Secretary appointed Lord Henry Belper to chair a committee to look into both fingerprint-ing and anthropometry (Sengoopta, 2003:171–183). The ensuing debate was really about how to file identification cards, and, despite the clear advantages of fingerprinting over Bertillon's system, the perception that fingerprinting was unproven continued to be a barrier to its introduction in Europe. One of the major reasons for the resistance to fingerprinting was the fact that Galton's main interest whilst he was developing his classification scheme was to link fingerprints to trace heredity, 'delineate differences between "races" and predict criminality and disease propensity' (Cole, 2002:100; also see Sengoopta, 2003:171–183). Galton's classification taxonomy, therefore, can be allied to scientific theories of criminality, some of which were explored in Chapter 3. Unfortunately, the association between fingerprinting as a technology to determine issues such as criminal heredity has largely been forgotten in most historical accounts of forensic investigations. Cole provides an insightful reason as to why this is:

> This selective amnesia is not accidental; rather it played a crucial role in establishing the legitimacy of fingerprinting in criminal investigation. Fingerprint examiners strengthened their authority by disassociating them-selves from their colleagues who speculated about the predictive powers of fingerprints.
>
> (2002:100)

Thus, there arose a twofold manifestation of fingerprinting in the late nineteenth and early twentieth centuries: on the one hand, fingerprinting and heredity and, on the other, fingerprinting and identification. What is interesting about this dichot-omy is that advocates of both positions were trying to prove diametrically oppos-ing ideas. In order for the idea of heredity to be empirically supported by fingerprints, it was necessary to argue that fingerprints between races, family members and so on were in fact *similar*; without similarity between prints, one could not logically argue for signs of inheritance. However, if fingerprints were to be used for identification purposes, it was imperative that *difference* was proven. The tension between these two positions was first expressed by Purkyne and was to 'plague the practice of fingerprint analysis for more than a century thereafter' (ibid.:105). Galton's attempt to establish the heredity of fingerprinting was not successful because he kept coming up against the uniqueness of each fingerprint. However, this did not deter others in the quest, as amateur and professionals throughout the world 'pursued ways of using fingerprint patterns to understand race, ethnicity, and character' (ibid.:110). The findings of this wide variety of research were not significant enough to develop into a fully fledged scientific research programme (ibid.:111), and by the 1920s scientists began to lose interest in fingerprints and moved 'onto other areas of research' (188). At the same time, another group of professionals were using fingerprints more successfully. These groups were police and prison officials, who viewed fingerprints not as a sign of heredity but as a 'convenient method of identifying the criminal bodies passing in rapidly increasingly numbers through their institutions' (ibid.:112). As such, law enforcement agencies were not concerned with the morphological research, as it tended to hinder the need for a practical and efficient classification system. In the 1930s, with more and more police and prison service personnel using fingerprint-ing with increasing success, the sheer weight of numbers of users and successes soon meant that *dactyloscopy* (the *scientific* study of fingerprint patterns) soon came to an end, and its use in forensic identification took over as the primary means by which fingerprinting was practically applied. However, the real test of forensic fingerprint identification was its evidential utility in the courtroom (ibid.:113).

In Europe, the first use of a fingerprint for forensic identification occurred in Paris when a bloody fingerprint was found at the scene of a strangled valet at a dentist's office. Ironically, it was Bertillon who photographed the bloody finger-print and checked his identification cards. He identified a recently released convict named Scheffer (ibid.:170) and, upon being presented with the evidence, Scheffer confessed to the crime, thus avoiding a lengthy and expensive trial. In the UK, Scotland Yard began using fingerprint identification in 1901, and shortly there-after police officers 'began performing forensic identifications' (ibid.:171). Cole (ibid.:171–173) suggests that one of the most influential practitioners who helped to test fingerprinting in a forensic setting was Inspector Charles Stockley Collins. Collins made his first 'forensic fingerprint identification in a burglary case in 1902' (ibid.:172). In this case, there was no strong attack on the fingerprint, which was accepted as proof that the accused was physically present at the crime scene. However, one of the major issues faced by the advocates of fingerprinting was that a number of cases ended in acquittals due to a lack of understanding and familiarity of fingerprinting amongst juries. Another core issue identified in these early debates, and one that resonates through contemporary debates between forensic experts, was just who the fingerprint experts should be. The *Deptford Murder Trial* involved the murder of a Deptford couple in 1905, in which detec-tives at Scotland Yard found a bloody fingerprint in a cash box. Inspector Collins testified at the Old Bailey that the print found belonged to Alfred Stratton (ibid.:173). Collins' method compared the *questioned mark* with a *known print* by 'finding and labeling matching ridge characteristics, or "points of similarity"' (ibid.:173). However, it was a trial in 1909 that firmly established the forensic utility of fingerprinting. In *Rex v Castleton,* Thomas Castleton's fingerprint was matched to a mark found on a candle at the scene. Upon conviction, Castleton appealed; but this was rejected with the appeals court 'establishing in law that defendants may be convicted on fingerprint evidence alone' (ibid.:177). This case, and many others besides, used the method of *matching* of samples to link evidence found at the scene with samples taken from suspects; and matching was a technique that was developed through the principle of exchange and trace evidence.

The reimagining of corpuscularianism – the advent of trace evidence

Around the same time as individuals were developing anthropometry and fingerprinting as systems of identification, one of the fundamental ideas of forensic science was created. No one can lay a better claim to being the founding father of forensic science than Edmond Locard (1877–1966). He, alongside Hans Gross, is perhaps the most famous and most commonly referenced in the histories of forensic science (see Nickell and Fischer, 1999; Pepper, 2005; Chisum and Turvey, 2007; Turvey, 2008; Houck and Siegel, 2010; Petherick *et al.*, 2010). Through his research on dust and microscopic particles, Locard produced what has become one of the core doctrines of forensic science – the *principle of exchange* (or exchange principle). Born in Saint-Chamond, France, in 1877, Locard graduated in medicine and law and became the director of the Lyon Institute of Forensic Medicine. He also created the first police forensic lab in Lyon (Inman and Rudin, 2000:44). Locard's research took an idea initially developed by Dr. Alexandre Lacassgne, who was Professor of Forensic Medicine at the University of Lyon and who highlighted the importance of *trace* and *transfer evidence* to his students. Specifically, he suggested to his students an idea that, up until then, had not been considered: '[t]he idea that the dust on clothing, or on people's ears, noses and fingernails, could provide information on the occupations and whereabouts of suspects' (Thorwald, 1966:281, cited in Petherick *et al.*, 2010:26).

The importance of Lassagne's work on microscopic particles, or trace evidence as it is now commonly known, is seen through the pioneering work of Locard, whose studies of dust and its usefulness in aiding criminal investigations is still being utilised over 100 years after its introduction. Locard himself is more humble about the origins of the principle of exchange, suggesting that 'the main idea, which was embryonic for a long time, has been hatched in many places simultaneously and no one can frankly attribute its paternity to himself' (Locard, 1930a:278). However, according to Petherick *et al.* (2010:27), Locard's work has often been 'misstated, misrepresented and misattributed over the years'. This confusion could be the result of poor translation, from Locard's native French to

English. Petherick *et al.* (ibid.:27–28) locate a rough translation from *La Police et Les Methodes Scientifiques* (1934):

> Searching for traces is not, as much as one could believe it, an innovation of modern criminal jurists. It is an occupation probably as old as humanity . . . the principle is this one. Any action of an individual, and obviously, the violent action constituting a crime, cannot occur without leaving a mark.
>
> (Cited in Petherick *et al.*, 2010:28)

In an article entitled 'The Analysis of Dust Traces, Part 1', Locard succinctly outlined the exchange principle when he stated that 'for the microscopic debris that cover our clothes and bodies are the *mute witnesses, sure and faithful, of all our movements and of all our encounters*' (Locard, 1930a:276 – original emphasis). This is perhaps the closest we can get to the original conceptualisation envisaged by Locard. The operationally useful idea within his exchange principle is the idea that *people leave marks*, or traces of themselves when undertaking crimes. If people left traces of themselves it soon became apparent that the actual environment in which a crime is committed could also produce trace elements that can be transferred between parties and locations. Therefore, Locard extended the concept of exchange by arguing that when two objects have been in contact, trace evidence will be exchanged between them. He argued that it was therefore necessary to detect, identify and recover these trace elements so they can be analysed to identify their source of origin (ibid.). Once this is achieved, it is possible to reconstruct the contacts between people and places and produce an overview and interpretation of the crime event that has taken place (Locard, 1930a, 1930b; Locard and Larson, 1930). The forensic usefulness of this was clear to Locard: the ability to recognise, document and examine the 'nature and extent of evidences traces and exchanges in a crime scene' (Petherick *et al.*, 2010:28), which enables us to track down and associate the suspect with the crime location, items of evidence and persons involved. Furthermore, the ideas of the principle of exchange and trace evidence imply that a certain level of evidentiary interpretation becomes the cornerstone of forensic science. The principle of exchange and evidentiary interpretation will be discussed in greater detail in Chapters 7 and 9.

The fundamental basis of Locard's principle of exchange was the analysis of traces of dust. For Locard, dust on things such as clothing and individuals was evidence of the contacts and interactions between individuals, objects and places. He locates the origin of the idea of using dust for discovering criminological evidence within Chinese legal medicine, and he also pays tribute to Hans Gross and Sir Arthur Conan Doyle as being two central influences on the work he and his colleagues undertook at the police laboratory of Lyon (1930a:276–277). In this research, Locard conceptualised dust as 'an accumulation of debris in a state of pulverization. This debris may originate from any special body, organic or inorganic' (ibid.:278). He noted that the importance of dust particles for forensic investigations lay in the fact that whilst this 'pulverized condition' destroyed the 'morphological state' that would usually be enough for us to recognise 'these objects by our senses or even with our instruments' (ibid.:279), this pulverization of inorganic or organic material did not reduce the object into molecules or atoms. Dust, therefore, still 'preserves sufficient distinctive characters, so that one is able, almost invariably, to identify its origin' (ibid.:280). However, in order to identify the origin of dust particles and its subsequent forensic uses, Locard proceeded to outline in depth the following issues: (i) the types of dust that existed; (ii) the objects that should be systematically examined for dust particles in the course of criminal investigations; (iii) the processes undertaken in the analysis of dust; (iv) a review of known (including his own) experimentation into dust particles; and (v) the applied uses of dust trace analysis in criminal cases. Readers are advised to examine the original three articles published in 1930 in *The American Journal of Police Science*, for it is within these three crucial works that Locard provides an excellent overview of the totality of his work on establishing the principle of exchange. Part C of Locard's first article, for instance, provides an overview of the objects that should be systematically examined for dust particles in the course of criminal investigations, which are outlined in Table 4.4 (ibid.:282–293).

An important element of Locard's, and other scientists' work on dust particles was its relationship to the technological and economic context of nineteenth-century and early-twentieth-century capitalist society. For example, George Dressy's report of the *Laboratory of Legal Medicine* (1884) 'noted that the eyebrows furnish interesting evidence of the individual's occupation, by the virtue of the dust they contain' (ibid.:285). Dressy provided a number of examples of occupations and the types of dust that accumulated in the eyebrows, including those in Table 4.5 (ibid.:286).

Even more comprehensive was the list of occupations and types of dust traces that could often be found under the fingernails. Locard took Villebrun's extensive study and added to the list of 'occupational dusts found around and beneath the nails' (ibid.:287). Locard identified 47 occupations and around 82 main categories of organic and inorganic dust particles that could be associated to specific occupations. The practical forensic uses of this information were soon to become obvious. If a murder victim was found to have specific traces of a particular dust

Table 4.4. Objects for the investigation of dust

Clothing	Eyebrows
Pockets	Nails
Shoes	Ears
Underwear	Nostrils
Skin	Weapons
Hair	Vehicles

Table 4.5 Eyebrow dust and occupations

Occupation	Primary dust trace particles
Railroad firemen and engineers	Powdered coal
Millers and bakers	Flour
Coppersmiths	Black dust of iron oxide and copper oxide
Plasterers, masons, bricklayers	Plaster, either dried or powdered
Locksmiths	Iron and copper filings
Prostitutes	Black dust of cosmetics; rice powder

on their body or clothing, or if specific dust particles were found at the scene of a burglary, *and* if the occupation of the murder victim or owner of the house was proven to be different, then a logical step would be to trace the particles to a specific occupation and start the investigation in that area.

Locard then went on to discuss three processes of analysing dust: (i) *sorting*; (ii) *microscopic examination*; (iii) and *microchemical examination*. The first process, *sorting*, could be achieved using a number of different methods including water sifting/separation and magnetic mounted needles (ibid.:293). However, Locard seems to have preferred direct sorting using a magnifying glass. The core reason for sorting was to 'separate out the grains whose origin is obvious . . . as well as any crystals that are of such size as to have preserved a recognizable form' (ibid.:293). Any particles not easily recognisable would then be grouped together if they possessed similar characteristics. The next stage, *microscopic examination*, was then used to qualitatively observe and classify the organic elements. Locard (ibid.:294) notes how microscopic examination of particles is based on the principles of crystallography.[27] The types of particles that came under microscopic examination for forensic purposes in Locard's lab included: *animal debris* such as microbes, ova and larvae, blood, fish scales, fats, muscular fibres and faeces (ibid.:294–297); and *vegetable debris* such as wheat, rye and barley flour, potato starch, seeds, pollen, mushroom spores and tobacco (Locard and Larson, 1930:401–410). It is interesting to note that, in the three articles on dust analysis, Locard does not mention the importance of *human debris*. The third process used by Locard was micro-chemical examination, which was used when microscopic analysis was not sensitive enough to identify the dust particle. Table 4.6 provides a list of micro-chemical tests for a range of textile fibres and their subsequent reactions with specific reagents, and this has been reproduced in full from Locard and Larson (ibid.:406).

So far, Locard had demonstrated the importance of dust, its collection and analysis. However, it was experimental research by others that really brought the forensic usefulness of dust to the forefront. In one such experiment reported by Locard and Larson (ibid.:416–417), Vuillemin and Parisot walked around the city of Nancy, in France, after it had rained heavily and 'drenched the soil'. Upon returning from their walk, they removed their shoes and examined the dust and

Table 4.6 Micro-chemical analysis

Textile fibres	Zinc chloride	Iodine and sulfuric acid	Ammoniacal copper oxide	Aniline sulfate	Phloroglucin
Cotton	Violet	Blue	Blue (solution)		
Linen	Violet	Blue	Blue (solution)		
Hemp	Violet	Blue	Blue (solution)	Often pale; often yellow-violet	Red
Jute	Brownish-yellow	Greenish-blue	Blue (solution)	Golden-yellow	Crimson
Nettle	Dirty violet	Dirty blue	Blue (solution)		
Manilla Hemp	Yellowish-brown			Yellow	Red
New Zealand linen	Yellow	Blue	Bluish	Yellowish	Pale red
Aloes	Yellow-bronze	Yellow-green interior and exterior	Bluish with marked swelling	Yellowish	Faint red
Coconut	Yellowish-brown			Bright yellow	Pale purple

mud that had accumulated on the soles, noting four specific types. From an analysis of the mud and dust they were able to 'reconstruct the exact itinerary' of where they had walked:

> So that one could, with certain complementary information, trace quite readily the route travelled ... Strassbourg Street, Orly Park, Strassbourg Street, Vic Street, Saverne Street, Lobau Boulevard, crossing of a railroad on a level with the street, the tow path along the canal, and returning by the same itinerary.
>
> (Ibid.:417)

Here we see an early link being made between evidence present through the principle of exchange and its possible usefulness in the reconstruction of events. Locard, therefore, was quick to realise the evidential utility of dust particles. In the third volume of *The Analysis of Dust Traces*, Locard reviewed cases from the courts where 'the analysis of dust has been of great assistance as circumstantial evidence' (1930b:496). These cases, taken from the research files of distinguished scientists such as Popp, Gross, Bayle, Parisot and Locard's police laboratory in Lyon (ibid.:496), are interesting not only for historical purposes but also because they demonstrate the early applied use of trace evidence in a forensic setting. For example, case 21 recounts the Vendel case, in which a 13-year-old girl had been raped. She accused a taxi driver who denied the claim. An analysis of her soiled underwear found stains that were thick and black. A microscopic analysis was undertaken and the dust particles were consistent with the 'oily dust found on automobile wheels' (ibid.:513). In order to ascertain whether the spots contained the necessary metal particles one would 'logically expect to find in the grease from automobile', the appropriate test was performed, and the Russian Blue reaction confirmed the existence of traces of iron metal particles.

Since these initial experiments and cases, Locard's exchange principle has become the bedrock of forensic science in respect of the applied collection and analysis of trace evidence (Inman and Rudin, 2000:44; Gallop and Stockdale, 2004:56–57; Weston, 2004:21–22; Houck, 2009:167–169; Houck and Siegel, 2010:54).

Summary

The aetiological development of forensic science has been very disparate, spanning many hundreds of years. Up until the nineteenth century, developments in forensic investigations could not be regarded as a coherent whole. Instead, many different microsites of knowledge developed with a number of individuals researching into a whole range of specific areas of science. This chapter provided a selective history of some of the core developments that can be linked to the overall epistemological and ontological development of forensic investigations and its links with scientific criminology. Forensic investigations have a long history, dating back to Chinese developments in medicine. Archeological evidence suggests that the Chinese used primitive forms of forensic science to investigate crime scenes as early as the third century BCE, although forensic history dates as far back as 3000–2000 BCE (Bell, 2008:23). The development of modern forensic investigations consists of a number of stages where fundamental ideas, methods and technologies were created, invented or discovered. These were then tested and developed so they could be applied to resolve criminal justice problems. However, there has to be a level of acceptance of the idea, method or technology amongst the scientific, police and legal communities. Aspects of these processes were illustrated by the development of key forensic investigative techniques surrounding identifying and measuring criminals, fingerprinting and trace evidence.

These three areas were the core advancements within forensic investigations during the Victorian period. The first important development concerned the identification and measurement of criminals. Here, theories of scientific criminology regarding evolutionary and biological determinism influenced the creation of practical methods of identification. For example, composite photography was used as an inscriptive device that attempted to visualise the degenerative criminality suggested by scientific criminology. Photography was used to highlight the physical differences that could distinguish criminals from each other and solve the problems of identifying habitual criminals. Alongside photography, measuring the 'criminal' became the main technique in the nineteenth century as a means to identify criminals. Through anthropometry, or the scientific measurement of the 'criminal body', a classification system was created that consisted of cards full of discernible information that, when used in conjunction with photographs, enabled the police to identify habitual offenders. The next major development for forensic investigations was the creation of a fingerprint classification scheme. Following from the fundamental idea that no two individuals bore the same prints, notable administrators and scientists sought to develop a fully formed taxonomy that included a method for classifying and labelling fingerprint patterns that could also be used for identifying individuals.

Finally, the nineteenth century saw the creation and development of what was to become *the* fundamental idea behind most of forensic science. Locard's principle of exchange, which examined the cross transference of trace evidence, brought scientific sophistication to criminal investigations. It soon became apparent to some practitioners that photography, anthropometry, fingerprints and the principle of exchange could all be extremely useful to the police in their developing role as criminal investigators.

Chapter 5

The beginnings of criminal investigation

> I am the last and highest court of appeal in detection
>
> (Sherlock Holmes, *The Sign of Four*, Chapter 1 – 'The Science of Deduction')

Introduction

The development of scientific criminology and forensic investigative techniques can also be linked to the development of the first professional police force, which came into being 'as a deeply contested institution in the early nineteenth century' (Reiner, 2010:67). Whilst the practical means to measure and identify criminals were hotly contested amongst the burgeoning scientific and social scientific disciplines, many criminal justice organisations and professionals embraced these new tools and techniques with pragmatic vigour in the fight against crime. As the previous chapter highlighted, practical measures largely developed as an administrative tool for colonial India (fingerprinting) or as a solution to the immense growth in police criminal records (anthropometry and photography). It is no coincidence that the utility of these techniques were accentuated by the creation of the first police force in the UK and the subsequent introduction of the detective branch (Morris, 2007). What is also clear is that these methods eventually played a key role in the hegemonic development of the police.

Since the introduction of the first professionalised, state-run police organisation in 1829, the police have become a dominant professional body with immense powers over its *citizens*. Today, in the twenty-first century, the police have not only *persuaded* us that they are necessary but they have also become mistresses of their own destiny, with the ability to influence and determine criminal justice policies and laws; which is a further blurring of the lines between Becker's (1963:147–164) 'rule creators' and 'rule enforcers'. This chapter examines the aetiological development of the police and their early links with investigating crime and forensic science. It begins by outlining a brief social history of the development of the police and discuss the role parameters that have traditionally been associated with the police. I also discuss some of the key social, economic and political contexts in which these developments took place. Concentrating mainly on the nineteenth century, I then move on to early forms of investigation and argue that, whilst a formalised structure was slow to develop, there were sporadic signs of some sophisticated forms of criminal investigations. In particular, pre-police modes of investigation provide evidence of a clear structure for investigating crime. I then move on to provide a brief history of the *pre-police* by looking at the Bow Street Runners of the eighteenth century, which were a precursor to the creation of the modern police force in Britain. By looking at the creation of first modern police force in 1829, I link criminal investigations to some of the earliest forms of forensic science and show how the end of the nineteenth century and the beginning of the twentieth century saw the creation of the forensic detective, who worked alongside the police and developed scientific techniques and methods that would change the landscape of forensic investigations in the twentieth century. I discuss some of the core pioneers in such practice, and I argue that it was the practical application, both at the *crime scene* and in the *courtroom*, that saw major developments in forensic practice – developments that fundamentally created modern crime scene investigation.

A social history of policing

Criminal investigations today are primarily under the professional dominance of the police. However, as various authors have suggested, the advent of numerous political and social programmes such as *community safety* programmes and *crime and disorder reduction partnerships*, the widening of the policing family including PCSO's (Police Community Support Officers) and the structural developments in new *public* and *risk* management, which has targeted specific offender populations, means the definition and role of criminal investigations have become increasingly unclear (Maguire, 2003:387; Reiner, 2010:3–36). Furthermore, definitions and roles are historically and culturally specific, meaning they are fluid and change depending on the social, political and economic climates in which they emerge. Such contexts are, of course, the *bread and butter* of the sociologist, historian, or criminologist interested in sociologically oriented criminology. However, they have rarely been considered in the plethora of texts on forensic science and criminal investigations, which are very much process oriented and tend to ignore contextual issues: a strange situation given that these processes are determined by *context*. It should be acknowledged that the social, political and economic context will often be a key factor that influences or even determines the strategic and operational elements of criminal investigations and, therefore, will ultimately determine a wide range of issues, such as the identification, interpretation and ordering of forensic information. Practitioners operate within these contexts on a daily basis, so knowledge of these contexts can be very important.

Police and policing parameters – controlling human nature?

Criminal investigations could be viewed as the core business of the *police*, especially in their role of *policing* society. These two ideas – *police* and *policing* – are not necessarily conterminous. Policing is a set of processes that has always been a universal feature of social relations (Reiner, 2010:4), and societies throughout history have always thought it necessary to *police* their members in order to ensure their own survival through the reproduction, growth and continuation of their cultural systems. In purely functionalist terms, the role of policing members of a society has always meant some form of social order maintenance (Spencer, 1896; Durkheim, 1982, 1984); and the ways in which social order was maintained varies greatly from age to age and society to society. The *police* on the other hand are a social institution that is 'not found in every society, and police organizations and personnel can have a variety of shifting meanings' (Reiner, 2010:4). The development of the police as a state-organised bureaucracy in the nineteenth century can be placed within the broader programme of developing government bureaucracies that Weber saw as part of the burgeoning dominance of capitalist economies (Weber, 1978, [1930]1992; Gerth and Mills, 1993) and which Durkheim (1984) saw as a progressive development from simple to complex societies and their transition from organic to mechanical solidarity. Historically, *policing* is a more robust notion than *police* as the police are usually associated with more complex societies, which tend to move away from the traditional notion of policing as embedded within localised social relationships 'and by citizen "volunteers" or private employees' (Reiner, 2010:6). Instead, police *organisations* tend to be found in more complex societies that have a developed specialised division of labour (Schwartz and Miller, 1964:166, cited in Reiner, 2010:6). It is somewhat bemusing that David Cameron's *Big Society* ideology in relation to crime control is effectively attempting to move back towards a pre-industrial concept of policing. We have yet to see the full implications of his plans, although one thing is certain – postmodernists will have to come up with a new term to cover this retro-progressive step. Perhaps *fashionably late postmodernism* could be the next inclusive catchphrase!

The ways in which the police developed their practices grew very much from the theories of human nature that were discussed in the Enlightenment period. In his usual eloquent and lucid way, Pinker (2003:5–13) notes how the original *blank slate* thesis (*tabula rasa*)[1] introduced by Locke was coupled with Dryden's concept and Rousseau's use of the *noble savage, and* Descartes' *ghost in the machine*[2] thesis; what philosophers call *empiricism, romanticism* and *dualism*. These ideas supported theories of human nature that have become so entrenched within the intellectual consciousness of modern society that they still impact upon a broad range of social arrangements, customs and government policies, including policies around policing citizens. For example, Dryden's concept of the *noble savage* captured the 'belief that humans in their natural state are selfless, peaceable, and untroubled, and that the blights such as greed, anxiety, and violence are the products of civilization' (ibid.:6). The Genevan philosopher Jean-Jacques Rousseau (1712–1778) used Dryden's noble savage to counter Hobbes' leviathan thesis, which contended that, without a common power, 'man' is in a constant condition of war, which is one of 'continual fear, and danger of violent death; and the life of man, solitary, poor, nasty, brutish, and short' (Hobbes, [1651]1957:185–186, cited in Pinker, 2003:7). Hobbes believed the only way that societies could escape this brutal existence was to surrender 'their autonomy to a sovereign person or assembly', which he called a *leviathan* (Pinker, 2003:7). Pinker also notes the interesting position that submission to the leviathan creates (ibid.:3):

> If people are noble savages, then a domineering leviathan is unnecessary. Indeed, by forcing people to delineate private property for the state to recognize – property they might otherwise have shared – the leviathan creates the very greed and belligerence it is designed to control. A happy society would be our birthright; all we need to do is eliminate the institutional barriers that keep us from it. If, in contrast, people are naturally nasty, the best we can hope for is an uneasy truce enforced by police and the army.

In short, policing through an institutionalised leviathan-esque police force has been a way to control the savage nature of humanity which has been created by the environmental conditions of civilised, capitalist society.

The role of the police in history

It is difficult to contemplate a society without a state sponsored and authorised police force; yet it is purely a modern phenomenon. In the period up until the 1066 Conquest, the UK commonly practiced the 'blood-feud and communal intervention' (Rawlings, 2003:41). Our early codes of law were primarily drawn up by Anglo-Saxon kings and were 'expressions of royalty authority', concerned with 'the codification of customary practice' and the re-articulation of 'the rights of the victim and the role of community. . . . into duties that were owed to the Crown' (ibid.:41). Looking through this historical prism, policing has often been connected to the notion of *law enforcement* (Rowe, 2008:5), especially the suppression of social disorder (Savage, 2007; Rowe, 2008; Reiner, 2010). Social disorder came to prominence as a major problem for the upper- and middle-class capitalist elite as social hierarchies, and the resultant inequalities they produced, advanced to become the natural state of affairs of the economic social relations created by industrial capitalism (Engels, [1845]1987; Marx, [1867]1990; Thompson, 1993). As the UK's stratified system of social classes developed through the intrinsic exploitation of the labour of the lower classes by the middle and higher classes, specialised police forces became a Durkheimian *mechanical*, state-sponsored, bureaucratic response to the problems caused by this exploitation.

In short, the police became state organised and sponsored 'specialists in coercion' (Reiner, 2010:32). It has full recourse to use force or violence over its citizens, and it's this role that has created much debate about the political nature of policing (Waddington, 1999; Savage, 2007; Reiner, 2010). For this current text, I view how the development of the modern police force has professionally organised policing in ways that 'responds to behavior and people it regards as deviant, problematic, worrying, threatening, troublesome or undesirable' (Cohen, 1985:1).

It would be a mistake to view the birth of policing as solely the result of the formation of the Metropolitan Police in 1829, for policing itself has a much longer aetiology. The creation of the Metropolitan Police Act 1829, which formed the Metropolitan Police, was the 'first unified body of state employees concerned primarily with social control' (Hobbs, 1989:18). Until 1829, policing was under-taken by a variety of individuals, usually appointed in a haphazard way based on economic and political interests determined by localised power networks. Hobbs' (ibid.:17–45) natural history of the police noted that, from around AD 900, a *constable* who was usually taken from the Norman high military office undertook policing. Over the next hundred years the high status rank associated with the constable was slowly demoted: eventually becoming the lowest rank and undertaking the most basic of tasks. However, it wasn't until around the Middle Ages that the link between parish constable, the state and social control began to establish itself. The Crown sanctioned the constable's authority and his main role was to keep the King's peace. This development is often linked to the Statute of Winchester in 1285 (discussed below). However, another ordinance of 1181, implemented by King Henry II and called the assize *of arms*, was a *call to arms* for locals, whereby the King made it obligatory for certain classes to have arms and swear an allegiance to the King. Another ordinance of 1252 updated the 1181 assize by appointing constables to summon men to arms, suppress breaches of the peace and deliver offenders to the sheriff. Pollock and Maitland (2010:595) outline the key difference between these two important ordinances:

> The original assize of 1181 had not treated the *villata* as an organized entity; it had required that individuals should have the armour suitable to their station. The ordinance of 1252 decreed that in every township a constable or two constables should be appointed, and a chief constable in each hundred to convene the *iurati ad arma*.[3]

The 1285 Statute of Winchester consolidated these earlier ordinances by establishing three measures that would link the police and policing to the State and introduced, in primitive form, the idea of a group of individuals authorised by the State to catch and arrest criminals (Hobbs, 1989:17–18). First, the role of *town watchman* was created. This was a position that supplemented the work of the parish constable and consisted of a *watch* of men who would guard the walls and boundaries of urban towns and villages. The watchman's primary function was to 'patrol the streets and maintain order by, for instance, arresting drunks and prostitutes' (Rawlings, 2003:45). These individuals had 'powers of arrest during hours of darkness' and would deliver any arrests to the parish constable, whose command they were under (Hobbs, 1989:18). There is some evidence that not everyone was welcoming of the night watchmen. According to Critchley, they were often thought to be 'contemptible, dissolute and drunken buffoons who shuffled along the darkened streets' (1978:30, cited in Reiner, 2010: 41). Rosenheim (1991:59, cited in Rawlings, 2003:45) notes how some people even refused to serve, for example, when 'John Callin attacked William Child in 1665 when Child told him it was his turn to serve'. The second measure introduced by the 1285 Statute was the revival of the ancient Saxon practice of *hue and cry*. It was inevitable that some individuals who were dealt with by the town watchmen would resist arrest, and the hue and cry was the pursuit of the *fugitive* by the entire local population. The hue and cry actually predated the 1285 Statute for it was originally part of England's Anglo-Saxon codes of laws. According to Riggs (1963:46, cited in Rawlings, 2003:41) the laws of Athelstan 'directed that a thief who fled "shall be pursued to his death by all men who are willing to carry out the king's wishes"'. The third and final measure introduced by the Statute of Winchester built upon the 1181 and 1252 *assize of arms* ordinances where 'every male between the ages of 15 and 60 was required to keep a hauberk and helme of iron, a sword, a knife, and a horse, while the poor were to have available bows and arrows' (Critchley, 1978:6, cited in Hobbs, 1989:18). Analogous to the hue and cry and assize of arms is the local English folk custom called *rough music*. Defined as 'a rude cacophony, with or without more elaborate ritual, which usually directed mockery or hostility against individuals who offended against certain community norms' (Thompson, 1993:467), rough music is a ritualised expression of hostility, involving a loud noise and usually dealt with issues of minor criminality or transgressions against morality, such as female adultery. Interestingly, this eighteenth- and nineteenth-century practice has survived into the twentieth and twenty-first centuries. I have argued elsewhere that the working-class Paulsgrove demonstrations that took place in August 2000, against a local and active child sex offender, followed the tradition of the rough music (Williams, 2004; Williams and Thompson, 2004a, 2004b; Thompson and Williams, 2014), despite the police, politicians, media and academics attempting to define these events as nothing more than mob mentality involving a bunch of *fishwives* (for example, see Silverman and Wilson, 2002).

All three of these measures signify the embryonic roots of modern forms of organised *policing* and a *police force*. Importantly, the social, political and economic contexts in which these measures were introduced and undertaken were localised and lacked any clear central organisation from the State. Styles (1987:21, cited in Hobbs, 1989:18) claims that the localisation of social control remained the same for around 500 years, and to a certain extent this is indeed true. However, it is also true that from the fourteenth century onwards there was a gradual movement towards the centralisation of power in relation to the policing of citizens. One visible manifestation of the move towards centralised control was the recognition in 1361 of Justices of the Peace (JPs) who were Crown appointed, heads of the localised justice system, and usually appointed the parish constable. The local JP was supposed to be 'the physical embodiment of an abstract body of law intended to represent universal standards of conduct and general public interest' (Hobbs, 1989:19). However, the reality was far darker than this romantic vision, as JPs were usually the Lord of the Manor and controlled the parish constables and town watchmen and thus supported specific ruling economic and political class needs and interests. In this respect, punishments for transgressions against these interests were dealt with harshly and included floggings, trans-portations and the death sentence for often trivial punishments (Foucault, [1977]1991; Garland, 1991). As there was a power differentiation between those investigating and those being investigated, it is not surprising that the working classes often suffered the most from this system of *justice*. They were the ones that were most likely to be identified as dangerous criminals, often charged with going against the two dominant prevailing ethical systems of *patronage* and *commercialism*. As Hobbs eloquently argues, many historical analyses of the police often ignore the 'entrepreneurial activities of magistrates as by-products of British society's preoccupation with wealth and property' (1989:20). In essence, the power-infused capitalist interest that ran our early criminal justice practice enabled 'magistrates to '"trade in justice"' (Landau, 1984, cited in Hobbs, 1989:20), based on their own economic interests and the interests of the capitalist elite. One famous example that illustrates the corruptness of the trading justices was a letter, dated 3rd July 1793, sent by Hatton Garden Police clerk W. Uptoon to the Home Department stating that 'had a canine brought a shilling in his mouth with a label for specifying his complaint, a warrant was readily granted' (cited in Cox, 2010:27). To a certain extent the power differential still exists in today's UK criminal justice system, as well as many other systems across the globe. One only has to think about the UK response to the 2011 London riots in terms of media coverage, stereotyping and profiling of the *chav* offender (Jones, 2011) as well as the sentences handed out to know that these offenders receive much harsher punishment for stealing £500 flat-screen televisions than the comparatively small number of bankers that have received custodial sentences for *losing* billions of pounds, corrupt trade practices, and wrecking the economy, which undoubtedly has negatively affected people's lives (Morrell *et al.*, 2011; Ministry of Justice, 2012).

The policing format briefly described above stayed roughly the same for 500 years. Indeed, the development of industrial capitalism and urbanisation in the nineteenth century meant State-sponsored and -organised policing would become more important than ever. Sociologists and historians have for many years researched and examined the social, economic and political contexts of the nineteenth century, so readers are advised to go to the following works for more factually accurate and in-depth accounts of the social, political and economic contexts in which policing, the police and criminal investigations developed:

- Frederich Engels – *The Condition of the English Working Class*;
- Karl Marx and Frederich Engels – *The Communist Manifesto*;
- Karl Marx – *Das Capital, Vols I, II and III*;
- Emile Durkheim – *The Division of Labour Within Society*;
- Max Weber – *The Protestant Ethic and the Spirit of Capitalism*;
- Henry Mayhew – *The London Underworld*;
- Henry Mayhew – *London Labour and the London Poor*;
- E. P. Thompson – *The Making of the Working Class*;
- E. P. Thompson – *Customs in Common*; and
- Willem Bonger – *Criminality and Economic Conditions.*

These texts, and many more like them, tell the story of the substantial changes to the European economic, social and political systems from the eighteenth century onwards and how these changes shaped the very foundations of contemporary economic and social relations. For the UK, capitalism brought about massive increases in population, migration towards cities, and huge developments in manufacturing industries such as cotton, coal, wood, metals, clothing, furniture, printing and stationery (Engels, [1845]1987; Hobbs, 1989:20–21; Thompson, 1993). As Hobbs suggests, the dynamics of this burgeoning and new economic and social structure presented a number of issues for the capitalist elite and, yet again, fits into the wider Victorian social discourse on *dangerous offenders* as discussed in Chapters 3 and 4:

> Those who made up London's casual work-force had few occupational reins upon their life-styles and consequently their moral and sexual habits along with their drinking and gambling were allowed to continue unfettered by the dull grind of factory life. As a consequence London's vast army of casual and unemployed workers was regarded generally as a threat due to its often obstructive habits, disregard for property, and its frequent manifestation as 'the mob'.
>
> (Hobbs, 1989:21)

There appears to be little qualitative difference between the perceptions of the working classes outlined above with those that the *Daily Mail* and *Daily Express* demonstrate on a daily basis in the twenty-first century! In the eighteenth and nineteenth centuries, with the population explosions in most of the large cities up and down England, crime was also seen to increase in these metropolises. As Reiner notes, it was in 1810 that the government 'began publishing annual figures of indictable committals for trial in England and Wales, which showed an apparently inexorable increase' (Philips, 1980:180, cited in Reiner, 2010:41). As a result, the constable and his watchmen came under increasing pressure, especially as they had also acquired a number of additional duties including 'dealing with minor disorder, carrying out warrants, and many more duties under the Poor Law regarding vagrancy' (Hobbs, 1989:22). As the role of constable and town watchman was part-time, the efficiency of the watch system obviously deteriorated as the pressures of responsibility and the number of cases increased. All of the issues pertaining to the development of capitalism and the resultant social inequalities, the increase in personal wealth and private property and the need to control an efficient workforce because of the subsequent social dislocation, demoralisation, crime and social conflict (Reiner, 2010:41) that capitalism created were the core drivers for the creation of the police and criminal investigations.

Early forms of investigation

The brief historical overview presented above does tend to suggest that policing and criminal investigations prior to the late nineteenth century lacked a proper structure and professional approach. Whilst this is certainly true with regard to a professionalised, centralised structure, it is certainly not the case that crimes were not investigated. Indeed, some of the more robust evidence points to the opposite. England's (1985) historical study, for instance, notes that regardless of whether the police existed or not, 'criminal investigation in some form was needed for the initial determination of facts about particular crimes before any further processes of criminal justice could be carried out' (105). Prior to the formation of the police, investigations were the 'direct responsibility of designated gentry officials, with assistance from constables responsible to them' (ibid.:105). Unfortunately, historical records are sparse, especially those kept by the assize courts, with the usual problems that beset written documents; as well as the fact that the Public Records Acts of 1877 and 1941 legislated for the destruction of records such as 'circuits of indictments, depositions, warrants, minute books, examinations, inquests and calendars' (ibid.:106). What we do know is that some records pertaining to serious crime, as recorded by magistrates' and coroners' investigations, have survived the march of time. England was able to access a number of records from the old Northern Circuit (comprising the counties of Cumberland, Yorkshire, Westmoreland and Northumberland), as well as some records from Oxford. Concentrating on the three types of criminal homicide that English law recognised at the time,[4] England reviewed 257 cases between 1800 and 1824. Within these cases, three discernible types of investigations, what England refers to as *modes of inquiry*, were identified, and these were the basis of an early form of investigative framework (see Figure 5.1).

Overseeing homicide investigations in pre-police times were the local *parish magistrates* and *county coroners*. However, magistrates were not *required* to investigate crimes, and tended only to do so if persuaded by individuals who initiated a private prosecution. For the most part, it was coroners who formally undertook investigations, and this was because coroners 'were required by law to

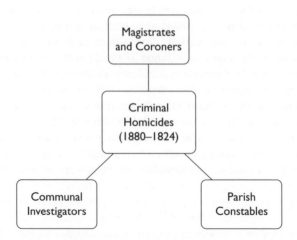

Figure 5.1 Pre-police modes of investigation

hold inquests on all suspicious or unusual deaths' (ibid.:113). The local magistrate would get word to his local county coroner, who would make the journey to the parish and undertake preliminary enquiries to assess whether an inquest was needed. England lists some of the elements that made up a typical murder inquest (ibid.:113):

- ordering an autopsy;
- organising the corpse for viewing;
- summoning witnesses and 23 jurors (taken from three or more parishes);
- arranging an assembly place; and
- alerting clerks and other attendants.

All this was organised without the availability of telephones or the Internet, which makes the speed at which coroners organised inquests very impressive. England (ibid.:113–114) calculates that, in around 78 per cent of homicide inquests, the time that elapsed between an officially known death and the inquest was two days. Most inquest reports began with a 'stately one-sentence preamble that served as a case fact-sheet' (ibid.:113), followed by three or more pages of sworn testimony. He also provides some evidence to counter the standard leftist and historical viewpoint that localised criminal justice practice was run by 'propertied men' in order to 'maintain their power and privileges' and use 'discriminatory law enforcement to keep the lower classes in line' (ibid.:114). Whilst there is no doubt that power differentials were at play within the criminal justice system and that this differential was based upon economic, political and cultural capital, England found that in over 350 provincial examinations and inquests he examined, except for a few cases, 'officials worked conscientiously to get at the truth through patient and thorough questioning' (ibid.:114). Officials running inquests would also occasionally adjourn the proceedings so constables could go off and 'seek independent verification of crucial testimony' and there was 'no general tendency to manipulate the collection of evidence' (ibid.:114).

The second *mode of inquiry* identified by England, was the use of *parish constables as investigators*. We have already seen how orthodox histories of the police and policing viewed the town watchmen and parish constables as bumbling, incompetent and drunken (Hobbs, 1989; Morris, 2007; Cox, 2010; Reiner, 2010). This romantic, idealised vision of localised investigative policing prior to the creation of the Metropolitan Police in 1829 has yet to be properly challenged. There is growing evidence to suggest that the constable was not always terrible at investigating crime, nor was it necessarily the case that crimes investigated were solely determined by the elite power base. The inclusion of constable testimony was common across many homicide inquests and consisted mainly of descriptions and details of the crime scene and statements 'made to the officers by witnesses and suspects' (England, 1985:115). In one case involving the cutting of the throat of 77-year-old Jane Milburn:

> The officer reported that he observed 'spats' of blood on the subject, whose arms appeared to have been recently washed. Searching the room, the constable found a clasp knife and a shoemaker's knife, and a bloody shirt that had been hidden in the folding bed.
>
> (Ibid.:115)

England (ibid.:105–124) also found that a number of these cases involved proper investigative methods; some of which involved the use of quite sophisticated methods of forensic crime scene analysis for the time:

> Two of the three cases in which constables' investigations are reported seem remarkable for the sophistication of their techniques. A pub ruckus near Bristol had culminated in an ambuscade stabbing of Isaac Gordon, a laborer. Seven men were implicated. At the roadside murder site three constables found shoe prints matching those of the suspect; they scooped up with a shovel and preserved another print which they placed for safekeeping with the governor of a local house of correction; nail patterns were matched to a second suspect; and even trouser marks made by sitting ambushers were studied.
>
> (Ibid.:116)

In another case, a Reading Catholic priest had been robbed and murdered. The constable and some local helpers, 'searching an adjacent field where three men had been seen lurking earlier, measured footprints and stride lengths and closely examined heel marks for distinctive nail patterns' (ibid.:117). Whilst the evidence provided by England is not conclusive, or even comprehensive proof, it does enough to suggest that not only was there a clear 'system' for investigations, 'the usefulness of constables in criminal cases might have been greater than the traditional evaluations of these functionaries would lead us to believe' (ibid.:116).

The final pre-police mode of inquiry incorporates a *communal* aspect to criminal investigators. When it comes to murder, twentieth and twenty-first centuries' fascination with the topic does not hold the patent. Many suspicious deaths in the seventeenth, eighteenth and nineteenth centuries often caused sensation amongst the local community. England (ibid.:117) notes how there 'certainly was occasional "public participation" in investigations by persons'. 'Public participation' included moving the corpse around the scene, handling physical evidence, speaking to suspects and undertaking searches. It was not uncommon for these individuals to testify 'about their observations' (ibid.:117). England's important historical research demonstrates the need for further research into pre-police forms of investigations. What England's important historical analysis demonstrates is that, prior to the introduction of the police in the UK in 1829, there was a clear structure to how investigations into homicides were conducted. However, as capitalist societies became increasingly modernised, criminal investigations also began to be modernised; and in order to do this a structured, professional system of individuals was needed to undertake investigations. This system became known as the police.

The pre-police

Perhaps the most significant step towards developing the first investigative police *force* came with appointment in 1729 of Thomas De Veil as Justice for Middlesex and Westminster. De Veil lived at No. 4 Bow Street, Covent Garden, which would eventually become the operational base for the Bow Street Runners. He soon established himself as an effective dispenser of criminal justice and acquired the 'reputation as the principal scourge of the criminal class' (Ascoli, 1979:33, cited in Hobbs, 1989:22). His work soon won him the coveted position of Court Justice, and over 17 years he was responsible for the execution or transportation of over 1900 of some of England's most dangerous criminals (Hobbs, 1989:22). Despite De Veil's successes, it was Henry Fielding (1707–1754) who put *policing as a trade* firmly on the political agenda. Fielding, the famous author, lawyer and Middlesex Judge succeeded De Veil in 1748, and he cemented the Court of Justice position as 'central to the apprehension and trial of London's criminals' (ibid.:23). Operating from the same house in Bow Street, Fielding, with his younger blind brother John, he brought together six ex-constables of Westminster to create a group of *thief takers* with the remit to 'act as a professional detective body, investigating crimes in and around the capital' (Cox, 2010:28). After some early successes with his *force*, Fielding petitioned the Duke of Newcastle, First Lord of the Treasury, for money to enable its continuation. In 1753 he was provided with £600 of government funding to further develop this system of policing and it was here that the Bow Street Runners were put on an official footing. The Fieldings received money from a number of 'clandestine government and administrative sources' which enabled them to 'administer justice to the poor', which sometimes included waiving of their fee (Emsley, 2010:20). The runners were sworn constables of Westminster, and by 1831 their number had risen to 11. The runners were also known as *thief takers* and much of the academic research on Fielding's group notes how there were numerous opportunities for runners to also 'trade in justice' through collecting fees for arrests (Hobbs, 1989:22). The more orthodox histories of policing (e.g. Reith, 1938, 1943, Ascoli, 1979 and Critchley, 1978, cited in Hobbs, 1989) tend to suggest that some of the runners died with rather large fortunes, as the fees and expenses for specific offences could be quite lucrative.[5] Such practices have been deemed to be corrupt,; however, Hobbs (1989:24) rightly points out the futility of those who attempt to apply a twentieth-century moral ideology to practices of the eighteenth and nineteenth centuries. Cox (2010) notes that what has been written on the Bow Street Runners is usually regurgitated from secondary sources 'with little or no investigation of the primary sources' which has resulted in 'a great deal of contradictory and often ill-informed opinion' (ibid.:2). For example, some have argued that the runners were taken from 'shadowy figures' with criminal backgrounds, whilst others have stated that they were 'men of unblemished character, proven fidelity and consummate bravery' (ibid.:2–3). Cox also highlights how the senior Bow Street personnel 'never referred to themselves as "runners," considering the term to be derogatory and demeaning' (ibid.:2). Furthermore, there is strong evidence to suggest that there were numerous attempts to ensure that runners were clearly differentiated from thief takers and other ranks of officers. For example, runners were actually called *Principal Officers of Bow Street* (hereafter POs), not Bow Street Runners (Emsley, 2010:21), and both Henry Fielding and his immediate successor, his brother John, 'viewed the Bow Street men as having a much wider remit than the infamous "professional" thief-takers such as Jonathan Wild or Stephen McDaniel' (Cox, 2010:29).

The POs were 'invited to investigate offences and detect offenders' and they were known to have in-depth knowledge of crime hotspots for 'offences such as pick-pocketing' (Emsley, 2010:21). They often ran down offenders, with some incidents ending in violence and injury to the PO, and also undertook an early form of 'stop and search' by keeping an 'eye out for people carrying suspicious packages, for known offenders and receivers' (ibid.:21). However, the work of the PO was not simply confined to London, as they also made themselves available to rural and urban provinces and in some cases were called upon to travel abroad to assist investigations. Fielding's brother, John, on taking over as Chief Magistrate in 1754, made a concerted effort to 'improve the methods of criminal investigation and detection outside London' (Cox, 2010:17). Thus, whilst still in their infancy, many POs did attempt to undertake investigations in a rational systematic way. As Emsley (2010:21–22) points out, this included asking questions, interviewing people and, in some cases, going undercover: for example, to catch a gang of poachers. On a few occasions they also used 'simple but effective forensic techniques'; for example, when one PO, 'Harry Adkins, tracked down the man who robbed and murdered a Staffordshire farmer in 1812' by matching 'a mark on the bullet taken from the victim with a bullet mould used by the killer' (ibid.:22).

Cox examined primary source information detailing 601 provincial cases involving the Bow Street officers and found that they were involved in a wide variety of criminal investigations including: arson/damage to property/threatening behaviour (93 cases or 15.47 per cent); murder/attempted murder (16.47 per cent); larceny (14.31 per cent); burglary (10.98 per cent); and robbery (10.15 per cent) (2010:105). He explains some of the reasons why local authorities turned to Bow Street for help in dealing with local crime:

> There may have been a localised epidemic of a particular type of crime, such as arson, and the parish constabulary were not experienced or capable of dealing with such matters over what could be a relatively large area. Similarly, crimes such as the murder of gamekeepers often occurred on large private estates and the landowner wanted to investigate the matter with the help of an outside agency which would not be intimidated by the local feelings of sympathy for the perpetrator.
>
> (Ibid.:143)

This evidence points to an interesting socio-economic influence in that POs were often *employed* by the wealthy or well connected to investigate crimes because the parish constable system was often deemed to be largely inadequate (ibid.:138–167). Plain-clothed Bow Street POs were therefore often called in by local elites to investigate a broad array of crimes to recover losses. Many orthodox versions of policing history discuss the runners as one of many factors driving police reform in the eighteenth and early nineteenth centuries (Reiner, 2010). The demise of the Bow Street Runners has been attributed to the loss of their investigative capacity in London (Morris, 2007:17), especially with the advent of Peel's *Bobbies*. Whilst there is some debate as to whether a *police force* existed prior to 1829, the historical evidence presented above strongly suggests that, whilst a fully formed, state sponsored, and organised professional police force was yet to develop, its embryonic form had slowly been taking shape over a number of centuries. This slow progress can be contrasted with the rapid social and economic changes and developments that took place in the nineteenth century; changes that would ultimately shape the context of modern policing and modern forensic criminal investigations. Before discussing the development of modern criminal investigations, and as an interesting aside to the history of criminal investigations, it is useful to take a look at the situation in early nineteenth-century France and the infamous Eugène-François Vidocq.

The case of Vidocq, born in Arras in 1775, and his links to France's Brigade de Sûreté are well documented but often ignored or barely mentioned in UK criminological texts on criminal investigations. This is strange given Vidocq's colourful history as a poacher, thief, convict and murderer; all of which eventually led him to become the head of the Paris Sûreté! Vidocq holds a special place in the history of criminal/forensic investigations, for he was a major influence in developing the detective department – he introduced what today would be the equivalent of the plain-clothed detective; he used police spies (the *mouchard*) to aid his detection rate; and he was one of the first individuals to use what John and Maguire (2007:200) call a 'sophisticated intelligence system of surveillance, using an innovative card index system of intelligence files on hundreds of people'. However, before he was made head of the Sûreté, Vidocq was a thief, joined the circus and then the army, before deserting and joining in the various criminal, adulterous and nefarious escapades associated with soldiers of fortune. He went to prison on numerous occasions but also escaped a number of times. He is also accredited with helping to con a rich Baroness out of her fortune, and he was wanted on suspicion of several murders. Sometime around 1809 Vidocq went to prison again, and it was here that he faced a difficult choice. His criminal past was about to catch up with him, and in order to survive the possible sentences for his crimes – death, transportation or a long prison sentence – Vidocq decided to become the equivalent of what today would be called a *supergrass*. The then head of the detective department of the Sûreté, Jean Henry, realising Vidocq's precarious position, called upon him to provide the 'names of escapees who were in custody under false names' (Morton, 2005:119). For 21 months Vidocq operated a double life: friend and star to inmates, impressed with his infamous ability to escape prison; and an informant to the police. Indeed, this pretence was gratefully facilitated by Henry who, in 1811, had *allowed* Vidocq to escape back to his wife, much to the applause and celebration of the convicts at *La Force*, thus cementing his reputation as an *insider* to the French criminal classes. Louis Canler, a police officer, sums up Vidocq's transition from criminal to police officer:

> M. Henry at length resolved to set him at liberty, on condition that he should act as denouncer, and each month supply the Préfecture with a settled minimum of criminals, under penalty of being sent back to Brest himself; he had a fixed salary of four pounds and a premium for each arrest.
>
> (Cited in Morton, 2005:126)

Foucault saw Vidocq's appointment to the police in negative terms. He saw it as the moment when 'the direct, institutional coupling of the police and delinquency took place: the disturbing moment when criminality became one of the mechanisms of power' (Foucault, [1977]1991:283). As with his poorly constructed *repression hypothesis* (Foucault, 1978, 1985) Foucault's historical analysis leaves a lot to be desired for it largely ignores people's experiential reality and the micro-contexts in which structures like the police operated, including the grass-roots needs of the local population. This can be summed up in the words of lawyer Antoine-Gérard Claveau, a critic of the repressive police force, who posed the following question:

> How do we discover the criminals if you do not employ scoundrels? It is a singular method. I'd rather call an arsonist to put out a fire or ask a known debaucher to guard the honour of my wife and daughter.
>
> (Cited in Morton, 2005:134)

One of the first post-prison supergrass roles undertaken by Vidocq was that of the spy and agent provocateur. Morton calls Vidocq a 'one-man forerunner of the post-Second World War English Ghost Squad' who were a 'squad of detectives allowed to mix freely, and often in disguise, with criminals to thwart their plans' (Morton, 2005:135); and Vidocq revelled in the role that was first outlined by Deseassart in his *Dictionnaire universel de police*. Acting as agent provocateur, Vidocq began to infiltrate the brothels and taverns in disguise; to use informers (usually other criminals); and to effectively engage in proactive intelligence gathering. Quite surprisingly, Vidocq also anticipated the findings of Lombroso some 40 years before the Italian doctor put forward his ideas on criminological positivism. He *profiled* physical characteristics of offenders, stating that there were *types* of offenders; for example, in describing Boudin, who was planning the murder of two elderly men, Vidocq notes that he was bow-legged, which was 'a deformity I have observed among several systematic assassins, as well as among many other individuals distinguished by their crimes' (cited in Morton, 2005:137).

Most orthodox histories of the English police rightly state that in England there was concern to not go down the route of the *Europeans*, the police in France being viewed as a military force like the Gendarmerie. Added to this was knowledge of Vidocq who, by and large, epitomised the international perceptions of the detective police in France as being predicated on the activities of a rogue and murderer. As the UK has always had a fractious relationship with France, the creation of the modern police was an attempt to move away from these contentious militaristic and criminal images of the Sûreté. Unfortunately, the Popay and Calthorpe Street affairs and the inquest into the beating to death of John Peacock Wood exposed the Metropolitan police as acting in precisely that fashion (Emsley, 2010:56–64).

The development of the modern police and criminal investigations

As the previous section demonstrated, the roots of policing and criminal investigations run long and deep. It is 1829, however, that is seen by many as pivotal in the development of the modern police and criminal investigations (see Emsley, 2003; Matassa and Newburn, 2007; Reiner, 2010). This was the start of what Morris identifies as being the *heroic period* (1829–1878) which, he argues, was the first major phase in the development of the modern police (2007:16–22); and it was the year when Robert Peel, then Home Secretary, decided that police personnel such as the Bow Street POs should be more organised. His vision was of a police force that comprised 'centrally controlled, uniformed watchmen with a rigid work discipline geared for supervising the streets and, in theory, for preventing rather than detecting crime' (Emsley, 2003:67). It is clear from this conceptualisation of the police that the investigative function was to play only a minor role, with *crime prevention* becoming the principal task. The clearest manifestation of this ideal was epitomised in the famous English *Bobby* patrolling his beat: with 'the careful checking of doors and windows, especially at night, the patrolling police constable would deter thieves' (ibid.:68). After fighting off some opposition from several directions, Peel successfully steered his Metropolitan Police Bill, introduced in April 1829; and in June the Bill was passed, creating the Metropolitan Police Act 1829. The first Metropolitan Police constables (PCs) 'took to the London streets in September' (ibid.:68). In the first ten years, these officers worked alongside the parish constables and Bow Street officers, and there is some evidence to suggest they 'conducted investigations' and 'detected offenders' (ibid.:69). However, much of their early work revolved around crime prevention, dealing with public disorder, which often meant controlling protests, drunkards, prostitutes and vagrants. Whilst this had very little to do with criminal investigations and even less to do with scientific criminology and forensic science, what I have discussed above does show that pre-1829 policing did include serious attempts to investigate many serious crimes. Morris argues that the *heroic period* was a distinct break from previous policing arrangements and is the beginning of the process of professionalisation of policing (and to some extent the centralisation of police powers).

Building upon previous legislation and social policy such as the Middlesex and Surrey Justices Act 1792 (Morris, 2007:16), outside of London, new forces were also established under the Municipal Corporations Act 1835 and the County Police Act 1839. In relation to 1829 though, the first recruits, numbering around 1,000, took to the streets of London on 29th September 1829. Over the following months 'many of these first recruits turned their back on the job and many more were dismissed' (Emsley, 2010:39). By May 1830, Peel's Bobbies had reached 3,000 in number, and were a uniformed body of men who patrolled the streets and were controlled from central government. The investigative nature of the Bobby was not as clear cut as it is today; with both reactive and proactive elements of criminal investigations meshed into the very function of patrolling. Instead, the main functions of the police in these early stages were maintaining public order, and policing crowds, demonstrations and riots; especially as the Chartist demonstrations from 1839 onwards led to the perception that the Metropolitan police was a 'national riot squad' (ibid.:52). In the first ten years since coming into existence, the Metropolitan police were a 'force for preventing crime by watching; the detection of crime was considered as secondary' (ibid.:63). However, this is not to say that some PCs did not engage in *forensic-like* investigations. For instance, in April 1850, PC Jesse Jeapes stopped and searched 21-year-old John Dismond. He found a number of items 'under Dismond's hat and in his clothing', including a screwdriver, which he 'was able to match to marks on a door that had been forced' (ibid.:59). Dismond was successfully prosecuted for burglary on the basis of the stop-and-search and forensic evidence. This case highlights that, whilst the macro-histories – such as the one presented by Morris (2007:15–40) – represent an important contribution to the history of criminal and forensic investigations, they sadly lack the micro-contextual analysis of the everyday experiential reality of criminal investigations, *in situ*, in the eighteenth and nineteenth centuries. It is clear that there were small pockets of officers engaged in simplistic forms of forensic investigation which, as we saw from examples such as the *Hsi Yuan Chi Lu* (Chapter 4), has a longer history than one might think. However, most of the examples listed in this and the previous chapters were of a rather *ad hoc* nature. It wasn't until the beginning of the 1840s that things began to change with the creation of specialised detective departments.

The invention of the detective

Despite these major developments, it wasn't until 1842 that detective departments were created. The Home Secretary sanctioned the Metropolitan Detective Department, and this was the first of its kind in the UK. The creation of the detective departments should not imply the invention of investigations; they merely represent the 'bureaucratisation and professionalisation' of the investigative function of the police (ibid.:17). As with most developments that take place within the police (see Chapter 6 for an expansion on this issue), the key driver for change was what Morris calls '*event-precipitated*' (ibid.:17); meaning that heightened visibility and reporting of a serious crime creates enough concern that changes to the structural arrangements of the criminal justice system soon follow. Morris argues that the Russell and Good murders of 1840 and 1842 were the precipitating events (Smelser, 1962) that led to the creation of the detective branch of the Metropolitan Police. In 1840, Lord William Russell was 'murdered by his valet, Courvoisier', and the subsequent investigation left 'much to be desired' (ibid.:17). The absence of an immediate arrest, as well as the fact that the victim was also the uncle of a recent Home Secretary, tipped the scales in favour of creating a group of specialist detectives. In the second case, on 3rd April 1842, Daniel Good committed a murder in Putney Park. He managed to escape from a police officer, went on the run and evaded arrest for an entire month, moving between different districts in London and Kent. The Good case showed up the faults of the communication systems within the police and the problems with offenders moving across different police jurisdictions: problems that were well known in other countries such as France, which 'forbade gendarmes to pursue criminals across district borders without express permission' (Morton, 2005:131). As a result, the detective branch was set up in August 1842. Frederick Wensley's autobiography as a detective in the Metropolitan Police shows the problems faced by Vidocq and the Paris Sûreté occurring some 70 years later in England:

> When I joined, an officer, except by definite instructions, was scarcely ever permitted to go outside his own division. The result was that criminals living in one district could, almost with impunity, commit crimes in others. A divisional superintendent did not like officers leaving his district to operate in another; and a local detective-inspector resented detectives from other districts 'poaching' on his division.
>
> (Wensley, 1931:39, cited in Morton, 2005:131)

What is somewhat alarming is that the trend in jurisdictional boundary ownership and maintenance has continued as a barrier to effective investigation into the twenty-first century, especially in the UK and the US; and this creates a whole range of problems for forensic investigations. The most obvious example to illustrate this is the problem of *linkage blindness* in cases of serial killing in the US, where cases committed by the same offender are not linked because they have crossed police districts and important physical evidence is not shared or communicated between two or more police forces (Keppel and Birnes, 2003). The UK has seen its fair share of problems with cross-force offenders such as the Yorkshire Ripper (Bilton, 2006) and the Soham murderer Ian Huntley (Bichard, 2004). From a forensic criminology perspective, such issues make the developments in offender profiling, crime analysis and geographical information systems even more important (see Chapter 8).

Returning to the nineteenth century, whatever importance Morris places on the Russell and Good cases, they were only two of many precipitating criminal events that caused concern amongst the general public, media, and politicians over the investigative function of the police. There were at least seven high-profile investigations that took place between 1831 and 1840 which raised concern over the ability of Peel's newly formed police force to adequately investigate crime. Cases such as the 1837 murders of Eliza Davis and Eliza Grimwood (separate crime events), the 1839 murder of watchmaker Robert Westwood (which included the theft of 80 watches and a fire, possibly to conceal both the murder and theft) and the 1840 murder of John Templeman all highlighted problems in the police investigations. Once the Russell murder had occurred, the media and public were *primed* for many years to the notion that the police would fail to apprehend the offender. This provided the necessary impetus for the creation of the detective branch, which gave recognition to this function as a crucial element in a core aspect of policing – the developing notion of crime control through the detection and prosecution of offenders – with the detective branch soon establishing ownership over this domain (Morris, 2007:16–20). Police commissioners were called in to advise the Home Secretary with respect to establishing a separate detective division. Perhaps the most influential commissioner was Richard Mayne (1797–1868) who, despite recognising the potential problems regarding supervision and control of a separate policing entity, made recommendations to the Home Secretary that a detective division should be created. Interestingly, Morris highlights that there 'seems to have been no substantive discussion in the Home Office, which approved the proposals within a week' (ibid.:18). The new detectives were taken from the ranks of the police (two inspectors and six sergeants) who had, for many years, already 'acted in a detective capacity' (ibid.:18). After the Fenian Clerkenwell explosion,[6] an 1868 Departmental Committee recommended the extension of the detective branch to every Metropolitan Police branch. These developments are important; however, it should be noted that the creation of the detective branch was only a simple political endorsement of pre-existing policing activities. Indeed, Morris (ibid.: 18–19) points to a rather lethargic take up of detective departments up and down the country.

In relation to the investigative methods and techniques used by detectives, these were rather *ad hoc* and pragmatic. There was no formal training, but, instead, informal apprenticeship was the norm. Mayne had pointed out in 1842 that 'the nature of crime in London at the time did not justify any complicated architecture for the response' (ibid.:18); and, in the year following the infamous 1877 Turf Fraud trials, where a number of senior and experienced detectives had been convicted of corruption, the 1878 Detective Departmental Committee heard evidence from the Metropolitan commissioner Edmund Henderson (1821–1896) who stated there was no need for specialist training: 'the real practical fact is that in 99 cases out of 100 cases of crime, the detection is most humdrum work, and it only requires just ordinary care and intelligence. You do not want a high-class mind to do it at all' (ibid.:20). Even more damning was the evidence of the Head Constable of Leeds, William Henderson, who stated that 'nineteen out of twenty of the detectives throughout the kingdom are very illiterate men' (Metropolitan Police, 1878: Q 3806, cited in Morris, 2007:20). Other commentators have noticed that, in the latter part of the nineteenth century, higher ranks of the police consisted of individuals who were 'unable to write, much less spell, a short report so as to be reasonably intelligible' (Jones, 1910:39, cited in Morris, 2007:20).

The 1868 committee brought in some new personnel with fresh ideas regarding criminal investigative practice. For instance, ex-Indian police officer, A. C. Howard was an enthusiastic advocate of the use of police diaries as both a method of control and supervision of detectives as well as directing detectives' work. The number of specialised detective departments steadily grew over the following years, and they were largely seen as an 'independent, self-referential satrapy within forces, the "firm within the firm"' (Morris, 2007:21). The notion of *difference* is important here; where the Sûreté wanted to create an entirely separate organisation of specialised detectives, it would take a further ten years and the Turf Fraud affair before anything resembling this would appear in England. Indeed, because of the independence exhibited by the early detectives, it wasn't long before it was found that effective supervision was not possible. The problem of institutional control over investigators was a major concern due to the long history of corruption linked to those who exercised state power. It was difficult to maintain control and supervise detectives, thus leading to both corrupt practices as well as allegations of corrupt practices. This is one of the reasons A. C. Dixon was brought in and advocated the use of diaries.

Morris (ibid.:21), perhaps a little harshly, argues that during the heroic period 'there was little evidence of scientific sophistication'; yet the few cases presented above and in the preceding chapters offer evidence to counter this claim. Furthermore, Morris' claims are only correct if he is comparing the techniques of the nineteenth century with contemporary techniques of forensic detection and investigation, and therein lies the problem: for, just as Hobbs (1989:24) criticised Reith for applying 'twentieth-century morality to an eighteenth-century scenario', the same can be said for Morris. Whilst *science* during the heroic period was still in its infancy, and scientific techniques and theories were still being developed, tested and falsified, these unsophisticated methods by twentieth-century standards were still sophisticated in terms of their historical, technological and cultural specificity. As mentioned in Chapter 2, if the sixteenth, seventeenth and eighteenth centuries could be regarded as the building of the scientific quest for knowledge through the Renaissance and Enlightenment projects, the nineteenth century was certainly the period where the ideas of Kepler, Galileo, Descartes, Kant, Leibniz and Newton (Reill, 2003; Gaukroger, 2009) continued to be developed. It would be better, therefore, to consider the heroic period (1829–1878) as the period where scientists pushed forward the science agenda through research testing of scientific ideas; where new ideas about nature and the order of things were thought up and tested; where the development of scientific societies and university science departments took place; and where the proliferation of both government and philanthropic funding of scientific research came about (Burke, 2008). Morris is right when he suggests that most scientific ideas were in their exploratory stage; and many people were suspicious of these ideas, not least because they appeared to be in direct contradistinction with religion. *Forensic* applications of science were linked to the natural or physical sciences, which usually meant a dead body and the deployment of a medical professional (Morris, 2007:21); and we can see this throughout history, which is littered with examples where a suspicious death has resulted in a *forensic-like* examination of the body and the crime scene. As most murders were committed using poison, knives and guns during this period, the toxicologist and chemist became quite useful to the police. The perceived utility of both forensic techniques and the experts that used them are important factors that still influence the application of forensics within the criminal justice system today. In particular, cases of poison raised many concerns regarding contamination issues, especially when the noted toxicologist Alfred Swaine Taylor, in testifying at the 1859 Smethurst case,[7] admitted that 'he found the presence of arsenic but only because of contamination from his own testing apparatus' (ibid.:21). The Home Secretary had no option but to grant a pardon to Smethurst because of the 'imperfection of medical science' (Parry, 1931:21–22, cited in Morris, 2007:21). The implication was obvious: if science was imperfect, it was open to manipulation and possible corruption, thus leading to miscarriages of justice. This perception was not helped by cases such as the Warwick poisoning trial, where 'expected standards of scientific proof could change over time' (Morris, 2007:21). Also of importance, linking this historical overview to present practice, was that even though scientific standards of proof varied quite dramatically during this period, it was the *way* it was presented in court rather than the actual validity of the *scientific technique or theory* that made people believe in it.

Regardless of the concerns over the abilities of science, the detective force were a group of tenacious individuals who did develop effective investigative practice; for example, some investigators included quite advanced 'intelligence assessments of motive and means' (ibid.:22). The continuing problem was still the fact that detectives were largely uneducated and there was no such thing as a training programme.

We don't need no education!

This situation changed dramatically in the last quarter of the nineteenth century, in what Morris (ibid.) calls the *organisational specialisation* period (1878–1932). The status of the investigative function of the Criminal Investigation Department (CID) was slow to gain acceptance, which also affected perceptions for the need for specialised training. Today, police training is extensive even for the lowest rank of police constable. For detectives, there is a myriad of specialised training available to the enthusiastic detective who wants to progress in the ranks, although some of this training is compulsory (see Chapter 6). The position in nineteenth-century England was completely different. As we saw earlier, Henderson gave evidence to the 1878 commission stating there was no need to have an educated and highly trained detective. Despite Henderson's obvious lack of vision, there were a number of key drivers for change that brought about significant developments within both criminal investigations and detective training.

Utilising Becker's concept of the *moral entrepreneur*, Howard Vincent was perhaps one of the most influential *rule enforcers* in creating a specialised force to conduct criminal investigations. In 1878 the creation of the first CID 'unified the divisional and central detective forces' (ibid.:21). On 8th April 1878, Charles Howard Vincent was appointed the first head of CID and, in order to distance himself from the term detective which had been discredited during the Turf Fraud trial that had so visibly highlighted detective culture as corrupt, Vincent was given the title *Director* (Jeyes, 1912:60, cited in James, 2011:82). According to Jeyes (1912:57, cited in James, 2011:82), Vincent was a vivacious individual who was determined to get the newly created position of Director. He brought 'new energy and more system to the investigative function' (Morris, 2007:22); perhaps the most innovative, long-standing and influential aspect was the introduction of what is now called the *proactive approach* (see Chapter 6). Vincent didn't wait for a complaint before starting an investigation (i.e. reactive policing); instead, he actively went searching for 'swindlers and thieves'. Another innovation of Vincent's was that he took over control of the *Police Gazette*, which had, up until then, been under the control of the POs at Bow Street. Vincent changed things around and used the magazine to increase the circulation of police criminal intelligence (ibid.:22). The *Police Gazette* was the first intelligence circular that included descriptions of wanted individuals; information or 'MO profiles' of specific offences (i.e. burglary); details of stolen property; as well as reviews of interesting and important cases. By increasing the intelligence knowledge and strength of the detective department, Vincent's detectives also vastly improved their criminal records filing system in line with the Bertillon developments discussed in Chapter 4. The subtitle of the *Police Gazette* harked back to the earlier forms of pre-policing, as shown in Figure 5.2.

Vincent was also one of the main rule creators behind the movement towards CID officers being drawn from the higher classes and elite. Up until Vincent's appointment, police recruits were largely taken from the working-class communities in which they served; and, though many came from the armed forces, few were *officers* (Hobbs, 1989; Wall, 1998; Emsley, 2003, 2010; Reiner, 2010). With the development of police forces up and down the country, 'it was clear to both the elite and the Home Office that better-educated recruits were needed' (James, 2011:82). Vincent was one of the first to benefit from the opening up of police recruitment to *commissioned officers*; however, the power was still with the politicians and stayed that way until 1884. Other innovations identified by James (ibid.:84) include:

- the introduction of a shift system of working;
- the supervision of officers through the ranks;

Figure 5.2 The Hue and Cry[8]

- appointing of 60 divisional detectives and 20 special patrols (for instance Special Branch emerged between 1881–1883 – also see Morris, 2007:23);
- creation of the rule whereby CID officers had to remain in the department throughout their careers; and
- maintaining of links with the Parisian Prefecture of Police.

Culturally, the detective was often met with derisory scorn, as James found in his background research into police intelligence:

> Mr. Bridge, the Hammersmith Police Magistrate 'chafed unmercifully' at a detective who appeared before him as a 'crime investigator' rather than as a detective (*The Era*, 1878, April 14th). Another, who styled himself as a 'criminal investigator' was told by a second Magistrate to 'Call yourself a constable, I suppose you are one' (*The Graphic*, 1880, September 4th).
>
> (Cited in James, 2011:83)

Another string to Vincent's bow was that he also 'published widely on legal and police matters' (James, 2011:84). In 1882 he published one of the first textbooks for the police entitled *A Police Code and Manual of Criminal Law*. James argues that Vincent's *Code* was the nineteenth-century equivalent of *doctrine* which, as we shall see in Chapter 6, has come to dominate the investigative environment in the twenty-first century (ibid.:84). He was also keen to break down barriers between uniformed officers and CID, especially when it came to taking cases away from uniformed police, stating to detectives that 'if they have any information which may secure the arrest of a criminal, they should communicate it to the officer who is placed in a position to work it out, instead of reserving it for themselves' (Vincent, 1886, cited in (James, 2011:88–89).

Given Vincent's significant influence on the development of investigative practice, it is perhaps surprising that more historical work has not been undertaken on his life and career; especially as he effectively kick-started the modernisation of criminal investigations by developing the organisational specialisation of the investigative function within the detective departments. Unfortunately, cases such as Jack the Ripper in 1888 did little to aid the reputation of the detective; the police force in general came across as particularly inefficient, and the Ripper avoided capture. What is also very surprising is that, despite his *Police Code* being used in Britain and throughout the British Empire for many years after his death in 1908, the British government still resisted the enhancement of Vincent's police training and development ethos. This can certainly be seen in the 1919 Desborough Committee, which recommended *against* specialist training for detectives. It was the opinion of the committee that detectives received enough training by way of 'experience and practical work' (Desborough, 1919: Part II, para. 115, cited in Morris, 2007:24). Such attitudes can also be linked to the insularity that many detectives felt because of the structural fact that the detectives' CID role was closed, they determined their own work standards, and their pay and pension were far superior to other uniformed police officers'. The attitude of superiority, including claims that the CID at Scotland Yard was 'the most efficient detective force in the world' (Fuller, 1912:27, cited in Morris, 2007:24), was soon challenged by a number of people; especially in respect of the detectives' use of 'backwards methodologies' (Fosdick, 1915:313, cited in Morris, 2007:24). Specialists in scientific methods and techniques soon proliferated and brought about the age of the forensic detective.

Integrating science within criminal investigations

Whilst many were impressed with the detectives themselves (see Fosdick, 1915, cited in Morris, 2007; also see Goddard, 1930a, 1930b), there was criticism that detectives had not caught up with the advancements in forensic science that had taken place between 1880 and 1930. As the previous section noted, there was much resistance to introducing specialised training for detectives; so it will come as no surprise that, from a macro-level analysis, there is the perception that this type of resistance was also seen in relation to using forensic science in criminal investigations. There was no standardised information on the most up-to-date techniques available, nor was there any national guidance on how and when forensic techniques could or should be used. Indeed, the work of Hans Gross (see below) was only translated from German to English in 1924, a full 31 years after its initial publication (Gross, 1962). However, despite all this, there is clear evidence of the integration of forensic science techniques with criminal investigations.

Crime laboratories

During the late nineteenth and early twentieth centuries, there was an increase in the provision of *crime detection laboratories* which were used for forensic and investigative purposes. Across Europe and in America, many photographic studios used by the police were expanded and developed into *scientific police laboratories* (SPLs). The first crime lab was developed by Locard in Lyon in 1910 and consisted of 'two attic rooms above the law courts' (Nickell and Fischer, 1999:12). Goddard, who visited Locard's SPL in 1929, offers the following observations:

> Considering Locard's reputation, a survey of his laboratory is disappointing. It contains very little equipment, is housed under the eaves of the Palais de Justice (this was true of *every* S.P.L. I visited, save that in London, which was in the basement), and what equipment it has appears crude and antiquated. But Locard himself is full of Divine Fire, and a conversation with him is a pleasurable experience. He has attempted – successfully – investigations of almost every conceivable nature, and written most entertaining books on

crime detection. His accomplishments, considering the means at his disposal, appear next to magical. [Original emphasis.]

(Goddard, 1930b:133)

Following Locard's success, the Los Angeles Police Department established a forensic laboratory in 1923 under the direction of August Vollmer (1876–1955). However, SPLs were not the only type of labs used for forensic purposes. Another type consisted of *Medico-Legal Institutes* (MLI). MLIs were largely under the directorship of medically trained doctors or natural scientists, all of whom had high levels of education qualifications (MD, PhD, etc.). In 1929, the Scientific Crime Detection Laboratory was established in Chicago. At the same time, Calvin Goddard[9] (1891–1955) undertook a systematic review of SPLs and MLIs across Europe (Goddard, 1930a, 1930b). Goddard's mission was to compare European techniques with those available in the USA; and, in doing so, he soon realised that his initial hypothesis, 'that the United States is, for the most part, immeasurably behind Europe in scientific methods of crime detection', was indeed correct (Goddard, 1930a:15). Goddard toured the cities of England, France, Spain, Switzerland, Italy, Romania, Hungary, Austria, Germany, Denmark and Belgium, and examined the provisions of both SPLs and MLIs for criminal investigations. In the latter part of the nineteenth century, and for most of the twentieth century, the character of the work undertaken by crime labs differed depending on whether it was an SPL or MLI. Goddard placed the work into the relevant labs as shown in Table 5.1.

Between 1930 and 1935, the US set up SPLs across the country largely as a result of Goddard's recommendations (1930b:145–155). For example, the FBI established the official United States Crime Laboratory in 1930 (Nickell and Fischer, 1999:14). In the UK, 1935 saw the creation of the Forensic Science Laboratory at Hendon, London.

Goddard's review of the facilities provides an interesting historical map of forensic practice in the first third of the twentieth century, and, whilst the work of Fosdick, Goddard and others points to a certain lack of integration between criminal investigations and forensic services, it is clear that the police were interested in and used such expertise. In fact, at the micro and meso levels of analysis, there is a great deal of historical evidence that points to pockets of police innovation and use of forensic techniques and expertise. Morris (2007:25–26) notes how local forces began using 'forensic experts' for a range of cases; for example, the Fenian bombing campaign of the 1880s provided the opportunity for J. C. Brown, a professor of chemistry in Liverpool, to provide expertise that gave vital evidence that convicted a bomb maker; whilst the Metropolitan police used ammunition manufacturers Eley to provide evidence regarding a bullet found in the brain of a murder victim (ibid.:25). Another example is that of gunsmith Robert Churchill who, building on the work of Goddard, privately developed the use of the comparison microscope for forensic purposes (Hastings, 1963, cited in Morris, 2007:25). In fact, ballistics is a good example of where

Table 5.1 The work of early crime laboratories

Type	Character of work	
Group 1 Scientific Police Studies	• Antiques (genuine or spurious) • Bombs • Explosions and Explosives • Fingerprints • Fingerprints (paternity) • Fires • Footprints • Forgeries • Glass • Handwriting (signatures, general and criminal) • Heels • Infernal Machines • Inks and Invisible Writings • Jewels (genuine or spurious) • Metals (etchings and other studies) • Money (metallic and paper) • Moulage and Molding • Paintings • Palm Prints Paper (fingerprints) • Postage Stamps (genuine or forged) • Post Marks (genuine or forged)	• Powder (guns) • Printing (date of and origin, etc.) • Rubber Stamps (genuine and criminal) • Seals (embossed and wax) • Shoe Prints • Shot (guns) • Soil Studies • Spots and Stains • Teeth • Textiles • Tire Prints • Tool Marks • Typewriters • Wads (gun) • Weapons
Group 2 Medico- Legal Institutes	• Abortions • Bones • Electricity • Gastric Contents • Hanging • Industrial Accidents • Infanticide • Lightning • Occupational Deformities	• Occupational Diseases • Paternity • Poisons (chemical) • Poisoning (food) • Psychiatry • Water Analysis • Wounds (gunshot, etc.)
Group 3 Variant[1]	• Adulterations (food, drugs, etc.) • Biological Tests • Bullets • Cerumen (aka earwax) • Dust • Faeces • Fingernails (scrapings)	• Hair • Haemoglobin • Larvae • Ova • Parasites • Serum • Urine

Note:
[1] The variant group consisted of either SPLs or MLIs, depending on which organisation was the 'more enterprising' (Goddard, 1930b:128).

technology and science meet to satisfy a human need: '[i]nventors draw upon pre-existing scientific and technological knowledge as they shape their inventions to satisfy some human want or need. Inventions, therefore, are fusions of an intellectual past with socioeconomic, functional future' (Basalla, 1999:113).

These and many other examples illustrate how, in the early part of the twentieth century, scientific practices, both internal and external to police expertise, were used to aid and reinforce criminal investigations. Whilst this was quite casual to begin with, the police began to borrow more and more from the available local experts. Many provincial forces often asked Scotland Yard for help; for example, Chief Inspector Walter Dew was sent to Salisbury to investigate the murder of a 12-year-old boy. Unfortunately, upon arrival he found that no 'effort had been made to preserve the scene' and the 'body had been washed . . . and a determined attempt . . . had been made to clear up all the bloodstains in the house' (Morris, 2007:26). The lack of knowledge of Locard's principle of exchange and the perceived gap between investigative expertise and actual detective practice was noticeable in this and many other cases. Perhaps one of the most important reasons for this, which was also a major challenge facing forensic *experts* in the early years of criminal investigations, was the cultural differences and practices between the police and scientists. For example, even as late as 1935, detectives were still offering resistance to using the scientific facilities at the Metropolitan laboratory. As one forensic scientist noted:

> It was the attitude of the detective. He reckoned that he was a failure if he needed to use science. . . . I think the detectives belonged to a profession of their own and believed they didn't need the help of scientists.
>
> (Cited in Ambage, 1987:82)

This situation was made worse by a number of 'medico-legal debacles, caused by squabbling doctors who placed ego some way ahead of facts', resulting in the reluctance of some juries to convict on medical or forensic evidence alone (Evans, 2006:24). For example, the famous Home Office pathologist Augustus Pepper had suffered because of 'luddite mulishness' in the 1908 case of Flora Haskell, who was accused of slashing her son's throat, only for the jury to ignore Pepper's blood spatter evidence and find her not guilty on the basis that 'such a heinous crime was morally incompatible with motherhood' (ibid.:24). It didn't help that scientific evidence and standards of proof were very fluid during this period, with clear differences and changes seen over a relatively small period of time (Morris, 2007:22); or that most juries yawned their way through scientific evidence (Evans, 2006:13). Eventually it took the medical profession and their useful scientific work at crime scenes to change such attitudes.

The coming of the forensic detective

Most people have heard of Sherlock Holmes, whether in the writings of Sir Arthur Conan Doyle (1859–1930), the numerous films from 1914 onwards, including the rather interesting modernist interpretations of the infamous detective played by Robert Downey Jnr. in recent films by Guy Ritchie, or Benedict Cumberbatch's incarnation in the BBC TV series *Sherlock*. Doyle (and his most famous work Holmes) is of particular interest to the history of forensic criminology; not only did he play in goal for Portsmouth FC, he was a practicing doctor and surgeon and was often consulted by the police on matters relating to criminal investigations, especially when a death occurred. The fact that he visited crime scenes and undertook what is equivalent today to a pathologist's examination of the body *in situ*, albeit less sophisticated, enabled Doyle to develop the deductive-forensic analysis of the pithy Holmes that invariably outshone and downright embarrassed police detectives:

> Gregson and Lestrade had watched the manoeuvres of their amateur companion with considerable curiosity and some contempt. They evidently failed to appreciate the fact, which I had begun to realise, that Sherlock Holmes' smallest actions were all directed towards some definite and practical end.
>
> 'What do you think of it, sir?' they both asked.
>
> 'It would be robbing you of the credit of the case if I was to presume to help you,' remarked my friend. 'You are doing so well now that it would be a pity for anyone to interfere.'
>
> (From *A Study in Scarlet,* Conan Doyle, 1986:22)

Of course, Holmes then proceeds to solve the case for the hapless detectives. Whilst Holmes was indeed a fictional character, he mirrored, in many places, a number of individuals who were engaged in real-life forensic investigations; who wrote practical texts on the application of science to criminal investigations; and who should go down in history as forever linking science, criminal investigations and criminology. Perhaps the most famous of these individuals was Dr. Johan (Hans) Gross (1847–1915), who was the first to formally and systematically link forensic science with criminal investigations. Born in Graz, Austria in 1847, Gross studied criminology and law and served as an examining magistrate of the Criminal Court at Czernovitz (Petherick *et al.*, 2010:24). Gross is most famous for producing the seminal 1893 text *Handbuch für Untersuchungsrichter, als System der Krimalistik* (*Criminal Investigation: A Practical Textbook for Magistrates, Police Officers and Lawyers*). This became *the* text for law enforcement agencies. He also coined the term *Kriminalistik* which has been adapted as the professional occupation *Criminalist* in the US. As a magistrate, Gross began to realise the failings of the criminal justice system, specifically in the areas of incompetent criminal investigators and inadequate criminal identifications based on 'flawed and biased eyewitness accounts' (ibid.:24). Knowing that people, at best, were unreliable or, at worst, downright malicious (Gross, 1962:36–69), Gross concentrated on setting an agenda for the systematic identification, recovery, analysis and interpretation of physical evidence. However, he was clear that these methods and techniques must be pertinent to the facts in hand of specific criminal investigations. In doing so, Gross became one of the first advocates of using systematic scientific methods in matters criminal. The success of Gross' *System der Kriminalistik* is unparalleled, reaching five editions and translated into eight languages by 1962. A quick scan through the contents of the fifth edition not only demonstrates how ahead of his time Gross was but also provides the epistemological format for many contemporary forensic science texts:

- The investigator
- Examination of witnesses and accused
- Inspection of localities
- Equipment of the investigator
- The scientific expert and the investigator
- The press
- Practices of criminals
- Slang expressions commonly used by thieves
- Construction and use of weapons

- Drawing and allied arts
- Footprints and other impressions
- Cryptography
- Theft
- Cheating and fraud
- Arson
- Road accidents
- The criminal records office
- International crime: Interpol

The contents of Gross' influential text highlights an important sociological issue that is developed through this current text: primarily that forensic techniques and criminal justice issues are linked to social and technological loci that cannot be divorced from broader cultural aspects. Whilst much of the science behind the techniques listed above has advanced since its publication, Gross' text is a testament to concept of the *forensic generalist*. Indeed, as Petherick *et al.* (2010:25) rightly suggest 'he changed the world with his multidisciplinary, scientific approach to criminal investigation and forensic analysis'.

In the UK, Sir Bernard Spilsbury (1877–1947) was another scientist who adapted *and* developed scientific methods for forensic purposes. Surprisingly, Spilsbury has been written out of much of the history of forensic science, especially from the dominant US texts. Even the most famous of British pathologists, Keith Simpson, in his biography *Forty Years of Murder*, when briefly discussing the work of Spilsbury, does so with a mildly envious tone (Simpson, 1978:22–28 and 77–79). This is remarkable given the forensic work he undertook on groundbreaking cases in the UK, which effectively created the modern CSI (Evans, 2006). A graduate of the prestigious University of Oxford, Chief Resident Pathologist at St. Mary's and then Home Office Pathologist, Spilsbury is accredited as being the first true crime scene investigator as well as inventing 'the role of the expert witness' (ibid.:5). What distinguished Spilsbury from the other scientists of the day was that he got *in the trenches*. Instead of being locked in a laboratory undertaking the type of *clean* experimental science advocated by Sir Francis Bacon, Spilsbury attended crime scenes and got *stuck in*:

> He clambered across muddy fields, stood knee-deep in icy water, bent his back into howling blizzards, wrinkled his nose over foul-smelling corpses, prepared to travel to any destination and endure any hardship in order to study the fractured detritus of death.
>
> (ibid.:5–6)

As a pathologist working at the dawn of the twentieth century, Spilsbury was often called to crime scenes involving suspicious deaths and, up until his suicide in 1947, was involved in some of the most intriguing and important cases of the early twentieth century. For instance, he played a crucial role in the case of Dr Crippen, an American homeopathic doctor who, alongside his mistress Ethel Le Neve, was accused of the murder of Crippen's wife, Cora (who often ran under the stage name Belle Emor). The case of Crippen introduced the nation and the jury to Spilsbury and medical science expert evidence. Cora Crippen had been reported missing in 1910, and, upon investigation by the police, Crippen proffered that she had returned to America where she 'had succumbed to double pleuropneumonia' (ibid.:8). Whilst the police did not believe his story, they wrote the case off as a domestic fight. However, two days after the initial visit, Chief Inspector Walter Dew returned to 39 Hilldrop Crescent only to find that Crippen and Le Neve had fled. Dew ordered a search of the property and, after three days of searching, severely mutilated and dissected body parts were discovered in the coal cellar (ibid.:14–15). After Crippen and Le Neve were located, Crippen argued that the body must have been there long before he moved into the property. This case was to be Spilsbury's first major test with a high-profile homicide for his main task was to try to ascertain if the body parts were indeed those of Cora Crippen. Spilsbury and Pepper agreed that the 'level of dissection suggested a killer with an above-average knowledge of human anatomy' (ibid.:15). Unfortunately for the killer, they had doused the body in 'slaked lime' instead of 'quicklime', with the former acting to preserve the flesh. This piece of good fortune led to Spilsbury isolating 'a patch of skin about 5½ × 7 inches, fringed with what appeared to be pubic hair' (ibid.:17). On this patch of skin 'was a strange horseshoe-shaped welt' which Pepper was convinced was an operation scar – and one that both he and Spilsbury hoped could positively identify the victim as Cora Crippen as she had undergone an hysterectomy whilst a teenager (ibid.:17). After eight weeks of painstaking analysis on the patch of skin, Spilsbury was able to conclude that 'the piece of skin *did* come from the abdomen, and the scar *did* correspond in position and type to the kind of incision made for a hysterectomy' (ibid.:24 – original emphasis). Spilsbury took centre stage at the trial and, as Evans (ibid.:26) points out, his performance as an expert on the stand 'highlights the fact that in the courtroom, as elsewhere, style matters'.

Spilsbury delivered and, whilst Le Neve was acquitted of any wrongdoing, Crippen was found guilty and was hung in November 1910.

Spilsbury was unique because he not only applied his in-depth knowledge of medicine and human anatomy to criminal cases, he undertook numerous experiments and research, kept in-depth index files on his research and cases, and was single-minded and meticulous in his work. During his lifetime, Spilsbury performed more than 25,000 autopsies, peaking at 1,000 per annum (ibid.:63). Other important cases dealt with by Spilsbury included: the *Brides in the Bathwater*, where George Joseph Smith committed three murders and made them look like drowning in order to obtain monies from the victims (ibid.:33–64); and the infamous *Butcher of Soho*, in which a package was discovered which contained four sacks full of body parts belonging to Madam Emilienne Gerard, and in which Spilsbury undertook a blood spatter analysis of 101 Charlotte Street as well as using the then relatively new precipitin blood test that had been created by Uhlenhuth in 1901 to catch Louis Voisin (ibid.:84–86). Another case of interest was of an apparent suicide in the military compound at *Sutton Veny*, where gun instructor Joseph Durkin was believed to have shot himself. Spilsbury was called in and when he asked for the officer's case notes he found the visual evidence did not tally with the claims of suicide. Spilsbury decided to reconstruct the alleged suicide in perhaps one of the first *in situ* experiments of crime reconstruction:

> Taking the rifle, he lay down on the rolled-out mattress and assumed the deceased's position. Despite being six feet two inches, he could scarcely reach the trigger with his little finger when the muzzle was touching his face. When he held the rifle another two inches away, he was physically unable to pull the trigger.
>
> (Ibid.:70)

This simple experiment provides an excellent example of the importance of linking scientific and theoretical knowledge with an investigator's understanding of the crime scene and for testing the logistics of the simplest of claims. One final case that also deserves mention is the case of the *Bungalow Murder* in 1924 (ibid.:122–150). Patrick Herbert Mahon was executed for the murder of Miss Emily Beilby Kaye in a bungalow on the Crumbles, near Eastbourne. He was caught after he went to the cloakroom at Waterloo station to pick up a Gladstone medical bag. Little did he know that the bag was under surveillance, and he was stopped by police and questioned. Upon opening the bag it was found to contain a cook's knife and articles of women's clothing that were heavily stained with blood. After police investigations lead them to the Crumbles bungalow, Spilsbury was called in to conduct the examination. In the second bedroom and inside a fibre trunk 'lay a headless human body, obviously female, minus limbs' (ibid.:138). Further investigations found bones amongst the ashes in the fire grates in the sitting and dining rooms. Mahon also confessed that he had boiled parts of the body and thrown the fragments from a train during different parts of the journey. Mahon was convicted of Miss Kaye's murder and executed on 3rd September 1924. Even that was controversial, for Spilsbury was asked to undertake the official autopsy in which he found that 'Mahon had been "doubly hanged"' (ibid.:146). The importance of this case is twofold: first, because it illustrated the poor understanding or even acknowledgement of the concept of contamination and trace evidence, epitomised in the police's response to Spilsbury's request that they bring all the remains from inside the bungalow to his 'ad hoc laboratory in the courtyard' (ibid.:138):

> What Spilsbury saw next appalled him. Without a second thought the officers merely rolled up their sleeves and grabbed hold of chunks of putrid flesh, tossing them in buckets, as if they were sorting fish on a quayside. . . . 'Are there no rubber gloves?' Savage looked at him blankly and explained that his officers never wore any form of protective gear when processing crime scenes.

The second reason this case is important relates to the lack of a proper understanding of crime scene practice. The fact that the police did not use proper equipment that minimised the possibility of the contamination and cross-transference of evidence gave Spilsbury an idea which grew into the creation of the *murder bag*. Largely due to the poor hygiene that he'd witnessed at the bungalow crime scene, Spilsbury undertook a thorough review of procedures. The main finding was that 'police officers were hopelessly ill-equipped for the efficient performance of their duties' (ibid.:148). In order to resolve this, Spilsbury got together with a Wimpole Street doctor called Aubrey Scott-Gillett and Detective Superintendent William Brown from Scotland Yard to create the first *murder bag* for detectives. This bag included 'rubber gloves, a hand lens, a tape measure, a straightedge ruler, swabs, sample bags, forceps, scissors, a scalpel, and other instruments that might be called for' (ibid.:149).

I have briefly outlined the work of Conan Doyle, Gross and Spilsbury, but there were of course many others. The late nineteenth and first third of the twentieth centuries saw many scientists and medico-legal pioneers develop a whole range of theories and tests that would later become standard practice for criminal investigators. As Evans (ibid.:23–24) rightly points out, these pioneers faced many difficulties: '[t]hey had no literature to consult, no comforting peer review to fall back on; basically they were flying by the seat of their forensic pants. Experiments were conducted in the dark.' What pioneers such as Spilsbury *had* to achieve for forensic science to become accepted was a meaningful foothold in the English courtroom (ibid.:24). Spilsbury not only achieved this but he also paved the way for future generations of investigators and forensic practitioners.

As well as the individuals mentioned briefly above, the beginning of the twentieth century saw an increase in the production of textbooks that were aimed at the application of scientific techniques to criminal investigations. Table 5.2 outlines two popular texts and their contents, which were typical of the texts that

Table 5.2 Early forensic investigative textbooks

Lucas, A. (1921). *Forensic Chemistry and Scientific Criminal Investigation.* (Contents taken from the 3rd edition published in 1931.)	Rhodes, H. T. F. (1931). *Some Persons Unknown: Being an Account of Scientific Detection.* (Contents taken from the 2nd edition published in 1936.)
• Blood stains • Clothing • Counterfeit coins • Documents • Dust, dirt, stains and marks • Explosives and explosions • Fibres, woven fabrics, string and rope • Finger prints • Fibres and insurance frauds • Firearms, cartridges and projectiles • Microscopy, photography and ultra-violet rays • Poisons • Preservation of the human body after death robbery from letters and parcels • Tobacco	• How the poisoner used to work • Modern poisoners and their detection • Three mistakes and their consequences • Some person or persons unknown • Verdicts from dust • The infallible finger-print • What the camera sees • The ultra-violet ray – the sixth sense of the laboratory • Forgers and others • The chemist versus the forger • The search with the microscope • Duly registered • Criminal psychology and detection • Bombs • The ordeal in court

were available to investigators during this period. These two works offer an insight into the level of integration of forensic science with criminal investigations at the beginning of the twentieth century. There were, of course, many other texts available, including: Jago's *Forensic Chemistry and Chemical Evidence* (1909); Mitchell's *Science and the Criminal* (1911) and *The Scientific Detective and the Expert Witness* (1931); Willis' *Circumstantial Evidence* (1912); and Osborn's *The Problem of Proof* (1922). We should also not forget Locard's *L'Enquete Criminelle de les Méthodes Scientifiques*.

Summary

As with Chapters 3 and 4, this chapter sought to provide a selective historical overview of some of the key developments within a specific area linked to forensic criminology. This time the emphasis was on the eighteenth- and nineteenth-century developments in the police, policing, criminal investigations and their links with early forms of forensic science. Up until the creation of the UK's first police force in 1829, policing was very much a localised affair and centred on town watchmen and reliance on the general public to help out whenever a hue and cry was needed. The scant historical information available suggests that, whilst investigative methods were basic and very unstructured, there are plenty of examples demonstrating attempts to use forensic strategies to uncover evidence to successfully trace and prosecute criminals. Such attempts, of course, do not match contemporary forensic techniques; but they do point to a period in history where a number of forensic pioneers, both investigators and scientists, came together and merged the developing area of science with the practice of criminal investigations and applied criminology.

The eighteenth and nineteenth centuries and the first 30 years of the twentieth century should be regarded as an important historical epoch, rich in developments that link to forensic criminology; and it was a period that started major changes that would affect the landscape of criminal and forensic investigations forever. Part 2 now considers the contemporary landscape of forensic criminology, by examining criminal investigations, crime reconstruction, crime scene examination and forensic evidence.

Part 2

Contemporary forensic investigations

Chapter 6

Investigating crime

Introduction

The commencement of a criminal investigation begins the process of collecting a range of material that is used in the reconstruction of a crime event. This process is often a long and arduous journey that can take years before a suspect is even brought to the courtroom. Alternatively, it can be a relatively short journey that is painless and takes just a few weeks to see through to a conclusion. Innes' (2003:113) depiction of criminal investigations as a form of *information work* is a useful analytical framework for understanding the journey that a criminal investigation takes in relation to forensic criminology and its links with forensic science. For Innes, a criminal investigation is 'concerned with the identification, interpretation, and ordering of information with the objective of ascertaining whether a crime has occurred, and if so, who was involved and how' (ibid.:113). This ordering of information forms the basis of crime reconstruction (Chisum and Turvey, 2007), producing a narrative of the crime event or events, which is tried and tested in a courtroom. This is where decisions are made as to what evidence collected on this journey is submitted and allowed, agreed or contested; and who, ultimately, is to blame for the crime. This constructed journey involves three core professions that all play a crucial role in constructing the crime narrative – *police, forensic investigators or scientists* and the *legal system*. As the police undertake most criminal investigations, this chapter is primarily about the police, the structural, organisational and legal frameworks in which they operate, and the role they play in information work. I start with criminal investigations purely for logical reasons because, in the majority of cases, this is the beginning of the forensic process. The role of forensics throughout this entire process is a strange beast, determined by and dependent upon a number of structural and organisational factors as well as more micro, localised technologies, knowledge and situational components (Jasanoff, 1997; Innes, 2003); all of which are housed within the context of a criminal investigation.

This chapter attempts to introduce the core practical components of undertaking criminal investigations, how forensic issues play a role, and how both criminal investigations and forensics are shaped by the wider political, economic, social and technological contexts in which they arise. Furthermore, this chapter examines the link between criminal investigations and how they aid in 'creating' and 'defining' the 'criminal'.

Creating modern criminal investigations

As we saw in Chapter 5, up until the 1930s the levels of training and scientific sophistication was relatively low, albeit with pockets of moral entrepreneurs trying to enhance both the reputation and the techniques of criminal investigations. This situation started to change and improved quite dramatically from 1933 onwards as the Home Office started to take a more proactive role in policing. Morris calls this the period of *central leadership* (1933 to 1980); a stage that began the movement towards the centralisation of power and control over criminal investigations (2007:27). Whilst the 1919 Desborough Committee recommended that the police should remain locally organised and controlled, A. L. Dixon, secretary of the committee, who 13 years later would head up police affairs, disagreed. Sometime around 1932, Dixon started a full examination of detective work and training (ibid.:28), eventually producing the 1938 *Report of the Departmental Committee on Detective Work and Procedure*, which ran into five volumes. It identified that there were approximately '2,600 detectives in England and Wales in 1933' (1,000 Metropolitan officers; 1,100 city and borough officers; and 450 county officers) (ibid.:28). Interestingly, at this time there were around 181 separate forces across England and Wales.

As previously mentioned, changes that take place in criminal investigations are usually 'kick-started' by either problems or unique developments within the investigative process and which take place in cases where there is high public and media interest. It is no surprise that the 1934 *Brighton Trunk Murders* was a major influence in this period, and this case highlighted the importance of the need to reinforce aspects of the investigative processes undertaken by detectives. In the Brighton case, a limbless and headless female torso was found in the trunk at Brighton's lost luggage office; the legs were found at St. Pancras; but the head and other bits of the body were never found (ibid.:26). The Metropolitan police became involved and, at one time, had 15 plain-clothes officers making house-to-house inquiries in an attempt to identify the victim by tracing the 800 women that had been reported missing at the time. Unfortunately, the victim was never identified (ibid.:26). Cases such as the Brighton Trunk murders would have been at the forefront of discussion in Dixon's committee, addressing the need to make recommendations to improve police practice and investigative efficiency. Whilst there were many important recommendations made in the 1938 report, two areas stand out as pertinent here. The first related to *detective training*. Formal training for detectives was still rather unstructured and *ad hoc*; and even Dixon conceded that 'nothing in the way of an accepted system of instruction, or doctrine, had been developed in respect of detective work' (Dixon, 1966:138, cited in Morris, 2007:28). He and his committee recommended the introduction of formalised training, consisting of a 'detailed syllabus for an eight-week full-time course' (ibid.:28). The second area related to forensics and its use in criminal investigations. The newly suggested detective course should take into consideration the following elements:

- need for 'systematic behaviour at crime scenes';
- systematic use of 'forensic aids';
- how to investigate offences;
- provision of an overview of the 'evidential requirements' for cases; and
- stressing the development and use of 'observational and human skills,' especially for 'interrogation' purposes.

As we saw at the end of the last chapter, there was already an established body of forensic scientific techniques that were available to the police. However, it should be acknowledged that the UK and USA were already behind other European countries (i.e. France and Germany) in integrating forensic sciences into the investigative process (Goddard, 1930a, 1930b). Across Europe and in the United States, forensic laboratories had been integrated across various law enforcement agencies. It took the UK several years to 'catch up', with the establishment of the Metropolitan Police laboratory in 1935 at Hendon Police College (Morris, 2007:29). Unfortunately, the ingrained ideology of CID, as identified by Ambage (1987:83), meant that many detectives felt that if you needed to use science you had failed as an investigator. This type of attitude, as well as the obvious differences between the cultures of scientists and police, created a situation where the laboratory withered because the CID starved it of cases by not providing the necessary four signatures required to refer cases to the lab. With the appointment of a new Head (Henry Holden), who was a botanist, and the new Commissioner Scott, the police laboratory was soon reinvigorated with new life and purpose, producing some innovative work (Morris, 2007). Up until the Second World War, other laboratories opened in Bristol, Birmingham, Cardiff, Nottingham and Preston.

After the second World War, with Britain depleted of resources and in desperate need of rebuilding (Osgerby, 1998), the British government, often see-sawing between leftist Labour ideology and rightist *laissez-faire* Conservatism, engaged in an dramatic expansion of the bureaucratic machinery of social control (Pearson, 1975; Cohen, 1985) that was in line with their impressive economic policies. Part of this expansion programme included the increase in control over the police and criminal investigations from central government. It is, therefore, the period after the Second World War where attempts were made to structurally formalise the police and provide a framework for identifying what modern police actually do.

What do the police actually do?

The history presented in Chapter 5 leads into a consideration of the contemporary role of the police. Unfortunately, pinpointing exactly what the police do is not as easy as it sounds. They have a vast remit when it comes to the roles and responsibilities, routinely engaging in a broad array of tasks and events, many of which could not be deemed investigative in any way shape or form (Reiner, 2010:7): for instance, directing traffic, controlling drunks in the local night-time economy (Hobbs, 1989; Hobbs *et al.*, 2003) or dealing with lost children. Even a large number of thefts are not 'investigated', and the police only get involved in order to provide a crime number necessary for insurance claims. In his research on criminal justice, Howard Packer (1968, cited in Davies *et al.*, 2005:23–25) identified two primary models of criminal justice – *Due Process* and *Crime Control* – and it is the crime control model that is most relevant to the role of the police. Crime control 'stresses the role of the system in reducing, preventing and curbing crime by prosecuting and punishing those who are guilty of offences . . . the police and prosecution agencies may interpret their role primarily as crime fighters responsible for ensuring that the guilty are brought to justice' (ibid.:25). Mawby notes how, in terms of function, both government policy and senior management focused on the crime control aspect of policing, whilst at the same time undertaking welfare and service roles (2003:17). Adding to the complexity of understanding police roles are the sociocultural differences across state jurisdictions. Mawby provides an overview of the different policing systems across the globe, noting how there is an extensive variation in the ways the police are structured and the roles they perform (ibid.:15–35). As previously mentioned the police 'are responsible for law enforcement, for investigating crime, arresting suspects and deciding whether or not to pass the case on to the CPS' (Davies *et al.*, 2005:142), and these core functions fit into a broader set of responsibilities (142–143):

- crime control and investigation;
- crime reduction;
- order maintenance;
- peace keeping;
- social service;
- emergency service; and
- state security.

It is difficult to conceptualise any other public service or organisation that is expected to cover such a broad array of roles as the police, although this comment is not intended to take anything away from the myriad of crucial tasks and responsibilities undertaken by other public agencies. It is also important to note that many of these responsibilities are shared with other agencies such as the fire and ambulance services. Furthermore, all the roles noted above link to criminal investigations, and the use of forensic techniques and tools co-occur in all these areas, albeit to different degrees and in different forms. For example, the State Security role will include intelligence gathering of forensic evidence used for proactive investigations to prevent terrorist attacks (for an example see 'Qaeda Plot to Attack Plane Foiled, U.S. Officials Say', *New York Times*, 7th May 2012). In a recent report entitled *Policing in 2020: A Summary of Discussions on the Future of Policing*, written by the independent think tank Policy Exchange, and in collaboration with PA Consultancy Group, it was found that policing in England and Wales was facing 'significant, wide-ranging changes on a scale not seen for decades' (Policy Exchange, 2011:8). Changes such as the phasing out of NPIA (the National Policing Improvement Agency), the creation of a new National Crime Agency and the introduction of elected Police and Crime Commissioners on the 15th November 2012, mean that, in the future, it may become increasingly difficult to pinpoint the roles and responsibilities of the police. For ease of analysis and linking with the overall aims and topic of this book, the rest of this chapter considers the criminal investigative role within the confines of the organisation of the police and their policing function and its links to forensics.

Understanding criminal investigations

One of the ways in which the modern idea of the police engages in 'policing' its citizens is through the investigation of crime. Stelfox (2009:1) and Rogers (2007:150) both place criminal investigation as one of the core functions of the police. However, as previously noted in Chapter 5, this function has not always been a core role of the police. Indeed, over the last 20 years the 'hallowed status' of criminal investigations has been constantly challenged by numerous official reports produced by a range of committees and commissions as well as high-profile cases of investigative failures, such as the cases of the Yorkshire Ripper Peter Sutcliffe and the murder of Stephen Lawrence (Maguire, 2003:386). For instance, the Audit Commission's (1993) *Helping With Enquiries: Tackling Crime Effectively* identified weaknesses in the practices of criminal investigations' crime management and made recommendations for improvement such as improving the definitional parameters of the work of Criminal Investigative Departments (CIDs), more effective management of police investigations and increasing the weight given to intelligence-led investigations (Savage, 2007:98–100). These regulatory, structural and organisational elements will heavily influence the nature of investigative work, therefore structuring the uses and application of forensic tools, techniques and evidence – which are discussed in more detail below.

One important thing to note is that the investigation of a crime leading to a case being prosecuted in court is actually *atypical*. If we look at the differences between the rates of offences as suggested by the British Crime Survey (BCS)[1] and police recorded crime and then look at those that are actually prosecuted, we see that the vast majority of crimes are not presented in a forensic setting (i.e. the court). So, for instance, BCS figures for 2009/10 put the number of crimes committed at 9.6 million, while police recorded crime was 4.6 million (Flately *et al.*, 2010:2). An examination of the CPS 2010 *case outcomes* statistics[2] shows they undertook 947,008 prosecutions. So, out of the suggested 9.6 million crimes that the BCS claim occur, only 9.86 per cent are prosecuted. For police recorded crime in 2009/10, the ratio is 5:1; that is, just over 20 per cent ended up in court in 2010. These figures do appear low and tend to counter popular cultural perceptions of the success rates of criminal investigations (Deutsch and Cavender, 2008). However, if we look at those that did make it to court, the success rate is relatively high with 85.77 per cent (812,290) of those 947,008 cases ending in a successful prosecution. Of course, these macro averages hide regional differences between police forces and some striking disparities in successful prosecutions between offence categories (Brantingham and Brantingham, 1984). There are many factors influencing these figures, most of which are discussed at various points below and throughout this text. The relatively low proportion of identified crimes to successful prosecutions is not a new phenomenon (Reiner, 2010:151–155) and has been a concern for many years. Over the last 20 years or so, some of this concern has translated into a pragmatic approach to the development of a structured understanding of criminal investigations. However, the problem of *identification* is far broader and goes back even further than many people even care to think about. Paul Kirk, the famous forensic scientist, succinctly summarised this issue in his discussion of what criminal investigations are:

> The central problem of the criminal investigator is the establishment of personal identity – usually of the criminal, sometimes of the victim. The investigator may use direct methods, or he may work indirectly through the identification of physical objects associated with the individual to be identified. . . . Philosophically, 'identity' refers to unique existence. A thing is identical only to itself, because it is an object with a separate existence, independent of all other objects, no matter how similar. . . . In the field of criminal investigation, the general use of the word 'identification' differs markedly from the classical philosophical concept, since 'identity' itself is differently defined. *Identification is the placing of an object in a class or group.* [Original emphasis.]
>
> (Kirk, 1974:9–10)

To put it even more simply, any definition of criminal investigations should incorporate the fact that police are attempting to do one or more of the following: ascertain if a crime has been committed; find out who the offender is; and build a case against the suspect (Horswell and Fowler, 2004:84).

Towards a definition

In the Royal Commission on Criminal Justice's report *The Conduct and Supervision of Criminal Investigations*, criminal investigations were defined as:

> the application of a set of standard procedures to reports or allegations that a crime has been committed. Most such reports emanate from members of the public (including commercial and other organisations) and most are fairly easily classifiable at the outset as complaints of a specific type of criminal offence. The investigations are 'reactive', or 'offence based', in the sense that police officers are expected to make appropriate inquiries into each individual complaint, completing forms to satisfy their supervisors that they have done so. Police handbooks usually present this process as a logical and systematic 'search for the truth': in the archetypical case, the investigator undertakes inquiries in order to (i) determine whether, in fact, an offence has been committed and (ii) gather sufficient evidence to establish a set of possible suspects, to eliminate those not responsible, and to support criminal charges against any who might be.
>
> (Maguire and Norris, 1992:7)

This definition explains criminal investigations that are *reactive*. However, criminal investigations can also be *proactive,* where you effectively start from the other end by targeting known and prolific offenders and use a range of strategies 'to discover and demonstrate their involvement in various offences, previously recorded or not' (ibid.:8). In short, criminal investigations can be defined and determined by their starting point and the techniques used to collect evidence (Stelfox, 2009:148), and this crude dichotomous *reactive/proactive* model is commonly recited as the two main types of criminal investigation (Stelfox, 2009; Monckton-Smith, *et al.*, 2013). Indeed, much recent research often uses this simple dichotomous framework in what can be described as a trend towards a sociocultural reification of these two systems without further erudition (Carson, 2007:407).

If we look at other non-legal definitions we find a number of similarities in the definitional elements. O'Hara and O'Hara (2003:5) suggests that criminal investigations have three aims – 'to identify and locate the guilty party and to provide evidence of his guilt'. Similarly, Swanson *et al.* (2003:28) argue that the objectives of investigations are: (i) to establish a crime was committed; (ii) to identify and apprehend the suspect; and (iii) to assist in the prosecution of the individual charged with the crime. Interestingly, they also include the recovery of stolen property as a function of criminal investigations. From a legal standpoint, criminal investigations are defined in Part II, Section 22 Criminal Procedure and Investigations Act 1996 (CPIA):

(1) For the purposes of this Part a criminal investigation is an investigation conducted by police officers with a view to it being ascertained –

    a.   whether a person should be charged with an offence, or
    b.   whether a person charged with an offence is guilty of it.

(2) In this Part references to material are to material of all kinds, and in particular include references to –

    a.   information, and
    b.   objects of all descriptions.

(3) In this Part references to recording information are to putting it in a durable or retrievable form (such as writing or tape).

This purely legal framework ensures that the police have the primary responsibility to undertake a professional criminal investigation in an attempt to determine the following: (i) whether a crime has been committed; (ii) whether criminal proceedings can commence; (iii) the identification of an individual or group of individuals responsible for the crime or crimes committed; and (iv) aiding in the prosecution of those responsible for the crimes committed (Rogers, 2007:150–151). The idea of undertaking a 'professional criminal investigation' is embedded within Section 23 CIPA, which places a statutory responsibility on the Secretary of State to produce a code of practice for criminal investigations. This code is discussed in more detail below, but it includes provisions designed to ensure: that all reasonable steps are taken and all lines of inquiry are pursued (s23[1][a]); that the recording of relevant information connected to the investigation is undertaken (s23[1][b]), retained (s23[1][c]) and is revealed to the defence (s23[1][e]); and that the accused is allowed to inspect the evidence against them (s23[1][f and g]). The primary aim of CPIA was to ensure a 'level playing field at a trial by placing a legal duty on investigators to disclose all the material they gather to both prosecution and defence' (Stelfox, 2009:67), so Part II s23[2] of CPIA is really a framework defining what an investigator does (Rogers, 2007:151–152). From the perspective of forensic criminology, professional criminal investigations as outlined in the provisions of CPIA, as well as the definitions discussed above, provide a pragmatic definitional parameter covering three valuable functions (Figure 6.1).

The first function is the gathering of evidence for reactive crime reconstruction. A crime occurs, is reported or identified and the police begin to gather evidence in relation to this matter. Regardless of whether the evidence is eventually used in court,[3] most investigators will attempt to gather as much relevant 'evidence' as they are able or need too. This is of course determined by a wide variety of factors including the nature of the crime (Tilley et al., 2007), the amount of resources

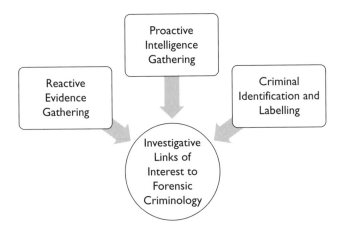

Figure 6.1 The functions of criminal investigations

allocated (Roberts and Willmore, 1993; McCulloch, 1996), as well as the decision-making processes involved in the management of the investigation (McCulloch, 1996; Tilly and Ford, 1996; Innes, 2003). The second important function for forensic criminology is that criminal investigations gather intelligence for crime prevention purposes, a process that comes under the heading of proactive investigations. Proactive policing has become embedded within the police, especially since the introduction of the *National Intelligence Model* (NIM) in 2004 (ibid.). Proactive policing grew out of the perceived concerns over the ineffectiveness of reactive policing, and attempts were made to focus more on the actions leading to a potential criminal act. In short, criminal investigations offer both reactive gathering of evidence as well as proactive gathering of intelligence that determines the direction that criminal investigation may take. They also have a bearing and influence on the trial process and outcome. As Carson notes (2007:407), these two models are typical ways to conceptualise current policing perspectives. However, there is also a third important function of criminal investigations. Reactive and proactive evidence and intelligence gathering is part of the journey to identify perpetrators of crime, with the ultimate objective being the *correct* identification and *successful* labelling of the 'criminal'. This idea has largely been associated with the *interactionist* paradigm, which grew in prominence in the 1950s and 1960s through work such as Lemert's *Social Pathology* (1951), Becker's *Outsiders* (1963), Wilkins' *Social Deviance* (1964), Erikson's *Wayward Puritans* (1966), Scheff's *Being Mentally Ill* (1966) and Young's *The Drugtakers* (1971). Many of these texts rightly pointed to the processes involved in the social construction of 'deviant' and 'criminal' populations, through the examination of what Becker called *moral entrepreneurial activity* and how such activity created an experiential framework (Goffman, 1986) for society to understand stigmatised folk devils. The labelling process, if successfully applied, initiates the full coercive power of the bureaucratic state, which includes a vast array of increased punishment and surveillance technologies, or what Wacquant (2009) refers to as the *penal dragnet* of the *carceral state*. However, few have paid attention to the role criminal investigations and forensic techniques play in this labelling process. Most texts on criminal investigations are very process oriented (e.g. see O'Hara & O'Hara, 2003; Sonne, 2006; Berg, 2008; Rowe, 2008; Stelfox, 2009; Monckton-Smith *et al.*, 2013) and tend not to consider the interactive relationship between the investigator, the physical and witness evidence collected, and the effects these processes have on the overall outcome of the constructed 'criminal'; a point I return to in the next chapter. This final element, then, is crucial from the standpoint of the forensic criminologist because it brings to it an alternative dimension and use of forensic information within the structured frame of criminal investigations. However, before a crime can be investigated it has to be detected.

Detecting crime

One of the most influential factors affecting the nature and direction of a criminal investigation, as well as the amount and type of information received or collected and the way the case is proceeded with, is how the crime is *detected* to begin with. To put it another way, detections are how the crime comes to the attention of the authorities. Although not an exhaustive list, Table 6.1 outlines some of the main ways crimes are detected (collated from O'Hara & O'Hara, 2003; Sonne, 2006; Rogers, 2007; Berg, 2008; Stelfox, 2009).

Table 6.1 highlights the fact that crimes are detected in a wide variety of ways, and each way produces both similar and dissimilar types of information that the police use for a range of intelligence and evidential purposes, for either tactical or strategic objectives. If we then add in the structural-bureaucratic framework of regulatory practice and 'cop culture' (e.g. see Waddington, 1999:97–120; Reiner, 2010:115–173), this issue becomes more complex, with a myriad of factors at any given time impacting upon the detection of crime. Furthermore, just because a crime is 'detected' does not necessarily mean it will result in (a) the undertaking of the investigative process including the collection of forensic evidence and (b) end up in the court room. According to recent detection figures in *Crimes Detected in England and Wales 2010/11*, out of the 4.15 million crimes recorded by the police in 2010/11, the sanctioned detection rate was only 28 per cent (1.15 million)[4] (Taylor and Chaplin, 2011:9). Sanctioned detections are detections that 'are associated with at least the potential for a sanction to be administered' (Tilley *et al.*, 2007:227); for example, where 'a suspect has been charged or summonsed, has had a fixed penalty notice issued or has had the offence taken into consideration by a court' (Stelfox, 2009:198). Non-sanctioned detections include 'all those that do not lead to any further action' (Tilley *et al.*, 2007:227). In 2004 the government introduced the sanctioned detection measure due to the fact that not all crimes detected resulted in the offender being brought to justice. Following the introduction of the *National Crime Recording Standard* in 2002,

Table 6.1 How crimes are detected

Type	Description
Caught in the act	• Stemming from police patrols and the original Beat Patrol system from 1829 • Visible presence where officers walk or drive around a geographical area and 'come across' crimes as they are being committed • Members of the public 'flag down' police officers and report crimes
Forensic evidence	• The discovery, identification, collection and analysis of physical and trace evidence • Evidence that links a suspect to the victim and/or crime location • The most commonly used types of physical evidence in criminal investigations include DNA and fingerprints
Witnesses	• Those with knowledge of the offence through directly witnessing: (i) the crime event (i.e. the reason 999 was created in 1937); (ii) the interaction between victim and suspect; or (iii) witnessing post-crime activity undertaken by the suspect, such as destroying evidence • Gathering of witness evidence through media appeals, house-to-house enquiries, snowball interviewing, anniversary appeals and 'stop checks'
Interviews with suspects	• Investigative interviewing where investigators search for information regarding crime events • Suspects may incriminate themselves • Other individuals may incriminate offenders • Offenders may want to clear up other offences whilst being investigated for other crimes – known as offences 'taken into consideration' (TIC)
Searches	• Through searches of persons, property and vehicles • Many stop-and-search enquiries uncover a wide range of criminal offences ranging from the possession of illegal drugs to dangerous weapons, through to more serious offences such as possession of explosives for the purpose of undertaking terrorist attacks
CCTV[1]	• Where crimes that occur in public spaces are recorded during their commission • Where police officers investigating crimes trace routes taken by victims that are recorded • Extensive network of CCTV coverage provides numerous opportunities for evidence
Given into custody	• A number of offenders are 'handed over' to the police by witnesses (citizen's arrest) or by individuals as part of their general duties – e.g. PCSOs, store detectives, security guards, etc. • Given into custody suspects can generate a lot of evidence that needs to be rigorously tested

(Continued)

Table 6.1 (Continued)

Informers	• Individuals who may have information relevant to a crime but are not offenders, victims or witnesses • Known as Covert Human Intelligence Resources (CHIS) – a person who establishes/maintains a relationship with someone for the purpose of gaining investigative information
Surveillance	• The undertaking of covert surveillance to gather both intelligence and evidence of criminal activity • Includes traditional forms such as 'stakeouts', 'following suspects', 'recording suspects' activities' (i.e. photographs and video/digital recordings)
Interception of communications	• Where intelligence is obtained through covert interception of telephone calls, letters and parcels • Interception of telephone calls is not usually admissible in court • Provides both tactical and strategic information for intelligence and law enforcement agencies
Communications/ electronic data	• Similar to interception of communications • Intelligence is also gathered by analysing communications/electronic data such as mobile phones, e-mails and text messages • Identification of networks or groups as part of criminal gangs and/or terrorist groups
Information from other agencies	• Crimes detected through information received form other agencies • List is potentially endless and includes: UK Border Agency; Secret Intelligence Service; MI5; HM Revenue and Customs; Department for Work and Pensions; Driver and Vehicle Licencing Agency (DVLA); Identity and Passport Service
Information from prison	• Witness statements from prisoners • Crimes committed whilst inside prison • Risk assessment, psychological and/or psychiatric reports from prison personnel
SARs (Suspicious Activity Reports)	• A financial report completed by an institution when it believes transactions may be linked to crimes • Administered by the Serious Organised Crime Agency (SOCA) (subsumed under the newly formed National Crime Agency)
Expert advisors	• Information from individuals who have a specific expertise • Expertise enables individuals to provide expert testimony in court over matters of relevance to the case • Includes engineers, psychiatrists, medical doctors, forensic scientists, etc.

Note:
1 Closed-circuit television

sanctioned detection rates rose steadily between the years 2004/05 and 2007/08; however, this rise can largely be linked to the introduction of *Cannabis Warnings* and *Penalty Notices for Disorder* in 2004/05 (Taylor and Chaplin, 2011:13), and this demonstrates how recording standards and crime classifications are related to what is crime is detected and whether the detected crime ends up in the 'forensic forum' of the courtroom. What is also of interest to the forensic criminologist is that there are different levels of sanctioned detections across offence categories. Figure 6.2 lists the percentage of sanctioned detections across offence groups for England and Wales in 2010/11.

On average, for all crimes recorded by the police for 2010/11, there is a sanctioned detection rate of just 28 per cent. This figure provides an important context for the application and use of forensics, as the implication of having such a low detection rate is that much forensic evidence does not even end up in a court case and certainly does not contribute to sanctioned detections. It also opens up the definitional question of whether 'evidence' that is not presented in court should be deemed as 'forensic' evidence at all.

There are a large number of factors that potentially impact upon whether a crime is detected and then investigated. Some of these factors are obvious; for example, whether the crime is actually reported. However, there are a number of subtle factors that also come into play, such as organisational priorities and the forensic strategies that are developed as part of criminal investigations as well as the forensic submissions to be analysed. For example, a study by Tilley and Ford (1996:20) found that in the 11,922 cases they reviewed, 42.4 per cent (5,056) of submissions were for drug offences. Even across borders and different country jurisdictions, drug submissions to forensic laboratories are commonly amongst the highest (Saferstein, 2007; Jackson and Jackson, 2011). The two primary reasons for this are the relative ease and quickness of the forensic procedure for ascertaining the chemical breakdown of drug compounds, as well as the simple fact that drug substances are easily identifiable and collected during the investigative process. We thus see a set of elements that clearly interact with each other to determine and produce the sanctioned detection rate. However, for those recorded crimes that are investigated, the actual criminal investigation process itself also fundamentally determines the detection rate; and this process operates within a particular structural framework.

Structural and organisational issues

The structural organisation of the police determines its functioning and the 'outcomes' it produces. Every individual that has been defined as a 'criminal' in court has been 'constructed' through the criminal justice process, which includes the police and criminal investigations (Jasanoff, 1997). This notion of the 'constructed criminal' should not belie the objective reality that individuals engage in real acts that harm people and property. The notion of 'construction' is meant to signify the idea that, whilst there is an objective reality to crime events,

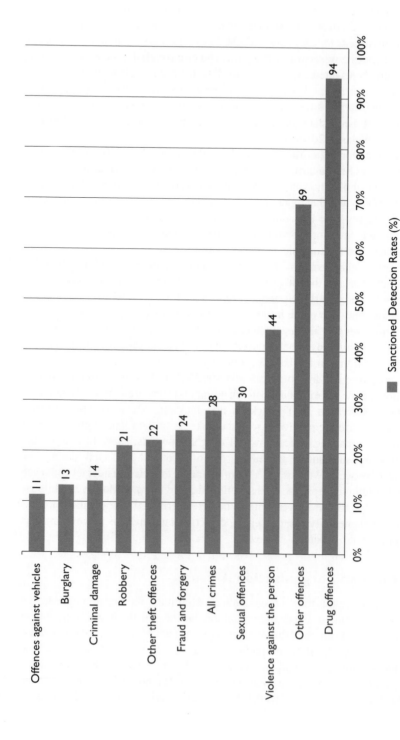

Figure 6.2 Sanctioned detection rates by offence group, England and Wales, 2010/11

Data Source: Taylor and Chapin, 2011.

these events have to be reconstructed from bits of information and material from the crime event, and that the labels and sanctions placed upon 'criminals' are wholly human-made (Chisum and Turvey, 2007). These 'bits' of information and material will be the main topic of the next chapter. In the meantime, the context of this material and the structure and processes in which it is created is the focus of the rest of this chapter. The organisation of the police largely depends upon the country it operates in, its legal system and its structure of governance. This means that, across the globe, there exists a rich and varied range of police forces and investigative processes. In England and Wales, two levels of governance – the *tripartite system* and *police forces* – determine policing and criminal investigations; and both of these structures, at the time of writing, operate using the National Intelligence Model.

The tripartite system

The first, and the overriding, system of governance is the *tripartite system*. Established by the Police Act 1964, the tripartite governance structure for policing consists of the Home Secretary, Police Authorities and Chief Constables (Jones, 2003; Davies *et al.*, 2005). Police authorities were composed of 'two-thirds elected representatives from local councils and one-third justices of the peace' (Davies *et al.*, 2005:151). Currently, there are police authorities for all 43 police forces in England and Wales as well as additional police authorities for British Transport Police, Civil Nuclear Police, and a Police Committee for the Ministry of Defence Police (see www.apa.police.uk/your-police-authority). Police authorities consist of 17 members (9 local councillors appointed by the local council and 8 independent members selected following local advertisements).[5]

According to Jones (2003), the Police Act 1964 attempted to resolve a number of 'tensions between national and local influences' that included unifying the dual system of governance[6] and clarifying powers of the 'local authorities, national government and chief constables in the framing and implementation of policing policy'. Whilst the 1964 Act divided the responsibility of governance of the police between the three aforementioned parties, local operational governance was placed in the hands of the chief constables. This tripartite system was supposed to develop into a more reciprocal, flat hierarchy with all three parties having influence, a 'voice', and responsibility over how the police operate, funding policies and their accountability. However, this involved further ambiguity between the three governance roles. For example, in practice, police authorities had little say or control over police policy or how police budgets were spent. Empirical research supports this, as Jones and Newburn (1994, cited in Davies *et al.*, 2005:151) found that policy developments such as crime prevention, private policing and the move to the civilianisation of certain administrative roles were 'increasingly determined by central government', with local police authorities having little influence over these developments. Such developments really started with the 1964 Act as it also established on a statutory footing the increasing dominance of centralised power through the broad 'array of powers' it provided to the Home Secretary (Newburn, 2003:92). In the report *A Force to be Reckoned With* by the Policing Reform Working Group for the Centre for Social Justice, it is argued that the 1964 Act was designed to 'ensure that no one party could dominate the other two in setting the agenda for policing in any given locality' (Policing Reform Working Group, 2009:26). The report further argues that the 'tripartite structure in its current form is not fit for purpose and needs to be rebalanced' (ibid.:26).

Since the 1964 Act, there have been a number of important changes that have attempted to update the system of governance. The Police and Magistrates' Court Act 1994 sought to reform the tripartite structure 'within a framework of national planning and performance management' (Jones, 2003:609). Enacted in July 1994, changes were made to the governance structure of all three parties. For example, local authorities gained independence from the local government structure and were 'responsible for publishing an annual "local policing plan" including specific national and local policing objectives, and associated performance targets' (ibid.:609). Chief constables were given freedom to 'use the overall budgets set by their police authorities' (Brain, 2010:227–228). According to Brain, it was the Home Secretary that gained the most, who now had the ability to 'set national objectives, performance targets, and codes of practice for police authorities' (ibid.:228). The Police and Magistrates' Court Act was short-lived, as it was soon replaced by the Police Act of 1996, which consolidated much of what was in the 1994 Act. However, it did make some important additions including the introduction of police authorities' *local policing plans*, which set out the police arrangements for the year. A more recent legislative change affecting policing and investigative governance was the Police Reform Act 2002, which introduced 'the national policing plan for 2003–2006', setting out 'the government's strategic priorities for the police service' (Davies *et al.*, 2005:152). This plan included promises to deliver on core issues affecting local communities – such as anti-social behaviour and disorder, volume-, violent-, street-, and drug-related crime – organised and serious crime, and increasing the number of offences successfully brought to justice (ibid., 2005:152). The most recent development in how the police is governed is the Police Reform and Social Responsibility Act 2011, which transferred control of police forces from police authorities to Police and Crime Commissioners; the first of which were elected in November 2012.

Police forces

The tripartite system oversees 43 police forces in England and Wales, and each force, whilst able to maintain a form of autonomy over its localised policing priorities and policies, is 'steered' from the centre by government control. At the

Table 6.2 Police forces in England and Wales

North East	**East Midlands**	**London**
Cleveland	Derbyshire	City of London
Durham	Leicestershire	Metropolitan Police
Northumbria	Lincolnshire	
	Northamptonshire	
	Nottinghamshire	
North West	**West Midlands**	**South East**
Cheshire	Staffordshire	Hampshire
Cumbria	Warwickshire	Kent
Greater Manchester	West Mercia	Surrey
Lancashire	West Midlands	Sussex
Merseyside		Thames Valley
Yorkshire and the Humber	**Eastern**	**South West**
Humberside	Bedfordshire	Avon & Somerset
North Yorkshire	Cambridgeshire	Devon & Cornwall
South Yorkshire	Essex	Dorset
West Yorkshire	Hertfordshire	Gloucestershire
	Norfolk	Wiltshire
	Suffolk	
		Wales
		Dyfed-Powys
		Gwent
		North Wales
		South Wales

time of writing, these forces were still in place; yet the spectre of cuts still hangs over them. Suggestions have been made that, in order to streamline policing and make efficiency savings, some forces will eventually be merged. Thus, the structure of today's police forces may be completely different in the future. Table 6.2 outlines the current police forces in England and Wales (Dhani, 2013:5).

The National Intelligence Model

A third and important framework for understanding the nature of criminal investigations is the development of *intelligence* and the National Intelligence Model (hereafter NIM). As we saw with the proactive and undercover approaches of Vidocq's Paris Sûreté and Vincent's CID officers, *agent provocateurs* have existed throughout policing history and have been used to gather intelligence on crimes, offenders and criminal gangs. Indeed, Grieve (2004, cited in John and Maguire, 2007:199) links police intelligence to the 'Chinese strategist Sun Tzu and his military treatise *The Art of War*, written 2,000 years ago, with its reference to spies and intelligence'. John and Maguire (2007:200) note that the development of modern intelligence systems and practices began in the 1970s and 1980s, placing the 1975 'Baumber Report' as a central influence, due to its call for a more systematic use of police intelligence. It was in this report that criminal intelligence was defined:

> The end product of a process often complex, sometimes physical, and always intellectual, derived from information that has been collated, analysed and evaluated in order to prevent crime or secure the apprehension of offenders.
>
> (ACPO, 1975: para. 32, cited in John and Maguire, 2007:200)

As we will see, as a main theme running through Chapters 7, 8 and 9, the process of turning 'intelligence' into evidence that reaches the evidential standards of the legal world, but also successfully identifies the right offender, is fraught with numerous difficulties and challenges; and NIM was perceived by many to be one method that could reduce these difficulties.

Whilst there are many influences that drove the development of NIM, the increasing frustration with reactive policing and its inability to 'achieve reductions in crime rates or increases in detection rates, despite increased investment in personnel and technology' (John and Maguire, 2007:201) frustrated many government and senior ranked police officials. The Audit Commission report *Helping with Enquiries* found that reactive policing was simply a 'band-aid' measure and that the police could not stem the tide, arguing that 'crime threatens to overwhelm them' (1993:40). Interestingly, one of the core problems, as perceived by the Audit Commission, government and senior police officers, directly relates to forensic issues. According to Maguire and John (1995:5, cited in John and Maguire, 2007:201), reactive policing methods often include an examination of the crime scene. Unfortunately, this does not always yield the necessary physical evidence required for positive identification of the offender, regardless of the perceptions generated by TV shows such as *CSI (Las Vegas)*, *CSI: Miami* and *CSI: New York*. In contrast to this, proactive intelligence gathering could 'yield powerful alternative forms of evidence' including: surveillance records; financial records; information from informants; police observations; and statements from undercover officers (John and Maguire, 2007:201). Other factors influencing the development of intelligence-led policing (John and Maguire, 2007:202–203; Ratcliffe, 2008) include:

- limitations on interviewing and confession evidence;
- advances in technology;
- increased focus on serious and organised crime; and
- pressures for more efficient and effective use of resources.[7]

I discuss the notion of intelligence and the five processes of the intelligence cycle in detail in Chapter 8, when examining techniques of crime analysis and crime mapping. For now, it is enough to briefly mention the five processes and the overall NIM as piloted in 2000 by what was then the National Criminal Intelligence Service.

Intelligence-Led Policing (ILP) has become the standardised policing practice for England and Wales, and thus determines the investigative process itself (John and Maguire, 2007; Ratcliffe, 2008; James, 2011). Because of this, it also has a direct influence on the uses (and abuses) of forensic practice, the types of offences that are prosecuted and the offenders that are produced as a result. ILP gained impetus due largely to the work of academics who tend to develop evidence-based criminological research using sophisticated analytical techniques (e.g. see Brantingham and Brantingham, 1984; Clarke, 1980; Clarke and Felson, 2004; Cornish and Clarke, 2008; Felson, 2008; Ratcliffe, 2008). However, this time policymakers were listening and realised that empirical-based ILP could be used as a management tool to direct police resources across a whole range of police management 'business'. In the NIM, this 'business' takes place over three tiers (ACPO Centrex, 2005; John and Maguire, 2007; Savage, 2007) as shown in Figure 6.3.

NIM's management processes are replicated at each level so that what informs local (level one) policing could, if relevant, inform national and international objectives as well. The basic idea within the NIM is to use business management ideas and parlance to create a more efficient police force, and this followed what was then New Labour's philosophy of governmental bureaucracy (Nash and Williams, 2008). Of course there are huge problems with attempting to apply an economic model to criminal justice, not least because public sector organisations like the police do not produce any direct wealth; they only spend it. Furthermore, there is a world of difference between the cultures and day-to-day running of criminal justice agencies, such as the police and probation services, as opposed to, say, a manufacturer of computers or cars. Despite the obvious problems with

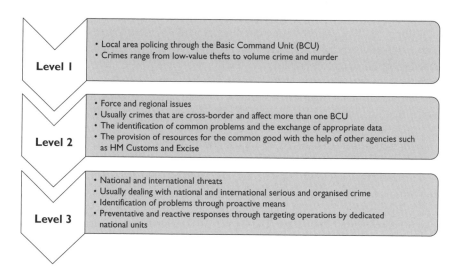

Level 1
• Local area policing through the Basic Command Unit (BCU)
• Crimes range from low-value thefts to volume crime and murder

Level 2
• Force and regional issues
• Usually crimes that are cross-border and affect more than one BCU
• The identification of common problems and the exchange of appropriate data
• The provision of resources for the common good with the help of other agencies such as HM Customs and Excise

Level 3
• National and international threats
• Usually dealing with national and international serious and organised crime
• Identification of problems through proactive means
• Preventative and reactive responses through targeting operations by dedicated national units

Figure 6.3 The three levels of NIM

what was to be called New Public Management (NPM), the government had already committed itself to this philosophy (Savage, 2007). The then Prime Minister Tony Blair put his trust in Patrick Carter, a businessman with 'experience of the private health care sector' (Raynor and Vanstone, 2007:75), who reviewed major parts of the criminal justice system (Carter, 2003). His report, *Managing Offenders, Reducing Crime: A New Approach* set in play the reorganisation of 'offender management' that brought the prison and probation services together under the structure of NOMS (National Offender Management Service) (see Nash and Williams, 2008 for a full review). All of this was under the umbrella term of NPM and, at the same time, policing through NIM was also being developed using the same ideology. The quote below, provided by John Orr, then Chairman of the Crime Committee, of ACPO in Scotland and also Chief Constable of Strathclyde Police, conveys the ingrained business management ideology within NIM:

> The Model has real value in that it clearly outlines the component parts of the intelligence process and clarifies terminology which is all too often misunderstood. Adoption of the Model throughout the UK will ensure commonality in working practices and an understanding of the intelligence requirements which will ensure greater effectiveness in the future.
>
> (NCIS, 2000:7)

NIM was designed to cover three important managerial needs, identified by what was then the National Crime Intelligence Service: first, the need to 'plan and work in co-operation with partners to secure community safety'; second, to 'manage performance and risk'; and finally, to 'account for budgets' (ibid.:7). With regard to the activities of the police, it sets a framework of requirements for patrolling, reactive, proactive and intelligence staff. Obviously it is useful to have a common structure with regard to working practices so as to ensure that a specific standard of investigative practice and intelligence gathering is undertaken; that is, as long as, at the same time, there is some flexibility built into the system to allow for the fluidity and vagaries of criminal investigations. However, it should be noted that this structure also frames the forensic work undertaken as part of the investigation process. Figure 6.4 has been reconstructed from *The National Intelligence Model* (NCIS, 2000) report and provides a visual overview of the core themes within NIM (ibid.:9).

This early conceptualisation of NIM, produced in 2000, was then introduced in the National Policing Plan 2003–06, and required 'all 43 police forces in England and Wales to adopt the NIM and be compliant with its procedures by April 2004' (John and Magure, 2007:210). The owner of the 'business' at each level is the Tasking and Co-ordinating Group (TCG) which, at the Basic Command Unit (BCU) level, comprises a superintendent chair, inspectors and other non-police business owners such as local authorities (NCIS, 2000; ACPO Centrex, 2005; John and Magure, 2007). As Figure 6.4 illustrates, the overarching policing aim

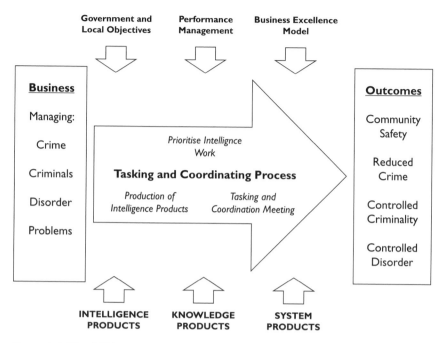

Figure 6.4 The NIM process

is the structured move from identified business objectives to tangible outcomes that can be measured. The achievement of the aims is through the development of four key intelligence products: strategic assessments, tactical assessments, target profiles and problem profiles (John and Magure, 2007:212). Strategic assessments set the long-term goals at each level, usually at six-monthly or yearly intervals, and these assessments are usually empirically based upon intelligence-led products such as crime analysis tools and techniques (see Chapter 8). Since the introduction of the Crime and Disorder Act 1998 and the Criminal Justice and Court Services Act 2000, local 'responsible authorities' have had a statutory requirement placed on them to produce multi-agency strategies regarding local crime and disorder priorities (Williams, 2004; Nash and Williams, 2008:108–119). As each force area has to contend with its own human and structural ecology (Park *et al.*, [1925]1967), this will usually produce different crime and disorder problems, which will result in different uses of forensics techniques.

NIM consists of 11 individual elements and these are discussed in detail in ACPO's (2005) main policy document, *Guidance on the National Intelligence Model*, and are summarised in Table 6.3. Each section of this document focuses on a single element of the NIM business process, and each element has a set of minimum standards associated with it, with a checklist provided at the end of each section. Forces must take appropriate action to ensure that they comply with all 135 standards within a given time frame.

Table 6.3 NIM minimum standards

Standard	Description	Examples
Element 1: Knowledge Assets	Knowledge assets are products that deal with the knowledge used by the organisation in its day-to-day running at all levels of NIM. All police staff must have access to and knowledge of these assets. The acquisition, maintenance and delivery of knowledge assets and training materials must be continually reviewed by the police service.	Current legislation and case law; codes of practice; manuals of standards and ACPO[1] guidance; force policies; briefing products.
Element 2: System Assets	System assets are the infrastructure that supports NIM. They provide the necessary systems and facilities for the secure capture, recording, reception, storage, linkage, analysis and use of information generated through policing activities. The police service must ensure their personnel has access to these systems using the 'need to know' principle.[2]	Physical security; security policies; sterile corridor; authorities management; effective briefing and debriefing; information exchange protocols.
Element 3: Source Assets	Source assets are the lifeblood of both investigative and intelligence systems. They can be any source of information that enable the efficient working of policing objectives at all levels of NIM.	Victims and witnesses; communities and members of the public; Crimestoppers; prisoners; forensic information; undercover operatives; surveillance product; and CHIS.[3]
Element 4: People Assets	Relates to all the staff of the organisation and how their roles and responsibilities contribute to the overall intelligence function. Each force and BCU relies on its human resources, so emphasis is on identifying roles, competencies and development that ensures a 'professional and efficient service delivery' (pg. 38).	Identification of key roles: e.g. heads of profession, intelligence manager; telecommunications SPOC[4]; source handler. Also, functions of intelligence such as: intelligence collection; support functions; tasking and co-ordination groups.
Element 5: Information Sources	Intelligence is built upon access to data obtained from a diverse range of sources. The right information management policies and procedures should be in place to ensure that the 'appropriate information is recorded and developed as intelligence' (pg. 46). This intelligence is then used in decision-making and risk management policies through the tasking and co-ordination process.	Information enters the police in three ways: (i) tasked collection; (ii) routine collection; (iii) volunteered information. Different types of information such as open and closed source data; crime, custody and command control records; and databases such as HOLMES/SCAS/NCF for profiling data.

Element 6: Intelligence, Information Recording	A requirement that accurate and relevant information is routinely and uniformly recorded onto standardised IT systems. NIM sets the requisite recording and evaluation processes that assesses the strength and validity of intelligence; it does so using skills, people and information technologies which results in further research and analysis. Four themes are relevant here: collecting and recording information; evaluating information and its authorisation as intelligence; accessing and disseminating intelligence; retaining or deleting information.	The use of the 5 x 5 x 5 evaluation method; use of intelligence codes and flags; information management and supervision codes; sanitisation and risk assessment protocols; data protection compliance; common data input standards; prioritisation of data input and research.
Element 7: Research, Development and Analysis	Where NIM recognises that intelligence is no good unless it is actionable. Sets out how research, professional development and skilled analysis create quality intelligence products. Sets out what is required for research, development and analysis, through intelligence unit structures, and the minimum standards for research and development.	Analytical options such as: crime pattern analysis; demographic and social trend analysis; network analysis; market profiles; criminal business profiles; risk analysis. Minimum standards include: access to technical support/surveillance equipment; standards for delivery of products; information exchange protocols; intelligence specialists and researchers trained to national standards.
Element 8: Intelligence Products	NIM uses four intelligence products that provide information on which strategic and tactical decisions are made. The Tasking and Co-ordination Group (T&CG) use intelligence products to make decisions and approve actions. This element deals with force policy dictating corporate standards, timing and circulation and business plans relating to intelligence products.	Four intelligence products are: strategic assessments; tactical assessments; target profiles; problem profiles.
Element 9: Strategic and Tactical Tasking and Co-ordination	Provides managers with a 'decision-making mechanism with which to manage their business strategically and tactically' (pg. 76). Enables the prioritisation of the deployment of resources based upon a thorough analysis of intelligence products. Establishes priorities for prevention, intelligence and enforcement around four key areas of: priority locations; subjects; crime/incident series; and high-risk issues.	T&CG policy; consistency in T&CG meetings throughout the force; engagement of stakeholders in strategic T&CG process; strategic and tactical assessment; daily management meeting with BCU.

(Continued)

Table 6.3 (Continued)

Standard	Description	Examples
Element 10: Tactical Resolution	T&CG manage and control the tactical resolution of identified crime and disorder problems. Access to a number of tactical options required; meaning that the nominated 'problem owner' must use these options to create a plan to resolve the problem' (pg. 86). Centres around three tactical options: prevention; intelligence; enforcement.	Various tactical options include: prevention (CCTV, neighbourhood watch); intelligence (surveillance, CHIS); enforcement (offender/ locality targeting, positive prosecutions policy). Also considers: investigative capability; tactical capability; tactical plans; and trigger plans.
Element 11: Intelligence, Operational Review	This standard ensures that lessons are learned and retained in the organisational memory. Allows performance issues to be measured. Operational reviews are commissioned by the T&CG, and these must establish what intelligence was required and if any new gaps have emerged.	Components of operational review include: debriefing records; authority review; impact assessments; audit trail; operational intelligence assessment; results analysis.

Note:
[1] Association of Chief Police Officers.
[2] The 'need to know' principle is defined as 'a security principle which states that the dissemination of classified information should be no wider than is required for the efficient conduct of business, and should be restricted to those who have authorised access' (ACPO Centrex, 2005:22).
[3] CHIS are Covert Human Intelligence Sources (ACPO Centrex, 2005:35).
[4] Single point of contact

NIM sets out a structured framework for the strategic and tactical operations of the police and other relevant stakeholders. It is a framework that sets out a *'business model* for policing, applying business process models to the world of policing' (Savage, 2007:117 – original emphasis). It also acts as a *national standards framework*, which has 'become very much part of the scenery of the performance culture within British policing' (ibid.:117–118). This culture has been increasing in scope and depth during the period Morris (2007:31–36) calls the *central initiative and control* period (1981 to present): a period in which the professionalisation of policing has gained a central role in how the police practice and manage policing in the twenty-first century.

Professionalising the investigative process

So far in this chapter, I have spent a great deal of time outlining the definitions and structures of contemporary policing in the UK. The reason for doing so is because the application of scientific ideas and techniques for forensic purposes operates within these structures. These techniques are, therefore, largely determined by such structures. The various definitions of criminal investigations point towards the idea that a criminal investigation is a sequential process with a number of different stages that investigators travel through on the way to a resolution. Despite the fact that each offence is unique, and each crime type has different components requiring different investigative and forensic techniques, most criminal investigations go through a standard set of procedures. For a simplistic model, O'Hara and O'Hara (2003:13) note how criminal investigations consist of three phases: (i) the suspect is identified; (ii) they are traced and located; (iii) facts are gathered to prove the suspect's guilt and these are presented in court. These stages are not mutually exclusive and are often fused during a process that is often very dynamic, fluid and constantly changing as new evidence comes in and further lines of investigative inquiry are taken. Investigative processes exist largely due to the *professionalising of police practice* (Rogers, 2007; Savage, 2007; Stelfox, 2007), which has developed incrementally over the last 20 years or so. However, these developments have not taken place in a vacuum, as there have been a number of drivers for change that have impacted directly on investigative practice.

Drivers for change

There are usually three core reasons why criminal investigations have come to be seen as an activity that needs professional development (Stelfox, 2007:630):

1   legal framework changes;
2   technological and procedural changes; and
3   miscarriages of justice and concerns of police effectiveness and conduct.

What should be highlighted is that none of these factors occurs in isolation; they are linked together in a complex symbiotic relationship. For example, a new technological development in a specific investigative technique will not only produce a procedural change, but it may also be necessary to alter the law so the new technique is admissible in court. Indeed, as will be shown in Chapter 11, the courtroom is the place where many scientific techniques demonstrate their forensic worth (Huber, 1991; Jasanoff, 1997; Golan, 2007). Another example of the link between these drivers is that many changes in the legal framework for criminal investigations were brought about after a number of miscarriages of justice and 'system failures' (Savage, 2007:23–43; Nash and Williams, 2008:158–177, 242–244). Savage argues that miscarriages of justice often destroy the legitimacy of agencies to 'deliver fair, transparent and accountable justice'; yet they can also produce 'reform which strengthens the right of citizens, and improves the accountability of those charged with administering justice' (2007:23). For example, the Maxwell Confait case in April 1972, in which three teenage boys were convicted of a mix of arson, manslaughter and murder on the basis of confession evidence (Newburn, 2003; Matassa and Newburn, 2007; Savage, 2007), was one of many cases of miscarriages of justice in which confession evidence through dubious interrogation techniques was discredited, specifically the Reid Technique developed in America (Gudjonsson, 2002). Two of the suspects in this case, Colin Lattimore and Ronald Leighton, both pleaded not guilty to murder, claiming that their written confessions were 'made under duress' (Savage, 2007:23; see Price and Caplan, 1977 for an in-depth overview of the case). Leighton was convicted of murder and Lattimore of manslaughter, and both appealed against their convictions. At the time of the criminal investigation, Leighton was 16 years old with a history of disobedience and aggressive and violent behaviour (Fisher, 1977:47). Whilst he was at Knotley House Approved School, 'intelligence testing resulted in the following scores: verbal scale 80, performance scale 86, full scale IQ 81 . . . limited intelligence and with a reading age of 9 years and 6 months' (ibid.:47). Lattimore, was 18½ in April 1972, and testing 'showed that his IQ was 66 and he was assessed as subnormal in terms of the Mental Health Act 1959' (ibid.:49). In 1974, their case was referred to the Court of Appeal, which quashed the convictions on the basis of: (i) expert evidence provided by the pathologist, which put the time of death approximately two hours before the fire and which provided an alibi for Lattimore; and (ii) a critical attack on the confessions, which highlighted poor interviewing practices by the police, especially in relation to processes involved in the interviewing of what are regarded today as vulnerable witnesses (Savage, 2007:24). Indeed it was the reliance on the confession in the Confait case that led to the Fisher Inquiry, ordered by the then Home Secretary Roy Jenkins, which investigated 'the circumstances leading to the trial' (Fisher, 1977:3). Conducted by Sir Henry Fisher, a high court judge, the inquiry identified the following problems (ibid.:19):[8]

> The Confait case has shown that it is possible to [sic]:
>
> (a) for a prosecution to proceed through all stages up to the start of the trial based on a time of death outside the brackets given by medical witnesses, without any attempt to clarify the medical evidence or to discover whether it was consistent with the case to be presented;
>
> (b) for a prosecution based wholly (or almost wholly) on uncorroborated confessions to proceed to trial without proper steps having been taken to seek evidence to support or contradict the evidence of the confessions;
>
> (c) that, although in a prosecution such as that of three boys there are five occasions when a dispassionate evaluation and analysis of the case could take place . . . there can be no assurance that those occasions will be used so as to lay bare discrepancies and weaknesses in the prosecution case;
>
> (d) for the pathologist to be given no opportunity to see other evidence relevant to time of death and reconsider his own estimate in the light of it.

Whilst there are many interesting facets to this case, the most relevant point to note is how the key recommendations made by Fisher concentrated on processes, procedures and rules surrounding the collection of witness evidence, as well as identifying areas where protection for persons interrogated could be improved, including: rights to communicate with a solicitor (sections 2.19–2.23, Fisher, 1977:14–16); the introduction of tape recording of interviews (section 2.24, Fisher, 1977:16); and amendments to judges' rules and administrative directions (section 2.25, Fisher, 1977:16–17). These recommendations then set the agenda for the *Royal Commission on Criminal Procedure*, known as the *Phillips Commission* (1981), and also led to the creation of the Police and Criminal Evidence Act 1984; perhaps one of the most important acts ever to have had an impact on policing and evidence collection in the UK.

A second major case to have dramatically changed the way the police investigate crime was that of the *Yorkshire Ripper*, Peter Sutcliffe, who was convicted of murdering 13 women between 1975 and 1980, as well as attacking at least 7 others. The police investigation into the murders involved a number of mistakes and problems, especially pertaining to information sharing and intelligence gathering. These problems resulted in missed opportunities to capture Sutcliffe, who was questioned by police but was released and went on to kill again. In May 1981, the then Home Secretary William Whitelaw ordered an inquiry into the police investigation of the Ripper case, which was conducted by Lawrence Byford who was Her Majesty's Inspector of Constabulary (Byford, 1981:5). The subsequent Byford Report had far reaching implications for policing, having uncovered numerous limitations and mistakes (see Table 6.4).

Table 6.4 Limitations of the Ripper investigation

Limitations	Overview
The Major Incident Room (Byford, 1981:144)	• Many of the limitations stemmed from the major incident room (MIR); • Problems with varying MIRs across the 43 police forces; • MIR reliance on manual card indexes but Sutcliffe was never regarded as a '"suspect" under the 'D'62 index system' as he was eliminated because of the 'Sunderland' letters and tape; • PNC[1] did not have facility for searching criminal names; • MIR operated under an inherently rigid system that was not able to adapt to the fluid and dynamic nature of a complex investigation; • MIR was persistently overwhelmed by workloads and information and staffing levels were not reviewed.
The Cross-Area Sighting Inquiry (Byford, 1981:144–145)	• As the victims were prostitutes, an assumption was made that the murderer was a client of the prostitutes. Police started to record vehicle registration numbers in red-light districts (the so-called 'punters index'); • Cross-area sightings (vehicles seen in red-light districts in two cities) and triple sightings (vehicles seen in three cities) produced 20,000 cross-area and 1,200 triple area sightings; • Sutcliffe was interviewed as his vehicle was logged in the cross and triple sighting samples. However, the interviewers were inadequately briefed due to 'poor index searching and the failure to locate previous papers within the MIR'; • MIR procedures were complex, there were problems with data handling and staff were incompetent, both of which increased the 'error rate'; • Sutcliffe should have been regarded as a prime suspect.
Tyre Marks and Vehicle Inquiry (Byford, 1981:145–146)	• Tyre marks were found at the scene and tread patterns were cast in an attempt to identify vehicles; • List yielded 53,000 and, by 1977, 20,000 vehicles remained to be examined, including Sutcliffe's; • Sutcliffe was interviewed on 2nd and 8th November 1977 and, had the wheels and tyres of his red Ford Corsair been closely examined, he would have been regarded as a suspect.
Description of Suspects, Photofits and Other Assaults (Byford, 1981:146)	• Internal review set up in 1978 to examine all reported attacks on women, but the criteria applied were too narrow 'so that a number of assaults with good descriptions or photofit pictures of suspects were not included'; • Senior detectives should have assembled photofit impressions from surviving victims as this would have identified the assailant as having dark hair and beard and without a Geordie accent (therefore not linked to the hoax phone call).

The Letters and Tape Inquiry (Byford, 1981:147)	• Between March 1978 and June 1979 the police received two anonymous letters and a tape recording from a native of Sunderland claiming he was the 'Ripper'. Major resources were allocated to tracing the author, wasting valuable time and resources; • Complete acceptance that the author was the killer was not justified by the evidence; • Public response and publicity given to these letters overwhelmed the MIR and its staff.
Police Interviews (Byford, 1981:147–149)	• Sutcliffe was interviewed by the police on 12 occasions; • There were a number of missed opportunities to challenge Sutcliffe, including incompetent interview techniques, failing to cross-reference information, or even check details; • Officers missed the opportunity to closely check Sutcliffe's tyre treads.
Media Relations (Byford, 1981:150)	• A civilian press officer was appointed to liaise with the press; • Poor media relations with the police as many media bypassed the press officer; • Media made spurious calls to the police to test the 'promptness of response' and 'outdated pictures were resurrected and republished as current information'.
Lack of Computerisation of Records (Byford, 1981:150–151)	• Increased use of computers would have improved storage and retrieval capabilities; • Two main problems with the MIR – (i) back record conversion; (ii) lack of computer technology; • A police officer with computer knowledge should have been appointed to the Ripper investigation; • The 'punters index' should have been more sophisticated.
Command Control and Resources (Byford, 1981:151–152)	• Senior detectives were not well equipped 'in management terms to control an inquiry of that size and scale'; • Lack of flexibility to resolve 'system failures'; • Poor delegation of authority which led to the 'overburdening of senior officers with mundane matters'; • Failure to adequately plan and assess the impact of new lines of inquiry.

Note:
[1] Police National Computer

Byford's inquiry had far-reaching implications for the management of criminal investigations and the use of intelligence in major inquiries. Unfortunately, his findings did not paint a flattering picture of UK policing, so William Whitelaw 'refused to publish Byford's penetrating report which stripped bare all the mistakes that were made' (Bilton, 2012:xxx). Instead, Whitelaw allowed for a brief four-page summary to be 'placed in the House of Commons library' and 'such was the confidentiality surrounding the report that it was printed privately outside London and not by Her Majesty's Stationery Office' (ibid.:xxx). Whitelaw classified the report as top secret, and so it remained for 17 years! Despite the attempts to bury the report, the first computerised incident room arrived in 1986, implementing many of Byford's recommendations, especially around the issues of data handling and management. Called HOLMES (Home Office Large Major Enquiry System), the new system gave the police the ability to store and process the huge amount of data that is inevitably created during a major inquiry: 'statements, messages and actions could be fed in and later printed out as documents when required by the Crown Prosecution Service' (ibid.:539–541). Bilton outlined the core benefits of HOLMES:

> HOLMES saved hugely on manpower costs when serious crimes became complex. Information stored on the computer could be searched with a high degree of subtlety; managers were better able to control resources during a major investigation. Data could be cross-indexed and the computer asked to isolate specific information or draw comparisons.
>
> (Ibid.:540)

Bilton (2012:540–541) also highlights the fact that, if an operational computer had been used, 'Sutcliffe would have been arrested in 1977 and subjected to rigorous questioning at a police station' (ibid.:541). In 2001, HOLMES2 became fully accredited by the Police IT Organisation (PITO) and operational in all forces across the UK. HOLMES2 was designed to provide the following (UNISYS, 2007:2):

- one system for major investigations and major disasters;
- one system to be used by all police forces and policing organisations throughout the UK;
- the ability to link systems together within different police forces in a real-time secure environment; this would assist in investigations which are across county boundaries and allow the provision of mutual aid to a force in a major disaster situation.

HOLMES2 became very successful, and has been used in some high-profile cases such as the 7/7 bombings in London. It has also been used in non-criminal cases such as the South Asian Tsunami in 2004. More recently, it was announced that the police were developing an upgrade to HOLMES2;

however, HOLMES 2020 was scrapped under the coalition governments funding cuts.[9]

Other cases/incidents that impacted upon the way policing operates in the UK include: the *Brixton Riots* (1981) and the subsequent *Scarman Report* (1982) into widespread disorder after a 'flashpoint' (Waddington *et al.*, 1989) occurred in which a stabbing took place of black youth Michael Bailey, with inaction by the police in terms of providing urgent medical attention; and the murder of *Stephen Lawrence* (1993) by racist thugs and the subsequent *Macpherson Inquiry* (1999) into the failure to act by the police through a botched criminal investigation, which led to a miscarriage of justice that, 19 years on, has only been partly resolved (Chakraborti and Garland, 2009; Chakraborti, 2010). What these and many other cases like them have in common is that a criminal case goes bad, becomes highly visible and results in a public inquiry that recommends major changes to strategic and operational protocols, as well as legal frameworks, which is often complemented by technological developments.

Since the introduction of Peel's Bobbies in 1829, policing in the UK has been governed by a plethora of legislation that determines the strategic, tactical and resource structures of the police. The law also determines the nature and structure of the investigative process and frames what the police are allowed to do. I have already discussed some of this legislation; for example, CIPA 1996, which provided a 'legal definition of criminal investigation and the role of the investigator' (Stelfox, 2009:34). It is not possible here to cover *all* the legislation and its full impact on policing for, as Table 6.5 demonstrates, the *key* legislation is numerous and rather complex.

Table 6.5 Police governance legislation

• 1792 Middlesex Justices Act	• 1996 Police Act
• 1824 Vagrancy Act	• 1996 Criminal Procedure and Investigations Act
• 1826 Oldham Police Act	• 1997 Police Act
• 1829 Metropolitan Police Act	• 1998 Crime and Disorder Act
• 1833 Lighting and Watching Act	• 1998 Human Rights Act
• 1835 Municipal Corporations Act	• 1999 Local Government Act
• 1839 County Police Act	• 2000 Regulation of Investigatory Powers Act
• 1839 Rural Constabulary Act	• 2000 Terrorism Act
• 1856 County and Borough Act	• 2001 Criminal Justice and Police Act
• 1936 Public Order Act	• 2002 Police Reform Act
• 1964 Police Act	• 2003 Criminal Justice Act
• 1984 Police and Criminal Evidence Act	• 2005 Serious Organised Crime Agency Act
• 1985 Prosecution of Offences Act	• 2006 Police and Justice Act
• 1994 Criminal Justice and Public Order Act	• 2011 Police Reform and Social Responsibility Act
• 1994 Police and Magistrates' Courts Act	

As briefly mentioned above, the Police and Criminal Evidence Act 1984 has had the most important influence on policing in the UK. It defined police powers (e.g. Part I, sections 1–6, powers to stop and search); laid down investigative procedures (Part II, sections 8–23, powers of entry, search and seizure); and defined suspects and others' rights (Part II, sections 24–33, powers of arrest; Part IV, sections 34–52, detention protocols; Part V, sections 53–65, questioning and treatment of persons by the police). The Prosecution of Offences Act 1985 established the Crown Prosecution Service (CPS), which took over the responsibility of prosecuting offenders from the police (ibid.:34). Another major piece of legislation is the Regulation of Investigatory Powers Act 2000, which is an Act:

> To make provision for and about the interception of communications, the acquisition and disclosure of data relating to communications, the carrying out of surveillance, the use of covert human intelligence sources and the acquisition of the means by which electronic data protected by encryption or passwords may be decrypted or accessed.[10]

Whilst many of these Acts set out legal rules and regulations for investigative conduct, others dealt with professionalising the police themselves.

PIP

Part II of the Police Act 1996 set the tone for the advanced professional development of the police. Section 39, for example, created the notion of *codes of practice*, whereby the Secretary of State could issue codes of practice relating to the discharge by police authorities of any of their functions. Section 2 of the Police Reform Act 2002 amended the 1996 provision by inserting Section 39A outlining that the codes of practice for chief officers may include components for 'promoting the efficiency and effectiveness of police forces'. The 2002 Act also introduced a *National Policing Plan*, which set 'out the government's strategic priorities for the police service' (Davies *et al.*, 2005:152). Another important area covered by the 2002 Act related to the regulation of procedures and practices. Section 7 stipulates that the Secretary of State, in conjunction with the Chief Inspector of Constabulary and the Central Police Training and Development Authority, may develop provisions whereby all police forces in England and Wales adopt particular procedures or practices (s7(1)a). Leading on from this in September 2005, ACPO, working with the National Centre for Policing Excellence (later subsumed under NPIA) and the Police Skills and Standards Organisation (now known as Skills for Justice) launched a national training and development programme entitled Professionalising Criminal Investigation Programme (PIP). According to the NPIA website:

> PIP is aimed at police officers and staff whose role involves them conducting or managing investigations, conducting interviews with victims and

witnesses, and interviewing suspects. The development and maintenance of investigative skills is at the heart of the programme.[11]

PIP, therefore, is a framework that trains and develops investigators in the professional practice of criminal investigation. Professional practice, as outlined by Flynn (1999: 34, cited in Stelfox, 2007:628), includes the forming of occupational competency standards, which are specialised knowledge and practices that professionals use to claim autonomy and ownership over specific problems (also see Cohen, 1985; Abbott, 1988). Stelfox (2007:628–630) and Morris (2007) both note how professional practice has been slow to develop within the police and this has been explained by the fact that investigative knowledge and practice has historically been located within the dialectic of *craft skills* (Innes, 2003:9–12; Stelfox, 2007:628); where investigative skills are developed 'on the job' and the most valuable skills 'were held to be those developed through natural instinct and experience' (Innes, 2003:9). The problems associated with this approach were threefold: (i) they were subject to local and individual variation; (ii) they could often result in corrupt practices due to 'light regulation'; and (iii) they were only viable when criminal investigations involved 'low levels of technical and procedural competence' (Stelfox, 2007:628). The craft skills dialectic echoes an earlier study by Hobbs (1989:183–217) who noted the importance of the 'entrepreneurial' qualities of detectives that were created through a fusion of police organisational-cultural artefacts that operated within the broader working-class community of East London, where officers had to pit their entrepreneurial wits against local villains.

PIP was seen as an attempt to move beyond this simple *craft model* of criminal investigations (Innes, 2003; Stelfox, 2007; Reiner, 2010). Whilst it sees local experience and knowledge (craft skills) as being necessary, PIP also recognises the importance of fusing these with an empirically based, scientific-style rationality; what Innes called a *dialectical synthesis of art and science* (Innes, 2003:9). The science aspect has been translated into the development of a 'cradle-to-grave training curriculum for investigators' (Stelfox, 2007:641), providing them with the necessary technical and legal knowledge required for today's criminal investigations. The PIP structure identifies 'four levels of investigators and includes details of who should operate at each level and what types of crime are typically investigated at each level' (Rogers, 2007:155). Table 6.6 outlines the roles, levels and types of training available within the PIP framework (NCPE, 2005:12; Rogers, 2007:155; Stelfox, 2007:641, 2009:40).

As Table 6.6 illustrates, at all levels the PIP model invests in the notion of professionalising police practice through career development training of all the technical and legal aspects relevant to criminal investigations, including how they are conducted and managed. What is also important is that the links with forensic issues are intertwined with the issues of criminal investigations. For example, the SIODP course incorporates training on how to coordinate the gathering of material (information, intelligence and evidence) and the effective recording and retention

Table 6.6 The PIP levels of investigation

Investigative level	Example of role	Typical investigative activity	Courses[1]	Course summary
Level 1	Patrol Constable/ Police Staff/ Supervisors	Investigation of Volume Crime	Initial Police Learning and Development Programme (IPLDP) Sexual Offences – Specially Trained Officer Development Programme (STODP)	Basic training course for all police officers for PIP level 1 Training for initial responders to sexual offences and the interview of complainants
Level 2	Dedicated Investigator, e.g. CID officer	Substantive investigation into more serious and problem offences including road traffic deaths	Initial Crime Investigators Development Programme (ICIDP) Initial Management of Serious Crime Course (IMSC)	Basic training course for all police officers for PIP Level 2 Aimed at Level 2 investigators who conduct or manage serious and complex investigations
Specialist Investigative Roles	Child Protection, Family Liaison, Major Crime	Child Protection, Special Branch, Family Liaison, Force Intelligence Bureau	Detective Inspectors Development Programme (DIDP) Linked to Level 1, 2 and 3 courses – e.g. the Specialist Child Abuse Investigator Development Programme (SCAIDP)	Trains officers to conduct complex investigations Trains those involved in the investigation of child abuse
Level 3	Senior Investigating Officer (SIO)	Lead investigator in cases of murder, stranger rape, kidnap or crimes of complexity, Category A, B, C	Senior Investigating Officers Development Programme (SIODP)	Provides training for those officers leading homicide and major incident investigations

Note:
[1] These are only a select few of the courses available within the PIP framework. For a list of all courses please refer to http://www.college.police.uk/en/10093.htm.

of material for use in major crime investigations, which of course includes the management of forensic strategies and physical evidence.

Investigative doctrine

The current professional practice most closely associated with supporting PIP is the Core Investigative Doctrine, which provides 'national guidance on the key principles of criminal investigation' (Stelfox, 2007:635). Developed by the National Centre for Policing Excellence (later incorporated within the NPIA), the core investigative doctrine 'focuses on the knowledge, skills and under-standing that investigators need to be operationally competent' (ibid.:635). It also sets out operational parameters for the process of criminal investigations used by the UK police, as illustrated by Figure 6.6, taken from the document *Practice Advice on Core Investigative Doctrine* (NCPE, 2005:48).[12] This process is a Weberian 'ideal type' model of the criminal investigative process. Weber utilised the 'ideal type' as a key term in his methodological orientation towards Western positivist thought and followed his desire to give the social sciences the same 'matter-of-fact approach with which the natural sciences approached nature' (Gerth and Mills, 1993:59). The ideal type method is a useful way to construct closely related elements, or 'types' that hold an empirical reality, into a logically precise conception. Ideal types are very useful for analytical purposes, especially when cultural constellations, such as criminal investigations, are being compared (Gerth and Mills, 1993:59–60). The constructed scheme only serves the purpose of offering an ideal means of orientation that floats somewhere between extreme and 'pure types'. There are numerous examples where contemporary behavioural and social scientists use 'ideal types' as analytical frameworks for the study of various phenomena – the only difference is that we call them *typologies* or *taxonomies*. For instance, in sex offender research and treatment in the US, child molesters under the care of psychiatrists and psychologists[13] at the Massachusetts Treatment Centre have been classified into four 'types' (fixated, regressed, exploitative and aggressive), which are determined by the level of fixation and the amount and type of contact (Bartol and Bartol, 2008). Other typologies that have been developed as ideal types include those for rapists (Groth, 1979); serial killers (Holmes and DeBurger, 1988); and burglars (Canter and Youngs, 2009).

The above schema is useful for demonstrating a clear sequential flow between the subcategories of the components of criminal investigations, all framed within three action types – *activities, decisions* and *outcomes*. Investigations start with the instigation of an investigation, which is triggered by a crime occurring and it being detected. An initial investigation is undertaken, and that usually generates some evidence (e.g. witnesses or physical evidence) upon which an evaluation is undertaken and decisions are made. Broadly speaking, two decisions occur at this point – no further action is undertaken, or further investigation is required. The next activity is suspect management, which includes the gathering

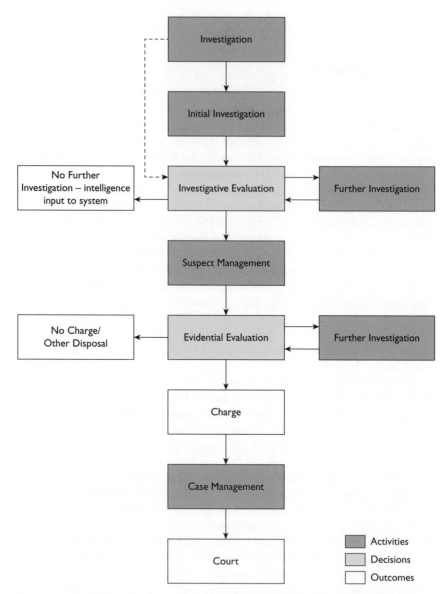

Figure 6.5 ACPO's Core Investigative Doctrine stages of criminal investigations

Reproduced from Authorised Professional Practice (APP) for Investigation with permission from the College of Policing Ltd.

and management of material in order to identify the suspect and interview strategies. Another evidential evaluation stage is undertaken where the same two decisions can be made (no charge or further investigation). If the police feel there is sufficient evidence then the suspect will be charged, which instigates the case management phase of the investigation, leading to the final stage, the court case. The stages identified in Figure 6.5 are obviously simplified and contain generic umbrella terms for each stage/process. Obviously, within each of these stages there are further complexities. The types of activities individual investigators engage in, the decisions they make and the outcomes that can be achieved will vary and depend on whether the investigation is reactive or proactive (NCPE, 2005:48). An investigative action is defined as 'any activity, which, if pursued, is likely to establish significant facts, preserve material or lead to the resolution of the investigation' (ibid.:77). There are generally two distinct types of investigative activity: the first is an array of actions that *trawl* for information; the second is a range of actions that are *specific lines* of enquiry. Both types of activities are common to criminal investigations, although trawling usually occurs at the beginning of the investigation, aiding the development of specific lines of enquiry at any given point throughout. Specific lines of enquiry differ from trawling 'because they are evidence specific and some information about the crime is needed in order to identify the most appropriate action' (ibid.:77). Advice provided by ACPO on developing investigative actions highlights that legal and ethical issues must be constantly considered. Investigators must also prioritise activities that are proportionate to 'the investigative response in accordance with force policies' (ibid.:77), which obviously creates the possibility of wide variation across the 43 police forces in England and Wales. Investigators do not usually use the terms actions or activities; instead, these notions are subsumed under the term *strategy*, where actions and activities create different types of investigative strategies:

- Scene strategy
- Forensic strategy
- Search strategy
- Victim and witness strategy
- Intelligence strategy

- Passive data generating strategy
- Trace/Interview/Eliminate strategy
- Communications strategy
- Covert policing strategy
- Suspect strategy

Scene strategy, for example, is crucial, as the management of the crime scene or scenes will impact heavily on the quality, quantity and integrity of the material gathered. The CSI effect (Podlas, 2006, 2009; Cavender and Deutsch, 2007; Smith *et al.*, 2007) has left an indelible impression that crime scene investigation and management is a specialised field involving highly trained experts (CSIs or SOCOs) using a number of scientific techniques to recover trace evidence. Whilst part of this image is true, 'much of what needs to be done in relation to crime scene examination can be done by any competent investigator' (Stelfox, 2009:126). Scene strategy will be discussed in greater detail in Chapter 9. Another example is the development of a victim and witness strategy. Victims and witnesses are often the cornerstone to any criminal investigation, especially when it comes to evidence presented in court (Rogers, 2007:162–164). The material provided by victims and witnesses often determines the success of an investigation, so investigators develop these strategies in order to increase the probability of success. In developing theses strategies, investigators should consider issues such as fast-tracking interviews, risk and witness assessments, witness support and the consideration of the witness as a scene (NCPE, 2005:84–92). The *Practice Advice on Core Investigative Doctrine* (ibid.) provides a full review of investigative strategies.

The core investigative doctrine can be linked to the broader intelligence-led developments within NIM, as outlined earlier in this chapter. James argues that 'in the modern era, the investigative environment has come to be dominated by 'doctrine' (2011:84). His extensive research into intelligence-led policing models also found that the proliferation of 'doctrine' overall 'has not been universally welcomed' (ibid.:28), with many claiming that policing 'doctrine' results in the increase of a bureaucratic matrix of complex rules, regulations and processes. For instance, in a letter to the Home Secretary Theresa May, Dr. Paul Knapman, the Westminster Coroner in charge of the inquest into the shooting of solicitor Mark Saunders by the police in May 2008, said 'the police red tape may have left them "unable to see the wood for the trees." He said that a "slavish adherence" to paperwork and guidelines risks was preventing officers applying "common sense" in life-and-death situations such as the siege in which Saunders died' (ibid.:28 and 247). A quick review of the numerous protocol and guidance manuals produced by ACPO confirms this: the *Core Investigative Doctrine*, for example, is 145 pages of guidance, processes and flow charts!

Regardless of the problems with the notion of a police 'doctrine', the core investigative doctrine does offer the investigator a useful sequential process that not only helps frame any type of criminal investigation but also provides guidance on how to develop appropriate investigative strategies. Overall, the purpose of developing these strategies is to identify what suitable lines of enquiry are to be taken, their overall objective and what is needed to achieve the set objective. Strategies are also action oriented in the sense that they result in the gathering of material which may lead to further lines of enquiry: they therefore determine the decisions that are made and the outcome of each line of enquiry.

Summary

This chapter examined some of the important developments in modern policing and outlined some definitional boundaries regarding the concepts of 'police' and 'policing'. It highlighted the fact that there is no clear consensus regarding what activities the police should undertake, although investigating criminal activity is often close to the top of the list. Understanding how criminal events are detected opens up numerous investigative pathways for identifying and collecting all kinds of evidence, which needs to be properly controlled and managed. The chapter then discussed the structural arrangements of UK policing; for example, examining the 'tripartite system' and how that operates within the 43 police forces in England and Wales. In recent years, the introduction of the National Intelligence Model has provided a structured process to the identification, analysis and prioritisation of localised crime and disorder problems, the outcomes of which are to enhance community safety, reduce crime and control criminality and disorder. The chapter then considered the means in which policing has become more professionalised over the last 30 years. It briefly outlined the important drivers for change that have had a major impact on the development of policing by examining changes to legal frameworks and some of the key case célèbres (the Yorkshire Ripper, Brixton Riots and Stephen Lawrence) that have dramatically altered the landscape of criminal investigations in the UK. Two of the most important developments have been the introduction of the PIP and Core Investigative Doctrine: the former to enhance police training within a structured framework of professional practice; the latter outlining a structured process for undertaking criminal investigations, through the introduction of the concept of 'strategies'. These investigative strategies create actions and activities that centre on identifying, collecting and analysing material that can be turned into evidence; some of which are used within a forensic setting and are examined in the next chapter.

Chapter 7

Information, material and evidence

Introduction

The structures and processes that were discussed in the previous chapter have been designed to provide some form of common framework to criminal investigations, regardless of the type of crime committed; although the work of Innes (2003) and Carson (2007) and many others illustrates the subtle differences between different criminal investigations. Furthermore, it was also noted that, whilst the structure and regulatory system of criminal investigations is quite rigid, it is flexible enough to allow for the numerous vagaries that could occur during the course of an investigation. Flexibility in investigative practice is crucial for another reason: the core task for those investigating a crime event is to find out what has happened and who the victims and offenders are. In order to do this, investigators reconstruct the crime by gathering bits of information, similar to putting together a 1,000-piece jigsaw puzzle. They try to figure out what has happened and get as close to the truth as they can; but, unfortunately, a *crime jigsaw puzzle* has numerous pieces missing from the box. The remaining pieces are scattered across different areas and need to be identified, collected and interpreted before a reconstructed narrative of the event or events is presented in court. This is all achieved through what Innes calls *information work* (Innes, 2003:113); and what links the police investigator, crime scene examiner, forensic scientist and legal agencies to these processes is information work. However, despite this link, each of these roles involves its own organisational cultural artefacts and processes; for instance, the investigator is usually a police officer, who operates within an organisational and regulatory framework (see Chapters 5 and 6), whilst the forensic scientist has a completely different perspective and set of practices (see Chapters 2, 3, 4 and 10). Regardless of any organisational differences, there has developed some common ground between the different individuals who are involved in the investigation of crime. This chapter is about that common purpose – the undertaking of information work.

Depending on the context in which it sits, the term *information* is interchangeable with data, evidence and material. From an academic/scientific perspective, data is the lifeblood of research and knowledge; criminological theories and knowledge are only as good as the data on which they are based, and it is best to choose a range of robust research methodologies with data and method triangulation (Denzin, 1971). For example, and as we have demonstrated elsewhere (Thompson and Williams, 2014), crucial evidential weaknesses in moral panic theory – perhaps one of the biggest *paradigms* in sociology and criminology over the last 40 years – ensures that moral panic *groupies* are chasing a myth. This chapter introduces the different types of information that are common to criminal investigations. It concentrates more on the physical aspects of forensic evidence for three obvious reasons: first, this text is about *forensic* criminology; second, information such as witness statements and victim/suspect interviews, whilst mentioned briefly here, have been subject to extensive research and writing, so there is little need to cover these subjects in too much detail (see Milne and Bull, 1999; Gudjonsson, 2002, 2007; Milne, *et al.*, 2007); and, finally, it is not possible to cover every pertinent subject in any meaningful depth in this introductory text, so I have chosen to concentrate mainly on physical evidence. Chapter 8 incorporates a broader range of intelligence information through the discussion of crime analysis.

Fundamentally, data, evidence, material or information, whatever concept you wish to use or abuse, is always at the centre of forensic criminology. This chapter starts by outlining some of the structural developments that have taken place in the twentieth and twenty-first centuries and which have made it possible for the collection of information and material to take place. It then examines some of the key concepts, ideas and debates that are important for understanding the forensic links to information, material and evidence, including: case construction and the different forms and types of information and evidence that exist. Following from this, a more detailed look at the current use and importance of trace evidence is discussed, which also introduces the importance of factors that affect the type of material that is collected. In particular, I examine the concepts of transference and persistence, also including an examination of evidence dynamics, which can change physical material. Finally, this chapter links trace evidence types with classifications of evidence.

Drivers for bureaucratic change

Before looking at information work, I start with a brief exploration of the history of why science and scientific detection methods have become so integrated within the police. This will provide context to the sociological analysis of the influences and drivers that fought against a very deeply ingrained ideology within the police that believed forensic science was not required and created the 'unnecessary expert' (Ambage, 1987:182). From the 1930s onwards, this widely held organisational ideology slowly began to be eroded by a few administrative 'rule creators' (Becker, 1963) who saw the benefit in creating not only a full training programme for detectives but also forensic sciences services to aid the detection and investigative activities of the police.

Structural conduciveness

The interwar period saw a broad range of planning and organisational activities undertaken by a wide range of government departments. This growth in bureaucratic governmental departments was a continuation of the enhancement of nineteenth-century government, embedded within the Passenger Acts which, MacDonagh argues, enabled the government to grow 'imperceptibly, naturally and with little premeditation' (1958, cited in Ambage, 1987:15). This process operated as follows:

> Executive officers began to undertake more systematic and truly statistical and experimental investigations. They strove to keep in touch with the inventions, new techniques and foreign practices relevant to their field. Later, they even called directly upon medicine and engineering, and the infant professions of research chemistry and biology, to find answers to intractable difficulties in composing and enforcing particular preventive measures; and once, say, ventilation mechanism . . . or the presence of arsenic in certain foods or drinks, had been clearly proved, the corresponding regulations passed effortlessly into law and, unperceived, the ripples of government circled ever wider.
>
> (MacDonagh, 1958:61, cited in Ambage, 1987:15)

Nineteenth-century governmental growth through increased regulations and their enforcement, mixed with application and planning activities in the interwar period, provided the structural conduciveness necessary for the creation of the Forensic Science Service and their integration with criminal investigations. The advent of the Second World War initially slowed this process down but, after its conclusion, provided new impetus for growth and development. Decimated by the Nazi bombing of many cities, with the British economy on the brink of collapse and the vast reduction in the workforce due to the death of so many soldiers, Britain undertook the huge task of rebuilding the country (Osgerby, 1998). Many of the UK's allied countries were in a similar position with the need to rebuild both the economy and their populations; and this was achieved in a number of ways that are sociologically relevant to forensic criminology. One of the first responses was to relax immigration laws, allowing more immigrants into the country, which occurred in both the UK and USA (ibid.:18). For instance, in Britain, estimated net immigration from the New Commonwealth increased from 2,000 to 94,900 between the years 1953 and 1962, with a peak of 136,400 entering the UK in 1961 (ibid.:118). Most of this new labour moved into big metropolitan cities such as London, Bristol, Birmingham and Manchester. An interesting observation that has been made over the years is that with the influxes of immigration, a strengthening of the social control mechanisms also occurs, as if there were some sort of organic relation between immigration and crime (Pryce, 1986). Stealth racist social control policies have existed since humans began paying attention to their *otherness*, so it should come as no surprise that the expansion of the penal dragnet, the formation of centralised regulatory framework for criminal investigations, also helped to drive the more systematic integration of forensic science with investigative practice.

At the same time these social and political changes were taking place, crime was also moving up the political policy hierarchy. After the Second World War the police service was reinforced and expanded greatly. In 1962, there were less than 85,000 police officers but, by the late 1970s, the number of police officers had increased to approximately 110,000; and, as of 31st March 2012, this number had increased to 134,101 full-time equivalent police officers in the 43 police forces in England and Wales (see Figure 7.1, from Berman, 2012).

As the numbers of police officers increased, so too did the number of crimes. Official police recorded crimes show a distinct pattern from the end of Second World War onwards, with a steady and sometimes dramatic increase in the number of crimes. Maguire (1997:159) notes how, since their inception in 1876, official crime figures remained relatively unchanged until the 1940s, but show a:

> sharp and sustained increase from the middle of the 1950s onwards. This saw a doubling of the figures within ten years (from roughly half a million crimes in 1955 to a million in 1964), another doubling over the next ten years, and yet another by 1990.

There are, of course, a number of reasons behind this quite dramatic change. Changes in technology, for instance, will often fuel changes to crime rates. As electricity became commonly available from the 1930s onwards, more and more technological advances became possible which, when turned into business opportunities, created the *need* for consumable household goods. From the late 1960s, consumables such as TVs, washing machines, cookers and vacuum cleaners also started to become more affordable and popular. Alongside these developments, there was also the increase in the availability and use of cars as technology advanced and costs were driven down, mainly due to the scientific management principles of Fordism (Shiomi and Wada, 1995). This was also the period where advances in music technology meant the creation of one of the constants in the cultural artefacts of youth. The first 7" single was introduced in 1952, and it soon became embedded within the culture of the younger generation, often a sign of rebellious teen angst (Osgerby, 1998:38). Record and cassette players soon became available – another must-have consumable for many households that could afford it. In short, with the increase in availability and cheaper cost of such consumables, more and more households began to own these items.

It is relatively easy to see the links between these developments and their influence on criminology, rising crime rates and forensic investigations. With increasing numbers of manufacturers using new technological developments in the manufacturing process, more goods and cheaper prices meant more items in

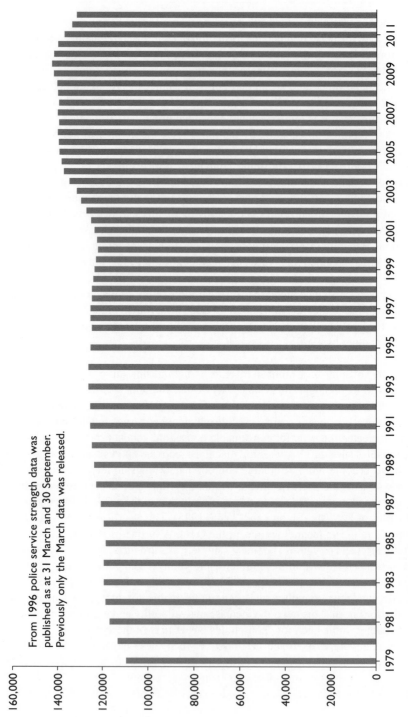

From 1996 police service strength data was
published as at 31 March and 30 September.
Previously only the March data was released.

160,000
140,000
120,000
100,000
80,000
60,000
40,000
20,000
0

1979   1981   1983   1985   1987   1989   1991   1993   1995   1997   1999   2001   2003   2005   2007   2009   2011

Figure 7.1 Police strength 1979–2012[1]

the home and in society in general. Many manufacturers began to keep records of the materials that went into their products and these materials were taken from the available resources of the planet. More material available to the public meant more potential areas of contact, exchange and transfer of material between victims, offenders and locations. If we then factor in the sociological fact that as societies develop they tend to move from mechanical to organic solidarity (Durkheim, 1982:97), which produces a more complex bureaucratic system that includes the need to develop a more complex system of rules and regulations, or laws, the result is both the increase in legal categories of crime and an increase in the need for someone to police them; a functionalist offshoot of Becker's concepts of *rule creators* and *rule enforcers* (1963:147–163). It is obvious that this will impact upon the crime rate: more legal categories of crime means more *crime* out there, and more police means more *crimes* will be detected; therefore more crimes recorded. As a society, we should not always be afraid of rising crime statistics, as that is often an indicator of a *more effective* justice system.

Centralisation and the development of the modern forensic scientist

There are two primary reasons why the identification of microscopic material and the information contained within such material became the core business of forensic science: *structural changes* taking place from central government, and the advent of the *forensic scientist*. The economic, business and social expansion from the late 1940s until the early 1960s stimulated growth and development in science. The most obvious forensic *discovery* of this age was, of course, the discovery by Crick and Watson of the double-helix DNA structure in 1953 (Watson and Crick, 1953); although the implications and relevance of this to forensic criminology and criminal investigations would not be realised for another 32 years. Other major advancements in gas and liquid chromatography methods also strengthened the position of science during the same period, brought on, largely because of the developments in the tools and machines used to undertake such analyses. Scientific and technological inventions and developments, therefore, 'are fusions of an intellectual past with a socioeconomic, functional future' (Basalla, 1999:113); and is not only that such inventions are shaped to satisfy 'some human want or need' (Schmookler, 1966, cited in Basalla, 1999:113).

This potent mix of economic, social, political and technological development saw the move towards central leadership in the area of criminal investigations and its use of scientific analysis (Morris, 2007:27–31). A review of some of the structural developments after the Second World War illustrates how they fuelled the rapid expansion of the role of science in criminal investigations, marking the beginnings of what we today call forensic science. If we take a snapshot look within the period Morris called *central leadership* (1933–1980) (ibid.:27–31), we find a broad range of developmental activities within science and detective work and a more general reorganisation of the police that brought about the structural conditions for the establishment of forensic science within the area of police investigations. Table 7.1 outlines some of these developments, although this list is not exhaustive.

There are many influential figures that have played a role in developing modern forensic science in the context of policing. Ambage (1987:17) suggests that, in the UK, the development of scientific methods of detection and their integration into the structure of the police was initially imposed from above, planned and implemented from central government and was largely a result of the activities of

Table 7.1 Inter- and post-war forensic developments

Date	Developments	Date	Developments
1931	Sir Arthur Dixon conference with Chief Constables to discuss creation of centralised detective training and 'police school'. Dixon establishes the 'detective committee'.	1950	The American Academy of Forensic Science (AAFS) was formed in Chicago, Illinois, and began publishing the *Journal of Forensic Science*.
1931– 1935	Four detective sub-committees established; sub-committee D, which dealt with 'scientific aids', establishes a framework for developing forensic science personnel and the integration of scientific detection methods into police investigations. The detective committee began work in 1933.	1951	F. H. Allen and colleagues identify the Kidd blood grouping system.
1931– 1960	Creation of forensic laboratories to aid police investigations. Labs were set up around the UK; for example, in Nottingham, Bristol and Cardiff.	1953	US Criminalist Paul Kirk publishes *Crime Investigation*, a comprehensive practical text on criminalistics and crime investigation.
1934	Establishment of the Criminal Research Laboratory in Bristol under the honorary directorship of police surgeon Dr. Burgess. In 1935 Professor Francis of the prestigious University of Bristol chemistry department is appointed head of the lab.	1953	Watson and Crick propose a double-helix structure for DNA.
1934	Special Services Fund established which provided funds for special activities including technical assistance to HM inspectors of constabulary	1958	A. S. Weiner and colleagues introduced the use of H-lectin to positively determine O blood type.

Date	Developments	Date	Developments
1934	Metropolitan Police College at Hendon established	1959	Hirshfeld first identified the polymorphic nature of group specific component (Gc).
1935	Metropolitan police laboratory opened at Hendon Police College	1959	Stuart Kind founds the UK Forensic Science Society in Nottingham on 30th October.
1948	Metropolitan police laboratory relocated to Scotland Yard. Results in a slight drop in the number of cases handled by staff.	1960	The first meeting of the British Academy of Forensic Sciences held.
1950	The Swiss criminalist Max Frei-Sulzer developed the tape lift method for collecting trace evidence.	1960	First issue of the *Journal of the Forensic Science Society* is published.

Arthur Dixon (later to become Sir). Dixon was 'Principal Assistant Under Secretary of State and head of the Police Department at the Home Office from 1919 to 1941' (ibid.:17); and it can be argued that his political 'moral entrepreneurial activities' were the main force behind modern forensic science and its links with policing. Dixon had a clear vision: to develop detective training; to make training a structured part of a police officer's career development; and to develop and implement the integration of forensic services into the police. He was a strong believer in the uses, nay necessity, of scientific methods for crime detection and spent a great deal of effort and energy in 'establishing a fully working Forensic Science Service and in convincing the police of the efficacy of scientific aids to the detection of crime' (ibid.:26). To this end, the creation of forensic science services 'was an inseparable part of the development of the police in England and Wales' (ibid.:6). The forensic science service was established during the 1930s and was part of the broader development in police *regional services* that was instigated by Dixon with the backing of the likes of C. T. Symons and Dr J. M. Webster (forensic science advisers); R. M. Howe (Deputy Assistant Chief Constable); Lord Trenchard (Commissioner); and Sir John Anderson (Permanent Under Secretary of State) (ibid.). This period of development requires a full historical analysis, as it is rich with both macro and micro influences that set the future course and structure of forensic investigations in the UK. At this juncture, it is enough to briefly mention some of the more influential factors that link police investigations, information and evidence. Perhaps the most important area was the creation of science laboratories across the UK from the 1930s onwards. Not only were labs set up all over the UK, including in major centres such as Nottingham, Bristol and Cardiff, but two were also established at Hendon Police College and the Home Office. However, Ambage (ibid.:i) notes how 'the path of development was strewn with pitfalls: with tensions and animosities; with successes and failures; and with personality clashes'.

As discussed at various points in Chapters 3, 4 and 5, up until the 1930s, the development, use and application of scientific methods for policing purposes was largely piecemeal and was concentrated in small pockets of individual *experts* who were sporadically called in by the police to assist them with their enquiries. The majority of these experts were medically trained doctors engaging in developing *forensic medicine*. Those with the most practical experience were usually doctors, who visited crime scenes and were able to provide analysis of wounds, blood spatter and the causes and mechanisms of death (ibid.:1–3; DiMaio and DiMaio, 2001). In fact, one of the early debates from the 1930s was about who would be better suited to head up the laboratories Dixon was creating as the first stage in developing a national forensic science service. There was some dispute as to whether medical doctors or scientists should head up the newly created science laboratories. This debate was located in attempts to move away from the early links with forensic science and medicine, epitomised in the work of the likes of Sir Arthur Conan Doyle and Sir Bernard Spilsbury. H. J. Wallis, who was one of the first full-time forensic scientists in England, suggests a number of reasons behind this debate:

> Sixty or more years ago, doctors were looked upon as being the fountainheads of scientific knowledge, something they wouldn't themselves claim now because both medicine and science have since got so specialised. But when police wanted scientific assistance in those days they tended to turn to pathologists. People like Sydney Smith at Edinburgh, for example, a lot of purely scientific work came into his laboratories from police forces in Scotland. So that in the 1930s forensic science, the application of science to crime detection, was finding its feet as a separate discipline. After that it grew away from medicine and now they are quite separate.
>
> (Wallis, personal interview 8th November 1983, cited in Ambage, 1987:3–4)

Ambage provides an interesting thesis on this development, arguing that the establishment of the Home Office forensic science service was one full of 'tensions'[2] engendered by the creation of the 'distinction between forensic science and forensic medicine, and forensic science and police techniques' (1987:4). Indeed, the establishment of regional Home Office laboratories and their applied use of forensic science techniques led the way towards the creation of the forensic scientist as a specialised occupation (ibid.:5). Once these conditions were created, scientists working closely with police advisors in an environment dealing primarily with criminal cases were able to develop scientific techniques of detection and even created specialisms where none had existed beforehand. Furthermore, from around 1942, forensic scientists played a key role in 'convincing the police of the efficacy of scientific aids to the detection of crime' (ibid.:26). These advances had a great influence on *information work* and its uses for catching criminals, as illustrated in the following review of caseload statistics for submissions to the labs during the period of development under discussion (see Figure 7.2). What gave scientists even more impetus was the creation of the two professional bodies that aimed to develop forensic science as a distinct occupation. The first was the Forensic Science Society (FSS), which was established by Stuart Kind on 30th October 1959 during a 'meeting between scientists, pathologists, police surgeons and police officers' (ibid.:285). The objectives of the FSS were to 'advance the study, application and standing of forensic science, and to facilitate cooperation among persons interested in forensic science throughout the world' (ibid.:284). Another professional body established at the same time as the FSS was the British Academy of Forensic Science (BAFS), which was founded to:

> encourage the study, improve the practice and advance the knowledge of Legal Medicine and Forensic Science. . . . [and] to do all such things as may be calculated to widen, improve and develop the education and knowledge both of those actively concerned in the pursuit of the forensic sciences and of the public.
>
> (BAFS Constitution, Item 2, cited in Ambage, 1987:284)

These two societies and their respective members created an atmosphere of inter-agency cooperation and development in relation to forensic detection and analytical methods. As the members of these two societies often worked in the newly created forensic laboratories, it wasn't long before advances in the number of cases were made. Looking at caseload statistics for the Metropolitan Police forensic science laboratory over a 15-year period between 1936 and 1951, with the exception of 1940, there is a quite dramatic increase during this period. In 1936 there were approximately 260 submissions to the laboratory, but this had grown to around 855 by 1951.

Comparing the Metropolitan Police lab with the caseload statistics of the forensic science service, figures for 1946 to 1950 show the follow submission levels: 1946 – 2,400 submissions; 1947 – 2,800; 1948 – 3,800; 1949 – 3900; 1950 – 3,700 (ibid.:233). After the end of the Second World War there was further investment in forensic laboratories, which began to see even more of an increase in forensic submissions.

Figure 7.3 illustrates the dramatic increase in the workload handled by the various forensic laboratories across the country. It is interesting to note that, in the years 1950 to 1960, provincial forces outstripped forensic caseloads of the Metropolitan Police's lab, usually by around 300 cases. In 1956, for instance, provincial forces' combined caseload was around 1,000 cases whilst the Metropolitan force's caseload was 650. Ambage (ibid.:245) notes that the disparity in figures was a 'fairly sensitive point with the scientists, who looked for a greater submission rate from the capital's forces'. He also discusses three reasons as to why this might have been the case. Firstly, disagreements over the

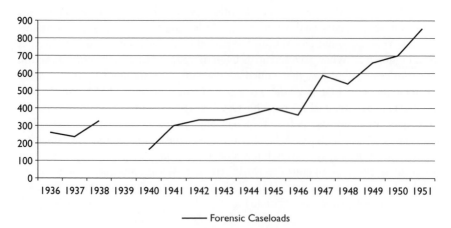

Figure 7.2 Metropolitan Police forensic science laboratory caseloads,
1936–1951

Data adapted from Ambage (1987:242–245)

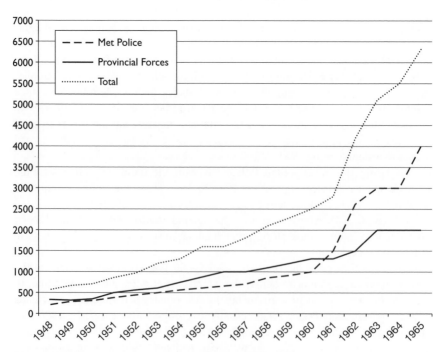

Figure 7.3 Comparative forensic caseloads, 1948–1965

Data adapted from Ambage (1987:242–245)

analysis of coroners' cases caused most consternation as most of these analyses were either cases that had no hope of criminal proceedings being undertaken or concerned private issues such as those relating to suicide (ibid.:245). The second reason for larger submissions from provincial forces related to the 'differences in the routine of bringing cases to court' (ibid.:250), with provincial police officers being more efficient in their use of forensic labs and wider issues such as attending training courses. Finally, the different systems used to prosecute those accused of drinking and driving also affected submission levels. Provincial forces were 'accustomed to sending samples of urine from suspected drunken drivers' (ibid.:251), so a greater number of analysis submissions led to greater caseload numbers. In 1961, a Metropolitan Police order was issued which gave authorisation for the 'taking of blood and urine samples in cases of drunk in charge' (ibid.:251). After the introduction of this order, forensic caseloads for the Metropolitan Police dramatically increased. For example, out of the 4,200 cases in 1962, '1837 analyses were carried out in prosecution for drinking and driving offences, and 1171 of these analyses had been submitted by the Metropolitan police' (ibid.:251).

This section has examined some of the structural factors that influenced the development of modern forensic science in the UK in the twentieth century. All of these actions were geared towards the creation of a highly centralised and structured policing agency with forensic investigative detection and analysis methods being developed to aid in the main task of policing – case construction.

Case (re)construction

After the preservation of life, *case construction* is one of the most important functions of the police. The very nature of reactive policing means that crime events are historical; they occur in the past and are investigated in the present. This means our understanding of them is *constructed* through a number of processes involving the identification of material or evidence and the information contained therein. These processes involve a number of key personnel including criminal investigators, crime scene investigators, forensic technicians, forensic analysts and forensic scientists; which creates a complex relationship between the evidence that is identified and its subsequent interpretation. The idea that criminal investigations are a constructed process, through interaction with the material and an individual's understanding of that material, is an important idea that runs through much forensic and investigative work. This section examines four important concepts crucial for any practical understanding of the constructed processes used within forensics and criminal investigations: *interactive and natural materials, reification and crime reconstruction.*

Interactive and natural materials

Police investigative work is geared towards the construction of a narrative of the crime event or events that have taken place, and that narrative is supported by data or evidence. It is therefore an obvious fact that police activities are *goal oriented*: the 'goal usually being the presentation of a strong case against the believed perpetrator' (Redmayne, 2004:6). As Redmayne outlines (ibid.:5–17), cases are 'put together'; they are constructed out of evidence that is generated through the information work of the police, crime scene investigators, forensic scientists and other relevant experts. The notion of construction is a familiar one to social scientists, especially those with knowledge of the social constructionist literature (Holstein and Miller, 1993; Best, 1995, 2001; Spector and Kitsuse, 2001; Loseke, 2003). This concept has been useful for sociologists and criminologists who are interested in how a society labels acts as deviant and criminal and how these social constructs tend to vary over time (Conrad and Schneider, 1992; Best, 1995; Rubington and Weinberg, 1995). For natural scientists, it is a concept that is a lot harder to swallow. As anyone who has attempted to use social constructionist arguments when engaging in a discussion with a *hard scientist* can tell you, trying to get them to view a *scientific truth* as a construct of human endeavor that '*changes*' is often difficult for them to even acknowledge or accept. They believe they are dealing with hard facts that *mother nature* has provided them, without realising (or wanting to admit) that their own methods and theories are human, *not* natural, constructs and therefore affect the *knowledge* that is produced. Even the most fundamental principles of our knowledge of nature are *constructed* using human cognitive processes that are unique to us. For instance, Redmayne (2004) utilises the concepts of *building* and *discretion* to demonstrate how scientists *build* scientific theories based upon evidence that is chosen by the scientists using their own methodological and theoretical *discretion*. There have been a number of sociological studies into laboratory science that have looked at the construction of scientific *fact*, including Knorr-Cetina's study on research into food proteins (cited in Redmayne, 2004:7). Another study that considered scientific knowledge as a construction is Latour and Woolgar's (1986) *Laboratory Life* which, amongst other things, considered the structure of a typical science laboratory and how researchers into a thyrotropin-releasing hormone were presented with a 'seething mass of alternative interpretations' from which they had to choose a single one.

Added to the complex notion of construction through building and discretion is Hacking's distinction between *interactive* and *natural* kinds (1999:103–117, cited in Redmayne, 2004:8). These two concepts are useful, especially for practical applications within forensic criminology, criminal investigations and forensic science. When dealing with natural kinds, material that has been created by and is present in nature, on Earth and in the universe, we need to consider that whilst such material exists as an objective *social fact* (Durkhiem, 1982:97), there is a part of the material that is constructed; and it is necessary to work out which *bit* has been constructed by humans. Redmayne succinctly summarises the natural kind in his discussion of quarks: '[i]f quarks exist, for instance, they are a natural kind. We cannot construct them: they simply exist or do not. But our *ideas about quarks, and even the concept 'quark', have been constructed by physicists*' (2004:8 – my emphasis).

Where science has made gigantic strides over the last 500 years is that it has engaged in a huge effort to reduce the constructed elements of natural kinds through rigorous processes of observation, recording, testing, and falsification/ verification; however, that's not to say that scientific natural kinds are devoid of human influence. Obviously the processes of *science* are a lot easier to undertake when you're dealing with natural objects, as they rarely change their physical properties, and their actions are not based upon a complex symbiotic relationship between biology, social environment and human thought processes (Blackburn, 1995; Andrews and Bonta, 2003; Bartol and Bartol, 2008).

The other *kinds* that exist are *interactive*, and these are a little trickier to deal with, as 'the entity interacts with our knowledge of it' (Redmayne, 2004:8). Sociological categories and subcategories such as social class/working class, gender/female, sexuality/homosexual are good examples of interactive kinds. They contain a *natural* element to them – for instance, biologically you may recognise yourself as a female – yet they also interact with their social environment at the same time. The shifting meanings of these kinds interact with developments within society, which accounts for differences in our understanding of these kinds across time and between different cultures. A very good contemporary example of this is Britain's horror and generally (non)understanding of honour killings. Redmayne (2004:8–9) notes how interactive kinds are linked to case building in the criminal justice system by way of investigative techniques such as investigative interviewing (Milne and Bull, 1999; Gudjonsson, 2007; Milne *et al.*, 2007) and legal categories such as 'rape' and 'theft' which are used to *frame* an interactive understanding of the crime event; the interaction being between the police and the suspect during police questioning. Expert evidence is also interactive, especially when presented in court, where it is discussed and where the interpretation of evidence is often *negotiated* through interaction between prosecution, defence and the judge or legal clerks.

The case of Sally Clark and Roy Meadow is a perfect example of how evidence can be used and interpreted on the basis of knowledge and our understanding of it: and this is the *constructed* aspect that always needs to be taken into consideration (see Case study 7.1). When it comes to physical evidence, on initial inspection it may appear that it does not fit with the concept of interactive kinds. Evidence such as DNA and fingerprints have proven quite robust over the years; placing this type of evidence within the natural kind category, although when it comes to fingerprints there is still a high level of construction involved; for example, when fingermark quality is assessed using the Bandey system (Bandey, 2004). However, natural kinds are also *part constructed* through human interaction. Redmayne, for instance, highlights how forensic evidence may play a role in the interaction between the material and our knowledge of it (Redmayne, 2004:9). As we will see in Chapter 11 with the Cowper case, the interpretation of forensic physical evidence certainly undergoes various forms of construction through a negotiated interaction between the physical evidence, an expert's interpretation of it and how the court processes, defines and uses that interpretation. If we look at a more recent case, we see how forensic science evidence, whilst not being completely interactive, can play a role in the process of negotiated interaction. Redmayne notes how the trial of the *Birmingham Six* illustrates how expert forensic evidence

CASE STUDY 7.1 SALLY CLARK AND BAD INTERACTIVE KINDS

The tragic case of Sally Clark is an excellent example of the potential problems with *interactive kinds*. Clark was convicted of murdering her two sons and jailed for life in 1999. Clark and her defence team always maintained that the two boys died of natural causes and proffered the explanation of Sudden Infant Death Syndrome (SIDS) as a possible reason. As Clark was the only individual with both boys at the time of their deaths, and it was believed that there was no other witness or physical evidence available, Clark was soon arrested for both murders. The prosecution and defence teams relied on a number of medical experts to provide argument and counterargument. In total, around nine specialists gave their *expert* opinion, which became very technical and difficult to follow. However, it was one expert that became pivotal to the case: Sir Professor Roy Meadow, a noted (and knighted) paediatrician and expert in child abuse, gave his expert opinion of the medical evidence relating to both deaths. Importantly, a section of his evidence was not of a medical nature at all, but consisted of statistical evidence regarding the likelihood and risk factor probabilities connected to SIDS. At the time of the trial, a government funded multidisciplinary study called *Confidential Enquiry into Sudden Death in Infancy* (CESDI) noted that, in a household with none of the identified three risk factors (i.e. smokers, low income and mothers age and parity), the likelihood of an incidence of SIDS was 1 in 8,543. Meadow suggested that the odds of two children from such an affluent family dying of natural causes were 1 in 73 million. He came to that conclusion using a poor probability calculation:

> Yes, you have to multiply 1 in 8,543 times 1 in 8,543 and I think it gives that in the penultimate paragraph. It points out that its approximately a chance of 1 in 73 million.
> (Para 96, 2003, EWCA Crim 1020).[3]

He even went on to compare this SIDS statistic and the Clark case with the chances of backing two Grand National winners at 80 to 1 for 2 consecutive years running (Para 99, 2003, EWCA Crim 1020)! He thus ruled out the possibility of SIDS (Para 58, 2003, EWCA Crim 1020). However, Meadow interpretation of the evidence was based upon a poor understanding of statistical probability, and the Royal Statistical Society even wrote to the Lord Chancellor to say there was no statistical basis for the figures quoted by Meadow. One of the core mistakes made by Meadow was his assumption of the independence between the risk factors; something which has not been proven. He assumed that the death of Clark's first child, Christopher, was independent of the death of her second child, Harry. His statistical *sleight of hand* would only be possible if the SIDS occurred randomly and *without* the existence of any underlying condition that would cause it. As Scheurer (2009) highlights 'it was simply not possible for anyone to assume that SIDS is caused by random factors which are wholly independent of one another'. Furthermore, as the second Appeal in 2003 identified, the report from which Meadow took his evidence also specified the following:

> the figures did not 'take account of possible familial incidence of factors other than those included' in the table. It ended with the warning: 'When a second SIDS death occurs in the same family, in addition to careful search for inherited disorder, there must always be a very thorough investigation of the circumstances – though it would be inappropriate to assume maltreatment was always the cause'
>
> (Para 101, 2003, EWCA Crim 1020).

What is also interesting is that, at the time of the trial, Meadow was writing the preface for the CESDI government report and used the preliminary findings of this study as the basis for his statistical interpretation. This point raises an important issue regarding the integrity and independence of experts. Professor Meadow was being paid and funded by his *employers*, the State, who were also prosecuting Clark. Meadows also stepped outside his area of expertise for he is a paediatrician and an expert in child sexual abuse, *not* an expert in statistics. After an unsuccessful appeal in 2000, Clark was eventually set free in 2003 with many believing she had been a victim of one of the most terrible miscarriages of justice in British history. Tragically, she died in 2007, reportedly due to being unable to recover from prison and being accused of murdering her children; at the time of her death she was battling an alcohol addiction.

can play a 'role in the process of interaction' (ibid.:9). In 1974, the IRA blew up two pubs in Birmingham, killing 21 and injuring more than 160. Within hours of the explosion, six Irishmen were detained and, after three days of interrogation, four of the men had signed confessions. At the trial, all six pleaded not guilty, claiming that the confessions had been beaten out of them. They also refuted the forensic evidence against them (Mullin, 1986). Mullin's excellent overview of this miscarriage of justice, *Error of Judgement* (1986), shows how the scientific evidence in both the investigation and trial was used for coercive means to elicit confessions, when the evidence was dubious to begin with. In particular, the forensic test conducted on the suspects' hands to look for the presence of explosives, known as the Griess Test,[4] produced an interesting interpretation of the meaning of a *negative result*. The scientist who undertook and interpreted the test, Dr Skuse, testified that if he obtained a positive result then 'he was ninety-nine per cent certain the suspects had been in contact with nitroglycerine' (ibid.:45). The results were reproduced in Mullin's investigation:

> The Greiss (sic) test on Richard McIlkenny's hands proved negative. So did those on Gerry Hunter. The sample under Billy Power's left hand was negative. The samples under his nails were negative. The sample from his right hand, however, turned pink immediately. . . . As far as Dr Skuse was concerned there was only one possible explanation. Bill Power had recently handled explosives . . . he obtained a strong positive reaction from Hill's right hand. . . . When he later did a Greiss test on the sample from Hill's left hand, the result was negative.
>
> (Ibid.:45)

Skuse also undertook further tests on the samples taken from the suspects. He subjected the samples to Thin Layer Chromatography (TLC) and Gas Chromatography/Mass Spectrometry (GCMS) which, at the time, were amongst the most advanced scientific methods used to determine the chemical composition of compounds. As these tests were more sensitive than the Griess test, one would have expected more conclusive, positive results; but (ibid.:165–167):

- positive Griess sample taken from Power was negative using TLC and GCMS;
- the TLC and GCMS tests on Walker were negative; and
- Skuse had tested his own hand before testing Walker and the positive result of nitrate could have been from his own contamination.

The forensic tests were argued over for hours, moving back and forth between 'Griess tests, mass spectrometry and thin layer chromatography, ammonium and nitrate ions, nitrates and nitrites' (ibid.:167). According to Mullin, Skuse was never asked to provide answers to a number of simple yet crucial questions: first, why there was a one-and-a-half-hour gap between his finishing with Paddy Hill (around 7.30) and Johnny Walker (at 8.55); second, why the majority of tests performed on the hands of the suspects were actually negative; third, it was not discussed in any detail which other substances would give a positive Griess test (ibid.:165–171). The expert witness for the defence, Dr Black, who was a retired Chief Inspector of Explosives at the Home Office, testified that there were a wide range of substances that would give a positive Griess test, such as nitrocellulose which was commonly found 'in lacquers, varnishes and paints on furniture in hotels and bars' (ibid.:168). The lacquer cover on playing cards also contained elements of nitrate and when these facts were taken into consideration within the context of the *Birmingham Six*'s arrest – on a train, playing cards – an alternative hypothesis should have been put forward. Because of the complexity of the forensic arguments involved in the trial, Mullin rightly argued that 'there was no possibility that the jury could have absorbed the complex arguments surrounding Dr Skuse's evidence' (ibid.:168). Their understanding of the forensic arguments presented, therefore, was based more upon the perceived stature of the experts: what is known as *reification*.

Reification

Reification is based on the simple premise that many scientific facts exist 'only within a wider web of assumptions and procedures' (MacKenzie, 1990:341, cited in Redmayne, 2004:10). What we think of as scientific facts have become so 'because the assumptions on which they rest are largely hidden' (Redmayne, 2004:10). DNA, for example, is based upon a 'web of assumptions and procedures' that include topics such population genetics, laboratory protocols and probability. Many of us do not even come close to understanding the complexities of such knowledge, hence the reliance on experts to show us the way. Latour and Woolgar's (1986) study illustrates the process of reification and how reification was endemic in the construction of Thryotropin-Releasing Factor Hormone (TRH).[5] Upon reviewing the core works on this compound, Latour and Woolgar found that:

> In spite of its 'outstanding' and 'dramatic' character, no more than a few lines are devoted to the discovery in works more than 1000 pages long. For most readers of these texts, knowledge of TRH is limited to these few lines.
>
> (Ibid.:108)

The authors then go on to demonstrate that in the 698 articles written on the subject by 1975, researchers would only have read some of the articles, and that the meaning and usage of the term TRH depended on the network or group using them. In short, the knowledge around the substance TRF and its synthetic derivative TRH was largely hidden. For example, by 1966, an almost pure form of TRF had been obtained; but this advance had to be stopped because of its impracticality as, in order to produce a small quantity of TRF, large quantities of brain fragments (hypothalamus) were needed (ibid.:127–128). Redmayne (2004:10–11) suggests that 500 tonnes of pig brains was required by one laboratory to produce just 1mg of TRH. The TRH scientific knowledge that subsequently became reified, therefore, was derived from this very small amount of material.

One of the obvious implications for scientific knowledge based upon the concept of reification is that it is open to testing and critical analysis. It is incumbent upon forensic criminologists, forensic scientists and criminal investigators to pull apart the assumptions of knowledge, especially when it is being used in criminal investigations and trials. Furthermore, whilst we must be careful not to place too strong a link, case construction parallels the concept of reification as it is often difficult to challenge the cases constructed by the police. As we have seen in the previous chapter, criminal investigations are constructed using a number of processes and regulations that enable a number of what Redmayne (ibid.:10–11) calls 'discretionary decisions' to be made by police. For the majority of this investigative process, these decisions remain hidden, with the interaction between suspects, witnesses and victims often predicated upon belief in the police's interpretation of events. With the advent of police investigative decision logs, the discretionary decisions that are made have become more transparent; yet much still remains hidden.

Crime reconstruction

Case construction, using natural and interactive kinds of evidence, and reification point to another concept that is important for understanding any practical aspect of forensic criminology. *Crime reconstruction* is defined as:

> The determination of the actions and events surrounding the commission of a crime. A reconstruction may be accomplished by using the statement of witnesses, the confession of a suspect, the statement of a living victim, or by the examination and interpretation of physical evidence.
>
> (Chisum and Turvey, 2007:2)

Crime reconstruction works well for deductive methods of criminal investigations and ideo-deductive and nomothetic techniques of criminal profiling (Chisum and Turvey, 2008:155–186). It is primarily concerned with interpreting physical evidence or information that is produced by the effects of actions and events pertaining to the crime. Where crime reconstruction differs from case construction is that the techniques and processes of crime reconstruction require the ability to put together 'a puzzle using pieces of unknown dimensions without a guiding picture' (ibid.:156), incorporating the application of scientific methodology to analyse physical, behavioural and witness evidence within the framework of analytical logic and critical thinking. The emphasis is on understanding the crime, whereas case construction has the broader aim of putting together a robust a case as possible to present to a jury and successfully prosecute those responsible for the crime. Usually, crime reconstruction is the overriding objective that helps achieve the aim of case construction, and it is the information that is identified, collected and analysed that makes this possible.

The different forms of information

As mentioned at the beginning of this chapter, police investigations and forensic analysis are concerned with information work. Innes defines information as 'data that has been ordered and communicated' (2003:113). This information is *encoded* by the ontological measures relevant to the information type contained within the substance. For example, atoms are made of extremely tiny particles called protons, neutrons and electrons, and scientists have designed an ontological classification system to fit with this composition; so the element carbon (pure and in its natural state) consists of 6 protons, 6 electrons and 6 neutrons, whereas sodium has 11 protons, 11 electrons and 12 neutrons (Gray, 2009). Scientists use such differences for identification purposes when measuring the chemical atomic structure of substances found at crime scenes (Saferstein, 2007; Jackson and Jackson, 2011). However, this is not the only form of information that exists and this section discusses the interplay between *information* and its three forms - *intelligence, knowledge* and *evidence.*

When it comes to information generated in the context of a police investigation, 'information is meaningful data of potential relevance to the investigative activities of the police' (Innes, 2003:113). As Innes points out, this information needs to be *selected* and *interpreted* in order for it to be meaningful in the context of a crime. This is a crucial point that Kirk originally made back in the 1950s in his first edition of *Crime Investigation*:

> Wherever he steps, whatever he touches, whatever he leaves – even unconsciously – will serve as silent evidence against him. Not only his fingerprints and his shoeprints, but also his hair, the fibres from his clothes, the glass he breaks, the tool mark he leaves, the paint he scratches, the blood or semen that he deposits or collects – all these and more bear mute witness against him. This is evidence that does not forget. It is not confused by the excitement of the moment. It is not absent because human witnesses are. *It is factual evidence.* **Physical evidence cannot be wrong; it cannot perjure itself; it cannot be wholly absent. Only in its interpretation can there be error.** [My emphasis and bold.]
>
> (1974:2)

It is here that any investigator must distinguish between *information* and *knowledge*. Robust forms of knowledge have usually gone through an extensive process of interpretation and testing before they are finally classified into a specific theory that belies any alternative interpretations. In short, knowledge is deemed to have acquired *factual status*. This does not mean knowledge cannot change for, as our understanding and technologies advance, new data will always eventually *update* knowledge, and knowledge in the context of forensic criminology 'makes a positive contribution to the investigator's understanding of the crime' (Innes, 2003:114). This is juxtaposed against information, which still has a level of ambiguity within it and 'can be subject to multiple interpretations'. '[I]nformation becomes knowledge when it is situated in a context established by other information available to investigators so as to facilitate understanding' (ibid.:114). This aspect has its origins in Beccaria's theories of criminal justice, commonly known as *classicism* ([1764]1986:26):

> When all the proofs of a fact depend equally upon a single piece of evidence, the number of proofs neither augments nor diminishes the probability of fact, for their total worth comes down to the worth of the one proof upon which they all depend. When the proofs are independent of one another, that is, when the pieces of evidence are supported by something besides each other, then the likelihood of the fact increases as more proofs are adduced, because the flaws in one proof have no bearing on the others.

In this sense, knowledge has a much firmer standing than information, because it is deemed to be more objective and *valid*, and part of the crime construction process involves turning information into knowledge. Stelfox (2009:93–97) includes in the list of knowledge useful to police investigations victim and witness accounts: offender accounts and informant accounts. However, he wrongly places intelligence under the same category when, in fact, intelligence is a distinct category.

Intelligence is the second form that information takes and can be defined as 'information that has been analysed with the purpose of creating a future field of action for the police, in order to generate further knowledge' (Innes, 2003:114). Generally, it has two functions: first, intelligence is used to 'make business decisions, such as setting organizational priorities, patrol patterns and suchlike' (Stelfox, 2009:95; also see John and Maguire, 2007); second, it is used to make operational decisions 'such as who to investigate, the best time to search a particular premises or where to locate a suspect for arrest' (Stelfox, 2009:95). This form of operational intelligence tends to include information pertaining to addresses, lifestyle, and social and criminal networks and often forms part of official criminal justice databases, such the Police National Computer (PNC), and is known as *closed source data*. Other sources of intelligence include *open source* data, which is data that is publicly available and includes electoral information, business ownership data (i.e. from Companies House) and records regarding births, marriages and deaths. The uses of closed and open source data are discussed in further detail in the following chapter.

The final form of information is *evidence*. Evidence is information specifically formatted 'according to legal discourse' and 'can be understood and represented in accordance with the rationale of the legal framework' (Innes, 2003:114). Evidence can take many forms and usually consists of physical and non-physical material. Innes (ibid.:114–115) identifies four broad classifications of evidence in respect to its legal or probative value. First, there is *direct evidence*, which is usually in the form of testimony from a witness who actually saw, heard, or touched the subject of the investigation. This type of evidence, if believed by magistrates or the jury, proves the fact at hand without the need for any inferences or presumptions (Durston, 2008:56). An example of direct evidence would be Bill witnessing Harry molest Sally. Second, there is *circumstantial evidence*, which is also known as indirect evidence. Circumstantial evidence relates to a series of facts which, by inferential and experiential reasoning, are deemed to be closely associated with the fact to be proved (ibid.:56–58). So, in the above scenario, Bill would witness Harry taking Sally into another room and hear specific noises that he would infer relate to sexual activities. He then sees Sally afterwards looking distraught with ripped clothing. He has not directly witnessed sexual assault but, from the noises, distressed look and clothing, his experiential reality infers an assault has taken place. The third type is *corroborative* which is evidence 'that tends to support a view already formed' (Innes, 2003:114–115). This type can be problematic as the investigative mindset of police officers often creates the situation where corroborative evidence is only used when it verifies the theories of the lead investigator, so they tend to only look for evidence of this kind whilst ignoring the evidence that provides alternative directions and suspects (see Turvey, 2008). The fourth type of evidence is *indicative*; that is, 'where it points strongly towards a particular individual' (Kind, 1987, cited in Innes, 2003:115).

These four forms of information follow a movement from the general to the specific and, along the way, go through a variety of filtering and interpretative processes that arrange the information in a framework specific to its functional form; whether it's used as knowledge, intelligence or evidence to inform a criminal investigation. Rogers (2007:161) calls this the *attrition of material*.

Figure 7.4 demonstrates that the police will only gather a proportion of the total amount of material generated from an offence. As Rogers (ibid.:160) notes,

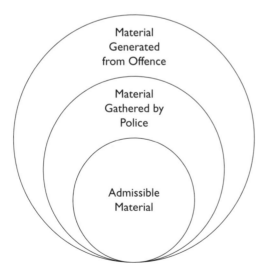

Figure 7.4 The attrition of material

'some physical material may be destroyed, some witnesses may not be located, some of the material will only be known to the offenders, etc.'. Furthermore, not all of the material collected by the police will meet the evidential test, so there will be a further reduction in the material that is eventually used in court. Therefore, as the investigation progresses, the amount of information that becomes *admissible evidence* is less than the amount gathered by the police, and considerably less than the total produced by the crime itself. Of course, the most important form, when it comes to developing the overarching narrative of a crime including identifying the right offender, is *evidence*; and there are different types and uses of evidence.

The efficacy of evidence

One of the problems highlighted in the literature into the 'CSI effect' is that TV crime programmes such as *CSI*, *Silent Witness* and *Waking the Dead* create the impression that most crimes are *detected* and *solved* primarily through the identification and analysis of physical evidence (Podlas, 2006, 2009; Cavender and Deutsch, 2007; Smith *et al.*, 2007). As we have seen in Chapter 6, there are many different ways crime is detected; and it is quite rare that the forensic analysis of physical evidence alone solves a crime. This idea tends to be supported by the limited amount of research undertaken on criminal investigations. In their brief review of the literature, Bradbury and Feist (2005:8) note that 'the majority of detected cases are *not* solved through the use of forensic evidence'. It is important then to provide some current context to the uses and availability of physical evidence. In one of the first attempts to examine the contribution of physical evidence to criminal investigations, Greenwood and Petersilia (1975:vii) came to the following conclusion:

> On how cases are solved: The single most important determinant of whether or not a case will be solved is the information the victim supplies to the immediately responding patrol officer. If information that uniquely identifies the perpetrator is not presented at the time the crime is reported, the perpetrator, by and large, will not be subsequently identified.

This research, known as the *RAND Report*, suggests that in 'combined crime types' the offenders' identity became known immediately in over 50 per cent of cases due to the following reasons:

> (1) the offender was arrested at the scene; (2) the victim or other witness identified him by name and address even though he was not arrested at the scene; or (3) he was identifiable by some unique evidence apparent at the crime scene, for example, a witness observed the license plate on the perpetrator's car or his employee badge number.
>
> (Ibid.:vii)

They also found that where the offender was not identifiable at the time of the initial police report, 'almost all are cleared as a result of routine police procedures' (ibid.:vii). When it came to collecting physical evidence, it was found that 'most police departments collect more physical evidence than can be productively processed' (ibid.:viii), and that it was rare that latent fingerprints provided the only basis for identifying a suspect. The conclusions of *RAND* tend to be supported by contemporary research, which again highlights the limited role of forensics. For example, Steer's (1980, cited in Bradbury and Feist, 2005:8) study of a 'sample of detections in the Thames Valley' police force, found very limited use of physical evidence, with only 0.9 per cent of offences (out of 340) 'detected as a result of fingerprint searches, with no other physical evidence categories listed' (ibid.:8).

UK research shows a slightly different pattern. Ramsay (1987, cited in Tilley and Ford, 1996:11) found that, in 330 cases analysed, forensic analysis from the Forensic Science Society made no contribution in 30 per cent (99) of investigations; meaning it aided in 70 per cent of cases. Tilley and Ford's (1996) and McCulloch's (1996) research into the police use of forensic science were the first attempts in the UK to try to measure the actual usage of forensic science and their successes within criminal investigations. For example, when it came to fingermarks found at the scene, Tilley and Ford (1996:16) reviewed figures from seven 'sample police forces' and found an average ratio of 1:3.2; so, for every 3.2 scenes examined, only 1 of the scenes produced fingermarks. However, finding a fingermark does not always translate into a successful identification or a useful elimination of suspects and victims. The authors also note that, in 1993, the national rates 'at which identifications were made in relation to scenes visited varied from 1:9.6 to 1:44, with an overall rate of 1:19 (National Conference of Scientific Support, cited in Tilley and Ford, 1996:16). McCulloch's review of the Scenes of Crime Information Management System (SOCIMS) found that in all the criminal investigations conducted in 1993, only 11,922 forensic science submissions were produced. Furthermore, these submissions are determined by a number of factors including the type of case and the structure of the police force itself.

The core problem with this research is that it is historical, and predates the significant developments that have taken place in crime scene investigation and forensic science over the last 15 years or so. However, it does provide us with some empirical evidence that suggests that forensic scientific analysis of evidence has different levels in both its use and evidential value. Such evidence is often used by police culture orthodoxy and academic commentators as a stick to beat *forensics* with, claiming that it's not as important as, say, interview evidence. Whilst this may be true for most criminal cases, part of the reason for this is due to the restrictions and policies regarding which crime scenes are attended. Not all scenes are attended by CSIs, so forensic evidence is not always collected. Moreover, the forensic strategy decisions made by CSIs and crime scene managers will determine the level and type of evidence collected at the scene (NPIA, 2012:34–51). What must be remembered is that, when it comes to forensic evidence, it is not necessarily the quantity that is important; rather it is the quality of the analysis and interpretation that is crucial. The House of Commons Science and Technology Committee note how forensic science plays a crucial role in unlocking the information from material and is therefore key to the efficient and effective running of the criminal justice system (House of Commons Science and Technology Committee, 2005a:8). In its report *Forensic Science on Trial*, the committee found:

> The main contribution that forensic science makes to the criminal justice system is the generation of intelligence to assist investigations: the provision of actual evidence to convict the guilty or exculpate the innocent represents a small, although very significant, part of its role.
>
> (Ibid.:8)

So, whilst forensic scientific evidence is a relatively small proportion of all evidence eventually used in court cases, its potential is huge in relation to aiding criminal investigations. Since the advent of DNA fingerprinting, this potential has increased dramatically: in 2002–03 'there were more than 21,000 detections in crimes where a DNA profile had been obtained, a 132% increase since 2000' (ibid.:9). So, whilst it is clear that non-forensic evidence, in particular witness testimony, is still the primary type of evidence collected, forensic evidence provides invaluable help to the overall investigative process and should not be undermined by those wishing to maintain their professional jurisdictional boundary (e.g. in the case of investigative interviewing).

Types of evidence

In the broadest of terms, there are two types of evidence – *physical* and *non-physical*. Houck (2004:166) notes that not all evidence is created equal and some items of evidence can be more relevant than others. A useful way to explain this is using Canter and Youngs' (2009) concept of the *continuum of trustworthiness*, which describes the idea that the information produced from evidence has different levels of robustness in relation to its factual accuracy but also its evidential and probative force. Looking at the four broad categories of investigative information, this can be placed on the trustworthy continuum in the following order: (i) crime scene material; (ii) victim statements; (iii) eyewitness statements; and (iv) suspect statements.

Non-physical material

Types (ii) to (iv) are regarded as the *non-physical* evidence usually produced through standard investigative police practice. Most of this of type of evidence consists of qualitative, textual information (Denzin and Lincoln, 2000; Gilbert, 2012) that has one or more of the following functions:

1   tells the narrative, or part of the narrative of the crime event;
2   provides useful information on the victim/victims and potential suspect/ suspects; and
3   provides identification information pertaining to victim(s) and suspect(s).

Non-physical evidence is formatted data and knowledge in relation to legal rules and regulations (primarily under legislation such as the PACE Act 1984, RIPA 2000, PJ Act 2006, etc.) and usually takes the form of statements or interview recordings that are transcribed and used in court. As Milne *et al.* (2007:65) note, 'interviewing is at the heart of any police investigation and this is the root of achieving justice in society'. As previously mentioned (see Chapter 6), key drivers for change in policing in the 1970s came off the back of the problematic nature of confession evidence and its links with high-profile miscarriages of justice, such as the *Guildford Four* and the *Birmingham Six* (Mullin, 1986), that then continued with the horrendous miscarriages pertaining to historical allegations of child sexual abuse in care homes, which were produced by police trawling and interviewing techniques (for example, at Bryn Estyn; see Webster, 2005 for a thorough exposé of these problems). When it comes to interviewing suspects, the introduction of PACE and its codes of practice (C, D and F) is still the most important development (Milne *et al.*, 2007:66). This kicked-started a fruitful interplay between 'academic research and practical policing' (ibid.:65); and, over the last 15 years, there has been an abundance of psychological research on how interview evidence is generated through criminal investigations (for example, see Milne and Bull, 1999; Gudjonsson, 2002, 2007; Fisher and Reardon, 2007; Milne *et al.*, 2007; Williamson, 2007). This research has resulted in changes to the way the police gather witness testimony. For example, seven *principles of investigative interviewing* were developed by the Home Office and made available in circular 22/1991 (ACPO, 2004:7–8):

1   The role of investigative interviewing is to obtain accurate and reliable information from suspects, witnesses or victims in order to discover the truth about matters under police investigation.
2   Investigative interviewing should be approached with an open mind. Information obtained from the person who is being interviewed should always be tested against what the interviewing officer already knows or what can reasonably be established.
3   When questioning anyone, a police officer must act fairly in the circumstances of each individual case.
4   The police interviewer is not bound to accept the first answer given. Questioning is not unfair merely because it is persistent.

5   Even when the right of silence is exercised by a suspect, the police still have a right to put questions.
6   When conducting an interview, police officers are free to ask questions in order to establish the truth; except for interviews with child victims of sexual or violent abuse, which are to be used in criminal proceedings, they are not constrained by the rules applied to lawyers in court.
7   Vulnerable people, whether victims, witnesses, or suspects, must be treated with particular consideration at all times.

The current service model that the police use for investigative interviewing is PEACE. This stands for (ibid.:8–9):

•   **Planning and preparation** – which discusses what to consider when planning for an interview;
•   **Engage and explain** – which is about the problems of getting started with an interview and establishing the ground rules;
•   **Account, clarification and challenge** – this deals with obtaining the interviewees account, and clarifying and challenging this account;
•   **Closure** – identifies considerations before closing an interview; and
•   **Evaluation** – considers what was achieved during the interview in relation to the overall investigation.

PEACE has been implemented in an attempt ensure the critical failure points associated with interviewing, such as leading questions (House of Commons, 2002a, 2002b), are minimised and do not produce false information. It also operates alongside other developments such as *Achieving Best Evidence in Criminal Proceedings* (Home Office, 2002), which provides guidelines to police and other agencies (e.g. social workers) on how to interview children and vulnerable witnesses. Whilst the PEACE structure is by no means perfect, for much depends on the level of training provided by the force as well as the individual skill of officers (see Clarke and Milne, 2001; Milne *et al.*, 2007), it has been a vast improvement on previous interview techniques and provides an excellent example of the usefulness of a synergy between academic research and practical policing; although, with the jurisdictional dominance of particular academic authors, and their very close links with the police, there is a distinct whiff of reification in the air.

Physical evidence

With current levels of theoretical and technical knowledge, and on the continuum of trustworthiness, crime scene material is seen as the most robust form of *evidence*. Often called physical evidence, this type potentially incorporates any material found on Earth. As mentioned in Part 1 of this current text, over the last 500 years natural philosophers and scientists have been cataloguing material found on Earth, concentrating their efforts on describing the physical and chemical structure of the elements and their subsequent compounds (Larson, 1971; Fortey, 2008; Gaukroger, 2009, 2010; Pavord, 2009; Magnus, 2012). The creation of our ontological categories of material leaves an incredibly large number of possible combinations of such material coming into contact during crime events. In order to reduce this complexity, scientists have created broad categories of where such material can be placed, which makes it slightly easier to analyse. For example, Saferstein (2007:70–71) identifies 21 categories of physical material that is can be found at the crime scene (see Table 7.2).

Most forensic science texts discuss these types of evidence in detail so there is no need for repetition here; however they sometimes use slightly different categories when describing them (see Fraser and Williams, 2009; James and Nordby, 2009; Houck and Siegel, 2010; Jackson and Jackson, 2011).

The importance of physical material that is identified as being relevant to the crime under investigation is that it can provide identification and comparison information, which can then be turned into investigative lines of enquiry that, if successful, lead to the material being turned into evidence. In this respect, there are two levels of use of physical evidence; and the crime scene investigator, forensic analyst, police investigator and legal advisors *should* all work together to bring these two levels together. Level one is *identification of the material and the information* contained therein. Level two involves turning the material and information into evidence that satisfies the *legal regulations surrounding evidence submissions and applicability*. Some of these issues are discussed in this current chapter, as well as Chapters 8, 9 and 10 (level one, e.g. a discussion of crime scene examination and forensic analysis methods); whilst Chapter 11 deals with level two (the legal construction of evidence). What is important to note here is that physical material does not always come fully formed (i.e. a pane of glass broken at the scene of a burglary); it is often that only traces of physical evidence are found at the scene. Not only that: whilst Kirk's axiom is true, that physical evidence does not perjure itself, it can have been affected by a large number of factors that change or alter both the form and meaning and therefore the final interpretation of the trace evidence.

Table 7.2 Categories of physical material

Blood, semen and saliva	Paint
Documents	Petroleum products
Drugs	Plastic bags
Explosives	Plastic, rubber, and other polymers
Fibres	Powder residues
Fingerprints	Serial numbers
Firearms and ammunition	Soil and minerals
Glass	Tool marks
Hair	Vehicle lights
Impressions	Wood and other vegetative matter
Organs and physiological fluids	

Trace evidence

For around the last 100 years, many criminalists, forensic scientists and criminal investigators have been using the microscopic analysis of trace evidence to aid the reconstruction of crimes. The analysis of trace evidence usually involves three core processes: first, the characterisation of the trace evidence found; second, the identification of what type of trace evidence has been found; finally, a comparison between different samples of trace evidence (Houck, 2004, 2009; Houck and Siegel, 2010). This final component is crucial to criminal investigations, as it links the three core factors of the *crime equation* together (Figure 7.5).

Defining trace evidence

The term trace evidence can be defined as 'as microscopic material recovered as evidence that is used to help solve criminal cases' (Grieve and Houck, 2004:1). It is regarded as *trace* due to the size and texture of the material found and the fact that it is 'easily transferred from one location to another' (Houck, 2009:166). Others have used similar definitional parameters; for instance, Nickell and Fischer (1999:54) suggest it refers to 'minute physical evidence that may be transferred from a criminal to a victim or crime scene'; whilst Jackson and Jackson (2008:448) state that trace is 'minute amounts of materials (such as glass shards, paint chips, hairs or fibres) that are inevitably transferred through contact between individuals, or between an individual and a physical location'. Kubic and Petraco (2009:327) include in their definition the 'qualitative or quantitative analysis of the minor or ultraminor components of a sample', which incorporates the idea of data and methodological triangulation.

From these definitions, three core components can be identified as being tied to the trace evidence concept. The first is that the material is *microscopic*. Trace evidence analysis was made possible because of the invention of the microscope;

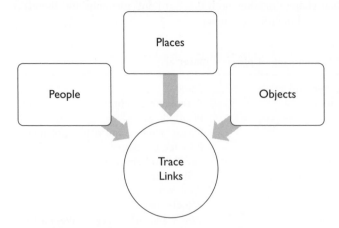

Figure 7.5 Trace evidence and the crime equation

with the first instrument using objective and ocular lenses produced around 1590 by Zacharias Janssen, and the first proper microscope developed by Anton van Leeeuwenhoek (Wilson, 1995; Nickell and Fisher, 1999; Ruestow, 2004). This new technology provided powerful magnification, allowing us to see beyond the observable informational base and into the hidden depths of nature in order to analyse the particles that make up physical objects on Earth (and the known universe). As the technology developed, so too did the types of microscopes, which now include the standard laboratory microscope, stereo binocular, comparison, polarised light and scanning electron microscopes (Kubic and Petraco, 2009:328). Each of these increasingly powerful machines allowed for the *microanalysis* of trace particles. As the visual analysis of properties became a reality, more and more information about physical objects and their particles became known to us and placed within the informational base of known human knowledge. It is therefore possible to use the microscopic analysis of trace evidence to examine, analyse, compare and identify a whole range of substances found at crime scenes, on victims and on suspects.

The second important component to the definitions is *contact*. In the majority of crimes, when objects and/or people interact during the commission of a crime, there is always some form of contact. The four principle areas of contact are:

1   between offender and victim;
2   between offender and environment;
3   between victim and environment; and
4   between offender, victim and environment.

The fact that there is usually some contact between one or more of the four areas cited above means that links can potentially be found between, say, a suspect, victim and the circumstances and context of the offence; and of course this is crucial for any successful investigation. However, before any links can be confirmed with physical evidence, the third aspect of the definition of trace evidence must occur: there needs to be some form of *transference*. With each contact, there is the potential for many pieces of material to be transferred between the different sources of the contact; and this duality of *contact* and *transfer* is the perhaps the fundamental component to Locard's principle of exchange. As we saw in Chapter 4, Locard's tenet is based upon the three components of the definition of trace evidence – *microscopic, contact* and *transfer* – after he discovered that dust particles could be analysed and linked to their likely source of origin (Locard, 1930a, 1930b). However robust Locard's principle appears on the surface, it should be noted that his maxim that *every contact leaves a trace* is not always true. Every contact does not necessarily lead to a transfer of evidence, and even if transfer does take place there are many factors that affect the level of transfer and whether there is enough material for comparisons to be made.

The amount and quality of trace evidence depends on the two ideas of *transfer* and *persistence*. Transfer relates to the actual process of the transfer of evidence through contact and is determined by factors such as the physical properties of the objects that have come into contact with each other, as well as the general laws of physics regarding mass, density, energy and motion (Saferstein, 2007:102–107). For example, the *amount of pressure applied* during the contact will determine the amount of material transferred; so 20 pounds of pressure should transfer more material that 1 pound of pressure. This can be useful for crimes such as violent assault as the amount of transferred material may provide an indication as to the force at which an individual was struck (Turvey, 2008). The *number of contacts* is also crucial, as 5 contacts between two objects will transfer less material than 15 contacts (Locard, 1930a, 1930b; Houck, 2004, 2009:166–169; Houck and Siegel, 2010:54–56). The physical properties of the material itself will also determine the ease with which the transfer takes place; for example, wet blood transfers more easily than dry concrete. This links to the *form* of the material, which in the parlance of physics is *matter*; and there are four core types of known matter – *solid, liquid, gas and plasma* (Saferstein, 2007:131). The form of the matter will affect the transfer and persistence; for example, liquids will obviously transfer more easily than solids, yet liquids will dissipate (an issue of persistence) more quickly than solids. The form of matter will also influence the amount of the item that is transferred; so one square centimeter of blood should transfer less than one square metre of blood (Houck, 2009; Houck and Siegel, 2010). These factors can be seen in Figure 7.6.

A key factor in relation to the transfer of material is the areas where transfer can occur, which brings in the notions of *primary* and *secondary* transfer, also known as *direct* and *indirect* transfer (Houck, 2004, 2009:166–169; Houck and Siegel, 2010:55–56). Direct transfer refers to evidence that has been transferred between

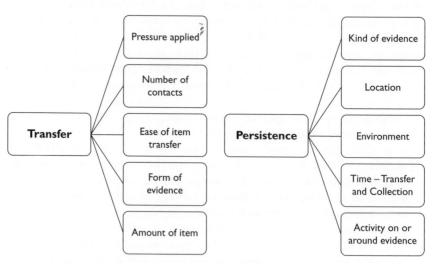

Figure 7.6 Factors affecting Locard's principle of exchange

Source: adapted from Houck and Siegel (2010).

two direct points, with no intermediary transfer points involved. For example, offender A assaults victim B, and during the assault victim B scratches her assailant. The resultant direct transfer is: skin from A transfers to the fingernails of B. Indirect transfer involves the same process but includes 'one or more intermediate objects – the evidence transfers from A to B to C' (Houck and Siegel, 2010:55). Case study 7.2 provides a good example of indirect transfer.

CASE STUDY 7.2 SARAH PAYNE AND THE COOLHAM SHOE

On 1st July 2000, eight-year-old Sarah Payne was abducted and murdered by Roy Whiting. Sarah's partially covered body was found in a West Sussex field on 17th July, and forensic estimations believed that she had been subjected to the elements and animals for over two weeks. The search and subsequent murder investigation became the largest investigation Sussex police had undertaken, and it had many interesting aspects to it – not least, the links with forensics. Specifically, what became known as the 'Coolham Shoe' played a central role in helping to convict Whiting. When police identified Whiting as a possible suspect, they examined his white van and, amongst the various items found, a clown curtain and red sweatshirt were recovered. They were also provided with intelligence from a member of the public, who claimed they saw a child's shoe at a junction in Coolham. Coolham, a hamlet in the Horsham District of West Sussex, is located at the crossroads of the A272 and B2139 roads. It is also approximately 20 miles from where Sarah was abducted and less than 10 miles from where her body was found (between Pullborough and Billinghurst). When the body of Sarah was discovered, and Whiting's van was searched, police could not find one of the shoes she was wearing. Understanding the importance of locating this shoe, the earlier sighting from the witness became one of the primary leads in the case. Despite several weeks passing since the sighting of the shoe, the senior investigating officers in charge of the case took a chance and went to the Coolham junction where, quite miraculously, they found Sarah's shoe a few hundred yards down from the junction. There were obvious signs of being run over by vehicles, but the shoe straps consisted of Velcro and, because of the tough nature of this type of material, a number of fibres were found still attached. Three main fibres were found: *a red fibre, a blue fibre* and a *multicoloured fibre*. Because of the distinctive nature of the multicoloured fibre, forensic analysts were able to individualise to the clown curtain found in Whiting's van, as well as making a positive match between the red fibre and Whiting's red sweatshirt and Sarah's blue sweatshirt. Figure 7.7 demonstrates the indirect transfer evidence that crucially linked Whiting to Sarah.

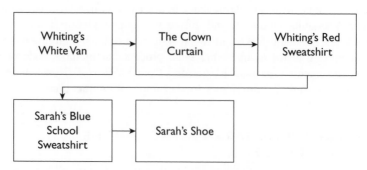

Figure 7.7 Indirect transfer of fibre evidence

Whilst direct transfer 'may be straightforward to interpret' (Houck and Siegel, 2010:55), indirect transfer potentially complicates matters considerably for crime scene investigators, detectives and forensic scientists. First, as the number of intermediary objects increases and spreads the evidence across several different areas, the amount transferred potentially decreases, making it difficult to establish links between people, objects and places (ibid.:55). Second, the contact between intermediary objects could involve unknown contact between offender A, and individual, object or place C, which has nothing to do with the crime event or events. How is it possible to know where to look for evidence if the contacts are unknown? Third, and on the flip side to this second point, evidence could be transferred from an external object or individual *onto* the crime scene or victim (ibid.:55). This is demonstrated by the famous US case of Wayne Williams who, in 1982, was found guilty of murdering Nathaniel Carter and Jimmy Payne. During the trial, evidence was introduced linking Williams to the murders of another ten boys and young men. This evidence included dog hairs and carpet fibres, all belonging to Williams, that were found on the bodies and/or clothing of numerous victims. Some of these dog hairs and carpet fibres were transferred via Williams to the victims (Saferstein, 2007:87–97).

The second major influence on the amount and quality of evidence transferred during a crime is *persistence* (see Figure 7.6) which relates to how long it will persist as it remains *in situ* before it is further transferred, collected as evidence, degraded, or lost. As with transference, the persistence of evidence depends upon a number of factors, some of which are similar to the factors already mentioned. Here factors relating to composition of matter play a role, such as mass, density, absorbance and weight. For instance, hairs persist less than paint (Houck, 2009:169). We must also consider factors external to the structure of the substance itself. The *location* and *environment* in which the evidence is transferred can determine the persistence of said material; for instance, is it open to the environment or protected from the elements? All possible weather factors such as rain, snow, sun, and dry can affect the persistence of trace. External crime scenes are notoriously difficult to gather appropriate evidence from, as weather conditions often interfere with trace evidence persistence, as in the case of attempting to undertake bloodstain pattern analysis outside when it is raining (Houck, 2004, 2009; Saferstein, 2007; Jackson and Jackson, 2011). Other factors affecting the persistence include the length of *time* between transfer and collection, which follows the general rule that the shorter the elapsed time usually means more evidence is available. This aspect has been clearly written into the investigative and forensic strategies developed by the police and is known as the *golden hour* rule, which is defined as 'the period immediately following the commission of an offence when material is in plentiful supply and readily available to the investigator (Rogers, 2007:161). The type of *activity* on or around the evidence is also crucial, as less activity leads to greater retention of evidence; again, this links closely to forensic strategies, which will be discussed in Chapter 9.

Particle memory

A useful question to consider is how case construction through the analysis of trace evidence is made possible? As it consists of the gathering of information about the crime event or events, we must look to information – and take a rather interesting tangential leap into the realm of quantum physics.

One of the sacred principles of physics is that information is never lost. It can be chopped up, scrambled, dissipated and shredded, but it is never lost. This idea underpins the concept of *unitarity*, which is an essential factor of unified theories of particles and forces and is located within the second law of thermodynamics (Hawking, 1988). All physical material on Earth consists of particles, which contain information about that material. For example, drug raids undertaken by the police often uncover trace evidence, or particles of substances, that need to be identified. Once an initial presumptive test is undertaken – for instance, the Marquis Color Test[6] – full confirmation is required so the substance is recovered and sent to the forensic laboratory for further testing (Christian, 2009; Houck and Siegel, 2010; Jackson and Jackson, 2011). The forensic analysts will use scientific techniques such as gas and liquid chromatography and infrared and mass spectroscopy (Christian, 2009:458–460) which unlock the information within the substance, including a breakdown of its chemical structure. In cases of rape and murder, a whole range of substances *could potentially* be transferred from one area to another; and identification of the substance and its source of origin aids in the reconstruction of the crime event or events. Logically, this idea within physics becomes extremely useful to the investigator of crime, especially when part of the investigation involves using information that is within one of the different forms of matter (Saferstein, 2007). As it is matter that always contains some form of information, particles found at crime scenes and on victims and offenders have the potential to provide both the identity of the material itself but also its format before it was *scrambled*. Of course, the aforementioned description is an oversimplification of the concept, for there exists the counter-theory that information can be lost (for example, Stephen Hawking's [1988] initial theories on information not existing in black holes). However, for the purposes of this text, it is enough to follow the basic principle, for it is commonly practiced within forensic science and, without it, there would be no practical use for the plethora of procedures and protocols regarding trace evidence.

This section has only briefly touched upon the issues relating to the quality and amount of trace evidence. However, this is enough to demonstrate that, when it comes to the physical evidence relied upon in criminal investigations, there are many factors that influence the type of evidence available for collection, what sort of information can be extracted from the evidence and the final interpretation and placing of the evidence in the overall narrative of the crime event. One of the most important factors impacting on these areas is what Chisum and Turvey (2008) call *evidence dynamics*.

Exchange evidence dynamics

Perhaps one of the overriding consistencies within forensic criminology is that it often yields imprecise results. Drilling down into the elements that make up the broader subject of forensic criminology, the same can be said of criminal investigations, forensic science and criminal trials, as all three are filled with potential evidentiary holes, sequential gaps and alternative possibilities (ibid.:166). It is therefore crucial that those involved in case construction, whether it's the police investigator, forensic analyst or trial barrister, understand how physical evidence can be affected by external forces which produce distortions in the evidence. This is known as *evidence dynamics* and is defined as 'any influence that adds, changes, relocates, obscures, contaminates, or obliterates physical evidence, regardless of intent' (Chisum and Turvey, 2007:161). The way evidence dynamics changes the nature of material will also have an impact on what type of information can be obtained, which of course influences the entire processes involved in criminal investigations. According to Chisum and Turvey (2007, 2008) an understanding of the range of external influences on physical evidence ensures critical thinking; and this means moving outside the sphere of the investigative mindset and not thinking that the *facts* are necessarily right or precise. This is also known as the *assumption of integrity* and is a useful concept because it describes the 'mistaken belief that taping off an area, limiting access, and setting about the task of taking pictures and making measurements somehow ensures the integrity of the evidence found within' (Chisum and Turvey, 2007:162). These actions are part of the overall processes of crime scene examination and will be discussed in Chapter 9. Their inclusion here is simply to highlight the fact that these practices often provide the faulty impression that the evidence at the scene has been protected and is unaltered (ibid.:162). In fact, evidence dynamics are often at work even before the crime happens for the routine activities of offenders and victims and the social and physical environment means that contact, transference and persistence issues are always at play and lots of the resultant *trace* potentially does not have anything to do with the crime event itself.

In their discussion of the factors affecting the forensic analysis of evidence for the purposes of crime reconstruction, Chisum and Turvey (ibid.:161–196) note two 'dynamic influences' that need to be considered. The first they label *pre-discovery* and the second *post-discovery*. Post-discovery effects on evidence will be discussed in Chapter 9, as they specifically relate to crime scene examination processing. Pre-discovery suggests that evidence will go through some or all of the following changes before the evidence is properly identified, recorded and transported from the scene for scientific analysis:

1   transference or the *creation* of the material;
2   changes due to time between crime event and detection – e.g. blood dries and bodies decompose;
3   changes due to environmental circumstances – e.g. rain, heat, snow, cold, wind;
4   alteration, destruction and further *creation* by officials – e.g. first officer(s) at scene; emergency service personnel; and
5   recognition or discovery of the *evidence* – e.g. often where evidence is identified through contact with personnel at the scene, such as stepping on the material.

There are potentially an infinite number of different combinations of pre-discovery evidence dynamics – the interaction between objects, individuals and environments – that could affect the form the evidence finally takes and the one that is used for interpretative purposes. However, for the analytical and practical purposes Chisum and Turvey (2007, 2008) have been able to reduce these infinite possibilities into nine broad categories, which are outlined in Table 7.3.

These categories are useful for understanding the complex nature of material objects and the role they play in the creation of material that is used in criminal investigations. This material still has a long journey to make before it ends up in a court room, for the information locked within can take different forms, and some of this information could be useless in relation to understanding the crime event. This is where crime reconstruction is useful again; for another function is to classify what the evidence is actually telling us.

Crime reconstruction classifications of evidence

As evidence is rarely discovered in its original, full format, it is identified and examined in a different mode. Any attempt at reconstruction needs to consider the role the evidence played in the commission of the crime and 'what it can establish regarding the events that have taken place' (Chisum and Turvey, 2008:160). In short, the evidence and how it is classified is framed around answering the who, what, when, where, how, and sometimes why questions' (ibid.:160). In order to

Table 7.3 Forms of evidence dynamics

Form	Description
Other Side of the Tape	Decisions are made as to where to place the cordon around a crime scene, and this can have an effect on the evidence. This is called the *limiting effect of crime scene boundaries*, as investigators may only focus on material within the inner or outer cordons, thus ignoring the possible evidence outside.
Crime Scene	There is the need to differentiate between the items/ objects that were pre-existing at the scene and material that is actual evidence and can inform the reconstruction process.
Offender Actions	The actions of an offender are often a factor in evidence dynamics. For instance, *precautionary actions* such as disguises, times of the day (i.e. the dark can obscure the offender), use of gloves, use of a condom, use of fire (see Turvey, 2008:212) can alter or change the evidence. In certain circumstances, offenders can engage in *ritualistic or fantasy* actions which alter the evidence. For example, the US serial killer Jeffrey Dahmer used some of the skulls and bones from his victims in a home-made coffee table (see Masters, 1993); other killers engage in mutilation or inserting objects into the body such as one offender who placed golf balls and a knife in a female victims' vagina in a case of domestic violence (Turvey, 2008:223–240). Finally, offenders engage in staging actions, where they alter the evidence on purpose to mislead the authorities or misdirect the investigation. Staged elements include staging the actual offence, so a murder looks like a suicide; scene location; weapons; removal or placing of items such as letters, notes, drugs, etc. (Turvey, 2008:241–271).
Victim Actions	The actions of the victim during the crime event can also alter the evidence. For instance, in the case of interpersonal violence or sexual assaults, the defensive actions, such as struggling or running, will increase the number of contacts and the likelihood of primary transfer.
Secondary Transfer	This is where the exchange of evidence between objects or persons occurs after the original exchange. For instance, evidence can also be transferred during the search process, such as hairs and fibres being transferred by investigators onto the crime scene.
Witnesses	Witnesses can also engage in post-offense or pre-discovery actions which can alter the nature and quality of the evidence.
Weather/ Climate	The natural elements such as temperature, precipitation and wind can affect the evidence, especially if the scene is outside and is subject to the weather and climate.

Form	Description
Decomposition	When it comes to organic carbon-based forms such as dead bodies decomposition will obscure, obliterate or mimic evidence.
Insect/Animal Activity	The actions of insects can alter evidence, as they can obliterate or alter wounds. For example, in blood pattern analysis there is a classification scheme that includes *altered,* which incorporates insect activity on and around the decomposing body (see James *et al.*, 2005).
Emergency Services Activity	The activities of the emergency services are predicated on the preservation of life, so many activities these services undertake lead to the altering or destruction of evidence. For example, fire suppression efforts will usually destroy much evidence.

answer some or all of these questions, investigators and forensic analysts will try to place the evidence in one or more categories of evidence classification (Figure 7.8).

Evidence is deemed to be *sequential* when it 'helps to establish when an event occurred or the order in which two or more events occurred' (ibid.:161). So, a fingerprint in the victim's blood (but not belonging to the victim) found on a door frame indicates that someone was at the scene after the 'bloodshed event'; or a 'footprint over tire track shows an individual person present subsequent to the vehicle passing' (ibid.:161). *Directional* evidence shows where the object came from and where it is going or went. For example, in cases of firearms discharge, the trajectory of the fired bullet is calculated by connecting two impact locations and measuring horizontal and vertical axes, perhaps using a laser line or trajectory

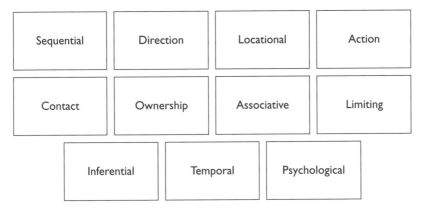

Figure 7.8 Evidence classifications

rod, to ascertain the direction or likely point of origin (Bevel and Gardner, 2008:157–167). Other examples include bloodstains, which can potentially identify the direction an individual was walking at the scene by examining the impact angle and directionality, also known as the gamma angle (ibid.:109–113); or where footprints determine the burglars directional actions. Evidence can also show where 'something happened, or where something was, and its orientation with respect to other objects at the location' (Chisum and Turvey, 2008:161). This is *locational* evidence and examples include the direction and orientation of a fingermark on a glass window of a car which demonstrates whether someone was inside the car or, in the case of fingermarks pointing downwards at the top of the window, indicates that someone was outside the vehicle and leaning into the car. Tool mark impressions on a window provide a possible entry point location, and therefore provide an area for crime scene examiners to investigate further.

Action evidence shows anything that happened during the crime event. To many, this may seem a tad absurd because of the assumption that all evidence is action evidence and is *ergo* useful. However, as Chisum and Turvey note (ibid.:162), 'misinterpretation of action evidence at any point during the reconstruction can provide for criminal charges brought against an innocent defendant'. If innocent people are wrongly accused, that means guilty people are going free; so identifying the right action evidence is important for justice. There are many examples of action evidence, some of which include (ibid.:163):

- bloodstains and patterns indicating a bloodshed event with possible injuries;
- broken glass with the majority of glass outside the window indicating that the window was broken from the inside; and
- wounds with sharp edges indicating a sharp force weapon such as a knife, sword or razor was used.

Of course, it should be highlighted that action evidence is heavily open to manipulation and can be staged.

Contact evidence has already been discussed in detail, for it is evidence that indicates two persons, objects or locations are associated, based upon Locard's exchange principle. Examples of contact evidence include trace evidence such as hairs, fibres, glass or paint. It can also include personal items at a residence indicating the number of occupants; for instance, two toothbrushes, towels and toiletry products. *Ownership* evidence is evidence that answers the *who* question as it includes items that belong to or are associated with an individual. This type of evidence includes *individuating forms* such as DNA, fingerprints, driving licences, credit cards, computers, mail, e-mail and written signatures. *Associative* evidence is usually a form of trace evidence that indicates 'certain or potential contact between persons or environments' (ibid.:163). Again, Locard's principle is used to identify common materials that indicate contact and can include evidence such as a bloody footprint, fibres, and gunshot residue. The general hope for any investigator would be to have collected a range of strong associative evidence so as to reduce the likelihood that the combination of associative evidence could be linked to another individual, what is known as the *product rule*, which is discussed in detail in Chapters 10 and 11 and relates to probability and statistical calculations used by forensic scientists (Lucy, 2005). Eighth on Chisum and Turvey's list is *limiting* evidence (ibid.:164). This concept is used to highlight that the nature and boundary of the crime scene, as identified by FOAs and CSIs, can limit the type and amount of material found. These personnel often establish both the primary and secondary crime scenes and make decisions regarding the inner and outer cordons. The *inferential* category relates to items that that may have been at the scene but not found, so inferences can be made as to the likely motive or offender fantasy element. For example, if a deceased female victim is found outdoors and her bra and underwear are missing, the inference could be there was a sexual motive behind the attack. However, caution must be exhibited with all forms of inferential reasoning as any assumptions made can be potentially misleading. In the aforementioned hypothetical example, the female victim may not have worn underwear on this occasion. The tenth type identified is *temporal* evidence, which is evidence that denotes the passage of time for actions that are relative to the commission of the crime (ibid.:165). Forensic entomologists, for instance, use the life cycle and activities of insects to provide useful information as to the timings between death and finding of murder victims (see Anderson, 2009; Gennard, 2012). Finally, *psychological* evidence can also be indicated by physical evidence. Crimes such as sexual assault, rape, and serial sexual murder often produce physical signs of acts committed by the offender to satisfy some personal need or motivation. Physical and sexual behaviours will often provide clues as to the offender's fantasy narrative (see Purcell and Arrigo, 2006 and Turvey, 2008).

Summary

This chapter examined some of the important issues in relation to information, material and evidence used within the framework of criminal investigations. In the UK, from around the 1930s onwards, Home Office officials began to plan for the systematic development and application of science methods and their integration into policing structures. The establishment of professional bodies, such as the Forensic Science Service and the British Academy of Forensic Science, as well as a number of forensic laboratories not only created the structural conduciveness for the creation of a new specialist occupation – the forensic scientist – but also increased the potential for research into physical evidence. To this end, it is important to understand that physical material contains information that needs to be unlocked, interpreted and placed within a classification scheme that makes it evidentially useful. To achieve this end, police and crime scene investigators and forensic analysts engage in crime reconstruction in order to construct cases against the perpetrators. What makes this task even more difficult is that there are a number of factors that will influence the form the material takes at the crime scene, *ergo* its interpretation as part of the reconstruction process. Evidence dynamics are at play even before the crime scene investigators identify evidence at the scene and must therefore be considered crucially important in understanding the crime event. Before information can be obtained from both people and material, that material must be identified and located, recorded *in situ* at the scene and transported to various laboratories for analysis. Police investigators and crime scene investigators undertake the majority of this work, and this is the subject of the next two chapters.

Chapter 8

Crime analysis and
crime mapping

Piss-Poor Planning Prevents Proper Performance
(Personal Communication, Research Officer for Wyre Forest,
31st January 2009)

Introduction

In the previous chapter, I examined the areas of information work that are
undertaken in relation to criminal investigations. This type of work tends to
revolve around the identification and collection of two generic types – physical
and non-physical. In Chapter 9, I examine in more detail the processes of
identifying and collecting physical evidence. This chapter considers the
importance of non-physical evidence and its relation and usefulness to forensic
investigations. One of the more practical subspecialties within academic
criminology is called crime analysis and crime mapping, which is a distinctive set
of criminological methods and theories, and up until the recent government
20 per cent slash-and-burn policies, crime analysis was one of the more steady
growth areas within criminal justice agencies in the UK. In particular, the police
service and Crime and Disorder Reduction Partnerships (CDRPs) had enjoyed
high levels of investment in recruitment, training and technology related to crime
analysis and crime mapping techniques (Boba, 2005; Chainey and Ratcliffe,
2005), which many regard as another tool in the crime prevention arsenal. As
discussed in Chapter 6, the introduction of the NIM brought about the pressing
need to develop intelligence *products* that could be analysed in a systematic way
in order to produce strategic and tactical crime prevention goals with measurable
outcomes (ACPO Centrex, 2005). Crime analysis and crime mapping tools have
become the dominant techniques used to achieve this end and to aid in both
proactive and reactive police investigations.

It is the purpose of this chapter to present an overview of crime analysis and
crime mapping. First, it outlines some basic definitional parameters of both concepts and discusses the core goals of crime analysis and crime mapping, showing
the ways in which these techniques aid in criminal investigations. Second, it
briefly examines the historical development of these two techniques and provides
an overview of the core criminological theories that underpin them. The final

section of the chapter reviews the core processes of crime analysis and crime mapping by reviewing the core issues, theories and tools utilised by both techniques. Before moving on to definitional issues, it is important to highlight the links to forensic criminology. The definition of forensic criminology supplied by Turvey and Petherick (2010:xxi), and expanded upon in the Introduction to this text, identified the applied use of research, theory and knowledge derived from criminology to address investigative and legal issues. Non-physical intelligence derived from proactive and reactive intelligence work fits within the remit of this definition. Crime analysis and crime mapping could rightly be placed as a subspecialty of forensic criminology because it uses crime data and police reports (including forensic/physical evidence) to study crime and respond to criminal justice problems. So, for instance, crime analysts use the characteristics of crime scenes, information about offenders and victimology reports in order to analyse patterns and trends in crime (Wortley and Mazerolle, 2008:1). Much of this information originates from the forensic realm, being a mixture of the physical, behavioural and witness evidence that results from the interplay between the victim, offender and context of the crime event(s) (see Scott, 1977).

Definitional parameters

As the work of crime analysts developed and became more permanently integrated within key sections of the criminal justice system, definitional parameters became increasingly important. Crime analysts working for the police service, for example, are guided by specific targets and measurable outcomes and therefore work within strictly defined parameters that make it fairly clear what is expected of them in their practical work. These types of parameters are often quite exclusive and have clearly defined operational boundaries. Academic definitions, on the other hand, tend to be inclusive. By way of illustration, consider the following three definitions of crime analysis:

> Crime analysis refers to the set of systematic, analytical processes that provide timely, pertinent information about crime patterns and crime trend correlations.
>
> (Emig *et al.*, 1980:v)

> Crime analysis is the systematic study of crime and disorder problems as well as other police-related issues – including socio-demographic, spatial and temporal factors – to assist the police in criminal apprehension, crime and disorder reduction, crime prevention, and evaluation.
>
> (Boba, 2005:6)

> Crime analysis involves the synthesis of police and other relevant data to identify and interpret patterns and trends in crime to inform police and judicial practice.
>
> (Cope, 2003:340)

The themes that are common in the above definitions are: *systematic and analytical processes*; providing *timely and pertinent information* about *crime patterns and crime trend correlations*; that use *socio-demographic, spatial and temporal factors*; and that aid in *criminal apprehension, crime and disorder reduction, crime prevention, and evaluation*. The relevance and usefulness of crime analysis for forensic criminology should be obvious. It provides empirical evidence of similar and linked crimes using police information such as crime reports, which, whilst predominantly consisting of non-physical evidence, can also include forensic/physical evidence (Ainsworth, 2001; Boba, 2005; Chainey and Ratcliffe, 2005; Wortley and Mazerolle, 2008). As with definitions of crime analysis, definitions of crime mapping are numerous. Consider the two definitions below:

> Crime mapping is the process of using a geographic information system to conduct spatial analysis of crime problems and other police-related issues.
>
> (Boba, 2005:37)

> Crime mapping is the direct application that comes from considering [this] inherent geography ... to help explain why crime occurs and most usually makes use of geographical information systems (GIS) to capture, analyze and visually interpret these geographical qualities.
>
> (Chainey, 2009:60)

Again, it is possible to identify a number of themes within these definitions. For example, most definitions state that crime mapping: uses *geographic information systems*; it provides a *spatial analysis of crime problems and other police-related issues*; and highlights the *geographic qualities of offending*; as well as enabling the *capture, analysis and visual interpretation of crime*. The core difference between the concepts crime analysis and crime mapping is that whilst crime analysis encompasses a broader range of methods and theories that utilise a myriad of data types, crime mapping is more focused and tends to use a specific type of data. It is perhaps easy to think of crime mapping as an analytical tool used for crime analysis. Despite the clear differences between the two, the terms crime analysis and crime mapping are often synonymous with each other. The reason for this synchronicity can be found by looking at their historical origins.

The development of crime analysis and crime mapping

The history and development of crime analysis and the placing of crime data (and other types of information) onto geographical maps has a long and interesting history. It was not until the 1960s and 1970s that Geographical Information Systems (GIS) emerged and were developed through applications 'such as planning for the US Census of Population in 1970 ... and from the national mapping agencies that began using technology to help automate their cartographic draughting' (Chainey and Ratcliffe, 2005:2). It is interesting to note that whilst

GIS has become more advanced due to rapid changes in computer technology, these developments are still based upon the simple idea that statistical data about crime locations and crime types can be visualised on a map.

Historical foundations and context

Crime analysis and crime mapping has its historical roots in the period where the growth in social statistics played a central role in developing sociological positivism (Davie, 2005; Rafter, 2009). Within this area, two central influences can be identified: (i) the growth of criminal statistics; and (ii) the mapping work of Charles Booth. The growth of criminal statistics in the nineteenth century created the opportunity to test theories, aid the criminal justice system and empirically ground social policies (Rafter, 2009:269). Andre-Michel Guerry (1802–1866), a French lawyer and statistician, organised the first annual collection of crime data in France. Guerry became part of France's Ministry of Justice project to create the first database on crime, which was called *Compte général de l'adminstration de la justice criminelle en France* (*General Account of the Administration of Criminal Justice in France*) (ibid.:270). What fascinated Guerry was the constancy of facts that were reproduced every year by the statistics collected and analysed. In perhaps his most famous of work – *Essai sur la statistique morale de France* (*Essay on the Moral Statistics of France*) – he defined his concept of *moral statistics* as:

> data aimed at the study of 'intellectual man' – his faculties, customs, and feelings. It is a field that embraces moral philosophy, politics, religion, legislation, history, literature, and the arts. In other words, he sees crime statistics as a means of understanding a broad range of human behaviour – of creating a sociology of man.
>
> (Ibid.:269)

One of the more controversial aspects of Guerry's work was his use of arrest statistics instead of conviction data. For Guerry, arrests represented a more accurate picture of the rate and type of crime that existed and could therefore be used for a more in-depth understanding of criminality (Guerry, 1833, cited in Rafter, 2009:270–271). He was one of the first individuals to map statistics of crimes, some examples of which include: property crimes reported per year in each province in France; the yearly average number of children born out of wedlock in each French province; and a map of crimes against persons in France. During the nineteenth century, there was an increase in the number of individuals producing this type of data; for instance, hygienist A. J.-B. Parent-Duchâtelet's (1790–1836) map of the origins of prostitutes in Paris. There is also an argument that the work of Guerry and others is an early form intelligence analysis for proactive and reactive policing; we certainly see the origin of the use of criminal statistics for policing and criminal justice purposes. However, Guerry was not the only one to develop criminal statistics. Aldophe Quetelet (1796–1874) followed up on Guerry's findings 're-emphasising the almost static nature of the annual figures and explaining . . . why numbers are better than individual cases when it comes to analysing criminal behaviour' (1835, cited in Rafter, 2009:269). Quetelet was a Belgian astronomer and mathematician, and he helped establish the quantitative tradition as well as attempting to insert criminal behaviour into a formal structure of causality (1825, cited in Rafter, 2009:273). In 1835 he wrote *Sur l'homme et le développement de ses facultés* (*On Man and the Development of his Faculties*), which set out to confirm the truth of the proposition that 'when we look at the human species en masse, we find order in the physical facts' (1935, cited in Rafter, 2009:277). He used the term *tendency to crime* to denote the probability of an individual committing crime, and he specifically considered the effects that variables such as the seasons, climate, gender and age had on this proclivity. For example, one conclusion he came to was that 'age is undoubtedly the cause that acts with the most energy to develop or dampen the tendency to crime' (1835, cited in Rafter, 2009:276). There were many other contributors that were involved in the development of criminal statistics, most notably: Joseph Fletcher (1813–1852), who from the 1840s statistically mapped social conditions in England and Wales and created models for the sociological investigation of crime (1849, cited in Rafter, 2009:278); Mary Carpenter (1807–1877), who in 1857 argued for the gathering of accurate statistics of the government's reformatories in order to properly evaluate research on crime control policies (1857, cited in Rafter, 2009:284); and Enrico Ferri (1856–1929), a follower of Lombroso, who in his famous *Criminal Sociology* (1898) advocated a positivist school of criminology, with criminal statistics being the 'most efficacious instruments for the study of crime' (Rafter, 2009:295). Ferri was a strong believer in crime prevention rather than deterrence, and he suggested that the best way of preventing crime was through statistical analysis, as it was only statistics that 'led us to the nature of crime as a social (as opposed to an individual) phenomenon' (Rafter, 2009:295).

The second major influence was the work of Charles Booth (1840–1916), who produced the phenomenal survey into life and labour in London from 1886 to 1903. Booth's work is especially relevant to crime analysis and crime mapping as he produced a number of maps of London onto which was placed a myriad of socio-demographic, criminal, religious and deprivation indices. More importantly, this groundbreaking work was the first of its kind to use a group of investigators in what can only be described as an early form of ethnographic analysis:

> The survey methodology was complex and original, as befitted such an ambitious exercise of empirical research. Booth attempted to understand the lives of Londoners through a tripartite investigation of their places of work and working conditions, their homes and the urban environments in which they lived, and through the religious life of the city. Investigators accompanied London School Board visitors, and policemen on their beats.

They interviewed factory owners, workers and trade union representatives at their places of work or in their homes. They visited ministers of religion and their congregations. The notebooks record the comments of interviewees and investigators and gathered data which was then used to generate statistical evidence of the living and working conditions of Londoners.[1]

Booth's work is testament to the spirit of scientific analysis and its use of empirically produced evidence to aid in the resolution of social problems. In this case it was an attempt to resolve problems before the criminal justice system became involved and further compounded the issue. In this respect, Booth was following the ideology ingrained in many of the Enlightenment philosophers' work, which attempted to facilitate the application of science and empiricism to enhance the social and economic circumstances and the health of members of society (Yeo, 2003; Snyder, 2006). Over the course of several key works, Booth developed a classification system of poverty, which he mapped across London. His most famous publications, *Maps Descriptive of London Poverty (1898-99)* and *Life and Labour of the People of London* (1902) represented one of the first systematic surveys of poverty in a UK major metropolitan city. With *Maps*, Booth and his researchers accompanied policemen on their beats across London and recorded what they saw on each street, their own interpretations of what they saw, as well as the policemens' own musings about their beat areas. Booth used a system of colour coding to identify the inhabitants of each street, ranging from the poorest and most criminal to the richest. Unfortunately, Booth's classification of the seven colour codes and the eight classes is not directly translatable (O'Day and Englander, 1993:47); however, the basic system started at: class A, consisting of the lowest class (e.g. occasional labourers, criminals and semi-criminals); class B, who were the very poor (e.g. defined as household earnings of less than 18s per week); class C were intermittent earners (18s to 21s per week); class D, which consisted of small regular earners (e.g. factory or dock workers, messengers and porters); class E, regular standard earners (22s to 30s per week); class F, higher-class labour (e.g. earnings in excess of 30s per week); class G, consisting of the lower middle class (e.g. shopkeepers, small employers, clerks and subordinate professional men); finally, class H, which were the upper middle class (ibid.).

The maps of Booth and his team, as well as the work of Guerry and the French social statisticians could easily be regarded as early examples of crime mapping. At the beginning of the twentieth century, the mapping of crime areas within the city became a key aspect of the dominant sociological explanations of crime and criminality. Through the unique and eclectic work of the Chicago School, the 'city' became a real-world laboratory which contained potent 'criminogenic forces' (Lilly *et al.*, 2011:40) and relocated pathology from the 'personal to the social plane' (Matza, 1990:47). Chicago School theorists used what were at the time sophisticated data and methodological triangulation techniques to examine the major problems within the city of Chicago. Merging statistical analysis with ethnography, life and oral histories, researchers used concepts such as social disorganisation and human ecology to map the different levels of poverty and crime across the city. Perhaps the most relevant study in relation to crime mapping and analysis is *The City* ([1925]1967) by Robert Park, Ernest Burgess and R. McKenzie. *The City* introduced the zonal hypothesis which identified areas in Chicago where youthful delinquents were found. The researchers divided the city into five concentric circles or zones; and zones further from the centre were less prone to delinquency, as they were neighbourhoods with higher socio-economic status and standards of living (Park *et al.*, [1925]1967; Blumer, 1984; Downes and Rock, 2007). The zones where crime was highest were labelled *transitional neighbourhoods*, where deviant and conventional values competed side by side; and these were neighbourhoods with the largest influx of immigration and migration and the poorest levels of housing and socio-economic status.

Current developments – databases, murder and crime science

Building on the important work discussed in the previous section, current developments in the techniques of crime analysis and crime mapping have increased rapidly over the last 40 years. These developments have largely been the result of intensive academic research, technological innovation and organisational innovation and reform. The majority of these developments have taken place in the final period identified by Morris (2007:31–35) as *central initiative and control*, and they are part of the professionalisation and reform of the police which took place from 1981 onwards (Morris, 2007; Savage, 2007; Brain, 2010). As highlighted in Chapter 6, this period saw an increase in the centralisation and professionalisation of training as well as the implementation of the Core Investigative Doctrine. The expansion of crime analysis can be seen as linked to these processes and are part of what Bottoms and Wiles (1997) see as an increase in new public management and the move towards capturing police performance and accountability. For example, the introduction of the National Crime Intelligence Service (NCIS) and the National Crime Squad (NCS, which later became the Serious Organised Crime Agency, or SOCA), as well as the National Police Improvement Agency (NPIA) and Professionalising Criminal Investigation Programme (PIP) can all be considered as important developments that influenced the growth of crime analysis (Cope, 2003:341). With the passage of the Crime and Courts Act 2013, SOCA became the new National Crime Agency (NCA) in 2013 (SOCA, 2013). The move towards greater accountability for the police has been applied through the lens of problem-oriented and intelligence-led approaches, and crime analysis supports this (Cope, 2003). For example, the ideology behind problem-oriented policing, as we have seen (see Chapter 6), suggests police switch emphasis away from responding to symptoms of problems and instead have a significant role in crime prevention and reduction (Ratcliffe, 2008). Thus, in order for core problems and their relevant components to be identified, some form of analysis needs to be undertaken. John and Maguire

(2007:201) note that the growth in intelligence-led policing occurred for the following reasons:

- perceived ineffectiveness of reactive policing;
- limitations on interviewing and confession evidence;
- advances in technology;
- increased focus on serious and organised crime; and
- pressures for more efficient and effective use of resources.

Intelligence-led policing has been greatly influenced by NIM and was developed initially under the NCIS. NCIS provided a blueprint for a business model for organisation of police responses to crime and, as Maguire (2003:387) notes, was based on the primary notion that the core business of policing is to collect relevant information to allow a clear and accurate identification and analysis of current and likely future problems. However, in order to collect relevant information, this information needs to exist and to be accessible, and this has been made possible due to the growth and development in computer-based technologies over the last 30 years and the creation of a range of *databases*. The identification and analysis of policing problems is much easier when computer database information systems are made available, are efficient and up to date, and the information is shared across different agencies. Whilst the list is not exhaustive, Table 8.1 outlines some of the key databases that crime analysts use.

Any one of these databases, and many more besides, can potentially be used to identify crime problems and enable the police to target areas and specific problems, following the ideologies of problem-oriented, intelligence-led policing, as well as NIM.

Linked to all the developments mentioned above, the tragic murder of TV presenter Jill Dando provided further impetus for the development of crime analysis and crime mapping, under the term *crime science*. On 26th April 1999 at around 11.30am, Jill Dando arrived home at Gowan Avenue, London and was

Table 8.1 Computer databases

Database	Description
PNC	The *Police National Computer* is the main computer system used by police across England and Wales. It went live in 1974 and contains (approximately): over 9 million 'nominal' (person) records; 52 million driver records; and 55 million vehicle records.
PIS	*Police Intelligence Systems* are individual for each UK police force and operate as the major database where crimes are recorded and intelligence on crimes, offenders and victims is generated. Examples include Guardian (Avon and Somerset police), and CRIMINTS (the criminal intelligence system used by the Metropolitan police).

Database	Description
QUEST	*Querying Using Enhanced Search Techniques* enables the search of the names in the database to identify suspects through the use of gathered information such as physical description and personal features.
VODS	*Vehicle Online Descriptive Search* allows users to search the vehicles database by search criteria such as registration, postcode and colour details to narrow the list to potential suspect vehicles.
ANPR	*Automatic Number Plate Recognition* is used to take a visual image of a number plate; the PNC scans thousands of numbers each hour, alerting police to any that are of interest.
CRIMELINK	An enhanced, web-based version of the *Comparative Case Analysis Tool* (CCA), which can be used to solve serious serial-type crimes by searching for similarities in incidents, helping investigators to identify patterns and links.
NDNAD	The *National DNA Database* was set up in 1995 and holds approximately 6 million profiles (10 per cent of the UK population). The NDNA stores patterns of short tandem repeats, and not the full genome profile of individuals. Individuals' skin or blood samples are permanently linked to the database.
HOLMES2	*Home Office Large Major Enquiry System 2*: this system is used by UK police forces for the investigation of major incidents. It provides an integrated intelligence management system and can handle vast amounts of material and information.
ViSOR	*Violent and Sex Offender Register* is a UK-wide system used to store and share information and intelligence on those individuals who have been identified as committing violent and/or sexual crime and posing a risk of serious harm to the public. Details of offenders' MO and their physical and demographic characteristics, as well as offence behaviours and victimology information, are stored on this system.
CHILDBASE	This database was developed by POLIT (The Paedophile Online Investigation Team) and is a database that helps identify victims of abuse, as well as the abusers themselves. As of 2005, the system contained approximately 220,000 photos and images of children being abused, which paedophiles have distributed on the net.
ACORN	*A Classification Of Residential Neighbourhoods* is a geodemographic tool for categorising some UK postcodes into a typology based upon socio-economic demographic information taken from the census. It can be used to link postcode and socio-economic data to geographic information systems such ArcGIS.
MULTIPLE INDICES OF DEPRIVATION	This database combines a number of indicators, chosen to cover a range of economic, social and housing issues, into a single deprivation score for each small area in England.

shot once in the head on her doorstep. The forensic analysis of the evidence at the scene and on the body found that 'a firearm had been pressed to her head when her assailant discharged the weapon' ([2007] EWCA Crime 2722, p. 2, section 2).[2] The obvious shock from the public and high media visibility put pressure on the investigators, and they identified a suspect who they thought was the correct murderer. Barry George was arrested on 25th May 2000, and on 29th May appeared at West London magistrates' court charged with her murder ([2007] EWCA Crime 2722, pp. 2–7, sections 4 and 7). On 23rd April 2001, George's trial began at the Old Bailey and the prosecution relied primarily on four pieces of evidence ([2007] EWCA Crime 2722, pp. 2–3, section 5):

1 An eyewitness claimed to have seen George at the scene of the crime four hours before the murder, although it was not a positive identification;
2 George's interview was characterised as 'containing repeated lies, in particular, as to his knowledge of and interest in Miss Dando';
3 The fact that he 'made considerable attempts to create a false alibi for the time of the shooting'; and
4 The similarity between the firearm discharge residue (FDR) that was found on the wound of the victim and the single particle (11.5 microns [approximately one-hundredth of a millimeter]) of FDR that was found in the pocket of George's Cecil Gee coat.

On 2nd July 2001, and after deliberating for 32 hours, the jury convicted George for the murder of Jill Dando with a 10:1 majority. Protesting his innocence, George appealed twice, first in July 2002, which was dismissed, and then again on 15th November 2007. Having spent six years in prison, the appeal was allowed on the basis of the *fresh evidence rule*, and the sentence was quashed ([2007] EWCA Crim 2722]. Unfortunately, that was not the end for George. He endured another trial for the murder in December 2007, again pleading not guilty; however, he was eventually acquitted of the charge on 1st August 2008. The Dando case represents a seminal example of how the combination of both physical and non-physical evidence can link together in an investigation to produce a miscarriage of justice; but, whilst *R v George* remains yet another black mark on the criminal justice system, something positive came from the presenter's death. After a £1 million donation made by the Trustees of the Jill Dando Fund on 26th April 2001 (which was the second anniversary of her death), the Jill Dando Institute of Crime Science, based at UCL (University College London), was established (Laycock, 2005:3). Nick Ross, Dando's co-presenter on the BBC programme *Crimewatch*, opened the institute and is also accredited with coining the term *crime science*. Following from this, in 2002, a number of academics came together to try to form a definitional system, which included (ibid.:3–25):

• an attempt to conceptualise and operationalise key concepts and their relationships to each other;

- a discussion around the dissatisfaction of theory and practice with an attempt to place emphasis on the individual criminal;
- consideration of non-offender methods of crime reduction; and
- an emphasis on concentrating on situational methods of crime prevention.

Crime science is outcome-focused, as it attempts to reduce crime, so the emphasis is placed very much on crime prevention methods. It is also based within what Packer called the 'crime control' model of criminal justice (1964, cited in Davies *et al.*, 2005), which emphasises *prevention* (stopping crime from happening) and *detection* (increasing efficiency in catching people). The crime control paradigm provides a social function of punishment, and it prioritises a number of elements: (i) the disregard of legal controls; (ii) the implicit presumption of guilt; (iii) high conviction rates; (iv) an emphasis on the unpleasantness of the criminal justice experience; and (v) provision of support for the police and their actions. Laycock (2005:6) also suggests that crime science is multidisciplinary in nature, as it utilises theories and methods of the physical, social, biological, and computer sciences. In doing so, crime science should follow the same methodologies, standards and values of the natural sciences, so that theories are explicit and testable and methods control for chance, bias, and other extraneous factors; which follows the randomised control trial (RCT) guidance laid out by the Campbell Collaboration.[3] Crime science developed at a time when the government placed great emphasis on protecting the public using advances in science and technology; for example, through groups such as the Home Office Scientific Development Branch (HOSDB), the Police Science and Technology Group (PSTG) and the Future Scanning Sub-Group (FSSG). Such groups consisted of members of *hard* science and engineering communities who acted as scouts in identifying scientific and technological innovations that were relevant to crime as well as developing links between the three fields of education, crime and justice, and social welfare (Smith and Tilley, 2005). These activities followed the government's science and innovation plan, which was outlined in the *Police Service Strategy 2010–2013* and suggested that 'robust research needs to be delivered in a way that equips officers with the knowledge they need to make decisions' (NPIA, 2010a:3). Because of the problems created by the world economic recession, policies have been put into place regarding reducing the costs of and maximizing the efficient use of the finite resources, what is often called the *more for less* strategy. Crime science, as seen through the lens of the Government's science and innovation strategy, considers how best the decreased resources can be used to reduce and prevent crime and 'stresses the importance of horizon scanning in setting priorities for research and development' (ibid.:6). In short, crime science looks at how science and technology can be used to produce efficient (i.e. cost-saving) crime prevention/reduction techniques and tools by looking at the holistic picture of crime. A useful mnemonic for this type of analysis is *PESTLE* – Political,

Economic, Social, Technological, Legal, Environmental – which is an analytical tool developed for the business world to:

> track the environment they're operating in or are planning to launch a new project/product/service etc. . . . It gives a bird's eye view of the whole environment from many different angles that one wants to check and keep a track of while contemplating on a certain idea/plan.
>
> http://pestleanalysis.com

By understanding the PESTLE factors that relate to crime, analysts can identify core crime and disorder problems and make suggestions as to where the police prioritise their resources to ensure efficient crime fighting. The science and innovation in the police service strategy uses crime science to harness sometimes radical, long-term scientific developments into a threefold approach of (Ekblom, 2005; Pease, 2005):

- **Coordination** – where different criminal justice and science organisations' goals and objectives align together to have maximum impact;
- **Collaboration** – where specialists from different sectors and disciplines work together, encouraging innovation and knowledge transfer; and
- **Challenge** – where investment in innovation is targeted to where it will deliver the strongest benefits.

In order to achieve all this, we must consider four important factors: what science can tell us about the nature of crime; what it can contribute to prevention; how science can support detection; and finally, how scientific method is applicable to crime reduction (Smith and Tilley, 2005). At the meeting in 2002, Ron Clarke suggested that a coherent theory should underpin crime science (Laycock, 2005:6).

Theoretical foundations

Crime analysis and crime mapping, like its parent discipline forensic criminology, utilises a multitude of theories and methods. It is this multidisciplinary approach that enables a richness of data and methodological triangulation that can be applied to the broad range of policing and crime and disorder problems. It includes the core theories suggested by Ron Clarke in 2002 (Laycock, 2005:6): *environmental criminology,* the *rational choice perspective, situational precipitators of crime, routine activity approach* and *crime pattern theory.* The following section provides only a broad review of these theories.

Environmental criminology

Environmental criminology is not a theoretical perspective per se but should be viewed more as an umbrella term in which a number of specific crime analysis and crime mapping theories are situated. It is, therefore, a group of theories that provides an integrated approach that cover the three domains of *theory, analysis* and *practice* (Wortley and Mazerolle, 2008:3). According to Brantingham and Brantingham 'environmental criminology argues that criminal events must be understood as confluences of offenders, victims or criminal targets, and laws in specific settings at particular times and places' (1991:2, cited in Wortley and Mazerolle, 2008:1). Where offender profiling primarily seeks to understand the offender and his or her behaviour, environmental criminology's task is to describe and understand crime patterns; as seen in Brantingham and Brantingham's (1984) seminal study which brought together a number of theories and applications to examine the interdependency between environmental influences and crime patterns. According to Wortley and Mazerolle (2008:2–3), the environmental perspective is based upon three premises:

1   Criminal behaviour is significantly influenced by the nature of the immediate environment in which it occurs. All criminal behaviour results from a 'person–situation interaction, with the environment playing an active role in the crime event'.
2   The distribution of crime in time and space is not random, due to the fact that criminal behaviour is dependent upon situational factors and determined by the crime location. Most crime is concentrated around crime opportunities and environmental factors that 'facilitate criminal activity'.
3   The adequate investigation and prevention of crime should rest on an understanding of the role of criminogenic environments and crime patterns. Resources can concentrate on particular crime problems and areas.

The first premise has its historical origins in the mapping of crime statistics in the early work of the Chicago School (see above). It also follows Scott's (1977) work on dangerous offenders, which details the interaction between offender, victim and context and circumstance. The context and circumstance of crime is the location and environment in which the crime takes place. The second premise is interesting, for it argues that behaviour, and more specifically criminal behaviour, is not random. The issue here is whether it is possible to identify structured patterns in order to understand and predict future patterns or types of criminal behaviour. This is, of course, reminiscent of the underlying epistemological philosophy of the natural sciences outlined in Chapters 2, 3 and 4. There is still much debate as to whether it is possible to accurately detect patterns of human behaviour, much of which is tied to criminological debates around assessment of risk and dangerousness (see Prins, 1995, 2010; Nash, 2006; Nash and Williams, 2008, 2010). For example, Harcourt's (2007) *Against Prediction* proffers an anti-actuarial thesis of *randomness* in relation to racial profiling in the US. Regardless of which paradigmatic belief one holds, environmental criminology has been quite successful in providing more empirically robust solutions to criminal justice problems such as crime prevention; which is the basis of the third premise.

Another important aspect introduced by Brantingham and Brantingham (1984:251–365, 1991) was their identification of three levels of analysis – *macro-*, *meso-* and *micro-spatial* patterns of crime. They argue that 'the spatial patterning of crime can be analyzed through a cone of resolution at many different levels' (1984:251). First was the lowest level, which they called macro-spatial patterns in crime (1991:251–296). This refers to a level of spatial resolution that examines world and national crime patterns (ibid.:251; Wortely and Mazerolle, 2008:3–4). This particular level of orientation involves the study of the distribution of crime between countries or, in contemporary terms, global comparative crime rates. It is thought that looking at the aggregate data of crime across these broad geographical areas enables the conceptualisation of environmental influences on crime; and, historically, macro-spatial analysis has its roots in the research of Guerry and Quetelet outlined above. The two data sources used in Brantingham and Brantingham's macro-spatial analysis were the United Nations Survey of Crime Rates and Crime Problems from the 1970s, and the International Criminal Police Organisation's (Interpol) database on recorded crime and criminal convictions, which they have been collecting since 1950 (1984:251). Using this information, they mapped crime across the world, demonstrating some interesting patterns in different rates for different crimes for different countries. For example, theft rates per 100,000 of the population were 1,580.3 for Western Europe, North America, and Oceania, and 1,302.8 for the Caribbean, compared with 153.1 for North Africa and the Middle East. On the other hand, rates for intentional homicide were 2.1 per 100,000 for Western Europe, North America, and Oceania compared with 6.7 for the Caribbean and 4.7 for North Africa and the Middle East (ibid.:252). The differences between the crime rates across the different world regions allows for some initial inferences about environmental contexts. For example, possible explanations for the very high theft rates within the Western Europe, North America, and Oceania and Caribbean areas could be explained by: (a) higher concentrations of consumable goods within the first region and; (b) high levels of tourism within the second region. Another example is that the rates from the UN crime survey 'noted a major difference in the relative crime mixes of nations at different stages of economic development' (ibid.:255). Still within the macro approach, Brantingham and Brantingham compared crime patterns between England, Canada, and the United States (ibid.:261–279). Their conclusions stated that world and international crime patterns 'persist over relatively long periods of time, and are, in some respects, consistent with one another' (ibid.:195).

The second level is the higher state of meso-spatial analysis. This involves the study of crime patterns within subareas of a city or, as Brantingham and Brantingham put it, 'intercity crime patterns' (ibid.:251). They compared crime rates between states/counties or cities within a particular country, as well inter-metropolitan crime patterns within both the USA and Canada (ibid.:279–285). They explained the reason for meso-level analysis as follows (ibid.:261):

> Geographic patterns at the world level of aggregation, however, mask underlying differences within nations ... the crime patterns of England,

Canada, and the United States resolve into regions with very different crime problems when examined at the county, province, or state level. Some regions have very high crime rates, and other regions have low crime rates. Crime mix also varies by region: some areas have problems with violent personal crime but not with property crime; some regions have property crime problems, but not violent crime problems.

The main point of moving to the higher level of analysis is to identify variability within regions, and this, therefore, opens up the possibility of statistical analysis utilising tests such as correlation, covariance, comparison of means and analysis of variance (Agresti and Finlay, 1997; Field, 2013). Whilst such tests cannot say much about individual motivations and reasons behind offending behaviour, they do demonstrate that crime is not uniformly distributed across urban space.

The third and final level of analysis identified by Brantingham and Brantingham (1984:332–365) is micro-spatial analysis. This level of analysis examines specific crime sites, focusing on 'building type and its placement, landscaping and lighting, interior form, and security hardware' (Brantingham and Brantingham, 1991:21–22, cited in Wortley and Mazerolle, 2008:6). The micro focus examines the immediate environment and how this influences the decisions and behaviour of individuals. Much of this focus is based upon the debates in psychology about what causes behaviour and, as such, introduces the concept of the *active individual*. This active individual, therefore, becomes part of the definition of criminal behaviour, which the Brantinghams give as 'a complex form of subjective spatial behaviour in which movement patterns depend on underlying spatial mobility biases, knowledge, and experience' (1984:332). They begin by describing the environment of a crime and conceptualise the environment for an individual as 'the totality of objects – people, places and things – that he or she comes in contact with and the relationships that influence his or her behaviour' (ibid.:333). The focus of analysis is between the environment and individual behaviour, and it is these two areas that are conceptualised and theorised at the micro-spatial level. In order to achieve this, Brantingham and Brantingham (ibid.:334–344) utilise two core models of the environment. First, they review the work of Gans (1972, cited in Brantingham and Brantingham, 1984:334), who divided the environment into the *potential environment* and the *effective environment*. The potential environment is the 'physically real', and is composed of non-manipulatable and manipulatable elements, such as climate (non-manipulatable) and buildings, roads and human-made structures (manipulatable) (Brantingham and Brantingham, 1984:334). For Gans, the potential environment is selectively interpreted through an effective environment which is made up of a social system or cultural norms and which helps to influence behaviour. Gans argues that because human activity is able to alter the manipulative physical environment – for example, through changes to buildings or the infrastructure – there is an *endless loop* between the potential and effective environments. Subsequently, there is symbiosis between individual behaviour/action and the environment, with both of these elements influencing each other (1972, cited in Brantingham and Brantingham, 1984:334). The second model of the environment used was Sonnenfield's work on geography, perception and the behavioural environment (1972, cited in Brantingham and Brantingham, 1984: 334–335). The *geographical environment* is the 'totality of all things in the universe' (1984:334) and is the objective reality that exists outside of the individual's inner world. The *operational environment* is the section of the geographical environment that has a direct impact on the individual. However, the individual may not be aware of this impact. The third type is the *perceptual environment*, which is a sub-part of the operational environment and is the awareness aspect of the individual's operational environment. This awareness is primarily learned through past experiences, indirect experiences and current events and is closely linked to Blumer's (1992) three components of symbolic interactionism. Finally, the behavioural environment is the section of the perceptual environment that 'triggers actions or responses, or the part of the environment toward which actions are directed' (Porteus, 1977:139, cited in Brantingham and Brantingham, 1984:334). For the purposes of forensic criminology, the behavioural environment where crime occurs is of most interest when attempting to understand the crime event for analysis and mapping purposes. Brantingham and Brantingham note five components of the behavioural environment for crime (1984:335–336):

1   *Physical setting* – the physical structure or the potential environment (Gans, 1972, cited in Brantingham and Brantingham, 1984:335); for example, buildings, roads and climate;
2   *Social setting* – the socio-economic conditions, group structures, and social networks that form the social setting for action;
3   *Psychological setting* – consists of the psychological and physical predispositions to commit crime;
4   *Legal setting* – the laws and policing patterns that result in the labelling of individual actions as criminal; and
5   *Cultural setting* – consists of the belief and values systems that influence and control behaviour.

For the micro-spatial aspect of the environmental perspective, accurate analysis and mapping of crime is contingent upon the examination of the interplay and interdependency between the physical and behavioural environments. The usefulness of this perspective for forensic criminology should not be underestimated, for, whilst the use of forensic analysis tells us much about what happened and who was involved in the crime event, full reconstruction can only occur when the context and understanding of why the crime occurred is included. Environmental criminology aids in providing this deeper context and understanding of the crime event. By way of an example, some empirical sociological studies of the 1960s and 1970s provide the necessary structural and environmental analysis and context of the processes that influenced individuals to commit crime.

CASE STUDY 8.1 WORKING-CLASS CRIMINALITY AND THE ENVIRONMENT

Peter Willmott's (1969) seminal study *Adolescent Boys of East London* was part of a small but highly significant flurry of sociological research around youth in the mid 1960s. Willmott considered a broad range of social and environmental elements that converged on a group of working-class adolescent boys growing up in Bethnal Green. He considered:

*   group and gang interactions;
*   personal relationships (i.e. girls, sex and marriage);
*   family and kinship networks;
*   school and work; and
*   delinquency and criminal activity.

Willmott used a range of empirical data collection and analysis methods; most importantly, he used diary records kept by the boys themselves, statistical and spatial data, as well as interviews (ibid.:187–220). One of the most interesting facets of Willmott's study was his analysis of the environmental conditions in which these adolescent lives and behaviours were shaped and influenced.

A core finding was the way that the changing environment – i.e. through changes to buildings and streets – determined the routine activities and behaviour of those living within. The move from the traditional working-class two-storey Victorian terraced cottages, 'low-browed and intimate, in patterned short streets with corner shops and pubs' (ibid.:15), to the 'soaring glass and concrete of the council flats' (16) not only changed the structure and layout of the street but also destroyed the old sense of the community. In many places these changes moved the working classes further away from the problems of previous generations; for example, problems of malnutrition and poverty. However, Willmott identified a number of effects that the changing environment had on the boys. For example, it was found that changes in local buildings and street formats meant that they spent less time locally and were not as tied to their locality as earlier generations (ibid.:23).

Despite its age, Willmott's *Adolescent Boys of East London* demonstrates how the spatial and structural local environment influences individual and group behaviour, including factors like routine activities and the propensity and opportunity to commit criminal acts.

Rational choice perspective

The rational choice (RC) perspective provides a theory for practice (Cornish and Clarke, 2008:21). It is a perspective that pays less attention to pontificating about criminal motivation and more attention to finding out about how crimes occur in order to develop practical ways to prevent them from happening. At its theoretical centre are the concepts of 'choice and decision-making, present-centredness, and the centrality of the crime event to continued criminal activity' (ibid.:21). Historically, the RC perspective has its roots in the classical school of criminology, with its emphasis on the 'individual criminal as a person who is capable of calculating what he or she wants to do' (Lilly *et al.*, 2011:20) – humans have free will and their actions are guided by hedonism. RC perspective is simply a more complex and detailed development of early classical ideas and comes from the dissatisfaction with the positivist, rehabilitative models that were dominant in the 1950s (in part), the 1960s and the 1970s. Within this paradigm, criminal behaviour was believed to be a result of individual pathology, an idea that gained much currency because of the medicalisation of deviancy that took place from the 1950s onwards (Pearson, 1975; Conrad and Schneider, 1992). Individuals who committed crime were believed to suffer from long-term biological predispositions and psycho-pathologies (Rafter 1997, 2009; Downes and Rock, 2007; Lilly *et al.*, 2011). The belief in this paradigm, which is not entirely unfounded, led to a large investment in research and treatment programmes in the hope of preventing the development of criminality (Cornish and Clarke, 2008:22).

Unfortunately, this approach meant that offenders were taken out of their environment and the context in which their offending took place and were relocated to total institutions (Goffman, 1991), 'treated', and then reinserted back into the community with 'varying degrees of support' (Cornish and Clarke, 2008:22). Unfortunately, research that concentrates on one area at the expense of another is more likely to produce a myopic understanding of criminality and is, thus, doomed to failure. The perceived failure of the rehabilitative model, however, produced two important outcomes, and these had a huge influence in the development of the RC perspective. First was the fact that relapse back into criminality was commonplace. The second was the identification of the effect that treatment environments had on individuals. Many were clearly affected by their treatment environments, which appeared to have an influence on their behaviour. This observation soon led to research that produced empirical evidence 'of the effects of the immediate environment on inmates' behaviour' which pointed to the 'influence of the current environment on behaviour' (see Sinclair, 1971 and Clarke and Martin, 1975, cited in Cornish and Clarke, 2008:22).

According to Cornish and Clarke (2008:22), this evidence and research resulted in an environmental/learning theory explanation of behaviour, which consisted of four key elements. The first element plays homage to positivistic notions of behaviour by arguing that, whilst an individual's 'emotional inheritance and upbringing play some part in delinquency', the major influence that determines behaviour is the *current environment* (Clarke and Cornish, 1983:37, cited in Cornish and Clarke, 2008:22). Judith Harris provides a wonderful thesis supporting this idea. In *The Nurture Assumption* (Harris, 1999), she argues that, when it comes to behaviour, the social environment including socio-economic status and exposure to social problems such as violence, drug and alcohol misuse has very little to do with children's behaviour. Harris provides a convincing argument that it is an individual's *current environment* and the *interaction between social networks* that provides the major determinant for behaviour. The second element is that the current environment provides the *cues, stimuli and reinforcements* for criminality, which includes states of emotion that might create a 'readiness to offend' if the opportunity lends itself to such action. If this readiness produces a criminal act, then it becomes part of the 'individual's behavioural repertoire' with reinforcement and opportunity becoming crucial to its maintenance (Cornish and Clarke, 2008:23). Third, is the principle of *consistency*: it was found that similar conditions would produce a similar crime event, so consistencies in behaviour were therefore dependent upon consistencies in an individual's environment. Finally, different types of criminal or delinquent acts 'do not serve equivalent functions' for the individual. Each act and function is acquired, developed and maintained by '*situational variables* specific to it, and it alone' (Cornish and Clarke, 2008:23).

One of the more important aspects of the RC perspective was that it highlighted the fact that criminal behaviour was more fluid and malleable that had previously been thought and that this fluidity was fundamentally tied to environmental and situational variables. Conceptualising criminal behaviour in this way enabled a way of thinking about how the environment might be manipulated to prevent crime, which led to the development of *situational crime prevention* practice, which started to use the notions of choice and decision-making. In this sense, RC theory was very much an attempt to think of, and provide practical solutions to, criminal justice problems. Cornish and Clarke highlight that the 'language of intentionality and choice is the discourse of the criminal justice system and of everyday life' (ibid.:23), so attempts were made get inside the offender's *head*, to try to identify their decision-making processes. In the mid-1980s these ideas brought together a convergence of different academic disciplines including: the sociology of deviance, criminology, economics, and cognitive psychology (Clarke and Cornish, 1985:149, cited in Cornish and Clarke, 2008:24).

> The picture that emerged was one of offenders as reasoning criminals, using cues present in potential crime settings to guide their decisions about whether (or not) to commit particular crimes and, if so, how to commit them.
>
> (Cornish and Clarke, 2008:24)

Rational choice theory has a six core concepts and four decision-making models embodying them (see Table 8.2). It is deemed to be a *heuristic device*

Table 8.2 The core concepts of rational choice

Concept	Description
Criminal behaviour is purposive	• Uses a simple theory of action;[1] • People have needs and desires and beliefs about how these can be fulfilled; • Beliefs guide actions that attempt to achieve these goals; • Action is therefore purposive; • Crimes are purposive and deliberate acts that are committed to benefit the offender; • Benefits include: money, sexual gratification, excitement, autonomy, admiration, revenge, control, material goods, etc.

Criminal behaviour is rational	• An individual's behaviour is deemed to be rational as most people select the best means to achieve their needs and desires;
	• Similar to Weber's (1978) notion of instrumental action – determined by expectations as to the behaviour of objects and human beings in the environment;
	• However, it is not perfect rationality but instead is guided by a number of principles that have specific functions:
	  – Intellectual functions – principle helps us organise our beliefs and chart our intellectual development;
	  – Interpersonal functions – interact with other people to reach a certain goal together (e.g. commit crime);
	  – Personal functions – principles help organise our own goals and desires (e.g. be healthy);
	  – Overcoming temptation – principles can aid in guiding non-action;
	• An action is rational when it is most effective and efficient in the attainment of a goal.

Criminal decision-making is crime specific	• Making decisions to commit crimes is often crime specific – i.e. it depends upon the crime; • Crime is a diverse range of behaviours – i.e. each crime has its own particular motives, purposes and benefits; • For each different crime a different set of beliefs, motives and cognitive processes may come into play; • Each crime event comes with its own specific circumstances, risks, efforts, rewards, activities undertaken and locations within which they take place; • It is important to distinguish the choices and decisions made in each crime event.

Criminal choices fall into two broad groups: 'involvement' and 'event'	• Need to distinguish between (a) *involvement decisions* and (b) *crime event decisions*;
	  – *Crime event decisions* are crime specific and are undertaken when preparing for, carrying out and concluding the crime event;
	  – *Involvement* decisions incorporate a rich range of variables from the criminal's career – e.g. initial involvement, continued involvement and desistence;
	• Decisions to consider include: the complexities involved in committing the crime, risks involved, skills required, alternatives to the crime in question, moral considerations, and the costs of discovery.

There are separate stages of involvement	• There are three broad stages of criminal involvement:
	  – *Initiation* – getting involved in crime, which can be influenced by a number of background variables including: personality and upbringing, lifestyle, education, needs and motives;
	  – *Habituation* – where the individual continues offending, which will be heavily influenced by their success and failure rates, and the impact these have on their lifestyle, needs and desires;
	  – *Desistence* – decisions to stop offending, which can equally be affected by those variables discussed in habituation;
	• Throughout both stages of involvement, an offender may be involved in a number of different forms of crime, with varying degrees of choices and decisions to be made simultaneously.

Criminal events unfold in a sequence of stages and decisions	• Need to identify and understand the sequence of stages and decisions made throughout the crime event; • Involves identifying the MO (*modus operandi*), and the opening and closing stages of the crime event; • Understanding the sequence and stages of physical, verbal and (if present) sexual core behaviours enables an understanding of decision- and choice-making processes.

Note:
[1] Weber (1978) identified four types of social action: (i) *Instrumentally Rational* – where action is determined by expectations as to the behaviour of objects in the environment and the behaviour of other human beings. Expectations are used as conditions or means for the actors' goal attainment; (ii) *Value Rational* – where action is determined by the conscious belief in the value of some ethical, aesthetic, religious or other form of behaviour, which is independent of prospects of success; (iii) *Affectual* – where action is determined by the actors' specific affective and feeling states; (iv) *Traditional* – which is action that is determined by ingrained habituation.

(which enables self-learning and discovery) rather than a standard criminological theory, and it proffers a way of looking at offender behaviour in its context.

When considering the ideas in Table 8.2, it is important to highlight that there will always be exceptions to the rule. For example, when considering the issue of rational choice and decision-making, there will sometimes be situations where an individual's ability to make decisions and act in a rational way are affected by mental health or psychological problems that these individuals suffer from. However, Maden (2007) suggests that we should not overemphasise the causal link between mental health and criminality. He argues that the majority of individuals who suffer from such problems are able to adequately manage their problems without resorting to crime. Furthermore, criminological research undertaken by Matza (1990) indicates that whilst it may appear that an individual has desisted from crime, oftentimes this resistance is short-lived and it is perhaps more advantageous to think about their choice and decision-making within the framework of Matza's delinquency and drift thesis.

Alongside the core concepts of rational choice, Cornish and Clarke (2008:29–37) developed five decision-making models 'to illustrate the decision processes for the three stages of criminal involvement, and for the crime event' (29). *Initiation* consists of the various background psychological and sociological factors that initiate and develop an interest in offending. Psychological and sociological theories tend to consider how factors influence values, attitudes and personality traits. So, for Cornish and Clarke's work on suburban burglary (1985, cited in Cornish and Clarke, 2008:29–31), background factors that influence experiential and learning processes include: *bio-psychological* factors such as temperament, gender and intelligence; an individual's *upbringing*, for example, *broken* home, poor education, and parental crime; and, finally, *social* factors including social class, ethnicity and social exclusion. Furthermore, current personal circumstances, such as whether someone is married, has a family to support, is in full employment, as well as their friendship networks will influence and effect initiation into offending. It will influence and in some cases determine needs and motives, opportunities and inducements as well as the range of perceived solutions available (both legitimate and illegitimate).

Habituation pays less attention to background factors and instead considers contemporary issues and situations (Cornish and Clarke, 2008:31). For example, the rewards of crime and new peer group relationships will become major influences in whether or not individuals continue along the pathway of criminality. The third decision-making model is *desistance*. Again, background factors are in the distance, with situational factors playing a more influential role. It is here that factors such as lack of success, brushes with the police and an increasing reluctance to take risks play 'important roles in decisions to desist' (ibid.:31). The fourth model concerns the *crime event* itself. According to Cornish and Clarke (ibid.:31), decision-making pertaining to committing the crime tends to concentrate on those situational factors that hinder or advance the crime event objective. For example, a major element identified by Cornish and Clarke (1985,

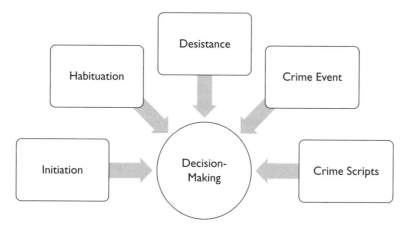

Figure 8.1 Core concepts of decision-making models

cited in 2008:34) in their study of suburban burglary is tied directly to environment and opportunity. If the property is easily accessible with low security and the right level of escape routes, then the crime event commences. However, if the area is unfamiliar and has some guardianship, such as neighbourhood watch or community wardens, the rational decision is to not commit the crime. The final decision-making model is the *crime script*, as it is often found that offenders are presented with a complex mix of decisions. All of these factors, however, operate within the context and situations in which offenders' find themselves.

Situational precipitators

According to Wortley (2008:48) rational choice is only half an explanation for the role of immediate environment for explaining the crime event. It must be remembered that these decisions are made in the individual's specific environment, where a multitude of cues and stimuli (situational precipitators) influence the decisions made. In short, there are numerous situational precipitators that affect the crime event. Indeed, the probability of a crime event taking place can be significantly increased by a variety of these situational precipitators. The importance of understanding these precipitators can easily be demonstrated by looking at the risk assessment paradigm, which has become the core business of a number of criminal justice agencies over the last 15 years or so (Nash, 1999, 2006; Nash and Williams, 2008, 2010). Assessing risk and developing risk management plans are often predicated upon an understanding of the situational context of offending behaviour, which includes examining the numerous situational precipitators which lead to offending (Kemshall, 2008; Nash and Williams, 2008; Williams, 2010).

Wortley (2008) outlines five aspects of situational precipitators and juxtaposes them against the notion of rational choices. He argues that precipitators are 'events and influences that occur prior to the contemplated behaviour' (ibid.:49). Rational choices, on the other hand, tend to emphasise events after the behaviour; for example, the probability of getting caught. Second, these events often act as stresses and pressures before the criminal behaviour takes place, and, more importantly, they act to initiate such behaviour. For rational choice theorists, the environment only enables the behaviour. A third aspect is that precipitators can 'supply or intensify the motivation for individuals to commit crime' (ibid.:49), whereas rational choice assumes that individuals already possess the will to act in a criminal way. Fourth, 'precipitators often (although not always) operate below consciousness' (ibid.:50). Making rational choices infers some form of conscious thinking on behalf of the offender. The fifth and final aspect is that precipitators are largely thought to be out of the control of individuals, whereas rational choices, because of their inbuilt consciousness form, are usually regarded as deliberate acts. For Wortley, and despite the fact he contrasts the two approaches, rational choice and situational precipitators are 'complementary stages of the offending process' (ibid.:50). In fact, there is somewhat of a symbiotic relationship between precipitators and opportunity. The epistemological roots of situational precipitators can primarily be found within psychology and, more specifically, the areas of *learning theory, social psychology, social-cognitive theory* and *environmental psychology*. According to Wortley (ibid.:51), each of these four theory streams explains one of the four types of precipitators that are prevalent in offending behaviour – *prompts, pressures, permissions* and *provocations* – and within each of these four precipitators there are four further subtypes. Wortley (ibid.:51) provides a matrix of precipitators and their corresponding elements, which has been reproduced in Table 8.3.

Whilst it is not necessary to examine these in any detail here, a brief overview would be useful. The taxonomy outlined in Table 8.3 shows that, within the four primary situational precipitators, there are a number of types that could affect the decision to commit a crime. For example, prompts such as a 'trigger' produce an involuntary, physiological response, eliciting an emotional response that could lead to action (ibid.:52). If an individual, for example, listens to a particular piece of music that reminds them of a loved one who has passed, the response may be that it makes them feel sad or even cry. Research into criminal behaviour has often examined the role of triggers; for example, Marshall (1988, cited in Wortley, 2008:52) found that one-third of rapists and child molesters surveyed stated they had been incited to offend by viewing pornography. Unfortunately, this means that around 66 per cent *were not* incited by watching pornography; a fact that is not often highlighted in such research. Another precipitator could be some form of *pressure* placed on the individual to offend, which links to research in social psychology (Eysenck, 1998). For instance, research into gangs demonstrates how conformity to gang initiations and activities provides pressure on individuals to

Table 8.3 Classification of situational precipitators of crime

Prompts	*Pressures*	*Permissions*	*Provocations*
Triggers e.g. weapons effect	Conformity e.g. gang crime	Minimising the rule e.g. culture of corruption	Frustration e.g. road rage
Signals e.g. gay-bashing	Obedience e.g. following corrupt superiors	Minimising responsibility e.g. alcohol-related crime	Crowding e.g. nightclub violence
Imitation e.g. copycat crime	Compliance/ defiance e.g. defying security staff	Minimising consequences e.g. 'petty' theft	Territoriality e.g. turf wars
Expectations e.g. pubs with violent reputations	Anonymity e.g. lynch mobs	Minimising the victim e.g. revenge against employer	Environmental irritants e.g. riots in heat waves

commit crimes (Cloward and Ohlin, 1960; Thrasher, 2000; Kontos *et al.*, 2003; Thornberry *et al.*, 2003; Klein and Maxson, 2006). Others commit crimes due to the *permission* precipitator; for example, when child sex offenders minimise the consequences of the abuse and its effects on their victims (Jenkins, 2003; Ward *et al.*, 2006), which links in with research into cognitive distortions. Finally, all sorts of crimes are situationally precipitated by *provocations*; for example, Kenneth Noye murdered 21-year-old Stephen Cameron in Kent, in 1996, after a road-rage incident (Farmer, 2013). This precipitator directly links to environmental psychology research.

Other theories

Other theoretical frameworks important for understanding criminal behaviour include the *routine activity approach* (RAA) and *crime pattern theory* (CPT). Cohen and Felson (1979) developed the routine activity approach and examined crime patterns and trends in terms of broad social forces. The problem was how to explain the post-war increase in crime rate in terms of changes in routine activities of everyday life that accompanied economic prosperity (Wortley and Mazerolle, 2008:11). Again, the roots of this theory can be traced back to the demographic research of Guerry and Quetelet and The Chicago School (Cohen and Felson, 1979; Wortley and Mazerolle, 2008:11). In basic terms, RAA puts forward the proposition that crime is caused by the convergence in space and time of a number of elements that Clarke and Eck (2005, cited in Felson, 2008:75; Scott *et al.*, 2008:234–236) called the 'problem triangle', which consists of two triangles with one inside the other. The first level, the inside triangle, includes three crucial elements if 'normal' crime is to occur (Felson, 2008:74):

1   potential offender;
2   crime target; and
3   absence of capable *supervisor*.

Outside of the inner triangle, three types of *supervisors* exist who control and regulate an individual's behaviour and activities. The first is the *handler* who supervises the offender; for example, a parent or neighbour (Scott *et al.*, 2008:235). Second is the *guardian* who supervises the target or place where the crime could occur; for example, a bouncer at a nightclub (Hobbs *et al.*, 2003) or the police (Scott *et al.*, 2008:235). Finally, the *manager* supervises the crime setting and 'regulates the functioning of a place'; for example, teachers, lifeguards, or airline flight attendants (ibid.:235). It is suggested that crime occurs when there is the absence of these factors, so solutions are found and tailored to fit the specific crime problem. The emphasis in RAA, therefore, is on the problem-solver, hence its usefulness for crime analysts. Because standard criminological theories provide little in terms of their practical usefulness when it comes to solving actual criminal justice problems (ibid.:234), theories such as RAA should be used in conjunction with the RC and SP approaches due to the emphasis on the situational aspects of the crime problem. However, there is also a need for a careful analysis of crime patterns.

Crime pattern theory attempts to understand crime patterns that are formed from the rich complexities of criminal events (Brantingham and Brantingham, 2008:78; see also Brantingham and Brantingham, 1984), which consist of a complicated tapestry of the law, offender motivation, target characteristics and the environmental backcloth. The theory asks what is perhaps a key question for NIM: how do we develop a clear cognitive structure for understanding crime patterns and develop crime reduction strategies? In doing so, it has developed the following aspects (Brantingham and Brantingham, 2008):

•   basic theoretical rules;
•   defined processes for combining those rules;
•   formally structured patterns; that are
•   referenced to observations of actual crime.

CPT places eight rules of offending and crime activity within a spatio-temporal context (see Figure 8.2, collated from Brantingham and Brantingham, 2008:80–88).

Rule 1 indicates how decision-making activities become regularised when they are regularly repeated, generating a crime template that, with each crime success, is followed, renewed and reinforced (Brantingham and Brantingham, 2008:80). *Rule 2* denotes the network of 'family, friends, and acquaintances' that have

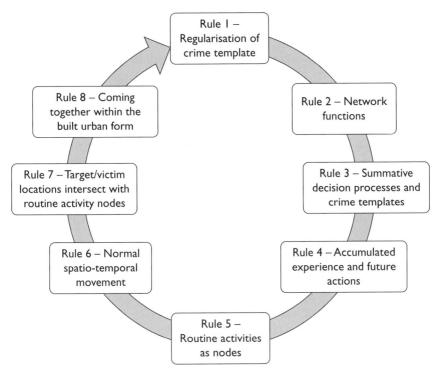

Figure 8.2 The rules of crime pattern theory

'varying attributes and influence the decisions of others in the network' (ibid.:81) and thereby influence crime behaviours. *Rule 3* considers the aggregate of individual 'decision processes and crime templates' which determine the typical patterns of criminal and non-criminal behaviour (ibid.:82). *Rule 4* suggests that when a trigger event occurs and the individual locates a victim or target that fits with the crime template, the resultant criminal act changes 'the bank of accumulated experience' and alters 'future actions' (ibid.:82). *Rule 5* highlights the fact that individuals undertake everyday routine activities such as going to school, university or work, going shopping or participating in leisure activities such as going to the gym. These tend to operate along set geographical places, labelled as *activity nodes* (ibid.:83). *Rule 6* denotes the 'normal spatio-temporal movement patterns' of individuals who commit crime, suggesting that the 'likely location for crime is near this normal activity' (ibid.:84). *Rule 7* suggests that the crime targets or victims 'intersect the activity spaces of potential offenders' (ibid.:87). Crime targets and victims, therefore, often (but not always) fall along the same spatio-temporal nodes of the offender. Finally, *Rule 8* highlights the fact that all the previous rules operate in a specific environmental context and that crime is 'created by high flows of people through and to nodal activity points' (ibid.:88). These eight rules help explain a whole range of issues relevant to the day-to-day work of crime analysts, as well as the police. For example, they provide context and understanding to the following four areas: (i) crime templates that reflect target/victim assessment; (ii) crime locations vis-à-vis spatio-temporal activity nodes and routine daily movement; (iii) crime concentrations found along pathways and activity nodes; and, finally, (iv) crime attractors and crime generators (Brantingham and Brantingham, 1984, 2008).

Crime analysis and mapping concepts and processes

Having outlined the historical development and theoretical underpinnings to crime analysis and crime mapping techniques, the remainder of this chapter is devoted to discussing the core ideas and components of the analysis and mapping process itself. It examines the analysis process and the types of data utilised within crime analysis as well as the common tools and techniques.

In principle, crime analysis is relatively easy to understand. As I have shown in Table 8.1, numerous police databases (and other agencies' databases) keep *information* based upon crime type (Douglas *et al.*, 1997; Stelfox, 2009), and this is usually the starting point for crime analysts. They examine multiple sources of data, extract the bits of information required and order them in some form of interpretive framework that changes information into *intelligence*, which allows for a criminal justice response to be developed. Figure 8.3 illustrates what crime analysts attempt to do. The left side depicts the pool of information whilst the right side is intelligence extracted by the crime analyst (CA). By way of illustration consider the follow example:

• An offender is stopped and searched on the street and is found to be in possession of 1/8 of cannabis.
• The same offender has a small cannabis factory set up in his basement with 15 cannabis plants growing using a hydroponics system.
• The same offender commits GBH against another drugs supplier who had recently moved into his area.

Their crime type classifies these different events, so these would be found within the police's *data pool* by offence. Thus, the first would be possession of a Class B drug; the second, possession with intent to supply; and the final type is GBH, which is a violent offence. Each crime is different but the crimes are *linked* because the same offender commits them. To get from crime stored as types (information – the left side of Figure 8.3) to a linked series (intelligence – the right side), the crime analyst must extract the information from criminal justice databases by reference to the criminal's activity and description. The resulting intelligence is then presented to the agency (or agencies) that has requested the information, and suitable responses are discussed. This is crime analysis.

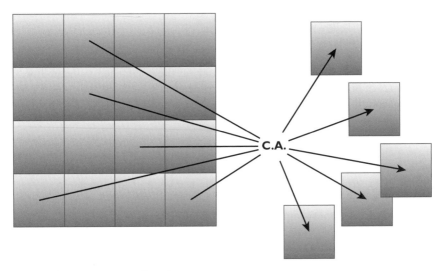

Figure 8.3 Extraction and analysis

This chapter began by outlining three definitions of crime analysis. Within all three definitions, crime analysis is seen as the systematic study of crime and disorder problems in order to assist in criminal apprehension, crime reduction and prevention, as well as crime evaluation (Boba, 2005:6). Boba's work is based on her working knowledge of the United States (ibid.:6), and she highlights that crime analysis involves the application of social science data collection and analysis techniques; for example, qualitative and quantitative research methodologies. She includes field research, 'observing characteristics of locations' (ibid.:6) as an example of analysts using qualitative research. However, in the UK it is extremely rare that crime analysts visit crime scenes. The majority of analysts utilise the relevant databases and recorded statistics to undertake their day-to-day tasks, and they do not visit crime locations;[4] which means they are effectively engaging in secondary data analysis (Innes *et al.*, 2005). Regardless of the differentiation between theory and practice, the central focus is to bring the research and analytical tools of academia to bear on practical problems that those in power deem to be important and need solving. Ignoring the constant ebb and flow of criminal justice policy and its close links with party politics, it is possible to identify some core areas where crime analysis and crime mapping is useful (see Boba, 2005; Chainey and Ratcliffe, 2005; Wortley and Mazerolle, 2008).

- **Repeat victimisation** – where patterns are identified as to the increased risk to those who have suffered crime;
- **Hotspots** – which identifies the concentration of incidents in particular places or categories of place;

- **Prolific offenders** – where patterns and concentrations of offending behaviour is tied to particular persons;
- **Hot products** – where the attractiveness of particular products as targets for theft are identified (i.e. mobile phones);
- **Hot classes of victim** – which focuses on the heightened vulnerability of types of persons to specific types of crime; and
- **Seasonality** – times of day, week or year when incidents tend to be more frequent.

Crime analysis and crime mapping techniques can be very effective in all these areas, and they deal with many different characteristics of crime and disorder. In doing so, crime analysis can incorporate a myriad of information types and truly follows what Denzin (1971) called data and methodological triangulation. Perhaps the three most important kinds of information used by crime analysts are *socio-demographic, spatial* and *temporal* (Boba, 2005; Chainey and Ratcliffe, 2005; Wortley and Mazerolle, 2008). *Socio-demographic* information consists of the personal characteristics of offenders, victims and groups; for instance, sex, age, ethnicity, income and education. Crime analysts use socio-demographic information at the micro level to search police databases for local suspects; they can also use this information on both meso and macro levels: for example, by identifying the characteristics of groups of offenders and how they relate to specific crimes. For example, they may be interested in identifying the socio-economic status of child sexual offenders between different boroughs in London, and they link that to the socio-economic status of victims' parents. *Spatial* information is also central to understanding the crime event for, as Chainey and Ratcliffe note, 'crime has an inherent geographic quality. When crime occurs, it happens at a place with a geographical location' (2005:1). Recent developments in computer and satellite technology, especially geographical information systems, have enabled a more sophisticated use of spatial analysis in crime analysis. Indeed, the visualisation of crime locations and their relationship to geographical features and socio-demographic information facilitates a deeper understanding of crime patterns and trends. As we have seen earlier in the discussion of Booth and the Chicago School, visual mapping of crime can also aid in developing criminological theory and understanding of the crime event. Finally, crime analysts on several different levels use *temporal* information. They may examine long-term patterns in crime trends 'over several years, the seasonal nature of crime, and patterns by month' (Boba, 2005:7). This is usually referred to by social scientists as longitudinal analysis. They may also examine mid-length and short-term patterns of crime; for example, patterns by days of the week and time of day or time between specific crime incidents. By identifying the aspects of time and location as well as socio-demographic information tied to the crime events that take place, crime analysts are able to assist the police and other agencies in criminal apprehension and crime prevention. The key, though, is the undertaking of the systematic analysis of crime using multiple data sources.

The analysis process

Even though crime analysis incorporates a broad range of data collection and analytical techniques, there is a clear crime analysis process, which is a general way that crime analysis is practiced. Boba (2005:9–13) identifies a five-step sequential process with feedback loops. The five steps are *data collection, data collation, analysis, dissemination of results* and *feedback to end users*, and these are shown in Figure 8.4, which illustrates that the process not only follows a sequential logic but also incorporates feedback loops that inform and update the analysis process. This is similar to the FBI's behavioural profile generation process (see Ressler *et al.*, 1995) and allows for the fluid nature of research/ investigation as every new piece of data/evidence on crime events that is identified during an investigation can be inserted into the analysis. Data *collection* requires a number of important steps to be undertaken. First, the data must be collected accurately and consistently, which is tied to the issue of data storage. Technological advances have made it easier to store and manage data more efficiently, although databases are beset by a number of problems such as: incorrect spellings and addresses, which when mapped could result in a data point being in open space or even in the middle of the ocean; the use of abbreviations and local aliases, which make geographical identification difficult; and incomplete records, which reduce the validity of the analysis, or halt the mapping of the offence (Boba, 2005; Chainey and Ratcliffe, 2005). Second, only relevant data should be compiled. It is often said that we live in the information age (Furedi, 2006), which has many benefits. Unfortunately, the downside is information overload. We are bombarded with large amounts of information so the question becomes which pieces of information are valid and which ones we should discard. Crime analysts have an array of data sources at their disposal, so they must make informed

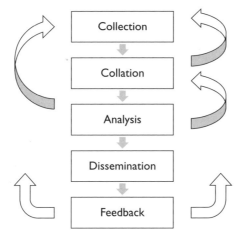

Figure 8.4 The crime analysis process

decisions as to which data is both relevant and accurate. They should not, therefore, collect aspects of data that are not relevant for investigative or legal purposes (Boba, 2005:10). Third, it should be compiled in a timely manner. It's no good undertaking research 6 or 12 months after the observations have been made, or the request for an analysis has been made. Fourth, the data should be stored for an adequate period of time to allow for effective analysis. Finally, it is important that the data be available in electronic raw form so it can be queried and downloaded.

The data that is collected for a crime analyst's use is normally taken from the official databases of various criminal justice agencies, as outlined in Table 8.1 above. These databases are not usually designed for analysis purposes, so it is often necessary for the crime analyst to alter the data so it is fit for whatever analytical purpose is desired. The second step is *collation*, which is the preparation of raw data from databases for analysis, and this consists of three components:

1 **Cleaning** – where mistakes and inconsistencies in the data are corrected (e.g. incorrect postcodes, poor/incorrect formatting of data, or imputing missing data);
2 **Geocoding** – where the data is combined with geographic data (e.g. latitude and longitude coordinates; or Eastings and Northings) so they can be analysed spatially; and
3 **Creating new variables** – where new variables are created from existing variables in order to facilitate more effective analysis.

Once the data has been collected and prepared, the *analysis* can be undertaken. Most data analysis will have terms of reference that tend to have flexible yet clearly defined boundaries. Upon receiving the terms of reference the crime analyst must then decide which analytical tools they should use. Typically, they utilise a number of statistical and visualisation techniques which are discussed below. The important part of the analysis sequence is that it often uncovers (a) previously unknown problems with the data and/or (b) missing pieces of data (ibid.:11). As this is a common occurrence, crime analysts have built into their process a number of feedback loops which enable them to go back to earlier stages and fix any problems they need to. Boba (ibid.:11) calls this the *data modification sub-cycle* and apart from fixing problems it also can affect the eventual outcome of the analysis.

The fourth part of the analysis sequence is *dissemination*. Just like any other type of scientific/academic research, the results are presented to a target audience. Because of the nature of crime analysis, the information is often presented to a broad range of criminal justice or *responsible authorities*.[5] Each of these groups will have a specific objective in mind when it comes to the *actionable outcomes* of the analysis. It is therefore important that crime analysts tailor their results to the audience in question. Results commonly take one or more of the following formats:

- report (e.g. Word document);
- presentation (e.g. PowerPoint);
- briefing;
- e-mail; and
- phone call.

What is crucial is that the format should contain all the necessary information that conveys the core results of the analysis that are pertinent to the terms of reference (ibid.:12). These results can then feed into specific investigations to help aid in the apprehension of offenders, or they can aid in preventing more general crime and disorder problems. They may also take the form of *intelligence products* as outlined by the NIM process (see Chapter 6). The main point of dissemination is to make recommendations for action, based on the inferences drawn from the data. Furthermore, results of crime analysis can contribute to the general stock of knowledge about crime and criminality, with local police agencies using micro and meso levels of crime analysis to 'form a body of knowledge, which is the goal of any social science' (ibid.:13).

The fifth and final part of the analysis sequence is the feedback or evaluation process. It is important that crime analysts get feedback from those who have received their findings. Types of feedback useful for the data modification cycle include 'feedback about the quality of particular analyses or reports, about the nature of the data analyzed, or about the usefulness of their analysis for decision making' (ibid.:13). Feedback often improves communication, focus, process, delivery and usefulness. Perhaps the most important reason for feedback is to assess the exact impact that the analysis has had on the identified problem, as well as the resultant action taken to address the issue. Overall, this five-stage process is relatively straightforward to follow but is often difficult to undertake. It should also be highlighted that the process outlined above is a generic one, and criminal justice agencies across the world tend to create bespoke analytical processes to suit the meso- and micro-environments in which they operate. For example, the Royal Canadian Mounted Police use CAPRA, which stands for Client, Acquiring (and analysing) information, Partnerships, Response and Assessment (RCMP, 2000, cited in Scott *et al.*, 2008:234). In the UK, crime analysts tend to use the SARA model.

The SARA model

SARA stands for *scanning, analysis, response* and *assessment*, and it is a model process used in problem-solving policing. SARA can be used to manage problems of all types of crime, disorder and substance misuse. An alternative model called

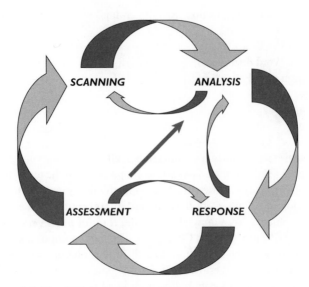

Figure 8.5 The SARA problem-solving model[6]

PROCTOR is also sometimes used (Problem, Cause, Tactic, Treatment, Output, and Result) (Read and Tilley, 2000:vi); here, however, I will concentrate on the SARA model. It was developed within and for problem-oriented policing and has been evolving over the last 20 years (Scott *et al.*, 2008:231). Figure 8.5 illustrates the SARA model as outlined in Clarke and Eck (2005).

The first stage is *scanning*. This is the stage where a problem is discovered and defined so action can be taken about it. Multiple sources of information are used to identify and define crime problems. Such sources include 'crime data, community members, elected officials and news media accounts' (Scott *et al.*, 2008:232; see also Read and Tilley, 2000:11). As the definition of what a *problem* is can be difficult to pin down, an operational definition that has emerged in recent years is that it is 'a recurring set of harmful events that the police are reasonably expected to handle' (Scott *et al.*, 2008:232). The core component here is *reoccurrence*, which means problems that are not likely to reoccur tend to be discounted from crime analysis processes. The second stage, *analysis*, involves collecting information about the problem in order to figure out ways to address it. This includes identifying the nature of the problem, the trends and series of crime and disorder, and geographical information including identifying problematic locations. Subsequently, inferences are made about the potential causes of the problem (Leigh *et al.*, 1996; Read and Tilley, 2000). This aspect of the SARA model is usually localised and follows Brantingham and Brantingham's (1984) micro-level spatial analysis. As Scott *et al.* suggest 'the objective is to know how the problem arises and locate pinch points that suggest ways of reducing the problem' (2008:233). Third is the *response* stage. Because crime analysis involves identifying a broad range of possible solutions that fit the results of the analysis, the analyst must identify the most appropriate option and then implement it. The final stage of the SARA process is the *assessment* stage. The whole point of SARA (and crime analysis more generally) is to be effective in solving, reducing and/or preventing crime. It is therefore important to judge the impact of the response to see if it actually worked. Scott *et al.* (ibid.:233) highlight three possible outcomes: (i) the problem has changed for the better; (ii) the problem has reduced; or (iii) the problem has become less harmful. As with the more general analysis process presented above, SARA is not a linear process. There are a number of feedback loops that act to update and alter all four components. For example, as new data is retrieved and examined in the analysis phase, the problem (scanning) may be redefined slightly.

Scott *et al.* (ibid.:234) note how the SARA model has become so widespread it has become the dominant analytical process utilised in the UK; however, they also highlight that this is problematic because it is not the only analytical process available to the police (see also Read and Tilley, 2000; Innes *et al.*, 2005). This is an unfortunate downside to the over-bureaucratisation of criminal justice processes as criminal justice agencies adopt processes that have become standardised at the expense of others. These processes, whilst creating defensible decision-making, can stifle innovation in practice, which I have demonstrated elsewhere through an analysis of serious further offending (SFO) (see Nash and Williams, 2008).

Crime analysis data

As Figure 8.4 illustrates, data collection and collation are perhaps the most important elements of the crime analysis process. In fact, crime analysts can spend more time collecting and preparing the data for analysis than on any other part of the process (Boba, 2005:75). Data is the most important aspect of any research and forensic practice: the techniques that are used in the analysis are determined by it; and the results and interpretations are based upon it. In fact, *the overall analyses and responses are only as good as that data the feeds it.* It is therefore important to understand a little bit about the nature and types of data commonly used within crime analysis. Data may consist of numbers, words, or images that represent the values of a variable (a measurable characteristic, object or system that is expected to vary): for example, crime type, date, time or location. As with general social science data, there are usually two broad types – quantitative and qualitative – and these include all sorts of information about:

- what crime has happened;
- where it has occurred;
- date and time of the offence;

- crime triangle information – e.g. victim characteristics, offender characteristics (if known); MO; and
- core verbal, physical and sexual (if relevant) behaviours committed during the crime event.

The next aspect to consider is the source of the data, defined by the NIM training manual as a person, organisation, or record from which information may be obtained (ACPO Centrex, 2005). There are two main sources of data. The first type is known as *open source* data, which is data that anyone can access. Examples of open source data include public records, newspaper reports, specific official government documents, Internet sources such as open-access networking sites (e.g. Facebook, MySpace, Twitter, etc.) and library and museum records. The second type is *closed source* information, which is information that is not open to the public. This includes criminal justice databases such as the PNC or any other bespoke crime reporting systems used by the police, probation or prison services; for example, crime analysts in the UK use iQuanta to access crime statistics.

It is important that the strength and validity of the information used in the analysis process is properly evaluated, and there are a number of different ways to evaluate information sources in the social sciences. For example, forensic criminologists will often utilise government statistics because they are produced by statisticians who utilise the necessary checks and balances (i.e. sampling distribution and error procedures), which ensure the figures produced are as accurate as they can be.[7] Alternatively, when dealing with qualitative information such as witness and victim statements, corroborating evidence could be used to either include or exclude such evidence. When it comes to police analysts, information that is used for intelligence purposes is evaluated using a $5 \times 5 \times 5$ intelligence report, and consists of grading information sources in three ways using five criteria (Spinelli and Sharma, 2007:16–17). The $5 \times 5 \times 5$ allows analysts to 'determine the reliability of the source and of the information provided, and the rank and role access to this $5 \times 5 \times 5$' (2007:16). The first element of the grading matrix is *source evaluation*, which grades the reliability of the source. The five criteria used here are:

1 **A** – Always reliable
2 **B** – Mostly reliable
3 **C** – Sometimes reliable
4 **D** – Unreliable
5 **E** – Untested source.

The second 5×-grading element is *intelligence evaluation*. This consists of the following five criteria:

1 known to be true without reservation;
2 known personally to source but not to officer;

3   not personally known to source but corroborated;
4   cannot be judged; and
5   suspected to be false or malicious.

The final 5×-grading element is related to the dissemination part of the analysis process as an important question that must be asked by all crime analysts: who can I disseminate this information too? Again, a five-point criterion is used to assess who can handle the information; this is referred to as its *handling code*, and is completed at the time of entry onto an intelligence system and reviewed upon its dissemination. The five grades are as follows:

1   May be disseminated to other law enforcement and prosecuting agencies, including law enforcement agencies within the EEA, and is EU compatible (no special conditions);
2   May be disseminated to UK non-prosecuting parties (authorisation and records needed);
3   May be disseminated to non-EEA law enforcement agencies (special conditions apply);
4   May be disseminated within the originating agency only; and
5   No further dissemination and refer to the originator. Special handling requirements imposed by the officer who authorised collection.

As Spinelli and Sharma's (ibid.:19) research highlights, the production of a 5 × 5 × 5 analysis should involve the creation of an intelligence log in the local crime reporting system. The evaluation of the source is important, largely because most crime analysis is *secondary data analysis*, which is the means of taking data that has already been recorded and collected by someone else, and using it for another purpose. The benefits of using this type of data analysis is that it is less time-consuming and doesn't cost as much to undertake; however, there are also many problems, which have been well documented in the methodology literature of the social sciences (see De Vaus, 2002; Gilbert, 2012). Some of these problems include: the person using the data will not have a full understanding of the original conceptualisation of the research question or how the variables were operationalised to produce the results being used; or there will often be a mis-match between the research question from the original research and the terms of reference of the secondary analysis. This often results in the data being manipu-lated to *fit* the analysis. For example, tools within SPSS (Statistical Package for the Social Sciences) allow for variables to be altered and excluded in order to *best fit* the analysis being undertaken (Field, 2013; Bryman and Cramer, 2011). Because of these two problems, it is imperative that crime analysts use secondary data carefully. Of course, there are various aspects within the collation and analy-sis parts of the analysis process that ensure such problems are minimised; and, in order to achieve effective collation and analysis, analysts use a number of tools, techniques and technologies.

Technology and tools

Crime analysis relies heavily on computer technology, and over the past 20 years or so there have been significant improvements in computer hardware and software. These technological improvements have led to extremely useful developments in the field of crime analysis and crime mapping; for example, Windows-based software programmes such as Word, Excel and Access. The computer hardware used for crime analysis is usually standard computers that are now common to many homes and businesses in the UK and that are used by most other forensic disciplines and criminal justice agencies. In recent years, developments to computer hardware and software have enabled the *computerisation* of criminal identification and intelligence records, making entering crime data and searching for crime types and suspects much more efficient, wildly surpassing the capabilities of the early Bertillon system. However, caution must exercised, as accessing databases is often time-consuming and full of problems. It is completely different from the world presented in TV shows such as *Criminal Minds*: where Agent Penelope Garcia is able to instantly access (or easily hack) all known databases in the universe (some of which don't actually exist); download all sorts of information (that isn't actually available); cross reference and analyse using all manner of algorithms (again that often don't exist); and then make what is seemingly the strongest of connections and inferences to catch the right bad guy or gal. In the real world, even if the relevant database does exist, its software is often different to the one the analyst is using; and to gain access to the information requires negotiation between agencies, which can sometimes take weeks, and a great deal of form-filling.

Examining the types of software that make crime analysis and crime mapping possible, it is noticeable that many different types exist. Indeed, because much of crime analysis uses quantitative data, basic software programmes such as Excel, Access and SPSS are used in the collation and analysis of crime trends and patterns. When it comes to crime mapping software, more advanced software has been developed which enables databases from Excel and Access to be imported and the crime data mapped, producing a visual representation of the spatial aspects of the crime events being analysed. There are numerous mapping software programmes on the market, and these are available to organisations, businesses or individuals who wish to undertake crime mapping. Typically the choice of which software to use is determined by a number of factors including:

- end user purposes, goals and objectives;
- the organisation's budget and strategic plan;
- knowledge of IT systems; and
- partisan IT-Politics.[8]

The crime analysis and crime mapping software packages that are commonly used include Rigel, Dragnet, I2, ViClas (the Royal Canadian Mounted Police's

Violent Crime Linkage System) and ArcGIS (which used to be known as ArcView). Each of these products, whilst offering slightly different functions, has the ability to analyse and visualise crime data. For example, Dragnet is a geographical prioritisation package, developed primarily by Canter at the Centre of Investigative Psychology (Canter, 2003:127–128; Canter and Youngs, 2009:404–405). Built upon 20 years of empirical research into environmental criminology and spatial behaviour of offender patterns, Dragnet uses a series of crime locations and prioritises the surrounding area in order to determine the most likely area of the offender's home or base of operation (Chainey and Ratcliffe, 2005:308). The software is extremely useful, not only for research but also operational purposes; for example, it provides an understanding of patterns and trends of spatial crime data. It is also useful for investigative work, as it enables the identification of crime hotspots on which the police can then focus their efforts in crime prevention. The software also allows the police to determine where the offender may live as well as providing details of other offenders living in that area. More recently, Canter and his team have developed the Interactive Offender Profiling System (iOPS), which is changing the way investigators think about and record crime, not to mention how investigations are carried out.[9]

Another example of analysis and mapping software is Rigel. Initially developed by Rossmo in his pioneering work on geographic profiling (2000:222–224), it is based around the Criminal Geographic Targeting model and 'incorporates an analytic engine, GIS capability, database management, and powerful visualization tools' (ibid.:222–223). It effectively enables the analyst to examine and analyse the core components of offending behaviour, outlined in the theoretical section above (e.g. environmental criminology, situational precipitators and crime pattern theory). Rigel is able to do all this because it 'incorporates mathematical models of known offending movement patterns and hunting behaviour, journey to crime distances and includes a method to calculate the relationship between sets of crime locations (e.g. contact, assault, release sites) and offender residence' (Chainey and Ratcliffe, 2005:306–307). Environmental Criminology Research Inc. offer a number of Rigel products including: Rigel Analyst, Gemini, Rigel Workstation, Rigel Profiler, Rigel Military Profiler. Rigel Analyst, for example, works alongside crime data and GIS software and provides mapping software that generates geographic profiles and includes features such as interactive geocoding, a direct crime data inputting facility, import and export functions, and visual and statistical analysis functions.[10] Whilst Rigel is a useful geographic profiling and mapping software package, it tends to use only spatial and temporal data. This does not allow for a more in-depth analysis of the core behaviours and actions undertaken during the commission of crime. However, other types of analysis software have been developed with that in mind; for example, many crime analysts in the UK utilise ArcGIS for crime analysis and mapping tasks, as the software provides criminal justice agencies with 'spatial analytics, modeling and visualization capabilities'.[11] ArcGIS comes with a *crime analyst* add-on that allows for the production of crime maps as well as modelling and forecasting tools. Of course, ArcGIS is used for a variety of analysis and mapping purposes and not just for crime analysis. For the purposes of forensic criminology, software programmes such as ArcGIS enable trends and patterns in any type of crime to be visualised onto a map.

There are, of course, a number of problems with such software, some of which are discussed below. However, regardless of which mapping software is used, they are all primarily based upon the principles of geographic information systems, so an understanding of GIS is crucial.

GIS

Geographic information systems (GIS) is 'a computer system for capturing, managing, integrating, manipulating, analysing and displaying data which is spatially referenced to the Earth' (McDonnell and Kemp, 1985:42, cited in Chainey and Ratcliffe, 2005:38). Since the 1960s, GIS has developed in a wide range of areas including: (i) technology; (ii) its uses; and (iii) research. It has also become an academic discipline in its own right (ibid.:2), especially for those who wish to move beyond the theoretical and paradigmatic tunnel vision that has infested much of criminological theory and which has filled criminology and sociology departments over the last 50 years. GIS as an academic subject is meant to be applied to real social problems facing society, and it is meant to be used in a forensic setting. In short, it is an applied approach. It is not political or ideological rhetoric, despite the unfortunate fact that the results can be (mis)used for political or ideological purposes. The rapidity of developments in GIS can be located in a number of disparate influences. For example, Chainey and Ratcliffe (ibid.:2) highlight the planning of the US Census of Population in 1970 as well as national mapping agencies, which started to use the developing technology to aid in their own organisational objectives. Technological developments in satellite imagery also aided in the rapid development and use of GIS, especially since the military were the first to develop a 'uniform system of measuring location, driven by the need for accurately targeting missiles' (ibid.:2). The military were also responsible for developing the first Global Positioning System (GPS).

According to Longley et al. (2001), these early influences were soon surpassed by the huge reductions in cost and developments in hardware technology that occurred in the 1980s. Alongside hardware reductions came improvements in operating systems, electronic storage and computer software. All of these areas have converged to enable the widening of uses of GIS to other areas including policing and crime reduction, fitting together with policy developments such as NIM and the developments in crime and intelligence analysis. Whilst such processes may be organised and developed separately, through organisational and policy innovation they can be used above and beyond their original purpose. However, because of this interconnectedness, early uses of GIS for mapping crime were often stifled or held back. Chainey and Ratcliffe (2005:2–3) point to four main reasons why this occurred. First, as with any new technology or technique, there were a number of *organisational and management problems* that needed to be faced, such as ensuring there was the necessary personnel and management oversight in place, which, in many places, has not been an easy task. Second, an issue with *sharing information* was a problem that had to be overcome, as many crime analysts undertake analysis for multiple end users and within a multi-agency framework. The sharing of information between different agencies has been a general, yet major, obstacle for the development of multi-agency working (see Nash, 2006; Nash and Williams, 2008). Therefore, problems with information sharing are not specific to crime analysts per se, but they form part of a broader bureaucratic problem within multi-agency frameworks and, historically, have been linked to the restrictive reading of the Data Protection Act.[12] Indeed, Nash and Williams (2008) highlight how poor communication and the sharing of information are one of the more common explanations for why serious further offences occur. The third issue that stunted the initial development and implementation of GIS was *technical problems*. Not only do you have to have the right personnel and training in place, you need to have the right technology, not only in terms of hardware and software but also the right type of databases (i.e. where the original crime data is recorded and stored and can be imported). The final obstacle is *difficulties with geocoding*. Before an analyst can use geographic information, the data must be geocoded (Chainey and Ratcliffe, 2005:3), which is defined as:

> the process of linking an address (e.g. an incident address or the address of an offender's residence) with its map coordinates so that (a) the address can be displayed on a map and (b) the GIS can recognize that address in the future.
>
> (Boba, 2005:88)

This has been one of the more difficult tasks to achieve due to problems such as incorrect or incomplete addresses being entered onto the initial recording system. Despite these four problems, Chainey and Ratcliffe (2005:3) claim that many of these issues have been resolved. Unfortunately, there are still remnants of them; for example, pockets of resistance against sharing information between agencies as well as continuing problems with geocoding. Chainey and Ratcliffe (ibid.:3) also note that many new problems have also emerged as crime analysis and crime mapping has become a central part of the intelligence gathering process. However, despite the problems over the last ten years, there has been a significant growth in mapping innovation, most of which has stemmed from the United States; in particular from the National Institute of Justice's Crime Mapping Research Centre (CMRC), renamed in 2002 as Mapping and Analysis for Public Safety (MAPS). This US government initiative influenced developments in crime mapping in many countries, including the UK, and the MAPS programme raised awareness of crime mapping through its seminars, conferences and publications (ibid.:3). In recent years, geographical information science has also developed, and a number of authors have suggested scientific development has overtaken the GIS systems side of things (Goodchild, 1992 and 1997, cited in Chainey and Ratcliffe, 2005:3).

Summary

This chapter has provided an introduction to crime analysis and crime mapping by examining its theoretical foundations, processes, tools and techniques. It is argued that crime analysis and crime mapping techniques are a useful recent addition to the forensic criminologists arsenal. If undertaken in the appropriate way, using the relevant scientific methodology and analytical processes at our disposal, it can produce a fairly robust and holistic understanding of the crime triangle (offender, victim, and circumstances, context and location). Not only does it provide empirical evidence that can be added to the stock of knowledge about specific types of crime and criminality, but it also allows for suitable localised responses to be developed. As forensic criminology is about using robust analytical techniques to resolve criminal justice problems, crime analysis and crime mapping can easily be incorporated into the broad range of techniques that can be called upon to achieve this goal. Crime analysis is also a relatively straightforward procedure to understand. In recent years within the criminal justice system, there has been a large investment in technology, personnel, education and training pertaining to crime analysis and crime mapping. Indeed, it had, until recently, been one of the highest growth areas within police and CDRP agencies in the UK. However, there are a number of problems associated with the processes. The difficulties tend to lie in the structural and organisational arrangements within which crime analysis is undertaken. For example, analysis results, interpretations and subsequent criminal justice responses are only as good as the data on which they are based, and this is determined by such things as the available reporting and recording systems and the quality of the information that is inputted on these systems. Having spent this chapter outlining how non-physical intelligence is used, the following two chapters consider physical intelligence and evidence and its uses to forensic investigations.

Chapter 9

Scientific support and crime scene examination

> Facts are stubborn things; and whatever may be our wishes, our inclinations, or the dictates of our passion, they cannot alter the state of facts and evidence.
>
> (John Adams)

Introduction

The analysis and mapping 'information work' that is undertaken by the police and crime analysts is also supplemented by the collection of physical evidence, which is either identified and collected through crime scene investigation or during standard police investigative procedures (e.g. a search of a property). Some of this material is transformed into evidence and used during the trial process, which labels the acts as 'criminal' and defines who the 'offender' is. The majority of criminology over the last century has focused only on the final 'criminal' product and how to assess and manage it. With a few exceptions (e.g. see Gilbert, 2006) criminologists rarely consider the way the investigative and trial processes use physical and non-physical evidence, through the means of 'inscriptive devices' (Latour and Woolgar, 1986; Sekula, 1986;), to construct the criminal product. This fully formed 'investigative-legal-image', consists of a complex interplay that is defined and negotiated by police investigators, crime scene examiners (CSEs), forensic scientists, solicitors and barristers; all of whom work within the complex structures and regulations I have outlined throughout this text. Regardless of whether the criminologist is interested in the 'Lombrosian' or 'Governmental' project (Garland, 1997:12–13), much research starts from the position of the 'criminal' as simply 'existing'. For example, researchers and practitioners who undertake the analysis of crime behaviours when using risk assessment tools such as OASys (the Offender Assessment System) or Risk Matrix are basing their pseudoscientific risk assessment and management plans on evidence that suffers from a number of problems (See Harcourt, 2007; Williams, 2010). In many cases the evidence that is used for risk management plans is incomplete and would have gone through several filters that decontextualises it. One such filter will be the actions of police, CSEs and forensic analysts. This chapter discusses these processes and how they affect the structure and nature of the evidence that is used to construct the 'criminal image'.

The approach to crime scene investigation appears overwrought and complex; however, these processes and structures have been put in place to ensure the most accurate and evidentially useful material is safely collected and transported for analysis. I start this chapter by examining the different terms, roles and structures that organise crime scene examination in the UK and which tend to operate around scientific services departments based within the police service. I then move on to discuss the role that national standards play, which includes a discussion of forensic strategies and how important they are in determining what types of evidence are collected at each crime scene. This leads on to a discussion of how crime scenes are examined, which includes: a definition of what crime scenes are; a review of the scientific method and its links with crime scene examination; a discussion of the core elements of crime scene processing such as the initial assessment, cordoning the scene, search strategies, preservation of evidence, contamination and the continuity of evidence, recording and documenting the scene and how forensic evidence is recovered.

Definitions, roles and structures

Definitions and terminology

As with most practical concepts, there are a number of terms that are used to denote the investigation of the crime scene, and these are often interchangeable. For instance, some authors use the term *crime scene investigation* (Pepper, 2005, 2010; Dutelle, 2011; Becker and Dutelle, 2013); some use *crime scene examination* (Weston, 2004; Monckton-Smith *et al.*, 2013); whilst others prefer the term *crime scene analysis* (Gardner and Bevel, 2009). Examining and processing a crime scene actually consists of all three: the scene is examined in light of the overall investigation, and an analysis is made as to the forensic strategies that should be applied, which determines what evidence is identified and prioritised for collection and removal from the scene. In short, crime scene investigation is at the heart of all forensic analysis (Pepper, 2005:2). If evidence is missed or incorrectly recorded or packaged at the scene, more often than not that evidence becomes useless (Weston, 2004:21). Gardner and Bevel define *crime scene analysis* as the evaluation of 'the context of the scene and the physical evidence found there in an effort to identify what occurred and in what order it occurred' (2009:1); whilst Dutelle (2011:4) uses the term *crime scene investigation* to denote 'the systematic process of documenting, collecting, preserving, and interpreting physical evidence associated with an alleged crime scene, in an effort to determine the truth relating to the event in question'. What is clear is that crime scene examination should be the application of scientific knowledge and methodologies to criminal investigations in order to help resolve legal problems. The main problem with this type of definition is the inclusion of the term 'scientific knowledge'. The majority of crime scene examiners (CSEs) are not trained forensic scientists, so the application of scientific knowledge is usually minimal. In effect, CSEs act as the practical link between police investigations and forensic scientists, and their key role 'is to identify and collect evidence, but not to analyse the evidence collected' (Monckton-Smith *et al.*, 2013:53). Instead, CSEs tend to be technologically proficient in key areas of what has been termed *police science*. As previously noted, Ambage (1987:3) points out that the distinction between forensic science and police science was an important one, despite the dividing lines being somewhat fluid. Police science encompasses areas such as fingermark recovery and analysis, photography, footwear and tool impression analysis and, whilst there are elements of scientific knowledge to some of this work, it is primarily technological work that is undertaken, and it is more akin to traditional detective work than forensic science (Monckton-Smith *et al.*, 2013:53). It is perhaps more useful to think of crime scene examination as a *series of systematic and methodical steps designed to identify and recover physical evidence to determine the series of events that occurred when a crime has been committed.* This definition is closer to the reality of crime scene examination in the modern era. For reasons of clarity, I will use the term crime scene examination and crime scene examiners (CSEs) throughout the remainder of this chapter, although this term is simply a personal preference, and other terms, such as scenes of crime officers (SOCOs) and crime scene investigators (CSIs), are just as valid. A review of the uses and applications of forensic science to criminal investigations is covered in Chapter 10.

As with police investigations, there are a range factors that influence crime scene work long before any individual steps onto a scene. Of these, one of the most important factors is the structural organisation within which crime scene examination operates, as this will determine a broad range of issues that are extremely important and affect the final nature of the evidence collected and analysed. Durkheim's notion of *social facts* is useful in explaining the structural and regulatory framework of crime scene examination as it has the capability 'of exerting over the individual an external constraint' and has 'an existence of its own, independent of its individual manifestations' (1982:59). Such investigative work is constantly constrained by the three types of social facts identified by Durkheim – *morphological, social institutions,* and *collective representations* (Durkheim, 1982, 1984). *Morphological* facts are those related to the morphological structure of society and its organisations; for example, population density (e.g. which affects the number of burglaries), technology (e.g. buildings and scientific equipment) and territorial organisation (e.g. police force geographical boundaries, scientific support divisions, etc.). *Social institutions* include the family, religion, economic, political and criminal justice institutions, and these are institutions that involve beliefs and practices. Finally, there are *collective representations*, which include anything involving moral concepts, religious dogmas, political or legal rules (Durkheim, 1982). The importance of these social facts in relation to crime scene examination is that they constrain and regulate CSEs, as they are invested with coercive power (ibid.; Thompson, 1992). For example, the majority of police forces in England and Wales have their own scientific support departments and personnel, and their attendance at crime scenes is determined by social facts such as resources, geographical location and force priorities (McCulloch, 1996). Thus, not all crimes reported result in a crime scene examination, and not all crimes produce forensically useful information that can be turned into evidence. The implication of this is that any forensic meaning or criminological understanding we glean from officially recorded crimes is usually restricted only to those scenes visited, which leaves an epistemological gap between the reality of crime events and those that are recorded and assessed. However, for crimes where the scene is attended by CSEs, it is important to consider the structure and organisation of scientific support in England and Wales.

The structure and roles of scientific services in the UK

Crime scene investigation is placed within the broader structure of scientific support within UK police forces (Beaufort-Moore, 2009:4–6). It is not possible to provide a single model of the morphological and institutional structures of scientific support, as each of the 43 police forces in England and Wales have different geographies, population densities and policing priorities. Whilst the government operates some level of central control and oversight over police forces, the Chief Constable in each area has the overall power and controls the budgets, including the forensic budget, and the new Police Crime Commissioners have full oversight. Each police force has its own in-house scientific services department (SSD), and, whilst there are individual differences between the forces, they provide specialist support in respect of forensic examination and recovery, as well as a range of photographic, enhancement, analysis and examination techniques. When it comes to the structure within the SSDs, the departments shown in Figure 9.1 are usually standard (see Weston, 2004; Beaufort-Moore, 2009; Dutelle, 2011).

Within this typical structure there are also a number of roles that make up the morphological structure of police scientific services. These roles are varied and consist of both police officers and civilian staff, the numbers of which are again determined by the structural facts, such as the police force, its jurisdictional area, population density, etc. However, there is usually the head of SSD, who oversees a team consisting of a deputy and the relevant unit managers (e.g. the fingerprint bureau manager). These individuals run teams consisting of crime scene managers (CSMs), CSEs, technicians (e.g. members of the high-tech crime department that do not visit scenes but review and compile evidence collected by CSEs), and submissions officers (e.g. for major crimes where there is the need for a designated officer to collate all exhibits that are submitted to court) (Beaufort-Moore, 2009:4–13). At the time of writing, for example, Hampshire had around 150 people working in its SSD, and around 25 per cent of those are police officers. Figure 9.2 outlines a typical structure for scientific services in the UK.

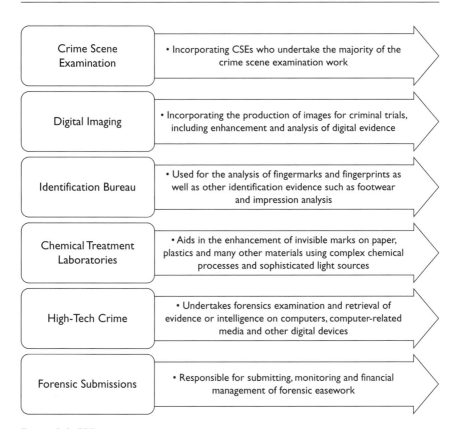

Figure 9.1 SSD units

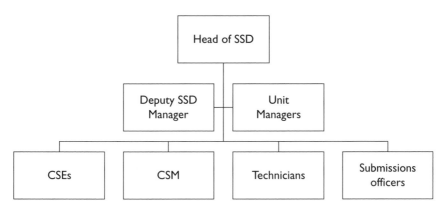

Figure 9.2 SSD roles

National standards, forensic strategies and submissions

What is clear from the previous section is that there is a structure and organisation to scientific services in the UK, and most police forces are organised in a similar fashion. These structures provide a framework within which forensic examination and the analysis of crime scenes is undertaken. On a practical level, this means that the organisational structures determine the actions and decision-making processes of CSEs even before they set foot on to a crime scene. Not only this, but regulatory frameworks also determine the work of crime scene examination, and, in the UK, national standards and the forensic strategy frameworks fulfill this important role.

National standards

Forensic investigation is framed within a range of national standards that set the minimum level of practice for forensic investigations, and, over the last 15 years or so, a number of key agencies have steered the development of forensic standards. Agencies such as the Forensic Science Service, the Forensic Science Regulator, ACPO and NPIA have all worked towards developing a nationwide strategy for forensic improvement within the area of police investigations. For example, within the NPIA's National Improvement Strategy for Policing, a number of learning, people and performance improvement programmes developed, some of which were specifically designed for forensic investigations. In another example, the ACPO/NPIA *quality standards project's* (QSP) second phase objective was to 'improve police forensics by implementing a national quality standards framework, better forensic processes and assured practitioners competence' (Hunter, 2010). This was to be under the shared vision of embedding 'a quality culture into forensics that will support continuous performance improvement and greater public confidence in policing' (Hunter, 2010). Two further projects were linked to QSP: the first being the ACPO-commissioned Forensics21 project, created to provide support to UK police forces in gaining accreditation to the ISO national standards which was being undertaken by the second project, known as the Forensic Quality Standards Project. Forensics21 consists of two phases. The first phase was completed in March 2010 and incorporated the following improvements to police forensic services:[1]

- the successful transition of the National DNA Database (NDNAD) into a 'police-owned', secure environment;
- reducing the average time to establish a fingerprint identification from 17 days to 2 days by the introduction of the remote transmission of crime scene marks;
- the delivery of the first National Footwear Reference Collection enabling forces to communicate footwear pattern links in a single intelligent language;

- a National Forensic Procurement Framework delivering more than £2 million cashable savings for forces; and
- a return on investment of 21 per cent or £4.1 million per year invested in Live Scan Technology.

Phase 2 of the project commenced in April 2010; its intention being to develop a number of projects including:[2]

- ADAPT (Accelerated DNA Profiling Technology);
- Operation Slingshot (Forensic Science Service Transition);
- National Forensic Procurement;
- eForensics;
- Protection of Freedoms Act implementation;
- Forensic Quality Standards; and
- National Footwear Database.

These projects came about because of the financial crisis hitting public sector budgets, creating the need to think more carefully about where to direct increasingly squeezed resources. As the need to find best value in forensic practice moves forward, the implementation of a national framework of forensic standards was the attempt to control and regulate practice. The two core ISO standards relevant to structuring of forensic practice in the UK are ISO 9001 and ISO 17025, and these relate to the accreditation and standards of laboratory work in the UK, which is examined in more detail in the following chapter. For crime scene examination, the NPIA's (2012) *Forensic Submissions: Good Practice Guide* sets the national standards.

Forensic strategies and submissions

In Chapter 7, the concept of case construction and crime reconstruction was introduced in relation to information work. Whilst these three concepts move beyond mere abstract thinking and enter into the practical world of criminal investigations, in recent years they have been framed more and more within the structure of *forensic strategies*. As with the development of national standards, the Forensics21 project was a key driver in developing national guidance on forensic submissions and strategies (NPIA, 2010b). Through the *Forensic Submissions National Trend Report*, data was collected from selected police forces using the methodology of 'the impact on detections from forensic submissions', the results of which identified 'a number of consistent trends' (NPIA, 2012:3). This research is of interest as there is a clear difference between a successful, positive result from a forensic examination and whether that examination results in a successful detection that yields some probative value in court. Again, economic constraints have forced stricter control over forensic budgets, leading ACPO and the NPIA to develop good practice guidance for forensic submissions and strategies. The latest version sets out guidelines that aid police forces 'in managing the submission process' and also assist in demonstrating 'the impact on policing budget cuts around submissions' (ibid.:6). By providing standards to all forces, the aim of the guidance is to produce a national framework for cost-effective and efficient forensic strategies and submissions that would 'provide a centralised submissions service for the force to ensure the requirements of the Criminal Justice System' (ibid.:7). Furthermore, through POLKA, the Police OnLine Knowledge Area,[3] a structured learning environment has also developed with online policing communities sharing, discussing and collaborating on a wide range of investigative practice including forensic submissions and strategies.

Section 4 of the *Forensic Strategies* document outlines the basic components for formulating forensic strategies with the overriding aim being to provide the best value 'from the available forensic resources' (ibid.:34). Forensic strategies are largely determined by forensic submissions officers, although the separation of roles between the CSE and forensic submissions and exhibits officer tends only to occur with more serious and publicly visible crimes such as rape, murder and major incidents such as terrorist attacks. For minor crimes, such as residential burglary or car theft, and *if* the CSE visits the scene, they usually act as submissions and exhibits officer all rolled into one. Whatever the specific arrangements for individual crime scenes, it is important that whoever develops the forensic strategy has 'detailed knowledge of the circumstances of the case so that consideration can be given to what kind of examinations may be carried out and what may be expected from them' (ibid.:34).

NPIA guidance points to three levels of propositions that should be considered when formulating forensic strategies. Each proposition level should, in theory, consider not only a prosecutorial position but also an alternative defence hypothesis, which is loosely linked to Popper's (2002) idea that the scientific method should strive for falsification over verification. It is questionable whether the CSE operates on a truly objective basis, testing both potential prosecutorial and defence propositions, due to the very simple fact that whilst CSEs have largely developed into a professional, civilian role (Baber and Butler, 2012:1), they are still part of the police structure, *ergo* they are invested with police culture (Waddington, 1999; Reiner, 2010). This raises important issues as to whether they are able to provide independent, objective assessments of crime scenes, as structural, cultural and external pressures will often impact on an individual's ability to make unpopular decisions: for instance, moving against a pre-existing investigative hypothesis from a superior officer (Gross, 1962; Kirk, 1974; Mullin, 1986; Maguire and Norris, 1992; Innes, 2003; Innes *et al.*, 2005; Gilbert, 2006).

The three levels of propositions are: (i) *evidentiary material*; (ii) *activities*; and (iii) the *actual offence*. Level one propositions relate to 'the source of evidentiary material' – for example, semen on victim X came from suspect A, which is known as the investigative and prosecutorial proposition; whilst the defence proposition would be that the semen on victim X came from another individual (Anderson *et al.*, 2005:96–131; NPIA, 2012:34). According to the NPIA, as level one propositions are evidence specific, it is not necessary to have all the contextual evidence surrounding the crime event. Level one propositions, therefore, tend to concentrate on answering *what* and/or *who* questions; and, in the case of physical evidence, identifying its class or individual characteristics (NPIA, 2012:34). Level two propositions on the other hand require more detail regarding the overall circumstances of the offence. These relate to both the activities undertaken during the commission of the crime event and the individual(s) involved (ibid.:34). For example, suspect A stabbed victim X in the neck is a prosecutorial proposition, whilst a defence proposition would argue that suspect A was not present when victim X was stabbed. Activity propositions should be related to the concepts of transference and persistence of trace evidence as they can provide the necessary evidence that links the suspect, victim and crime scene (as outlined in Chapter 7). Finally, level three propositions relate to the actual offence; for instance, where the prosecutorial proposition states that 'A assaulted B, with a defence proposition being A had nothing to do with the assault of B' (ibid.:35). This type of proposition usually relates directly to those which are considered by a jury during the trial process, so the NPIA guidance stipulates that the higher the propositional level, the more probative value is 'added by the scientific evidence' (ibid.:35). What this means in practical terms is that materials recovered from a crime scene should be those that have the potential to yield the most relevant information vis-à-vis the case being investigated. Interestingly, experimental research conducted by Baber and Butler (2012), which compared the search strategies of novices (first-year undergraduate forensic science students) with experienced CSEs, found that novices explored the scene in terms of the objects contained within, whereas experts considered the evidence analysis that can be performed as a consequence of the examination and which would yield the highest probative value. The development of the appropriate forensic strategy is therefore crucial for maximising the forensic yield of evidence, so the NPIA and ACPO have provided four broad criteria for forensic strategists to follow (NPIA, 2012:35):

1   Material recovered from a scene is determined by an intelligent assessment of the potential probative value that evidence could yield in relation to the investigation.
2   While making submission decisions, officers should consider the different strengths inherent within different types of evidence.
3   Submission decisions should also take into consideration the circumstances of each case as well as wider police force policies including budgetary constraints and strategic and operational crime priorities linked to NIM.
4   Consideration should also be given to all material evidence as potentially becoming important during the course of the investigation.

It should be noted that these four criteria are not strict, dogmatic rules as they allow for the 'submissions officer's professional discretion' (ibid.:35). However, these criteria tend to frame the CSEs' processes as they enter and undertake their crime scene examination. If we look at other jurisdictions across the world, similar attempts have been made to provide standards for crime scene examination. For example, Wilson-Wilde *et al.* (2011:333–334) note how the Australia New Zealand Policing Advisory Agency's National Institute of Forensic Science (NIFS) established a 'project to set up a sustainable mechanism for the development and maintenance of standards, across a broad science and technology base that is relevant to general law enforcement, and the forensic science community' (333). From this project developed a strategic framework for forensic standards, consisting of four core standards: (i) collection; (ii) analysis; (iii) interpretation; and (iv) reporting (ibid.:333–334). Standards (ii) to (iii) relate specifically to forensic science and are discussed in the following chapter. Standard (i), however, is directly linked to crime scene examination, and encompasses the collection standards labelled recognition, preservation, recording, collection, packaging, transport and storage (ibid.:334).

The components of crime scene examination

As was previously shown, information work uses various types of material which is transformed into information and evidence in order to reconstruct the crime event under question and build a case that is presented for criminal adjudication (Innes, 2003; Sutton and Trueman, 2009). When it comes to forensic evidence, the majority of the material that produces forensically useful information is identified and collected from the crime scene, suspects and victims. This evidence, then, is crucial, as it not only provides the basis for the direction the investigation takes, its lines of inquiry and developing a suspect pool, but it also provides the 'proof' of the case that has been reconstructed and is presented in the courtroom. In short, the actions of the forensic investigators at the crime scene help determine the final outcome of the case; and it's for this reason that procedures regarding processing the crime scene have developed over the last 60 years (Kirk, 1974; Gardner and Bevel, 2009; Dutelle, 2011).

Defining the crime scene

Perhaps the first important issue to determine is what is meant by the term 'crime scene'. As Miller notes (2009:167), the 'only thing consistent about crime scenes is their variety'. Crime scenes are initially determined according to the location of the original criminal activity and can be classified as either primary or secondary scenes. A primary scene is the site of the 'original or first criminal activity' and the secondary scene relates to any subsequent activity undertaken in the commission of the same crime event (ibid.:167–168). Dutelle utilises a simple, yet effective, working definition of a crime scene as 'anywhere evidence may be located that will help explain events' (Ragel, 2002, cited in Dutelle, 2011:13). Gardner and Bevel (2009:1) raise an important point when they suggest that the term 'scene' should be used instead of 'crime scene'. They argue that, when it comes to the initial inspection and evaluation, the term scene should be used, as the CSE has yet to confirm the fact that it is indeed the scene of the crime, and 'that decision is not always apparent until after the analysis' (ibid.:1). Oftentimes the crime scene is not simply a geographical location such as a room, flat, or house but can also include the staging and planning areas; the paths of entry and exit to and from the primary scene; and the paths between the primary and any other scenes (Beaufort-Moore, 2009; Miller, 2009; Trueman, 2009a). These types of crime scenes are often referred to as *macroscopic* as there are often multiple scenes with different structural dynamics. Apart from the physical structure of the environment in which a crime event occurs, a crime scene is also determined by a number of *microscopic* factors, such as the type of crime committed, the behaviour of the offender and victim during the crime, and the available objects/ material at the crime scene (Fisher, 2005; Pepper, 2005; Beaufort-Moore, 2009; Dutelle, 2011). For example, a rape victim attacked in a park will yield the following multiple macroscopic and microscopic crime scenes:

- the attack site at the park;
- possible entry and exit points;
- the victim and the victim's wounds;
- the victim's clothing;
- the suspect's home or places they visit; and
- the suspect and the suspect's clothing.

What the above discussion illustrates is that it is difficult to provide an overarching definition that covers the intricacies of different crime scenes. Ultimately, it is the adaptation to the context of the scene or scenes that determines and defines their type. Despite this complexity and differentiation, structured processes such as national standards and forensic strategies aid CSEs in maximising the gathering of material and its probative usefulness.

A systematic process

Briefly turning back to crime reconstruction, Chisum and Turvey (2008:159) suggest six processes which offer a useful framework of analysis when trying to place material, and the information contained within, into a reconstructed crime narrative. However, it should be remembered that, when it comes to the processing of the scene, only 'some of the actions and sequences of events are being established' (ibid.:155): it is not the entire scene that is being reconstructed – it is an incomplete picture. These six processes are as follows:

1 **Observe** – identification of evidence of events occurring at the crime scene and related clues;
2 **Determine** – decide what can be learned of events from each observation;

3 **Postulate** – ask yourself and your investigative team what the clue or observation means in light of the crime;

4 **Propose** – develop alternative explanations for events;

5 **Eliminate** – provide a critical analysis of the alternatives through the use of logic, critical thinking and experimentation (aiming at falsification); and

6 **Sequence** – review the events and evidence until the picture is completed.

Gardner and Bevel (2009:37–72) provide another useful conceptualisation of crime scene examination by outlining a seven-stage *event analysis* process. The first step is to *collect data*; consisting of identifying material at the crime scene, with four specific questions that must be asked of each item found: (i) What is the material?; (ii) What is its function (vis-à-vis the crime event)?; (iii) How does it relate to other items found at the scene (e.g. has it 'interacted' with other items, or have other items 'interacted' with it)?; and finally (iv) What does the item tell us about the timing and sequencing of the crime event(s)? During the data collection stage, CSEs should not blindly consider all items at the scene but try to make decisions about which material is more relevant to the crime event under investigation and which can also provide the most probative value; for instance, regarding identification evidence (ibid.:41–45). Stage two of the process is the *establishment of the event segments* (ibid.:45–60), which is described as 'a specific action that is identifiable based on one or several pieces of evidence' (45). For example, if there is a bloody footprint, the direction of which is moving away from the body at the scene of a murder, then this tells us someone other than the victim was present after the bloodshed event. CSEs and forensic analysts often use event segments when conducting blood spatter analysis (see James *et al.*, 2005; Bevel and Gardner, 2008; Turvey, 2008). The event segments are 'snapshots' which are the pieces of the crime event puzzle, so it is important that the CSE identifies as many as possible. Third, it must be established which *event segments are related* to one another (Gardner and Bevel, 2009:60–61; also see Chisum and Turvey, 2008; Dutelle, 2011). Going back to the jigsaw puzzle analogy, if you had identified all 1,000 pieces of the jigsaw, the next stage is to see how the pieces fit together. It is here that the CSE should focus on 'trying to understand different areas or activities that occurred during the incident' (Gardner and Bevel, 2009:60). So if we follow a hypothetical example of a stabbing of a male youth in the chest, in an alley off a street in Bristol where bins are kept, and involving a gang of six individuals (four males and two females); there are numerous event segments that could be identified, and their relationships to each other could include any of the following:

• **The male victim's (MV) stabbing event** – MV's coat, jumper and t-shirt exposed to the bloodshed event (i.e. number of wounds, weapon angle, ripped clothing and bloodstains);

- **Activity involving the male offenders (MO1 ... MO*n*)** – blood spatter on the jeans and trainers of the male offenders; fibre transfer evidence of MV's torn clothing; fingerprints on knife;
- **Activity involving female offender (FO ... FO*n*)** – fibre and hair transfer evidence; and
- **Activity involving the scene** – large amount of blood spatter on the floor and wall of the alley; spatter on the bins; knife found at scene.

The fourth step is to find the *sequencing of the event segments* (Gardner and Bevel, 2009:68; also see Chisum and Turvey, 2008; Dutelle, 2011). This entails looking 'for sequencing information' (Gardner and Bevel, 2009:61) and includes identifying 'three relative chronology relationships between the various event segments' known as *terminus post quem, terminus ante quem,* and *terminus peri quem. Terminus post quem* (TPQ), or 'limit after which', means that an event segment has occurred after another event segment, an example of which is the identification of fresh tool-mark impressions on a car-door lock and a smashed car window. Logic would dictate that the car thief tried to break in through the door and failed (event segment A) so instead broke the window (event segment B). *Terminus ante quem* (TAQ), or 'limit before which', denotes that an event segment happens before another segment. For instance, in the above hypothetical stabbing case, blood found on the floor, wall and bins in the alley (event segments B, C and D) automatically means that a 'bloodshed event' (James *et al.*, 2005) has occurred (event A). Finally, *terminus peri quem* (TPeQ), which can be defined as 'several actions appear to be simultaneous to one another' (Gardner and Bevel, 2009:64) or 'a statement of near simultaneous actions' (62). Whilst TPQ and TAQ are extremely useful for sequencing the event segments, TPeQ is closely aligned to contemporary crime scene examination for the principle of exchange often produces simultaneous event segments. In the case of the car thief smashing the window, the breaking of the glass, shards of glass transferred to the floor inside the car and the floor directly below the window, and glass fibres transferred to the offender's clothing are nearly simultaneous events. The fifth stage involves an *analysis of all possible sequences and the auditing of background information* (ibid.:68–70). As highlighted in Chapter 7, oftentimes, there are a number of event segments that are missing during any investigation, and sometimes information from that crime event will be missing. The CSE must, therefore, 'audit' the information, taking out the irrelevant pieces that do not aid in the reconstruction of the crime event(s). Unfortunately, it's not easy making the correct auditing decisions, which is why the decision logs used in UK policing have become important (see NCPE, 2005; Stelfox, 2009). Step six involves creating a *final order of the events* based on the event segment sequence (Gardner and Bevel, 2009:70). It is important that, upon final presentation, the correct order of events is identified, and this usually 'organically evolves' through the process of the investigation. Finally, stage seven consists of building an inscriptive device

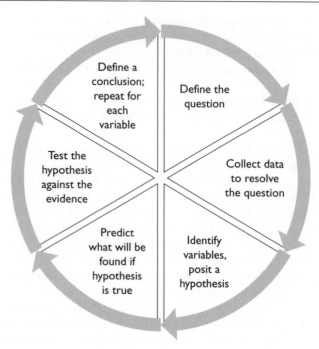

Figure 9.3 The scientific method

(Latour and Woolgar, 1986) of the events; for example, a *flow chart of the incident that validates the sequence* (Gardner and Bevel, 2009:70–71). The graphic is used to 'recognize, understand, and demonstrate the overall sequence' of the crime (ibid.:70) and starts at stage four of the process. New event segments (material and information) that are identified and analysed can potentially change the sequence and order so the graphic must be continuously updated and revised.

What the CSE in the above seven-stage process is trying to follow is the scientific method, as applied within an investigative framework, as outlined in Figure 9.3 (ibid.:19).

The above processes need to be strictly followed by the CSE if they are to provide the most accurate reconstruction of the crime using the available and most relevant material. Once these processes have been implemented, the CSE needs to identify which of the three outcomes outlined in Table 9.1 fits with the material examined from the scene.

The qualities of a good investigator

Hans Gross (1962:15–19) outlined three core qualities that he believed were essential to becoming a good, efficient police investigator. These qualities are also important for crime scene examiners. Gross suggests that that, apart from

Table 9.1 Possible outcomes of crime scene processing

Outcome	Description
Supported	• Where hypotheses regarding the crime event are consistent with physical evidence. This is largely based upon known circumstances and favours a particular explanation over any alternatives proffered.
Inconsistent	• Where the hypotheses of the crime event are eliminated or disproved by physical evidence and the known circumstances. This is where the theory about the crime is out of alignment with particular facts.
Inconclusive	• Where the theory of the crime is not disproved or eliminated by physical evidence and the known facts. Inconclusive evidence often addresses alternatives that remain untested or produce examinations of evidence where the results are inconclusive.

the normal qualities they should possess, 'indefatigable zeal and application, self-denial and perseverance, swiftness in reading men and a thorough knowledge of human nature, education and an agreeable manner, an iron constitution, and encyclopedic knowledge' (ibid.:15), they should also possess the qualities of *energy, self-denying power* and *accuracy*. A CSE must have a constant supply of energy, for energy feeds the investigative spirit and, in the face of a 'hot-headed, refractory, and aggressive' offender or a 'difficult, complicated or obscure case' (ibid.:15), energy enables the CSE to keep going in the face of adversity. Second, self-denying-power represents the idea that 'virtue is its own reward' (ibid.:16), and that CSEs should not consider public success but should simply concentrate on an honest examination of the crime scene. Finally, the CSE must adhere to the idea of absolute accuracy and must not be 'content with mere evidence of third parties or hearsay when it is possible for him . . . to ascertain the truth with his own eyes or by more minute investigation' (ibid.:16). Thus, when undertaking the processes outlined above, attention to detail and the exactness of the work is crucial. The application of the scientific method suggested in Figure 9.3 is a way to ensure accuracy for CSEs, and it also reduces the potential for mistakes:

> A thousand mistakes of every description would be avoided if people did not base their conclusions upon premises furnished by others, take as established fact what is possibility, or as a constantly recurring incident what has only been observed once.
>
> (Ibid.:17)

The attributes outlined by Gross over a century ago are still relevant to today's CSE. Dutelle (2011:25–26) lists the crucial attributes required for CSEs as being:

an enjoyment and passion for life-long learning (continuing education); an eye for detail; good communication skills; intuition; relevant knowledge of methods for locating and preserving evidence; and confidence as an expert witness. These skills, and many others besides, are combined with the systematic approaches identified above to produce specific ways for processing the crime scene.

Processing the scene

The overriding consideration for all actions undertaken at the scene is maintaining the *chain of continuity*, which is also known as the *chain of quality, chain of evidence* or *chain of custody* (Barclay, 2009:356–357; Beaufort-Moore, 2009: 25–26, 42–43; Trueman, 2009b: 57–58; Houck and Siegel, 2010:36; Dutelle, 2011:24; Monckton-Smith *et al.*, 2013:69–70). It must be demonstrated that the *integrity* of the evidence is maintained and properly recorded and thus provides honest 'accountability of an exhibit' (Trueman, 2009b:58). Continuity starts at the moment the material is recognised as being potential evidence, and 'from then on its location and movement must be accountable and documented until it is presented before court and until its disposal is authorized' (ibid.:58). The 'chain' should show who has had direct or indirect contact with the evidence and include such information as: times and dates for each contact (the 'link' in the chain); under what circumstances each contact is made; and what changes are made to said evidence (Dutelle, 2011:24). Attempts to maintain the chain of continuity have led to the development of procedures similar to some of the principles of scientific management, including standardisation of protocols and methods of crime scene management (Shiomi and Wada, 1995). In the UK, the standardisation of crime scene management has led to the *five building blocks* principle, which Beaufort-Moore (2009:26–37) suggests is a useful framework for approaching the investigation of crime scenes. These five principles are: (i) to preserve life; (ii) to preserve scenes; (iii) to preserve evidence; (iv) to identify victim(s); and (v) to identify witnesses. Principles (ii) to (v) are geared towards maintaining the quality of the evidence, and this is done for three core reasons: first, so there can be no question as to the authenticity of the evidence – i.e. the information contained within demonstrates what it is claimed it demonstrates; second, so there can be no suspicion that the evidence used in a trial has been contaminated – i.e. so it can be identified as originating from the crime scene and/or the suspect or victim in connection with the crime under investigation; and, finally, to ensure that a full record of the continuity of possession is maintained – i.e. so only authorised and relevant individuals have accessed the material recovered and analysed (Beaufort-Moore, 2009:25–26; Trueman, 2009b; Houck and Siegel, 2010; Dutelle, 2011). The processes of crime scene examination detailed in this section are therefore tailored towards the maintenance of the chain of quality. Operating within the national standards and rules governing police investigations and the collection and submission of evidence (some of which were outlined in Chapters 6 and 7), when it comes to physical evidence, CSEs engage in four

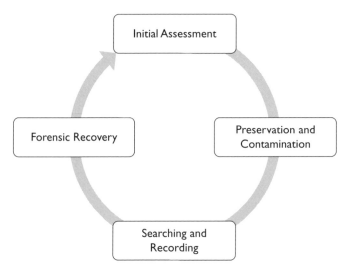

Figure 9.4 Maintaining the chain of continuity

broad categories of actions. These four areas primarily relate to building block principles (ii) and (iii) but, of course, lead to the identification of victims and suspects (building blocks iv and v).

Within each of these broad areas, many tasks are undertaken in order to ensure the highest possible quality of the evidence that is examined in the forensic laboratory and which might end up as part of the case file submitted to the CPS.

Initial assessment

Hans Gross highlighted that the first thing to do when arriving at the scene is to 'quietly and attentively' take 'stock of the situation' (1962:78). Obviously, crime scene examination begins with the arrival at the scene and early decisions, and actions taken at this stage immediately affect future actions and what is eventually recovered from the scene. However, before proceeding to some of the processes undertaken by CSEs, it is important to note that they are not usually the first individuals at the scene, so any actions undertaken prior to their arrival must be identified and considered, as they potentially determine the course of action they take (Cook and Tattersall, 2008; Trueman, 2009a). Apart from offenders and victims, there are usually three other groups that potentially impact upon the crime scene prior to the arrival of the CSE: witnesses, the first officer attending (FOA) and emergency service personnel. For example, most crime scene investigators are called out to scenes by someone else, which is usually the FOA; and it is the FOA that usually sets the initial cordon and takes the first details of the incident (Cook and Tattersall, 2008; Beaufort-Moore, 2009:26–27; Trueman,

2009a:21–35; Dutelle, 2011:63–80; Becker and Dutelle, 2013:28–31). However, it has been suggested that this in itself is problematic. Research into the level of forensic awareness amongst practitioners such as FOAs notes the lack of the most basic understanding of doctrines such as Locard's principle of exchange or the chain of quality. For example, in 2005, the House of Commons Science and Technology Committee reported on the results of an inquiry into the viability of the then proposed GovCo model for the Forensic Science Service. Recommendation 27 (House of Commons Science and Technology Committee, 2005a:85) noted concerns over the provision of forensic science education in the UK, whilst recommendation 32 highlighted the need for forensic awareness to become 'embedded in the wider police, rather than being confined to those in specialist roles or who have had specific training' (ibid.:86). Unfortunately, this problem is not new and goes back even further. In 1987, accounts firm Touche Ross reported that 'police management of scientific support was "generally poor"' and that 'forensic science was being applied in an undesirably scattershot fashion to criminal investigations' (Lawless, 2011:5). Nine years later, research by Tilley and Ford (1996) and McCulloch (1996) highlighted that, whilst 'external provision of forensic science, and the management of scientific support within police forces have been implemented' (Tilley and Ford, 1996:v), a basic understanding of forensics amongst FOAs was still severely lacking. Tilley and Ford also found that there 'was a widespread lack of awareness within the police service about forensic science itself . . . which inhibits the optimal usage of forensic science' (ibid.:v). Things, of course, have improved over the last 26 years, but it *is* telling that the concerns raised by Touche Ross and the Tilley/Ford and McCulloch studies were echoed in 2005 through the Science and Technology Committee. As it stands at the time of writing, provision for basic forensic training for police trainees plays only a minor role in their initial training course.

Regarding the third group, in cases of injury or fire, the emergency services will more often than not attend the scene before the CSE is called; and they, like police officers, will operate on their primary function of preservation of life – preserving the crime scene will be a distant second. As such, emergency service actions at the scene could impact on the evidence; this was briefly discussed in Chapter 7 through the concept of evidence dynamics (Chisum and Turvey, 2008). What this pre-arrival activity means for the CSE is important, for it determines the nature of some of the material *in situ*, which can affect the decisions made at the scene and the types of material collected for analysis. Because of this pre-arrival activity, the CSE must begin with an initial examination, or a 'walk-through', of the scene. The walk-through enables the CSE to get a feel for the environment, the layout of the scene and the structures and objects within that scene in order to start developing the appropriate forensic strategy. It also allows the investigator to 'correct if need be the impression that he has already formed about the case on its first being reported, and modify his plans accordingly' (Gross, 1962:78). This idea has been written into the Core Investigative Doctrine (NCPE, 2005:62), which outlines the ABC approach in Figure 9.5 (see also Cook and Tattersall, 2008; Beaufort-Moore, 2009:25).

Assume nothing	**B**elieve nothing	**C**hallenge everything

Figure 9.5 The ABC approach

In the C element, we could also include *check, clarify* and *corroborate*. Trueman notes the importance of the initial examination for any investigation when he suggests that 'if the assessment is carried out carefully then everything else will fall into place and all pertinent evidential material will be identified recorded and recovered' (2009b:46). The initial assessment also includes a health and safety check to ensure that the CSE is not putting their own, or anyone else's, health and safety at risk. It may be necessary at times to crawl and clamber around buildings, including roofs and attics where the possibility of injury increases. The health and safety check is known as a *dynamic risk assessment* and includes identification of any possible dangers on the scene that could result from the recovery of evidentially useful material (Weston, 2004; Cook and Tattersall, 2008; Beaufort-Moore, 2009; Trueman, 2009b; Dutelle, 2011). Other risks at crime scenes include dust particles and other air pollutants – for example, pathogens, chemicals and gases – as well as a whole myriad of objects that could cut or injure personnel on the scene. All CSEs are issued with 'various items of personal protective equipment (PPE) and clothing' (Trueman, 2009b:47), such as gloves, crime scene suits, masks, etc.; which not only reduces the risk of contamination of evidence but also serves as a form of protection from hazardous materials (Houck and Siegel, 2010:41–45). The dynamic risk assessment should also include a safe recovery strategy and will, of course, be dependent upon the circumstances of the crime. Volume crime risk assessments may not take any longer than a few minutes whereas more serious or major crimes require much longer preparation and assessment time (Cook and Tattersall, 2008; Beaufort-Moore, 2009; Trueman, 2009b; Dutelle, 2011).

Once a dynamic risk assessment has been completed, the CSE can then begin to identify *key evidence areas*, and these tend to be identified through the initial assessment information provided by FOAs, the aggrieved party and the CSEs own review of the situation. They are areas where the CSE should target their initial scene preservation and recovery strategies as they *should* yield the most forensically useful information (Nickell and Fischer, 1999; Fisher, 2005; Berg, 2008; Cook and Tattersall, 2008; Beaufort-Moore, 2009; Trueman, 2009b; Dutelle, 2011; Becker and Dutelle, 2013).

Preservation of the scene

During the initial assessment, the CSE must also *confirm, cordon, secure* and *control* the scene, which may mean altering what the FOA has set up (Nickell and

Fischer, 1999; Weston, 2004; Pepper, 2005; Berg, 2008; Cook and Tattersall, 2008; Beaufort-Moore, 2009; Trueman, 2009b; Dutelle, 2011; Becker and Dutelle, 2013). The CSE must *confirm* the details of the incident and briefly interview, if possible, those who have been at the scene to find out what actions they have undertaken which may affect the nature of the evidence. Second, if in place, they must review the initial *cordon* and its placement and determine whether it needs to be altered in any way. A cordon is crucial because it determines the area that is searched for evidence and can often be affected by what Chisum and Turvey (2007, 2008) call *the other side of the tape* problem. The cordon establishes the crime scene and this is dependent upon the nature of the incident, so minor volume crimes such as theft from a vehicle parked in the car park of a local cinema would not require a cordon; but if the same vehicle had a dead body within, then cordons would be required (Berg, 2008; Cook and Tattersall, 2008; Beaufort-Moore, 2009; Trueman, 2009b). It is very important that the right scene is identified and correctly cordoned, as case studies and anecdotal evidence from CSEs suggest that time after time FOAs fail to identify the correct scene and cordon off the wrong area. In some cases, crime scenes are obvious; in other cases, they are more difficult to ascertain, especially if the scene is outdoors (Cook and Tattersall, 2008:122–128; Beaufort-Moore, 2009:29). As trace evidence is microscopic, it can be destroyed, lost, transferred or contaminated, so identifying the right scene and placing a valid cordon (or perimeter) is important for minimising these potential risks. Where they are required, officers cordon off anything that may be potentially relevant. For more serious crimes, two cordons are used – *outer* and *inner* cordons. The *outer cordon* excludes anyone but police officers and relevant forensic personnel, acting as a control zone for authorised personnel but also a buffer just in case important trace evidence is overlooked within the outer cordon zone. The most useful forensic material is often found in the *inner cordon*, and this is where CSEs undertake their most intensive activities (Cook and Tattersall, 2008:125; Trueman, 2009a:29; Dutelle, 2011:68–69). It is also 'the immediate area of the incident, usually sited around the body or attack site' (Beaufort-Moore, 2009:30), so it is important that the entry and exit points taken by the offender are identified early on, so they can be secured. The general rule is that, in the early stages of a criminal investigation, the bigger the cordon the better; but obviously this presents many problems when trying to investigate crime in urban areas. If the area is densely populated, is in a public place (i.e. street or shop), or is in a residential area, then achieving an effective and controlled cordon is operationally difficult. The larger the area the more complex it is, with all sorts of possible areas where evidence can be transferred, hidden or simply dumped. Urban areas provide a geographical area with a complex mix of residential houses, flats, maisonettes, shops, parks, schools, churches, hospitals, pubs and so forth (Trueman, 2009a:29). Added to the problem of environmental complexity, there will be numerous items that also make up the scene such as dustbins, outhouses, bushes and so forth.

From a legal standpoint, Cook and Tattersall (2008:127–128) note that the power to cordon and secure areas is not clear cut, as there is scant statutory power or authority conferred to the police for the setting up of cordons (for example, see section 11(i) of *DPP v Morrison*, [2003] EWHC 683 Admin). Sections 8, 18, 23 and 32 of PACE, provide the police with the powers to access and secure premises for the purposes of searching; but the only direct statutory authority regarding cordons in English law is under section 33 of the Terrorism Act 2000:

> 33.—(1) An area is a cordoned area for the purposes of this Act if it is designated under this section.
> (2) A designation may be made only if the person making it considers it expedient for the purposes of a terrorist investigation.
> (3) If a designation is made orally, the person making it shall confirm it in writing as soon as is reasonably practicable.
> (4) The person making a designation shall arrange for the demarcation of the cordoned area, so far as is reasonably practicable —
> (a) by means of tape marked with the word 'police', or
> (b) in such other manner as a constable considers appropriate.

However, this only applies to suspected acts of terrorism. In *DPP v Morrison* ([2003] EWHC 683 Admin),[4] the Director of Public Prosecutions (DPP) challenged the successful appeal of Clive Winston Morrison. Morrison was convicted in a magistrates' court under the Public Order Acts of 1986 and 1996 for challenging the police's right to stop him entering a cordoned area of a shopping mall, which had a public right of way. Besides the issue of conviction, the crucial point for the DPP was to challenge the decision of Judge Latham and the lay justices of Wood Green Crown Court, who found that the police had wrongfully assumed they had the 'lawful power to set up and maintain a cordon' ([2003] EWHC 683 Admin, section 12(2):3). Lord Justice Kennedy and Mr Justice Hooper found that, whilst there is no statutory authority apart from the aforementioned section 33 of the Terrorism Act 2000, common law practice does provide the necessary legal support for police to cordon areas to secure and preserve evidence (Cook and Tattersall, 2008:127). They found that the Wood Green Crown Court was wrong to uphold the appeal of Morrison and that 'the Metropolitan Police on the evidence in this case had no lawful power or authority to close the public right of way over private premises by a cordon and forcibly prohibit the Defendant from using that right of way on foot against his will' ([2003] EWHC 683 Admin, section 4(1):2). Furthermore, under PACE 1984 Section 116 (6b), the police have the right to arrest individuals for 'serious interference with the administration of justice or with the investigation of offences or of a particular offence', and section 117 outlines the 'power of a constable to use reasonable force in the exercise of his or her power'. From a practical perspective, police are allowed to assume that, for the most part, the general public will cooperate when it comes to restricted access to public crime scenes; and anecdotal evidence from crime scene officers suggests that, even then, there can be some flexibility regarding the circumstances under which access to certain areas of cordoned scenes is granted; for example, if a home owner needs to collect a pet.

Once the scene has been properly identified and cordoned, it is important to identify and establish a common approach path (CAP) and rendezvous point (RVP) (Cook and Tattersall, 2008:124; Beaufort-Moore, 2009:31–32; Trueman, 2009a:29–33). The CAP should be used by everyone entering and exiting the scene and, if possible, should avoid the entry and exit points taken by the offender so as to reduce the likelihood of evidence destruction or contamination. It is 'the route into and out of the crime scene for all those subsequently attending the scene' (Beaufort-Moore, 2009:31), and this is usually from the outer perimeter tape of the crime scene to the victim or key area of the crime. The RVP is an area where CSEs and other relevant personnel can meet to discuss findings and forensic strategies *in situ* whilst the scene is still fresh; it is also where a relevant officer maintains the scene log and allows access to the scene (Cook and Tattersall, 2008:124). It is crucial that there is easy access for personnel and that the RVP is out of sight from the general public and scrutiny of the media. Cordons, the CAP and the RVP help investigators *secure* and *control* the scene, so it is crucial that only authorised personnel have access to scenes and that this access is controlled. This is achieved using the scene log (Nickell and Fischer, 1999:24; Beaufort-Moore, 2009:31; Trueman, 2009a:32–33). Where the incident requires it, the scene log should be instigated at the earliest convenience; and anyone entering or leaving the crime scene must take the CAP route and have their presence recorded on the scene log. An amusing story from the United States and reported in the *Metro* shows us why.

CASE STUDY 9.1 BATMAN AND CONTAMINATION[5]

This amusing case involves Michigan resident Mark Wayne Robinson. Robinson's pastime was to dress up as Batman, the 'Caped Crusader' and fight crime. On this particular crime-fighting mission, Robinson refused to leave the scene of a roadside accident, stating that he wanted to help police look for the driver who had left the scene. The police were trying to use a canine unit to pick up the scent of the driver. Unfortunately, Robinson's presence at the scene kept 'screwing up the scent', making it confusing for the dog and difficult for the police to track the offender. This interesting example highlights the problems with contamination of crime scenes and illustrates why cordons and their control are crucial. In the end, the police had to arrest the Caped Crusader, the second time he had been arrested for interfering with a police investigation.

As a minimum, the scene log should include: 'the details of all those entering or leaving the scene; the time of arrival and departure of such personnel; the purpose or role at the scene; telephone contact details; the person's signature' (Beaufort-Moore, 2009:31). The record must be precise and exact, it must follow the standardised rules and procedures laid down by law, and it must be able to withstand the highest level of scrutiny, especially legal questioning and testing (Nickell and Fischer, 1999:24–25; Weston, 2004:46; Pepper, 2005:110–111; Trueman, 2009a; Dutelle, 2011:66–71). There are a number of reasons why these procedures are in place and are extremely important, and all of these relate to the problem of contamination.

Contamination

The preservation of the scene and all the elements discussed above is effectively an attempt to 'stop time': to 'freeze' as much of the scene as is humanly possible, so that all the material therein is as close to the state it was originally in, or transformed into, through the process of the crime event. When it comes to evidence, the primary consideration 'is whether trace material found on one set of items did in fact come from the source proposed for them' (Gallop and Stockdale, 2004:80). After that, it is crucial to ensure that the material in question could not have arisen as a result of contamination. The factors relating to the chain of continuity discussed so far in this chapter are all geared towards reducing the possibility of contamination, so this is a serious and central issue for criminal investigations. Contamination can be defined as when something occurs which adds 'to the sample, accidentally or deliberately. This can occur for example, by an officer sneezing over material that potentially bears DNA; the officer's DNA can then contaminate the stain' (Beaufort-Moore, 2009:45; see also Trueman, 2009b; Pepper, 2010; Dutelle, 2011). Contamination, therefore, is to make something impure or corrupt through the process of *contact* or *mixture* or a combination of both. *Mixture contamination* usually involves the process of mixing particles, chemicals or substances into evidence, which alters the forensic interpretation and probative value of the evidence. A famous example of mixture contamination is the 1859 trial of Dr Thomas Smethurst, who was charged with poisoning his pregnant mistress, Isabella Bankes. At his trial, toxicologist Professor Arthur Taylor proclaimed that, through his analysis of her vomit and stools, he had found arsenic in her body. After Smethurst was initially convicted of her murder, doubts arose as to the veracity of the forensic medical evidence. Professor Taylor later admitted that it was possible that the traces of arsenic came from his own lab instruments, which had not been properly cleaned; so the Home Secretary threw out the case and Smethurst was released (Evans, 2006:3; Morris, 2007:21). Contamination potentially negates the evidence collected, leaving it inadmissible in court; and with more sophisticated technologies being developed that are able to detect increasingly smaller amounts of trace evidence, contamination has become perhaps the core concern for CSEs. The ISO and national standards briefly discussed above align both crime scene and laboratory processes in order to ensure that any possible contamination is minimised; and it goes without saying that all the procedures and equipment used for crime scene examination are also there to reduce the likelihood of contamination (Weston, 2004; Beaufort-Moore, 2009; Pepper, 2010).

Not all contamination involves the mixture of physical properties. Contact contamination occurs through *secondary cross transference*, where physical material from one area – for example, fibres from a crime scene – is inadvertently transferred to another area by a third party or action not directly related to the original crime event (Beaufort-Moore, 2009:45; Trueman, 2009b:59; Monckton-Smith *et al.*, 2013:47–49). This usually occurs when the FOA and/or emergency personnel enter scenes, and most police officers have 'funny' anecdotal evidence of when they accidentally contaminated a scene. One detective, for instance, when he was first promoted to CID at the grade of Detective Constable, attended a murder scene that involved a stabbing. The body lay in the kitchen and there was some blood pooling around the body and passive spatter trail leading from the doorway. Having called for the CSEs and coroner, he went into the dark lounge and sat down on the sofa awaiting their arrival; he suddenly felt wet, got up, turned on the light and realised he was covered in the victim's blood, for the main bloodshed event had occurred on the sofa.[6] Cross-contamination then, changes the whole dynamic of the material and its subsequent interpretation and admissibility. Again, the murder of 8-year-old Sarah Payne in July 2000 provides a good example of the potential problems with *contact contamination*.

CASE STUDY 9.2 CONTAMINATION AND SARAH PAYNE

In 2001, the trial of the man accused of murdering Sarah Payne uncovered the issue of contact contamination of evidence. A single blond hair was located on a red sweatshirt found in Roy Whiting's van, and subsequent DNA analysis confirmed the hair belonged to Sarah. With the advent of DNA analysis, it has become harder for suspects, solicitors and barristers to deny having any contact with victims. Barristers and solicitors have, therefore, become adept at creating the strategy of attacking the integrity of the evidence; and possible cross-contamination is often used as a way to discredit DNA evidence. During the trial of Whiting, it was suggested that the hair that allegedly placed Sarah in his van could have been cross-transferred through poor crime scene packaging procedures. Raymond Chapman, the forensic scientist leading the team that undertook the main forensic analysis of the Payne evidence, testified that '55 items of evidence sent to his examination team included not only the vital red sweatshirt, but also two hairbrushes from the Payne family home' (*The Guardian*, 29th November 2012). It was also noted that some of the packaging, which contained the evidence, was poorly sealed with the sticky side of the tape showing in places. This sticky edge contained 'several hairs, including a long, fine strand which had similar visual characteristics to the one found on the sweatshirt'. Part of the prosecution's case rested on proving a link between Whiting and Sarah, which meant proving that Sarah had been in the white van owned by Whiting and identified by Sarah's brother Lee on the day of her abduction. The main evidence linking Sarah and her attacker was the hair found on the red sweatshirt that was found in the van, as illustrated by Figure 9.6.

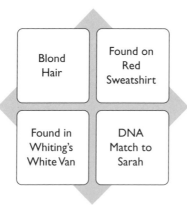

Figure 9.6 Payne-Whiting forensic link

As the evidence bags that contained the sweatshirt and the two hairbrushes were placed in the same area (which was a poor mistake to make), it was suggested that the hair could have been transferred because of the poor quality of the packaging, storage and transfer procedures. Sally O'Neill, the QC defending Whiting, argued that one of Sarah's hairs could have become attached to the bag and then transferred to the sweatshirt, which Chapman agreed under oath could have happened, although he insisted it was 'unlikely'. Despite the problem with packaging, storage and transference of evidence, Whiting was convicted of the murder of Sarah and is currently serving a life sentence.

The case of Sarah Payne demonstrates the importance of procedures and protocols when it comes to minimising contamination. It also highlights the fact that physical material must be handled and processed in a way that prevents, or at least reduces, the likelihood of any change taking place between the time it is removed from crime scene and received into the forensic laboratory, and that contamination can occur at any time (Gallop and Stockdale, 2004; Weston, 2004; Saferstein, 2007; Beaufort-Moore, 2009; Trueman, 2009b; Dutelle, 2011; Jackson and Jackson, 2011). Contamination is further linked to the concepts of transfer and persistence, that were discussed in Chapter 7, for the type and amount of material as well as the conditions and context in which it exists will also have an impact upon the likelihood of contamination. Gill and Clayton's (2009:29–56) discussion of DNA profiling in the UK identifies three useful possible areas where contamination can take place: *adventitious* (before the crime event); *crime scene contamination* (from the crime event to the moment material is recovered and transferred); and *laboratory contamination* (with the laboratory):

> Before and after a crime event there is the potential for adventitious transfer of cells. Note the term contamination is reserved for transfer of DNA *after* the crime event. Adventitious transfer and laboratory contamination usually involve low levels of DNA.
>
> (Ibid.:46)

Contamination is not the only way changes are made to the evidence that compromise the integrity of this evidence. Evidence suffers from breakage, evaporation, accidental scratching or bending and loss through improper or careless packaging (Miller, 2009; Houck and Siegel, 2010; Dutelle, 2011; Jackson and Jackson, 2011). Fundamentally, what investigators should be trying to achieve is the maintenance of the integrity of the evidence. This is achieved by keeping the item in its original condition as found at the crime scene.

Searching the scene

Once the scene is secured and controlled then the search can begin, and this is the start of the information work (Innes, 2003). CSEs will undertake a specific *scene approach sequence*, which includes building an accurate picture of what has occurred through the process of gathering initial information on the crime event under investigation (the initial assessment phase outlined above). CSEs gather information from the incident log, the FAO and the aggrieved party (if present), which should provide a preliminary overview of the crime event (Miller, 2009; Trueman, 2009b; Dutelle, 2011; Jackson and Jackson, 2011). This information should provide enough detail for the CSE to make their assessment of the scene and to develop the relevant bespoke forensic strategies which determine where they prioritise the search for evidence and what type of evidence they look for (Miller, 2009; Beaufort-Moore, 2009; Trueman, 2009b). However, it should be noted that this process is fluid and should not be solely determined by the information provided by those first on the scene but also the CSE's own observations following the ABC approach outlined above.

When it comes to the basic principles of scene examination the *GAME* approach is a useful pneumonic to apply. First, ensure that there is *Good lighting*: anyone who has watched *Crime Scene Investigation (Las Vegas)* could be forgiven if they thought that the majority of crime scenes were undertaken in the dark, with moody UV lighting for added dramatic and cool effect. However, this representation goes against the fundamental basics of good lighting. Crime scenes should be well lit to ensure both the health and safety of those working the scene but also for the more obvious reason that CSEs need enough light to see the scene properly, enabling the identification and recovery of key material. To put it simply, you can't recover what you can't see. Second is *Awareness*: being alert and aware at the scene is important for both health and safety and evidence identification purposes. As previously stated, health and safety includes being aware of the potential risks at the scene. However, awareness is just as important when it comes to searching for and identifying evidence. The third principle is the *Methodical search*. This will be dealt with in more detail in the following section, but undertaking a systematic and methodical search of the identified crime scene so the entire area is covered is a fundamental principle of crime scene examination. Finally, having an *Enquiring mind* is a necessity for any investigation and is linked to engaging in logical and critical thinking when it comes to crime reconstruction (Chisum and Turvey, 2007), which involves searching for evidence that both verifies and falsifies any current investigative hypotheses. Gross was perhaps the first to highlight the importance of good crime scene searching: or what he called the *inspection of localities*: 'In a judicial inspection of localities it is necessary to conform to a sort of technical formula in the method of procedure, and this formula is acquired only by conscientious preparation and dispassion' (Gross, 1962:76).

This *technical formula* consists of a systematic methodical search that ensures nothing is missed and all areas of the crime scene are covered. Over the years, a number of search techniques have developed which have taken the spirit of Gross's technical formula, creating search strategies that can be applied and adapted to fit the specific dynamics of crime scenes. Whilst search patterns are bespoke, and fitted to the specific circumstances of the investigation, Miller argues that search patterns 'share a common goal of providing organization and systematic structure to ensure that no items of physical evidence are missed or lost' (2009:179). Unfortunately, much of the current UK literature on crime scene examination and management provides insufficient space and time when it comes to reviewing crime scene search patterns. For example, two of the 'market leader' texts in crime scene examination (Sutton and Trueman, 2009; Beaufort-Moore, 2009) do not even mention the different search patterns, which is surprising given that many of the authors are ex-practitioners. Even the more established UK texts such as White's *From Crime Scene to Court* (2004, 2010) and Pepper's *Crime Scene Investigation* (2005, 2010) fail to adequately discuss the issue, although Pepper's text does include a diagram of 'a typical search pattern' (2005:15).

In order to find a reasonable overview of searching patterns, we have to turn to our American counterparts, whose breadth and depth of available forensic literature is far in advance of the UK's. Most of this literature points to at least six geometric crime scene search methods (O'Hara and O'Hara, 2003; Saferstein, 2007; Berg, 2008; Miller, 2009; Dutelle, 2011). The first method is known as the *link method* and is based on linkage theory and similar to the snowball sampling method in the social sciences. The basic idea is that one type of evidence leads to another type and so on, and this tends to be the most logical and common search method, useful for large, small, indoor and outdoor scenes (Miller, 2009:179–180). The other five methods are outlined in Table 9.2.

Each of the methods outlined in Table 9.2 has its own advantages and disadvantages, as some are better suited to indoor scenes, and some for outdoor scenes. These techniques can also be combined, so the CSE can adapt the appropriate search strategies in keeping with the situation identified in the initial crime scene assessment. It is important to note that whilst the primary reason for undertaking a methodical search is to find evidence, this collection must not be indiscriminate and should be directed towards establishing one or more of the following (O'Hara and O'Hara, 2003:50):

1   the *corpus delicti* (the 'body of the crime', or the fact that a crime has been committed);
2   the *modus operandi* (how the crime was committed);
3   the identity of the guilty.

A secondary reason for undertaking a crime scene search is to provide a complete map, including all the contextual elements and objects, that freezes the scene in time from the moment the search begins. This aspect links into the necessity of reducing the possibility of contamination and maintaining the integrity of the scene and evidence found therein. In order to achieve this, a number of techniques for recording the scene have developed, all of which are intended to capture the crime scene.

Recording the scene

Next to identifying and collecting evidence, recording the scene is the most important task undertaken during crime scene examination. As Miller highlights, documenting the scene is the most time-consuming activity undertaken, and the purpose is to 'permanently record the condition of the crime scene and its physical evidence' (2009:172). There is a simple reason as to why recording the scene is so important: it cannot be taken to the lab, analysed and then replicated in the courtroom. Even in major incidents such as the 7/7 bombings in London, as the crime scenes were part of sections of London's public transport system, they had to be cleaned up so normal service could be resumed. However, the wheels of justice turn very slowly, as do some types of scientific analysis, often taking

Table 9.2 Crime scene search methods

Type	Pattern	Description
Line Method		• Search along a single line trajectory that is usually linear; • Works best on large, outdoor scenes; • Usually requires a search coordinator or is run by a POLSA (Police Search Advisor); • Can include volunteer searchers.
Grid Method		• As for the line method but is a double-line search; • More methodical and effective, but also more time-consuming.
Zone Method	A B C D	• Based on searching in clearly defined areas; • An area is divided into smaller areas, which breaks the scene down into manageable sections; • Makes searching and processing easier and is useful for search warrants; • Includes: entry and exit points; specific rooms of a building such as a living room or bedroom; • Each is searched as if it were an independent scene in its own right.
Wheel Method		• A limited technique that is best used on small, circular crime scenes;
Sprial Method		• These can be either inward or outward spirals; • Has limited applications; • Best used on crime scenes without physical barriers such as water and large, open expanses of land;

months and sometimes years for cases to reach the courtroom. Because of the time delay between crime scene examination and the evidence being presented at trial, all the elements used for recording the scene act as an aid to memory, enabling the prosecution and defence to produce a version of the crime event, using the relevant crime scene documentation. As already stated, the different varieties of crime scene documentation are *inscriptive devices* (Latour and Woolgar, 1986) that turn the physical structure of the crime scene, and any material found within it, into figures, diagrams and photographs that are usable by all relevant organisations of the criminal justice process.

The logical starting point for recording the scene would be after the initial crime scene assessment has been made and the scene has been secured. However, if the scene is outdoors and the possibility of bad weather makes it likely that evidence will be lost, altered or contaminated then it's crucial that the recording process begins as soon as possible (Beaufort-Moore, 2009:34). Obviously, some of the decisions and processes that have already been outlined above will determine the nature and extent of what is recorded; for example, the area that is cordoned will set the boundaries of the scene to be examined *ergo* what is recorded. Alongside the physical area, a further issue that should be considered is what is actually recorded. As previously discussed, forensic strategies are developed and these strategies include identifying areas where evidence that yields the most probative value can be recovered. However, if this process is followed when it comes to recording the scene, documentation of the scene will be incomplete. In terms of what should be recorded, it is perhaps useful to think that all evidence found and collected will be presented in court so full documentation of the scene is desirable, which fits with criterion four of the NPIA's guidance on forensic strategies (2012:35). In order for a clear representation of the scene and its forensic evidence to be presented in court, and which clearly outlines all three levels of prosecutorial propositions (evidence, actions and offence), various inscriptive devices are used that come under the umbrella term of *scene documentation*.

Scene documentation

As Dutelle notes, 'there is an adage in police work that "if it's not written down, it didn't happen"' (2011:115). Scene documentation consists of any inscriptive device that is created during the recording of the crime scene and potential evidentiary material, which is undertaken as part of the process of crime scene examination. These devices act as a permanent record of the crime event (remembering of course that it is only a part record of the entire crime event). Interestingly, they also operate on several chronological levels: they are constructed in the *present* as a reconstruction of the *past,* and are used for a *future* purpose (i.e. a criminal trial). It is therefore important to remember that scene documentation used to inform the jury in criminal cases is only a constructed picture, some parts of which are either missing or have been extrapolated using inferential reasoning; and it should not be taken for granted as being a full and accurate record of events.

There are two main types of scene documentation that are commonly used at most scenes: (i) *photography* and (ii) the *crime scene report* (Weston, 2004; Pepper, 2005; Saferstein, 2007; Beaufort-Moore, 2009; Miller, 2009; Trueman, 2009b; Dutelle, 2011; Jackson and Jackson, 2011). However, it should be highlighted that within these two broad types exist a number of other inscriptive devices and information that are used to aid in the recording of the scene. Depending on the specific circumstances of the crime being investigated, scene documentation could include: detailed information of all people present at the scene (Beaufort-Moore, 2009:31; Trueman, 2009b:52–53); which specific tasks they have been allocated to undertake; details of the risk assessment, including the health and safety survey (Trueman, 2009b:52–55); details of the visual examination and initial assessment of the scene (Dutelle, 2011:115–116); sketches of the scene and evidential material located and recovered (including measurements), as well as a record of the cordons where possible (Dutelle, 2011:116–127); basic details of photographs taken (a full record is usually kept as a separate digital image log); what presumptive tests have been conducted, including the location and results; details of all evidence recovered, including exhibit references and packaging details (i.e. barcodes and batch numbers) (Trueman, 2009b:51–52; Dutelle, 2011:105–115). I expand on these issues for the remainder of the chapter.

Photography

Photography has a long and rich history so there are hundreds of texts devoted to the technology and techniques behind taking photos. As previously stated in Chapter 4, photography also has close links with the development of criminology and forensic investigations, as the mugshot was used for identification purposes. During the same period, of course, photographs of crime scenes began to appear; and, over the last 120 years, this has developed to become one of the primary features of crime scene examination. Entire texts have been written solely on the topic of crime scene photography (see Duncan, 2010; Robinson, 2010, 2013), so this section provides only a brief overview of some of the core issues and processes that are pertinent to photographing a crime scene.

Photography and digital imaging can be defined as 'the act of recording light or reflected light from an object or group of objects and recording that image on media' (Jones, 2009:195). Traditionally, the media was photographic film but, with the advent of digital cameras, the recording media now preferred is a memory card (an electronic chip). The purpose of crime scene 'still photography', as opposed to video recording, is 'to provide a true and accurate pictorial record of the crime scene and physical evidence present' (Miller, 2009:176). In doing so, it records an overview of the scene, which includes its geographical location and context, as well as documenting the minutiae of the objects and evidence found in the inner and outer cordons. Obviously, the photographs depict the scene as it appears once the CSE has secured the area, so pictures of evidence may include changes that have occurred due to the actions of FOAs, emergency personnel and witnesses. As previously stated, it is crucial for CSEs to identify such actions through their initial assessment using the ABC approach. Photography also enables future and multiple examinations of the scene long after it has been cleaned and returned to its normal state. Forensic analysts will often use photographs of the scene to place into context the evidence they have been sent and also to ensure their interpretations fit with the 'dynamics' and 'physics' of the scene. Finally, photography serves 'as a permanent record for any legal concerns' (ibid.:176), and it's for this last reason that photographs must include images that provide the 'best possible documentation and reproduction of the reality present at the moment in time when the scene was photographed' (Dutelle, 2011:105). Clear and accurate representations are therefore the cornerstones for successful crime scene photography. However, photography is not just about the image, but it also provides evidence of the context of the interaction between the victim, offender and location:

> Photographs can be instrumental in recording the victim's lifestyle and personality; the topography and socioeconomic conditions surrounding the crime scene; and much more which is important to any investigator or analyst who is unable to visit the crime scene.[7]

Contemporary crime scene photography in the UK is primarily undertaken by CSEs trained in forensic photography, using professional equipment (Crowe, 2009:69–95); although in cases where scenes of crime are not visited by CSEs but are attended by the police, the FOA may take some basic pictures on his or her mobile phone or small digital camera. Today, most CSEs carry with them advanced equipment which includes: Digital Single Lens Reflex cameras (D-SLR); 18–35mm zoom lens and 60mm macro lens; flash gun; tripod; scales (in millimetres); and, of course, spare batteries (ibid.:71). D-SLRs have become an important tool for CSEs due to their versatility, advanced quality and reduced cost; so most police forces in the UK choose to use D-SLRs.

There are some general principles that are usually followed when it comes to crime scene photography, and Dutelle (2011:105–115) invokes the theme of 'visual storytelling' in order to explain these principles. Photos should set the scene to the 'story' of the crime event and also include snapshots of all the relevant information (i.e. objects and evidence) that is used to illustrate, affirm and answer the key questions (who, what, when, where and how) of the constructed narrative presented in court. Before the CSE starts taking the main scene photographs, the first photo should be a *photo identifier,* which is often a preprinted sheet consisting of details such as the case number, the date the photographs were taken, the address where they were taken, and the name and badge number of the photographer (Robinson, 2010:306–307). A list of all digital photos is usually created, and this is known as either a *digital log sheet* or a *photo memo sheet*. The information contained on the memo sheet includes: sequential numbering of each photo; lighting conditions; F-number;[8] and a description of the photograph, including its location and context vis-à-vis the scene (ibid.:308–309). This memo sheet can then be linked to both the actual photographs produced as well as the crime scene report and exhibits entered for submission to any subsequent court case. These procedures are important, as they follow the regulations around continuity of evidence by creating a clear audit trail.

Once these initial steps have been carried out, the CSE is ready to start taking photographs. In doing so, they have to be aware that these photos must be relevant to the visual storytelling aspect, as some of the photographs taken will be shown to a jury. It is important, therefore, that each individual item (evidence) is related to the crime scene (ibid.:313). Robinson (ibid.:19–49) links crime scene photography to the three composition cardinal rules that have been developed in professional photography. The first rule is known as *fill the frame*, which follows the simple yet effective rule: 'if something is important enough to photograph, fill the frame with it' (ibid.:24). This rule has been designed so as to not lose the primary object in a sea of background objects and colour. Rule number two is *maximise the depth of field*. The depth of field is 'the variable range, from foreground to background, of what appears to be in focus' (ibid.:35). When photographing a scene, it is important that the entire scene and evidence within the scene is in focus. Factors such as the F/stop choice, lens choice and the camera-to-subject distance can all affect the depth of field (ibid.:156–166). Finally, the third cardinal rule is *keep the film plane parallel* or, in today's digital camera parlance, *keep the digital sensor parallel* (ibid.:39–46); and this simply means 'keep the back of the camera parallel to the subject; keep the length of the lens perpendicular to the subject; keep the front lens element parallel to the subject' (ibid.:39). These three cardinal rules of photography are also followed by CSEs when they photograph crime scenes.

CSEs create three core types of photos that follow a specific sequence and ordering: *overall, midrange* and *close-up* photographs. The first type is the *overall* photograph (ibid.:313–329; Dutelle, 2011:108), also known as long-range macro photographs. These types of photographs link the individual evidence to the crime scene, and they also provide a link between the crime scene itself and its relationship to its general surroundings (Robinson, 2010:313). In most circumstances, overall photographs will be taken from the standing height of the photographer and will provide a long-range overview of the scene, from multiple angles. Furthermore, if a witness at the scene has provided a statement claiming to have seen something pertinent, the CSE should take a photograph of that object, providing a permanent record of the witness's vantage point (ibid.:314).

When it comes to overall photos, two types are taken: *external* and *internal*. External overall photographs relate directly to outside crime scenes and the immediate surrounding environment, including public areas such as parks, streets, buildings and shopping/leisure areas (ibid.:314–323). For example, if there has been a suspected rape in a park next to some public toilets, then the overall photographs taken would include: the rape site, possible entry and exit points that both offender and victim took (if known), the toilet building, as well as an aerial photograph of the entire park. Internal overall photographs relate to indoor scenes, although it is still necessary to take some external shots of the building, again, in order to place the scene in the context to its local surroundings. For example, if there has been a suspected murder of an individual in their three-bedroom, two-storey house, with the body found in the kitchen, then external shots of the house from as many different angles as possible (usually front and back) including location markers such as street signs would be taken. Internal overall photographs would include the kitchen itself, from different angles (i.e. if there is more than one entry/exit point, pictures would be taken from all of these points). This type of shot would also include a picture of the body *in situ*.

Once the overall photographs have been taken, the next stage is to begin to focus in on the objects of evidence that are relevant to the crime under investigation. The second type of photographs taken are called *mid-range* photographs (ibid.:329–336). When close-up photographs are shot, the frame is filled with just the object, so it is important to be able to identify where that object was located in the scene. Mid-range shots provide this context, linking the item to the crime scene, and they should be taken directly after the overall shots are finished. Of course, overall photographs, where possible, should also include a long-range shot of any items of evidence for which mid-range and close-up shots are taken (ibid.:305–365). In the hypothetical murder example outlined above, the CSE will focus more closely on the body and the immediate surrounding area; for instance, a shot of the floor around the body and perhaps the kitchen cabinets next to where the body is lying, etc. If the suspected murder weapon were found next to the body then the CSE would try to get the body and weapon in the same shot. The general rule for a mid-range shot is that it includes two items: 'a fixed feature of the scene and an item of evidence' (ibid.:330); and, for the most part, the shot must be taken using the 'natural perspective' rule.[9] One further point to make is that it is customary for mid-range shots of evidence to be immediately followed by a close-up photograph of said evidence before moving on to to other mid-range shots; or, as Robinson puts it, 'once an item of evidence has been selected to be documented, its midrange photograph is taken, followed by close-up photographs of the same item of evidence' (ibid.:329).

The third type of photograph, then, is the *close-up*. This type of shot should link directly with the mid-range photographs, they should follow cardinal rule number one (fill the frame), and there are a number of different types of close-up photos taken. Firstly, the 'as found' or 'in situ' type (ibid.:336) denotes a close-up photograph of the evidence as found at the scene and before any alteration of the evidence itself or any movement of anything in the scene has taken place. Once these initial photographs are taken, a second type – the 'fully labelled scale' – is taken, and this is where the object is photographed with a scale alongside. This is done in order to provide some sense of size of the evidence as some items cannot be appreciated without the scale (e.g. shoe mark impressions). The fully labelled scale provides evidence of the chain of continuity, and it also helps if the image has been enlarged for the purposes of analysis (i.e. comparison against a known item of evidence) (ibid.:338). Finally, the 'altered' close-up is taken. Once the evidence has been photographed *in situ* and with a labelled scale, it can be moved and examined in closer detail. This is done as there may be important markings or aspects to the evidence that were on the bottom side and that were hidden from camera view; for example, an object found next to a murder victim may have blood on the underside, inferring that the object was dropped onto the blood after the bloodshed event (ibid.:3401–341). As Robinson (ibid.:340) notes, the altered close-up may be the only opportunity to document important aspects of the evidence before they are destroyed by the removal and packaging procedures undertaken by the CSE.

Overall, crime scene photography plays a crucial role in documenting evidence *in situ* and provides a visual account of the scene, objects and evidence therein. This inscriptive device is then used by a number of individuals as the case moves through the criminal justice process, becoming part of the final narrative of the crime event that is presented in court.

Crime scene report

As well as taking photographs, CSEs produce handwritten crime scene reports that document their examination of the scene, and these notes are usually taken at the same time as the photographs. The taking of effective notes of all actions undertaken and all items found during the crime scene examination is crucial as they effectively create written documentation of the $5 \times WH \times H$ principle[10] (Cook and Tattersall, 2008:118–119). As the time between the original crime scene examination and the trial can be anywhere from weeks to years, crime scene reports also act as an aid mémoire to remind CSEs what they did, what evidence was found, where it was located and how it related to the overall context of the crime. It is because of their aid mémoire function that scene reports must be written contemporaneously, with notes being taken as the actions are done, so as to avoid the problems related to memory loss. Other functions for crime scene reports include: being used as intelligence – for example, identifying general MO patterns for burglaries in specific areas; acting as an evidence submission itself; and, finally, being used for reference when giving evidence in court (Miller, 2009; Dutelle, 2011; Jackson and Jackson, 2011). The contents of the crime scene report and the extent of the notes taken will be determined by a number of factors including: the type of crime and crime scene being examined, the number of scenes involved, the size of the scene, the number of CSEs involved, and the context of individual CSE's responsibilities. Regardless of these factors, there are some identifiable items that are usually included in the scene report (see O'Hara and O'Hara, 2003; Miller, 2009; Dutelle, 2011; Jackson and Jackson, 2011; Becker and Dutelle, 2013):

- *Initial briefing and assessment information* – which includes information on who reported the incident, the time and date reported, location of the scene, the time and date when the scene was attended, any actions undertaken by the FOA and emergency services since attending the scene, details of the likely type and nature of incident, an initial assessment of the likely events that have taken place, the roles and locations of those involved, and details of the initial cordon and its review (including, if any changes have been or need to be made). Details of the risk assessment of the scene should also be noted.
- *Crime scene control* – a record of all identities of individuals entering and leaving the scene must be maintained, which should include the time and date when people enter and leave. A record should also be taken of the roles allocated to each individual on scene.
- *Actions* – detailed descriptions of all actions undertaken at the scene from all personnel involved, which should be in chronological order with all dates and times recorded. All actions include items such as search and recovery strategies, photographs taken and items of evidence identified.
- *Images* – as previously discussed, a log of images taken is created, and these are included and linked to references on the scene report.
- *Sketches* – a hand-drawn detailed sketch of the scene, which should include a basic outline of the structure and layout as well as items of furniture within it. The sketch should also show any important/crucial items of evidence discovered and incorporate units of measurements of the overall structure of the crime scene (e.g. room and window sizes); the size of key objects and items of evidence in relation to two fixed points of reference at the scene, which can be either triangular or rectangular in nature (e.g. a murder weapon with a measurement from fixed points such as the corner of two walls).
- *Evidential items and forensic recovery* – the report should list all items that are identified as evidence, including the location *in situ* at the scene, and detailed notes should be taken of the forensic recovery strategy used for each item. All of this should be in the same chronological order as it occurred on scene. Every item of evidence should also be assigned a separate reference number, and a note of the batch and barcode numbers to the packaging should also be taken (see the discussion on packaging below).
- *Presumptive tests* – CSEs should note whether any presumptive tests have been undertaken, and include details such as the type of test used and on what evidence, as well as the result (e.g. if a suspected blood mark is found, then a test such as Kastle Myer would be undertaken and the result recorded – i.e. pink result equals a positive trace of blood).
- *Environment* – notes should be taken throughout regarding the environmental and weather conditions at the scene, including any changes that take place during the crime scene examination.

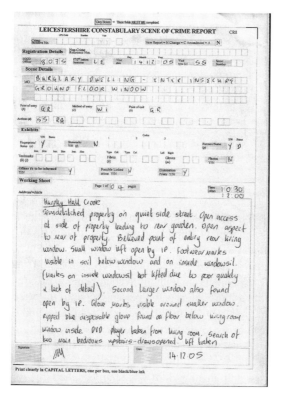

Figure 9.7 The crime scene report

Source: Courtesy of ex-crime scene manager Paul Smith, University of Portsmouth, and Barbara Ann O'Donoghue and Kenneth Andrews of Leicestershire Constabulary Scientific Support department.

To sum up, the crime scene report is a record of all direct actions undertaken during the processing of a crime scene; and, whilst the CSE follows clear guidelines and occupational standards, they are still able to be flexible in their approach to each individual scene. Information work and investigative actions are intrinsically linked when it comes to crime scene examination. Unfortunately, there has been little research into the number and types of actions undertaken during crime scene examinations, so it is difficult to provide a full analysis of this aspect. However, research by Innes (2003:132–143) provides some empirical analysis of the actions undertaken during murder investigations. Using diachronic and synchronic tracking analysis,[11] Innes found that four key types of actions are undertaken during murder investigations which produce the information used by investigators: *suspect-focused, victim-focused, forensic-focused* and *information-focused actions*. He found that during the course of an investigation, the focus 'of attention of the investigation subtly shifts between specific issues' (ibid.:133), with the first four days being the period where the most focused activities of the police and CSEs are carried out. Furthermore, Innes' diachronic analysis demonstrated how the initial investigative actions are targeted towards 'identification information' (ibid.:138), which is certainly a priority for CSE activities; and these activities help alter the content of the information which, in turn, changes the activities as each stage of the investigation progresses. Because of this, the crime scene report is often referred to during the trial for, under section 139 of the Criminal Justice Act 2003 (the use of documents to refresh memory), a person giving oral evidence in criminal proceedings may refresh their memory from any document made at an earlier time.

Forensic recovery

The final part of the crime scene examination process is the forensic recovery of items. This is extremely important and must follow strict procedures that, despite being subject to human error, have been designed for two purposes. The first purpose is to reduce the likelihood of contamination through the cross-transference of foreign material, with the second being to ensure the chain of continuity and integrity of the evidence. It is perhaps obvious that the forensic recovery of items is bound together with the principles of continuity and contamination, as this evidence has to be removed from the scene and fully analysed at another location. This, of course, entails movement of the item, which means other individuals become involved in the 'chain'. It is crucial that a record is kept of all items, who has been in contact with them and for what purpose; and this record is kept from the moment items are identified and recovered from the scene through to their transportation to the relevant laboratory for analysis and to the moment they are submitted as evidence to a court room (O'Hara and O'Hara, 2003; Barnett, 2004; Gallop and Stockdale, 2004; Beaufort-Moore, 2009; Miller, 2009; Trueman, 2009b; Dutelle, 2011; Jackson and Jackson, 2011; Becker and Dutelle, 2013). Fundamentally, the CSE must be able to testify that the 'exhibit offered in evidence is the same object' they 'discovered at the crime scene' (O'Hara and O'Hara, 2003:82). Items may be taken from the scene and individuals at the time of the initial crime scene examination, or they may be collected from individuals and the homes of suspects and victims at a later stage in the investigation (Beaufort-Moore, 2009). When CSEs recover evidence they undertake a systematic procedure that consists of the following steps (O'Hara and O'Hara, 2003:82–103):

1   Protection;
2   Collection and Preservation;
3   Identification; and
4   Storage and Transportation.

The first step is to *protect* the evidence as soon as it is identified. This is important because certain types of evidence are so fragile that any 'slight act of carelessness in handling can destroy their value as clues and remove the possibility of obtaining from them any information which would further the investigation' (ibid.:83). Items such as fingermarks and biological evidence, for example, need immediate protection and preservation to ensure degradation is kept to a minimum. Items of evidence should be protected from damage, which can be caused by negligence, accident or deliberate actions such as intentional damage or theft. These problems can occur at the crime scene, during transportation from scene to the lab, in the lab itself and, finally, when the exhibit is transported from the scene to the courtroom. The second stage is *collection* and *preservation*. Many errors that lead to the contamination of evidence occur at the point of collection; for example, errors relating to ensuring that the right packaging is used and that this packaging is sealed correctly. The general rule of packaging is that material must be 'preserved in a manner that will maximize the potential for evidence recovery' and 'ensure that the item cannot suffer any damage, alteration, loss or destruction' (Beaufort-Moore, 2009:51). The item that is being collected determines the type of packaging used, and broadly speaking there are three main types: (i) paper bags and cardboard boxes; (ii) polythene bags and rigid polythene containers; and (iii) nylon bags (Trueman, 2009b:60–65; Beaufort-Moore, 2009:51–56). For example, it would not be appropriate to package a knife in a brown paper evidence bag; instead polythene knife tubes should be used (Beaufort-Moore, 2009:51–57; Trueman, 2009b:60–67). Clothing, on the other hand, is usually packaged in brown paper bags. Once the item has been packaged, it must be properly sealed, which again depends on the type of evidence and packaging used. For instance, if a presumptive test on a suspected blood mark proves to be positive, then four swabs are usually collected (wet, dry, background and control samples) from the same swab batch (with sequential bar codes/batch numbers), and placed in tamper-evident bags that have an adhesive strip and are marked with hazardous material tape. Brown paper bags are used if the evidence is clothing or footwear, and these are sealed by folding over the top corners and edge. The top edge is then folded again and secured using tape. The stitched bottom and sides are also taped to ensure that microscopic particles are not lost, which increases the integrity of the evidence, and each taped area should be initialed by the CSE who has packaged the item (Beaufort-Moore, 2009:52). Case study 9.2 provides an excellent example of the problems associated with packaging that has been incorrectly sealed.

Once the item has been correctly packaged, the CSE should ensure that it is labelled; and this relates to the third process, *identification*. Evidence should be properly marked for identification as this aspect begins the chain of continuity. The first stage is to assign a number to each item collected (usually in a logical and sequential order), which is logged on the scene report and becomes the reference for tracing the continuity of the item and also linking any personnel who have had contact with it. This number is part of a broader range of information that is written on the outside of the packaged item. Each type of packaging contains a label, which includes information such as: name and signature (of the

CSE who collected and packaged the item); officer badge number; date and time (of when the evidence was collected); location details (i.e. where the item was seized); case reference number; item reference number (which should be the same number as on the crime scene report); description of the item; exhibit reference number; and spaces for all persons who come into possession of an item of evidence (name, position, date, time and signature). The label details, which are constantly referred to as the evidence progresses from crime scene to courtroom, forms the basis of the chain of continuity and provides the necessary audit trail regarding every individual who has collected, handled and analysed the item of evidence (O'Hara and O'Hara, 2003; Barnett, 2004; Gallop and Stockdale, 2004; Beaufort-Moore, 2009; Miller, 2009; Trueman, 2009b; Dutelle, 2011; Jackson and Jackson, 2011; Becker and Dutelle, 2013). In the case of tamper-evident bags and swabs, these tend to come in batches with specific batch numbers and/or barcode numbers. If used, these numbers should be recorded on the scene report as well. Finally, all items collected and packaged at the scene must be adequately *stored* and *transferred* to the appropriate holding and/or lab facility which, of course, depends on the forensic strategy developed by the CSE and, where relevant, crime scene manager. Not all items collected from the scene are submitted for analysis, so a forensic submission strategy is developed that should aim to maximise the probative yield of forensic evidence. This topic is dealt with in the following chapter.

Summary

The examination of the crime scene is *the* major component to many criminal investigations and the information work that is undertaken. The majority of evidence that is submitted for forensic analysis comes from the initial crime scene examination, which is only available at one moment in time, so it is crucial that CSEs follow the correct standard operating procedures and regulations. These procedures have been developed primarily for the maintenance of the continuity and integrity of physical evidence in order to avoid contamination through the problems of cross transference discussed in Chapter 7. These processes are also framed within the wider scientific method, which calls for a systematic and logical process involving critical thinking and the testing of hypotheses through the verification and falsification of data. The CSEs, in conjunction with police, use items found at the crime scene to both reconstruct the events under investigation and create hypotheses to answer the important $5 \times WH \times H$ method of problem solving (see Cook and Tattersall, 2008). However, it is with the analysis of forensic evidence that the falsification or verification of investigative hypotheses occurs, and this enables investigators to provide a more accurate reconstruction of the crime event under investigation.

Part 3

Failsafe forensics

Failsafe forensics

Chapter 10

Forensic science and detection methods

Introduction

The organisational and operational *free-for-all* that currently exists when it comes to the provision of forensic science in the UK deserves an entire chapter of its own. However, this is not the aim of this chapter. Whilst there is some minor *scene setting* that examines the history and current structure and organisation of forensic science provision in the UK, the majority of this chapter is devoted to the key ideas, concepts and theories relevant to understanding the application of forensic science in criminal investigations. As previously defined, forensic science is any science that is used in the service of criminal justice (Jackson and Jackson, 2008:1); or, alternatively, it is the study and practice of the application of science to the purposes of law (Nickell and Fischer, 1999:1). This chapter examines these methods and practices. It begins with a discussion of the difference between the roles of the forensic scientist and police technician, introduces the case assessment model and explores the structures of analysis, which include the scientific method and a forensic science developmental framework. A brief review of the core ideas behind scientific analysis and detection methods precedes a more in-depth look at the techniques of visual examination (what is called pattern matching), absorption and emission rates and chemical reactions. Finally, a discussion of the core concepts of identification and individualisation as well as a much-needed critical review of the epistemological basis and problems with these concepts rounds off the chapter.

Forensic science in the UK

The primary consumer of forensic science in the UK is the police force; however, wealthy defendants may often instruct independent forensic consultants to work on their behalf, as in the US case of O. J. Simpson and the UK case of Sion Jenkins, a famous miscarriage of justice (Jenkins and Woffinden, 2008). In recent years, the use of forensics has expanded its parameters into civil cases, especially in the area of tort litigation (see Kennedy, 2013). Whilst recognising the importance of these developments for the forensic criminologist, this section concentrates its discussion on traditional criminal cases led by the police.

Historically, it has been impossible to compile an accurate understanding of the exact amount of forensic science provision in the UK. In the 1980s and 1990s, forensic science was largely provided by the following agencies/ departments (House of Lords Select Committee on Science and Technology, 1993): Forensic Science Service, which included its Central Research and Support Establishment at Aldermaston (FSS); Metropolitan Police Forensic Science Laboratory (MPFSL); Metropolitan Police Forensic Science Laboratory (MPFSL); Strathclyde Police Forensic Science Laboratory (Glasgow) (SPFSL); Lothian and Borders Police Forensic Science Laboratory (Edinburgh) (LBPFSL); Grampian Police Forensic Science Laboratory (Aberdeen) (GPFSL); the Northern Ireland Forensic Science Laboratory (NIFSL); DRAFED – Defence Research Agency, Forensic Explosives Department; and TPSFL – Tayside Police Forensic Science Laboratory (Dundee). The House of Lords Select Committee on Science and Technology undertook a review of the provision of forensic science in the UK in its 1992–93 session and found that it was impossible to compile a complete set for 1980 and 1985; some laboratories were unable to provide financial information; others were unable to provide a breakdown of their expenditure, staffing or workload into the categories requested (ibid.:56). However, the committee was able to provide some information on the number and types of cases, as well as the number of exhibits these cases produced (Tables 10.1 and 10.2).

What is also interesting is the ratio of exhibits to cases. Many criminal cases produce more then one exhibit and exhibits are often *products* created by the forensic scientist (see Cook *et al.*, 1998a, 1998b). It is important therefore to have an understanding of both caseloads and the number of exhibits they create. These are outlined in Table 10.3 and have been sorted in order of highest to lowest ratio values.

As Table 10.3 demonstrates, the number of exhibits created by case type is highest for serious crimes such as murder (an average of 28.81 exhibits per case) and sexual offences (13.87). Interestingly, cases that involve *documents* rank second at 15.96. The types of forensic products produced here could range from fingermarks on documents to handwriting forgeries for fraud cases. Whilst these figures are quite old, and they are complicated by the fact that police in-house services are usually not included, they provide some historical context to the caseloads of those involved in forensic science provision in the UK. Furthermore, if we take a look at overall expenditure figures we can gain some picture of how the cost has changed dramatically over time. For instance, total expenditure costs of forensic science in the UK, including Scotland and Northern Ireland, in 1985 and 1991 was £20,772,518 and £42,346,900 respectively; an increase in 6 years of 48.48 per cent (adjusted for 1991 prices) (House of Lords Select Committee on Science and Technology, 1993:48). The figure for total expenditure in 2005 was £400,000,000. Adjusting for inflation between 1991 and 2005, there has been an increase in expenditure of 313.16 per cent, with the overall cost increasing from £42,346,900 to £400,000,000 (or 844.58 per cent)!

Table 10.1 Number of forensic science cases, 1991

Laboratory	FSS	MPSFL	LGC	DRAFED	SPFSL	LBPFSL	GPFSL	TPFSL	NIFSL	Total
Explosives	110	42	0	111	~	8	0	~	480	751
Arson/Fire	959	291	0	0	194	54	55	~	632	2,185
Burglary	4,101	599	0	0	~	66	236	~	172	5,174
Alcohol Technical Defence	1,398	~	0	0	~	7	17	~	~	1,422
Theft	1,040	312	0	0	~	26	58	~	171	1,607
Criminal Damage	467	39	0	0	~	10	36	~	49	601
Traffic	453	312	0	0	~	16	72	~	261	1,114
Tachograph	236	~	0	0	26	0	0	~	~	262
Grievous Bodily Harm	1,029	451	0	0	~	83	34	~	191	1,788
Murder	682	330	0	0	55	13	0	~	266	1,346
Robbery	547	594	0	0	~	29	128	~	92	1,390
Sexual	1,669	844	0	0	~	83	97	~	166	2,859
Drugs	12,839	7,573	1,621	0	5,376	1,178	1,133	~	475	30,195
DUI Drugs	694	~	0	0	~	~	0	~	31	725
Sudden Death	1,642	61	0	0	~	369	0	~	654	2,726
Unclassified/Other	720	156	90	0	2,609	58	64	619	606	4,922
DUI Alcohol	16,336	4,484	0	0	676	205	1,039	~	1,817	24,557
Documents	1,939	408	518	0	~	0	289	~	154	3,308
Firearms	1,302	1,119	0	0	~	4	19	~	671	3,115
Total	48,163	17,615	2,229	111	8,936	2,209	3,277	619	6,888	90,047

Source: data from House of Lords Select Committee on Science and Technology (1993).

Table 10.2 Number of forensic science exhibits, 1991

Laboratory	FSS	MPSFL	LGC	DRAFED	SPFSL	LBPFSL	GPFSL	TPFSL	NIFSL	Total
Explosives	660	390	0	1,102	~	~	~	~	4,765	6,917
Arson/Fire	5,603	867	0	0	569	~	~	~	2,570	9,609
Burglary	36,114	3,228	0	0	0	~	~	~	1,127	40,469
Alcohol Technical Defence	1,769	~	0	0	~	~	17	~	~	1,786
Theft	5,225	903	0	0	~	~	~	~	523	6,651
Criminal Damage	3,306	170	0	0	~	~	~	~	345	3,821
Traffic	2,064	601	0	0	~	~	~	~	931	3,596
Tachograph	664	~	0	0	163	~	~	~	~	827
Grievous Bodily Harm	11,023	2,817	0	0	~	~	~	~	1,319	15,159
Murder	24,164	8,092	0	0	~	~	~	~	6,524	38,780
Robbery	6,841	2,562	0	0	~	~	~	~	1,043	10,446
Sexual	26,842	10,015	0	0	~	~	~	~	2,804	39,661
Drugs	36,459	17,318	7,146	0	8,607	2,915	~	~	1,053	73,498
DUI Drugs	810	~	0	0	~	~	~	~	31	841
Sudden Death	5,716	483	0	0	~	1,590	~	~	1,518	9,307
Unclassified/Other	2,762	415	944	0	30,688	5,052	7,347	3,816	1,176	52,200
DUI Alcohol	16,336	4,523	0	0	706	~	1,039	~	1,818	24,422
Documents	36,975	4,443	9,878	0	~	~	~	1,071	415	52,782
Firearms	4,339	1,446	0	0	~	~	~	91	3,955	9,831
Total	227,672	58,273	17,968	1,102	40,733	9,557	8,403	4,978	31,917	400,603

Source: data from House of Lords Select Committee on Science and Technology (1993).

Table 10.3 Ratio of number of exhibits to number of cases, 1991

Type	Total Exhibits	Total Cases	Ratio
Murder	38,780	1,346	28.81
Documents	52,782	3,308	15.96
Sexual	39,661	2,859	13.87
Unclassified/Other	52,200	4,922	10.61
Explosives	6,917	751	9.21
Grievous Bodily Harm	15,159	1,788	8.48
Burglary	40,469	5,174	7.82
Robbery	10,446	1,390	7.52
Criminal Damage	3,821	601	6.36
Arson/Fire	9,609	2,185	4.40
Theft	6,651	1,607	4.14
Sudden Death	9,307	2,726	3.41
Traffic	3,596	1,114	3.23
Tachograph	827	262	3.16
Firearms	9,831	3,115	3.16
Drugs	73,498	30,195	2.43
Alcohol Technical Defence	1,786	1,422	1.26
DUI Drugs	841	725	1.16
DUI Alcohol	24,422	24,557	0.99
Total	**400,603**	**90,047**	**4.45**

Source: data from House of Lords Select Committee on Science and Technology (1993).

In 2012 the FSS closed, bringing to an end an embarrassing episode of political and civil service mismanagement. It was reported that the reason behind the closure was the FSS's operating losses, estimated to be around £2 million per month,[1] and the projected shrinking of the forensics market (House of Commons Science and Technology Committee, 2011a:3, 2013a:8). Despite many experts and practitioners strongly protesting against the closure of the service (see House of Commons Science and Technology Committee, 2011a, 2011b, 2011c, 2011d, 2013a, 2013b; Silverman, 2011a, 2011b, 2011c), their rational arguments and evidence bounced off the coalition Government's impenetrable privatisation agenda as if there were some form of invisible deflector shield protecting Whitehall's free-market zone of arrogance. With its closure, forensic science in the UK has become a haphazard, *ad hoc* system that currently has no organisation or direction. In previous chapters, I have devoted a great deal of time to both the structure and regulations of criminal investigations and crime scene management, and how these are tied to overriding operational *strategies* identified by the relevant criminal justice agency. Unfortunately, at the time of writing, the UK government *has no long-term strategy for forensic science provision*. This is both bemusing and concerning. When asked by the House of Commons Science and Technology Committee (see 13th March 2013) to explain the government's forensic strategy, Jeremy Browne, the Minister of State for Crime Prevention, responded that there was no need for one, as the *free market* would dictate forensic provision without the need for such a strategy! It seems wildly contradictory that a government, who believes in the free-market, doesn't think business strategies are important. The current state of forensic science provision in the UK is just as concerning.

More recently, and up until 2012, police laboratories, the FSS and a small number of private firms (which are known as forensic service providers, or FSPs) undertook the provision of forensic science in the UK. The majority of what could be called forensic science analysis was conducted at one of the five main FSS laboratories in Solihull, Huntingdon, Lambeth, Wetherby and Chepstow, and in privately run labs such as LGC[2] and Cellmark. The FSS was a 100 per cent government-owned, contract-operated organisation, and it worked on over 120,000 cases per year, employing around 1,300 scientists (House of Commons Science and Technology Committee, 2011a:9). It provided services across England and Wales to all police forces; the Crown Prosecution Service; the Serious Organised Crime Agency; the Ministry of Defence Police and Guarding Agency, British Transport Police, and HM Revenue and Customs. The FSS also assisted 'more than 60 countries worldwide with services including consultancy, training services, systems and databasing technology and casework' (ibid.:9). In addition to the laboratory work of the FSS and private firms, police forces across the UK have their own scientific support departments as described in Chapter 9. These departments do not engage in scientific analysis per se, although chemical treatment and fingerprint departments could lay some claim to scientific status. A review of the forensic services market in 2005 estimated that police in-house services accounted for 52 per cent of the market; 45 per cent were undertaken by external providers (which included the FSS); and 3 per cent were individual forensic practitioners (House of Commons Science and Technology Committee, 2005a:12). The cost of this provision to the police was around £400 million, or 0.04 per cent of total police expenditure. In real terms, in 2004–05, police in-house forensic services cost £208 million; £180 million went to external providers; and £12 million to individual providers. The market share for the FSS in 2005 was around 85 per cent, or £153 million, but by 2010 their market share had declined to 60 per cent (House of Commons Science and Technology Committee, 2011a:5), largely because of an increase in *outsourcing* of forensic products to the likes of FSPs such as LGC and Cellmark; however, this increase was also due to internal forensic spending which rose to 56.4 per cent (House of Commons Science and Technology Committee, 2013a:10). The trend towards a decreasing market share for the FSS and an increasing one for both internal and external forensic service providers gave support to the decision to get rid of an organisation that was once a world leader in forensic science.

Since the closure of the FSS in 2012, the landscape of forensic provision in the UK has changed dramatically. With private firms taking on more forensic science contracts, this closure, as well as the changes to the police's in-house scientific support departments, means that gauging the extent and nature of forensic science practice and provision within the UK is difficult. A *small remnant* of the FSS does remain in the guise of Forensic Archive Ltd, which looks after the archives of the FSS (ibid.:3); however, it is envisaged that this will become redundant in time. When the decision was made to close the FSS, the government expected that FSPs would pick up the 'FSS's 60% share of the external forensics market' (House of Commons Science and Technology Committee, 2011a:17), although this logic has since been heavily criticised by the *House of Commons Science and Technology Committee* (see 2011a; 2013a; 2013b; and 2013c). Unfortunately, the closure of the FSS, and the move towards the *free-marketisation* of forensic sciences (see Roberts, 1996; Lawless, 2011) has not dissipated the decade-long 'constant flux' in forensic science provision in the UK (House of Commons Science and Technology Committee, 2013a:3). Indeed, much of the evidence provided by forensic science experts and practitioners at the various House of Commons Science and Technology Committee (2011a; 2011b; 2013a; 2013b) and Silverman (2013a; 2013b; 2013c) inquiries support Lawless' thesis that neo-liberal free-market initiatives have actually exposed forensic science *actors* to new risks; for example the closure of the FSS. Perhaps the most unfavourable evidence against the government, however, is their lack of forensic strategy and the fact that they are unable to collate even the most basic of figures regarding the current cost of forensic science to the public purse (House of Commons Science and Technology Committee, 13th March 2013[3]; also see House of Commons Science and Technology Committee, 2013a:8–10). The committee were extremely damning of the Minster in this regard:

> The Minister's response to the question of value for money reflected that he had not prepared for the evidence session, and in particular had not read our previous report nor the evidence we had received for this inquiry. Throughout the evidence session with the Minister we were disappointed at his disregard of his responsibility towards a parliamentary select committee.
>
> (ibid.:8)

It appears that the problems with obtaining accurate and reliable figures on forensic science provision in the UK, as described by the 1993 committee, are still prevalent 20 years on (ibid.:8). One particular area that skews any attempt at producing accurate costs is police in-house forensic services. Between 2005–06 and 2010–11, internal forensic spending 'rose from 46.5 per cent to 56.4 percent of total police forensic expenditure' (ibid.:10), leading to accusations that with the forced *20 per cent* budgetary cuts and closure of the FSS, the police have increased their in-sourcing of forensic services, thereby creating a decline in the external forensic market. However, the government and ACPO have consistently denied these allegations, and all attempts by the House of Commons Science and Technology Committee to try to explore this issue have been met with the usual resistance with the government stating that it did not 'compile details of police

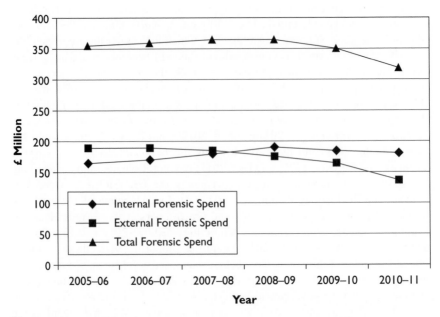

Figure 10.1 Police forensic spend in England and Wales, 2005–2011

Source: data from House of Commons Science and Technology Committee, 2011.

expenditure as it is up to individual Police Authorities and Chief Constables to decide how best to spend their money' (ibid.:10). Even a Freedom of Information (FoI) request made by Diana Johnson MP failed to provide 'insight into forensic expenditure of police forces, revealing inconsistent accounting practices between forces that made reliable comparisons and aggregation impossible' (ibid.:10). Despite these problems, some extrapolations can be made; for instance, Figure 10.1 provides a comparative look at internal, external and total police forensic spending from 2005 to 2011 (ibid.:15).

Whilst such figures provide some support to the idea that there is a dwindling forensic market, it is extremely difficult to accurately assess the impact of the recent changes to the structure of forensic provision in the UK. What is certain is that, at the time of writing, the UK has no central forensic strategy; and, whilst the forensic regulator Andrew Rennison and his team do their utmost to try to keep in place a professional forensic science system, it is worrying that the government's current reliance on the belief in free-marketisation and its inability to consider evidence, or even the need for a forensic strategy, will seriously undermine the future of forensic science in the UK.

The scientist v. the police technician

As Chapter 4 highlights, with the creation of techniques of identification such as fingerprinting, and its wholesale use in police investigations at the turn of the twentieth century, the police began to rely more and more on forensic evidence. One by-product of this was the development of what some have called *police science*; and, historically, crime scene investigators and *in-house* police analysts engaged in this whenever they visualised and developed a crime scene fingermark and then compared that to a known fingerprint; or when a crime scene footwear or tool-mark impression was *matched* to the items connected to a suspect. Police science techniques and roles can be contrasted with those of the external scientist who is usually asked to contribute their scientific expertise to a criminal case. It has also been suggested previously that there is a clear split between the roles and techniques of *forensic science* and *police science* (Ambage, 1987). Ambage's historical work indicates that these two organisational cultures often clashed over jurisdictional boundaries, with forensic scientists undertaking work for the police in a sometimes hostile, competitive and non-collegiate environment. As others have demonstrated (Reiner, 2010), the police are a powerful and influential organisation, whose culture, power base and policy reach far exceed that of any other criminal justice organisation in the UK. Historically, then, forensic scientists have often played second fiddle to the police, and these roles have become further complicated over the last 40 years with the creation of the police's own laboratories and the creation of the crime scene investigator role.

It is important to note the differences between *police science* and the *forensic scientist*, which is still a useful demarcation to make. As discussed later on in this current chapter, and which also links with the work discussed in Chapters 8 and 10, a great deal of forensic work is conducted by police or civilian officers engaging in police science. In recent years, the issue of the link between police science and forensic science has been raised (Millen, 2000).

A case assessment model

Before examining some of the key ideas and concepts used by scientists in the analysis of evidence found in the course of a criminal investigation, it might be useful to introduce an operational forensic science decision-making process that embodies the principles of Bayesian inference (Cook *et al.*, 1998a, 1998b). The fundamental essence of forensic science is the 'drawing of rational and balanced inferences from observations, test results and measurements' (Cook *et al.*, 1998a:152), and this process involves *interpretation*. How we interpret results has constantly evolved over time and, in recent years, the Bayesian paradigm has come to the forefront in forensic science (Robertson and Vignaux, 1995; Aitken and Taroni, 2004). Thomas Bayes (1702–1761) was a Presbyterian minister in Tunbridge Wells from 1731. He was also an excellent mathematician who established a mathematical basis for inductive probability inference (Adam, 2010).

His rule, known as Bayes' Theorem, Bayes' Law or Bayes' Rule, is a means of calculating, from the number of times an event has not occurred, the probability that it will occur in the future; and this was set out in an *Essay Towards Solving A Problem in the Doctrine of Chances* (1763) which was published posthumously in the *Transactions of the Royal Society of London*. To put it another way, Bayes' Theorem is a mathematical formula used for calculating conditional probabilities; and the interpretation of forensic science evidence leans heavily towards the realms of conditional probabilities. This is explained in greater detail in Chapter 11: for now, it is enough to mention that the 'essential feature of Bayesian inference is that it permits the move from prior (initial or pre-test) to posterior (final or post-test) probabilities on the basis of data' (Aitken and Taroni, 2004:72).

Before its closure in 2012, the FSS, working with scientists and academics from numerous disciplines, established a model for forensic casework. The aim was to enhance 'cost-effectiveness of its casework activities' and this fitted with the FSS's introduction of *products*, which are defined as 'an activity; the time taken for it; the cost; the standards to which the activity adheres; the expected outcome; and the chargeable unit' (Cook *et al.*, 1998a:152). As a result of this work a Case Assessment and Interpretation Model (CAIM) was developed. Cook *et al.* (ibid.:152) outline its main objective, which was 'to enable decisions to be made which will deliver a value for money service meeting the needs of our direct customers and the criminal justice system' (see Figure 10.2).

The first phase – *customer requirement* – involves determining what the customer *needs*, and this means having access to case information (ibid.:153). Good communication between the customer (e.g. the police) and the scientist is essential, as a good understanding of the case circumstances is required so that the scientist can develop a framework for the kinds 'of examinations [that] may be carried out and what may be expected from them' (Cook *et al.*, 1998a:153). This presents a rather awkward problem for those wishing to undertake any scientific analysis, as the scientific method (which is discussed below) should include error and bias rates. One of the main ways scientists assess for error and

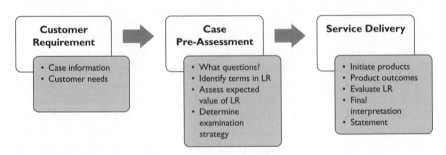

Figure 10.2 The case assessment and interpretation model

Note: LR is likelihood ratio

bias is through blind testing; unfortunately, this would involve having no knowledge of the case. One of the ways around this is to make greater use of experimental studies, which include error rates, as well as using control samples alongside questioned (crime scene) and known (suspect/victim) samples of evidence. What is certain, in this first stage, is that the scientists should take a balanced view of the case and ensure that they not only evaluate the police's version but also concentrate on alternative hypotheses. In terms of a criminal trial, this boils down to the *prosecution proposition* versus the *defence proposition*, although these are not easy to develop or prove. In another paper, Cook *et al.* (1998b) outline the three broad levels of propositions that can be identified within forensic casework, and these will be discussed in greater detail below.

The second stage in CAIM is *case pre-assessment*, and this involves the sharpening up of the formulation of the propositions to be tested and identifying key questions and determining the examination strategy. This is also where the scientist begins to think in terms of quantifiable *likelihood ratios* (the LR in Figure 10.2). For example, if the proposition that an individual burgled a house and gained entry by smashing the window is true, the scientist should think in terms of: 'I would expect to find "X" amount of glass shards on the offenders clothing' if the suspect is indeed the offender. Later on, this proposition will be turned into a likelihood ratio, 'which is central to the Bayesian formulation of interpretation' (Cook *et al.*, 1998a:153), and takes the form:

Probability of the evidence if defence proposition is true

This enables the scientist to approach the case in a balanced non-directional way and allows for the expectations to 'be turned into a probability distribution for the expected weight of evidence' (ibid.:153).

The final phase is *service delivery*, and this relates to the main part of the examination and the creation of the forensic *product*. Service delivery includes initiating the products (undertaking the analysis) and identifying their outcomes (analysis results), which are then assigned the relevant likelihood ratios. These ratios provide an indication as to the direction and strength of the product results in relation to either prosecution or defence propositions. Likelihood ratios are calculated using the following probability equation (Adam, 2010):

$Pr(Q|C)$

Where:
Q = quantity
C = prosecution proposition to be evaluated
C = defence proposition to be evaluated

When conducting this calculation, the scientist must take into account a number of factors, including: the transference and persistence qualities of the object under examination (i.e. the amount of material transferred and whether it lasts); background information regarding the suspect or victim (i.e. do their routine activities relate to the types of material that could have been transferred); specific scientific research and surveys that have tested the transference and persistence levels of the material as well as reporting probability and error rates (Robertson and Vignaux, 1995; Cook *et al.*, 1998a, 1998b; Aitken and Taroni, 2004; Lucy, 2005; Jackson and Jackson, 2011). I expand upon these issues in a later section and include an example of its application. For now, CAIM offers a structured framework for analysis that is fluid and dynamic enough to cope with the vagaries of criminal investigations. It also provides a counterargument against 'accusations of post hoc rationalisation of findings' (Cook *et al.*, 1998a:154), for the scientists have formulated expectations before any examinations and analyses have taken place. However, it should be noted that, when reporting the findings, it is 'not usual practice for scientists to report numerical LRs' (ibid.:155). Instead, a verbal scale is invoked which provides a 'notion of support qualified by terms which are loosely equivalent to a numerical LR scale' (ibid.:155). Terms such as *weak, moderate* and *strong* are attached to the term *support* for prosecution and defence propositions. The only exception is the reporting of DNA profiles.

Whilst the case assessment and interpretation model is not fully accepted or operationalised in all forensic laboratories (both police and private), it sets out a process that, if adhered to, offers a 'framework for sound decision making in terms of impartiality, scientific rigour and the need to be cost-effective' (ibid.:156). The overriding structure, though, is always the application of the scientific method.

Structures for analysis

Each of the scientific disciplines that make up the forensic sciences has its own methods and practices, as well as its strengths and weaknesses. Furthermore, the level of scientific development varies from discipline to discipline and in the degree to which they follow 'the principles of scientific investigation' (National Research Council of the National Academies, 2009:111). Observance of scientific principles lies at the cornerstone of scientific knowledge and is what makes this type of evidence far stronger than evidence that does not rely on such principles. Specifically, when the court admits and relies on forensic evidence in criminal trials, it does so because of the extent to which the forensic science discipline is founded upon a robust scientific methodology, accurate analysis of evidence and a standardised system of reporting its findings (ibid.; author unknown, *Science and Justice*, 2009; Wilson-Wilde *et al.*, 2011). However, it is not simply a matter of following a rigorous methodology; analysts must also be aware of the cognitive biases that affect interpretation and 'adopt procedures and performance standards that guard against bias and error' (National Research Council of the National Academies, 2009:111). Science has built its reputation on its use of empirical evidence that is tested and examined using the scientific method. Whilst there has been some philosophical debate around the epistemological basis of science, primarily from religious zealots and fanatics (Hitchens, 2007) and those who *believe* in mysticism and magic (Pavord, 2009), what marks science out is the belief in applying rigorous logic and critical thinking to the analysis of tangible evidence using a standardised method.

The scientific method

Isaac Newton famously defined the scientific method as 'the body of techniques for investigating phenomena, acquiring new knowledge, or correcting and integrating previous knowledge. It is based on gathering observable, empirical and measurable evidence subject to specific principles of reasoning' (Newton, [1687]1729). The presumption is that physical matter will behave in consistent patterns, given the same external forces exerting pressure on them, and this enables scientists to understand patterns and behaviour through 'careful comparison and systematic study' (National Research Council of the National Academies, 2009:112). Scientific knowledge is incrementally produced through a logical *series of steps*, which includes:

- the *observation and recording* of data through specific collection methods that are themselves tested for accuracy;
- the *development of hypotheses* which test and measure the strengths and weaknesses of the data using analysis methods that help to falsify or verify the hypotheses;
- the drawing of *inferences* about the causal relationships generated from the data analysis; and
- identification of *limits of the knowledge* (e.g. the precision of the observations, collection and analysis methods, bias and error rates).

It is important to acknowledge that these steps are not simply undertaken once: for scientists must ensure that they 'continually observe, test and modify the body of knowledge' (ibid.:112). To this end, science does not claim to know absolute truth. Instead, it produces truth incrementally through discoveries or by testing theories repeatedly, and most discoveries and tests take place in natural settings or under laboratory conditions. In the lab, scientists are able to control the conditions of the tests, and this enables them to 'isolate exclusive effects and thus better understand the factors that influence certain outcomes' (ibid.:112). The important *buzzwords* for science then, are *standardisation* and *reproducibility*. The collection, analysis, interpretation and reporting methods should be standardised so they can be compared and reproduced in order for others to test theories and create robust knowledge.

When it comes to the day-to-day practical work of forensic science, analysts follow these simple principles and methods; but there are some minor differences: first, whilst they do observe and record data, this data has usually been collected by someone else; second, instead of formulating and testing hypotheses, they carefully prepare and analyse samples and interpret the results in a straightforward manner. Despite these minor differences, forensic analysts still follow the basic guiding principles of science outlined above.

Forensic science standards

In addition to the application of a rigorous scientific methodology, those practicing forensic science should operate within a structured framework of common standards. As discussed in Chapter 9, IOS standard 17025 was established which set out the 'general requirements for the competence of testing and calibration laboratories' (ibid.:114). Unfortunately, this standard was not specifically designed for forensic applications (Wilson-Wilde *et al.*, 2010:e333). To address this problem, in 2010, the Australia New Zealand Policing Advisory Agency National Institute of Forensic Science (NIFS) established a project 'to set up a sustainable mechanism for the development and maintenance of standards' (Wilson-Wilde *et al.*, 2010:e333). The resultant standards cover the four core areas of forensic science and are outlined in Figure 10.3.

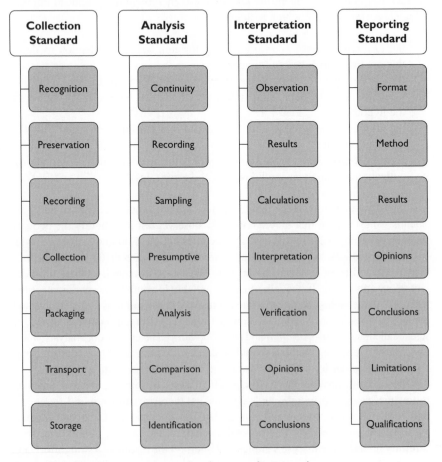

Figure 10.3 The forensic science development framework

Source: adapted from Wilson-Wilde *et al.*, 2010:e333–e334

In the UK, with the exception of forensic pathologists, most forensic scientists are not usually involved in the collection standard (this was discussed in the previous chapter), although an individual investigation may specifically require a specialist to attend the crime scene and collect evidence. For most cases, material is sent to the laboratory for analysis, so the scientist is primarily involved in the analysis, interpretation and reporting standards outlined above. For example, to maintain continuity, once the *evidence* has been received into the laboratory, the technician or scientist will sign the packaging as well as keep his or her own record. Depending on what type of analysis is being conducted, they will then take necessary samples from the material received and undertake the relevant presumptive and analytical tests (see below). Once the initial analysis has been completed on the *questioned sample*, the analyst will undertake a comparison with a *known sample*; for instance, in a drug investigation, a known sample of heroin would be kept in the laboratory and its component parts (class and individual characteristics) compared to those of the questioned sample to see if there is a *match*; or a questioned sample of blood found at crime scene will be compared to an arrested suspect's known DNA profile (Jackson and Jackson, 2011). Once a comparison has been achieved, *identification* of the material may be possible. See below for an expansion on this process.

Once the material has been identified, the information contained within must be interpreted; and this involves a number of steps. The first two stages comprise *observation* of the class and individual characteristics and the *results* of these observations. When it comes to interpreting evidence, the majority of forensic analysis involves *calculating* a score that should give an indication as to the strength, or *probative weight*, of the evidence. Probative weight, or probative force, refers to an item or body of evidence that 'answers the question: "How strong is this evidence in favoring or disfavoring some penultimate probandum[4] in the case at hand?"' (Anderson *et al.*, 2005:71). Different material will have different levels of weight, and this strength is determined by a number of factors that are examined throughout the remainder of this chapter. For the time being, once the observations, results and calculations have been made, there should follow some form of *interpretation* (Wilson-Wilde *et al.*, 2010:e333–e334). The data may show *X* result with a probative weight of *Y*, but what does that mean in respect to the broader investigation? How do the findings support or disfavour a particular investigative hypothesis or line of enquiry? Interpretation should provide meaning to the observable facts, even if that meaning is positive or negative. Once the analyst has provided an interpretation of the results, this should move to the process of *verification*, which could involve the retesting of the material or asking another analyst to double-check the results. The final two stages involve *opinions* being formed and final *conclusions* being reached (Wilson-Wilde *et al.*, 2010:e333–e334).

The final standard relates to how the results of the analysis are *reported*. For many years now, forensic science reporting standards have been mixed, with some scientists being more methodical and comprehensive than others (Faigman *et al.*,

2010; Wilson-Wilde *et al.*, 2010). One of the reasons the scientific method has been so successful in pushing the boundaries of our knowledge is because of the standardisation of the way it reports its findings. The importance of having a structured reporting standard is so others can follow the analysis and results; so they can replicate the studies to test the theories; and so they can compare other individuals' findings against their own. The reporting standard suggested by NIFS consists of outlining a clear *format* for discussing the *method*, *results*, and *opinions* reached, as well as the *conclusions* adopted. The report should also include a section on the *limitations* of the methods, results, and conclusions and a review of the *qualifications* of the analyst so external parties can confirm that they have the relevant knowledge for conducting the tests and interpreting the results. Wilson-Wilde *et al.* (2010:e334) note that, whilst there are no set international standards in forensic science, the ones developed for NIFS in Australia 'have the potential for international adoption or may form the basis for the development of international standards'. Furthermore, the standards outlined above should only be considered as an *ideal type* (Weber, 1978), and it should be acknowledged that standards of practice will vary from organisation to organisation and from country to country. Unfortunately, it is not clear where CAIM sits with the standards set out in Figure 10.3. Regardless of which process is used, the criminal investigators' main concern is to establish the personal identity of the offender. Oftentimes, this means using indirect methods such as the identification of physical objects associated with the individual to be identified (Kirk, 1974:9). The majority of forensic science deals with this type of analysis, which is referred to as the *forensic identification sciences* (FIS) (Saks and Faigman, 2008), and includes key physical evidence such as *DNA*, *fingermarks/prints*, *handwriting*, *bite marks*, *voiceprints*, *tool marks*, *firearms*, *tyre prints* and *footwear marks*. FIS is defined as those subfields that involve pattern matching in an effort to associate a crime scene mark or object with its source (ibid.:150). In order to achieve this aim, a number of scientific analysis and detection methods can be utilised.

Analysis and detection methods

The scientific analysis of substances can be broken down to either *microscopic* or *instrumental* techniques, which involve either the *separation* or *identification* of the component parts of the substance. Some techniques, therefore, can separate a substance and identify its individual elements; yet this does not mean that the substance itself can be identified, or *individualised*. Other primarily microscopic techniques can explore only the structure of the substance. As all material on Earth is made of specific combinations of elements that are the building blocks of the three types of matter found on Earth (solid, liquid and gas), forensic scientists are able to utilise the known taxonomic knowledge to try to identify the material found at crime scenes, on victims and offenders. As previously discussed, each element and compound contains *information* that acts as identifying markers that are specific to that type of material, and numerous analytical techniques enable scientists to unlock and interpret that information. Broadly speaking, quantitative and qualitative information are the two basic categories used by scientists and police analysts when examining trace material identified during criminal investigations. Qualitative information relates to the identity of the material and requires the determination of the numerous properties that make up that material. Quantitative information requires the determination of the percentage of the components of the material under examination and is usually accomplished by the precise measurement of a single property of that material. In most cases, qualitative identification should precede any attempt at quantitation.

Most qualitative and quantitative analytical techniques consist of one of the following three areas: (i) *visual examination* of the material and its structure; (ii) the rate at which the *substance absorbs or emits energy*; and (iii) how a substance *chemically reacts* when another substance (usually a reagent) is added. However, as scientific knowledge progresses, so too do the analytical techniques. It is not necessarily the case that all three areas will be applied to the examination of one type of material, as a single method or a combination of two of the above techniques might provide the information required by the analyst. The type and number of analytical techniques used, therefore, is determined by a number of factors that include:

• the type of substance being examined;
• what information is required by the criminal investigator; and
• the quality and quantity of the material recovered for analysis.

Obviously, before any material is analysed by the police technician or forensic scientist, Locard's *principle of exchange* must have occurred. As discussed in previous chapters, microscopic material can be transferred between the offender, victim and crime scene. Whilst this does not happen every time a crime occurs (due to context, transference and persistence), when it does, material is left that can possibly be identified and provide the necessary *links* that answer the what, when, where and who questions in criminal investigations.

Visual examination – the microscope

Once there is contact and transference, trace evidence must be visualised and its component parts measured. Such microscopic traces are often undetected by the *naked eye*; for example, latent finger marks need to be *visualised* through the application of techniques such as powdering in order for them to become visible, which then allows for their recovery and an analysis of the patterns to take place. Other trace material is larger and might be visible to the naked eye yet requires further enhancement to be able to analyse its component parts so identification of the object and its source can be undertaken. The most common tool used in this regard is the microscope, which is 'an optical instrument that uses a lens or a combination of lenses to magnify and resolve the fine details of an object'

(Saferstein, 2007:180); and, as Bell and Morris suggest (2010:1), these are devices that 'move light from a source, through a sample where interactions take place, and then to the eye or a camera'. In the late sixteenth century, several Dutch lens makers designed devices that magnified objects, and in 1609 Galileo perfected the first device known as a microscope (Wilson, 1995; Ruestow, 2004). Further developments include the concept of compound microscopy, which was invented by Dutchmen Zaccharias Janssen and Hans Lipperhey when they placed different types and sizes of lenses in the opposite ends of tubes and found that small objects were enlarged (Wilson, 1995; Ruestow, 2004). The creation of the microscope opened up the world of observation and profoundly altered the thinking of natural philosophers. The *interior* of nature was suddenly accessible, and this led to a vast expansion in the observational and experimental sciences (Wilson, 1995); all of which led to a conception of science as an objective and procedure-driven mode of inquiry that enabled scientists in the eighteenth, nineteenth and twentieth centuries to advance the epistemological and ontological basis of knowledge of substances/objects, animals/mammals and plant species. Furthermore, the microscope has become the most commonly used piece of technology and is standard in all scientific labs, especially those dealing with forensic analysis. Today, there are numerous types of microscopes available to the scientist, some of which include: the stereo binocular microscope, the compound binocular microscope and the digital microscope. All of these types of scopes use the visible light section of the electromagnetic spectrum, which is projected onto the object under examination by an illuminator and is then magnified through a combination of objective lenses, eyepieces, and a condenser (Kubic and Petraco, 2009:327–333; Bell and Morris, 2010:27–34). Since the invention of microscopy, scientists have continued to develop more and more sophisticated ways of observing and measuring material. They now call upon a host of techniques such as X-ray diffraction, spectrophotometry and microspectrophotometry, spectroscopy (atomic, infrared and Raman), and liquid and gas chromatography (for a review of these methods please see Saferstein, 2007; Houck and Siegel, 2010; Jackson and Jackson, 2011). All of these methods and technologies have been designed to identify the elements involved in the composition of material (i.e. atomic spectroscopy); or, to put it another way, to observe the *hidden information* contained within the material, which is beyond the somewhat limited visible spectrum of human beings. These techniques all use and manipulate electromagnetic radiation to delve into the interior of nature.

Absorption and emission interactions

Scientists use the different absorption and emission rates of *electromagnetic radiation* to identify substances found at crime scenes and on victims and offenders (see Saferstein, 2007; Houck and Siegel, 2010; Jackson and Jackson, 2011). Electromagnetic radiation (EMR) refers to 'various types of energy in the form of waves' (Houck and Siegel, 2010:99) and can be described in terms of a

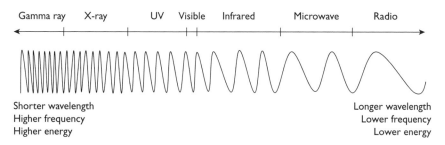

Figure 10.4 The electromagnetic spectrum

stream of *massless* particles, called *photons*, each travelling at the speed of light. As EMR travels, it spreads out as it goes so there are different types and levels of energy waves, which make up what is called the *electromagnetic spectrum* (Saferstein, 2007; Houck and Siegel, 2010). The level of energy is determined by the wavelength, which is the 'distance between two corresponding peaks or valleys and is denoted by the Greek letter λ'; and its frequency, which is 'number of waves that pass a given point in one second . . . and is denoted by the Greek letter ν' (Houck and Siegel, 2010:100). So, a shorter wavelength is travelling faster and has a higher frequency and higher levels of energy, whilst a lower wavelength has a lower frequency and lower levels of energy (Saferstein, 2007; Houck and Siegel, 2010). Figure 10.4 represents the electromagnetic radiation within the known universe. Examples of objects using different levels of EMR include AM and FM radio waves, aircraft communication, microwave ovens, TV remotes, night vision goggles (infrared), UV light from the sun, airport scanners and dentist X-ray machines, and positron emission tomography scan machines (known as the *PET Scan* which uses gamma rays). The light radiation that humans and animals are sensitive to is known as the visible light spectrum and, as Figure 10.4 illustrates, this is only a small proportion of all EMR in the known universe (Houck and Siegel, 2010).[5]

It should be mentioned that substances do not absorb all visible light; instead, a substance 'selectively absorbs some frequencies and reflects or transmits others' (Saferstein, 2007:147), depending on the structure of the composition under investigation. On the basis of this theory, scientists developed ways of bombarding matter with different levels of EMR as different types of substances, due to their unique composition, have different levels of absorption and emission rates.[6] The absorption phenomenon is the basis for *spectrophotometry* which is an analytical technique used in chemical identification. As Saferstein notes, spectrophotometry 'measures the quantity of radiation that a particular material absorbs as a function of wavelength or frequency' (ibid.:147). Whilst it is difficult to predict with certainty all the frequencies at which a substance will absorb a particular level of EMR, what scientists do know is that the frequency of the absorption of photons of radiation 'corresponds to the energy requirement of the substance' (ibid.:147).

As different substances have different energy requirements, it follows that they have different absorption frequencies. These differing levels act as *identifying markers* for the component parts of the material under examination, and these are matched against known ontological taxonomies. For example, the 'UV absorption spectrum of heroin shows a maximum absorption band at a wavelength of 278 nanometers' (ibid.:149). It follows that, because substances consist of different types of chemical compositions which each have their own unique energy requirements, there are different techniques for identifying and measuring this information. It is also important to recognise that some analytical techniques are not suitable for particular types of material. For example, testing a volatile explosive material such as nitroglycerine would normally entail using gas chromatography (Jackson and Jackson, 2011:365): just to ensure that the analysts do not become trace material themselves.

In order to identify which technique is the best one to use, an understanding of analytical chemistry and physics is necessary. Saferstein (2004 and 2007) notes that a useful starting point is to identify whether the substance to be examined is *organic* or *inorganic*. Organic substances are defined as those that 'contain carbon, commonly in combination with one or more of the following elements: hydrogen, oxygen, nitrogen, chlorine, phosphorous, or other elements' (Saferstein 2007:132). As carbon constitutes less than 0.1 per cent of the Earth's crust, it logically follows that non-carbon substances are usually prominent at crime scenes. Inorganic substances consist of non-carbon material such as iron, steel, aluminium and copper, as well as inorganic chemicals such as pigments in paints and dyes (ibid.:160–161). Whilst it is not possible here to examine in depth the entire organic and inorganic techniques available, Table 10.4 highlights some of the more established methods used.

What is important to note is that these techniques have all been through years of testing and refinement, and have reached the level of being accepted/accredited

Table 10.4 Core analytical techniques

Field of matter manipulation	Examples of techniques	Field of matter manipulation	Examples of techniques
Light and Matter	Spectrophotometry Molecular fluorescence Infrared spectroscopy Raman spectroscopy Mass spectroscopy Atomic spectroscopy (absorption and emission) X-ray diffraction	Separation	Liquid chromatography Gas chromatography High-performance liquid chromatography Thin Layer Chromatography (TLC) Electrophoresis

by the scientific community. They have also been accepted in court, which follows different evidential thresholds and rules (Faigman *et al.*, 2010, 2012); and which is discussed at greater length in Chapter 11.

Whenever an analyst uses one of the above techniques to unlock the information intrinsic to the substance being examined, this information is translated into something that is visual or readable. Thus, we must return to the previously stated notion of the *inscriptive device*, which turns the information contained within physical material into a form of visual medium that becomes the scientific 'arte*fact*' (Latour and Woolgar, 1986). Examples of inscriptive devices include: pictures (e.g. from photographs and microscopes); bar and line charts and histograms (e.g. atomic spectroscopy results); or numerical information in the form of composition percentage rates. As many scientists still agree with the idea that the book of nature is written in mathematics; visual graphs, charts and numbers are the most common forms of inscriptive devices used to convey the information within substances examined and interpreted by forensic scientists. However, it is important to acknowledge that the abstract nature of mathematics can never fully describe nature because the natural world 'is one of infinite varieties and complexities, a multidimensional world' (Capra, 1991:35).

Chemical reactions

The final broad type of technique used on crime scene objects is the introduction of an external substance that chemically reacts with the material to produce (or not produce) some effect that can be measured. The reaction of the *examined substance* when interacting with the *added substance* is useful to the scientist and/or police analyst in two key ways. The first area mainly concerns the use of *presumptive tests*. These are tests that apply a chemical substance to an identified testing sample, which then reacts to provide either a positive (present/+) or negative (not-present/−) result. Such tests are normally used to test substances suspected to be illegal, such as drugs, or substances at crime scenes that are thought to be blood. For example, colour and spot tests, such as the Cobalt Thiocyanate test for cocaine or the Duquenois-Levine reagent for marijuana, help establish the *possibility* that the drug is present. When it comes to serological[7] evidence, a common presumptive blood test used by crime scene examiners is the Kastle Meyer (KM) test, which introduces the chemical indicator phenolphthalein. The chemical reagent interacts with the peroxidase activity of haemoglobin and turns pink when there is a positive result, *ergo* there is a trace of either human or animal blood present. Unfortunately, some vegetable material such as potatoes and horseradish can produce a positive result, so Hemastix strips may be preferred, which turn green in the presence of blood (Saferstein, 2007:354). The benefits of presumptive tests are that they are easy to use and require only a small amount of training; they are sensitive to trace amounts; they aid in narrowing the possibilities and help decide which tests to do next; they can be used on relatively large areas; and they can locate evidence not visible to the naked eye (see Nickell and Fischer, 1999; Cole, 2004; Spalding, 2009; Houck and Siegel, 2010). However, it is also important to acknowledge that presumptive tests only provide preliminary results, and there is always the risk of producing a *false positive*. False positives occur when there is a positive result from a test (i.e. a pink KM result), but further testing confirms that the substance is not present. This occurs when the examined substance reacts to the chemicals in the reagent, or the chemicals in the reagent itself react to produce a positive result. Because of the possibility of false positives, all positive presumptive tests should be followed up by the relevant *confirmatory test* such as the ones outlined in Table 10.4; although other confirmatory tests exist – for instance, the Teichmann and Takayama tests (for blood) (Spalding, 2009:269–271).

The second way in which chemicals are used in the analysis of material identified during criminal investigations is in the processes of *enhancement* and *visualisation*. As previously mentioned, some crime scene material is outside the visible light spectrum, so it needs to be *enhanced* so that it can be seen. It should be obvious that the enhancement and visualisation is required to fulfil two of the requirements of the scientific method – observation and measurement. Chemical treatment and fingerprint departments use a number of techniques to chemically treat material in order to enhance the properties for analysis, and these are most commonly used for developing fingermarks or impression marks, or to identify areas that are possibly DNA-rich. The enhancement processes involve any combination of the following interactions between: the chemical constituents occurring in natural latent fingermarks (i.e. sweat oils); some contamination materials found in the environment; and the relevant enhancement substance (Jackson and Jackson, 2011). The Scientific Development Branch of the Home Office has outlined the various ways in which chemicals are used for fingermark enhancement in its *Fingerprint Development Handbook* (2005) and the *Fingerprint Source Book* (2013). These techniques are numerous and include the application of chemicals such as: acid black, violet or yellow; gentian violet; iodine; ninhydrin; DFO (1,8 Diazafluoren-9-One); powders (e.g. magnetic and aluminium); radioactive sulfur dioxide; superglue; and vacuum metal deposition (Home Office Scientific Development Branch, 2005). Of course, the choice of chemical used depends on a number of important variables, some of which include:

- the *type of material* being examined – e.g. paper, plastic, metal, rubber, fabric, wood, blood, etc.;
- the *colour of the material* – e.g. the colour of the substance should not be the same as or similar to the material or background being examined;
- the *porous nature* of the material – e.g. porous, non-porous, smooth, rough, etc.;
- the *type of analysis/information* required – e.g. one test may destroy the possibility of further testing by destroying the material under examination; and
- The *available resources* – e.g. the crime under investigation might not warrant expensive tests being performed.

Ninhydrin, for instance, is a chemical reagent that reacts primarily with the amino acids in fingermarks 'to provide coloured or fluorescent reaction products' (ibid.:85). If appropriate to use, Ninhydrin has been found to produce immediate visible fingermarks, and it is simple to use and cost-effective. Another process used is *vacuum metal deposition* (VMD). This technique is used by some police forces to visualise finger and palm marks and, in some cases, to identify areas on clothes where DNA analysis can be focused. VMD 'utilises vacuum coating technology for the thermal evaporation of metals and deposition of thin metal films' (ibid.:125). To begin with, a thin coating of gold is deposited on the item being examined, and a coating of zinc that gives a visible grey deposit follows this. VMD works due to 'disturbances in the physical and chemical nature of the surface', which are revealed because of the 'different rates of growth of the zinc metal film' (ibid.:125). Whilst the running and maintenance costs are quite high, training someone to operate the machine only takes a couple of hours, and, more importantly, the VMD method does not affect DNA or ballistics analysis, which other methods such as superglue have been known to do (ibid.). Of course, the VMD machine is only a fraction of the technology that is available to scientists. Other machines include cyanoacrylate fuming cabinets; ESDA machines such as electrostatic imaging systems and humidifiers; and thermal fingerprint developers.

This discussion provides only the briefest glimpse into the types of scientific analysis that most forensic scientists commonly use when they examine items regarded as evidence by police investigators. They play various roles in the analysis outcome process outlined in Figure 10.3. However, it is important to acknowledge that these techniques only touch the surface of the complexity of the scientific analysis of matter. There are many sub-fields within each of the core analytical techniques and, oftentimes, whilst having the basic practical knowledge of standard techniques, forensic scientists specialise in specific techniques or areas. The primary aim of all these analytical techniques, of course, is to identify the examined material and link to the crime scene, suspect and/or victim. In order to achieve this, forensic scientists frame their findings in terms of two concepts called *identification* and *individualisation*.

Identification and individualisation

As we have already seen, forensic science is concerned with the analysis, identification and interpretation of physical evidence. The previous section described some of the analytical tools and technologies used in this process; this section looks at the notion of *identification* and *individualisation*. As Faigman *et al.* (2010:34) point out, there are two 'different connotations associated with the term *identification*'. The first is a process of placing an item into a category, such as identifying an animal as a cat; and in the second sense, one may identify something as a blue Honda Civic (ibid.:34; also see Saks and Koehler, 2005, 2008; Saks and Faigman, 2008). However, being able to identify the class of an object rarely satisfies the forensic scientist. They require a higher level of discrimination that moves beyond simple categories. It is not sufficient to identify a blue Honda Civic as the type of car that killed someone in a hit-and-run; what scientists need to know is whether a particular blue Honda Civic, to the exclusion of all others, was involved in the hit-and-run. Forensic scientists use the concept of *individualisation* to extend the level of discrimination to 'unique', and the term denotes the 'process of placing an object in a unit category, which consists of a single unit' (Faigman *et al.*, 2010:34); for example, a specific configuration of alleles of an individual's DNA. In short, individualisation implies uniqueness whereas identification does not. Kirk (1974:9–17) was one of the first scientists working on criminal cases to highlight the need to distinguish between the concepts of identification and individualisation. He defined identification as 'the placing of an object in a class or group' (ibid.:10) and individualisation as 'identifying a unique strand or unit to the object within that class or group (10–11).

These are important concepts which need to be distinguished as they are often confused and misused. The police, solicitors, barristers and the courts tend to have conflicting expectations as to what science can provide, and, for the most part, this conflict originates from a misunderstanding of these two concepts (Faigman, *et al.*, 2010:29). Identification tells us what the material or substance is likely to be whilst individualisation implies a uniqueness that can be traced to the source of origin. As most of the analytical techniques described above involve the comparison of identified material in order to associate this material with a suspect and/or victim, the concepts of *class characteristics* and *individual characteristics* are useful in determining either identification or individualisation. As a general rule, material where only class characteristics have been identified places the discrimination squarely within the concept of *identification*, whereas material with individual characteristics can be said to have *individualised* levels of discrimination. The term class characteristics denotes general characteristics 'that separate a group of objects from a universe of diverse objects' (Faigman *et al.*, 2010:30; also see Nickell and Fischer, 1999; Saks and Koehler, 2005, 2008; Saks and Faigman, 2008; Jackson and Jackson, 2011); for example, a sole pattern on a shoe or the colour blue. The identification of class characteristics tends to be the starting point for most forensic analysis, and it is used as a screening tool for eliminating large numbers of objects that do not share 'the characteristics common to all members of that group' (Faigman, *et al.*, 2010:30; also see Jackson and Jackson, 2011). So, for investigative purposes, if a witness of a hit-and-run claims to have seen a blue Honda Civic, this screens out, or excludes, the majority of non-blue and non-Civic cars. The three class characteristics in this hypothetical scenario are the colour (blue), make (Honda) and model (Civic), and the police investigator applies a 'fundamental mathematical foundation to this type of elimination' (Faigman *et al.*, 2010:30; also see Nickell and Fischer, 1999; Saks and Koehler, 2005, 2007, 2008; Saks and Faigman, 2008; Jackson and Jackson, 2011): a simplified version of Boolean algebra (which involves *either/or* logic). This means that any vehicle that is not blue or a Honda Civic can be eliminated from police enquiries. However, it should be noted that the witness might be wrong (they may have seen a grey Toyota); which means the investigator should look for corroborating evidence such as traces of paint on the victim or at the scene.

Individual characteristics are 'those exceptional characteristics that may establish the uniqueness of an object' (Faigman *et al.*, 2010:30; also see Saks and Koehler, 2005, 2007, 2008; Saks and Faigman, 2008; Houck and Siegel, 2010). Taken in isolation, individual characteristics may not fully individualise an object, so the uniqueness required for individualisation may include an ensemble of individual characteristics; for example, a vehicle identification number (VIN), which is unique to each car. Table 10.5 gives a few examples of class and individual characteristics.

The skill in forensic analysis lies in the ability to recognise these two different types and not to confuse them. Whilst most natural scientists understand the difference between class and individual characteristics, for their epistemological and ontological knowledge consists of the comprehensive taxonomies relevant to their subject/expertise, in some circumstances, this is not easy to accomplish; for example, in the 'area of handwriting examination' (Faigman *et al.*, 2010:32). It can be even more difficult for police officers, solicitors, barristers, the courts and juries to distinguish between these two types of characteristics, and this can be fatal when it comes to administering true justice (Jasanoff, 1997; Redmayne, 2004; Golan, 2007). Each characteristic *part* of the material that is examined within the context of criminal investigation is assigned a *weight*, which equates to the strength of that material, and the *strength* of an item is directly related to two factors. The first factor is the type of material being examined, which again links back to the level of epistemological and ontological knowledge of that material and the information contained within its constituent parts. The level of robust scientific information that can be accessed varies depending on the type of material and techniques used to examine it. For instance, consider the two examples outlined in Table 10.6.

Table 10.5 Class and individual characteristics

Class Characteristics	Individual Characteristics
Fingerprint patterns (e.g. loop, whorl, arch)	Ridge ending, bifurcation, dot
Number of lands and groves of a firearm	Striations on the surface of a fired bullet
Thickness of a shard of glass	Irregular fracture margin
Width of a prying tool (e.g. screwdriver)	Striations within the tool-mark
Tread pattern of an automobile tyre	Cuts and tears acquired through use

Source: Faigman *et al.*, 2010:32

Table 10.6 Information and matter

Aluminum	Footwear Impression
We know the following:	We know the following:
• Atomic structure (e.g. number of electrons, protons and neutrons) • Crystal structure (e.g. face centred cubic) • Atomic radius – 118pm • Atomic weight – 26.9815386 • Density – 2.7g/cm³ • Melting point – 660.32°C/1220.6°F • Boiling point – 2519°C/4566°F • Electronegativity – 1.61 • % in universe – 0.0050% • % in sun – 0.0060% • % in Earth's crust – 8.1% • % in ocean – 0.00000050% • % in humans – 0.000090%	• Tread pattern and measurements • Identified 'unique' marks (however finding the source of origin – i.e. individualisation – is another matter) We may know the following: • Make of footwear • Place of manufacture

This clearly demonstrates the importance in understanding not only the type and range of information available to the analyst, but that this information greatly varies along a continuum from weak to strong. In the example in Table 10.6, a forensic analyst should have greater confidence in the aluminium evidence than the footwear impression.

The second factor that affects the *strength* of the evidence is other types of material and the role they play in understanding the crime event. For example, a few fibres found on a victim of sexual homicide and traced to a mass-produced duvet that can be purchased all over the country in Tesco and Asda supermarkets is weak evidence with little chance of individualising to a suspect. However, if that same suspect has a dog and rolled the victim up in a carpet and transported the body in his or her car, and hairs and fibres were found on the victim that *matched* to the three sources, the evidence becomes slightly stronger against the suspect. This is known as the *product rule* and is discussed in greater detail below.

Individual characteristics are caused by a combination of one or more of three possible forces (Faigman, *et al.*, 2010:32). They arise as *natural phenomena* or, more specifically, in the form of the elements that make up all matter on Earth. Unfortunately, natural phenomena are poorly understood outside of the area of natural science, despite the fact that many police officers, crime scene investigators, solicitors, barristers, courts and juries have to make important decisions using them. The natural origins of fingerprints, for example, are often misunderstood, especially when it comes to the matching process (see Bandey, 2004). Second, they may result from the *manufacturing process*. These processes are understood

Figure 10.5 Damaged fingerprint

This is a print of the author's left middle finger. It shows the damage that occurred when the finger was accidentally sliced open over 16 years ago. Note the diagonal line that cuts through the fingerprint (just above the arrow line), altering its natural pattern. This is a clear example of how damage through wear and tear, whether accidental or intentional, can alter the *natural* characteristics of an object, thereby creating a unique *individual* characteristic. Obviously, there may be other individuals who have similar damage but the probability of someone living in the same area and having an identical injury can be very low.

but are 'unintentional in their expression, such as marks associated with the machining of tools' (Faigman *et al.*, 2010:32). Finally, individual characteristics are created through the *career and history* of an item. As items are used, they take on individual characteristics based upon use and abuse/wear and tear, so it is sometimes possible to individualise an item if it has a unique mark created through its everyday use. Examples of this type include impression marks from tools and footwear, or damage to a fingerprint (see Figure 10.5). Overall, when the analyst is comparing material, they will begin with identifying the class characteristics to see if there is a basic match before moving onto the individual characteristics, which basically acts an analysis filter. It is pointless for an analyst to continue with the comparison when a fingermark fragment found at a crime scene holds a whorl pattern while the suspect's fingerprints only contain arches.

It should be remembered of course, that material found at a crime scene is only useful if it can be identified and then linked to a person or place, and, in order to achieve this, a crucial factor is required. There needs to be a *taxonomic system* that defines and labels the material under examination and provides a reference point on which the analysis can be based. As stated in Chapter 2, the taxonomic mission of the natural scientists from the Enlightenment onwards has created our epistemological and ontological knowledge of all the known (or available) organic and inorganic material that exists on Earth. Forensic scientists or police analysts, in their quest to identify and characterise trace material found at crime scenes, constantly access this knowledge. We know with a relatively strong level of certainty what specific type of hair belongs to a specific type of dog or cat; and we can identify where drugs originate from in the world, because we can analyse mineral composition in soil and the elements in pesticides (i.e. different parts of the world have different mineral compositions and use different types of pesticides; see Jackson and Jackson, 2011). This knowledge does not necessarily provide us with conclusive proof, but it can provide useful evidence for criminal investigations. However, the question still remains as to whether this translates to a level of probative weight that helps identify and convict the right person; and this is the topic for the remainder of this chapter as well as Chapter 11.

In recent years there have been various challenges to the concept of individualisation (Saks and Faigman, 2008; Saks and Koehler, 2008) with the forensic sciences coming under increasing scrutiny (Budowle *et al.*, 2009). These criticisms have largely been ignored in the forensic science textbooks, despite the fact that they are both valid and necessary if forensic evidence is to continue to be used to decide the fates of individuals caught up in the criminal justice process. It is also useful to examine these in terms of future research into the probability and error rates of transference and persistence of all sorts of trace evidence. These challenges need to be taken seriously, and explained fully to the police and the courts, as they have the potential to undermine the links made between offender, victim and location of crimes. If we remind ourselves that individualisation implies uniqueness and is 'the process of placing an object in a category which consists of a single, solitary unit' (Thornton and Peterson, 2008: 150), we need to unpack what this actually means. To imply uniqueness means you exclude all other possible sources, and the reality is that this is a lot more difficult than it sounds. Even if we take into account DNA profiling, which, despite its shaky early foundations (Sekar, 1998), has considerably improved the evidential basis on which its statistical probability is determined, we are left with the uncomfortable fact that the majority of forensic science knowledge is based upon 'the irrational reliance on unspecified, unsystematic "experience" coupled with plausible-sounding arguments' (Saks and Faigman, 2008:150). Saks and Faigman (ibid.) and Saks and Koehler (2008) outline two broad problems with what they label as the *individualisation fallacy* within the forensic identification sciences (FIS) – *scientific failures* and *illusory judicial oversight*. I examine illusory judicial oversight in Chapter 11, as this links with the court and legal processes. For the remainder of this chapter, I examine the scientific failures behind what Saks and Faigman call the 'nonscience forensic sciences'. First is the *no basic-science origins* problem. Forensic science claims to be the application of science to resolve criminal justice problems, yet, as Saks and Faigman suggest, 'this description does not fit the subfields of forensic science that are concerned with individualization' (2008:152). The point here is that when forensic analysts make the claim that no two firearms produce the same bullet casing striations, or that an individual's fingerprints are unique to them, these claims are not based on the epistemological knowledge of conventional science. Furthermore, such claims have not gone through the rigorous testing procedures of the scientific method, and 'even a cursory review of major university course catalogs quickly reveals that nothing could supply a knowledge base for the forensic identification services' (ibid.:152). More importantly, academic scientists rarely take up forensic issues, and most of the forensic identification sciences 'missed the school bus', as they were not developed within the university system and its institutionally based practices which promote a 'culture of scientific curiosity and adventure' (ibid.:152). Instead, FIS have been developed and integrated within the police apparatus (see Chapters 3, 4 and 5) and are largely the 'instrument of law enforcement' controlled by police technicians. Whilst these might be hard-working and well-intentioned technicians, they do not subject their methods to 'systematic empirical testing before being offered as testimony': or, as Cole (2007, cited in Saks and Faigman, 2008:152) suggests, 'they followed a testify-first-validate-later approach'. Cole even goes as far as arguing that, even after the Second World War, latent fingerprint identification 'was still not based on scientific research at all. Instead, it was based on anecdote, experience, and nineteenth-century statistics' (Cole, 2002:257).

The problem with the lack of scientific basis extends to further problems with the science behind FIS. The second is the *absence of empirical testing*. There is a disturbing lack of empirical evidence to support much of the evidential claims made about numerous types of forensic evidence. Saks and Faigman (2008:157) use forensic ondontology (bite-mark evidence) and handwriting evidence as examples of the lack of rigorous empirical research underpinning claims, and they call for more systematic, proper research and empirical testing to be undertaken in all of the forensic disciplines (ibid.:157). This leads to a third problem: the fact that there is *little use of the scientific method*. The authors highlight the fact that the standard scientific method of testing procedures to determine which methods produce the most accurate results, and undertaking 'systematic experiments on different training procedures to determine which work best' (ibid.:158), are largely absent from the 'nonscience forensic sciences'. The most problematic issue however is directly tied to the paradox of forensic case assessment. When outlining CAIM earlier, it was suggested that forensic scientists should have access to case information in order to determine the best forensic products to construct for the customer (Cook *et al.*, 1998a). Unfortunately, this tends to be in opposition to conventional scientific studies, which are designed to 'maximize the contribution of the phenomenon under study and minimize the contribution of expectations and biases' (ibid.:158). The majority of forensic analysts are part of the police investigation – some are even members of police organisations – and receive case information that has not been constructed to minimise expectations and biases. It is even suggested that most forensic scientists do not employ the procedures designed to avoid observer effects, as many used to believe that they are not affected by such issues (Risinger *et al.*, 2002:12–21, 27–42). Risinger *et al.* (ibid.:3) include a wonderful quote by Roy Hazlewood, a now retired member of the FBI's Behavioural Sciences Unit, who was responding to a question concerning the conduct of the investigation into the alleged responsibility of Clayton Hartwig for the 1989 explosion of the centre gun turret on the *USS Iowa*: 'This is a criminal investigation, sir. You are asking about bias controls, which refers to research.'

Recent research casts doubt on the claims that observer effects are not present in forensic analysis (see Dror *et al.*, 2006). For example, Dror *et al.* (ibid.) found that around 80 per cent of fingerprint examiners changed their initial opinions when the researchers introduced incorrect contextual information, and this research is supported by case after case of misidentified fingermarks; for example, the Madrid terrorist bombing, in which the FBI laboratory *matched* a fingermark found on a bag of detonators to Oregon lawyer Brandon Mayfield, only to withdraw their match result after the real owner of the fingermark, an Algerian national, was identified by the Spanish National Police. The FBI convened a two-day review panel to determine how such an error was made: '[s]everal panelists cited overconfidence in the power of IAFIS and the pressure of working on a high-profile case as contributing to the error. Some panelists stated that verification was "tainted" by knowledge of the initial examiner's conclusion' (US Department of Justice, 2006:3–4). In short, the very act of knowing information can affect the outcome of what we are trying to measure as well as its interpretation. In quantum mechanics, this is known as the *Heisenberg Uncertainty Principle*.

The lack of the application of conventional scientific studies relevant to the Heisenberg principle leads on to a fourth problem: that of *error management*. A cursory glance over most scientific research would suggest that scientists are obsessed with error. Most of these studies are filled with incomprehensible statistical results because statistics deals with uncertainty and error (Robertson and Vignaux, 1995; Agresti and Finlay, 1997; Aitken and Taroni, 2004; Lucy, 2005; Adam, 2010; Faigman *et al.*, 2012). Courts tend to have difficulties in comprehending the notion of *error rates*, despite the fact that science always has some error associated with it, whether it's in the form of mistakes made by the researcher or in the test methods themselves (Faigman *et al.*, 2012:61–65). Thus, research studies 'report probability levels, specify confidence intervals, present error bars on graphs and so on' (Saks and Faigman, 2008:158). Unfortunately, up until recently, most forensic scientists pretended that error rates did not exist in

Figure 10.6 The Heisenberg Uncertainty Principle

This principle holds that increasing the accuracy of measurement of one observable quantity increases the uncertainty with which another conjugate quantity may be known. In layman's terms, this means even if we shot one photon particle of light at a moving object, in doing so, we change (observer effects) the position and motion we're trying to measure.

Source: Photo courtesy of Jonas Claesson, www.jonasclaesson.com

their work; as can be seen in the case *U.S. v. Allen (2002)*, where a forensic expert testifying about footwear identification techniques claimed 'that the error rate of the process itself' was zero (cited in Saks and Faigman, 2008:158). As Saks and Faigman (2008:159–160) point out, there is no such thing as a 'zero error rate or failure rate in practice', and claims to the contrary contradict proficiency testing. Furthermore, in the small number of studies on pattern matching, there is some convincing evidence to suggest that the zero error rate is a fallacy, especially if you consider the ironic fact that most FIS relies on the subjective interpretation of the assessor.

The fifth and final problem with the science behind FIS is perhaps the most important and can be described as the *impossibility of individualisation* (ibid.:154–157). Textbook after textbook on forensic science or criminalistics includes sections on the concept of the individualisation of physical evidence (Nickell and Fischer, 1999:2–4; Inman and Rudin, 2000; Houck, 2009:169–171; Saferstein, 2009:72–78; Houck and Siegel, 2010:57–61; Faigman *et al.*, 2010:34–39; Jackson and Jackson, 2011). Saks and Koehler (2008) call this the *individualisation fallacy*, and they argue that the courts and juries are gerrymandered into claims that forensic scientists have found *uniqueness*. Most of these claims can be traced back to the nineteenth century and the growth in scientific criminology and positivist sociology (Davie, 2005; Rafter, 2009; Tierney, 2011) and, in particular, to the work of French statistician Quetelet who hypothesised that *nature never repeats* and offered the product rule of probability theory to suggest great odds against such repetition, which was then famously put into practice through Bertillon's anthropometric system and which became the bedrock of fingerprint identification systems (Cole, 2002; Saks and Faigman, 2008; Saks and Koehler, 2008; also see Chapters 3 and 4 of this current text). Indeed, *Harper*'s headline in the 1910 edition boldly claimed that 'only once during the existence of our solar system will two human beings be born with similar finger markings', and the 1911 edition of *Scientific American* claimed that 'two fingerprints would be found only once every $\times 10^{48}$ years' (Maltoni *et al.*, 2003:257). Unfortunately, the repeated *individualisation* claims of forensic scientists and criminalists have not been empirically verified so, at this moment in time, the *scientific basis* for this claim does not exist. Even worse, such claims are in contraposition to how nature actually works. Nature is full of repeating patterns and commonalities, such as identical twins and fractal patterns, and to insist that nature never repeats is based upon a logical fallacy 'filled with assertions supported by little more than intuition, anecdote, and *ipse dixit*'[8] (Saks and Faigman, 2008:155). Such ideas and reasoning are frighteningly akin to *faith-based beliefs* such as mystical, religious and political ideologies, and it has been well documented where that has led the world (Hitchens, 2007).

Since Kirk (1974:9–17) first introduced the notion of individualisation, forensic scientists and criminalists have turned this hypothetical construct into *the* central aspect of their practice and, to illustrate this, Saks and Koehler (2005:892) use the notion of *discernible uniqueness*. The discernible uniqueness assumption stipulates that 'markings produced by different people or objects are observably different. Thus, when a pair of markings is not discernably different, criminalists conclude that the marks were made by the same person or object' (ibid.:892). This belief can clearly be seen throughout the courts as numerous cases contained phrases such as 'to the exclusion of all others in the world'. For example, in *U.S. v. Green* (405 F.Supp.2d 104, D.Mass. 2005), the firearms examiner testified that they were 'able to identify the unknown weapon "to the exclusion of every other firearm in the world"' (cited in Saks and Koehler, 2008:4). Unfortunately, this is not the only case where such strong claims have been made (for examples see Saks and Koehler, 2005, 2008; Saks and Faigman, 2008). Whilst the notion of individualisation has no theoretical or empirical foundations, its constant application to criminal justice cases needs explaining. Saks and Koehler (2005:892; 2008:4) proffer three reasons as to why the discernible uniqueness assumption has become a popular strategy:

1   It enables criminalists and forensic scientists to make bold/strong and definitive conclusions.
2   It relieves criminalistics and forensic scientists of the 'rigors of developing measures of object attributes and collecting population data on the frequencies of variations in those attributes' (Saks and Koehler, 2008:4).
3   It exempts forensic science sub-fields from 'determining the proper statistical model for estimating random match probabilities, calculating those probabilities in actual cases, and explaining to judges and juries the extent to which different objects could share a common set of observable characteristics' (ibid.:4).

These three issues make the claim to individualisation more and more difficult to accept. However, there are some positive developments. In 2005, Saks and Koehler published 'The Coming Paradigm Shift in Forensic Identification Science' in the journal *Science*, in which they suggest that a change to the discernible uniqueness paradigm was occurring. The authors note how various challenges to this idea have come through developments in DNA typing (e.g. the discovery of wrongful convictions and the 'model for scientifically sound identification science'); changes to legal admissibility standards for expert evidence and testimony; and the growth in 'studies of error rates across the forensic sciences' (2005:892–895). Only time will tell as to whether these changes bring about practical substantive changes to the forensic identification sciences. What is interesting is that these developments actually echo Kirk's original conceptualisation of individualisation: for he stated that 'there is an indefinite number of degrees of identification' with each degree, or factor, narrowing the pool of class characteristics and making individualisation to a unique source not a guarantee but a possibility (1974:10–11). Kirk's *degrees of identification* thesis directly relates to issues of interpretation and probative weight that are attached to evidence; which is the subject of the next chapter.

Summary

Forensic science in the UK has gone through some major changes since the coalition government came to power in 2010. Whilst it is clear that the FSS could not maintain losing £2 million per month due to poor/mismanagement, the fact that the government feels that there is no need for a forensic strategy, as *free-market-economics* solves all societal ills, should be concerning for those who actually pay attention to the immense distress caused to millions because of globalisation. In the UK, a mix of police technicians/analysts, forensic scientists and a small number of independent consultants provides forensic provision. Regardless of the roles involved in the analysis of physical evidence, the primary aim of forensic science is to identify physical evidence using indirect methods such as the 'identification of physical objects associated with the individual to be identified' (ibid.:9). This has been labelled as the *forensic identification sciences* and covers most types of physical evidence that can be transferred between offender, victim and the crime location. Forensic scientists have developed two important concepts in which they can place the results of their analyses: class characteristics and individualisation; and these two concepts help frame the conclusions drawn by the analyst. Of course, the ideal situation is to be able to individualise physical evidence to one unique source; however, the reality is somewhat different. Saks and Faigman (2008) have produced a convincing argument that, with the exception of DNA profiling, it is not possible to individualise with the current state of epistemological and ontological knowledge in the field of forensics. Because of this, forensic scientists assign *probability weights* to their findings, and it's the use of probability and forensic science evidence in the courtroom that I now turn my attention to in the final chapter.

Chapter 11

Forensics on trial

Introduction

The information work undertaken during a criminal investigation (Chapters 6, 7 and 8), which is collected by CSEs (Chapter 9) and analysed by forensic scientists, analysts and technicians (Chapter 10) is directed towards the successful identification and prosecution of the individual who has committed the crime under investigation. When this information work is presented to the court as the narrative of the crime event, its function is to tag, define, identify, describe, and emphasise the 'criminal' (Tannenbaum, 1938:19): in other words, the courtroom process is the labelling of the 'criminal body'. Forensic evidence, in its reconstructed form, aids in the labelling process; however, the very nature of this reconstruction is fraught with numerous difficulties. I have already introduced problems with the concepts of individualisation and probative weight, and this current chapter expands upon these issues in relation to their application in criminal trials. It examines how science and the legal system, despite their well-known differences, interact to test and develop each other's methodologies, frames of reference and rules of engagement. For the most part, despite the rigorous methodologies and testing used by scientists, the courts can and have rejected *new* scientific ideas when they do not follow the evidential rules set out by law. This chapter examines this process by examining the relationship between science and the law; the development of the scientific expert and the problems associated with expert testimony produced within the adversarial framework; and the reasoning strategies used by scientists when presenting their evidence to the court and jury.

Science and the legal system

It is important to acknowledge that the two most authoritative institutions in modern Western culture are science and law (Golan, 2007:1); and the relationship between these two institutions is crucial when understanding the acceptance and application of scientific evidence for resolving criminal justice problems (Jasanoff, 1997; Golan, 2007). What is of special interest to forensic criminologists is the way that scientific knowledge is mediated, contested and constructed within the legal framework. In her excellent study *Science at the Bar* (1995), Jasanoff examines how science and the courts 'interact with each other in the face of technological innovation and political change' and 'our society is increasingly defining itself through conflicts that are at once scientific, technological, and legal' (1995:xiii). Scientific claims are highly contested and are contingent upon localised legal circumstances. The legal context 'shapes the representation of legally relevant scientific claims' and this includes determining the 'standards for what counts as valid science' (Jasanoff, 1997:xiv). Scientific evidence is filtered and critically assessed through the *adversarial* approach, which is a legal system where two advocates represent their parties' positions and an impartial person and/or group of persons, usually a judge and 12-person jury, attempt to determine which side is telling the truth. Because of these filters, scientific evidence is often afforded stronger weight by the courts and juries. Jasanoff (ibid.:43) suggests that this is because most judges are generalists without any specialised knowledge of scientific methods and theories and that juries often have an even lower level of scientific sophistication; or worse, those jury members that have specialist knowledge are instructed by judges not to use their expertise in case deliberations. These important issues highlight the existence of what Saks and Koehler (2008:161) call the *cultural divide* between science and the law. Science operates using an autonomous framework of validation and control (i.e. standardised methodologies and peer review), which are not 'subjected to the law's normative concerns or institutional practices' (Jasanoff, 1997:6). Furthermore, Jasanoff (ibid.:7–9) highlights binary contrasts between the two institutions, shown in Table 11.1.

Whilst there is an element of truth to these cultural differences, Jasanoff also notes how law and science 'are in fact mutually constitutive' and that they 'jointly produce our social and scientific knowledge, and our relationships with technological objects' (1995:8). This link is largely made through the role of fact-finding:

> Each tradition claims an authoritative capacity to sift evidence and derive rational persuasive conclusions from it. The reliability of observers (or witnesses) and the credibility of their observations are of critical concern to both legal and scientific decisionmaking.
>
> (Jasanoff, 1997:8)

Table 11.1 Cultural divisions between law and science

Law	Science
Does justice	Seeks the truth
Is prescriptive	Is descriptive
Emphasises process	Emphasises progress
Emphasis on settling disputes fairly and efficiently	Emphasis on getting the facts right

The sifting of evidence in legal fact-finding tends to take the form of a ritualised courtroom drama, where scientific ideas are subject to further 'conceptual and rhetorical filters' (1995:8). This tends to centre on the prosecution and defence expert witnesses, who apply their scientific knowledge and understanding to the interpretation of the evidence. From this perspective, science is as much a constructed entity as any other form of human endeavour or institution and is, therefore, not 'an independent, self-regulating producer of truths about the natural world' (Jasanoff, ibid.:xv). Instead, science is a 'dynamic social institution, fully engaged with other mechanisms for creating social and epistemological order in modern societies' (1995:xv). This claim can be verified by considering case examples of the interplay between science and the law; and the Cowper case is one of the earliest cases that provides an excellent illustration of this.

Murder, autopsies and drowning dogs

The Cowper case was one of the first trials to make use of what today would be called 'expert testimony' and 'forensic science evidence'. As Knights argues:

> the case was to have far-reaching implications, not just for Hertford, for through it and its aftermath it is possible to reconstruct the extraordinary ferment of ideas that constitute England's early Enlightenment – the process by which long-accepted beliefs, institutions, prejudices, and customs were fundamentally challenged and sometimes overturned.
>
> (2011:13)

On 14th March 1699, Sarah Stout's body was found floating in a mill pond in Hertford (ibid.), and the subsequent trial exposed the key features of contingencies of place, localised scientific knowledge and global scientific practices. Speculation about the cause of death soon spread across the village, and within three hours of the discovery, suicide was rumoured to be the cause of death, due to the fact that 'she was with child' (ibid.:10). The post-mortem found that Sarah had drowned and a coroner's inquest recorded a verdict of suicide as Sarah was found 'not being of sound mind' (ibid.:11). Mary Stout, Sarah's mother, refused to accept the verdict and her subsequent actions in getting the case re-examined is similar to the contemporary crusades of the Lawrence and Zito families in refusing to accept the structural and institutional failures of the localised criminal justice system (Rock, 2004; Nash and Williams, 2008). Mary Stout had her daughter exhumed six weeks after her death, and a second post-mortem was performed, which, as Knights (2011:11) points out, was very unusual. A team of new doctors, supplementing the original two, performed the second autopsy, and they ruled out death by accident or suicide. The last person to see Sarah alive was Spencer Cowper, and he was arrested on 18th July and tried for her murder. Breaking down the complexities of the case, three identifiable micro-contextual themes emerge – *local factions*, *core questions*, and *scientific evidence and experts*.

As previously stated, whilst physical evidence is supposed to be objective and cannot perjure itself (Kirk, 1974:2), human analysis and interpretation of evidence is not. It is often influenced and determined by influences that commonly determine human behaviour – beliefs, prejudices, values, norms and group affiliations and pressures (Eysenck, 1998). The Cowper case is no exception. For instance, upon the discovery of Sarah's body, Mary Stout asked one of the town's doctors, John Dimsdale, to examine the body. Dr Dimsdale had been reluctant to undertake this task as he was part of a 'faction within the town who were bitter rivals of the Stouts and their local patrons, the Cowpers' (Knights, 2011:11). Dr Dimsdale's father, for example, was the town's mayor and was 'instrumental in orchestrating an attack on the political interests of both the Stouts and Cowpers' (ibid.:11). However, he bowed to pressure and with the help of Dr Camlin, physician to the Cowpers, examined Sarah Stout. The examination of the victim was undertaken to answer the primary question of a how Sarah died; however, it should also be seen as being part of a number of wider questions about fact, truth and knowledge.

When it comes to the second theme, and as we saw in Chapter 2, at the heart of the Enlightenment period were debates about what was fact and how facts could be verified (ibid.:14). For example, Comte ([1865]2009) had created a way to view how societies developed and changed the way they viewed how the natural world worked. At the centre of the philosophy of the Enlightenment was the attempt to find out how humans acquired knowledge, how it was possible to distinguish truth from error and what authorities and experts could be trusted (Knights, 2011:14). The search for truth and the problems of knowledge were specific areas of concern to the courtroom, and, by looking at the Cowper case, different ways of exploring and presenting evidence by the prosecution and defence can be identified. The core forensic questions within this case related to Sarah Stout's body and the autopsies performed, all of which fundamentally tried to establish the cause, mechanism and manner of death. At the heart of this was whether dead bodies sink or float; and the Cowper case is a seminal example of the interplay between new forms of knowledge and expertise and their acceptance and use in court.

Sarah's body was found floating, and it was noticed that there was froth around her mouth and nostrils and that there was 'a great settlement of blood' behind her left ear. Upon examining her body, Dr Dimsdale found swelling on the side of Sarah's neck, and she was black on both sides and between her breasts (ibid.:11). When Sarah's body was exhumed and examined by Dr Coatsworth and Dr Philips, they found her stomach and guts full of wind, and an examination of the uterus found it to be 'perfectly free and empty' (cited in Knights, 2011:12). Coatsworth and Philips then examined the stomach, breast and lungs and found they were all dry, noting how well preserved the internal organs were. All of the evidence pointed away from drowning: 'this women could not be drowned, for if she had taken in water, the water must have rotted all the Guts' (Knights, 2011:12). This was all confirmed by John Dimsdale senior, who also examined the body, as well as the coffin; all of which he found were dry.

The evidence collected from the two post-mortems involving the two teams of doctors eventually led all but one of them to agree that she had not been drowned. The only dissenting voice was Dr Camlin, who refused to change his original opinion of death by drowning. The scientific evidence came down to two issues: first, the fact that several witnesses testified to seeing her floating 'on or near the surface, and little water was seen to come from it when pulled from the river' (ibid.:17); second, the fact that there was no fermentation or destruction of the internal organs, all of which were intact and bone dry. As with many contemporary forensic cases, scientific experts often play an important role in presenting knowledge to help determine the truth. The Cowper case was unique for its time because it used a number of experts on both prosecution and defence sides. The prosecution put forward the medical evidence, with Dr Coatsworth testifying that if someone was alive and then jumped into a body of water, they would swallow a great deal of water, as 'everybody that is drowned is suffocated by waters passing down the Wind pipe into the Lungs' (ibid.:17). He was convinced, therefore, that a body that had been in the water for many hours would be full of water. Several more doctors confirmed the notion that a body without water in it 'was dead before it was put into the water' (ibid.:17). However, according to Knights (ibid.:17), the most interesting evidence came from sailor Edward Clement. Clement's experience included a number of battles where he had seen dead bodies thrown overboard, all of which floated. He testified that there was 'a certain Rule that those that are drowned sink, but those that are thrown overboard do not' (ibid.:18). The evidence presented by the prosecution was 'sensational'; however, Knights' historical reconstruction shows that the case for the defence was even more so (ibid.:18–34).

A central issue between the prosecution and defence in the Cowper case, and something which reverberates throughout today's criminal justice system, is whether science can offer 'a clear solution to the problem of establishing truth' (ibid.:18–19). In 1699, the doctors for the prosecution prepared to do battle against the best anatomist in Europe, William Cowper (no relation to Spencer) (ibid.:19). Cowper used Enlightenment (Baconian) experimentation and observation to produce rational explanations and verifiable facts. For instance, he conducted experiments by drowning three dogs to see how much water would enter the body. The results of these rather cruel experiments led Cowper to conclude that very little water 'had penetrated the lungs and that there was none at all in the stomach' (ibid.:19). Cowper used the experiments as evidence in court to suggest that the prosecution's case was wrong. Furthermore, he argued that a small amount of water mixing with air would be converted into froth and that it was the froth 'that blocked the windpipe and caused suffocation' (ibid.:19). As Knights argues:

> Cowper's testimony signalled the growing importance both of scientific experimentation–the method of establishing truth advocated by the

Royal Society and its followers–and of forensic evidence in criminal cases. At stake in the trial was the question of how truth could be determined and proven.

(2011:20)

The defence wanted to destroy the scientific conclusions of the prosecution so, to support William Cowper's findings, they brought other renowned doctors to confirm his findings. For example, Samuel Garth and Hans Sloane, who later became the founder of the British Museum (Fortey, 2008), both gave evidence on behalf of the defence.

The case of Sarah Stout and Spencer Cowper demonstrates the importance of the context of crime events and that evidence is constructed and interpreted within 'localised environments' (Jasanoff, 1997; Golan, 2007; Knights, 2011). The new scientific knowledge that was being used was developed within a structure that Raj notes as being based upon circulation and locality common to early modern science (2010:513–517). Raj notes how the development and movement of early modern scientific ideas and practices were infested with contingencies of place, which incorporated localised centres of knowledge which were circulated 'across large distances or across geographically close, but professionally distinct, communities, resulting in reconfigured knowledge forms or practices' (2010:515–516). The concept of circulation is important here. Markovits *et al.* (2003:1–22, cited in Raj, 2010:515) highlight the importance of circulation as something more than mere mobility, stressing that it 'implies an incremental aspect and not the simple reproduction across space of already formed structures and notions'. Instead of a centre-periphery model, then, we must consider that the development of knowledge within society, especially scientific knowledge, consists of mutations that are determined by interactions within specific localities. These 'interactions' are perhaps most crucial at the crossroads where scientific expert testimony meets the legal system.

Legal types of evidence

As Chapters 6–10 of this text discuss, evidence that is used in criminal investigations is subject to a number of filters that are built into criminal justice processes. The final filter is the rules of evidence, and these regulate and influence the submission, admissibility, and framing of the evidence that is presented in court, which includes forensic evidence. These rules have been carefully constructed, some over many years, through both legislation (also known as statute law) and common law decisions by judges (Bingham, 2011:42–46; Durston, 2008). As the burden of proof in criminal trials is on the prosecution, and *Ferguson v. The Queen [1979, 1 ALL ER 877]* reinforced the parameters of 'satisfied beyond all resonable doubt' (ibid.:128), evidence submitted must be used solely for the facts in hand. Obviously, during a case, many different forms of evidence can come into play in order to determine the facts. The main types of evidence used include (ibid.):

- character evidence;
- hearsay evidence;
- confession evidence;
- opinion evidence; and
- corroboration and identity evidence.

Forensic evidence cuts across the categories of hearsay, opinion and identity evidence. Interestingly, forensic evidence can be viewed as multiple hearsay evidence due to the fact that it is produced by an intermediary who has not directly observed the scene yet acts as a witness to the events (Durston, 2008:247–248). However, sections 114 to 136 of the Criminal Justice Act 2003 set out various conditions where such evidence can be admissible in criminal trials.

When it comes to opinion evidence, there is a general rule in criminal and civil litigation that witnesses must only speak to facts. Personal opinions – that is, any inferences drawn from the facts – are not usually permitted. Since the early 1700s, witnesses were discouraged from providing opinion and were encouraged 'to swear to nothing but what they have seen or heard' (Nelson, 1717, cited in Durston, 2008:469). However, as scientific and technological knowledge became increasingly important for deciding the facts of cases, an exception to this general rule soon appeared, which forms the basis of scientific expertise. Durston (2008:470) outlines the role that expert evidence plays in the broader area of opinion evidence:

> If scientific, technical, or specialized knowledge will assist the tribunal of fact to understand other evidence adduced in a case, or help it to determine facts in issue, a witness who is deemed by the court to be qualified as an expert may provide evidence in the form of an opinion, provided it is within his field of competence.

It must be acknowledged that just because evidence is scientific, technical or specialised, it does not always equate to valid knowledge. Unfortunately, problems can and do occur when it comes to this type of opinion evidence, and over the years there have been many cases where opinion evidence has been presented in court which is actually weak, or even false. For example, in the scandalous Cleveland sexual abuse debacle in 1987, 121 children were taken from 57 families due to a diagnosis by the paediatrician Marietta Higgs and social worker Judith Richardson (Thompson and Williams, 2014:189). Higgs used the Reflex Anal Dilation (RAD) test, which was 'accepted in courts as evidence of assault because they had been promoted in medical journals'; despite the fact that none of the signs of sexual assault (e.g. perihymenal erythema and scarring) had been scientifically verified. Indeed, Thompson and Williams argue that the RAD test findings 'merely reflected the consensus amongst a small group of self-appointed medical experts in the US' (ibid.:189). When proper controlled tests were finally undertaken, it was found that 'most turned out to be normal, common, anatomical variations in children's genitalia (McCann *et al.*, 1990a, 1990b). When RAD test results were combined with opinion evidence produced by experts in the now discredited disclosure therapy, courts blindly accepted the claims as evidence of the cycle of abuse (Thompson and Williams, 2014:189–190). This example, and many others like it, should act as a warning that scientific expert testimony can be open to a number of manipulations based upon the ideological beliefs and agenda of the experts themselves.

Scientific experts

The Cowper case also illustrates how scientific evidence can be heavily contested, especially when it comes into contact with the legal system, and how expert opinion is crucial for deciding the tribunal of fact. As scientific and technological ideas began to rapidly develop from the seventeenth century onwards, there was growing need for regulation, and the legal system had trouble keeping up with new forms of knowledge; especially when prosecution and defence advocates were able to provide contradictory expert testimony on issues of science and technological advancements (Jasanoff, 1997; Golan, 2007). The cultural divide that separates the institutions of law and science also compounded this situation. This section briefly examines some of these issues and discusses how scientific expert testimony developed.

The practice of using specialised information from 'skilled persons' in legal proceedings has been commonplace since the fourteenth century (ibid.:42). For example, an English judge in 1554 noted that "'if matters arise in our law which concern other sciences or faculties, we commonly apply for the aid of that science or faculty which it concerns'" (Golan, 2007:18). Despite early uses of experts, it wasn't until the nineteenth century that these skilled persons became fully recognised expert witnesses. UK and American courts saw the widespread use of expert witnesses, especially in matters relating to new forms of scientific knowledge and technological innovation (Jasanoff, 1997). In this period the law was a 'major patron' of science, and it fulfilled this function through numerous means that included: underwriting scientific progress; allowing a forum for expert testimony; providing a lucrative sideline in counselling; and influencing broader debates in standardisation, accuracy and reliability in scientific studies (ibid.; Golan, 2007). In essence, the legal system played, and still plays, a crucial role in legitimating expertise around notions of agency, causality, rights, responsibilities and blame (Jasanoff, 1997:xiv).

The coming of the expert

It is difficult to know for sure when the first expert witnesses were used, and numerous texts point to different origins. For instance, as we have already seen,

Knights (2011) points to the Cowper case in 1699 as clearly including expert witness testimony within an adversarial framework. The Cowper case represents a typical historical case relevant to forensic criminology for it involved the criminal act of murder and a dispute over the determination of the cause, mechanism and method of death. However, the majority of the early cases that used scientific expertise and helped develop the expert witness were not criminal in nature. The majority involved products liability, nuisance litigation, patents, medical malpractice and environmental litigation (Jasanoff, 1997:26–39; Golan, 2007:52–106); all of which signified the fast-changing nature of scientific and technological innovations as capitalism and urbanisation took hold in many Western countries. These developments, as Golan argues, 'introduced, sometimes within days and weeks of their discovery or invention, novel forms of knowledge claims into courts' (2007:2). Thus, Jasanoff (1997) and Golan (2007) consider *Folkes v. Chadd (1782)* as the starting point for the 'rise of expert testimony in the modern Anglo-American legal system' (Golan, 2007:5). Also known as the *Wells Harbour case*, this case primarily concerned finding what had caused the decay of the Norfolk harbour, and involved numerous trials and 'men of science' which pitted the emerging Newtonian Philosophers against men of experience and of the law (ibid.:7). This case has been expertly examined and reviewed by Golan (ibid.:6–51), so there is no need to replicate it here. However, it is important to highlight some of its relevant issues. The first point is that both the plaintiff and defendant hired several highly regarded scientists such as Robert Mylne and John Smeaton to provide expert testimony for their respective sides. This caused some very heated discussions around the scientific credibility of the observations made by both sets of experts, most of which appeared to centre on the differences between the Newtonian philosopher's understanding of natural laws (i.e. an inductive approach to understanding nature) and the practitioners' method of observations *in situ* and the application of deductive forms of reasoning. This mirrored the clear cultural divide between law and science, as epitomised by Chief Justice Gould's strict adherence to the approach of law:

> His logic, the logic of Common Law, was Baconian. It disdained abstract explanations, suspected elegantly constructed theories, and stressed the necessity for direct observational data in processes of proof. Hypotheses were but preliminary means of directing further observation and measurements.
>
> (Ibid.:39)

This was contrary to the position laid out by Lord Mansfield in the first trial, which set the principal precedent of calling experts as *partisan witnesses* and, for a further two centuries, maintained that the law should not favour one science over another, and should use all kinds of science in legal proceedings (ibid.:6–7). Gould, on the other hand, maintained that the 'law should exclude from the courtroom certain expert opinions for not being scientific enough' (ibid.:49).

Another important issue that was brought to the fore in the Wells Harbour case was the fact that the expert witnesses had exclusive privilege to pronounce an opinion regardless of whether they had 'observed the facts of the case directly or not', which highlighted that there existed, by the end of the eighteenth century, 'a class of persons, i.e., those skilled in matters of science, who, though they personally knew nothing about the circumstances of the case' were able to provide an expert opinion on it (ibid.:43). For the first time, inductive reasoning, using Newtonian philosophers' application of natural laws, was utilised in legal proceedings to provide evidence of the unknown short- and long-term effects of the new technologies being used across the recently modernised Western world. This, coupled with the adversarial environment in which such evidence was framed, created disagreement, conflict and sometimes hostility between scientific experts and became one of the most striking problems for nineteenth-century science and their attempts to gain the status of 'professional men' (Jasanoff, 1997; Golan, 2007). This can be illustrated by looking at numerous cases of the period, some of which included: *Severn, King and Co. v. Imperial Insurance Company (1820)*, which concerned a dispute over the cause of a fire at a sugar factory and the refusal of the insurance company to pay for repairs because the sugar refining process used was a 'new' technology – the effects of which, the insurance company argued, were to blame for the fire (Golan, 2007:54–70); *The Great Copper Trial, 1833*, which was a nuisance litigation issued towards John Henry Vivian's Hafod copper works, and its destruction of the local environment because of its smelting procedures and the toxic 'smog' these procedures created (71–76); and *Regina v. Spence*, another piece of environmental nuisance litigation concerning the production of alum and the discharge of sulfurous acid gas and sulfurated hydrogen gas into the local environment, which was the first legal attempt to prosecute the chemical industry (76–80). In each of these examples, as well as numerous patent litigation cases involving new production technologies, the adversarial nature of criminal and civil litigation brought many different scientific experts to court, which led to numerous problems that affected the status of both science and the scientific expert.

The problems with expert witnesses

The adversarial format of justice creates conditions where experts are pitted against each other, not necessarily in the search for truth, but for the advancement of a position that is bought and paid for by the side that has acquired their expertise. Unfortunately, the buying and selling of scientific expertise on the free market has also created numerous problems, many of which were identified and debated through the cases mentioned above (Jasanoff, 1997; Golan, 2007). The most immediate problem, which started in the nineteenth century and has continued into the present day, is the issue with conflicting theories and experimental results. New scientific ideas, procedures and technologies often produce differences in opinion regarding their short- and long-term effects, risks to the public and environment as well as alternative theories and experimental results. For the most part, these differences rarely become public knowledge and stay within the confines of academic institutions and journals, which are hardly read outside the specialism of the academic discipline (see Harris, 1999; Abbott, 2001). This is a necessary and healthy part of science and the robust development of its epistemological and ontological foundations. Theories are proposed; hypotheses developed to verify and falsify; theories are reconfigured as new/more data becomes available; and all this is peer assessed and debated in books, journals and at conferences. However, when science is used in legal proceedings, the adversarial framework exploits these divisions as scientific testimony is manipulated as a *tool* by prosecution and defence barristers, who isolate the experts in the witness box and attack their research methodologies and findings. They also attempt to attack their credibility by pitching expert against expert. In many cases in the nineteenth and twentieth centuries, experts became quasi-advocates for either the defence or prosecution councils, each arguing their scientific vantage point, which had the effect of actually confusing juries and presenting contradictory evidence on experimental results connected to the cases they were testifying in (Golan, 2007). The outcome was not only a widespread distrust of science, but also the creation of *partisan advocacy*, which further destroyed the belief in the objective status of science, as it was perceived that scientific expertise was for sale; a situation which was further exacerbated when scientific experts publicly attacked each other's evidence in the witness box (Jasanoff, 1997; Golan, 2007). Partisan advocacy opened up a number of further issues that directly affected the status of scientific expertise and its use in court.

The first problem is what Jasanoff (1997:45–47) calls the *commodification of the expert*. As more and more legal cases relied on technical evidence, lawyers began to pay for any expert testimony that 'presented as the truth or the best approximation to it', as long as the testimony helped their client (ibid.:45). In the twentieth and twenty-first centuries, the price of such expertise skyrocketed with some experts earning over £200,000 for an individual case, although it should be highlighted that many charged modest fees and some even work *pro bono*. Despite this, the high cost of expertise illustrates not only the 'commercial calculations that govern the use of expertise in the legal system' (ibid.:46) but also that such experts were out of reach of the poorer members of society, leading to vast inequalities in the balance of justice. Whilst Jasanoff rightly highlights the commodification of expertise as an important contemporary issue, Golan's work acknowledges that this was not always the case. He notes that in the second round of *Severn, King and Co. v. Phoenix Insurance*, the jury again found in favour of the plaintiffs, and the insurance company was required to pay all costs. However, at the time, it was not clear 'what legal basis there was for the compensation of men of science' (Golan, 2007:68); which enabled the insurance company to deny compensation to those scientists involved for the experiments conducted, as they were not a recognised group of professional men. This opened up an interesting debate about the legal status of 'men of science', with Judge

Dallas arguing that scientists were simply 'men of skill' who 'derived their expertise from their own private experience and were not entitled to be compensated for loss of time' (ibid.:70). Today, this situation has rightly changed, with proper recompense for expenses and time provided to experts by the criminal justice system. However, the fact that more wealthy clients can *purchase* better expertise attests to the inequalities that are inherent in Western criminal justice systems, as was seen in the O. J. Simpson case in 1995 (Jasanoff, 1997:44–46; Golan, 2007:3). Furthermore, the fact that, when it comes to access to forensic science expertise, the die are loaded towards prosecutorial propositions exacerbates even further the injustice in justice.

A second issue raised by both Jasanoff (1997) and Golan (2007) is the *pressure of advocacy*. As previously stated, the legal system shares with science the 'search for truth'. However, as anyone who has practiced criminal law and civil litigation will know, the 'rules and devices of adversary litigation as we conduct it are not geared for, but are often aptly suited to defeat, the development of the truth' and that 'truth and victory are mutually incompatible for some considerable percentage of attorneys trying cases at any given time' (Frankel, 1975:1036–1038, cited in Jasanoff, 1997:47). Logically it makes sense that, when it comes to criminal trials, the adversarial framework is designed to permit parties to conceal the truth from the court, especially when defence barristers know their client is guilty, and thus engage in strategies that 'subverts and distorts truth for the sake of winning' (ibid.:48). In this respect, there is a real temptation for what Meier calls 'aggrandisement' (1986:273, cited in Jasanoff, 1997:48), where experts downplay other contradictory scientific knowledge and exaggerate their own position or scientific paradigm.

The third problem is the *reluctant expert*: many scientists 'are often unwilling to play the expert witness game' (Jasanoff, 1997:49). Legal strategies often go against the objective impartial observer ideology that most scientists adhere to, which is further compounded by legal argumentation. Not all scientists wish to make the strong decisions about scientific findings that is demanded by the court, as any expert worth their salt will understand the uncertainty in all scientific data and should provide a guarded answer as to the probative strength of the evidence. Indeed, some barristers suppress 'inconvenient or inconsistent observations' in scientific evidence, which 'presents an insurmountable ethical obstacle' for scientists (Jasanoff, 1997:49). A further deterrent to providing expert evidence is the very strong belief that public disagreement with peers and colleagues 'brings discredit on one's discipline' (ibid.:49). The types of quarrelling that take place with adversarial legal entanglements can create a large amount of negative publicity for the scientists' fields, increasing the pressure on the experts and making them more and more reluctant to become witnesses.

The final problem is *science made for courts*. Scientific experts are often called upon by the legal establishment to discuss new forms of scientific knowledge and techniques; and are sometimes asked to make decisions 'before the scientific community has generated data reliably confirming or failing to confirm a particular causal claim' (ibid.:50). There exists, therefore, a time lapse between the law's need for scientific knowledge and science's ability to produce such knowledge, and, because of this, there is a growing legal influence on the production of new scientific knowledge and techniques. For example, some forms of early DNA typing evidence compiled by private laboratories and used in criminal cases was later seen as unacceptable and indefensible (ibid.:51).

Scientific reasoning in court

Many of the problems associated with expert evidence discussed above can be circumvented, or at least minimised, through the strategies used by scientists to describe their findings in court. These strategies include expressions, Bayesian theorem and probabilities, and this section briefly reviews these areas of scientific reasoning.

Opinion expressions

Forensic scientists use a wide range of words and expressions to convey their results to investigators, courts and other pertinent groups. In their review of 100 case files, Satterthwaite and Lambert (1989) found 33 different expressions used to convey evidential the strength of the items examined. It is important to note that no real consensus exists as to the *real* evidential strength of each expression, meaning that there could exist different probative values for the same expression (Anderson *et al.*, 2005; Jackson, 2009). Because of this, the courts and juries can often get confused as to the meaning of the scientific findings but also the weight of that evidence vis-à-vis the tribunal of fact. Thus, it is important to not only know the core expressions used by forensic scientists but also to understand what that opinion means and how the scientist arrived at such an opinion (Jackson, 2009). The core expressions used by scientists when expressing their opinion evidence in court include those shown in Figure 11.1

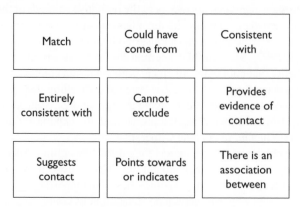

Figure 11.1 Opinion expressions of forensic scientists

Source: adapted from Jackson (2009:420–428).

Perhaps the most commonly used term is *match*, and this is used to denote when two sets of observations and/or measurements correspond (ibid.:421–422). As previously discussed, a great deal of material found at crime scenes is in its partial or microscopic form, particles of which are transferred between crime scene, victim and the offender. In order to provide the necessary links between these three elements, scientists take questioned and reference samples from these three factors and try to match them. However, it is not always that simple. Matching often involves the comparison of a set of elements such as shapes, colours, spatial patterns and complex numbers, and, whilst there might be a good degree of correspondence between the factors intrinsic to the known and unknown material, there may also be some degree of difference, which can be either quantitative or qualitative. The experience and knowledge of the analyst, as well as the level of case information provided by investigators, will largely determine how this difference is interpreted (Saferstein, 2007; Jackson, 2009; Jackson and Jackson, 2011). However, it is important to avoid confusion over the term 'match' as two matching samples may be interpreted as sharing the same *origin* (i.e. from the same source), yet the scientist may only wish to convey to the courts and jury that the samples share the same attributes (i.e. they are the same material/item but not from the same source).

The term *could have come from* appears to be an obvious and uncomplicated phrase. If a match is declared between a questioned and reference sample, the obvious inference one could make is that the questioned sample could have come from the same source as the reference sample (Jackson, 2009:422–423). It should be noted that the comparison process might have highlighted both similarities and differences between both samples. Therefore, an assessment of the factors affecting similarity and difference between the sample attributes may enable the forensic scientist or police analyst to form the 'could have come from' opinion. However, this type of opinion is an inductive inference and is created using the relevant quantitative data on the prevalence and spread of attributes of the material under analysis; which is then turned into probability score, for example, by providing a likelihood ratio (Aitken and Taroni, 2004; Redmayne, 2004; Lucy, 2005; Adam, 2010; Faigman *et al.*, 2012). Unfortunately, this can lead to one of the biggest problems with expressions such as 'could have come from', as there is often a lack of assessment of the evidential base and value of the evidence. This can lead to the phrase being applied to materials that are both common and rare, which can cause uncertainty amongst the court and jury members. In order to combat such confusion, it has been suggested that more qualification is required in order that the true evidential worth can be properly and clearly communicated (Jackson, 2009).

The third phrase, *consistent with*, is akin to the previous phrase but requires the expert to base their analysis and findings on more knowledge than would be required to simply say 'could have come from'. For example, if a forensic scientist observes a small amount of blood spatter on a suspect's trousers, they may express the opinion 'the findings are consistent with the wearer of the trousers having hit the victim repeatedly with the iron bar found at the scene' (ibid.:423). As with the previous phrase, there is little or no assessment of the evidential weight of the observations. One way around this is to add the qualifying word *entirely*. This subtle nuance is an attempt to lend more weight or the perception of a greater probability to the conjecture 'consistent with'. *Cannot exclude* is another common phrase used, and denotes when the forensic scientist or police analyst observes that the results have not eliminated an investigation hypothesis or proposition that a questioned sample originates from a particular source linking offender, victim and crime scene (ibid.:424).

The terms *provides evidence of contact* and *suggests contact* attempt to give some evidential weight to Locard's principle of exchange. However, and as previously discussed, contact could mean a number of things. For example, consider the following potential areas of contact in the scenario of a burglary by means of breaking and entering through a window (taken from Jackson, 2009:424–425):

- contact with fragments of glass as they showered the person breaking the window (i.e. blowback);
- contact with fragments of glass as they showered over people in the vicinity of the breaking window;
- contact with broken glass as a person walked through the fragments on the floor;
- contact with broken edges of the window as a person climbed through; and
- contact through lifting property that was covered in fragments from the broken window.

All of these (and possibly more) movements suggest contact. However, there is little scientific research that examiners can call upon to use for comparison with the evidence under examination (Saks and Koehler, 2007, 2008). Finally, the expressions *points towards or indicates* and *there is an association between* are phrases that are often used and are open to a wide interpretation. They can convey a very close relationship between two samples, but this could mean that they either share the same origin or they have been touching. Alternatively, the terms could also mean that the two samples analysed were from the same large production batch or that they have been in the same vicinity at the same time at some point in the past (Jackson, 2009:425–426).

These expressions, and many more (see Jackson, 2009:426–428), whilst seemingly innocuous ways to communicate an expert's opinion, can be innocently delivered by scientists or manipulated by barristers within the adversarial framework, thereby creating the illusion that the evidence is a lot stronger than it actually is. This can have a profound effect on how the jury perceives the physical evidence that is presented to it and, ultimately, determines the outcome of the trial. Because of the 'perceived status' of scientific experts, they can play an essential and sometimes decisive role in settling issues in both criminal and civil litigation. The downside to this is that such evidence could 'be used to bolster or to legitimize a preconceived conviction based on non-scientific evidence . . .

[and] may serve to lend an aura of scientific respectability to the legal decision-making process' (Broeders, 2009:90). To try to minimise this, the expressions used by forensic scientists are usually accompanied by some form of statistical calculation, which should provide the probative weight regarding the tribunal of fact under consideration.

Bayesian theorem and probabilities

Bayes' theorem is widely regarded as a robust and logical means of inductive reasoning and is rapidly becoming the most commonly used method in the forensic sciences (Aitken and Taroni, 2004; Redmayne, 2004; Lucy, 2005; Adam, 2010; Faigman *et al.*, 2012). It uses conditional probability, which measures the probability of an event given that another event has occurred, and provides a way in which new evidence can be incorporated into the forensic scientist's construction of a final opinion. In essence, conditional probability is an update of the probability of an event based on new information, which is why it can be useful to scientists and analysts who are working with the police during an investigation, which, as we have seen, is a fluid and dynamic process where new information is identified during the natural course of an investigation (see Chapters 7 and 9 of this text; also see Innes, 2003; Lucy, 2005; Adam, 2010). By new information I mean observations made and evidence collected at the crime scene; new information collected through the course of police enquiries; as well as the results of scientific tests undertaken on the material received. This flexibility is extremely useful for forensic scientists because Bayes' theorem allows for conditional probabilities to be incorporated, which enables the modification of probabilistic events. The probability of an uncertain event taking place can therefore be constantly updated as new information is added. To this end, forensic scientists tend to use Bayes' theorem as the first framework to categorise opinions as either *investigative* or *evaluative*.

Physical evidence is basically the observations made by the forensic scientist or police analyst during the course of their examination of case material. There is a range of factors that can influence these observations, some of which include: the shape, size and condition of items from the suspect, victim and crime scene; the presence of extraneous material on the items; the shape, size and condition of this extraneous material; results of any analyses of the materials; and any other observations within the scientist's domain of expertise. Furthermore, these factors also determine what weight the scientist or analyst can assign to the evidence. What we are effectively dealing with is the probability of events occurring during the commission of a crime, which produces the combinations of materials found at the scene, on the victim and offender. These events are therefore rephrased as observations made by the scientist or analyst, so it is important to have a good understanding of probability. Table 11.2 outlines some of the more important Bayesian probabilities that are used to communicate findings to the courts and juries.

Table 11.2 Forensic probabilities

Key:
E = observations
H = uncertain event that is being investigated
Pr = probability of
I = background information

Prior Probability	The prior probability of a proposition (H) given some background information (I) but before any scientific evidence (E) is presented	Written as a the probability equation Pr[H/I]
Explanations	Explanations put forward after the scientific evidence (E) has been acquired and given some conditioning background information (I)	Written as H1..n|E,I
Likelihood	The probability of obtaining the scientific evidence (E) given that a proposition (H) is true, and given some background information (I)	Written as Pr[E|H, I]
Likelihood Ratios (perhaps the most important for Bayes' theorem and forensic science opinion forming)	This is the ratio of probability of the scientific evidence (E) given that a prosecution proposition (Hp) were true; and the probability of the evidence given its complementary, alternative (defence) proposition (Hd) were true; and given some background information (I)	Written as Pr[E|Hp,I]/ Pr[E|Hd,I]
Posterior Probability	The probability of a proposition (H) given some background information (I) and given some scientific evidence (E)	Written as Pr[H|E, I]

Source: adapted from Aitken and Taroni (2004), Lucy (2005) and Adam (2010).

As Cook *et al.* (1998a:154–156) highlight, forensic scientists usually report numerical likelihood ratios (LR), the exception being DNA cases. However, numerical values can still be confusing, especially when mathematical terms such as 'to the *Nth* power' are introduced. In order to communicate the scientists' opinion regarding the weight of evidence to a lay jury, experts use verbal qualifiers that 'are loosely equivalent to a numerical LR scale' (ibid.:155). Such qualifiers include:

* moderate support for defence proposition;
* moderate support for prosecution proposition;
* weak support for prosecution proposition;
* weak support for defence proposition;
* strong support for prosecution proposition; and
* strong support for defence proposition.

Of course, these verbal qualifiers will depend on the available background episte-mological knowledge of the material under consideration; and, as Saks and Koehler (2007, 2008) suggest, the empirical evidence in much of the forensic identification sciences does not validate many of the strengths associated to that material, and this is communicated in court. Table 11.3 outlines a number of hypo-thetical cross-examination exchanges that can take place with forensic experts.

Despite these linguistic *sleights of hand*, it is fundamental to the interests of justice that the forensic scientist must reach an agreement with the police, prosecution, defence and the court regarding their opinions and propositions.

Table 11.3 Verbal responses in court

Question	Answer	Translation
Is this situation unusual?	I have never seen a similar instance.	You don't know what I have seen and what I haven't, so I can say this and get away with it.
What is the basis of your opinion?	My 26 years of experience in the field.	It's really a surmise on my part. I believe it to be true, but I can't really tell you why I think that. It's really more of an impression that I have than anything else but I can't say that it's a surmise or a vague impression.
Can you tell us how many cases of this type you have examined	Many hundreds.	I don't know, and I certainly don't know how many of them would support my current position, and I might not be able to tell even if I went back and pulled the files.
Can you supply us with a list of all cases?	Oh no, I don't think so. They go back many years.	No way. You don't have any way of smoking those cases out of me, and even if I was ordered to do so, I could come up with plenty of reasons not to comply.
Can you supply us with the raw data on all those cases?	I don't think so. Some of them were when I was in my previous job. And some might be on microfilm. And it would take weeks or months to locate all of them.	Not a chance.
Were those cases subjected to independent scrutiny for technical correctness?	All of them were reviewed by my supervisors. I don't have any reason to believe that their review wasn't adequate.	No. And also, now you're going to have to argue with those nameless, faceless supervisors that I have alluded to but haven't identified.

Source: Faigman *et al.*, 2010:45–46).

This is achieved by framing their probabilities in terms of a hierarchy of issues and propositions.

Hierarchy of issues and propositions

As the analysis of physical evidence by scientists and police analysts is framed by the case details and requirements of the lead investigating officer, it is important that evidence presented in court links to the relevant tribunal of fact. Scientists often use two concepts to frame both their analysis but also the presentation of facts in court. The first is called the *hierarchy of issues* (HOI) which are identified from the crime scene, witness, victim reports and so forth (Jackson, 2009:434–444). HOI is the precursor to the *hierarchy of propositions* (HOP) (ibid.:434–442), which is discussed in greater detail below.

Once a crime has been reported, discovered or detected, it is necessary to set out the issues pertinent to case, and these issues usually take four main forms – *sub-source*, *source*, *activity*, and *offence*. In order to illustrate these issues, consider the scenario of a female who alleges that a suspect in custody raped her, ejaculated inside her vagina and did not use a condom (adapted from Jackson, 2009). In conjunction with the investigating officer, the scientist must identify the following HOIs. First, is the identification of *sub-source* issues, which have been made possible due to advances in techniques such as DNA typing (Jackson and Jackson, 2011). In this hypothetical case, the obvious sub-source issues would be the generation of DNA profiles and a linked identification to both the alleged victim and suspect. The issues would therefore be framed as the following questions: Is the DNA from the suspect? Is the DNA from the alleged victim? Sub-source issues are related to *source* issues, which is the next level. The source issues in this example would be whether the semen is from the suspect and whether the vaginal cells are from the alleged victim. In this specific case, the sub-source issues answer the source issues. The third level relates to the activities that are alleged to have taken place during the crime. These are much easier to present to juries, as lay individuals understand these more than sub-issues, which tend to consist of a great deal of technical jargon. In the suspected rape example, the *activity* issue is whether the suspect had intercourse with the victim. However, in certain circumstances this could open up the issue of consent. This is where other contextual information needs to be considered. For example, if the suspect was a stranger, and broke into the victim's home, and then the evidence already stated could be combined with other evidence, such as broken glass (i.e. entry point), or footwear impression (i.e. did he enter through a garden window), it is likely that the victim did not consent. However, if the suspect is known to the victim, and met her for sex in a hotel room, consent becomes an issue; and this can be determined not just by the physical evidence, but other facts such as witnesses and pre-offence behavioural interactions between the suspect and victim. Finally, the offence issue deals with whether the suspect is the rapist, the answer of which is derived from answering the previous levels (Jackson, 2009).

It is important to acknowledge that, whilst the investigator will want the forensic scientist to develop HOIs that fit with his or her investigation, thereby following the prosecution propositions, if the forensic scientist or police analyst is to be truly objective, they should also form a second set of opinions that follow a defence hierarchy of issues. The reason for this is that HOIs must be converted into pairs of competing propositions that follow the prosecution and defence cases that are presented in court. However, it should be noted that pre-trial disclosure of evidence between both parties could result in HOIs being conceded and agreed upon as facts, so the issues and propositions do not even get to court (Durston, 2008:54–56).

As with HOIs, the *hierarchy of propositions* (HOP) addresses the same issues (i.e. sub-source, source, activity and offence). If the Bayesian framework is robustly and logically constructed on the basis of the evidence collected as part of the investigation, it can help determine what knowledge and understanding is required to answer the prosecution and defence propositions. To allow forensic scientists to give opinions that are robust and reliable, they use probabilities that are set against the propositions. However, it should be noted that reliable probabilities require reliable datasets that accurately reflect the incidence of particular events in an appropriate population (Aitken and Taroni, 2004; Redmayne, 2004; Lucy, 2005; Adam, 2010; Faigman *et al.*, 2012). In the hypothetical rape case discussed above, the reliable datasets in question would be biometric, genetic and demographic datasets (Jackson, 2009). Thus, for the alleged rape example the following LRs can be determined:

- **Activity:**
  Hp – The suspect did the activity in question – the suspect had sexual intercourse with the woman.
  Hd – The suspect did not do the activity – the suspect did not have intercourse with the woman.
- **Source:**
  Hp – The questioned sample (E) came from this source – the semen (E) came from the suspect.
  Hd – The questioned sample (E) came from some other source – the semen (E) came from some other person (unrelated to the suspect).
- **Sub-source:**
  Hp – The test result (E) came from this source – the DNA profile (E) came from the suspect.
  Hd – The test result (E) came from some other source – the DNA profile (E) came from some other person (unrelated to the suspect).

Once this is done, all that is left is to present the *opinion* to the court. However, generating explanations is a very open-ended and creative process, and experienced examiners will have better knowledge of possible explanations than inexperienced examiners. However, there are some potential problems with this claim. Experience is useful when accompanied by 'good mental cataloguing and recall of experiences' (Jackson, 2009: 438; Gross, 1962;). But there is still the potential of observer bias that may create *tunnel vision* in seeing only those things that explain preconceived ideas: the 'generation of propositions and alternatives is driven by an understanding of the key issues in the case, based on the requirements of the police, prosecution, defence and the courts' (Jackson, 2009:438). So the probabilities of the scientific evidence given the truth of each of these propositions will be informed by:

- what the scientist knows and understands about finding evidence;
- the truth of different suggestions; and
- whatever relevant data are available.

More generally, the hierarchy of issues and propositions provides structure that directs the scientist to the appropriate data and knowledge, which is then presented in court to try to aid the tribunal of fact.

Summary and future directions

This final chapter provided a snapshot of some of the core issues related to the presentation of evidence in court. The law acts as a form of gatekeeper to forensic evidence, both regulating but also aiding in its construction through cases. It defines and sets the boundaries as to what is legally acceptable and can be used to resolve criminal justice problems. Legal rules of evidence and its submission have developed over hundreds of years and as a result of statute law and common law decisions given by judges. Since the 1400s the law has recognised the need for specialists to provide help in matters of fact that deal with scientific and technological forms of knowledge. However, it wasn't until the late eighteenth century that legal cases regarding the nature and extent of expert testimony began to debate these issues in any meaningful detail. Unfortunately, the initial result of the debates in cases such as *Folkes v. Chadd (1782)* was to negate much of the optimism and belief in scientific knowledge that had developed since the Enlightenment. Case after case in the nineteenth century created the perception of scientific experts being *guns for hire*, which belied the objective, factual nature of science. The adversarial system turned scientist against scientist, attacking each other's theories, claims and evidence in open court, which was reported to the outside world. This led to a great deal of distrust in scientific evidence and created a plethora of problems with expert testimony. Golan (2007) highlights that some commentators defined this situation in entirely negative terms, claiming that the reputation of science would be destroyed by the adversarial conditions of criminal trials. However, whilst this was true to a certain degree (see Morris, 2007), Golan rightly notes that a healthy science is one that is debated and critically evaluated through peer assessment of research methodologies, data analysis and research findings. What many saw as the destruction of scientific knowledge was actually a healthy and fully functioning science operating Popper's (2002) falsification model.

Perhaps one of the most important aspects of scientific evidence presented in contemporary courtrooms is that of probative weight. The strength that a particular piece of physical evidence has in relation to not only the overall case but how it links the offender, victim and crime scene, is a crucial question that can create confusion and miscarriages of justice. Harris (2012) notes that the status and mysticism surrounding forensic science in the twenty-first century creates the circumstances in which evidence is given much stronger weight by experts than the known empirical data allows for. Over the last 100 years or so, this has caused numerous miscarriages of justice because the courts and juries have been blinded by science and technical jargon. Scientists, however, have moved towards resolving some of these issues by introducing Bayesian theorem and probabilities as a means to provide a better indication as to the appropriate strength that should be given to specific forms of evidence. These probabilities have been framed within the development of hierarchies of issues and propositions that allow scientists to frame their results in terms of the relevant case details from both the prosecution and defence points of view. Unfortunately, there has been little research undertaken as to the extent that scientists, who are usually commissioned by the police, objectively assess both prosecution and defence propositions. This point leads me to finish this text by briefly considering some future directions that forensic criminology could take in developing a sub-field within the academic disciplines of criminology and criminal justice.

The area of forensic criminology is fertile for future research and development, despite the fact that investment in forensics has become a casualty of the Government's austerity measures. By placing forensics within a social science framework, Fradella et al.'s (2007) vision of broadening the criminological and sociological understanding of forensic science and its application to resolving criminal justice problems has come to fruition. However, more could and needs to be done. It is certain that the addition of forensics to academic courses such as criminal justice and criminology has further enriched the subject by breaking the myopic, paradigmatic stranglehold that sociological and psychological explanations have had on criminology since the 1920s; which can only be a good thing. Whilst most forensic science textbooks provide current undergraduate and postgraduate students and interested parties with comprehensive overviews of the core forensic science techniques and how they can be applied in the fight against crime, what is lacking is both a critical review of these procedures as well as a sociological understanding of their effects on the criminal justice system and society in general. Future research could be directed in any one of the following areas:

- As Saks and Koehler (2007, 2008) argue, urgent research is required on empirically validating many of the techniques used in the forensic identification sciences. Whilst research in this area has improved since the publication of their articles, more work needs to be undertaken to develop datasets on fingermarks and fingerprints, footwear and tool-mark impressions, blood spatter analysis and hair and fibres. Such research could then be used to strengthen current probabilities and error rates, which, as we have seen, are crucial for assigning probative weight.

- One fruitful area of research could be a sociological analysis of the construction and interpretation of physical evidence from crime scene to the courtroom, building on Innes' (2003) and Fielding's (2006) work.
- Further research could be conducted on the interactions between the law and science, building on the work of Jasanoff (1997) and Golan (2007) but specifically directed towards the construction of forensic science evidence and its presentation in court.
- A greater understanding of the psychology of expert evidence within the adversarial system and its effects on juries could also help towards understanding miscarriages of justice.

With the resources of the Conservative-dominated coalition government being as they are, the possibility of this type of research being undertaken lies primarily within the university system. The potential for universities to engage with local criminal justice agencies such as the police and scientific support departments is unlimited, and this has started to happen in recent years. The area of forensic criminology is ripe with research potential, and, with universities and criminal justice agencies collaborating together, we may see a return to the good old days when universities engaged in the advancement of ideas and not just the creation of future bricks in the wall.

Notes

Chapter 1 Introduction

1 This list is not exclusive, as there are many reasons why social scientists face difficulties when trying to develop a forensic thread to educational programmes.

2 However, I will return to this theme in Chapters 6, 7, 9, 10 and 11, for knowledge degradation relates to the viability of a core type of evidence used in criminal investigations – the witness, suspect and victim statements.

3 Roughly translated, *Kriminalistik* actually means 'criminology'.

4 Whilst I am an advocate of the destruction of academic silos, I also appreciate that science and academia operate in the 'real world', with social, cultural and political constraints as well as economic and budgetary restrictions that ultimately affect the knowledge that is produced.

5 Unfortunately, this author's 16-year experience of researching and teaching in an academic environment has confirmed that academics rarely move out of their self-imposed and often very narrow 'comfort zones'.

6 For the full list of training courses provided by the NPIA see *Professional Development Guide 2009/10: People & Development* – available online at www.npia.police.uk/en/docs/Professional_Development_Guide.pdf.

7 For a greater understanding of the types of offences that are committed in prisons, which are mostly examined using the term 'adjudications', please refer to HM Inspectorate of Prisons' *Inspection Reports*. These can be found at www.justice.gov.uk/publications/inspectorate-reports/hmi-prisons/prison-and-yoi.

8 The QAA benchmarks for criminology consist of: (i) a set of defining principles; (ii) the nature and extent of criminology – for example, 'to develop and enhance its methodological and technical expertise' (QAA, 2007:3); (iii) subject knowledge and understanding; (iv) subject-specific and other skill sets; and, finally, (v) benchmarks on teaching, learning and assessment. For a full list and description of criminology benchmarks for higher education programmes, see QAA (2007).

9 Many higher education academics will recognise this problem, which is largely an outcome of this authors' feedback when asking students to read a broader range of eclectic academic sources.

10 This includes the advancement of knowledge and science only if it can be patented and turned into an economically viable commodity. For an interesting take on this aspect of society, see Laughlin's (2008) thesis on the criminalisation of knowledge.

11 This is the Higher Education Funding Council for England.

12 In the UK the funding of higher education tends to come from four key sources: (i) student loans; (ii) a student's Local Education Authority; (iii) HEFCE; and (iv) privately or from family funds. At the time of writing, HEFCE funding received

by universities was equivalent to around £5,000 per student. With HEFCE funding practically being taken away, universities have had to find alternative funds; hence the increase in fees.

13 Available online at www.independent.co.uk/news/education/education-news/50-universities-to-charge-9000-2270359.html (accessed 11th January 2013).

Chapter 2 Constructed knowledge and the philosophy of science

1 Currently Offender Group Reconviction Scale Version 3, or OGRS3 for short.

2 Burke defines the early modern period 'as the centuries from Gutenberg to Diderot . . . from the invention of printing with movable type in Germany around the year 1450 to the publication of the Encyclopedie from the 1750s onwards' (2008:11).

3 SPSS is Statistical Package for the Social Sciences (ironical given psychology's recent wholesale move over to *science* faculties in universities).

4 The atomic number is determined by the number of positively charged protons in the nucleus of every atom of that element. This determines the chemical properties of an element.

5 Shutterstock (2014) *Color Periodic Table of the Elements* by laschi. Available online at: www.shutterstock.com/cat.mhtml?lang=en&search_source=search_form&version =llv1&anyorall=all&safesearch=1&searchterm=periodic+table#id=120549517&src= 6pN1tUiBf-bzfaoL9Gg2AQ-1-17 (accessed 4th February 2014).

6 Heraclitus of Ephesus was a pre-Socratic Greek philosopher who believed in ever-present strife and change within the universe. He also believed in the *unity of opposites* and that all entities that exist are characterised by contrary properties.

7 *Novum organum scientiarum* translates as 'new instrument of science' and was a reference to Aristotle's work *Organon*.

8 Taxonomy can be defined as the science, laws or principles of classification. It deals with classifying *things* into established categories according to their observed similarities. As Fortey argues, 'a unit of classification is a taxon (the plural is taxa), and that is why the business of naming them is taxonomy' (2008:48).

9 The *corolla* is the petals of a flower that form an inner floral envelope.

10 The *calyx* is the sepals of a flower that form the outer floral envelope that protects the developing flower bud.

11 Kepler's first law stipulates that the orbits of planets take the form of elliptical curves (Synder, 2006:51–52).

12 Taken from CERN's Convention; a mission statement that was laid down in 1954. Available online at http://public.web.cern.ch/public/en/About/Mission-en.html (accessed 11th January 2013).

Chapter 3 The beginnings of scientific criminology

1 For a more in-depth analysis of these issues in the USA, see Boyer (1992) and Morone (2003); the UK collections by Rowbotham and Stevenson (2003, 2005) provide a useful broad sociological context of the same issues.

2 This is also a crucial point for understanding the development and practices of forensic science and criminal investigations (see Chapters 4 and 5).

3 Although I am using the term *dominant*, it should be noted that whilst there is clear historical evidence to suggest the dominance of one paradigm or set of ideas over another, this in no way is meant to suggest these were the only explanations of crime and criminality in the nineteenth century.

4 National Library of Medicine (1956) *Io. Baptistae Portae Neapolitani De humana physiognomonia libri IIII*, by Giambattista della Porta. Available online at www.nlm.nih.gov/exhibition/historicalanatomies/Images/1200_pixels/porta_p59.jpg (accessed 4th February 2014).

5 Wikipedia (2006) Typical illustration in a nineteenth-century book about Physiognomy (on the left: "Utter despair", and on the right: "Anger mixed with fear"). Available online at http://en.wikipedia.org/wiki/File:Physiognomy.jpg (accessed 4th February 2014).

6 Wikipedia (2005) This is an illustration and definition of "phrenology" from *Webster's Dictionary* circa 1900. Available online at http://commons.wikimedia.org/wiki/File:1895-Dictionary-Phrenolog.png (accessed 4th February 2014).

7 Wikipedia (2009) Phrenology diagram. From *People's Cyclopedia of Universal Knowledge* (1883). Available online at http://en.wikipedia.org/wiki/File:Phrenology Pix.jpg (accessed 4th February 2014).

8 Survival of the fittest was actually a term coined by Herbert Spencer in 1865. Spencer was an English Philosopher and Sociologist, and Charles Darwin used his ideas (Davie, 2005:84).

9 There is some debate about whether or not individuals working in this era could be called *criminologists*. On the one hand, the alienists were not primarily concerned with a distinct criminological project (Garland, 1997); on the other hand, the work carried out by the likes of Thomson and Wilson could be regarded as distinctly criminological (Davie, 2005).

10 It is not just the *Forensic Criminology* (2010) text, but also Turvey's work on *Criminal Profiling* (2001, 2008), which consistently emphasises critical thinking and analysis of evidence/data.

11 Which could be described as a person displaying eccentric behaviour and mental characteristics that approach the psychotic.

12 The political criminal, according to Lombroso, is motivated by economic and social fanaticism. They also share similar characteristics to the criminal of passion (Lombroso, 2007:313–315).

13 The 'Occipital bone is situated at the back part and base of the cranium' (Gray, [1858]2012:24). Within the occipital is the *Foramen Magnum*, which 'transmits the medulla oblongata and its membranes, the spinal accessory nerves, the vertebral arteries, the anterior and posterior spinal arteries, and the occipital-axial ligaments'. On each side of the foramen are *Condyles* and 'behind each condyle is a fossa' (ibid.:25).

Chapter 4 The beginnings of forensic investigation

1 Sumer was the ancient region of what is now part of modern Iraq (Bell, 2008:23) and is also referred to as Mesopotamia.

2 In 1975 several Chhin tombs were uncovered at Shui-hu-ti near Yun-meng in Hupei. Tomb 11 consisted of 1,155 bamboo slips 'bearing records of legal cases' (Gwei-Djen and Needham, 1988:364).

3 As Bell has rightly pointed out, biology 'remained hidden under the coattails of medicine until the Renaissance' period (2008:37).

4 Fire assay is a chemical process in which the material is subjected to high heat (as in fusion, scorifying and cupellation).

5 Sublimation is the process through which a solid substance is changed into a vapour or gas (through heating) without passing through a liquid phase and typically forms a solid deposit again when cooled.

6 Distillation is the purification of a liquid by heating it until it vaporises, then cooling the vapour and collecting the residual liquid, which is separate from the original liquid.

7   Pyrolysis is decomposition of organic materials brought about by high temperatures and is irreversible.
8   Habitual Criminals Act, 1869 (32 and 33 Vic. c.99).
9   Louis-Jacques-Mandé Daguerre invented the daguerreotype process in France. It is a direct-positive process, creating a highly detailed image on a sheet of copper plated with a thin coat of silver without the use of a negative. Available online at http://memory.loc.gov/ammem/daghtml/daghome.html (accessed 19th April 2012).
10 An *ambrotype* was an early method of photography that employed a glass negative and was developed by James Ambrose Cutting (Cole, 2002:20).
11 Cabinet Magazine online (2004). *Life on the Bell Curve: An Interview with Theodore Porter*, by Paul Fleming and Theodore Porter. Available online at http://cabinetmagazine.org/issues/15/fleming2.php (acessed 4th February 2014).
12 The Dismal Science Project (2002). *Common Themes in Ruskin and Galton: "Mythologizing the world by physiognomizing it"*, by Sandra J. Peart and David M. Levy. Available online at http://edwardmcphail.com/dismal_science/criminals_v_normal.jpg (accessed 4th February 2014).
13 Biometrics is the science and technology of measuring and analysing biological data and includes technologies that measure and analyse human body characteristics, such as DNA, fingerprints, eye retinas and irises, voice patterns, facial patterns and hand measurements.
14 The meaning is taken from Zoology and Medicine and means consisting of *bone*.
15 Bertillon, A. (1889). *Alphonse Bertillon's instructions for taking descriptions for the identification of criminals and others, by means of anthropometric indications.* Translated by Gallus Muller. Whitefish MT: Kessinger Legacy Reprints.
16 Available online at http://jimfisher.edinboro.edu/forensics/bertillon1.html#_ftn1 (accessed 12th July 2011).
17 Rhodes, H. T. (1936). *Some persons unknown: being an account of scientific detection.* London: John Murray.
18 Bertillon, A. (1889). *Alphonse Bertillon's instructions for taking descriptions for the identification of criminals and others, by means of anthropometric indications.* Translated by Gallus Muller. Whitefish MT: Kessinger Legacy Reprints.
19 *Commentatio de examine physiologico organi visus et systematis cutanei*, 1823, p 59.
20 Herschel, W. J. (1916). *The origin of finger-printing.* London: Oxford University Press.
21 Identity cards ceased to be valid legal documents in the UK with the ascension of the Identity Documents Act 2010.
22 Inner or radial loops are loops that enter and exist on the side towards the thumb. Outer or ulnar loops are those that enter and exist on the side of the finger toward the little finger (Houck and Siegel, 2010:489).
23 Galton, F. (1895). *Fingerprint directories.* Whitefish MT: Kessinger Legacy Reprints.
24 Henry's composites were hybrid types such as *central pocket loops, lateral pocket loops, twinned loops* and *accidentals* (Henry, 1900:33–45; Cole, 2002:82).
25 Upper-case letters were used to denote the index fingers only (Cole, 2002:82).
26 At the time of writing, Henry's text is available online at www.clpex.com/Information/Pioneers/henry-classification.pdf. (accessed 10th April 2013).
27 Crystallography is the science of the arrangement of atoms in solids, with all elements having an identifiable crystal structure.

Chapter 5 The beginnings of criminal investigation

1   *Tabula rasa*, or 'scraped tablet' is commonly associated with John Locke (1632–1704). The term surfaces, suggests we are born as blank surfaces and that it is through

learning and socialisation that we fill our blank canvass full of knowledge, theories and understanding of the world around us. *Tabula rasa* has been used by the social sciences and humanities to explain all sorts of behaviour (Pinker, 2003:6). This idea was also used by Sherlock Holmes when stating the following: 'I consider that a man's brain originally is like a little empty attic, and you have to stock it with such furniture as you choose' (Conan Doyle, 1986:16).

2 The ghost in the machine denotes the duality of humans, consisting of a *mind* and *body*, and the separate functioning of both (Pinker, 2003:8–9).

3 Which roughly translated means 'a call to arms'.

4 These were murder, manslaughter and suicide (England, 1985:110).

5 For example, John Sayer's estate was said to be worth £30,000; John Townsend's £20,000 (see Hobbs, 1989 and Emsley, 2003).

6 In 1867 senior Fenian arms agent Richard O'Sullivan-Burke was arrested and held on remand in Clerkenwell Prison (London). In an attempt to rescue him, the Fenians blew a hole in the wall of the prison. Unfortunately, they also blew up a number of tenement houses opposite the prison, killing 12 and injuring at least 90. The 1868 committee was set up a year later to discuss the 'Irish problem' as well as capturing mainland dissidents and sympathetic activists, in which the police were of course involved.

7 Dr Thomas Smethurst was accused of poisoning his wife, Isabella Bankes. The theory put forth by the prosecution in 1859 was that he committed the crime in order to abort the baby his wife was carrying. The reason for this was that he was already married, to Mary Smethurst and was trying to cover up this marriage.

8 Wikipedia (2013). *Part of front page of Police Gazette; or, Hue and Cry. Published by Authority. No. 371. Saturday, August 6, 1831.* Available online at http://commons.wikimedia.org/wiki/File:Police_Gazette_or_Hue_and_Cry_6_August_1831.jpg (accessed 4th February 2014).

9 Goddard was an ex-US Army Colonel who was amongst the first to develop methods for the individualisation of weapons and ballistics: he 'used the comparison microscope for this as well as for comparing the firing-pin marks on shell casings' (Nickell and Fischer, 1999:11).

Chapter 6 Investigating crime

1 Now known as the Crime Survey for England and Wales.

2 For CPS performance statistics see www.cps.gov.uk/publications/performance/case_outcomes/#a021 (accessed 18th July 2012).

3 Following the original Latin use of forensics as connected to the forum, or in the courtroom.

4 The sanctioned detection rate is the number of sanctions divided by the number of crimes.

5 At least one of these members must be a magistrate. The Metropolitan Police Authority has 23 members due to its size. See www.apa.police.uk.

6 Prior to the 1964 Act, this was between Chief Constables and Watch Committees in urban areas, and a chief responsible to a committee of magistrates in rural areas.

7 This is especially important, even for the most basic of investigative operations undertaken by the police. With the effects of the worldwide economic recession and the reduction in policing budgets of up to 20 per cent, as well as the closing of the Forensic Science Service in 2012, the amount of money available to investigations is often a crucial factor determining the investigation and forensic strategy, even before a crime scene has even been attended.

8 The Fisher Inquiry – www.official-documents.gov.uk/document/hc7778/hc00/0090/0090.pdf (accessed 23rd April 2013).

9 See www.mirror.co.uk/news/uk-news/database-used-for-hunting-serial-killers-140564 (accessed 30th April 2013).
10 www.legislation.gov.uk/ukpga/2000/23/pdfs/ukpga_20000023_en.pdf (accessed 30th April 2013).
11 www.npia.police.uk/en/10093.htm (accessed 18th July 2012). The NPIA has since been subsumed under The College of Policing.
12 At the time of writing this was available from www.ssiacymru.org.uk/media/pdf/6/c/Core_Investigation_Doctrine_Interactive_1_.pdf (accessed 18th July 2012).
13 I have controversially placed psychology under the heading of 'social science' as I am a strong believer in the fact that just because someone 'does statistics' within the discipline of psychology does not make them a scientist by any stretch of the imagination.

Chapter 7 Information, material and evidence

1 Berman, G. (2012). *Police Service Strength*. London: House of Commons.
2 Ambage suggests that during the interwar period of development: 'differences of opinion with regard to occupational interests and authority, tensions and even open hostilities, together with areas of agreement, were drawn out by the establishment of the laboratories' (1987:4).
3 The evidence for this case is largely taken from the second Court of Appeal judgment in the case of R v Sally Clark (2003, EWCA Crim 1020). Available online at www.bailii.org/ew/cases/EWCA/Crim/2003/1020.html (accessed 25th September 2012).
4 The Griess Test is a specific chromophoric (light absorption colouration) test that is used to test for the presence of nitrate compounds that are used in explosives. The Griess reagent (of which there are a few; e.g. 3 per cent sulfanilamide and 0.3 per cent N-(1 naphthyl)ethylenediamine dihydrochloride dissolved in 5 per cent phosphoric acid) is applied to a surface, such as hands, producing a pinkish/purple colour (Rowe, 2009:425–426).
5 TRH is a substance that is used for setting up new bioassays (Latour and Woolgar, 1986:108).
6 The Marquis Colour Test uses the chemicals formaldehyde and concentrated sulfuric acid. Heroin, morphine and most opium-based drugs will turn the solution purple. Amphetamines will turn it orange-brown.

Chapter 8 Crime analysis and crime mapping

1 Taken from the London School of Economics' *Charles Booth Online Archive*, http://booth.lse.ac.uk/static/a/3.html (accessed 30th August 2011).
2 The following is taken primarily from the Court of Appeal (Criminal Division) transcript of Barry George v R, Case No: 200703209B5, [2007] EWCA Crim 2722, 2007 WL 3389439; available online at http://login.westlaw.co.uk/maf/wluk/app/document?&suppsrguid=ia744cc630000013eda09febe603cee56&docguid=I9B185D60972D11DC8A0AFD288BB994A7&hitguid=ICBFEC76094D111DC8128C8875111AC63&rank=1&spos=1&epos=1&td=1300&crumb-action=append&context=15&resolvein=true (accessed 25th May 2013).
3 The Campbell Collaboration is an international research network that prepares and disseminates high-quality systematic reviews of social science evidence (see www.campbellcollaboration.org).
4 Personal communication with Research Officer (crime analyst), for Wyre Forest, 31st January 2009.

5 Section 5 of the Crime and Disorder Act 1998 set out statutory requirements regarding the responsible authorities that take the lead in Crime and Disorder Reduction Partnerships (CDRPs). At the time of writing, responsible authorities included: the police service, local authority, fire and rescue services, and the probation service.
6 Clarke, R. V. and Eck, J. E. (2005). *Crime analysis for problem solvers in 60 small steps*. Washington DC: Office of Community Oriented Policing Services, US Department of Justice.
7 This claim does not deny the problems associated with official statistics (for example, see Coleman and Moynihan, 1996; Dorling and Simpson, 1999; Best, 2001).
8 Partisan IT-Politics denotes when finance and IT departments push specific hardware and software products into the wider organisation. In the majority of cases, this software and hardware is the only choice available to staff members, regardless of its suitability. In some cases, consideration of these issues can become quite heated, as organisations have signed what is effectively monopolistic contracts with computer hardware and software companies.
9 See www.ia-ip.org/index.php?page=iops (accessed 19th November 2012).
10 See www.ecricanada.com (accessed 19th November 2012).
11 See www.esri.com/industries/public-safety/law-enforcement/arcgis-system.html (accessed 19th November 2012).
12 Personal communication DCI Mark Ashthorpe, February 2010.

Chapter 9 Scientific support and crime scene examination

1 www.npia.police.uk/en/10432.htm (accessed 1st March 2012).
2 www.npia.police.uk/en/10432.htm (accessed 3rd March 2012).
3 POLKA 'is an online platform created to facilitate efficient communication and information sharing across the Police Service and partner agencies' (NPIA, 2012:7).
4 *DPP v Morrison* ([2003] EWHC 683 Admin), available online at http://login.westlaw.co.uk/maf/wluk/app/document?&suppsrguid=ia744c09a0000013f0e37a4c5adbccd31&docguid=I9AFF21C0E42711DA8FC2A0F0355337E9&hitguid=I9AFEFAB0E42711DA8FC2A0F0355337E9&rank=1&spos=1&epos=1&td=179&crumb-action=append&context=5&resolvein=true (accessed 30th May 2013).
5 See http://metro.co.uk/2012/10/04/interfering-batman-mark-wayne-williams-arrested-for-refusing-to-leave-crime-scene-592654/ (accessed 8th December 2012).
6 Personal communication, DCI, 12th February 2007.
7 Taken from the Iowa division of the International Association for Identification – www.iowaiai.org/crime_scene_photography_requirements_of_criminal_investigative_analysis.html (accessed 8th June 2013).
8 The F-number in photography links to the concept of exposure. Exposure can be defined as the 'product of the intensity of image forming light reflecting from the subject and passing through the lens and the time this light is allowed to impinge on the film or sensor' (Crowe, 2009:72). It is expressed as $E = I \times T$ (where E = exposure; I = intensity; T = time or shutter speed). The F-number is the lens aperture, which controls the intensity of light (see Crowe, 2009; Jones, 2009; Duncan, 2010).
9 The natural perspective rule is defined as 'the viewpoint of the scene that has the photographer standing at full height' (Robinson, 2010:313). The exception to the natural perspective rule is when an aerial photograph is taken from an elevated position; or when the photographer has to move down to ground level to reach a hidden piece of evidence; for example, under a piece of furniture.
10 This principle relates to the who, what, when, where, why and how questions that should be asked and answered during any forensic investigation.

11 Diachronic tracking maps how information work and the actions undertaken change and develop over a period of time. Synchronic tracking 'supplements and complements this analysis by showing how, in such movements, the content and qualities of the information are transformed' (Innes, 2003:139).

Chapter 10 Forensic science and detection methods

1 The figure of £2 million per month was a common point made by the government to justify their intent to 'wind down' the FSS. However, when the evidence behind this figure was actually challenged it was found to be £1.58 million (House of Commons Science and Technology Committee, 2013a:7).

2 In one of the 15 forensic labs across the UK; see www.lgcgroup.com/contact-us/.

3 Available online at www.parliamentlive.tv/Main/Player.aspx?meetingId=12841 (accessed 14th November 2013).

4 In the law of evidence, the *probandum*, sometimes referred to as the *factum probandum*, is the fact to be proved.

5 Light which is detected by the human eye consists of wavelengths ranging from 780 nanometers (7.80×10^{-7} m – red) down to 390 nanometers (3.90×10^{-7} m – violet).

6 Absorption of radiation (which is commonly referred to as light or energy) by an atom, causes an electron to jump into a higher orbit around the proton and neutron nucleus; whilst the emission of radiation by an atom is caused by an electron falling back to a lower (or original) lower orbit. As each element is made up of different numbers of protons, neutrons and electrons, each element has distinctive absorption and emission levels.

7 The term serology denotes 'a broad scope of laboratory tests that use specific antigen and serum antibody reactions' (Saferstein, 2007:348). Serological evidence includes: blood, semen and saliva.

8 *Ipse dixit* relates to the 'bare assertion fallacy'; or 'he himself said it'.

References

Abbott, A. (1988). *The System of Professions: An Essay on the Division of Expert Labour.* Chicago: The University of Chicago Press.

Abbott, A. (2001). *Chaos of Disciplines.* Chicago: The University of Chicago Press.

ACPO (2004). *National Investigative Interviewing Strategy.* London: ACPO.

ACPO Centrex (2005). *Guidance on the National Intelligence Model.* Wyboston: Centrex/NCPE.

Adam, C. (2010). *Essential Mathematics and Statistics For Forensic Science.* Chichester: Wiley-Blackwell.

Agar, J. (2008). What happened in the sixties? *The British Journal for the History of Science, 41* (2), 567–600.

Agresti, A. and Finlay, B. (1997). *Statistical Methods for the Social Sciences* (3rd ed.). New Jersey: Pearson Education Inc.

Ainsworth, P. B. (2001). *Offender Profiling and Crime Analysis.* Cullompton: Willan Publishing.

Aitken, C. and Taroni, F. (2004). *Statistics and the Evaluation of Evidence for Forensic Scientists* (2nd ed.). Chichester: John Wiley & Sons Ltd.

Ambage, N. V. (1987). *The Origins and Development of the Home Office Forensic Science Service, 1931–1967.* Unpublished PhD Thesis, University of Lancaster, UK.

Anderson, G. S. (2009). Forensic entomology. In S. J. James and J. J. Nordby (Eds), *Forensic Science: An Introduction to Scientific and Investigative Techniques* (pp. 137–165). Boca Raton: CRC Press.

Anderson, R. (2004). Forensic toxicology. In P. C. White (Ed.), *Crime Scene to Court: The Essentials of Forensic Science* (2nd ed., pp. 318–349). Cambridge: The Royal Society of Chemistry.

Anderson, T., Schum, D. and Twining, W. (2005). *Analysis of Evidence* (2nd ed.). Cambridge: Cambridge University Press.

Andrews, D. A. and Bonta, J. (2003). *The Psychology of Criminal Conduct* (3rd ed.). Cincinnati: Anderson Publishing Co.

Association of Forensic Science Providers (2009). Standards for the formulation of evluative forensic science expert opinion. *Science and Justice, 49* (3), 161–164.

Audit Commission (1993). *Helping with Enquiries: Tackling Crime Effectively.* London: Audit Commission.

Baber, C. and Butler, M. (2012). Expertise in crime scene examination: Comparing search strategies of expert and novice crime scene examiners in simulated crime scenes. *Human Factors: The Journal of Human Factors and Ergonomics Society, 54* (3), 413–424.

Baber, C., Smith, P., Cross, J., Hunter, J. and McMaster, R. (2006). Crime scene investigation as distributed cognition. *Pragmatics and Cognition, 14* (2), 357–385.

Bacon, F. ([1620]2009). *Novum Organon Scientiarum*. Kindle Edition.

Bal, R. (2005). How to kill with a ballpoint: Credibility in Dutch forensic science. *Science, Technology and Human Values, 30* (1), 52–75.

Bandey, H. L. (2004). *The Powders Process, Study 1: Evaluation of Fingerprint Brushes for Use with Aluminium Power*. London: Home Office Police Scientific Development Branch.

Barclay, D. (2009). Using forensic science in major crime inquiries. In J. Fraser and R. Williams (Eds), *Handbook of Forensic Science* (pp. 337–358). Cullompton: Willan Publishing.

Barnett, K. (2004). Marks and impressions. In P. C. White (Ed.), *Crime Scene to Court: The Essentials of Forensic Science* (2nd ed., pp. 82–114). Cambridge: The Royal Society of Chemistry.

Barnett, P. D. (2000). The role of forensic science professional organisations in the new millennium of accreditation, certification, registration and standardization. *Science and Justice, 40* (2), 138–142.

Bartol, C. R. and Bartol, A. M. (2008). *Criminal Behaviour: A Psychosocial Approach* (8th ed.). New Jersey: Pearson Education Ltd.

Basalla, G. (1999). *The Evolution of Technology*. Cambridge: Cambridge University Press.

Bashford, A. and Levine, P. (Eds) (2012). *The Oxford Handbook of the History of Eugenics*. Oxford: Oxford University Press.

Bayne, S. and Carlin, M. (2010). *Forensic Applications of High Performance Liquid Chromatography*. Boca Raton: CRC Press.

Beaufort-Moore, D. (2009). *Crime Scene Management and Evidence Recovery*. Oxford: Oxford University Press.

Beaver, K. M. (2010). The promises and pitfalls of forensic evidence in unsolved crimes. *Criminology and Public Policy, 9* (2), 405–410.

Beccaria, C. ([1764]1986). *On Crimes and Punishments*. Indianapolis: Hackett Publishing Company.

Becker, H. (1963). *Outsiders: Studies in the Sociology of Deviance*. New York: Macmillan Publishing Co.

Becker, P. and Wetzell, R. F. (Eds) (2009). *Criminals and Their Scientists: The History of Criminology in International Perspective*. Cambridge: Cambridge University Press.

Becker, R. F. and Dutelle, A. W. (2013). *Criminal Investigation*. Burlington, MA: Jones and Bartlett Learning.

Bell, S. (2008). *Crime and Circumstance: Investigating the History of Forensic Science*. Westport, CT: Praeger Publishers.

Bell, S. and Morris, K. (2010). *An Introduction to Microscopy*. Boca Raton: CRC Press.

Ben-Yehuda, N. (2002). *Sacrificing Truth: Archeology and the Myth of Masada*. New York: Humanity Books.

Berg, B. (2008). *Criminal Investigation* (4th ed.). New York: McGraw-Hill.

Berger, P. (1991). *Invitation to Sociology: A Humanistic Perspective*. London: Penguin Books Ltd.

Berger, P. and Luckmann, T. ([1966]1991). *The Social Construction of Reality: A Treatise in the Sociology of Knowledge*. London: Penguin Books Ltd.

Bergslien, E. (2006). Teaching to avoid the CSI effect: Keeping the science in forensic science. *Journal of Chemical Education, 83* (5), 690–691. doi: 10.1021/ed083p690.

Berman, E. (1986). Science policy snapshot: Science policy research division, Congressional Research Service. *Science and Technology Studies, 4* (1), 32.

Berman, G. (2012). *Police Service Strength.* London: House of Commons.

Bernal, J. D. (1969). *Science in History, Volume 1: The Emergence of Science.* Middlesex: Pelican Books.

Bertillon, A. (1889). *Alphonse Bertillon's Instructions for Taking Descriptions for the Identification of Criminals and Others, by Means of Anthropometric Indications.* Translated by Gallus Muller. Whitefish: Kessinger Legacy Reprints.

Best, J. (Ed.). (1995). *Images of Issues: Typifying Contemporary Social Problems.* New York: Aldine De Gruyter.

Best, J. (2001). *Damned Lies and Statistics: Untangling Numbers from the Media, Politicians, and Activists.* Berkely, CA: University of California Press.

Bevel, T. and Gardner, R. M. (2008). *Bloodstain Pattern Analysis: With an Introduction to Crime Scene Reconstruction.* Boca Raton: CRC Press.

Bichard, M. (2004). *The Bichard Inquiry Report.* HC653. London: The Stationery Office.

Bilton, M. (2012). *Wicked Beyond Belief: The Hunt for the Yorkshire Ripper.* London: Harper Press.

Bingham, J. (2010). Mark Saunders inquest coroner: 'Jargon' hampering police 'common sense', *The Daily Telegraph* 8th October. Available online at www.telegraph.co.uk/news/uknews/law-and-order/8050495/Mark-Saunders-inquest-coroner-jargon-hampering-police-common-sense.html (accessed 21st July 2012).

Bingham, T. (2011). *The Rule of Law.* London: Penguin Books.

Black, E. (2004). *Ware Against The Weak: Eugenics and America's Campaign to Create a Master Race.* New York: Thunder's Mouth Press.

Blackburn, R. (1995). *The Psychology of Criminal Conduct: Theory, Research and Practice.* Chichester: John Wiley & Sons Ltd.

Blumer, H. (1984). *The Chicago School of Sociology: Institutionalization, Diversity, and the Rise of Sociological Research.* Chicago: The University of Chicago Press.

Blumer, H. (1992). *Symbolic Interactionism.* California: University of California Press.

Boba, R. (2005). *Crime Analysis and Crime Mapping.* Thousand Oaks, CA: Sage Publications Inc.

Bonger, W. A. ([1916]2012). *Criminality and Economic Conditions.* Charleston, SC: Forgotten Books.

Bonger, W. A. (1936). *An Introduction to Criminology.* London: Methuen and Co. Ltd.

Bottoms, A. E. and Wiles, P. (1997). Environmental criminology. In M. Maguire, R. Morgan, and R. Reiner (Eds), *The Oxford Handbook of Criminology* (2nd ed., pp. 305–359). Oxford: Oxford University Press.

Bourdieu, P. (2000). *Distinction: A Social Critique of the Judgement of Taste.* London: Routledge.

Bowen, R. T. (2010). *Ethics and the Practice of Forensic Science.* Boca Raton: CRC Press.

Boyer, P. (1992). *Urban Masses and Moral Order in America, 1820–1920.* Cambridge, MA: Harvard University Press.

Bradbury, S. and Feist, A. (2005). *The Use of Forensic Science in Volume Crime Investigations: A Review of the Research Literature.* Home Office Online Report 43/05. London: Home Office.

Brain, T. (2010). *A History of Policing in England and Wales from 1974.* Oxford: Oxford University Press.

Brake, M. (1980). *Sociology of Youth Culture and Youth Subcultures: Sex, Drugs and Rock 'n' Roll?* London: Routledge and Kegan Paul Plc.

Brantingham, P. and Brantingham, P. (1984). *Patterns in Crime*. New York: Macmillan Publishing Company.

Brantingham, P. and Brantingham, P. (1991). *Environmental Criminology*. Prospect Heights, IL: Waveland Press.

Brantingham, P. and Brantingham, P. (2008). Crime pattern theory. In R. Wortley and L. Mazerolle (Eds), *Environmental Criminology and Crime Analysis* (pp. 78–93). Cullompton: Willan Publishing.

Bristow, E. (1977). *Vice and Vigilance: Purity Movements in Britain Since 1700*. London: Gill and Macmillan Ltd.

Broeders, T. (2009). Decision-making in the forensic arena. In H. Kaptein, H. Prakken and B. Verheij (Eds), *Legal Evidence and Proof: Statistics, Stories, Logic* (pp. 71–92). Farnham: Ashgate Publishing Ltd.

Brown, M. (2003). Ethnology and colonial administration in nineteenth-century British India: The question of native crime and criminality. *The British Journal for the History of Science, 36* (2), 323–340.

Bryman, A. and Cramer, D. (2011). *Quantitative Data Analysis with IBM SPSS 17, 18 and 19*. Hove, East Sussex: Routledge.

Bryson, B. (2010). *Seeing Further: The Story of Science and the Royal Society*. London: Harper Press.

Budowle, B., Bottrell, M. C., Bunch, S. G., Fram, R., Harrison, D., Meagher, S., Oien, C. T., Peterson, P. E., Seiger, D. P., Smith, M. B., Smrz, M. A., Soltis, G. L. and Stacey, R. B. (2009). A perspective on errors, bias, and interpretation in the forensic sciences and direction for continuing advancement. *Journal of Forensic Science, 54* (4), 798–809.

Bunge, M. (2006). A systematic perspective on crime. In P. H. Wikstrom and R. J. Sampson (Eds), *The Explanation of Crime: Context, Mechanisms and Development* (pp. 8–30). Cambridge: Cambridge University Press.

Burbridge, D. (2001). Francis Galton on twins, heredity and social class. *The British Journal for the History of Science, 34* (3), 323–340.

Burke, P. (1994). *Popular Culture in Early Modern Europe* (2nd ed.). Farnham: Ashgate Publishing Limited.

Burke, P. (2008). *A Social History of Knowledge: From Gutenberg to Diderot*. Cambridge: Polity Press.

Burleigh, M. (2001). *The Third Reich: A New History*. London: Pan Books.

Burnell, P. (2010). 'Dangers' of a free market in forensic science. *BBC News*. Available online at http://news.bbc.co.uk/1/hi/uk/8400097.stm (accessed 17th September 2010).

Burrows, J., Tarling, R., Mackie, A., Poole, H. and Hodgson, B. (2005). *Forensic Science Pathfinder Project: Evaluating Increased Forensic Activity in Two English Police Forces*. Home Office Online Report 46/05. London: Home Office.

Byford, L. (1981). *The Yorkshire Ripper Case: Review of the Investigation of the Case by Lawrence Byford, Esq., CBE., QPM., Her Majesty's Inspector of Constabulary*. London: Home Office.

Caddy, B. (1986). *Uses of Forensic Sciences: The Proceedings of the Conference held in Glasgow in April 1986*. Edinburgh: Scottish Academic Press.

Caddy, B. and Cobb, P. (2004). Forensic science. In P. C. White (Ed.), *Crime Scene to Court: The Essentials of Forensic Science* (pp. 1–20). Cambridge: The Royal Society of Chemistry.

Campbell, E. (2009). Reading/writing autopsy: A dirty theory of the science of death. *Science as Culture, 18* (3), 313–331.

Canter, D. (2003). *Mapping Murder: The Secrets of Geographical Profiling.* London: Virgin Books.

Canter, D. and Youngs, D. (2009). *Investigative Psychology: Offender Profiling and the Analysis of Criminal Action.* Chichester: John Wiley & Sons Ltd.

Capra, F. (1991). *The Tao of Physics: An Exploration of the Parallels between Modern Physics and Eastern Mysticism.* London: Flamingo.

Carson, D. (2007). Models of investigation. In T. Newburn, T. Williamson and A. Wright (Eds), *Handbook of Criminal Investigations* (pp. 407–425). Cullompton: Willan Publishing.

Carter, P. (2003). *Managing Offenders, Reducing Crime: A New Approach.* (Correctional Services Review) London: Home Office.

Cavender, G. and Deutsch, S. K. (2007). CSI and moral authority: The police and science. *Crime, Media, Culture, 3* (1), 67–81.

Ceci, S. J. and Buck, M. (2009). *Jeopardy in the Courtroom: A Scientific Analysis of Children's Testimony.* Washington: American Psychological Association.

Chainey, S. and Ratcliffe, J. (2005). *GIS and Crime Mapping.* Chichester: John Wiley & Sons Ltd.

Chakraborti, N. (2010). *Hate Crime: Concepts, Policy, Future Directions.* Cullompton: Willan Publishing.

Chakraborti, N. and Garland, J. (2009). *Hate Crime: Impact, Causes and Responses.* London: Sage Publications Ltd.

Champod, C. and Chamberlain, P. (2009). Fingerprints. In J. Fraser and R. Williams (Eds), *Handbook of Forensic Science* (pp. 57–83). Cullompton: Willan Publishing.

Chisum, W. J. and Turvey, B. E. (2007). *Crime Reconstruction.* Burlington, MA: Elsevier Academic Press.

Chisum, W. J. and Turvey, B. E. (2008). An introduction to crime reconstruction. In B. E. Turvey, *Criminal Profiling: An Introduction to Behavioural Evidence Analysis* (3rd ed., pp. 155–186). Burlington, MA: Elsevier Academic Press.

Christian, D. R. (2009). Analysis of controlled substances. In S. J. James and J. J. Nordby, *Forensic Science: An Introduction to Scientific and Investigative Techniques* (pp. 457–487). Boca Raton: CRC Press.

Clarke, C. and Milne, B. (2001). *National Evaluation of the PEACE Investigative Interviewing Course.* Police Research Award Scheme, PRAS/149. London: Home Office.

Clarke, J. (1980). *Permissiveness and Control: Fate of the Sixties Legislation – Conference Proceedings.* Basingstoke: Macmillan.

Clarke, R. V. and Felson, M. (Eds) (2004). *Routine Activity and Rational Choice. Advances in Criminological Theory: Volume 5.* New Brunswick, NJ: Transaction Press.

Clarke, R. V. and Eck, J. E. (2005). *Crime Analysis for Problem Solvers in 60 Small Steps.* Washington DC: Office of Community Oriented Policing Services, US Department of Justice.

Cloward, R. A. and Ohlin, L. E. (1960). *Delinquency and Opportunity.* New York: Free Press.

Cohen, A. (1956). *Delinquent Boys: The Culture of the Gang.* London: Routledge and Kegan Paul.

Cohen, L. E. and Felson, M. (1979). Social change and crime rate trends: A routine activity approach. *American Sociological Review, 44*, 588–608.

Cohen, S. (Ed.). (1971). *Images of Deviance*. London: Penguin Books Ltd.

Cohen, S. (1972). *Folk Devils and Moral Panics: The Creation of the Mods and Rockers* (2nd ed.). Oxford: Blackwell Publishers.

Cohen, S. (1985). *Visions of Social Control*. Cambridge: Polity Press.

Cohen-Cole, J. (2007). Insitituting the science of mind: Intellectual economies and disciplinary exchange at Harvard's Centre for Cognitive Studies. *The British Journal for the History of Science, 40* (4), 567–597.

Cole, M. (2004). Drugs of abuse. In P. C. White (Ed.), *Crime Scene to Court: The Essentials of Forensic Science* (2nd ed., pp. 293–317). Cambridge: The Royal Society of Chemistry.

Cole, S. A. (2002). *Suspect Identities: A History of Fingerprinting and Criminal Identification*. Cambridge, MA: Harvard University Press.

Cole, S. A. (2010). Forensic identification evidence: Utility without infallibility. *Criminology and Public Policy, 9* (2), 375–379.

Coleman, C. and Moynihan, J. (1996). *Understanding Crime Data*. Maidenhead: Open University Press.

Comte, A. ([1865]2009). *A General View of Positivism*. Cambridge: Cambridge University Press.

Conan Doyle, A. (1986). *The Illustrated Sherlock Holmes: Complete Works*. Hertfordshire: The Leisure Circle.

Conrad, P. and Schneider, J. (1992). *Deviance and Medicalization: From Badness to Sickness*. Philadelphia: Temple University Press.

Conze, E. (1935). *The Scientific Method of Thinking: An Introduction to Dialectical Materialism*. London: Chapman and Hall Ltd.

Cook, R., Evett, I. W., Jackson, G., Jones, P. J. and Lambert, J. A. (1998a). A model for case assessment and interpretation. *Science and Justice, 38* (3), 151–156.

Cook, R., Evett, I. W., Jackson, G., Jones, P. J. and Lambert, J. A. (1998b). A hierarchy of propositions: Deciding which level to address in casework. *Science and Justice, 38* (4), 321–239.

Cook, S. (2005). Late Victorian visual reasoning and Alfred Marshall's economic science. *The Birtish Journal for the History of Science, 38* (2), 179–195.

Cook, T. and Tattersall, A. (2008). *Blackstone's Senior Investigating Officers' Handbook*. Oxford: Oxford University Press.

Cope, N. (2003). Crime analysis: Principles and practice. In T. Newburn (Ed.), *Handbook of Policing* (pp. 340–362). Cullompton: Willan Publishing.

Cornish, D. B. and Clarke, R. V. (2008). The rational choice perspective. In R. Wortley and L. Mazerolle (Eds), *Environmental Criminology and Crime Analysis* (pp. 21–47). Cullompton: Willan Publishing.

Couvalis, G. (1997). *The Philosophy of Science: Science and Objectivity*. London: Sage Publications Ltd.

Cox, D. J. (2010). *A Certain Share of Low Cunning: A History of the Bow Street Runners, 1792–1839*. Cullompton: Willan Publishing.

Cressey, P. G. (2008). *The Taxi-Dance Hall: A Sociological Study in Commercialized Recreation and City Life*. Chicago, IL: University of Chicago Press.

Crosland, M. (2003). Research schools of chemistry from Lavoisier to Wurtz. *The British Journal for the History of Science, 36* (3), 333–361.

Crowe, C. (2009). Police photography. In R. Sutton, K. Trueman (Eds), *Crime Scene Management: Scene Specific Methods* (pp. 69–95). Chichester: John Wiley & Sons Ltd.

Cummins, H. and Kennedy, R. W. (1940). Purkinje's observations (1823) on finger prints and other skin features. *The Journal of Criminal Law and Criminology, 31* (3), 343–356.

Dahrendorf, R. (1959). *Class and Class Conflict in Industrial Society.* London: Routledge and Kegan Paul.

Davie, N. (2005). *Tracing the Criminal: The Rise of Scientific Criminology in Britain 1860–1918.* Oxford: The Bardwell Press.

Davies, C. (1975). *Permissive Britain: Social Change in The Sixties and Seventies.* London: Pitman Publishing.

Davies, M., Croall, H. and Tyrer, J. (2005). *Criminal Justice: An Introduction to the Criminal Justice System in England and Wales* (3rd ed.). Harlow: Pearson Education Limited.

De Giustino, D. (1975). *Conquest of Mind: Phrenology and Victorian Social Thought.* London: Croom Helm Ltd.

De Maistre, J. (1998). *Examination of the Philosophy of Bacon: Wherein Different Questions of Rational Philosophy are Treated.* Quebec: McGill-Queens University Press.

De Vaus, D. (2002). *Surveys in Social Research* (5th ed.). London: Routledge.

Denzin, N. K. (1971). The logic of naturalistic inquiry. *Social Forces, 50* (2), 166–182.

Denzin, N. K. and Lincoln, Y. S. (2000). *Handbook of Qualitative Research* (2nd ed.). Thousand Oaks, CA.: Sage Publications Inc.

Derksen, L. (2010). Micro/macro translations: The production of new social structures in the case of DNA profiling. *Sociological Inquiry, 80* (2), 214–240.

Deutsch, S. K. and Cavender, G. (2008). CSI and forensic realism. *Journal of Criminal Justice and Popular Culture, 15* (1), 34–53.

Dhani, A. (2013). *Police Service Strength: England and Wales, 30 September 2012.* HOSB: 01/13. London: Home Office.

DiMaio, V. J. and DiMaio, D. (2001). *Forensic Pathology* (2nd ed.). Boca Raton: CRC Press.

Dorling, D. (2011). *Injustice: Why Social Inequality Persists.* Bristol: The Policy Press.

Dorling, D. and Simpson, S. (1999). *Statistics in Society: The Arithmetic of Politics.* London: Arnold.

Douglas, J. E., Burgess, A. W., Burgess, A. G. and Ressler, R. K. (1997). *Crime Classification Manual.* San Francisco: Jossey-Bass Publishers.

Downes, D. (1966). *The Delinquent Solution: A Study in Subcultural Theory.* London: Routledge and Kegan Paul.

Downes, D. and Rock, P. (2007). *Understanding Deviance: A Guide to the Sociology of Crime and Rule Breaking* (5th ed.). Oxford: Oxford University Press.

Dror, I. E., Charlton, D. and Péron, A. E. (2006). Contextual information renders experts vulnerable to making erroneous identifications. *Forensic Science International, 156,* 74–78.

Duncan, C. D. (2010). *Advanced Crime Scene Photography.* Boca Raton: CRC Press.

Durkheim, E. (1982). *The Rules of Sociological Method and Selected Texts on Sociology and Its Method.* New York: The Free Press.

Durkheim, E. (1984). *The Division of Labour in Society.* London: Collier-Macmillan.

Durston, G. (2008). *Evidence: Text and Materials.* Oxford: Oxford University Press.

Duster, T. (2006). The molecular reinscription of race: Unanticipated issues in biotechnology and forensic science. *Patterns of Prejudice, 40* (4–5), 427–441.

Dutelle, A. W. (2011). *An Introduction to Crime Scene Investigation.* Sudbury, MA: Jones and Bartlett Publishers.

Eddy, M. D. (2004). Scottish chemistry, classification and the late mineralogical career of the 'ingenious' Professor John Walker (1779–1803). *The British Journal for the History of Science, 37* (4), 373–399.

Elliott, P. and Daniels, S. (2006). The 'school of true, useful and universal science'? Freemasonry, natural philosophy and scientific culture in eighteenth-century England. *The British Journal for the History of Science, 39* (2), 207–229.

Emig, M. N., Heck, R. O. and Kravitz, M. (1980). *Crime Analysis: A Selected Bibliography.* Washington D.C.: National Institute of Justice.

Emsley, C. (2003). The birth and development of the police. In T. Newburn (Ed.), *Handbook of Policing* (pp. 66–83). Cullompton: Willan Publishing.

Emsley, C. (2005a). *The English and Violence Since 1750.* London: Hambledon and London.

Emsley, C. (2005b). *Crime and Society in England, 1750–1900* (3rd ed.). Harlow, England: Pearson Education Limited.

Emsley, C. (2010). *The Great British Bobby: A History of British Policing from the 18th Century to the Present.* London: Quercus.

Engels, F. ([1845]1987). *The Condition of the Working Class in England.* London: Penguin Books.

England, R. W. (1985). Investigating homicides in Northern England, 1800–1824. *Criminal Justice History, 6*, 105–124.

Erikson, K. T. (1966). *Wayward Puritans: A Study in the Sociology of Deviance.* London: John Wiley & Sons Ltd.

Evans, C. (2006). *The Father of Forensics: The Groundbreaking Cases of Sir Bernard Spilsbury, and the Beginnings of Modern CSI.* New York: Berkley Books.

Eysenck, M. (1998). *Psychology: An Integrated Approach.* Harlow, Essex: Pearson Education Limited.

Faigman, D. L., Saks, M. J., Sanders, J. and Cheng, E. K. (2010). *Modern Scientific Evidence: The Law and Science of Expert Testimony, Volume 4, Forensics 2010–11.* Eagan, MN: Thomson Reuters-West.

Ekblom, P. (2005). How to police the future: Scanning for scientific and technological innovations which generate potential threats and opportunities in crime, policing and crime reduction. In M. J. Smith, and N. Tilley (Eds), *Crime science: New approaches to preventing and detecting crime* (pp. 27–55). Cullompton: Willan Publishing.

Faigman, D. L., Blumenthal, J. A., Cheng, E. K., Mnookin, J. L., Murphy, E. E. and Sanders, J. (2012). *Modern Scientific Evidence: The Law and Science of Expert Testimony, Volume 1, Statistics and Research Methods 2012–13.* Eagan, MN: Thomson Reuters-West.

Farmer, B. (2013). M25 road rage killer Kenneth Noye fails in attempt to have minimum jail term cut, *The Independent*, 12th March. Available online at www.independent.co.uk/news/uk/crime/m25-road-rage-killer-kenneth-noye-fails-in-attempt-to-have-minimum-jail-term-cut-8531315.html (accessed 31st May 2013).

Felson, M. (2008). Routine activity approach. In R. Wortley and L. Mazerolle (Eds), *Environmental Criminology and Crime Analysis* (pp. 70–77). Cullompton: Willan Publishing.

Field, A. (2013). *Discovering Statistics Using IBM SPSS Statistics* (4th ed.). London: Sage Publications Ltd.

Fielding, N. (2006). *Courting Violence: Offences Against the Person Cases in Court.* Oxford: Oxford University Press.

Fielding, N. and Thomas, H. (2001). Qualitative interviewing. In N. Gilbert, *Researching Social Life* (2nd ed., pp. 123–144). London: Sage Publications.

Finn, J. (2009). *Capturing the Criminal Image: From Mug Shot to Surveillance Society.* Minneapolis: University of Minnesota Press.

Finnegan, D. A. (2005). Natural history societies in late Victorian Scotland and the pursuit of local civic science. *The British Journal for the History of Science, 38* (1), 53–72.

Fisher, B. A. (2003). *Techniques of Crime Scene Investigation* (7th ed.). Boca Raton: CRC Press.

Fisher, H. (1977). *Report of an Inquiry by the Hon. Sir Henry Fisher into the Circumstances Leading to the Trial of Three Persons on Charges Arising Out of the Death of Maxwell Confait and the Fire at 27 Doggett Road, London SE6, Vol. 1.* London: Her Majesty's Stationery Office.

Fisher, R. P. and Reardon, M. C. (2007). Eyewitness identification. In D. Carson, B. Milne, F. Pakes, K. Shalev and A. Shawyer (Eds), *Applying Psychology to Criminal Justice* (pp. 21–38). Chichester: John Wiley & Sons Ltd.

Flannery, D. J., Vazsonyi, A. T. and Waldman, I. D. (Eds) (2007). *The Cambridge Handbook of Violent Behaviour and Aggression.* Cambridge: Cambridge University Press.

Flately, J., Kershaw, C., Smith, K., Chaplin, R. and Moon, D. (2010). *Crime in England and Wales 2009/10: Findings from the British Crime Survey and Police Recorded Crime* (3rd ed.). London: Home Office.

Fleck, L. ([1935]1981). *Genesis and Development of a Scientific Fact.* Chicago: University of Chicago Press.

Fortey, R. (2008). *Dry Store Room No. 1: The Secret Life of the Natural History Museum.* London: Harper Press.

Foucault, M. ([1977]1991). *Discipline and Punish: The Birth of the Prison.* London: Penguin Books Ltd.

Foucault, M. (1978). *The History of Sexuality, Vol I: An Introduction.* London: Penguin Books.

Foucault, M. (1985). *The History of Sexuality, Vol II: The Use of Pleasure.* London: Penguin Books.

Foucault, M. (1994). *The Order of Things: An Archeology of the Human Sciences.* London: Routledge.

Fradella, H. F., Owen, S. S. and Burke, T. W. (2007). Building bridges between criminal justice and the forensic sciences to create forensic studies programs. *Journal of Criminal Justice Educations, 18* (2), 261–282.

Fraser, J. and Williams, R. (Eds) (2009). *Handbook of Forensic Science.* Cullompton: Willan Publishing.

Fraser, J. and Williams, R. (2009). The contemporary landscape of forensic science. In J. Fraser and R. Williams, *Handbook of Forensic Science* (pp. 1–20). Cullompton: Willan Publishing.

Fritze, R. H. (2009). *Invented Knowledge: False History, Fake Science and Pseudo-Religions.* London: Reaktion Books Ltd.

FSS (2003). *The Scenes of Crime Handbook: Version 4.* Chorley: Forensic Science Service.

Furedi, F. (2006). *Where have All the Intellectuals Gone?* (2nd ed.). London: Continuum.

Furedi, F. (2009). *Wasted: Why Education Isn't Educating.* London: Continuum.

Gaensslen, R. E. (2009). Fingerprints. In S. J. James and J. J. Nordby, *Forensic Science: An Introduction to Scientific and Investigative Techniques* (pp. 355–376). Boca Raton: CRC Press.

Gallop, A. and Stockdale, R. (2004). Trace and contact evidence. In P. C. White (Ed.), *Crime Scene to Court: The Essentials of Forensic Science* (2nd ed., pp. 56–81). Cambridge: The Royal Society of Chemistry.

Galton, F. (1892). *Fingerprints.* London: Macmillan and Co.

Galton, F. (1895). *Fingerprint Directories.* Whitefish: Kessinger Legacy Reprints.

Gardner, R. M. and Bevel, T. (2009). *Practical Crime Scene Analysis and Reconstruction.* Boca Raton: CRC Press.

Garland, D. (1991). *Punishment and Modern Society: A Study in Social Theory.* Oxford: Oxford University Press.

Garland, D. (1997). Of crimes and criminals: The development of criminology in Britain. In M. Maguire, R. Morgan and R. Reiner (Eds), *The Oxford Handbook of Criminology* (2nd ed., pp. 11–56). Oxford: Oxford University Press.

Gascoigne, J. (2009). The Royal Society, natural history and the peoples of the 'New World(s)', 1660–1800. *The British Journal for the History of Science, 42* (4), 539–562.

Gaukroger, S. (2009). *The Emergence of a Scientific Culture: Science and the Shaping of Modernity 1210–1685.* Oxford: Oxford University Press.

Gaukroger, S. (2010). *The Collapse of Mechanism and the Rise of Sensibility: Science and the Shaping of Modernity 1680–1760.* Oxford: Oxford University Press.

Gennard, D. (2012). *Forensic Entomology: An Introduction* (2nd ed.). Chichester: John Wiley & Sons Ltd.

Gerth, H. H. and Mills, C. W. (1993). *From Max Weber: Essays in Sociology.* London: Routledge.

Gibson, M. S. (2009). Cesare Lombroso and Italian criminology. In P. Becker and R. F. Wetzell (Eds), *Criminals and Their Scientists: The History of Criminology in International Perspective* (pp. 137–158). Cambridge: Cambridge University Press.

Gilbert, N. (1993). Research, theory and method. In N. Gilbert, *Researching Social Life* (pp. 18–31). London: Sage Publications.

Gilbert, N. (2006). *Courting Violence: Offences Against the Person Cases in Court.* Oxford: Oxford University Press.

Gilbert, N. (2012). *Researching Social Life* (3rd ed. reprinted). London: Sage Publications Ltd.

Gill, P. and Clayton, T. (2009). The current status of DNA profiling in the UK. In J. Fraser and R. Williams (Eds), *Handbook of Forensic Science* (pp. 29–56). Cullompton: Willan Publishing.

Goddard, C. (1930a). Scientific crime detection laboratories in Europe. Part I. *The American Journal of Police Science, 1* (1), 13–37.

Goddard, C. (1930b). Scientific crime detection laboratories in Europe. Part II. *The American Journal of Police Science, 1* (2), 125–155.

Goffman, E. (1986). *Frame Analysis: An Essay on the Organisation of Experience.* Boston, MA: Northeastern University Press.

Goffman, E. (1991). *Asylums: Essays on the Social Situation of Mental Patients and Other Inmates.* London: Penguin books Ltd.

Golan, T. (2007). *Laws of Men and Laws of Nature: The History of Scientific Expert Testimony in England and America.* Cambridge, MA.: Harvard University Press.

Golinski, J. (2005). *Making Natural Knowledge: Constructivism and the History of Science.* Cambridge: Cambridge University Press.

Gray, H. ([1858]2012). *Anatomy: Descriptive and Surgical.* London: Bounty Books.

Gray, T. (2009). *The Elements: A Visual Exploration of Every Known Atom in the Universe.* New York: Black Dog and Leventhal Publishers Inc.

Greenwood, P. W. and Petersilia, J. (1975). *The Criminal Investigation Process Volume I: Summary and Policy Implications.* Santa Monica, CA: The Rand Corporation.

Gribble, L. R. (1933). *Famous Feats of Detection and Deduction.* London: George G. Harrap and Co. Ltd.

Grieve, M. and Houck, M. M. (2004). Introduction. In M. M. Houck (Ed.), *Trace Evidence Analysis: More Cases in Mute Witnesses* (pp. 1–26). Burlington, MA: Elsevier Academic Press.

Gross, H. (1962). *Criminal Investigation: A Practical Textbook for Magistrates, Police Officers and Lawyers* (5th ed.). London: Sweet and Maxwell Limited.

Gross, R. (2005). *Psychology: The Science of Mind and Behaviour* (5th ed.). London: Hodder Education.

Groth, A. N. (1979). *Men who Rape: The Psychology of the Offender.* New York: Plenum Press.

Gudjonsson, G. H. (2002). *The Psychology of Interrogations and Confessions: A Handbook.* Chichester: John Wiley & Sons Ltd.

Gudjonsson, G. H. (2007). Investigative interviewing. In T. Newburn, T. Williamson and A. Wright, *Handbook of Criminal Investigation* (pp. 466–492). Cullompton: Willan Publishing.

Gwei-Djen, L. and Needham, J. (1988). A history of forensic medicine in China. *Medical History, 32,* 357–400.

Hall, A. R. (1954). *The Scientific Revolution, 1500–1800: The Formation of the Modern Scientific Attitude.* Boston, MA: Beacon Press.

Hall, M. C. (Ed.). (2010). *The Washing Away of Wrongs: Song Ci* Raleigh: Lulu Books.

Hall, S. and Jefferson, T. (Eds) (1975). *Resistence Through Rituals: Youth Subcultures in Post-War Britain.* London: Routledge.

Haour, G. and Mieville, L. (2011). *From Science to Business: How Firms Create Value by Partnering with Universities.* Basingstoke: Palgrave Macmillan.

Harcourt, B. E. (2007). *Against Prediction: Profiling, Policing, and Punishment in an Actuarial Age.* Chicago: University of Chicago Press.

Haringey Local Safeguarding Children Board (2009). *Serious Case Review: Baby Peter, Executive Summary.* London: Haringey LSCB.

Harris, D. A. (2012). *Failed Evidence: Why Law Enforcement Resists Science.* New York: New York University Press.

Harris, J. R. (1999). *The Nurture Assumption: Why Children Turn Out The Way They Do.* London: Bloomsbury Publishing Plc.

Harvey, D. (1990). *The Condition of Postmodernity: An Enquiry into the Origins of Cultural Change.* Oxford: Blackwell Publishers Ltd.

Hawking, S. (1988). *A Brief History of Time: From the Big Bang to Black Holes.* London: Bantam Books.

Hebdige, D. (1979). *Subculture: The Meaning of Style.* New Jersey: Transaction Books.

Heering, P. (2008). The enlightened microscope: Re-enactment and analysis of projections with eighteenth-century solar microscopes. *The British Journal for the History of Science, 41* (3), 345–367.

Henry, E. R. (1900). *Classification and Uses of Finger Prints.* London: George Routledge and Sons Ltd.

Herschel, W. J. (1916). *The Origin of Finger-Printing.* London: Oxford University Press.

Hewitt, R. (2010). *Map of a Nation: A Biography of the Ordinance Survey.* London: Granta Publications.

Hitchens, C. (2007). *God is Not Great.* London: Atlantic Books.

HM Inspectorate of Constabulary (2002). *Under the Microscope Refocused: A Revisit to the Thematic Inspection Report on Scientific and Technical Support.* London: HMIC.

Hobbs, D. (1989). *Doing The Business: Entrepreneurship, the Working Class and Detectives in the East End of London.* Oxford: Oxford University Press.

Hobbs, D. (1995). *Bad Business: Professional Crime in Modern Britain.* Oxford: Oxford University Press.

Hobbs, D., Hadfield, P., Lister, S. and Winlow, S. (2003). *Bouncers: Violence and Governance in the Night-Time Economy.* Oxford: Oxford University Press.

Hobsbawm, E. J. (1965). *Primitive Rebels: Studies in Archaic Forms of Social Movement in the 19th and 20th Centuries.* New York: W. W. Norton and Company.

Hobsbawm, E. J. (2012). *Uncommon People: Resistance, Rebellion and Jazz.* London: Abacus.

Holmes, R. (2009). *The Age of Wonder: How the Romantic Generation Discovered the Beauty and Terror of Science.* London: Harper Press.

Holmes, R. M. and DeBurger, J. (1988). *Serial Murder.* Thousand Oaks, CA: Sage Publications Inc.

Holstein, J. and Miller, G. (Eds) (1993). *Reconsidering Social Constructionism: Debates in Social Problems.* New York: Aldine De Gruyter.

Home Office (2002). *Achieving Best Evidence in Criminal Proceedings: Guidance on Interviewing Victims and Witnesses, and Using Special Measures.* London: Home Office.

Home Office Scientific Development Branch (2000). *Fingerprint Development Handbook.* Heanor, Derbyshire: Heanor Gate Printing Limited.

Home Office Scientific Development Branch (2005). *Fingerprint Development Handbook.* Heanor, Derbyshire: Heanor Gate Printing Limited.

Hoover, J. E. (1931). Criminal identification. *The American Journal of Police Science, 2* (1), 8–19.

Hoover, J. E. (1931). The national division of identification and information. *The American Journal of Police Science, 2* (3), 241–251.

Horrocks, S. M. (2007). The internationalization of science in a commercial context: Research and development by overseas multinationals in Britain before the mid-1970s. *The British Journal for the History of Science, 40* (2), 227–250.

Horswell, J. and Fowler, C. (2004). Associative evidence – the Locard exchange principle. In J. Horswell, *The Practice of Crime Scene Investigation* (pp. 75–85). Boca Raton: CRC Press.

Houck, M. M. (Ed.) (2004). *Trace Evidence Analysis: More Cases in Mute Witnesses.* Burlington, MA: Elsevier Academic Press.

Houck, M. M. (2009). Trace evidence. In J. Fraser and R. Williams (Eds), *Handbook of Forensic Science* (pp. 166–195). Cullompton: Willan Publishing.

Houck, M. M. and Siegel, J. A. (2010). *Fundamentals of Forensic Science* (2nd ed.). Burlington, MA: Academic Press.

House of Commons Health Committee (2003). *The Victoria Climbié Inquiry Report: Sixth Report of Session 2002–03*. London: The Stationery Office Limited.

House of Commons Home Affairs Committee (2002a). *The Conduct of Investigations into Past Cases of Abuse in Children's Homes: Fourth Report of Session 2001–02, Volume I*. London: The Stationery Office Limited.

House of Commons Home Affairs Committee (2002b). *The Conduct of Investigations into Past Cases of Abuse in Children's Home: Fourth Report of Session 2001–02, Volume II*. London: The Stationery Office Limited.

House of Commons Science and Technology Committee (2005a). *Forensic Science on Trial: Seventh Report of Session 2004–05, Volume I*. London: The Stationery Office Limited.

House of Commons Science and Technology Committee (2005b). *Forensic Science on Trial: Seventh Report of Session 2004–05, Volume II, Oral and Written Evidence*. London: The Stationery Office Limited.

House of Commons Science and Technology Committee (2005c). *Forensic Science on Trial: The Government Response to the Committee's Seventh Report 2004–05, First Special Report of Session 2005–06*. London: The Stationery Office Limited.

House of Commons Science and Technology Committee (2011a). *The Forensic Science Service: Seventh Report of Session 2010–12, Volume I: Report, Together with Formal Minutes, Oral and Written Evidence*. London: The Stationery Office Limited.

House of Commons Science and Technology Committee (2011b). *The Forensic Science Service: Seventh Report of Session 2010–12, Volume II: Additional Written Evidence*. London: The Stationery Office Limited.

House of Commons Science and Technology Committee (2011c). *The Forensic Science Service: The Government Response to the Seventh Report from the House of Commons Science and Technology Committee Session 2010–12 HC 855*. London: The Stationery Office Limited.

House of Commons Science and Technology Committee (2011d). *The Forensic Science Service: Government Response, Oral and Written Evidence*. London: The Stationery Office Limited.

House of Commons Science and Technology Committee (2013a). *Forensic Science: Second Report of Session 2013–14, Volume I: Report, Together with Formal Minutes, Oral and Written Evidence*. London: The Stationery Office Limited.

House of Commons Science and Technology Committee (2013b). *Forensic Science: Second Report of Session 2013–14, Volume II: Additional Written Evidence*. London: The Stationery Office Limited.

House of Lords Select Committee on Science and Technology (1992). *Forensic Science: Evidence Received after 31 July 1992, Session 1992–93*. London: HMSO.

House of Lords Select Committee on Science and Technology (1993). *Forensic Science: Session 1992–93, 5th report*. London: HMSO.

Hoyle, C. (2012). Victims, the criminal justice procesess, and restorative justice. In M. Maguire, R. Morgan and R. Reiner (Eds), *The Oxford Handbook of Criminology* (5th ed., pp. 398–425). Oxford: Oxford University Press.

Huber, P. W. (1991). *Galileo's Revenge: Junk Science in the Courtroom*. New York: BasicBooks.

Hunter, P. (2010). Forensics21 – Quality Standards Project update. Paper Presented 15th June 2010.

Huff, T. E. (2003). *The Rise of Early Modern Science: Islam, China and the West* (2nd ed.). Cambridge: Cambridge University Press.

Hunter, M. (2007). Robert Boyle and the early Royal Society: A reciprocal exchange in the making of Baconian science. *The British Journal for the History of Science, 40* (1), 1–23.

Hunter, M. (2009). *Boyle: Between God and Science.* New Haven: Yale University Press.

Ignatieff, M. (1978). *A Just Measure of Pain: The Penitentiary in the Industrial Revolution, 1750–1850.* New York. Pantheon Books.

Inman, K. and Rudin, N. (2000). *Principles and Practices of Criminalistics: The Professions of Forensic Science.* Boca Raton: CRC Press.

Innes, M. (2003). *Investigating Murder: Detective Work and the Police Response to Criminal Homicide.* Oxford: Oxford University Press.

Innes, M., Fielding, N. and Cope, N. (2005). The appliance of science? The theory and practice of crime intelligence analysis. *British Journal of Criminology, 45* (1), 39–57.

Jackson, A. R. and Jackson, J. M. (2008). *Forensic Science* (2nd ed.). Harlow, Essex: Pearson Education Ltd.

Jackson, A. R. and Jackson, J. M. (2011). *Forensic Science* (3rd ed.). Harlow, Essex: Pearson Education Ltd.

Jackson, G. (2000). The scientist and the scales of justice. *Science and Justice, 40* (2), 81–85.

Jackson, G. (2009). Understanding forensic science opinions. In J. Fraser and R. Williams (Eds), *Handbook of Forensic Science* (pp. 419–445). Cullompton: Willan Publishing.

James, A. (2011). *The Influence of Intelligence-Led Policing Models on Investigative Policy and Practice in Mainstream Policing 1993–2007: Division, Resistance and Investigative Orthodoxy.* Unpublished PhD Thesis, London School of Economics.

James, S. H., Kish, P. E. and Sutton, T. P. (2005). *Principles of Bloodstain Pattern Analysis: Theory and Practice.* Boca Raton: CRC Press.

James, W. ([1907]1912). *Essays in Radical Empiricism.* New York: Longmans, Green and Co.

Jasanoff, S. (1997). *Science at the Bar: Law, Science and Technology in America.* Cambridge: Harvard University Press.

Jenkins, P. (2003). *Beyond Tolerance: Child Pornography Online.* New York: New York University Press.

Jenkins, S. and Woffinden, B. (2008). *The Murder of Billy-Jo.* London: John Blake Publishing Ltd.

John, T. and Maguire, M. (2007). Criminal intelligence and the National Intelligence Model. In T. Newburn, T. Williamson and A. Wright (Eds), *Handbook of Criminal Investigation* (pp. 199–225). Cullompton: Willan Publishing.

Johnson, S. D., Bowers, K. J. and Pease, K. (2005). Predicting the future or summarisng the past? Crime mapping as anticipation. In M. J. Smith and N. Tilley (Eds), *Crime science: New approaches to preventing and detecting crime* (pp. 145–163). Cullompton: Willan Publishing.

Jones, D. W. (2008). *Understanding Criminal Behaviour: Psychosocial Approaches to Criminality.* Cullompton: Willan Publishing.

Jones, O. (2011). *Chavs: The Demonization of the Working Class.* London: Verso.

Jones, P. (2009). Forensic digital photo imaging. In S. H. James, J. J. Nordby, (Eds), *Forensic Science: An Introduction to Scientific and Investigative Techniques* (3rd ed., pp. 193–210). Boca Raton: CRC Press.

Jones, S. (2001). *Criminology* (2nd ed.). London: Butterworths.

Jones, T. (2003). The governance and accountability of policing. In T. Newburn (Ed.), *Handbook of Policing* (pp. 603–627). Cullompton: Willan Publishing.

Kaptein, H., Prakken, H. and Verheij, B. (Eds) (2009). *Legal Evidence and Proof: Statistics, Stories, Logic.* Farnham: Ashgate Publishing Ltd.

Keith, B. (2006a). *Report of the Zahid Mubarek Inquiry, Volume 1.* London: The Stationery Office.

Keith, B. (2006b). *Report of the Zahid Mubarek Inquiry, Volume 2.* London: The Stationery Office.

Kemshall, H. (2008). *Understanding the Management of High Risk Offenders.* Maidenhead: Open University Press.

Kennedy, D. B. (2013). Evolving practice parameters of forensic criminology. In S. J. Morewitz and M. L. Goldstein (Eds), *Handbook of Forensic Sociology and Psychology* (pp. 1–20). New York: Springer.

Keppel, R. D. and Birnes, W. J. (2003). *The Psychology of Serial Killer Investigations: The Grisly Business Unit.* San Diego, CA: Academic Press.

Kirk, P. L. (1974). *Crime Investigation* (2nd ed.). New York: John Wiley & Sons Ltd.

Klein, M. W. and Maxson, C. L. (2006). *Street Gang Patterns and Policies.* Oxford: Oxford University Press.

Klinkner, M. (2009). Forensic science expertise for international criminal proceedings: An old problem, a new context and pragmatic resolution. *The International Journal of Evidence and Proof, 13* (2), 102–129.

Knights, M. (2011). *The Devil in Disguise: Deception, Delusion, and Fanaticism in the Early English Enlightenment.* Oxford: Oxford University Press.

Kontos, L., Brotherton, D. C. and Barrios, L. (2003). *Gangs and Society: Alternative Perspectives.* New York: Columbia University Press.

Kornblith, H. (1995). *Inductive Inference and its Natural Ground: An Essay in Naturalistic Epistemology.* Cambridge, MA: The MIT Press.

Koslicki, K. (2008). Natural kinds and natural kind terms. *Philosophy Compass, 3* (4), 789–802. DOI: 10.1111/j.1747-9991.2008.00157.x.

Kubic, T. A. and Petraco, N. (2009). Microanalysis and exmaination of trace evidence. In S. H. James and J. J. Nordby (Eds), *Forensic Science: An Introduction to Scientific and Investigative Techniques* (3rd ed., pp. 327–354). Boca Raton: CRC Press.

Kuhn, T. S. ([1962]1996). *The Structure of Scientific Revolutions* (3rd ed.). Chicago: The University of Chicago Press.

Larson, J. L. (1971). *Reason and Experience: The Representation of Natural Order in the Work of Carl Von Linné.* Berkley, CA: University of California Press.

Latour, B. (2008). A textbook case revisited – knowledge as a mode of existence. In E. J. Hackett, O. Amsterdamska, M. Lynch and J. Wajcman, *The Handbook of Science and Technology Studies* (pp. 83–112). Cambridge, MA.: The MIT Press.

Latour, B. and Woolgar, S. (1986). *Laboratory Life: The Construction of Scientific Facts.* Princeton, NJ: Princeton University Press.

Laughlin, R. B. (2008). *The Crime of Reason: And the Closing of the Scientific Mind.* New York: Basic Books.

Lawless, C. J. (2011). Policing markets: The contested shaping of neo-liberal forensic science. *British Journal of Criminology, 51* (4), 671–689.

Laycock, G. (2005). Defining crime science. In M. J. Smith, and N. Tilley (Eds), *Crime Science: New Approaches to Preventing and Detecting Crime* (pp. 3–26). Cullompton: Willan Publishing.

Leigh, A., Read, T. and Tilley, N. (1996). *Problem-Oriented Policing: Brit Pop.* London: Home Office.

Lemert, E. (1951). *Social Pathology: A Systematic Approach to a Theory of Sociopathic Behaviour.* London: McGraw-Hill.

Lifton, R. J. (2000). *The Nazi Doctors: Medical Killing and the Psychology of Genocide.* New York: Basic Books.

Lightman, B. (Ed.). (1997). *Victorian Science in Context.* Chicago: The University of Chicago Press.

Lightman, B. (2002). Huxley and scientific agnosticism: The strange history of a failed rhetorical strategy. *The British Journal of the History of Science, 35* (3), 271–289.

Lilly, J. R., Cullen, F. T. and Ball, R. A. (2011). *Criminological Theory: Context and Consequences* (5th ed.). Thousand Oaks, CA: Sage Publications.

Locard, E. (1930a). The analysis of dust traces. Part I. *The American Journal of Police Science, 1* (3), 276–298.

Locard, E. (1930b). The analysis of dust traces. Part III. *The American Journal of Police Science, 1* (5), 496–514.

Locard, E. and Larson, D. J. (1930). The analysis of dust traces. Part II. *The American Journal of Police Science,* 1(4), 401–418.

Lombroso, C. (2007). *Criminal Man.* Translated by M. Gibson and N. Hann-Rafter. Durham, NC: Duke University Press.

Longley, P. A., Goodchild, M., Maguire, D. J. and Rhind, D. W. (2001). *Geographic Information Systems and Science.* Chichester: John Wiley & Sons Ltd.

Loseke, D. (2003). *Thinking about Social Problems: An Introduction to Constructionist Perspectives.* New York: Aldine De Gruyter.

Lucas, A. (1931). *Forensic Criminology and Scientific Investigation.* London: Edward Arnold and Co.

Lucy, D. (2005). *Introduction to Statistics for Forensic Scientists.* Chichester: John Wiley & Sons Ltd.

McCann, J., Wells, R., Simon, M. and Voris, J. (1990). Comparison of genital examination techniques in prepubertal girls. *Pediatrics. 85* (2), pp. 182–187.

McCann, J., Wells, R., Simon, M. and Voris, J. (1990). Genital findings in prepubertal girls selected for nonabuse: A descriptive study. *Pediatrics. 86* (3), pp. 428–439.

McConville, M., Sanders, A. and Leng, R. (1993). *The Case for the Prosecution: Police Suspects and the Construction of Criminality.* London: Routledge.

McCulloch, H. (1996). *Police Use of Forensic Science. Police Research Series. Paper 19.* London: Home Office.

MacLeod, J. (2004). *Ain't No Makin' It: Aspirations and Attainment in a Low-Income Neighbourhood.* Colorado: Westview Press, Inc.

Maden, A. (2007). *Treating Violence: A Guide to Risk Management in Mental Health.* Oxford: Oxford University Press.

Magnus, P. D. (2011). No grist for Mill on natural kinds. Available online at www.academia.edu/2801850/No_grist_for_Mill_on_natural_kinds (accessed 26th February 2012).

Magnus, P. D. (2012). *Scientific Enquiry and Natural Kinds: From Planets to Mallards*. Basingstoke: Palgrave Macmillan.

Maguire, M. (1997). Crime statistics, patterns, and trends: Changing perceptions and their implications. In M. Maguire, R. Morgan and R. Reiner (Eds), *The Oxford Handbook of Criminology* (2nd ed., pp. 135–188). Oxford: University of Oxford Press.

Maguire, M. (2003). Criminal investigation and crime control. In T. Newburn (Ed.), *Handbook of Policing* (pp. 363–393). Cullompton: Willan Publishing.

Maguire, M. (2007). Crime data and statistics. In M. Maguire, R. Morgan and R. Reiner (Eds), *The Oxford Handbook of Criminology* (4th ed., pp. 241–301). Oxford: Oxford University Press.

Maguire, M. and Norris, C. (1992). *The Conduct and Supervision of Criminal Investigations. Research Study No. 5*. The Royal Commission on Criminal Justice. London: HMSO.

Manier, E. (1986). Social dimensions of the mind-body problem: Turbulence in the flow of scientific information. *Science and Technology Studies, 4* (3/4), 16–28.

Mannheim, K. (1936). *Ideology and Utopia: An Introduction to the Sociology of Knowledge*. London: Routledge and Kegan Paul.

Marx, K. ([1867]1990). *Capital, Volume 1*. London: Penguin Books Ltd.

Marx, K. and Engels, F. ([1892]1987). *The Communist Manifesto*. London: Penguin Books Ltd.

Masters, B. (1993). *The Shrine of Jeffrey Dahmer*. London: Hodder & Stoughton Ltd.

Matassa, M. and Newburn, T. (2007). Social context of criminal investigation. In T. Newburn, T. Williamson and A. Wright (Eds), *Handbook of Criminal Investigation* (pp. 41–67). Cullompton: Willan Publishing.

Matza, D. (1990). *Delinquency and Drift* (2nd ed.). Piscataway, NJ: Transaction Publishers.

Maudlsey, H. (1884). *Body and Will: Being an Essay Concerning Will in its Metaphysical, Physiological and Pathological Aspects*. New York: Appleton and Company.

Mawby, R. I. (2003). Models of policing . In T. Newburn (Ed.), *Handbook of Policing* (1st ed., pp. 15–40). Cullompton: Willan Publishing.

May, L. S. (2011). *Crime's Nemesis*. Landisville, PA: Coachwhip Publications.

Mayhew, H. ([1851]1985). *London Labour and the London Poor*. London: Penguin Books.

Mayhew, H. ([1862]2005). *The London Underworld in the Victorian Period: Authentic First-Person Accounts by Beggars, Thieves and Prostitutes*. New York: Dover Publications Ltd.

Merton, R. K. (1968). *Social Theory and Social Structure* (3rd ed.). London: Collier-Macmillian.

Mill, J. S. ([1843]2011). *A System of Logic*. Kindle Edition.

Mill, J. S. ([1879]2012). *Utilitarianism*. London: Longmans Green and Co.

Millen, P. (2000). Is crime scene investigation forensic science? Are crime scene investigators forensic scientists? *Science and Justice, 40* (2), 125–126.

Miller, M. T. (2009). Crime scene investigation. In S. H. James and J. J. Nordby (Eds), *Forensic Science: An Introduction to Scientific and Investigative Techniques* (pp. 167–192). Boca Raton: CRC Press.

Milne, B. and Bull, R. (1999). *Investigative Interviewing: Psychology and Practice*. Chichester: John Wiley & Sons Ltd.

Milne, B., Shaw, G. and Bull, R. (2007). Investigative interviewing: The role of research. In D. Carson, B. Milne, F. Pakes, K. Shalev and A. Shawyer (Eds), *Applying Psychology to Criminal Justice* (pp. 65–80). Chichester: John Wiley & Sons Ltd.

Ministry of Justice (2012). *Statisical Bulletin on the Public Disorder of 6th to 9th August 2011 – September 2012 Update.* London: Ministry of Justice.

Monckton-Smith, J., Adams, T., Hart, A. G. and Webb, J. (2013). *Introducing Forensic and Criminal Investigation.* London: Sage Publications Ltd.

Morone, J. A. (2003). *Hellfire Nation: The Politics of Sin in American History.* New Haven: Yale University Press.

Morrell, G., Scott, S., McNeish, D. and Webster, S. (2011). *The August Riots in England: Understanding the Involvement of Young People.* London: NatCen. Available online at www.gov.uk/government/uploads/system/uploads/attachment_data/file/60531/The_20 August_20Riots_20in_20England_20_pdf__201mb_pdf (accessed 15th October 2012).

Morris, B. (2007). History of criminal investigation. In T. Newburn, T. Williamson and A. Wright (Eds), *Handbook of Criminal Investigation* (pp. 15–40). Cullompton: Willan Publishing.

Morton, J. (2005). *The First Detective: The Life and Revolutionary Times of Vidocq, Criminal, Spy and Private Eye.* London: Ebury Press.

Mullin, C. (1986). *Error of Judgement: The Truth Behind the Birmingham Bombings.* London: Chatto and Windus.

Nair, S. P. (2006). Science and the politics of colonial collecting: The case of Indian meteorites, 1856–70. *The British Journal for the History of Science, 39* (1), 97–119.

Nash, M. (1999). *Police, Probation and Protecting the Public.* London: Blackstone Press.

Nash, M. (2006). *Public Protection and the Criminal Justice Process.* Oxford: Oxford University Press.

Nash, M. and Williams, A. (2008). *The Anatomy of Serious Further Offending.* Oxford: Oxford University Press.

Nash, M. and Williams, A. (Eds) (2010). *Hanbook of Public Protection.* Cullompton: Willan Publishing.

National Research Council of the National Academies (2009). *Strengthening Forensic Science in the United States: A Path Forward.* Washington, D.C.: The National Academies Press.

Naylor, S. (2005). Introduction: Historical geographies of science – places, contexts and cartographies. *The British Journal for the History of Science, 38* (1), 1–12.

NCIS (2000). *The National Intelligence Model.* London: National Crime Intelligence Service.

NCPE (2005). *Practice Advice on Core Investigative Doctrine.* Cambourne: National Centre for Policing Excellence.

Newburn, T. (2003). Policing since 1945. In T. Newburn (Ed.), *Handbook of Policing* (1st ed., pp. 84–105). Cullompton: Willan Publishing.

Newburn, T. (2007). Understanding investigation. In T. Newburn, T. Williamson and A. Wright (Eds), *Handbook of Criminal Investigation* (pp. 1–10). Cullompton: Willan Publishing.

Newburn, T., Williamson, T. and Wright, A. (Eds) (2007). *Handbook of Criminal Investigation.* Cullompton: Willan Publishing.

Newton, I. ([1687]1729). *The Mathematical Principles of Natural Philosophy, to which is Added Newton's System of the World* (Trans. Andrew Motte). Kindle Edition.

Nickell, J. and Fischer, J. J. (1999). *Crime Science: Methods of Forensic Detection.* Kentucky: The University Press of Kentucky.

Nowotny, H., Scott, P. and Gibbons, M. (2001). *Re-Thinking Science: Knowledge and the Public in an Age of Uncertainty.* Cambridge: Polity Press.

NPIA (2010a). *Science and Innovation in the Police Service 2010–2013.* London: National Police Improvement Agency.

NPIA (2010b). *Forensics21 Update.* London: National Police Improvement Agency.

NPIA (2012). *Forensic Submissions: Good Practice Guide.* London: National Police Improvement Agency.

O'Day, R. and Englander, D. (1993). *Mr. Charles Booth's Inquiry: Life and Labour of the People in London Reconsidered.* London: Hambledon Continuum.

O'Hara, C. and O'Hara, G. (2003). *Fundamentals of Criminal Investigations* (7th ed.). Springfield, IL: Charles C. Thomas Publisher Ltd.

Osgerby, B. (1998). *Youth in Britain since 1945.* Oxford: Blackwell Publishers.

Pareto, V. (1935). *The Mind and Society: Vol I.* London: Richard Cape Publishers.

Park, R. E., Burgess, E. W. and McKenzie, R. D. ([1925]1967). *The City: Suggestions for Investigation of Human Behaviour in the Urban Environment.* Chicago: University of Chicago Press.

Parsons, T. (1967). *The Structure of Social Action, Vol. I: Marshall, Pareto, Durkheim.* New York: The Free Press.

Pavord, A. (2009). *Searching for Order: The History of the Alchemists, Herbalists and Philosophers who Unlocked the Secrets of the Plant World.* London: Bloomsbury Publishing Plc.

Pearl, C. (1955). *Girl with the Swansdown Seat.* London: Frederick Muller.

Pearson, G. (1975). *The Deviant Imagination: Psychiatry, Social Work and Social Change.* Basingstoke: The Macmillan Press Ltd.

Pearson, G. (1983). *Hooligan: A History of Respectable Fears.* London: The Macmillan Press.

Pearson, K. ([1919]2007). *The Grammar of Science.* Kindle Edition.

Pepper, I. K. (2005). *Crime Scene Investigation: Methods and Procedures.* Maidenhead: Open University Press.

Pepper, I. K. (2010). *Crime Scene Investigation: Methods and Procedures* (2nd ed.). Maidenhead: Open University Press.

Petherick, W. and Ferguson, C. E. (2010). Criminal profiling. In W. Petherick, B. E. Turvey and C. E. Ferguson (Eds), *Forensic Criminology* (pp. 177–218). San Diego: Elsevier Academic Press.

Petherick, W. and Turvey, B. E. (2008). Criminal profiling: The scientific method and logic. In B. E. Turvey, *Criminal Profiling: An Introduction to Behavioural Evidence Analysis* (pp. 43–74). Burlington: Elsevier Academic Press.

Petherick, W., Turvey, B. E. and Ferguson, C. E. (Eds) (2010). *Forensic Criminology.* San Diego: Elsevier Academic Press.

Pinker, S. (2003). *The Blank Slate: The Modern Denial of Human Nature.* London: Penguin Books Ltd.

Plummer, K. (Ed.). (1992). *Modern Homosexualities: Fragments of Lesbian and Gay Experiences.* London: Routledge.

Podlas, K. (2006). 'The CSI Effect': Exposing the media myth. *Fordham Intellectual Property, Media and Entertainment Law Journal, 16* (2), 429–465. Available online at http://heinonline.org/HOL/Page?handle=hein.journals/frdipm16anddiv=16andg_sent=1andcollection=journals (accessed 15th January 2011).

Podlas, K. (2009). The 'CSI Effect' and other forensic fictions. *Loyola of Los Angeles Entertainment Law Review, 27* (2), 87–125. Available online at http://heinonline.org/HOL/Page?handle=hein.journals/laent27anddiv=10andg_sent=1andcollection=journals (accessed 15th January 2011).

Policing Reform Working Group (2009). *A Force to be Reckoned with*. London: The Centre for Social Justice.

Policy Exchange. (2011). *Policing in 2020: A Summary of Discussions on the Future of Policing*. London: Policy Exchange.

Pollock, F. and Maitland, F. W. (2010). *The History of English Law Before the Time of Edward I, Vol I*. Indianapolis: Liberty Fund Inc.

Polsky, N. (1971). *Hustlers, Beats and Others*. Harmondsworth: Penguin.

Popper, K. (2002). *The Logic of Scientific Discovery*. London: Routledge.

Price, C. and Caplan, J. (1977). *The Confait Confessions*. London: Marion Boyars Publishers.

Prins, H. (1995). *Offenders, Deviants or Patients?* London: Routledge.

Prins, H. (2010). Dangers by being despised grow great. In M. Nash, A. Williams (Eds), *Handbook of Public Protection* (pp. 15–39). Cullompton: Willan Publishing.

Pryce, K. (1986). *Endless Pressure: a Study of West Indian Lifestyles in Bristol*. Bristol: Bristol Classical Press.

Purcell, C. E. and Arrigo, B. A. (2006). *The Psychology of Lust Murder: Paraphilia, Sexual Killing and Serial Homicide*. Burlington, MA: Academic Press.

Purkyne, J. E. (1823). *Commentatio de examine physiologico organi visus et systematis cutanei*. Breslau, Prussia: University of Breslau Press.

QAA (2007). *Criminology*., QAA. Available online at www.qaa.ac.uk/Publications/InformationAndGuidance/Documents/criminology07.pdf (accessed 24th July 2012).

Quine, W. V. (1969). *Ontological Relativity and Other Essays*. New York: Columbia University Press.

Quinney, R. (1970). *The Social Reality of Crime*. London: Little Brown and Company.

Rafter, N. (1997). *Creating Born Criminals*. Chicago: University of Illinois Press.

Rafter, N. (2004). The unrepentant horse-slasher: Moral insanity and the origins of criminological thought. *Criminology, 42* (4), 979–1008.

Rafter, N. (2008). *The Criminal Brain: Understanding Biological Thoeries of Crime*. New York: New York University Press.

Rafter, N. (Ed.). (2009). *The Origins of Criminology: A Reader*. London: Routledge.

Ratcliffe, J. (2008). *Intelligence-Led Policing*. Cullompton: Willan Publishing.

Rawlings, P. (2003). Policing before the police. In T. Newburn (Ed.), *Handbook of Policing* (1st ed., pp. 41–65). Cullompton: Willan Publishing.

Raynor, P. and Vanstone, M. (2007). Towards a correctional service. In L. Gelsthorpe and R. Morgan (Eds), *Handbook of Probation* (pp. 59–89). Cullompton: Willan Publishing.

Read, T. and Tilley, N. (2000). *Not Rocket Science? Problem-Solving and Crime Reduction. Crime Reduction Research Series Paper 6*. London: Home Office.

Redmayne, M. (2004). *Expert Evidence and Criminal Justice*. Oxford: Oxford University Press.

Reill, P. H. (2003). The legacy of the scientific revolution: Science and the enlightenment. In R. Porter, *The Cambridge History of Science, Volume 4: Eighteenth-Century Science* (pp. 23–41). Cambridge: Cambridge University Press.

Reiner, R. (2010). *The Politics of the Police* (4th ed.). Oxford: Oxford University Press.

Ressler, R. K., Burgess, A. W. and Douglas, J. E. (1995). *Sexual Homicide: Patterns and Motives*. New York: The Free Press.

Rhodes, H. T. (1936). *Some Persons Unknown: Being an Account of Scientific Detection*. London: John Murray.

Ribaux, O., Baylon, A., Roux, C., Delémont, O., Lock, E., Zingg, C. and Margot, P. (2009). Intelligence-led crime scene processing. Part I: Forensic Intelligence. *Forensic Science International, 195* (1–3), 10–16.

Risinger, D. M., Saks, M. J., Thompson, W. C. and Rosenthal, R. (2002). The *Daubert/ Kumho* implications of observer effects in Forensic Science: Hidden problems of expectation and suggestion. *California Law Review, 90* (1), 1–56.

Roberts, M. J. (1983). The society for the suppression of vice and its early critics, 1802– 1812. *The Historical Journal, 26* (1), 159–176.

Roberts, P. (1996). What price a free market in forensic science services? *British Journal of Criminology, 36* (1), 37–60.

Roberts, P. and Willmore, C. (1993). *The Royal Commission on Criminal Justice: The Role of Forensic Science Evidence in Criminal Proceedings. Research Study No. 11.* London: HMSO.

Robertson, B. and Vignaux, G. A. (1995). *Interpreting Evidence: Evaluating Forensic Science in the Courtroom.* Chichester: John Wiley & Sons Ltd.

Robinson, E. M. (2010). *Crime Scene Photography.* Burlington, MA: Academic Press.

Robinson, E. M. (2013). *Introduction to Crime Scene Photography.* Waltham, MA: Academic Press.

Rock, P. (2004). *Constructing Victims' Rights: The Home Office, New Labour, and Victims.* Oxford: Oxford University Press.

Rogers, C. (2007). Criminal investigations. In C. Rogers and R. Lewis, *Introduction to Police Work* (pp. 149–166). Cullompton: Willan Publishing.

Rose, M. H. (1987). Science as an idiom in the domain of technology. *Science and Technology Studies, 5* (1), 3–11.

Rossmo, K. D. (2000). *Geographic Profiling.* Boca Raton: CRC Press.

Rowbotham, J. and Stevenson, K. (2003). *Behaving Badly: Social Panic and Moral Outrage – Victorian and Modern Parallels.* Aldershot: Ashgate Publishing Ltd.

Rowbotham, J. and Stevenson, K. (Eds) (2005). *Criminal Conversations: Victorian Crimes, Social Panic, and Moral Outrage.* Columbus: The Ohio State University Press.

Rowe, M. (2008). *Introduction to Policing.* London: Sage Publications Ltd.

Rowe, W. (2009). Firearm and tool mark examinations. In S. James and J. Nordby (Eds), *Forensic Science: An Introduction to Scientific and Investigative Techniques* (pp. 407– 438). Boca Raton: CRC Press.

Rubington, E. and Weinberg, M. (1995). *The Study of Social Problems: Seven Perspectives.* Oxford: Oxford University Press.

Rudwick, M. J. (1997). *Georges Cuvier, Fossil Bones, and Geological Catastrophes.* Chicago: The University of Chicago Press.

Ruestow, E. G. (2004). *The Microscope in the Dutch Republic: The Shaping of Discovery.* Cambridge: Cambridge Unievrsity Press.

Ryan, A. (1970). *The Philosophy of the Social Sciences.* London: Macmillan and Co. Ltd.

Saferstein, R. (2007). *Criminalistics: An Introduction to Forensic Science* (9th ed.). New Jersey: Pearson Education.

Saks, M. J. and Faigman, D. L. (2008). Failed forensics: how forensic science lost its way and how it might yet find it. *Annual Review of Law and Social Science, 4*, 149–171.

Saks, M. J. and Koehler, J. J. (2005). The coming apradigm shift in forensic identification science. *Science, 309* (5736), 892–895.

Saks, M. J. and Koehler, J. J. (2007). The individualization fallacy in forensic science evidence. Available online at http://works.bepress.com/cgi/viewcontent.cgi?article=100 0andcontext=michael_saks (accessed 28th June 2013).

Saks, M. J. and Koehler, J. J. (2008). The individualization fallacy in forensic science evidence. *Vanderbilt Law Review, 61* (1), 199–219.

Savage, S. (2007). *Police Reform: Forces for Change.* Oxford: Oxford University Press.

Schaffer, G. (2005). Like a baby with a box of matches: British scientists and the concept of 'race' in the inter-war period. *The British Journal for the History of Science, 38* (3), 307–324.

Scheff, T. J. (1966). *Being Mentally Ill: A Sociological Theory.* New York: Aldine De Gruyter.

Scheurer, V. (2009). Convicted on statistics. Available online at http://understanding uncertainty.org/node/545 (accessed 29th April 2014).

Schickore, J. (2006). Misperception, illusion and epistemological optimism: Vision studies in early nineteenth-century Britain and Germany. *The British Journal for the History of Science, 39* (3), 383–405.

Schneer, C. J. (1960). *The Search for Order: The Development of the Major Ideas in the Physical Sciences from the Earliest Times to the Present.* London: The English Universities Press Ltd.

Scott, M., Eck, J., Knutsson, J. and Goldstein, H. (2008). Problem-oriented policing and environmental criminology. In R. Wortley and L. Mazerolle (Eds), *Environmental Criminology and Crime Analysis* (pp. 221–246). Cullompton: Willan Publishing.

Scott, P. (1977). Assessing dangerousness in criminals. *British Journal of Psychiatry, 131*, 127–142.

Sekar, Satish (1998). *Fitted In: The Cardiff 3 and the Lynette White Inquiry.* Southall: The Fitted In Project.

Sekula, A. (1986). The body and the archive. *October, 39*, 3–64.

Selcer, P. (2008). Standardizing wounds: Alexis Carrel and the scientific management of life in the First World War. *The British Journal for the History of Science, 41* (1), 73–107.

Sellin, T. (1937). *Research Memorandum on Crime in The Depression.* New York: Social Science Research Council.

Sellin, T. (1938). *Culture, Conflict and Crime.* New York: Social Science Research Council.

Sengoopta, C. (2003). *Imprint of the Raj: How Fingerprinting was Born in Colonial India.* Basingstoke: Macmillan.

Shane, S. and Schmitt, E. (2012). Qaeda Plot to Attack Plane Foiled, U.S. Officials Say. *The New York Times*, 7th May. Available online at www.nytimes.com/2012/05/08/world/middleeast/us-says-terrorist-plot-to-attack-plane-foiled.html (accessed 7th July 2012).

Shapere, D. (1986). External and internal factors in the development of sciences. *Science and Technology Studies, 4* (1), 1–9.

Shapin, S. (1982). History of science and its sociological reconstructions. *History of Science, 20*, 157–211.

Shapin, S. (1992). Discipline and bounding: The history and sociology of science as seen through the externalism-internalism debate. *History of Science, 30*, 333–369.

Shapin, S. (1998). *The Scientific Revolution.* Chicago: The University of Chicago Press.

Shaw, C. R. (1966). *The Jack-Roller: A Deliquent Boy's Own Story.* Chicago: The University of Chicago Press.

Shiomi, H. and Wada, K. (Eds) (1995). *Fordism Transformed: The Development of Production Methods in the Authomobile Industry.* Oxford: Oxford University Press.

Silverman, B. (2011a). *Research and Development in Forensic Science: A Review.* London: The Stationery Office Limited.

Silverman, B. (2011b). *Review of Research and Development in Forensic Science: University Responses.* London: The Stationery Office.

Silverman, B. (2011c). *Review of Research and Development in Forensic Science: Other Responses.* London: The Stationery Office.

Silverman, J. and Wilson, D. (2002). *Innocence Betrayed: Paedophilia, The Media and Society.* Cambridge: Polity Press.

Simoes, A. (2004). Textbooks, popular lectures and sermons: The quantum chemist Charles Alfred Coulson and the crafting science. *The British Journal for the History of Science, 37* (3), 299–342.

Simpson, K. (1978). *Forty Years of Murder: An Autoboigraphy.* London: Harrap Limited.

Smelser, N. (1962). *Theories of Collective Behaviour.* London. Routledge & Kegan Paul Ltd.

Smith, M. (2010). Architects of Armageddon: The Home Office scientific advisers' branch and civil defence in Britain, 1945–68. *The British Journal for the History of Science, 43* (2), 149–180.

Smith, M. J. and Tilley, N. (Eds) (2005). *Crime Science: New Approaches to Preventing and Detecting Crime.* Cullompton: Willan Publishing.

Smith, S. M., Patry, M. W. and Stinson, V. (2007). But what is the CSI effect? How crime dramas influence people's beliefs about forensic evidence. *The Canadian Journal of Police & Security Services, 5* (3/4), 187–195.

Snyder, L. (2006). *Reforming Philosophy: A Victorian Debate on Science and Society.* Chicago: The University of Chicago Press.

Soloway, R. A. (1990). *Demography and Degeneration: Eugenics and the Declining Birthrate in Twentieth-Century Britain.* Chapel Hill, NC: The University of North Carolina Press.

Sonne, W. J. (2006). *Criminal Investigation for the Professional Investigator.* Boca Raton: CRC Press.

Spalding, R. P. (2009). The identification and characterization of blood and bloodstains. In S. H. James, J. J. Nordby (Eds), *Forensic Science: An introduction to Scientific and Investigative Techniques* (3rd ed., pp. 261–284). Boca Raton: CRC Press.

Spector, M. and Kitsuse, J. (2001). *Constructing Social Problems.* New Brunswick, NJ: Transaction Publishers.

Spencer, H. (1896). *The Study of Sociology.* New York: D. Appleton and Company.

Spinelli, G. and Sharma, B. (2007). A paper-centred information system: Effectiveness and quality implications in UK police intelligence units. *Journal of Convergence Information Technology, 2* (3), 11–21.

Stelfox, P. (2007). Professionalizing criminal investigation. In T. Newburn, T. Williamson and A. Wright (Eds), *Handbook of Criminal Investigation* (pp. 628–651). Cullompton: Willan Publishing.

Stelfox, P. (2009). *Criminal Investigation: An Introduction to Principles and Practice.* Cullompton: Willan Publishing.

Stevens, A. (2011). *Drugs, Crime and Public Health: The Political Economy of Drug Policy.* London: Routledge.

Stockdale, R. (2000). Joined-up science. *Science and Justice, 40* (2), 131–133.

Sutherland, E. H. (1956). *The Professional Thief.* Chicago: The University of Chicago Press.

Sutherland, E. H. (1983). *White Collar Crime.* New Haven: Yale University Press.

Sutherland, E. H. and Cressey, D. R. (1960). *Principles of Criminology* (6th ed.). Chicago: J. B. Lippincott Company.

Sutton, R. and Trueman, K. (Eds) (2009). *Crime Scene Management: Scene Specific Methods.* Chichester: John Wiley & Sons Ltd.

Swanson, C. R., Chamelin, N. C. and Territo, L. (2003). *Criminal Investigation* (8th ed.). New York: McGraw-Hill.

Szasz, F. M. (1974). The many meanings of history, part I. *The History Teacher, 7* (4), 552–563.

Tannenbaum, F. (1938). *Crime and the Community.* Boston, MA: Ginn and Co.

Taroni, F. and Aitken, C. G. G. (1998a). Probabilistics reasoning in the law, part 1: Assessment of probabilities and explanation of the value of DNA evidence. *Science and Justice, 38* (4), 165–177.

Taroni, F. and Aitken, C. G. G. (1998b). Probabilistics reasoning in the law, part 2: Assessment of probabilities and explanation of the value of trace evidence other than DNA. *Science and Justice, 38* (3), 179–188.

Taylor, D. (2005). Beyond the bounds of respectable society: The 'dangerous classes' in Victorian and Edwardian England. In J. Rowbotham and K. Stevenson (Eds), *Criminal Conversations: Victorian Crimes, Social Panic, and Moral Outrage* (pp. 3–22). Columbus: The Ohio State University Press.

Taylor, I. and Taylor, L. (1973). *Politics and Deviance.* London: Penguin Books Ltd.

Taylor, I., Walton, P. and Young, J. (1994). *The New Criminology: For a Social Theory of Deviance.* London: Routledge.

Taylor, P. and Chaplin, R. (2011). *Crimes Detected in England and Wales 2010/11.* London: HMSO.

Thomas, W. I. and Znaniecki, F. (1958). *The Polish Peasant in Europe and America.* New York: Dover Publications.

Thompson, B. (1989). *PornWars: Moral Panics, Pornography and Social Policy.* Paper presented to the American Society of Criminology, Reno.

Thompson, B. (1994a). *Soft Core: Moral Crusades Pornography in Britain and America.* London: Cassell.

Thompson, B. (1994b). *Sadmomasochism: Painful Perversion or Pleasurable Play?* London: Cassell.

Thompson, B. and Williams, A. (2014). *The Myth of Moral Panics: Sex, Snuff and Satan.* New York: Routledge.

Thompson, E. P. (1991). *The Making of the English Working Class.* London: Penguin Books.

Thompson, E. P. (1993). *Customs in Common: Studies in Traditional Popular Culture.* New York: The New Press.

Thompson, J. (2000). The way ahead. *Science and Justice, 40* (2), 152–154.

Thompson, K. (1992). *Readings from Emile Durkheim.* London: Routledge.

Thornberry, T. P., Krohn, M. D., Lizotte, A. J., Smith, C. A. and Tobin, K. (2003). *Gangs and Delinquency in Developmental Perspective.* Cambridge: Cambridge University Press.

Thornton, J. I. (1994). Courts of law v. courts of science: A forensic scientist's reaction to Daubert. *Shepards Expert and Scientific Evidence, 1* (3), 475–485.

Thrasher, F. M. (2000). *The Gang: A Study of 1,313 Gangs in Chicago.* Peotone, IL: New Chicago Press.

Tierney, J. (2010). *Criminology: Theory and Context* (3rd ed.). Harlow: Longman.

Tilley, N. and Ford, A. (1996). *Forensic Science and Crime Investigation. Crime Detection and Prevention Series Paper 73.* London: HMSO.

Tilley, N., Robinson, A. and Burrows, J. (2007). The investigation of high-volume crime. In T. Newburn, T. Williamson and A. Wright (Eds), *Handbook of Criminal Investigation* (pp. 226–254). Cullompton: Willan Publishing.

Trueman, K. (2009a). First officer attending. In R. Sutton and K. Trueman (Eds), *Crime Scene Management: Scene Specific Methods* (pp. 21–35). Chichester: John Wiley & Sons Ltd.

Trueman, K. (2009b). The role of the scenes of crime officer. In R. Sutton and K. Trueman (Eds), *Crime Scene Management: Scene Specific Methods* (pp. 37–68). Chichester: John Wiley & Sons Ltd.

Turner, S. (1986). The sociology of science in its place: comment on Shapere. *Science and Technology Studies, 4* (1), 15–18.

Turner, S. (2008). The social study of science before Kuhn. In E. J. Hackett, O. Amsterdamska, M. Lynch and J. Wajcman (Eds), *The Handbook of Science and Technology Studies* (pp. 33–62). Cambridge, MA.: The MIT Press.

Turvey, B. (2001). *Criminal Profiling: An Introduction to Behavioral Evidence Analysis* (2nd ed.). San Diego: Elsevier Academic Press.

Turvey, B. E. (2008). *Criminal Profiling: An Introduction to Behavioural Evidence Analysis* (3rd ed.). San Diego: Elsevier Academic Press.

Turvey, B. E. and Petherick, W. A. (2010). Preface. In W. Petherick, B. E. Turvey and C. E. Ferguson (Eds), *Forensic Criminology* (pp. xix–xi). San Diego: Elsevier Academic Press.

Tyler, R. T. (2006). Viewing CSI and the threshold of guilt: Managing truth and justice in reality and fiction. *The Yale Law Journal, 115* (5), 1050–1085.

UNISYS (2007). *Holmes2 Case Study.* Available online at www.holmes2.com/holmes2/whatish2/HOLMES2.pdf (accessed 30th April 2013).

Urbach, P. (1987). *Francis Bacon's Philosophy of Science: An Account and a Reappraisal.* La Salle, IL: Open Court.

US Department of Justice (2006). *A Review of the FBI's Handling of the Brandon Mayfield Case.* Office of the Inspector General Oversight and Review Division.

Van Doren, C. (1991). *A History of Knowledge: Past, Present and Future.* New York: Ballintine Books.

Van Wyhe, J. (2002). The authority of human nature: The Schädellehre of Franz Joseph Gall. *The British Journal for the History of Science, 35* (1), 17–42.

Veblen, T. (1919). The intellectual pre-eminence of Jews in modern Europe. *Political Science Quarterly, 34* (1), 33–42.

Vold, G. B. (1958). *Theoretical Criminology.* Oxford: Oxford University Press.

Wacquant, L. (2009). *Punishing the Poor: The Neoliberal Government of Social Insecurity.* Durham, NC: Duke University Press.

Waddington, D., Jones, K. and Critcher, C. (1989). *Flashpoints: Studies in Public Disorder.* London: Routledge.

Waddington, P. A. (1999). *Policing Citizens.* London: UCL Press Ltd.

Wakefield, A. (2011). Undertaking a criminological literature review. In P. Davies, P. Francis and V. Jupp (Eds), *Doing Criminological Research* (2nd ed., pp. 78–98). London: Sage Publications.

Wall, D. (1998). *The Chief Constables of England and Wales: The Socio-Legal History of a Criminal Justice Elite.* Aldershot: Dartmouth Press.

Wallerstein, I. (2001). *Unthinking Social Science: The Limits of Nineteenth-Century Paradigms* (2nd ed.). Philadelphia: Temple University Press.

Ward, T., Polaschek, D. L. and Beech, A. R. (2006). *Theories of Sexual Offending.* Chichester: John Wiley & Sons Ltd.

Watson, J. D. and Crick, F. H. (1953). Molecular structure of nucleic acids: A structure for deoxyribose nucleic acid. *Nature, 171,* 737.

Weber, M. ([1930]1992). *The Protestant Ethic and the Spirit of Capitalism.* London: Routledge.

Weber, M. (1978). *Economy and Society, Vol I.* Berkeley, CA: University of California Press.

Webster, R. (2005). *The Secret of Bryn Estyn: The Making of a Modern Witch Hunt.* Oxford: The Orwell Press.

Weston, N. (2004). The crime scene. In P. C. White (Ed.), *Crime Scene to Court: The Essentials of Forensic Science* (2nd ed., pp. 21–55). Cambridge: The Royal Society of Chemistry.

White, P. C. (Ed.) (2004). *Crime Scene to Court: The Essentials of Forensic Science* (2nd ed.). Cambridge: The Royal Society of Chemistry.

White, P. C. (Ed.) (2010). *Crime Scene to Court: The Essentials of Forensic Science* (3rd ed.). Cambridge: The Royal Society of Chemistry.

Wiener, M. J. (1994). *Reconstructing the Criminal: Culture, Law and Policy in England, 1830–1914.* Cambridge: Cambridge University Press.

Wigelsworth, J. R. (2008). Bipartisan politics and practical knowledge: Advertising of public science in two London newspapers, 1695–1720. *The British Journal for the History of Science, 41* (4), 517–540.

Wilkins, L. (1964). *Social Deviance: Social Policy, Action and Research.* London: Tavistock Publications.

Wilkinson, R. and Pickett, K. (2010). *The Spirit Level: Why Equality is Better for Everyone.* London: Penguin Books Ltd.

Williams, A. (2004). *'There ain't No Peds in Paulsgrove': Vigilantes, Social Control and this Misapplication of Moral Panic Theory.* Unplished PhD Thesis, University of Reading.

Williams, A. (2010). An epistemological chasm? Actuarial risk assessment through OASys. In M. Nash and A. Williams (Eds), *The Handbook of Public Protection* (pp. 133–161). Cullompton: Willan Publishing.

Williams, A. and Thompson, B. (2004a). Vigilance or vigilantes: The Paulsgrove riots and policing paedophiles in the community. Part I: The long slow fuse. *The Police Journal, 77* (2), pp. 99–119.

Williams, A. and Thompson, B. (2004b). Vigilance or vigilantes: The Paulsgrove riots and policing paedophiles in the community. Part II: The lessons of Paulsgrove. *The Police Journal, 77* (3), pp. 199–205.

Williamson, T. (2007). Psychology and criminal investigation. In T. Newburn, T. Williamson and A. Wright (Eds), *Handbook of Criminal Investigation* (pp. 68–91). Cullompton: Willan Publishing.

Willmott, P. (1969). *Adolescent Boys of East London.* London: Penguin Books Ltd.

Wilson, C. (1995). *The Invisible World: Early Modern Philosophy and the Invention of the Microscope.* Princeton, NJ: Princeton University Press.

Wilson, E. O. (2006). *From So Simple a Beginning: The Four Great Books of Charles Darwin.* New York: W. W. Norton and Company.

Wilson, J. Q. and Herrnstein, R. J. (1998). *Crime and Human Nature: The Definitive Study of the Causes of Crime.* New York: The Free Press.

Wilson-Wilde, L. M., Brandi, J. and Gutowski, S. J. (2011). The future of forensic science standards. *Forensic Science International: Genetics Supplement Series, 3* (1), 333–334.

Wirth, L. (1956). *The Ghetto.* Chicago: The University of Chicago Press.

Withers, C., Higgitt, R. and Finnegan, D. (2008). Historical geographies and provincial science: Themes in the setting and reception of the British Association for the Advancement of Science in Britain and Ireland, 1831–c.1939. *The British Journal for the History of Science, 41* (3), 385–415.

Wolfgang, M. E. and Ferracuti, F. (1967). *The Subculture of Violence: Towards an Integrated Theory in Criminology.* London: Tavistock Publications.

Wood, K. (2006). Making and circulating knowledge through Sir William Hamilton's Campi Phlegraei. *The British Journal for the History of Science, 39* (1), 67–96.

Wortley, R. (2008). Situational precipitators of crime. In R. Wortley and L. Mazerolle, (Eds), *Environmental Criminology and Crime Analysis* (pp. 48–69). Cullompton: Willan Publishing.

Wortley, R. and Mazerolle, L. (Eds) (2008). *Environmental Criminology and Crime Analysis.* Cullompton: Willan Publishing.

Yeo, R. (2003). *Defining Science: William Whewell, Natural Knowledge and Public Debate in Early Victorian Britain.* Cambridge: Cambridge University Press.

Young, J. (1971). *The Drugtakers: The Social Meaning of Drug Use.* London: MacGibbon and Kee.

Young, J. (1999). *The Exclusive Society: Social Exclusion, Crime and Difference in Late Modernity.* London: Sage Publications.

Young, J. (2002). Critical criminology in the twenty-first century: Critique, irony and the always unfinished. In K. Carrington and R. Hogg (Eds), *Critical Criminology: Issues, Debates, Challenges* (pp. 251–274). Cullompton: Willan Publishing.

Zagorin, P. (2001). Francis Bacon's concept of objectivity and the idols of the mind. *The British Journal for the History of Science, 34* (4), 379–393.

Index